"In *Baptist Political Theology* Tommy Kidd, Paul Miller, and Andrew Walker bring together leading Baptist scholars who mine the riches of Baptist history and thought to inform our current cultural moment and to answer pressing ethical questions. The chapter titles are as inviting as their authors are impressive, but the content within each chapter is what makes this volume so worthwhile. This book comes with my highest recommendation."

—**Jason K. Allen**, president, Midwestern Baptist Theological Seminary

"No one will ever accuse me of being a Baptist, but I can and do appreciate many of the insights that Baptists have contributed to political theology. This impressive collection brings together many of today's sharpest Baptist thinkers to reflect on the historical sources of and future challenges to Baptist political thought without papering over the various strengths and weaknesses. It's a resource for the entire church."

—**Ryan T. Anderson**, president, The Ethics and Public Policy Center

"Opinions abound about what it means to be 'Baptist,' and that is perhaps no truer than when we try to define Baptist beliefs about politics. This collection of essays helps us on the road to defining Baptist political theology in ways that are historically informed and theologically aware."

—**Matthew Emerson**, professor of religion and dean of theology, arts, and humanities, Oklahoma Baptist University

"*Baptist Political Theology* is a masterful effort to describe and explain the collective historical experience of the people called Baptists as they interacted with various civil governments and wrestled with the role Baptists and their moral convictions should and should not play in civil society. The result is a cornucopia of critical information that will inspire readers as they discover a surprisingly well-developed tradition of Baptist political theology. This should serve as a valuable guide for all people who believe that Christian moral perspectives should be part of the conversations about societal moral standards. *Baptist Political Theology* should be a standard textbook in all Baptist and evangelical seminaries and colleges and will richly reward all interested readers who delve into its pages."

—**Richard Land**, president emeritus, Southern Evangelical Seminary

"There's never been a greater need in America for smart Christian political theology, and Baptists are central to the present and future of American Christian life. Baptists were also central to shaping early American democracy, especially religious liberty. This new volume on Baptist political theology from leading Baptist scholars is timely and relevant to all Americans who want constructive religious engagement in public life."

—**Mark Tooley**, president, The Institute on Religion and Democracy

"The great Protestant denominations emerging from the sixteenth century each have had unique methods of acting 'in the world, but not of the world.' Protestants have always cultivated a rich and varied engagement with the culture, and Baptists in particular. Kidd, Miller, and Walker have marshaled a constellation of contemporary Baptist luminaries to scatter light on Baptist perspectives on the changing currents of human interaction over the past four centuries. This is emphatically not a collection of stories in an *acta sanctorum*, but an honest, careful, and thought-provoking volume that studiously measures the contours of a tried, noble, and indispensable Christian tradition."

—**John D. Wilsey**, associate professor of church history and philosophy, The Southern Baptist Theological Seminary

"*Baptist Political Theology* offers us a chance to explore ideas that connect Baptist theological orientations to political perspectives. Both political scientists and theologians should welcome this exploration."

—**George Yancey**, professor of social sciences, Baylor University

BAPTIST POLITICAL THEOLOGY

BAPTIST POLITICAL THEOLOGY

Thomas S. Kidd, Paul D. Miller,
and Andrew T. Walker

ACADEMIC
BRENTWOOD, TENNESSEE

ISBN: 978-1-0877-3613-6

Dewey Decimal Classification: 230.6
Subject Heading: BAPTISTS--DOCTRINES \ DOCTRINAL
THEOLOGY \ CHRISTIANITY-- POLITICAL ASPECTS

Unless otherwise noted, all Scripture quotations are taken from the
Christian Standard Bible®, Copyright © 2017 by Holman Bible
Publishers. Used by permission. Christian Standard Bible® and CSB®
are federally registered trademarks of Holman Bible Publishers.
Scripture quotations marked CJB are taken from the Complete Jewish
Bible (CJB) by David H. Stern. Copyright © 1998. All rights reserved.
Scripture quotations marked KJV are taken from the
King James Version (public domain).
Scripture quotations marked KJVA are reproduced by permission of
Cambridge University Press, the Crown's patentee in the UK.
Scripture quotations marked NLT are taken from Holy Bible, New
Living Translation, copyright © 1996, 2004, 2015 by Tyndale House
Foundation. Used by permission of Tyndale House Publishers,
Inc., Carol Stream, Illinois 60188. All rights reserved.
Scripture quotations marked RSV are taken from the Revised Standard
Version of the Bible, copyright © 1946, 1952, and 1971 the Division of
Christian Education of the National Council of the Churches of Christ in
the United States of America. Used by permission. All rights reserved.

The web addresses referenced in this book were live and correct at the
time of the book's publication but may be subject to change.

Cover design by Darren Welch.

Printed in the United States of America

28 27 26 25 24 23 VP 1 2 3 4 5 6 7 8 9 10

CONTENTS

Part Two

Introduction

By Thomas S. Kidd, Paul D. Miller, and Andrew T. Walker

When we have spoken of this volume to others, one of the standard replies has been one of befuddlement, then eventually, intrigue: a book on Baptist political thought? The confusion, on the surface, seems justified.

The Possibility of a Baptist Political Theology

Of the traditions of political theology emerging from the Reformation, Baptists are not usually the first to come to mind—or, to state it more bluntly, they are sometimes thought to have virtually no discernible political theology that is not first grounded within the broader penumbra of Protestant political theology. In contemporary Protestantism, few would aver that Baptists have done much by way of reflecting on statecraft and the common good.

This volume arises from at least two convictions. First, as Baptists committed to our tradition, we believe that responsible theological reflection demands rigorous application of Baptist principles to the public arena. This need, we believe, is especially prescient, as America flirts with illiberalism from both the Left and the Right. Baptist thought, in general, immunizes against authoritarianism and illiberalism, since it believes the domains of church and state each have their own distinct, yet overlapping roles to play. Neither can be totalizing over the other.

Second, we are under the conviction that there is more to the possibility of a Baptist political theology than first meets the eye. Are we saying that Baptists are the lodestar of Protestant political thought? No. But we are saying that, properly understood and classified, Baptists have more political outworkings to their theology than is first assumed. It is not an accident, after all, that religious liberty arises with such fervency from the Baptist tradition. Baptist theologians and ethicists would strenuously argue, for example, that keeping the jurisdictional boundaries of temporal institutions and redeemed institutions clear offers massive scaffolding for religious liberty as a political doctrine.

What Is a Baptist?

But to speak of a Baptist political theology, it is necessary to ground these ideas within the larger distinctives of Baptist identity. While whole tomes have been devoted to the subject of Baptist distinctives, for our purposes, let us include the following chapters as the essential foundation from which to build a Baptist political theology. Most of the ideas herein are distinctive to Baptists; some are shared by other Protestants, but their unique combination alongside other particulars is another distinctive Baptist trait. The ordering is intentionally sequential.

Conversion. Baptists have traditionally taught that people must be regenerated to be considered authentically Christian. Becoming a Christian does not happen by tradition, culture, affiliation, or group identity. Each member of a Baptist church is to know a time in his or her life when the Holy Spirit drew him or her to repentance and salvation.

Soul competency. Although somewhat less prioritized than in former times, soul competency speaks to the nature of individuals standing before

God in their own persons. Soul competency speaks to the foundation of individual persons needing to reckon with their own fate before a holy God, such that no intermediary can disrupt or alter the condition of the person's soul.

Believer's baptism. Building on the logic of conversion, upon the open proclamation of one's faith in Jesus Christ, persons are to have their whole selves immersed in baptismal waters, signifying the dying of the former self to sin and being raised to newness of life following the pattern of Jesus's own resurrection.

Local church membership. In traditional baptistic formula, a prerequisite to formal membership in a church and taking the Lord's Supper is that one has been regenerated and baptized. Upon their membership in the local church, Baptist Christians are to see their membership in the local church as their participation in the redeemed family of Christ. To grow in holiness, members of Baptist churches are to practice holiness and are subject to church discipline if patterns of wanton sin flare.

Local church autonomy. Baptist churches are considered autonomous in that each is self-governing and not accountable to any ecclesiastical hierarchy. Authority within the local church is vested in the congregation's members, who, in some models, delegate decision-making to an ordained set of elders.

Sola Scriptura. As heirs of the Reformation, Baptists pledge their highest fidelity to Scripture as the authoritative deposit of faith. Each Baptist Christian is to read his or her Bible and be familiar with its contents as an authoritative guide to doctrine, ethics, and personal holiness. Baptists have traditionally rejected the Catholic elevation of tradition to the level of Scripture as a source of authority, the Anglican elevation of tradition and reason, and the Wesleyan elevation of reason, tradition, and experience.

Looking at the broad contours of Baptist distinctives, then, several themes seem to emerge related to political life and political communities. For one, on the nature and purpose of political authority, Baptists look to the Bible's teachings on the nature of human fallenness and the ordination of government. Baptist theology is not to be confused with pacifism or anarchy. We believe the state has a positive role to play in the administration of justice. Second, owing to our aspiration toward a democratic polity, Baptists have tended to value local determinations in matters of faith and life. This, in a way, correlates to a principle of subsidiarity. Rather than deferring matters to a managerial class of experts (whether ecclesiastical or political), an inherent populism undergirds Baptist identity. Third, in matters of social ethics, Baptists would lay claim to the Bible as the authoritative guide for defining what constitutes proper social ordering (at least in the areas where the Bible offers a fairly clear application). Principles of human dignity, religious liberty, racial harmony, the priority of the natural family, and care for the poor and the unborn would each equally emanate from biblical teaching.

Dilemmas and tensions do persist, however, in Baptist political theology. For starters, there is a historically justified suspicion of political power. One reason for this owes to Baptist history. In Anglo-American history, especially before the twentieth century, Baptists have, traditionally, been those dispossessed of power and, thus, leery of the government getting too large and too powerful. To make matters worse, Baptists can point to a myriad of historical examples where state power allied with religious bodies led to persecution against our forebears. It would seem only natural, then, that Baptists would register caution toward the state. This has led, however, to the paucity of political theology elsewhere, particularly an undeveloped doctrine of statecraft and the positive stewardship of power for good ends.

Due to their Reformation roots and their attitude toward Scripture, Baptists have also tended toward the development of public ethics on solely scriptural grounds. This, of course, is not problematic on its own since Scripture is the final rule and measure for the Christian life. But the cultivation of a political ethic on narrow biblical grounds has tended toward an incipient sectarianism in forging a Baptist public ethics, especially considering the tradition lacks any positive natural law theory of its own. This, in turn, has generally led to an undeveloped understanding of the common good and of the Baptists' relationship to sound political order.

But on matters where Baptists shine—in particular, religious liberty— you will find no greater advocate than Baptists. This timeless political principle is the extension of Baptist theology and Baptist identity (as a people defined by their dissent against unjust authority) into the public domain.

Historical Overview

Baptists have dissent hardwired into their spiritual history. The legacy of dissent and persecution tells us a great deal about why most Baptists have not embraced a Christian establishmentarian political theology. We can trace the origins of the early modern Baptist movement to the unfolding English and Continental Reformations in the sixteenth and seventeenth centuries. Baptists were deeply informed by the Reformed tradition, but with a major difference: they practiced believer's baptism instead of infant baptism, which was the norm for Catholics and virtually all other Protestant groups besides Baptists. Of course, Baptists believe the baptism of believers by immersion was the original practice of the New Testament church. They note that no indisputable instances of infant baptism are recorded in the book of Acts or the rest of the Bible. Instead, the typical sequence in Acts, the record of the church's history after Christ's ascension, is that people old enough to understand the gospel repent, believe, and then receive baptism.

Most Baptists would concede that by the early fifth century of church history, and the time of Augustine, infant baptism was becoming the new standard practice of Christian churches. The historic debates over the meaning of baptism do not concern us here; suffice it to say that by a century after Augustine, infant baptism had become nearly the universal practice in Christian churches, except for converts who had never received baptism as children. This commitment to pedobaptism endured in most traditions even after the beginning of the Reformation in 1517 in Germany. But on the Continent, groups disparagingly called "Anabaptists" (or rebaptizers) appeared in the wake of Martin Luther's stand against the corruptions of Rome. Luther, Calvin, and the other Reformers were calling the church back to New Testament simplicity. But how far should the Reformation go? Anabaptists argued that the ritual of baptism had also become corrupt over the course of church history and that it was time to get back to its original, biblical meaning.

Most Protestants regarded the Anabaptists as dangerous radicals, while Catholics derided the Anabaptists as the logical endpoint of Protestant extremism. The baptism of infants into the protective canopy of the church was so central to European Christian culture that withholding children from baptism seemed cruel and cavalier. Revulsion against the Anabaptists inevitably led to disdain and persecution, even before the Anabaptist debacle at Münster in Germany in 1534. There, Dutch prophet and visionary Jan Bockelson (John of Leiden) ruthlessly presided over a fanatical communistic experiment that enforced common property, embraced polygamy, and mandated the execution of Bockelson's rivals. After proclaiming himself a messiah, Bockelson was finally dislodged by German authorities and, eventually, was tortured to death in Münster. The Anabaptists were far better represented by leaders such as Menno Simons (leader of the "Mennonites"), but memories of Münster's horrors served as a convenient way to tar Anabaptists and English Baptists by association for centuries to come.

The English Baptist movement developed almost a century after the beginnings of Continental Anabaptist dissent, but it grew from the same root of Reformation thought. In England, the Reformation's origins were deeply political, rooted in King Henry VIII's decision to break from the Roman Catholic Church in 1534. But other English Reformers wished to see the Reformation further extended into church polity and doctrine. Ultimately, the desire for further reform fed into the "Puritan" movement, which was also a term of derision for "hot" Protestants who wanted to shape the Church of England into an exemplar of Reformed faith and practice. Other, more radical English Protestants had no confidence in reforming the Anglican Church, choosing instead to separate from it and hold illicit, independent meetings. Establishmentarians saw these "Separatists" as even more dangerous than the Puritans, and the Separatists often fell under harsh persecution. Some Separatists became familiar with Anabaptists and Mennonites in nearby Holland, including their convictions about baptism and the separation of church and state. Some of the English Separatists, including the Gainsborough, England, congregation of Separatist minister John Smyth, relocated to Amsterdam in the early 1600s, fleeing from persecution. The extent of Smyth's Mennonite influences is debated, but by 1609, Smyth denounced infant baptism as "the most unreasonable heresy of all Antichristianism."[1] He decided to baptize himself as a believer and then baptized the rest of his church members. One of Smyth's congregants, Thomas Helwys, soon split with the Amsterdam congregation and took some of his supporters back to England, where they began meeting in the north of London around 1612. Historians regard these events as the beginnings of the English Baptist movement.

Both the Anabaptist and Baptist traditions would influence the historic trajectory of the Baptist faith outside of Europe, not least in North America. Baptists were present in the American colonies almost from the beginning, but the most visible controversy first involved Baptist principles centered on the arch-dissenter Roger Williams in the mid-1630s. Williams, though a type of Puritan or Separatist himself, rejected Puritan Massachusetts's strictures about theological uniformity. Eventually he was expelled from Massachusetts and went on to found the colony of Rhode Island in 1636. Williams affiliated with the Baptist movement long enough to help establish America's first Baptist congregation in Providence, Rhode Island, in 1638. The erratic Williams never felt comfortable with any denomination, so his Baptist sojourn did not last. But Williams's convictions about liberty of conscience and his connection to America's first Baptist church turned him into a fixture of the history of Baptist political theology. Massachusetts, for its

---

[1] John Smyth, *The Character of the Beast*, or *the False Constitution of the Church* (1609); repr. W. T. Whitley, ed., *The Works of John Smyth*, 2 vols. (Cambridge: Cambridge University Press, 1915), vol. 2, in Joseph F. Early Jr., *Readings in Baptist History: Four Centuries of Selected Documents* (Nashville: B&H, 2008), 2.

part, went on to ban the Baptists in 1645 as "the troublers of churches in all places."[2]

When Baptists made inroads among the African American and Afro-Caribbean populations in the 1770s, it only heightened the connection between Baptist life and a culture of dissent. The Silver Bluff Church in South Carolina, a Baptist congregation, became the first enduring African American–led church in America around 1773. African American churches of many denominations took on a reputation among white observers as hives of sedition and resistance. This was especially the case with the "brush arbor" meetings that secretly sprang up across the plantation South and the Caribbean in the early 1800s. In 1831, the connection between slave unrest and Baptist piety became fixed with the twin outbreaks of Nat Turner's rebellion in Virginia and the so-called Baptist War in Jamaica. Turner was a lay Baptist preacher, and Samuel Sharpe, the leader of the Jamaican slave uprising, was a Baptist deacon. Sometimes at cross-purposes with white Baptist political advocacy, African American and Afro-Caribbean Baptist dissent became fixed more than a century before Martin Luther King Jr. became arguably the world's most famous proponent of Baptist political theology. Baptists in America and other parts of the world have sometimes envisioned themselves as part of a "moral majority," but the more common stance in Baptist history has been that of a dissenting minority, of strangers and pilgrims on the earth.

What Makes Baptist Political Theology?

The distinctive Baptist contribution to political theology is the doctrine of religious freedom and disestablishment. You will find some mention of religious freedom in almost every chapter of this book. But why? And what

---

[2] A. H. Newman, *A History of the Baptist Churches in the United States*, The American Church History Series, ed. Philip Schaff et al. (New York: Christian Literature Publishing Co., 1894), 127.

does religious freedom mean for the whole body of political theology? Is it the only thing we have to say about politics?

An inner logic connects adult baptism, conversion, religious freedom, and disestablishment. Baptism is a ritual that marks the entry of a penitent person into the church community by symbolizing the washing away of sin, the death of the old self and resurrection of the new self. Such a ritual has no meaning for infants or children who have no awareness or understanding of sin, repentance, or the gospel of Jesus Christ. No one can enter the kingdom of God apart from a conscious, inward, informed turning away from sin and toward Christ—a turning that we call repentance and faith. And if people cannot enter the kingdom, they should not be counted full members of the local church, which is an embassy of the kingdom. The church should strive to have a membership made entirely of regenerate Christians, baptized adults who have made a public profession of faith and covenanted together to hold one another accountable for walking in holiness.

By the same logic, no adult can be coerced into the kingdom—or the church—at the point of the sword. Our doctrine of baptism and the church is the seed from which grows an entire panoply of implications about the state. The state may coerce someone into attending the right church, uttering the right creed, and even comporting their behavior to the appearance of outward righteousness—none of which makes the least contribution to a person's actual salvation. We call this the doctrine of "soul competency," the idea that each person is accountable to God for himself or herself and no other authority is ultimately able to effect another's salvation. It is pointless for the state to use its tools, which touch outward behavior, to try to compel inward belief.

Worse, it is dangerous. The state has an educative function. When it passes laws, it habituates people to believe, even if unconsciously, that those laws reflect standards of good and evil. When the state makes laws endorsing, establishing, or regulating religion, it teaches people to rely on the state's judgment, rather than the church's or the words of Scripture, for their salvation. Imagine a citizen goes to church and recites a creed because the state tells him to. That citizen is at grave risk of believing he is a Christian because he is performing the appropriate deeds—without any reference at all to the saving work of Christ on the cross. State-endorsed (and, much more so, state-mandated) religion always has strong tendencies toward a religion of works. And there are further dangers, including the long history of states hijacking religion to use as propaganda for whatever political purpose the ruler has in mind. State religion cheapens religion, turning religious authorities into cheerleaders and boosters of the status quo, with all its injustices, and of whomever exercises power, regardless of what that power is used for. State religion has no prophetic witness and no independent voice.

The idea of religious freedom and disestablishment is one of the most revolutionary ideas in world history. Virtually every state in history allied with a religion or, when they banned conventional religion, invented new ones (like communism). The Baptist doctrine of religious freedom amounts to a claim that every state in history got it wrong. It would be breathtaking in its audacity, except for subsequent history in which religious freedom spread worldwide and vindicated the belief that states and churches relate best when they are institutionally and jurisdictionally separate. Every state on earth has (at least on paper) agreed to the Universal Declaration of Human Rights, article 18, which affirms that "everyone has the right to freedom of thought, conscience and religion; this right includes freedom to change his religion or belief, and freedom, either alone or in community with others and in public or private, to manifest his religion or belief in teaching, practice, worship and observance."[3]

Does the Baptist political witness end there? Do we have anything else to say? In fact, religious freedom and disestablishment, as revolutionary ideas, cannot but have far-reaching consequences throughout the full range of cultural, social, and political issues. Most importantly, religious

---

[3] United Nations, Universal Declaration of Human Rights, article 18, un.org, accessed October 27, 2022, https://www.un.org/en/about-us/universal-declaration-of-human-rights.

freedom and disestablishment mean the state has limited jurisdiction. There are matters over which it has no legitimate authority. Religious freedom and disestablishment are thus intrinsically opposed to totalitarianism and, at least, highly suspicious of softer forms of authoritarianism. Totalitarian government is sinful and anti-Christian by its very nature; authoritarian government with no check on its power is inherently dangerous and carries the potential for overstepping its bounds. Baptists should be the first to warn against the encroaching power of states that try to grow beyond their rightful boundaries.

That means Baptists are naturally sympathetic to forms of government that recognize their own limits, have checks on their power, and respect the religious rights of their people. That natural sympathy is reinforced by Baptists' own practice of congregational autonomy and self-government. Baptists practice self-government among themselves, which habituates them to its rhythms in society at large. That is why, in practice and in history, Baptists are almost exclusively republicans and democrats (with a small *r* and a small *d*) who believe in some version of representative government and in civil and political rights. That is not quite the same as saying that Baptists believe the Bible mandates democracy. We respect the authority of the Bible enough to reserve our strongest conclusions for what is explicit and clear in Scripture. But for Baptists, the logic linking biblical revelation to religious freedom and congregational autonomy and, thence, to free government is simpler and stronger than for any other Christian tradition. We have always thrown in our lot with free government. Most Christian traditions in the modern era support basic civil and political rights and find biblical support for them in the idea that all humans bear God's image and have coequal moral worth. But Baptists add our distinctive doctrine of religious freedom and disestablishment, an additional bulwark against authoritarianism and a cornerstone of free government.

This is an especially needful truth to revive today. We live amidst an upsurge in nationalist sentiment and rising authoritarian powers, which bring twin dangers to the right relationship of church and state. On the one hand, nationalism has historically almost always come tinged with religious rhetoric, religious symbolism, and even religious demagoguery. Statesmen know the power of religion, and if they can tap into that power and redirect it to themselves, they will. On the other hand, in reaction, nationalists' opponents often blame religious institutions and religious leaders, equate religion with the political agenda they oppose, and seek to shrink, ban, or silence religion in the public square. That means religion is in danger of hijacking by one side and proscription on the other; of being used and manipulated; and of being ignored, sidelined, and neglected.

In this context the Baptist political witness is crucial. More than any other Christian tradition, we can insist on the importance of disestablishment and warn of the dangers of being co-opted by those in power—at the same time and with the same framework that we insist on the vital necessity of religious freedom and a robust and vocal Christian presence in the public square. Christians must advocate for justice, peace, and flourishing—our Lord commands it of us—which means we must be active, present, and free to believe and speak. We must also insist on the state's limitation and the church's independence, which means our presence in the public square is never an effort to take it over in the name of serving it.

We have traveled a great distance from the seemingly small matter of believer's baptism. But that is the legacy of revolutionary ideas. They work their way through the architecture of ideas and recenter relationships in new ways. And the Baptist revolution in religious freedom and disestablishment—in free government and republicanism—is not done yet.

Outline of This Book

This book unfolds in two parts. The first part, chapters 1–16, are historical. We review the life, writings, and political involvement of key figures in Baptist history, including Roger Williams, Isaac Backus, Carl Henry, and more. We also review Baptist involvement in key historical eras and episodes, including seventeenth-century Britain, the American

Revolution, the US Civil War, and the Social Gospel movement of the early twentieth century. This part of the book is a summary of Baptist historical political theology, reviewing the road we have traveled, what our political witness has been, what we have gotten right and what we have not. We review our history to learn from it and to understand the story into which we are stepping.

The second part, chapters 17–27, are essays on contemporary issues, including bioethics, environmentalism, sex and gender, and war and peace. This is a collective effort at applied political theology, taking the principles that animated our political witness in preceding centuries and asking what light they shed on the social, cultural, and political issues of the twenty-first century. Not every issue is new. We revisit and update conversations about natural law and religious freedom—issues that have been under discussion in Baptist thought for centuries, but about which there are still things that need saying.

Some readers may wonder why we chose the topics, individuals, and historical periods that we did. The answer, as with any volume of this scope and ambition, is a little idiosyncratic and a little editorial. When we first conceived of this project (in Dallas over coffee on the sidelines of the Ethics and Religious Liberty Commission's annual summit in October 2019), it was a trilogy that included virtually everything imaginable. We aspired to edit a systematic and comprehensive treatment of the history, development, and contemporary contribution of Baptist political theology. Then it was a real proposal in front of an editor, after which it quickly was reframed as a single volume of some three dozen essays focusing on Anglo-American history and contemporary topics of prominent concern. Like all edited volumes, it subsequently went through a series of invitations to potential authors, followed by a long process of negotiation and haggling as we came to a series of concrete commitments and deadlines. At each step along the way, the project morphed and evolved, conforming to the limits of who was available, how much time we had, and of course, our publisher's word count.

The final product is a result of a long process involving dozens of people—whose work we deeply appreciate. With the number of contributors involved, any one person's involvement does not imply his or her agreement with any other chapter or contributor. Not all contributors affirm the Southern Baptist Convention's *Baptist Faith and Message 2000*, and even we, the editors, do not affirm every judgment and every conclusion found herein. But we believe this scholarship helps shed light on the history and contemporary practice of Baptists in the public square.

Together, we hope this volume is a road map, showing from where we have come, what road we have traveled, and where we think our road leads next. It is a map that covers a very large terrain of history, theology, and politics. We doubt you would have picked up this book unless such subjects already interest you. But we take a highly specific road through this terrain, the road charted by Baptists through the tumult of modernity and postmodernity. We think it a road worth following and invite you to walk with us on the journey.

PART ONE

1

The Reformation and Early Development of Baptist Political Theology

By Dustin Bruce

In 1644, seven baptistic congregational churches within the greater London area formulated and distributed a document titled "A Confession of Faith of Seven Congregations or Churches of Christ in London, Which Are Commonly but Unjustly Called Anabaptists."[1] While historians have long speculated that the timing of this entrance onto the public stage by English Particular Baptists was prompted by increasing hostility toward Separatists, Matthew Bingham has convincingly argued that these seven churches were responding to an invitation by the Westminster Assembly to bring forward their reasons

---

[1] For the text of the document, see William L. Lumpkin, *Baptist Confessions of Faith*, ed. Bill J. Leonard, rev. ed. (Valley Forge: Judson, 2011), 131–59.

for dissenting from the established practice of baptizing infants.[2] As Bingham stated, "By submitting their own confession of faith for public evaluation, the seven London churches were declaring that their congregations and ministers were as valid as those established and ordained by the national church."[3]

The Westminster Assembly had been appointed by the "Long Parliament" through an ordinance issued on June 12, 1643, for the purpose of reforming the English state church. As a creation of the state, the English legislature determined which divines would be invited to participate, as well as which members of parliament would fill the thirty slots set aside for their involvement. As dissenters from the English state church, these early Baptists were not merely seeking to define themselves over against the ecclesiology of the Church of England, but to challenge the reigning political theology as it had come to be developed during the English Reformation. The following essay seeks to survey the church-state synthesis of Western Europe present since the early medieval period, before giving special attention to the English Reformation as the immediate context from which the Baptist movement was birthed.

The Medieval European Political Context

The Reformation of the sixteenth century brought both a religious and political transformation of the European world. Since the Edict of Thessalonica in 381, political life had been wed to the Christian church in an official capacity. Christendom, as it came to be known, developed from the merging of the two swords: the sword of the state, whether Roman or otherwise, and the sword of the Word of God, as mediated through the church. While this merger of church and state was always

---

[2] Matthew C. Bingham, *Orthodox Radicals: Baptist Identity in the English Revolution* (New York: Oxford University), 56–61.

[3] Bingham, 58.

fraught, it nevertheless held for centuries as the de facto context of the majority of Europe.

The first significant challenge to the concept of Christendom occurred in the early fifth century when barbarian invaders laid siege to Rome.[4] Because Christians had begun to associate the strength of the church with the strength of the Roman state, many were distraught upon hearing of Alaric's sack of Rome in AD 410. This widespread sense of desperation, along with accusations from pagans that Christians were to blame for Rome's demise, prompted Augustine of Hippo (354–430) to write his magisterial *City of God*. For Augustine, Christians should not be overly distraught by the destruction of any earthly political entity, because the church can never be identified with a human political institution. Every Christian belongs to two cities: a city of man and the city of God.

With the progressive weakening and eventual breakup of the Roman Empire, political entities became more localized and varied across Europe and the Mediterranean. Feudal kingdoms and powerful city-states dotted the landscape of the once unified Roman Empire. Only in the eastern half of the empire did a version of the Roman Empire survive, centered in Constantinople (modern-day Istanbul). While the glories of old Rome were no more, medieval Europe perpetuated a version of Christendom that made the Roman Church the primary unifying factor of European society. There is perhaps no better example of the merger between church and state in the medieval period than the coronation of Charlemagne as Holy Roman Emperor on Christmas Day in AD 800 by Pope Leo III.

The late medieval European political context witnessed the rise of nation-states, which often strained but did not break the religious unity of Europe centered around the authority of the Roman Catholic Church and her bishop, the pope. Struggles for power between monarchs and the Roman hierarchy were not uncommon, as regents such as the French and

---

[4] Peter Brown, *The Rise of Western Christendom*, rev. ed. (West Sussex, UK: Wiley-Blackwell, 2013), 93–106.

English kings sought to consolidate their wealth and authority over against an increasingly influential church hierarchy. While these power struggles often stressed the fabric of European religious life, it would be the work of Reformers such as Martin Luther and Ulrich Zwingli that would ultimately rend the garment of Christendom.

Church and State in the Lutheran Reformation

In the popular imagination, the spark of Reformation was lit on October 31, 1517, as Martin Luther (1483–1546) nailed his Ninety-Five Theses to the chapel door in Wittenberg, Germany. Luther, an Augustinian monk and professor of theology at the local university, had taken aim at the selling of indulgences, a practice of the late medieval Roman Catholic Church that he considered out of step with Scripture. Intended as a call for debate over the theology and practice of the church, Luther's Ninety-Five Theses spread like wildfire across German lands, enabled by the recent technological innovation of the printing press.

Through his study of Scripture and church history, Luther had come to redefine God's message of salvation as occurring "by faith alone" and reduced religious authority as ultimately deriving from "Scripture alone."[5] The German Reformer rejected papal authority and the papacy rejected him by issuing a papal bull in June 1520 that censured much of Luther's teaching and demanded he recant within sixty days or face excommunication. After declaring the originator of the papal bull the Antichrist and offering multiple defenses of his teaching, Luther was formally excommunicated from the Roman Catholic Church in 1521.

At this point, Luther had not only run afoul of the papacy but also of important secular rulers as well. In April 1521, Luther was summoned to appear before the Holy Roman Emperor, Charles V, at the Diet of Worms.

---

[5] Mark Greengrass, *Christendom Destroyed: Europe 1517–1648* (New York: Penguin), 5–6.

After defending himself against accusations of heresy and refusing to recant, Luther was condemned as a heretic and, therefore, an outlaw by the imperial diet. To preserve his life, Luther was rushed from the city of Worms to be "kidnapped" by friendly forces and hidden away at the Wartburg Castle. While posing as a knight named Junker Jörg, Luther spent most of a year translating the New Testament into German.

The condemned Luther received such protection due to his relationship with Frederick the Wise, the Elector of Saxony, a man he is reported to have never spoken to in person. Frederick had founded the University of Wittenberg in 1502, and Luther had become the star faculty member of the burgeoning institution since arriving in 1512. As the elector of the wealthy region of Saxony, Frederick's support was vital to the rule of Charles V as Holy Roman Emperor. With such leverage, Frederick offered critical protection to Luther and the early Protestant movement.

As Protestantism took hold, the role of the magistrate came to the forefront of questions about how society should be ordered. While Luther's theological vision maintained the presence of the "two swords" as medieval Christendom had, the fracturing of ecclesiastical authority resulted in the state increasing its role.[6] Luther's hopes for an improved Christendom can be seen as early as 1520, when Luther published three significant writings that argued for a new vision of German society. In his *To the Christian Nobility of the German Nation Concerning the Improvement of the Christian Estate*, the reformer addressed the secular rulers in Germany with an appeal to reenvision their authority as those entrusted by God with the welfare of their state. In the text, addressed to Emperor Charles V and the nobility of Germany, Luther argued that since the religious authorities had failed to bring about necessary reforms, the secular rulers now had the responsibility to bring about the needed changes. He was clear, however, that he was not ascribing the state authority over the religious sphere. As Christians themselves, the German rulers had the right to push for reform

---

[6] Greengrass, 7.

within the church. As Christians with power and influence, they had an obligation to do so.[7]

In his appeal to the German rulers, Luther described three walls constructed by the Roman hierarchy for their protection. First, since spiritual authority is higher than secular authority, secular rulers could make no claim of jurisdiction over the church. Second, only the pope possesses definitive authority to interpret Scripture. Third, there was the claim that only the pope could summon a council. With these three walls firmly in place, the burden lay with the secular rulers to bring about reforms aimed at the health of the church. Luther recommended calling a council to institute the needed reforms, not so that the secular authorities could seize spiritual authority but correct it.[8] The Council of Nicaea, he reminded his readers, was called for by the emperor Constantine.

While Luther called for reform based on theological and ecclesial grounds, his *To the Christian Nobility* also built on long-standing complaints that the Roman church took advantage of the German peoples, leaving them economically weaker. Germans were left poor so that the vast bureaucracy of the Roman church could grow rich and the pope could go "about in such a worldly and ostentatious style that neither the king nor emperor can equal or approach him."[9] The German princes bore a responsibility to protect the people from such "rapacious wolves."[10]

In his 1523 work, *Temporal Authority: To What Extent It Should Be Obeyed*, Luther articulated a vision for how secular authority ought to be understood by Christians. According to Luther, God established two

---

[7] James M. Estes, "Introduction to *To the Christian Nobility of the German Nation Concerning the Improvement of the Christian Estate*," in *The Roots of Reform*, ed. Timothy J. Wengert (Minneapolis: Fortress, 2015), 369–70.

[8] Estes, 372.

[9] Martin Luther, "To the Christian Nobility of the German Nation Concerning Improvement of the Christian Estate," in *The Roots of Reform*, ed. Timothy J. Wengrert (Minneapolis: Fortress, 2015), 393.

[10] Luther, 397.

regimes within the world: the spiritual and the temporal. As he explained in a 1526 work, *Whether Soldiers, Too, Can Be Saved*, God has "erected two different governments among people: one spiritual, governed by his Word, without the sword, through which people become pious [good] and just so that they obtain eternal life with its righteousness. . . . The other is the secular government ruled by the sword, so that whoever will not become pious and just through the Word to eternal life, nevertheless will be compelled through the secular government to be pious and just before the world."[11]

In the mid-1520s, circumstances associated with the Peasants' War, a popular uprising of peasants that started in the Black Forest in May 1524, pushed Luther to develop his understanding of secular authority in new ways.[12] While numerous factors were at play leading up to the rebellion, leaders of the Peasants' War cited Luther's evangelical ideas as a reason for their revolt. While Luther initially tried to respond in moderation with his *Admonition to Peace* (1525), events spiraled out of control, and to justify severe action on the part of the civic rulers, Luther produced his infamous treatise *Against the Robbing and Murdering Hordes of Peasants* (1525). According to the German reformer, the call to uphold the social order amid rebellion warranted violent action to be taken by the magistrates.[13] By siding decisively with the princes during this tumultuous time, Luther had ensured the "evangelical clergy would effectively become servants of the state."[14]

---

[11] Martin Luther, "Whether Soldiers, Too, Can Be Saved," in *Luther's Works*, ed. Helmut T. Lehmann and Robert C. Schultz (Minneapolis: Fortress, 1526), 99.

[12] James M. Estes, "Introduction to On Secular Authority: To What Extent Should It be Obeyed," in *Christian Life in the World*, ed. Hans J. Hillerbrand, The Annotated Luther (Minneapolis: Fortress Press, 2017), 85–86.

[13] Carter Lindberg, *The European Reformations*, rev. ed. (Malden: Wiley-Blackwell), 156.

[14] Andrew Pettegree, *Brand Luther* (New York: Penguin Random House), 244.

Church and State in the Swiss Reformation

While Luther led the Reformation within German lands, an associated but distinct reform movement gained traction within Swiss territories. These two manifestations of Protestantism would develop distinct theological emphases and articulate political theologies suited for their different contexts. Whereas German lands were primarily divided into separate territories controlled by princes, the Swiss Confederation was divided into cantons, city-states with their surrounding territories. While both German and Swiss regions officially fell under the authority of the Holy Roman Empire, the Swiss Confederation had loosened its ties to its Hapsburg overlords considerably during the fifteenth century.[15] From within this distinct political environment, Ulrich Zwingli would establish a trajectory of leading state-sponsored religious reform that others such as John Calvin would continue.

Ulrich Zwingli (1484–1531)

Whereas Luther's call for reformation centered around the publication and distribution of the Ninety-Five Theses, Zwingli's protest against the errors and abuses of late medieval Roman Catholicism came to be associated with the 1522 "Affair of the Sausages."[16] Christoph Froschauer, a local printer working to prepare a new edition of the epistles of Paul, broke the Lenten fast by serving sausages to twelve hungry laborers. Authorities arrested Froschauer for his disregard of the publicly mandated fast. Zwingli, who had been present for the occasion but did not partake of the sausages, responded with a sermon, "On the Choice and Freedom of Foods," on March 23, 1522. The sermon was soon expanded into a pamphlet, where

---

[15] For an overview of the Swiss Confederation during the period leading up to the Reformation, see Regula Schmid, "The Swiss Confederation before the Reformation," in *A Companion to the Swiss Reformation*, ed. Amy N. Burnett and Emidio Campi (Leiden: Brill, 2016).

[16] Lindberg, *European Reformations*, 161.

Zwingli argued that since the Lenten fast was neither commanded nor prohibited in Scripture, Christians were free to either eat or not eat meat during Lent.

Zwingli had been called to serve as pastor of the Great Minster in Zurich in 1518, largely based on his reputation as a preacher.[17] A trained humanist, the Swiss reformer had received a bachelor's and master's degree at the University of Basel before serving as a parish priest in Glarus from 1506 to 1516 and a chaplain within a monastery in Einsiedeln from 1516 to 1518. Having gained notoriety for his learned exposition while at Einsiedeln, when he began his public ministry in Zurich on January 1, 1519, Zwingli departed from the established practice by beginning a series of connected expositions through the whole text of Matthew's gospel. Rather than preach the traditional text based on the church's calendar, the pastor of the Great Minster would choose an entire book that he felt to be relevant to his congregation and then exposit the book in its entirety week after week.

Zwingli's very appointment provides insight into the context in which the reformer developed his political theology. Zurich, a city of about 6,000 in the sixteenth century, was located within the diocese of Constance, one of the largest in the Holy Roman Empire.[18] Due to the size of the diocese and Zurich's distance from the bishop's headquarters in Constance, the Swiss canton had achieved practical independence to run its affairs since the late fifth century.[19] As such, Zwingli's invitation to assume the pulpit of the Great Minster came not from Hugo von Hohenlandenberg, the bishop of Constance, but from the town council of Zurich.

Two councils governed the city of Zurich.[20] The Great Council was composed of 162 members drawn from the twelve craft guilds and

---

[17] Lindberg, 164.

[18] Lindberg, 165.

[19] Bruce Gordon, *Zwingli: God's Armed Prophet* (New Haven: Yale University, 2021), 46.

[20] Lindberg, *European Reformations*, 165.

constables. The Small Council numbered fifty members taken from a similar pool of eligible men. The Small Council tended to the day-to-day affairs of Zurich, but since half of the membership changed every six months, there was always the possibility for volatility. Two *Bürgermeisters* chaired the councils for six-month terms.[21] On occasion the two councils would combine to form the Council of Two Hundred, primarily to arbitrate matters of foreign policy.[22] Whereas Luther had primarily concerned himself with the favor of one man, the elector of Saxony, Zwingli's context demanded he persuade a civic government controlled by the two councils.

While Zwingli called for reforms in his preaching and teaching, the city councils controlled the pace of such reforms by calling for two public disputations to be held so that they might hear from proponents and opponents of reform. The first public disputation was held on January 29, 1523, at the Zurich town hall. The bishop of Constance and other clergy were invited to meet before the Zurich Council of Two Hundred to speak to the future of religious life in the city. The bishop did not attend, unwilling to legitimize this unprecedented action with his presence. Bruce Gordon, capturing the significance of this unusual movement, stated that the "theology and governance of the Church were being removed from the episcopal courts and universities and placed in the city hall."[23] The disputation was weighted in favor of reform with the debate occurring in German rather than Latin and Scripture being put forward as the standard by which the council would judge the outcome. In preparation, Zwingli wrote his Sixty-Seven Articles, which affirmed salvation by faith alone and the authority of Scripture while disavowing numerous late medieval Roman Catholic beliefs and practices as unbiblical. Zwingli's arguments carried the day, and the Council of Two Hundred instructed all clergy within its jurisdiction to preach only from biblical texts. The disputation was a positive development

---

[21] Gordon, *Zwingli*, 46.

[22] Technically, the Council of Two Hundred was composed of 212 members.

[23] Gordon, *Zwingli*, 89.

for the burgeoning Reformed movement, but a development that came under the authority of the civic rulers of the city.

For the Swiss reformer, depending upon the city government to legislate reform of the church flowed from a political theology that understood both the civil magistrate and the church as two aspects of the Christian covenant community.[24] As Baker put it, Zwingli "held to a single sphere rather than to Luther's doctrine of the two kingdoms. Zwingli argued that the elders of the New Testament were the equivalent of the magistrate of his day. The council of the Christian city thus rightfully ruled both the civil community and the church, which were virtually identical."[25] By implication the civic leaders and ministers were to cooperate for the religious good of the Christian community.

Very much a Swiss patriot himself, Zwingli spent the last years of his life pursuing alliances with other Protestants and seeking to further the cause of reform within the Swiss Confederation. By 1531 tensions between the Protestant and Roman Catholic cantons had peaked, and a Zurich-led economic blockade was instituted against those cantons who refused to allow Protestant preaching.[26] The Roman Catholic cantons responded with force, surprising Zurich with a much larger army in the second battle of Kappel. Committed to the cause of reform and Zurich, Zwingli accompanied the forces to battle, intending to serve as a chaplain but armed, nevertheless. Injured during the rout of Zurich's army, Zwingli's identity was discovered by the opposing army. Struck with a final blow, Zwingli's body was quartered and burned with dung the following day. Zwingli was dead, but the cause of reform within Swiss lands was not. Other Protestant leaders would continue to build upon Zwingli's vision for a reformed Protestantism.

---

[24] Andries Raath and Shaun De Freitas, "Calling and Resistance: Huldrych Zwingli's (1484–1531) Political Theology and His Legacy of Resistance to Tyranny," *Koers: Bulletin for Christian Scholarship* 67, no. 1 (January 2012): 3.

[25] J. Wayne Baker, "Zwinglianism," in *The Oxford Encyclopedia of the Reformation*, ed. Hans J. Hillerbrand (New York: Oxford University, 1996), 324.

[26] Lindberg, *European Reformations*, 186.

John Calvin (1509–1564)

The most prominent reformer associated with the Reformed Protestant movement was the Genevan reformer, John Calvin. A second-generation reformer, as compared to Luther and Zwingli, Calvin was able to build upon the work of his predecessors even as he advanced the cause of reform. A native of France, Calvin spent most of his years in Geneva as a refugee of sorts, only being granted citizenship five years before his death. For most of his life, Calvin maintained an uneasy relationship with the civic authorities, both French and Swiss. Such was the context in which he developed his political theology.

In 1536, while traveling through the Swiss city of Geneva, Calvin was conscripted to lead reform efforts in the city by Guillaume Farel (1489–1565). Two months prior, the General Council of Geneva had voted to pursue reform within the city largely under the influence of Farel.[27] Calvin, who reluctantly accepted Farel's demand that he stay and lead reform, had been living in Basel for some time after being forced to flee from Paris in 1533 upon being implicated as the probable author behind a mildly evangelical address given by his friend and rector at the University of Paris, Nicolas Cop (1501–1540). By the time of his arrival in Geneva, Calvin had released his first edition of *Institutes of the Christian Religion* (1536) but remained a relatively unknown figure. Over the following years, the reputation of Calvin and his new home would grow among Reformed Protestants.

The structure of the civil government in Geneva was like Zurich's in that two councils largely controlled civic affairs and, by 1527, the religious affairs of the city as well.[28] By 1530, Farel and others had stirred the city

---

[27] Francis Higman, "Farel, Guillaume," in *The Oxford Encyclopedia of the Reformation*, ed. Hans J. Hillerbrand (New York: Oxford University, 1996).

[28] Matthew J. Tuininga, *Calvin's Political Theology and the Public Engagement of the Church: Christ's Two Kingdoms* (Cambridge: Cambridge University), 62–63.

with calls for reform. When the bishop of the city sought to intervene, the Small Council deposed him, and by May 1536, the decision to abolish the Mass and canon law was affirmed by the General Council of the city. When Calvin agreed to stay in Geneva and serve as one of the pastors of the newly Reformed church there, the city government had grown accustomed to exercising control over ecclesial matters for some time.

Calvin's first period of service in Geneva proved to be a famously troubled season for the young pastor. While the issues at play cannot be solely attributed to differences surrounding Calvin's political theology and that of the town's magistracy, differences on how the state and church relate to one another certainly stand at the center of the reasons for his dismissal in 1538.[29] The most contentious issues involved the discipline and order of the church in Geneva. For the young reformer, that the worship and discipline of the church should be in the hands of the clergy seemed beyond dispute.[30] However, in most of the reforming Swiss cities and particularly in the influential military protector of Geneva, Bern, religious authority remained in the hands of the civic authorities. Furthermore, much of the Genevan citizenry protested trading the religious rule by a bishop for a new version of religious rule by a handful of Protestant pastors.

The conflict came to a head when the Council of Two Hundred ordered the city's pastors to conform to the Bernese practice of offering unleavened bread for the Lord's Supper. Calvin and Farel vocally opposed the Council's ruling, and on Easter Sunday 1538, the two pastors refused to offer the Lord's Supper to their congregations, flouting the Council's instructions to comply with Bern's wishes and resulting in their own expulsion. Through these actions, as Tuininga stated, it became clear to the city officials "that they did not understand the distinction between the commonwealth and

---

[29] Tuininga, 65.
[30] Lindberg, *European Reformations*, 241.

the church in the same terms as Calvin did."[31] Given three days to leave the city, Calvin fled to Strasbourg, where he served for three years as a pastor of a French-speaking congregation under the oversight of Martin Bucer (1491–1551).

By the mid-1540s, the Genevan magistrates were recruiting Calvin to return to the city and continue the work of reform.[32] Having made a pleasant life in Strasbourg, he was initially hesitant but finally heeded the call to return, resuming his ministry in Geneva in September 1541. In one sense, Calvin downplayed the events of the past several years of his life, choosing for his sermon the exact text of Scripture he had left off at before his banishment. But in another sense, Calvin learned from his previous trials, negotiating the right to draft a set of ecclesiastical ordinances for the city, which would formalize a path for institutional reform of the church in Geneva. Submitted to the magistrates weeks after his return, Calvin's proposals were approved with only minor changes and enacted into law by city officials.

While Calvin found himself in a much stronger position within Geneva, conflict over where the authority to exercise church discipline ultimately derived from would continue to be a source of strife between the Genevan authorities and their famous reformer. Under Calvin's leadership, a consistory of pastors was formed to judge potential cases of church discipline. However, the civil authorities maintained that the power to excommunicate members of the Genevan church ultimately rested in their hands. The conflict remained until 1555, when the Genevan Council of Two Hundred affirmed that the consistory's authority over church discipline stood supreme.[33] Four years later, Calvin was finally granted formal citizenship by Genevan authorities, allowing him to officially become part of the city he had so long served.

---

[31] Tuininga, *Calvin's Political Theology*, 65.
[32] Lindberg, *European Reformations*, 247.
[33] Tuininga, *Calvin's Political Theology*, 80.

Church and State in the English Reformation

The English Reformation, the more immediate context from which the early Baptist movement originated, borrowed significantly from the Lutheran and Reformed Protestant movements but unfolded within a quite different state context. Early calls for reform were issued by William Tyndale (1494–1536) and others in the early 1520s as Lutheran and Reformed writings began circulating within English circles. However, the reformation of the English church would only gain traction at the behest of the monarch, King Henry VIII.

Henry VIII (r. 1509–1547)

Henry was born the second son of Henry VII (1457–1509), becoming the heir apparent to the English crown upon the death of his brother, Arthur, in 1502. Not only did Henry take Arthur's place in royal succession, but he also married his brother's wife, Catherine of Aragon. His brother had only been married to Catherine for about six months when he died, and the pope granted a special dispensation for Henry to marry his brother's wife, partially upon the grounds that the marriage had not yet been consummated. After failing to produce a male heir with Catherine, Henry concluded their marriage was cursed by God and sought to have Pope Clement VII (1478–1534) rescind the dispensation issued by his predecessor that had allowed the two to marry.[34]

The pope concluded that the appeal did not have a strong basis in canon law, but more important, the Vatican was threatened by Charles V

---

[34] Hans J. Hillerbrand, *The Division of Christendom: Christianity in the Sixteenth Century* (Louisville: Westminster John Knox), 211. Henry's reasoning was based upon Lev 20:21, which states, "If a man marries his brother's wife, it is impurity. He has violated the intimacy that belongs to his brother; they will be childless."

(1500–1558), Catherine's nephew, whose canons were trained on the papal city. Henry, realizing the denial was political, initiated a debate among the religious scholars of England and the Continent. For several years, experts and lawyers debated the "king's great matter" without drawing firm conclusions. Finally, the scholar Thomas Cranmer (1489–1556) recommended that the issue of a man marrying his brother's wife should be submitted to the scholarly divines to be examined based on the authority of Scripture. Rather than have Henry continue suffering due to papal politics, his conscience could be quieted on the basis of Holy Scripture.

With all attempts at having Henry's marriage annulled by the pope having come to naught, the king replaced Cardinal Thomas Wolsey as his chancellor with Sir Thomas More. Thomas Cromwell (ca. 1485–1540) also expanded his influence at court and began enacting Cranmer's plan to secure Henry's divorce.[35] Cromwell was also advocating that the English crown replace the pope as the supreme religious authority in England, an idea Cranmer had also voiced.

By 1531, Henry was taking steps toward a break from Rome. First, in early 1531 Henry placed the clergy under a praemunire, which prohibited any papal or foreign assertion against the king's supremacy.[36] In 1532, he pushed through legislation known as the Submission of the Clergy, which forbade the clergy to pass any laws without the king's permission. When the archbishop of Canterbury, William Warham, died in 1532, much of the groundwork had been laid for breaking from Rome.[37] However, Henry would need a new archbishop of Canterbury, and Thomas Cranmer was his obvious choice.

---

[35] Lindberg, *European Reformations*, 302.
[36] Leslie Williams, *Emblem of Faith Untouched: A Short Life of Thomas Cranmer* (Grand Rapids: Eerdmans, 2016), 32.
[37] Williams, 33.

Cranmer's Reformation

While Henry was heading toward a break from the authority of the church at Rome, the English monarch was not intending to depart from Roman Catholic theology and practice. Even so, he had several Protestant sympathizers close to him, including Anne Boleyn. For his part, Cranmer appeared to be a traditionalist when it came to doctrine. But while serving as the English ambassador to the court of Charles V, the soon-to-be archbishop of Canterbury had come through a reformation of his own. While in Nuremburg, now famous for hosting the post–World War II trials, Cranmer befriended the leading reformer of that city, Andreas Osiander. The Nuremburg pastor had been the only German reformer to come out in favor of Henry's annulment (Luther had recommended bigamy). And while Cranmer had not found Lutheran writings persuasive in print, his opinion shifted during his time in the German city. Cranmer "return[ed] to England a Protestant enthusiast,"[38] having seen the actual Reformation in practice. Moreover, it was not only doctrine the Englishman received from Osiander, but he married the German reformer's niece as well.

After Cranmer arrived back in England in January 1533, the next five months saw the creation of a new queen, a new heir, and a "new" church.[39] Anne Boleyn had become pregnant in early December 1532 with the child we would come to know as Queen Elizabeth I. On January 25, 1533, the king and Anne married. Now Henry's marriage to Catherine had to be undone. On April 7, Parliament passed the Act in Restraint of Appeals, which effectively prohibited Catherine from appealing a decision to Rome. A trial then began on May 10, 1533, to determine the legitimacy of Henry's first marriage. On May 23, a decision was announced. Cranmer declared that the "pretended matrimony of Henry, king of

---

[38] Williams, 164n31.
[39] Williams, 36.

England, and Katherine the queen, hath been and is none at all; being prohibited by both the law of God and nature."[40] The two were no longer allowed to live together and were free to remarry. Ironically, Henry was threatened with excommunication if he refused to comply with the ruling he had worked so hard to secure. On May 28, Cranmer judged Henry and Anne's marriage as lawful. She was officially crowned queen on June 1. Elizabeth was born on September 7; conceived out of wedlock, she was now the rightful heir. Catherine was stripped of her title; Mary, her only living child with Henry, was declared a bastard; and the two of them were forced to remain in England, an act that certainly contributed to their further humiliation.

Pope Clement VII drew up a sentence of excommunication for Henry on July 11, 1533, but waited for several months before sending it, hoping he could regain influence in England. His efforts were to no avail. By April 1534, Parliament had ratified the Act of Supremacy, making the English monarch the "supreme head" of the English church.

While the English church was now separated from the papacy, a two-party religious system was effectively operating within the church.[41] Henry VIII had firm control, but both Protestant sympathizers and papal sympathizers vied for influence. Apart from the reign of Elizabeth I, this situation would lead to decades upon decades of turmoil.

As archbishop of Canterbury, Cranmer would seek to lead the English church through these deep divisions, guided by two primary convictions: first, the authority of Scripture over any other authority, and second, the royal supremacy of the English crown.[42] Cranmer's vision of an English church that existed under the authority of the state would eventually be challenged as unwise and unscriptural by Separatists and ultimately by Baptists. Such challenges, however, would not gain momentum for decades.

---

[40] Williams, 39.
[41] Williams, 41.
[42] Williams, 41.

Edward VI (r. 1547–1553)

At age nine, Edward VI ascended the throne. Under his rule—or, more accurately, under the leadership of his advisors—Edward quickly established the Reformation in England.[43] His uncle, Edward Seymour, had been appointed lord protector and Duke of Somerset. He immediately ended the prosecution of Protestants and repealed most of the heresy laws, including the Six Articles. Given this newfound freedom, many English Protestants returned to their homeland. Scholars from the Continent, such as Peter Martyr Vermigli and Martin Bucer, were invited to serve in English universities. By this time, the primary reforming influence on the English had shifted from Lutheran to Reformed.

The primary architect of the English Reformation was Cranmer.[44] Clerical marriage flourished, much to Cranmer's personal approval. He released the first edition of a prayer book in 1549 with the aim of setting the tone for the English Reformation. In 1552, the prayer book was revised and reissued to remove any ambiguities that allowed for Roman Catholics to worship according to it. The Book of Common Prayer sought to avoid extremes in doctrine and liturgy while ultimately upholding Protestant doctrine. In 1553, Cranmer produced a statement of faith for the English church with the Forty-Two Articles. In the doctrinal statement, Cranmer sought to balance Lutheran and Reformed doctrine. His work did not initially last long, but it formed the basis of the Thirty-Nine Articles, which were issued by Elizabeth and continue as the doctrinal statement of the Church of England.

Tragically for the cause of the English Reformation, the sickly Edward VI died of tuberculosis on July 6, 1553. And after a failed attempt to insert Edward's cousin, Lady Jane Grey, as queen, the crown fell to Edward's eldest sister, the scorned Roman Catholic Mary Tudor.

---

[43] Lindberg, *European Reformations*, 306.
[44] Lindberg, 307.

The Reign of Bloody Mary (r. 1553–1558)

Just as many feared, Mary Tudor's ascension to the throne meant a temporary end to the progress of the English Reformation. Ironically, Mary's overwhelming concern for Roman Catholicism would ultimately help strengthen the Protestant cause.[45]

Mary, the daughter of Catherine of Aragon, sought to bring the English people out from a state of mortal sin by bringing them back into alliance with the pope. Politically, she failed to realize she was made queen only out of English loyalty to the Tudor lineage. Her eagerness to restore Catholicism resulted in her allying the English with the Spanish, primarily through a marriage to her cousin, Prince Philip of Spain. Furthermore, she relied heavily on her cousin, Cardinal Reginald Pole, to restore and enforce Roman Catholicism in the land.

Cranmer, whom Mary blamed for much of her troubles, was arrested and jailed for treason in November 1553. Cardinal Pole would follow him as archbishop of Canterbury, and in late 1554, official reunification with Rome was complete. The Mass was restored, Parliament repealed the anti-papal legislation, and the old heresy laws were reinstated. With a legal basis for the persecution of Protestants now in place, Mary and Pole inspired heresy trials that led to the burning of around 300 Protestants, including Cranmer.

Due to Mary's brutality, hundreds of Protestants fled to continental Europe, most landing in Reformed cities like Geneva. The way these Reformed communities were structured proved quite influential on the English. The order of worship and society witnessed on the Continent left the English eager to bring further reformation back to England. These English refugees would soon see an opening for such reform. Mary's health was in serious decline by the fall of 1558, and after naming Elizabeth as her successor, she died in November of that year.

---

[45] Lindberg, 308.

Elizabeth I and the Via Media

Elizabeth embarked on her forty-five-year reign over the English people at the end of 1558. Under her leadership, England would turn permanently Protestant and become a leading nation of Europe.[46]

Elizabeth sought to establish a "middle way" in England and thus avoid the extremes that had not only characterized the reigns of her siblings, but also were beginning to result in various wars of religion throughout Europe. Like her father, she kept both Catholics and radical Protestants in check by forging a *via media* that would characterize the Anglican church. What was most important for Elizabeth was outward conformity. She famously admitted that she did not wish to "make windows into men's souls."[47]

In 1559, what came to be known as the Elizabethan Settlement was begun. In April of that year, Parliament passed the Act of Supremacy, which confirmed Elizabeth as the supreme governor of the English church. Furthermore, a third edition of the Book of Common Prayer was issued with some minor changes to allow for vestments and a return of the communion table to the center.

In 1563, Parliament approved the Thirty-Nine Articles as the official doctrinal statement of the English church. This was a minor revision to Cranmer's Forty-Two Articles. However, they remained overtly evangelical: advocating justification by faith and allowing for clerical marriage. Lindberg explains that "the retention of Catholic vestments and liturgy allowed the traditional, illiterate person to experience Anglican worship much as he or she had experienced Catholic worship. At the same time, the use of English instead of Latin allowed the literate Protestant to hear a Reformation

---

[46] Lindberg, 310.

[47] Mark Konnert, *Early Modern Europe: The Age of Religious War, 1559–1715* (n.p.: Broadview, 2006; Toronto: University of Toronto Press, 2008), 137. Citations are to the UTP edition.

message in the sermons and prayers set within a Reformed theology framed by the Thirty-Nine Articles."[48]

While Elizabeth forged a remarkable consensus and left an indelible mark upon the English people through her long reign, there were also many radical Protestants offended by the *via media* of the English church. For the "Puritans," as they would come to be known, the Church of England was "but halflie reformed" and needed to be further purified of all Roman Catholic vestiges.[49]

Conclusion: The Legacy of State-Controlled Reform and *Via Media* for Early Baptists

Upon the death of the childless Elizabeth I, James VI of Scotland inherited the English throne, becoming James I of England, beginning the Stuart dynasty, and uniting all of England, Scotland, and Ireland under one monarch for the first time. While there was great anticipation among the English Puritans that James I would pursue further reformation of the English church, the reform-minded English would ultimately be disappointed. Although James I had grown up within a Presbyterian church context in Scotland, he preferred the structure and approach of the Church of England. His response to the Puritan movement has often been summarized by his belief "no bishop, no king." For James I, the episcopal hierarchy reinforced the monarchial system of government, and he had every intention of maintaining both.

Within a context that affirmed the English regent as the supreme authority for the English church, Puritans continued to push for further reform of the church to little avail. Many would conclude they could no longer

---

[48] Lindberg, 312.

[49] William Fuller, "Booke to the queene," cited in Patrick Collinson, *The Elizabethan Puritan Movement*, Routledge Library Editions: Puritanism, vol. 3 (1967; London: Routledge, 2021), 29.

wait for the civil and ecclesiastical authorities to bring the changes the more Puritan-minded saw as necessary. A movement of Separatists emerged, eager to pursue a "Reformation without tarying for anie,"[50] even if that meant forming churches outside the state church of England. The reign of James I's son, Charles I (1600–1649), only exacerbated tensions, leading ultimately to his own execution following the English Civil War.

As the early English Baptists gradually emerged from within the English Puritan and Separatist movement, the conviction that the state should have no jurisdiction over their religious belief and practice was nothing short of radical. Since the earliest days of Luther's reform efforts, the magistracy had played a defining role in breaking from Roman Catholicism and forging a new Protestant church. Baptists would remain Protestant, indebted to the likes of Luther, Zwingli, and Calvin for their theological contributions. But Baptists would call for a new relationship to form between the civil sphere and the church. As Timothy George has stated, "For Baptists the great doctrines of the Reformation were refracted through the prism of persecution and dissent which informed their intense advocacy of religious liberty and the separation of church and state."[51] By grasping how closely church and state had functioned together to bring about the Reformation, one understands how significant of an action it was for a small group of Baptists to challenge the reigning political theology of the Reformation both at the Westminster Assembly and beyond.

---

[50] See Robert Browne, *A Treatise of Reformation without Tarying for Anie* (1582), https://archive.org/details/atreatisereform00socigoog/page/n6/mode/2up.

[51] Timothy George, "The Reformation Roots of the Baptist Tradition," *Review and Expositor* 86 (February 1989): 10.

2

British Baptist Origins: From Thomas Helwys to Andrew Fuller

By Michael A. G. Haykin

Portions of this article were taken or adapted from Michael A. G. Haykin, "Resisting Evil," *Baptist Quarterly* 36, no. 5 (1996): 212–27. DOI: 10.1080/0005576X.1996.11751987. Used by permission.

During the first few years of the American War of Independence, John Sutcliff (1752–1814), fresh from his studies at the Bristol Baptist Academy and ministering in a struggling Baptist cause at Shrewsbury, Shropshire, received a number of letters of encouragement and advice from James Turner (d. 1780), the pastor of Cannon Street Baptist Church in Birmingham.[1] Turner, who was twenty-five years older

---

[1] For a study of Sutcliff's life and ministry, see Michael A. G. Haykin, *One Heart and One Soul: John Sutcliff of Olney, His Friends and His Times* (Durham, UK:

than Sutcliff, seems to have taken the latter under his wing and acted as a kind of spiritual mentor to him. The advice and comments in Turner's fascinating letters cover a broad range of issues from infant baptism to the nature of the pastoral office, from detailed descriptions of the annual meetings of the Baptist association, to which Cannon Street belonged, to observations on the ministry of such Anglican evangelicals as William Romaine (1714–1795). Given the seriousness of the military conflict that was raging in North America, it is not surprising that there are also some occasional references to this war.

For instance, writing to Sutcliff on December 7, 1775, Turner told his young friend that he had been reading numerous pieces about the conflict, including one by the Methodist leader John Wesley (1703–1791) and another by Caleb Evans (1737–1791), who was well known to Sutcliff since he was the tutor at the Bristol Baptist Academy. Turner especially urged Sutcliff to get hold of a pamphlet titled *Americans Against Liberty*, which he personally regarded as "unanswerable," but he was interested in knowing what Sutcliff thought of it. However, Turner was quick to add that he would not at all be disappointed if Sutcliff failed to find a copy, for, he said, "we have work enough on hand without Politics." And a few months later he admitted that "as to politics, they are too great a mystery for my capacity."[2] Despite these remarks, Turner still took the time to read about and reflect on the political affairs of the day. On January 13, 1776, for instance, he informed Sutcliff that he had been thinking further about Wesley's *A Calm Address to Our American Colonies*. Turner did not find the Methodist leader's reflections on the American conflict convincing: "He's a nothing," he bluntly told his friend, "both in politics & Religion."[3]

Evangelical, 1994). For a very brief sketch of Turner's ministry at Cannon Street, see James Hargreaves, *The Life and Memoir of the Late Rev. John Hirst* (Rochdale, UK: Joseph Littlewood, 1816), 345.

[2] James Turner, *Letter to John Sutcliff, December 7, 1775* (Oxford University Angus Library, *Sutcliff Papers*); Turner, *Letter to John Sutcliff, March 19, 1776*.

[3] Turner, *Letter to John Sutcliff, January 13, 1776*.

In claiming there were more pressing concerns than political reflection and involvement, Turner was echoing the viewpoint of many Particular Baptists of his era. True to their seventeenth-century roots, they were conscious that the extension of God's kingdom does not come through political decree or "the authority of the magistrate."[4] Nevertheless, Turner's evident refusal to live in ignorance of the political scene is also characteristic of eighteenth-century Baptists. And this too was part of their heritage. For instance, *The Second London Confession of Faith*, first issued in 1677 and then adopted twelve years later as the doctrinal standard of Particular Baptists in England and Wales, unequivocally affirmed that it is entirely "lawful for Christians" to be involved in the political affairs of the nation, in particular, "to accept, and execute the office of a magistrate."[5] The following essay seeks to detail this dual perspective regarding politics by looking at a number of authors between Thomas Helwys and Andrew Fuller who were key to the origins and establishment of an English Baptist political tradition. This tradition treasured religious liberty, viewed the church and state as separate realms mandated by God, but refused to demonize the political realm as some in the tradition of Anabaptism had done in the era of the Reformation.

"Blessed liberty": Thomas Helwys

This tradition of political theology is usually taken to originate with *A Short Declaration of the Mystery of Iniquity* (1612) by the English General

---

[4] William Carey, *An Enquiry into the Obligations of Christians, to Use Means for the Conversion of the Heathens* (1792; Oxfordshire, UK: Baptist Missionary Society, 1991), 103.

[5] *The Second London Confession of Faith*, 24.2, in William L. Lumpkin, *Baptist Confessions of Faith*, rev. ed. (Valley Forge: Judson, 2011), 281. The way in which eighteenth-century Baptists were far from being politically quietistic is detailed in James E. Bradley, *Religion, Revolution and English Radicalism: Non-conformity in Eighteenth-Century Politics and Society* (Cambridge: Cambridge University, 1990).

Baptist Thomas Helwys (ca. 1550–ca. 1616).[6] Along with John Smyth (ca. 1570–1612), Helwys had established a congregation in the town of Gainsborough, Lincolnshire, that was not part of the Church of England. They refused to accept anyone into the membership of the church unless that person could give a credible testimony of saving faith. Their congregation was part of several churches, now known as Separatists, who were seeking to return to what they understood as a biblical ecclesiology and who had given up the hope that the state church could ever be truly reformed along biblical lines.

In the course of 1607, though, pressure by state authorities to conform to the established church grew severe enough to prompt Smyth and Helwys to seek refuge for their congregation in Holland, which was a haven of religious freedom at the time. Having relocated their Separatist congregation to Amsterdam by 1608, Smyth and Helwys continued to search the Scriptures for the New Testament blueprint of church life. They became convinced that their infant baptism in the Church of England was invalid since the Church of England was not a true church. As they searched the Scriptures on baptism, they were led to Baptistic convictions, and when Smyth despaired of finding someone to administer the rite of baptism, he baptized himself and then baptized Helwys and the rest of their small congregation. Sadly, Smyth and a number of the congregation subsequently left this fledgling body of English Baptists for a Dutch Mennonite community when Smyth and Helwys came to differing convictions regarding Christology and the administration of the ordinances, leaving Helwys to lead the congregation back to England around 1612.[7] Helwys's *The Mystery of Iniquity* seems to have been published in Amsterdam before this return to England. In fact, the book may

---

   [6] "Thomas Helwys was . . . the bold architect of Baptist polity." See William R. Estep Jr., "Thomas Helwys: Bold Architect of Baptist Policy on Church-State Relations," *Baptist History and Heritage* 20, no. 3 (July 1985): 32.
   [7] Estep, "Thomas Helwys," 27–30.

well have led to Helwys's subsequent arrest and death in a London prison around 1616.[8]

For the modern reader, much of *The Mystery of Iniquity* is not easy to read since the book not only espoused the standard Puritan critiques of the Roman church and the episcopacy of the Church of England,[9] but also contained a bitter attack on all of the Puritans who had stayed within the English state church as well as the pedobaptist Separatists who had set up independent congregations as "false prophets."[10] Having once been a Separatist before his embrace of Baptist convictions might explain the severity of Helwys's remarks about the Separatists: their congregations were those of "infidels or unbelievers that are not joined to Christ, and have not put on Christ by baptism."[11] The book has been remembered in the Baptist tradition, though, because of Helwys's celebrated assertion that "men's religion to God is between God and themselves. The king shall not answer for it.

---

[8] For studies of the theological development of John Smyth and Thomas Helwys, see B. R. White, *The English Separatist Tradition from the Marian Martyrs to the Pilgrim Fathers* (London: Oxford University, 1971), 116–141; B. R. White, *The English Baptists of the Seventeenth Century*, A History of the English Baptists, vol. 1, rev. ed. (London: Baptist Historical Society, 1996), 15–23; Estep, "Thomas Helwys," 24–34. See also Anthony B. Cross, "Baptists, Peace, and War: The Seventeenth-Century Foundations," in *Baptists and War: Essays on Baptists and Military Conflict, 1640s–1990s*, ed. Gordon L. Heath and Michael A. G. Haykin, Canadian Baptist Historical Society Series, vol. 2 (Eugene: Pickwick Publications, 2015), 12–16 and Marvin Jones, *The Beginning of Baptist Ecclesiology: The Foundational Contributions of Thomas Helwys*, Monographs in Baptist History, vol. 6 (Eugene: Pickwick, 2017).

[9] Thomas Helwys, *A Short Declaration of the Mystery of Iniquity*, ed. Richard Groves, Classics of Religious Liberty, vol. 1 (Macon: Mercer University, 1998), 5–30.

[10] Helwys, 65 and 91. Brian Haymes has rightly commented on Helwys's work: "*The Mystery of Iniquity* . . . is generally polemical, sometimes sarcastic, and makes for hard reading" ("On Religious Liberty: Re-reading *A Short Declaration of the Mystery of Iniquity* in London in 2005," *Baptist Quarterly* 42, no. 3 (July 2007): 199). Although, see also H. Leon McBeth, *English Baptist Literature on Religious Liberty to 1689* (New York: Arno, 1980), 30.

[11] Helwys, *The Mystery of Iniquity*, ed. Groves, 94.

Neither may the king be judge between God and man. Let them be heretics, Turks [that is, Muslims], Jews, or whatsoever, it appertains not to the earthly power to punish them in the least measure."[12]

What is notable about this remark is that very few in his world or era upheld such a radical idea of religious liberty. But, for Helwys, it was derived from his conviction that "an earthly sword is ordained of God only for an earthly power, and a spiritual sword for a spiritual power."[13] Helwys sent a copy of his book to the monarch, James I (1566–1625), with a handwritten note penned on the flyleaf of the book in which he boldly—many in that day would have said recklessly—told the king, "The king is a mortal man & not God, therefore hath no power over the immortal souls of his subjects, to make laws & ordinances for them, and to set spiritual lords over them. If the king have authority to make spiritual lords & laws, then he is an immortal God and not a mortal man."[14]

According to Helwys, his central desire in the book was that his monarch might allow his people to "enjoy . . . blessed liberty to understand the Scriptures with their own understanding and pray in their public worship with their own spirits."[15] Indeed, as Barrie White has noted, an often-overlooked goal of Helwys's book was to persuade James I "to dismantle the whole of the power of the state establishment of the episcopal church."[16]

Although Helwys's fervent appeal for religious liberty as well as universal religious toleration has been deeply appreciated and heralded by Baptists from the Victorian era to the present day, this appeal was largely forgotten between his day and the close of the Georgian era. Thus, for

---

[12] Helwys, 53.

[13] Helwys, 35.

[14] Helwys, "Inscription" to his *The Mystery of Iniquity*, ed. Groves, vi. Spelling and capitalization have been modernized.

[15] Helwys, *The Mystery of Iniquity*, ed. Groves, 44.

[16] Barrie White, "Early Baptist Arguments for Religious Freedom: Their Overlooked Agenda," *Baptist History and Heritage*, 24, no. 4 (October 1989): 6.

example, when Joseph Ivimey (1773–1834) published the first volume of *A History of the English Baptists*, he specified that a key reason for drawing up this history was the fact that "English Baptists were the first persons who understood the important doctrine of Christian liberty, and who zealously opposed all persecution for the sake of conscience."[17] His discussion of Helwys, though, was negligible and said nothing about Helwys's advocacy of religious toleration.[18] Seven years later, Adam Taylor (1768– 1832), in his history of the General Baptists, did mention the General Baptist defense of religious liberty in words quite similar to those of Ivimey, but he linked it to a piece titled *Persecution for Religion Judg'd and Condemn'd: In a Discourse between an Antichristian and a Christian*, which was published anonymously by the General Baptists in 1615.[19] In fact, only five extant copies exist of the 1612 edition of *The Mystery of Iniquity*, and the work was not published again until 1935 when it appeared in a facsimile edition.[20] Moreover, given the fact that within a century of the founding of the General Baptists, the denomination was in dire straits theologically—many congregations were moving in the directions of either Unitarianism or heterodox Christology during the Georgian era— the organic influence of Helwys on immediate subsequent Baptist political theology is further diminished.

---

[17] Joseph Ivimey, *A History of the English Baptists* (London, 1811), 1:vi.

[18] Ivimey, 1:122–23, 125.

[19] Adam Taylor, *The History of the English General Baptists* (London, 1818), 1:90: "The principal glory of this piece, is the manly, and explicit avowal which the authors make of the true principles of Christian liberty, at a time when they were either unknown or opposed, by almost every other party." See Jones, *The Beginning of Baptist Ecclesiology*, 8–9, who believes that Taylor is referring to *The Mystery of Iniquity*. Adam Taylor was the nephew of the famous General Baptist leader Dan Taylor (1738–1816).

[20] For details of the locale of these five copies, see Haymes, "On Religious Liberty," 215, n. 2. See also the remarks of Groves, "Introduction" to Helwys, *The Mystery of Iniquity*, xxxiv.

"Subject to all civil powers": William Kiffen

Who, then, is at the fountainhead of seventeenth-century English Baptist political thought? If one figure is to be named, it would have to be the London Particular Baptist leader William Kiffen (1616–1701), whose life spanned most of the seventeenth century.[21] Kiffin had rejected Anglican arguments for the idea of a state church by 1638 and within a year had joined a body of believers that eventually became known as Devonshire Square Baptist Church in London. By 1642, he was chosen as their pastor. During the political turmoil of the British Civil Wars (1638–1651) and then the establishment of the Commonwealth (1649–1660), Kiffen became a key leader of the Particular—that is Calvinistic—Baptists, who grew from seven London churches in 1644 to roughly 130 congregations throughout the British Isles and Ireland on the eve of the Restoration of the monarchy in 1660. In the mid-1640s the Presbyterian merchant Josiah Ricraft attacked him as "the grand ringleader" of the Baptists,[22] while an anonymous publication from 1659 has the unforgettable description of him as the "ordained Mufti of all heretics and sectaries."[23]

---

[21] For the life of Kiffen, see especially William Kiffen, *Remarkable Passages in the Life of William Kiffin*, ed. William Orme (London: Burton and Smith, 1823); Barrie R. White, "William Kiffin—Baptist Pioneer and Citizen of London," *Baptist History and Heritage* 2, no. 2 (July 1967): 91–103, 126; Ronald Angelo Johnson, "The Peculiar Ventures of Particular Baptist Pastor William Kiffin and King Charles II of England," *Baptist History and Heritage* 44, no. 1 (Winter 2009): 60–71; Michael A. G. Haykin, "'By the Compass of the Word': The Life and Piety of William Kiffen—A Quatercentenary Appreciation," *The Evangelical Quarterly* 88, no. 4 (2016/2017): 367–79. Also see the tremendous resource on Kiffen's life in Larry J. Kreitzer, *William Kiffen and His World*, vols. 1–7 (Oxford: Centre for Baptist History and Heritage, 2010–2020). I have followed Kreitzer's lead regarding the spelling of Kiffen's name.

[22] Josiah Ricraft, *A Looking Glasse for the Anabaptists and the Rest of the Separatists* (London: Peter Cole and John Hancock, 1645), title page.

[23] Anonymous, *The Life and Approaching Death of William Kiffin* (London: 1659), 2.

Kiffen played a leading role in the drawing up of *The First London Confession of Faith* in 1644, which gave the early Particular Baptists an extremely clear and self-conscious sense of who they were, what they were seeking to achieve, and how they differed from other Puritan bodies at this time.[24] Since Kiffen and his fellow Baptists had been accused of denying the lawfulness of political authority, the final six articles of the *Confession*, Articles XLVIII–LIII,[25] responded by affirming the lawful supremacy of "the King and Parliament," whom subjects are obligated to defend "with our persons, liberties, and estates, with all that is called ours."[26] Nonetheless, if these authorities were to demand obedience in matters that violated key aspects of the Christian faith, believers must

> walk in obedience to Christ [. . .] even in the midst of all trials and afflictions, not accounting our goods, lands, wives, husbands, children, fathers, mothers, brethren, sisters, yea, and our own lives dear unto us, so we may finish our course with joy: remembering always "we ought to obey God rather than men,"[27] and grounding upon the commandment, commission, and promise of our Lord and Master Jesus Christ, who as he has power in heaven and earth, so also has promised, if we keep his commandments which he has given us, to be with us to "the end of the world"[28]: and when we have finished our course, and "kept the faith," to give us the "crown

---

[24] On the role and importance of this confession, see B. R. White, "The Doctrine of the Church in the Particular Baptist Confession of 1644," *Journal of Theological Studies* 19 (1968): 570–90 and his "The Origins and Convictions of the First Calvinistic Baptists," *Baptist History and Heritage* 25, no. 4 (October 1990): 39–47.

[25] The final two articles are both mistakenly numbered LII.

[26] *The Confession of Faith of Those Churches Which Are Commonly (Though Falsely) Called Anabaptists* (London: 1644), Article XLIX.

[27] Acts 5:29 KJV.

[28] Matt 28:19–20 KJV.

of righteousness," which is laid up for all that "love his appearing,"[29] and to whom we must give an account of all our actions, no man being able to discharge us of the same.[30]

The affirmation of the apostles in Acts 5:29 to obey God rather than human authorities and the commission and commandment of Christ in Matt 28:19–20 to go to the nations, make disciples, and baptize these disciples—an important ecclesial text for these early Baptists—undergirded the determination of Kiffen and his fellow Baptists to be obedient to God's commands to evangelize, baptize believers, and plant churches, no matter the cost. It is noteworthy that this obedience was also placed in an eschatological setting: at the Last Judgment, Kiffen and his friends will have to give an account of why they did, or did not, obey what were clear commands of Scripture.

With the establishment of the republican Commonwealth after the execution of the king, Charles I (1600–1649), Kiffen and many of his fellow Particular Baptists showed themselves to be strong supporters of the ruler of England, Oliver Cromwell (1599–1658), and the Cromwellian regime.[31] This was out of loyalty to what they saw as the God-ordained authorities, satisfaction with Cromwell's policy of toleration, and a deep-seated fear of anarchy. However, there were several Particular Baptists, especially in the army in Ireland, who were highly vocal in their criticism of Cromwell after his dissolution of Parliament in December 1653. Kiffen, with two other London Baptist leaders, John Spilsbury (1593–ca. 1668) and a Joseph Sansom, wrote to their Irish Baptist brethren in January 1654, urging them to "consult with that blessed rule of truth which you profess to be your guide, [. . .] for that expresseth no other thing to Christians but exhortations to be

---

[29] 2 Tim 4:7–8 KJV.

[30] *Confession of Faith*, Article LI.

[31] Richard D. Land, "Doctrinal Controversies of English Particular Baptists (1644–1691) as Illustrated by the Career and Writings of Thomas Collier" (PhD diss., Oxford University, 1979), 257.

subject to all civil powers, they being of God, and to pray for all that are in authority, that under them we may live a godly and quiet life in all godliness and honesty."[32] This letter by Kiffen, Spilsbury, and Samson was especially critical of what has been termed the Fifth Monarchy movement, a group of individuals who believed that the prophecies of Daniel 2 were going to be literally fulfilled in their lifetime and that Christ's millenarian kingdom was shortly to be established. While one wing of the Fifth Monarchy movement was moderate, nonviolent, and made up of "harmless Bible students," others had definite revolutionary tendencies and were convinced they should take an active, even violent, role in the fulfillment of the prophecies of Daniel.[33] Open and widespread adherence to these views would have had harmful repercussions for the Baptist movement. Seeking to counteract the influence of the Fifth Monarchists on the Irish Baptists, the latter were urged by Kiffen, Spilsbury, and Samson to reflect upon the fact that the Calvinistic Baptists in the British Isles had a marvelous opportunity to "give a public testimony in the face of the world, that our principles are not such as they have been generally judged by most men to be, which is, we deny authority, and would pull down all magistracy."[34] Another critical moment came in May 1658, when, at the meeting of the Western Association of

---

[32] William Kiffen, John Spilsbury, and Joseph Samson, *Letter [to the Irish Baptist Association], January 20, 1654,* in John Nickolls Jr., ed., *Original Letters and Papers of State Addressed to Oliver Cromwell* (London: William Bowyer, 1743), 159. The spelling of this quote has been modernized.

[33] On the Fifth Monarchists, see Andrew Bradstock, *Radical Religion in Cromwell's England: A Concise History from the English Civil War to the End of the Commonwealth* (London: I.B. Tauris, 2011), *passim*; Martyn Whittock, *When God Was King: Rebels & Radicals of the Civil War & Mayflower Generation* (Oxford: Lion Hudson, 2018), 123–38. The words "harmless Bible students" are those of White, *English Baptists*, 102.

[34] Kiffen, Spilsbury, and Sansom, *Letter* in Nickolls Jr., ed., *Original Letters*, 159–60. On the relationship of the Particular Baptists to the Fifth Monarchy movement, see especially Louise Fargo Brown, *The Political Activities of the Baptists and Fifth Monarchy Men in England During the Interregnum* (New York: Burt Franklin, 1911); White, *English Baptists*, 84–87, 99–101; Marilyn A. Hartman, "'For Christ

Baptist churches in Dorchester, Dorset, some individuals who were sympathetic to the subversive politics of the Fifth Monarchy movement sought to convince the representatives of the churches in the Association to publicly espouse the ideals and goals of this party. Kiffen, who was present with other representatives from the churches in London, successfully persuaded the Western Association not to commit itself in this direction.[35]

It is noteworthy that the Cromwellian republic of the 1650s was marked by a significant measure of religious freedom for all Protestants. In fact, American Baptist pioneer Roger Williams (ca. 1603–1683) once heard Cromwell maintain in a public discussion "with much Christian zeal and affection for his own conscience that he had rather that Mahumetanism [i.e., Mohammedanism or Islam] were permitted amongst us, than that one of God's Children should be persecuted."[36] Rightly did Martyn Lloyd-Jones once call Cromwell the "father of religious tolerance" in England.[37] However, the Anglican hierarchy who came to power with Charles II (1630–1685) after the Restoration of the monarchy tended to view the various religious groupings outside of the established church as political rebels and disturbers of the peace of the nation. Their view seemed to find confirmation in January 1661, when Thomas Venner (1608–1661), a lay preacher attached to a congregation in Swan Alley, London, and a cooper by profession, led an armed revolt to overthrow Charles II. For three days sections of London streets were terrorized by the violence of Venner and his Fifth Monarchist followers, who were convinced that Christ's kingdom was to be ushered

---

and the People': The Ideology of the Good Old Cause, 1653–1660" (PhD diss., Indiana University, 1977), 82–91; Bradstock, *Radical Religion*, 22–24.

[35] White, *English Baptists*, 88.

[36] Roger Williams, "To the truly Christian Reader" in *The Fourth Paper, Presented by Maior Butler, to the Honourable Committee of Parliament, for the Propagating the Gospel of Christ Jesus* (London: G. Calvert, 1652), ii.

[37] D. Martyn Lloyd-Jones, *From Puritanism to Nonconformity*, 2nd ed. (Wales: Bryntirion, 1991), 25. See also Herbert Butterfield, *Historical Development of the Principle of Toleration in British Life* (London: Epworth, 1963), 9–17.

in by such bloody means. Over forty people were killed in street fighting, with Venner himself killing at least three or four people. Unrepentant to the end—he was hanged, drawn, and quartered on January 19, 1661—Venner affirmed his allegiance to "King Jesus" and that what he had done had been for "the propagation of his [i.e., Christ's] Government and Rule, and for the advancement of his Kingdom."[38] Venner had links through his Swan Alley congregation with a number of Baptist leaders, and it is not surprising that one immediate consequence of the uprising was the imprisonment of a large number of Baptists, who, despite their attempts to distance them- selves from Venner, were now regarded as dangerous to the peace of Charles II's kingdom, along with others like the Quakers and Congregationalists.[39] Over the next twenty-seven years, persecution of dissent was the order of the day. Most Baptist elders spent some time in prison (including Kiffen), and not surprisingly, several Baptists, frustrated by the political situation, were caught up in plots to overthrow the government. Ronald Angelo Johnson has demonstrated that it was Kiffen who enabled the Baptists to navigate the treacherous political shoals of this era through his moderate convictions regarding obedience to the government.[40] As Kiffen and his fellow Particular

---

[38] *The Last Speech and Prayer with Other Passages of Thomas Venner* (London, 1660 [sic]), 5. For the life of Venner, see Richard L. Greaves, *Deliver Us from Evil: The Radical Underground in Britain, 1660–1663* (Oxford: Oxford University, 1986), 50–57. For the mindset of those involved in the Venner uprising, see Bernard Capp, "*A Door of Hope* Re-opened: The Fifth Monarchy, King Charles and King Jesus," *Journal of Religious History* 32 (2008): 16–30.

[39] *Behold a Cry! Or, a True Relation of the Inhumane and Violent Outrages of Divers Souldiers, Constables, and Others, Practised upon Many of the Lord's People, Commonly (though Falsly) Called Anabaptists, at Their Several Meetings in and about London* (London, 1662), 1–5; Michael R. Watts, *The Dissenters: From the Reformation to the French Revolution*, vol. 1 (Oxford: Clarendon, 1978), 222–23. Among the Baptists arrested were Hanserd Knollys (1599–1691) and Vavasor Powell (d.1670). See Thomas Crosby, *The History of the English Baptists* (London, 1739), 2:91.

[40] Cross, "Baptists, Peace, and War," 21–24; Johnson, "Peculiar Ventures," 60–71.

Baptists told the king right after the Venner insurrection, "We can say this, and prove it to all the world, that it hath been our profession, and is our real practice to be obedient to magistracy in all things civil, and willing to live peaceably under the government established in this nation: For we do believe and declare magistracy to be an ordinance of God, and ought to be obeyed in all lawful things. A civil magistracy is an ordinance of God set up by God."[41]

"We may glory in our loyalty": John Gill

In 1772, when Robert MacGregor (died ca. 1805), pastor of Woolwich Baptist Church, Kent, happened to reflect on the relationship that had existed between the Particular Baptists and the British government for much of that century, he declared with some measure of pride that his denomination had been consistently characterized by appreciative support for the government of the land. "We may glory in our loyalty," he stated, "for I never yet heard a single Baptist being concerned in any tumult, rebellion, or civil commotion, against the present royal family."[42] The "present royal family" were the Protestant Hanoverians, who had occupied the throne since George I (1660–1727; r. 1714–1727). The most serious threat to their rule during the period surveyed by MacGregor had occurred at the time of the Jacobite uprising in 1745–1746, when Charles Edward Stuart (1720–1788), supported by the French, had landed in Scotland and subsequently invaded

---

[41] William Kiffen et al., *The Humble Apology of Some Commonly Called Anabaptists, in Behalf of Themselves and Others of the Same Judgement with Them: With Their Protestation against the Late Wicked and Most Horrid Treasonable Insurrection and Rebellion Acted in the City of London. Together with an Apology Formerly Presented to the Kings Most Excellent Majesty* (London: Henry Hills, 1660 [1661]), 18.

[42] Robert MacGregor, *The Christian Minister's Reasons for Baptizing Believers Only* (London: M. Lewis, 1772), iv. For this quote, I am indebted to O. C. Robison, "The Particular Baptists in England, 1760–1820" (PhD diss., Oxford University, 1963), 389–90.

England in the hope of regaining the throne for the House of Stuart. His grandfather, James II (1633–1701), a confirmed Roman Catholic, had been forced to flee the country in the Glorious Revolution of 1688–1689, which placed the Dutch Protestant William of Orange (1650–1702) on the British throne as William III. The Particular Baptists, who had suffered greatly under the Stuarts, as previously noted, were quick to support the Hanoverians, whom they regarded as the God-appointed rulers of the English realm. On October 31, 1745, for instance, several Particular Baptist churches in the city of London and throughout the country held a fast on "account of the rebellion in Scotland" and prayed for deliverance from the very real possibility of a Stuart victory. Little Wild Street Baptist Church in London even organized its own volunteer militia and used its churchyard as a parade ground.[43]

The thinking that lay behind this support is well seen in the political theology of John Gill (1697–1771), who was the pastor of the premier London Baptist cause, which met at Goat Yard, Horsleydown, and then later at Carter Lane, Southwark. Gill was a voluminous author, whose commentary on the entire New Testament, his deeply learned *Exposition of the New Testament*, published in three folio volumes between 1746 and 1748; its companion, his four-volume *Exposition of the Old Testament* (1763–1766); and his magnum opus, *A Complete Body of Doctrinal and Practical Divinity* (1769–1770), formed an essential part of the library of most eighteenth-century Particular Baptist ministers.[44] Now, Gill maintained that the

---

[43] Henry Spyvee, *Colchester Baptist Church: The First 300 Years, 1689–1989* (Colchester: Colchester Baptist Church, 1989), 27; Robison, "Particular Baptists," 396; Joseph Ivimey, *A History of the English Baptists*, vol. 3 (London: B. J. Holdsworth, 1823), 239, 251–52.

[44] The standard biographical sketch of Gill is John Rippon, *A Brief Memoir of the Life and Writings of the Late Rev. John Gill, D. D.* (London: John Bennett, 1838). For more recent studies of Gill and his theology, see Graham Harrison, "Dr. John Gill and His Teaching," Annual Lecture of The Evangelical Library (London: Evangelical Library, 1971); George M. Ella, *John Gill and the Cause of God and Truth* (Durham: Go Publications, 1995); Michael A. G. Haykin, ed., *The Life and*

respective duties of rulers and ruled arise from a relationship that is "founded in consent, agreement, and covenant." Whatever the primal force that drove men together in this way—be it out of "mutual fear," as Thomas Hobbes (1588–1679) had imagined, or because human beings are by nature sociable creatures, as Aristotle (384–322 BC) had thought—Gill was persuaded that the government of "free and well-regulated states" was rooted in an agreement by which rulers consented to govern according to fundamental laws and their subjects agreed to obey "their lawful commands, and to support their government."[45] This assertion was certainly not original to Gill. The London Baptist was in fact drawing upon a tradition that reached back to such Huguenot activists as Philippe Duplessis-Mornay (1549–1623) and Puritan authors immediately before and during the British Civil Wars, who argued that the political authority which rulers exercise is rooted in the consent of those subject to it. As John Locke (1632–1704), the political philosopher who more than any other acted as the conduit by which these ideas reached the eighteenth century, later summed up this viewpoint: "Men being by Nature, all free, equal and independent, no one can be put out of this Estate, and subjected to the Political Power of another, without his own Consent."[46]

Gill also held that there were occasions when rulers, who have been acting unlawfully and pursuing a course of evil, may be lawfully resisted. As he noted in some remarks on Rom 13:2 ("Whosoever therefore resisteth the

---

Thought of John Gill (1697–1771): A Tercentennial Appreciation (Leiden: E. J. Brill, 1997); and Timothy George, "John Gill" in *Theologians of the Baptist Tradition*, ed. Timothy George and David S. Dockery, rev. ed. (Nashville: Broadman & Holman, 2001), 11–33.

[45] John Gill, *A Complete Body of Doctrinal and Practical Divinity* (1839; Paris, AR: Baptist Standard Bearer, 1989), 984. Gill has misunderstood Aristotle's thinking about the origins of human society. I am indebted to Prof. John W. Seaman for drawing this to my attention.

[46] John Locke, *Two Treatises of Government* 2.8.95, ed. Peter Laslett, Cambridge Texts in the History of Political Thought (Cambridge: Cambridge University, 1988), 330.

power, resisteth the ordinance of God" [KJV]): "This [phrase] is not to be understood, as if magistrates were above the laws, and had a lawless power to do as they will without opposition; for they are under the law, and liable to the penalty of it, in case of disobedience, as others; and when they make their own will a law, or exercise a lawless tyrannical power, in defiance of the laws of God, and of the land, to the endangering of the lives, liberties, and properties of subjects, they may be resisted."[47]

Such resistance might require violence. So, for example, Gill believed that the Glorious Revolution was justified and in full accord with the will of God. It was only right, therefore, to resist with military force any attempts to recapture the throne for the descendants of James II. Some comments that Gill made upon Psalm 25 in early December 1745 reveal the Baptist preacher's views in this regard. Gill believed David composed this psalm during the rebellion of his son Absalom, and thus, the enemies of whom David spoke in the opening and closing verses are to be understood as rebellious subjects. Commenting on Ps 25:3b ("Let them be ashamed which transgress without cause" [KJV]), Gill likened these rebels whom David had to face to the followers of Charles Stuart, "a parcel of perfidious treacherous wretches" who had "risen up against" a "rightful sovereign King George [II]." For such, he said, "we should pray, as David did for his enemies, that they might be ashamed; that they may fail in their attempts and designs, and be brought to deserved punishment."[48] It bears stressing, though, that while Gill allowed for the possibility of violent resistance to a tyrannical government—as in the case of the Glorious Revolution, where James II, seen as a religious tyrant, was deposed—it is quite evident that it was not a possibility he chose to develop. His lengthiest discussion of the respective duties of magistrates and subjects was in *A Complete Body of Doctrinal and Practical Divinity* (1769).

---

[47] John Gill, *An Exposition of the New Testament*, vol. 2 (1809; Paris, AR: Baptist Standard Bearer, 1989), 553. See also Gill, *Complete Body*, 987.

[48] John Gill, *An Exposition of the Old Testament*, vol. 3 (1810; Paris, AR: Baptist Standard Bearer, 1989), 632–33.

It was largely taken up, though, with the dynamics of being a loyal subject to the government and not with those of legitimate revolution.[49]

"Our resistance is glorious": Caleb Evans

Under the first two Hanoverian sovereigns, George I and his son George II (1683–1760), Baptist ministers were almost without exception unequivocal in their praise and support of the government. However, the 1760s to the 1780s witnessed among the Baptists, along with other Dissenters, a growing disenchantment with the government of the king, George III (1738–1820). The principal reason for this disenchantment and support of the American cause was undoubtedly the conflict in North America over taxation, political representation, and the sovereignty of the British Parliament. Yet James E. Bradley has pointed out that there was also a more strictly theological reason at work: at the heart of the Particular Baptist experience were deep convictions regarding the biblical necessity of congregational polity and the misguided nature of the concept of a state church.[50] As John Ryland Jr. (1753–1825) stated with regard to the latter at the time of his ordination in 1781 to the pastoral oversight of the Baptist cause in Northampton: "I believe that Jesus Christ the crowned King of Zion is the alone Head of the Church—that neither Kings, Queens, nor Parliaments have any right to determine Controversies about matters of Faith, nor to appoint rites and ceremonies in the Church."[51] Under the press of the events leading up to and surrounding the American Revolution, this traditional Baptist opposition to Anglicanism became overt and outspoken and further fostered a reorientation of political attitude toward the government.

---

[49] Gill, *Complete Body*, 983–88.

[50] Bradley, *Religion, Revolution, and English Radicalism*, 57–59. See also Robison, "Particular Baptists," 401–4.

[51] John Ryland Jr., "A Confession of Faith Delivered by John Ryland Junior of Northampton at His Ordination to the Pastoral Care of the Church in College Lane, June 8, 1781" (Bristol, UK: Bristol Baptist College), 18.

Representative of this change in attitude was Caleb Evans (1737–1791), a tutor and eventually principal at Bristol Baptist Academy.[52] The shape of Evans's political thought is probably best seen in his controversy with John Wesley over the American Revolution, "the most publicized clerical debate" of the day.[53] Near the beginning of the debate, which was sparked by the publication of Wesley's *A Calm Address to Our American Colonies* (1775), the Methodist leader confessed that he had been reared "in the highest notions of passive obedience and non-resistance," that is, the conviction that even if the monarch is guilty of grave offenses, a subject must be willing to accept civil penalties for any act of disobedience to his or her monarch. For someone holding to this perspective, both active resistance to one's sovereign and outright rebellion are obviously impermissible.[54] Nevertheless, even though Wesley continued to be devoted to the monarchy to the end of his life, by the time he uttered these sentiments he had actually come to believe in a monarchy that was subject to definite limitations and that guaranteed human liberty.[55] However, this change of perspective was not readily apparent in his *Calm Address*. There, Wesley affirmed that the British government had every right to tax the American colonies even though the colonists had no elected representatives in the House of Commons. Driving Wesley was a deep-seated fear of republicanism and the apprehension that

---

[52] On the life and ministry of Caleb Evans, see especially Norman S. Moon, "Caleb Evans, Founder of the Bristol Education Society," *Baptist Quarterly* 24 (1971–1972): 175–90; Roger Hayden, *Continuity and Change: Evangelical Calvinism among Eighteenth-century Baptist Ministers Trained at Bristol Academy, 1690–1791* (Chipping Norton: Nigel Lynn, 2006), 120–41.

[53] Bradley, *Religion, Revolution, and English Radicalism*, 127–28.

[54] John Wesley, *Letter to William Legge, the Earl of Dartmouth, June 14, 1775*, in *The Letters of the Rev. John Wesley, A. M.*, ed. John Telford, vol. 6 (1931; London: Epworth, 1960), 156; Leon O. Hynson, "Human Liberty as Divine Right: A Study in the Political Maturation of John Wesley," *Journal of Church and State* 25, no. 1 (Winter 1983): 57n1.

[55] Hynson, "Human Liberty," 57–85; Robert Hole, *Pulpits, Politics and Public Order in England 1760–1832* (Cambridge: Cambridge University, 1989), 22–24.

a few "determined enemies to the monarchy" in England were seeking to engineer a revolution in both England and America. Those whom Wesley regarded as duped by the anti-monarchial propaganda of these men needed to know, however, that "no governments under heaven are so despotic as the republican; no subjects are governed in so arbitrary a manner as those of a commonwealth."[56]

The sale of this pamphlet was phenomenal. Within months 40,000 copies of it had been printed, and Wesley's seemingly anti-democratic statements brought down a storm of criticism upon his head.[57] Consider, for example, the letter of James Turner referred to at the beginning of this essay, in which Turner mentioned to John Sutcliff that he had been thinking about the *Calm Address*. Immediately before this remark, Turner commented that with regard "to passive obedience & nonresistance I believe 'em to be abominable to the last degree." These two remarks are probably meant to go together. In other words, Turner's reading of Wesley's *Calm Address* was that it was a defense of "passive obedience & nonresistance," and as such, he found it "abominable" to the nth degree.[58] Turner's fellow Baptist, Caleb Evans, went more public in his critique of Wesley's position. Constrained by what he described as "conscientious motives and the fear of God,"[59] the Bristol Baptist published a twenty-four-page open letter under the pseudonym of "Americanus" in early October 1775. The main thrust of the letter, the most widely read of the various replies to the Methodist leader, was that taxation without representation is nothing

---

[56] John Wesley, *A Calm Address to Our American Colonies* in *The Works of the Rev. John Wesley, A. M.*, 3rd ed., vol. 11 (London: 1830), 86–87. On Wesley's fear of republicanism, see Allan Raymond, "'I fear God and honour the King': John Wesley and the American Revolution," *Church History* 45 (1976): 316–28.

[57] W. M. S. West, "Methodists and Baptists in Eighteenth Century Bristol," *Proceedings of the Wesley Historical Society*, 44 (1984): 163.

[58] Turner, *Letter to John Sutcliff, January 13, 1776.*

[59] Caleb Evans, Letter to John Sutcliff, October 23, 1775 (J. R. L. English Ms 369–71, John Rylands University Library of Manchester).

less than slavery. If Wesley's views on the conflict in North America arose from a fear of republicanism, Evans wrote with a concern that the overall drift in Wesley's argumentation was toward a revival of the "old Jacobite doctrine of hereditary, indefeasible, divine right, and of passive obedience and non-resistance."[60] Substance was given to Evans's concern by Wesley's frank denial that the origin of political authority is in the citizenry of a nation. To Evans, whose political views had been profoundly shaped by his reading of "the immortal Locke," such a denial contradicted his fundamental belief that, under God, the people, and the people only, are the source of power.[61]

Did Evans's employment of Lockean political categories entail a loss of a distinctively Baptist voice, a subversion of Baptist ideas by those of the Enlightenment? Not at all. Baptist convictions regarding the locus of governmental authority can be traced back to the seventeenth century, when Baptist authors like William Kiffen wrestled with the locus of authority in the local church. On the basis of Matt 18:17 and 1 Cor 5:4, the *First London Confession* had affirmed that "Christ has . . . given power to his whole Church to receive in and cast out, by way of Excommunication, any member; and this power is given to every particular Congregation, and not one particular person, either member or Officer, but the whole."[62] The members of the local church acting together have the authority and power

---

[60] Caleb Evans, *A Letter to the Rev. John Wesley, Occasioned by His Calm Address to the American Colonies* (Bristol: William Pine, 1775), 11. Evans mentions the same concern at the end of this letter: *Letter to the Rev. John Wesley*, 24. On the publication of Evans's *Letter to the Rev. John Wesley*, see Frank Baker, "The Shaping of Wesley's *Calm Address*," *Methodist History* 14 (1975–1976): 7. On Evans's response to Wesley, see also Donald H. Kirkham, "John Wesley's *Calm Address*: The Response of the Critics," *Methodist History* 14 (1975–1976): 13–23, *passim*.

[61] Wesley, *Calm Address* in *Works of the Rev. John Wesley*, 90; Evans, *Letter to the Rev. John Wesley*, 11. For Locke's influence on Evans, see Bradley, *Religion, Revolution, and English Radicalism*, 133–34. Evans described Locke as "immortal" in his *Letter to the Rev. John Wesley*, 4.

[62] *Confession of Faith*, Article XLII.

to receive new members into their midst as well as to excommunicate those who refuse to walk under Christ's lordship. Furthermore, "every Church has power given them from Christ for their better well-being, to choose to themselves meet persons into the office of Pastors, Teachers, Elders, Deacons."[63] It was also stressed that "none other have power to impose" leaders on the congregation from the outside. While later editions will limit the names of the leaders of the congregation to "elders" and "deacons," there would be no retreat from the fact that "the ministry was . . . firmly subordinated to the immediate authority of the covenanted community."[64] B. R. White has pointed out that these early Baptists maintained a jealous concern for congregational autonomy out of a deep desire to be free to obey Christ and not be bound by the dictates of men and human traditions.[65] Undergirding this was a profound concern for God's freedom to be Lord of his church. They regarded human religious traditions not sanctioned by God's Word as affronts to God's sovereign freedom and violations of his prerogatives.[66] Eighteenth-century Baptist political theology such as that of Evans took this principle of congregational authority and applied it to the larger political realm and found in the language of Locke a natural ally.

Responding to Evans's attack with a published vindication of Wesley was the latter's key lieutenant, John W. Fletcher (1729–1785), vicar of Madeley in Shropshire. Fletcher sought to uphold Wesley's perspective as thoroughly scriptural, rational, and constitutional as well as to demonstrate that Evans's views were deficient in all three of these areas. In fact, Fletcher went beyond Wesley to assert that the monarch, "whether we have a vote for parliament men or not, has both a right, and a power to dispose, not only of our money,

---

[63] *Confession of Faith*, Article XXXVI.

[64] White, "Doctrine of the Church," 581; see also White, "Origins and Convictions," 46.

[65] White, "Doctrine of the Church," 584.

[66] Philip E. Thompson, "People of the Free God: The Passion of the Seventeenth-Century Baptists," *American Baptist Quarterly* 15:3 (1991): 226–31.

but also of our liberty and life."[67] Reflecting Wesley's fear of republicanism, Fletcher accused Evans of dabbling in "dangerous politics," which had a manifest tendency to encourage sedition and stir up "groundless discontent."[68]

Evans lost no time in replying with a lengthy rebuttal to Fletcher's vindication, for Evans believed that "a nobler cause, next to that of religion, I cannot undertake. It is the cause of liberty."[69] He reviewed the controversy to that point in time, undertook a fresh defense of his argument that "to be taxed without being represented was the quintessence of slavery," and sought to show that his beliefs were in full harmony with the Scriptures.[70] After having stated that he revered the authority of the "oracles of truth" above all others, Evans indicated that he was quite prepared to accept Fletcher's position if the latter could demonstrate it from the Word of God. However, the Baptist author confidently affirmed that although he had been accustomed to reading the Bible from early childhood, he had yet to find in it the "principles of political slavery" that Fletcher so passionately asserted were there. Evans saw nothing in God's Word that commanded him to stand passively by and not oppose "tyranny, oppression, and all manner of evil." For instance, Evans postulated, were he to be stopped by a highwayman with pistol in hand and asked to hand over his money, not

---

[67] Claude L. Howe Jr., "British Evangelical Response to the American Revolution: The Baptists," *Fides et Historia* 8 (1976): 39. Fletcher was not the only evangelical leader who continued to assert a position that Wesley had outgrown. The lay preacher William Mason (1719–ca. 1790), for instance, insisted in 1776 that rebellion against the ruling powers was always a sin and, if persisted in, could lead only to damnation (Howe, "British Evangelical Response," 24). On Mason, see Simon Lewis, "Devotion and Polemic in Eighteenth-Century England: William Mason and the Literature of Lay Evangelical Anglicanism," *Huntington Library Quarterly*, 82, no. 3 (2020): 379–406.

[68] Bradley, *Religion, Revolution, and English Radicalism*, 158.

[69] Caleb Evans, *A Reply to the Rev. Mr. Fletcher's Vindication of Mr. Wesley's Calm Address to Our American Colonies* (Bristol: W. Pine, 1776), 3. This reply runs to 103 pages.

[70] Evans, 30.

an infrequent occurrence on eighteenth-century British roads, if he thought he could effectually resist such a theft, he would. It might be imprudent to resist, but certainly it was never sinful. Again, Evans argued, if the "Grand Turk," that is, the sultan of the Ottoman Empire, were to invade Great Britain, he would "chearfully [*sic*] risk [his] fortune and [his] life" to avoid living in servitude under a Muslim master. Where a person's "just rights" and "unalienable privileges" were at stake, physical resistance was not at all sinful. In both illustrations, resistance was being offered to an unlawful authority, which Evans sought to distinguish from a lawful one: "If a lawful authority, our resistance is sinful in a very high degree; but if it be an unlawful authority, our resistance is glorious."[71]

The majority of British Baptists at the time had apparently been in general agreement with Evans's views. At the close of the war, the London Baptist John Rippon (1751–1836) wrote to James Manning (1739–1791), then president of Rhode Island College (renamed Brown University), that he knew of only two Baptist pastors in Great Britain who had not favored "the side of the Americans in the late dispute. We wept when the thirsty plains drank the blood of your departed heroes, and the shout of a king was amongst us when your well-fought battles were crowned with victory."[72] One of these two pastors was undoubtedly the arch-conservative John Martin (1741–1820), pastor of Grafton Street Baptist Church in Soho, London, of whom it was said that "when he lifted up his feet, he was always careful to put them down again in the same place."[73] Not surprisingly,

---

[71] Evans, *Reply to the Rev.*, 51–55. For further discussion of Evans's views, see Howe, "British Evangelical Response," 37–41; West, "Methodists and Baptists," 164–65; Hole, *Pulpits, Politics and Public Order*, 28; Bradley, *Religion, Revolution, and English Radicalism*, 121–92, *passim*.

[72] William G. McLoughlin, *New England Dissent 1630–1833: The Baptists and the Separation of Church and State*, vol. 1 (Cambridge: Harvard University, 1971), 583. See also the remarks of Howe, "British Evangelical Response," 35–37.

[73] This description is that of Andrew Fuller and is cited by A. C. Underwood, *A History of the English Baptists* (London: Carey Kingsgate, 1956), 164. On Martin's views, see Howe, "British Evangelical Response," 43–44. As Bradley has noted

the response of most Baptists to the American War of Independence confirmed the British establishment in their opinion that Baptists, as well as other Dissenting bodies, were nefarious radicals bent upon the overthrow of the monarchy and the government.[74] And the opening stages of the next major political convulsion of the Western world, the French Revolution, only served to provide additional confirmation to the conservative forces in Great Britain that the Baptists and their fellow Dissenters were seriously courting treason.

"Cordial friends": Andrew Fuller

When the French Revolution began, English Dissenters, among others, were gripped by a naive enthusiasm for what was happening in France. For instance, Joseph Kinghorn (1766–1832)—who became the pastor of St. Mary's Baptist Church, Norwich, only a few months before the opening salvos of the Revolution in June and July of 1789—wrote to his father, David Kinghorn (d. 1822), in August 1789, the month after the storming of the Bastille (July 14), "I rejoice with all my heart at the destruction of that most infamous place the Bastille."[75] Another Norwich Particular Baptist minister, Mark Wilks (d. 1819), began a sermon on July 14, 1791—the second anniversary of the storming of the Bastille—with the provocative statement "Jesus Christ was a Revolutionist." He went on to inform his congregation that the French Revolution "is of God and that no power exists or can exist, by which it can be overthrown."[76] Robert Hall Jr.

(*Religion, Revolution, and English Radicalism*, 123, notes 4–5), the phenomenon of loyalist Dissenters like Martin has yet to be studied.

[74] James J. Sack, *From Jacobite to Conservative: Reaction and Orthodoxy in Britain, c. 1760–1832* (Cambridge: Cambridge University, 1993), 200–201.

[75] C. B. Jewson, "Norwich Baptists and the French Revolution," *Baptist Quarterly* 24 (1971–1972): 209.

[76] Mark Wilks, *The Origin and Stability of the French Revolution* (Norwich, 1791), 5–7, cited Robert Hole, "English sermons and tracts as media of debate on

(1764–1831), the most celebrated Particular Baptist preacher of the early nineteenth century, was equally enthralled by what was taking place in France. In a famous tract that went through several pirated editions, *Christianity Consistent with a Love of Freedom* (1791), Hall stated, "Events have taken place of late, and revolutions have been effected, which, had they been foretold a very few years ago, would have been viewed as visionary and extravagant; and their influence is yet far from being spent. [. . .] The empire of darkness and of despotism has been smitten with a stroke which has sounded through the universe."[77] Such sentiments proved to be utterly naive and uninformed, for right from the start the powerhouse behind the Revolution had been violence. As one of the moderate revolutionaries had remarked, "There must be blood to cement revolution."[78] In 1793 and 1794 the Revolution descended into a vortex of unspeakable violence and totalitarian terror. During this period, known to history as the Reign of Terror, at least 300,000 were arrested, and some 17,000 people were executed by the guillotine. Many others died in prison or were simply killed without the benefit of a trial. French revolutionary armies sought to spread the ideals of the Revolution to neighboring nations. While these Revolutionary ideals abolished various outdated medieval traditions, they

---

the French Revolution 1789–99" in Mark Philp, ed., *The French Revolution and British Popular Politics* (Cambridge: Cambridge University, 1991), 23–24.

[77] Robert Hall Jr., *Christianity Consistent with a Love of Freedom* in *The Works of the Rev. Robert Hall, A. M.*, ed. Olinthus Gregory and Joseph Belcher, vol. 2 (New York: Harper and Brothers, 1854), 37. For a study of Hall's attitude toward the French Revolution, see especially Dominic Aidan Bellenger, "The Persecution Chalice: Three Reactions to the French Revolution" in his ed., *Opening the Scrolls: Essays in Catholic History in Honour of Godfrey Anstruther* (Bath: Downside Abbey, 1987), 154–59.

[78] Attributed to Manon Philipon Roland; see Simon Schama, *Citizens: A Chronicle of the French Revolution* (New York: Alfred A. Knopf, 1989), 859. I am indebted to Schama's perspective on the Revolution, especially the summary in *Citizens*, 851–61.

plunged the continent into a war that lasted until 1815. Not surprisingly Baptists like Kinghorn and Hall became increasingly critical of what was taking place in France. By April 1798, Kinghorn was convinced that "all those notions of liberty which the French Revolution very generally raised a few years ago are at an end, they [the rulers of France] are the tyrants not the deliverers of men."[79] Hall's views had likewise been transformed. In a sermon titled *Modern Infidelity Considered, with Respect to Its Influence on Society* (1800), a work that made Hall something of a celebrity in England, Hall spoke of divine revelation having undergone "a total eclipse" in France, "while atheism, performing on a darkened theatre its strange and fearful tragedy, confounded the first elements of society, blended every age, rank, and sex in indiscriminate proscription and massacre, and convulsed all Europe to its centre."[80]

Baptist sermons preached in England during this time of war and horror that touched upon the realm of politics were thus frequently centered around the duties of believers to the government and the importance of loyalty.[81] A good example of such a sermon is one titled "Christian Patriotism," which was preached in 1803 by Andrew Fuller (1754–1815), pastor of Kettering Baptist Church, Northamptonshire, a man who has been well described as "the soundest and most creatively useful theologian" the English Particular Baptists ever had.[82] Not long before Fuller's delivery of "Christian Patriotism," the Treaty of Amiens (March 27, 1802), which had secured an uneasy peace in Europe for close to fourteen months, collapsed as open hostilities resumed between France and Great Britain.

---

[79] Cited Jewson, "Norwich Baptists," 215.

[80] Robert Hall Jr., *Modern Infidelity Considered, with Respect to Its Influence on Society* in *Works of the Rev. Robert Hall*, 1:47.

[81] For Baptist examples of such sermons and tracts, see Samuel Pearce, *Motives to Gratitude* (Birmingham: James Belcher, 1798); Thomas Blundell, *The Duty of Christians to Civil Government* (Dunstable: J. W. Morris, 1804).

[82] Underwood, *History of the English Baptists*, 164.

Almost immediately Napoleon Bonaparte (1769–1821) and his French generals committed themselves to extensive preparations for the invasion of England. Although these preparations would occupy much of Napoleon's energy for the next two years, events were at their most critical during the latter months of 1803, when invasion seemed an imminent certainty. Fuller's sermon, based upon Jer 29:7—"Seek the peace of the city whither I have caused you to be carried away captives, and pray unto the LORD for it: for in the peace thereof shall ye have peace" (KJV)—sought to help the members of his congregation determine their Christian duty during a time of grave national crisis.

The first section of the sermon is devoted to outlining the historical context in which the prophet Jeremiah spoke these words. The Babylonian king Nebuchadnezzar had taken into captivity a significant number of Judah's nobility along with their king, Jeconiah (aka Jehoiachin). Certain false prophets who had also been taken into captivity were encouraging the king and his nobles to expect a speedy return to the land of Palestine. Jeremiah, though, knew differently. Seventy years were to elapse before the return of the captives. Meanwhile, they should accept their lot, put roots down in their new home, and above all seek and pray for the peace of Babylon. If such was God's intent for men and women who were enslaved by the very nation for which they were to pray, then, Fuller asked his congregation, ought not they to seek the good of their native land, a land where they were protected by "mild and wholesome laws, administered under a paternal prince; a land where civil and religious freedom [were] enjoyed in higher degree than in any other nation under heaven?"[83]

Fuller understood God's command to his ancient people to "seek the peace"—or "prosperity," as Fuller translated the word *shalom*—of Babylon to be a call to British Christians of his day to be "patriots, or lovers of our

---

[83] Andrew Fuller, "Christian Patriotism" in *The Complete Works of the Rev. Andrew Fuller*, ed. Andrew Gunton Fuller, rev. ed., vol. 1 (1845; Harrisonburg: Sprinkle, 1988), 202–3.

country."[84] Thus, Fuller believed that the day in which he was living called for British Christians to be actively involved in repelling a French invasion. But he was not about to endorse carte blanche concerning every war in which his country engaged. As he declared near the close of his sermon, "If my country were engaged in an attempt to ruin France, as a nation, it would be a wicked undertaking; and if I were fully convinced of it, I should both hope and pray that they might be disappointed."[85]

Finally, Fuller argued that there is one other duty believers of his day owed to the British state, and that was to pray for the safety of their nation:

> You are aware that all our dependence, as a nation, is upon God; and, therefore, [we] should importune his assistance. After all the struggles for power, you know that in his sight all the inhabitants of the world are reputed as nothing: he doth according to his will in the army of heaven, and among the inhabitants of the earth; and none can stay his hand, or say unto him, What doest thou? [. . .] but in general the great body of a nation, it is to be feared, think but little about it. Their dependence is upon an arm of flesh. It may be said, without uncharitableness, of many of our commanders, both by sea and land, as was said of Cyrus, God hath girded them, though they have not known him.[86] But by how much you perceive a want of prayer and dependence on God in your countrymen, by so much more should you be concerned, as much as in you lies, to supply the defect. "The prayer of a righteous man availeth much" [James 5:16].[87]

Fuller was very conscious that the safety of the British people ultimately did not depend on their military might, even though many of Fuller's fellow

---

[84] Fuller, 203–4.
[85] Fuller, 206–7.
[86] See Isa 45:5.
[87] Fuller, "Christian Patriotism," 208.

citizens believed it did and were trusting in their armed forces. No, it is a sovereign God who rules over the affairs of men and nations, and all his holy purposes will stand. This lack of a genuine dependence upon God on the part of many of the British, though, should not lead believers to stand aloof from their neighbors and merely condemn them as godless. Rather, Fuller argued, they should give themselves even more assiduously to prayer.

A politically focused sermon such as this one was unusual for Fuller. Generally, he avoided politics as he was fearful his fellow Baptists would get entangled in the political webs of his day. He thus cautioned John Fountain (1767–1800), a missionary to India: "All political concerns are only affairs of this life with which he that will please him, who hath chosen him to be a soldier, must not entangle himself."[88] As his sermon "Christian Patriotism" made clear, however, when he delineated his position on the relationship between church and state, it was in many ways identical to the moderate views of Kiffen and Gill. In Fuller's apt words, when "the civil power [. . .] maintains the great ends of government, [it] ought, at all times, to be able to reckon upon religious people as its cordial friends."[89] This description of church-state relations as that of "cordial friends" well captured the tradition that William Kiffen hammered out in the turmoil of the seventeenth century, which, via especially the thought of Baptists like John Gill, had come to rich expression in the thinking of Andrew Fuller during an era of unprecedented revolution, war, and political upheaval.

Coda

Baptist arguments regarding the sanctity of the individual's conscience and, therefore, his or her fundamental right to religious liberty—arguments that were hammered out on the anvil of the tumult of the seventeenth and

---

[88] Andrew Fuller, *Letter to John Fountain, March 25, 1796,* cited in Haykin, *One Heart and One Soul,* 247.

[89] Fuller, "Christian Patriotism," 205.

eighteenth centuries, an era in which the union of the state and church was a given for many—inevitably made the English Baptists of that time seem to be subversive radicals. Indeed, during the American War of Independence, the viewpoint of Caleb Evans regarding liberty, which was shared apparently by numerous English Baptists, seemed to confirm the conviction of others in the British Isles that the Baptists were dangerous and seditious revolutionaries. However, the principal Baptist attitude with regard to the political realm is best seen in the patient reflection and argument of men like William Kiffen, John Gill, and Andrew Fuller, who enabled their communities to retain a firm grasp on their fundamental conviction about religious freedom while avoiding the politicization of their communities.

3

Roger Williams

By James Calvin Davis

If we measure a thinker's importance to a tradition by his self-identification with it, then Roger Williams barely rates in the history of Baptists in America, for he associated with a Baptist church for less than a year. In terms of impact on the tradition, however, few thinkers are more important to Baptist political theology than Williams, whose commitment to religious liberty and the separation of church and state was formative for later generations of Baptist thinkers and activists and for the political culture of the United States. Because he offered a *theological* defense of religious liberty, Williams represents an essential historical resource for that American doctrine, an important complement to the Enlightenment-influenced political philosophies to which we more commonly look for inspiration.

Contexts

Roger Williams (ca. 1603–1683) was a British Puritan minister and a theological activist, and his concern for religious liberty derived directly from his

73

Puritan-Calvinist commitments. To be a Puritan in the seventeenth century meant commitment to a set of theological priorities exemplified by the work of John Calvin. Puritans emphasized reliance on God's sovereignty and the sufficiency of divine grace for salvation. They believed in original sin as an apt description of the human condition and the reason human beings need God's saving intervention. They subscribed to the controversial doctrine of predestination, declaring confidently that God knows before time whom he will save (and presumably, whom he will not). And they lifted up Scripture as the supreme authority for Christian faith and life, making biblical study an important preoccupation of Puritan clergy and laity alike.

Among their theological convictions, the Puritans were committed to an ecclesiology that caused consternation for leaders in the Church of England. Most Puritans accepted that the visible church was a mixture of God's elect and the reprobate, but they believed the church had a responsibility to remain as pure as possible in its teachings, worship, and moral practice. In fact, it was this drive to purify the Church of England that gave the Puritans their pejorative nickname. The Puritans were concerned that the Church of England (which split from the Roman Catholic Church in the 1530s in a famous dispute between Henry VIII and Pope Clement VII over the king's desire for a new wife) had not distanced itself sufficiently from Catholic practices, particularly in worship. They objected to the requirement of clergy to wear vestments, the focus on liturgical ceremony at the expense of preaching and moral standards, and the hierarchical structure of church authority. In contrast, they subscribed to a vision of the church where authority was relatively local and shared between clergy and lay elders, the preaching of Scripture was the center of worship, and moral performance of all church members was strictly policed. Their constant critique of the Church of England was taken as a direct challenge to the institution's leaders, including the monarch.

While we cannot say for certain, Williams was likely born in Smithfield in 1603, the same year Queen Elizabeth I died and James VI of Scotland ascended to the English throne as James I of England. Because he was coming from Scotland, where Calvinist Presbyterianism flourished as the national church, Puritan agitators in the Church of England were optimistic that James's ascension would benefit their efforts to rid the established church of Catholic vestiges and augment Calvinist theological, liturgical, and moral reforms. Those hopes were soon dashed, however, for James's first priority was the assertion of royal authority in the church, and he quickly tired of the Puritans' challenges. Through the first decades of the seventeenth century, James's relationship with the Puritans became increasingly antagonistic, and Puritan agitators were subjected to more regular intervals of persecution.

In this environment, Williams was born and raised.[1] Little evidence suggests that his family was Puritan, but by the time Williams made his way to Pembroke College at Cambridge, he seems to have become a committed Puritan. Cambridge was intellectual training ground for Puritanism, and Williams fell in with them. He emerged from his Cambridge training thoroughly Calvinist in theological orientation and ecclesial principle. Upon graduation in 1629, he followed the path of other Puritans and refused to take ordination to a parish position, where he would be under constant pressure to conform to Anglican theology and practices. Instead, he became an estate chaplain to Sir William Masham of Essex, a Puritan sympathizer who became his protector and benefactor. During this same time, Williams met and married Mary Barnard, who would be his partner for the remainder of his life.

If Williams and his fellow Puritans thought James I was bad for the Calvinist cause, the ascension of James's son Charles in 1625 ushered in a more intense period of persecution, so much so that some Puritan communities actively considered emigration. Some went to Holland for a time, but the New England colonies were particularly attractive as a place where

---

[1] The biographical sketch in this chapter is especially indebted to Ola Elizabeth Winslow, *Master Roger Williams: A Biography* (New York: Macmillan, 1957), and Edwin S. Gaustad, *Liberty of Conscience: Roger Williams in America* (Valley Forge: Judson, 1999).

Puritans could practice their kind of church and serve as a "city on a hill" (Puritan leader John Winthrop's enduring phrase) for the reform of English church and society. An initial band of Puritans took off for Massachusetts Bay in 1630, and a year later, Williams and his wife followed. Governor Winthrop warmly greeted Williams, whom he described in his journal as a "godly minister" with impeccable Puritan credentials.[2] Soon after he arrived in Massachusetts, Williams was offered a ministerial position at the prestigious Boston church.

His response to that invitation was the beginning of his turbulent relationship with Boston authorities. Williams turned down the offer because he believed the Boston church insufficiently rejected the errors of theology and practice in the Church of England. Williams was a Separatist, a brand of Puritan that believed the only way for true Christians to remain pure was to reject the apostate mother church and constitute local communities of faithfulness independent of the Church of England. The Puritans who landed south of Boston at Plymouth—those Puritans we refer to as "Pilgrims" today—were Separatists, and Williams lived with them a while after he burned his bridges in Boston. For most of his time in Massachusetts Bay, however, Williams associated with the church in Salem, which also sympathized with his radical Separatist principles.

While in Salem, Williams was implicated in other controversies that contributed to his souring relationship with Boston authorities. He objected to the use of oaths in public settings, and he taught that women should be veiled in church. His Separatist principles were invoked by local opponents of the Christian cross in the English flag so that when they defaced the flag by cutting out the cross, Williams was blamed. He insisted that local native tribes had rightful ownership of the land on which English colonists settled so that their permission and adequate compensation—not just the English king's decree—was required before the English could claim it as

---

[2] John Winthrop, *The Journal of John Winthrop*, ed. Richard S. Dunn and Laetitia Yeandle (Cambridge: Belknap,1930), 34.

their own. Most enduringly, Williams objected to the conflation of religious and political authority in Massachusetts, arguing that clergy should not have direct influence in civil matters, and civil magistrates should keep out of church affairs.[3]

What began as a promising reputation in New England quickly deteriorated, and after repeated instruction not to publicly share his controversial beliefs, the Massachusetts General Court reached the limits of their patience with Williams and banished him from the colony in 1636. He was supposed to have been put on a ship back to England (where Royalists would certainly have imprisoned him), but after being tipped off about his banishment, Williams fled into the winter wilderness. Aided by Native American friends, Williams made his way to the Narragansett Bay and, after purchasing land from the local sachem, established the town of Providence. Providence soon became a haven for dissenting refugees from Massachusetts like him.

In his banishment, Williams had time and energy to begin a letter exchange with John Cotton, a prominent Puritan minister whom the Boston church hired when Williams turned them down. Williams believed that Cotton was a principal architect of his banishment and that he was exiled not for civil crimes but for his religious beliefs. Whether this charge was entirely true is hard to say, but Cotton stridently disagreed with both Williams's indictment of him and his understanding of his offense. Because Williams believed that he was convicted based on religious beliefs and

---

[3] Williams himself gives an account of the charges against him, at least as he understood them, in *Mr. Cotton's Letter Lately Printed, Examined and Answered*, 1644. See James Calvin Davis, ed., *On Religious Liberty: Selections from the Works of Roger Williams* (Cambridge: Belknap, 2008), 48–49. All subsequent references to Williams's writings (except his *A Key into the Language of America*) will be from documents in this volume, abbreviated *ORL*. Another point of some disagreement was slavery. Williams had a mixed record on slavery. He did oppose (at least once in writing) the idea of slavery theoretically as a violation of people's dignity, but he did not consistently call for the abolition of racial slavery. Late in his political leadership in Rhode Island, he endorsed slavery as a punishment for Native Americans captured in King Philip's War.

that a clergyman had instigated the conviction, the conflation of religious conformity and political power soon became the major point of contention between him and Cotton. The result was a series of extended correspondence in which Williams spelled out the foundational elements of his commitment to religious liberty and the separation of religious and civil authority. Williams's part in this exchange—published on trips to England in 1644 and 1652 as *The Bloudy Tenent of Persecution, for Cause of Conscience* and *The Bloudy Tenent Yet More Bloudy*—represents his major contribution to both Baptist political theology and American political history.

While he was in England on those two trips (aiming to secure a charter and political security for Rhode Island and Providence Plantations), Williams participated in debates over religious liberty during the English Civil War, and the shorter treatises he wrote for those occasions remain important additions to his corpus. When he was not in England, Williams was a leader of his fledgling colony. He served for many years as its chief officer, and the responsibilities of governing affected his understanding of religious liberty by sharpening his understanding of the balance between individual liberty and social obligations. In a colony full of religious dissenters, he had to entertain claims of "conscientious objection" in response to obligatory taxes and conscripted participation in the militia needed to ward off Native American attacks. Williams's response to these invocations of religious liberty lent nuance to his own, as he acknowledged the complex relationship between liberty and the common good.

Williams had to deal with other kinds of social discord that sometimes accompanied the exercise of religious freedom, and his struggles with Nonconformist Quakers in Rhode Island tested the limits of both his patience and his commitment to liberty. In the seventeenth century, the Quakers were known for their peculiar theology (including a resistance to religious authority and an antinomian commitment to the "inner light" in all people) and their penchant for publicly challenging social mores. Quaker provocateurs interrupted religious meetings with shouting, refused to greet fellow citizens with accepted honorific titles, grew their hair long as a challenge to cultural expectations of modesty, and occasionally ran through town naked as a sign of spiritual enlightenment. When Rhode Island hung out its shingle as a haven for religious Dissenters, the Quakers arrived in droves, and they soon aggravated other members of the Rhode Island towns. Massachusetts leadership looked upon the Quaker episode in Rhode Island with a mixture of horror and humor, perhaps entertained that Williams himself had to deal with the social consequences of his dangerous doctrine of religious freedom (see the "Controversies" section, below). Later interpreters have suggested that Williams's impatience with the Quakers represented a retreat in his commitment to religious liberty, but in reality his insistence on debating the Quakers modeled the only proper recourse for engaging religious disagreement. Discourse, not coercive force, was the appropriate weapon in a war of ideas.

In the context of his political career in Providence, Williams's role in the establishment of the first Baptist church in America is comparatively small. Convinced that the Baptist insistence on "believer's baptism" and local church autonomy was consistent with his vision of a pure and separate church, he settled in with the Baptists in Providence for a time as a charter member of their first congregation in 1638. Within a year, however, he apparently decided that this group of Christians was not sufficiently rigorous either, and he split from them as a matter of Separatist theological scruple. Williams would remain theologically isolated for the remainder of his life in Providence, even as he was politically immersed. When he died, likely around 1683, it was said he would take communion with no one other than his wife.

Texts and Tenets

While Williams was in England securing the first charter for Rhode Island and Providence Plantations, his correspondence with John Cotton found its way to a sympathetic publisher. (Williams denied any hand in its publication.) The back-and-forth began (at least as we have manuscript evidence to confirm) with a letter from Cotton outlining Williams's errors.[4] Williams then responded in a treatise straightforwardly titled *Mr. Cotton's Letter Lately Printed, Examined and Answered*. This rebuttal to Cotton illustrated what Williams believed to be the points of contention between them, and it reflected the principles that animated Williams's disagreement with Massachusetts authorities. The main principled difference between them was ecclesiological, namely the importance Williams placed on complete separation from an impure and apostate Church of England. The second conviction that divided them, however, was political, and it served as Williams's bequest to American social philosophy: religious liberty and the separation of civil and religious authority.

The most famous text to be published during Williams's first return to England was *The Bloudy Tenent of Persecution, for the Cause of Conscience*, in which he laid out, with sometimes excruciating elaboration, his arguments for opposing the conflation of religious and civil authority. *The Bloudy Tenent of Persecution* was written as a dialogue between Truth and Peace, both of which Williams believed were at risk in a society that assumes political coercion is necessary to ensure good religion. He would continue the literary technique and the laborious level of argumentative detail in his sequel, which he called *The Bloudy Tenent Yet More Bloudy*, published in 1652. (In between these two treatises, Cotton responded point by point to *The Bloudy Tenent* with his own text, *The Bloudy Tenent, Washed, and Made White in the Bloud of the Lambe*.) Cotton died that same year, and their verbal duel ended. In addition to these two major treatises, Williams published smaller occasional pieces as part of the debates over religious liberty in England. *Queries of Highest Consideration* was written in 1644 as an anonymous response to both Presbyterians and Independents vying for control of the established church in the early period of the Civil War. Early the next year, he would publish *Christenings Make Not Christians*, which contained

---

[4] See "To Roger Williams" in Sargent Bush, *The Correspondence of John Cotton* (Chapel Hill: University of North Carolina, 2018), 211–25.

his objections to European efforts at mass conversion of Native Americans. Implicit in this text, too, were the dual principles of ecclesial purity and freedom of conscience. Upon his second return to England in 1652, he published *The Fourth Paper Presented by Major Butler*, a concise summary of his views on religious liberty offered in support of similar arguments from a member of Cromwell's army. This same year saw the publication of *The Examiner Defended*, in which Williams came to the defense of Sir Henry Vane, a prominent Puritan politician and a proponent of religious liberty in both England and New England. In 1652 Williams also published *The Hireling Ministry None of Christ's*, his rejection of state financial support for clergy, which he saw as a clear violation of the necessary separation of church and state and an unacceptable imposition on minority communities forced to pay for religious leaders not their own.

In each of these two bundles of texts, one in 1644 and one in 1652, Williams laid out his major arguments for religious freedom. Despite using the term, Williams was advocating for more than toleration, or a voluntary benevolence toward religious minorities on the part of an established or majority religion. Toleration puts the freedom of religious belief and expression at the mercy of a ruler's good graces, and it fails to challenge the presumption of political authority over matters of religious conviction. Rather than mere toleration, Williams argued for "absolute soul-freedom," liberty in matters of religious belief, speech, and practice that he believed all citizens deserved.[5] Perhaps unique in his time, Williams argued for religious freedom for Jews, Catholics, Muslims, and atheists in Protestant-dominated England and New England, making his call for religious freedom more expansive and principled than, for example, John Locke's.[6]

---

[5] *The Fourth Paper Presented by Major Butler*, ORL, 234.

[6] See, for instance, *Queries of Highest Consideration*, ORL, 79; *The Bloudy Tenent*, ORL, 86; and *The Fourth Paper*, ORL, 235–36. As we will see, Williams did not defend the rights of these groups out of some ambivalence regarding religious convictions. He shared his Protestant contemporaries' assumptions about Jews' complicity in Christ's death, Catholics' enslavement to "popish" direction, and

His belief in religious freedom as a human right was rooted in his understanding of the conscience. For Williams, conscience was an internal "reflection or looking back on a [person's] mind or spirit upon itself."[7] The exercise of the conscience is the internal evaluation of our thoughts, words, and actions. More theologically, he understood it to be "the secret checks and whisperings" within a person that channeled the voice of God. Through the "smiting [and] accusing" of the conscience, a person experiences the judgment of God, even if they misunderstand its divine prescriptions.[8] According to Williams, this faculty of "self-conviction" by which persons "smite and wound themselves" is a universal capacity in every properly functioning human being.[9]

Because religious conviction is a matter of conscience, argued Williams, to force a person to believe or behave contrary to conscience is to subject that person to traumatic assault. Williams considered the injury to conscientious conviction so harmful that he used metaphors of sexual violence to describe it, regularly referring to the coercion of conscience as "soul rape."[10] He also rejected coercion in matters of religious conviction because he doubted that it would work. Williams considered persuasion, not force, the only effective means to convince a person to alter their religious beliefs. Force might successfully lead to outward conformity, but it does not persuade and change conviction. In fact, sometimes force hardens the conscience by

---

atheists' future in hell. Nonetheless, he rejected the notion that political authorities had any jurisdiction in the enforcement of religious convictions, and he maintained that members of these groups could be faithful political citizens despite their erroneous religious beliefs. Compare Williams's position with Locke's defense of restrictions on Catholics, Muslims, and atheists, justified (in his mind) by their lack of political trustworthiness. See John Locke, *A Letter Concerning Toleration* (Buffalo: Prometheus Books, 1990), 63–64.

[7] *George Fox Digged out of His Burrowes*, ORL, 268.

[8] *The Bloudy Tenent*, ORL, 104–5.

[9] *The Bloudy Tenent Yet More Bloudy*, ORL, 185.

[10] See *The Bloudy Tenent Yet More Bloudy*, ORL, 205.

demonstrating the lack of moral integrity in an opposing religious perspective that underwrites the use of coercion and violence.[11]

Indeed, Williams believed the confusion of civil and spiritual matters— and the conflation of civil and spiritual power—led to the degradation of both Christianity and civil government. On the religious side, Williams argued that the enforcement of uniformity in Christian belief and practice violated "the spirit and mind and practice of the Prince of Peace." Jesus Christ, he insisted, "is not delighted with the blood of men, but shed his own for his bloodiest enemies, that by the word of Christ no man for gainsaying Christ or joining with his enemy Antichrist should be molested with the civil sword."[12] The cross is the ultimate symbol of the nonviolent, noncoercive nature of Christ's gospel and kingdom. In fact, Williams defied his opponents to find one place in Scripture, "one footstep, print, or pattern in this doctrine of the Son of God," that called for the coercion of religious belief or enforced religious uniformity.[13] He did not expect them to succeed, for in his reading of "the last Will and Testament of Christ Jesus, we find not the least title of commission to the civil magistrate (as civil) to judge and act in the matters of his spiritual kingdom."[14]

Civil enforcement of religion leads to a degradation of Christian faith because civil protection compromises the church's integrity, makes it complicit in the use of violence, and leads it to moral laxity. As a Protestant, Williams believed that corruption in the medieval church was a particularly potent illustration of this judgment, but he also thought it true of royal

---

[11] For Williams's insistence that coercion simply leads to hypocritical conformity rather than genuine reform, see *The Bloudy Tenent, ORL*, 114 and 119. For his fear that coercion sometimes makes it harder to convince a conscientious dissenter of the error in their ways, see *The Bloudy Tenent Yet More Bloudy, ORL*, 224. In both texts, Williams also makes the point that coercion reflects badly on Christian religion (*ORL*, 114 and 216, respectively).

[12] *The Bloudy Tenent, ORL*, 126–27.

[13] *Queries, ORL*, 78.

[14] *The Fourth Paper, ORL*, 233.

patronage in the Church of England in his day. In fact, Williams was convinced that the church was its holiest when it was persecuted. He wondered aloud "whether Christianity did ever so flourish as when the people of God, in the first three hundred years of Christ, had no might but that of Christ's spiritual weapons," arguing that Constantine's political establishment of Christianity as the official religion of the Roman Empire was the beginning of the end for the Western church.[15]

But the separation of civil and spiritual matters is just as important for civil society, argued Williams, for he was convinced that religious persecution caused significantly more political conflict than religious pluralism and dissent. According to Williams, it is not religious diversity that causes civil strife, but the effort to coercively silence it. For evidence, he pointed to recent European history:

> The cry of the whole earth, made drunk with the blood of its inhabitants, slaughtering each other in the blind zeal for conscience, for religion, against the Catholics, against the Lutherans, etc. What fearful cries within these twenty years of hundreds of thousands of men, women, children, fathers, mothers, husbands, wives, brothers, sisters, old and young, high and low, plundered, ravished, slaughtered, murdered, famished! And hence these cries, that man fling away the spiritual sword and spiritual artillery . . . and rather trust for the suppressing of each other's God, conscience, and religion . . . to an arm of flesh and sword of steel![16]

Coercion in matters of religion, said Williams, violates "the common principles of all civility" and "kindles the devouring flames of combustions and wars in most nations of the world."[17] He declared that "there is no doctrine, no tenant so directly tending to break the cities' peace as this

---

[15] *The Examiner Defended, ORL,* 241.
[16] *The Bloudy Tenent, ORL,* 92–93.
[17] *The Bloudy Tenent Yet More Bloudy, ORL,* 224–25.

doctrine of persecuting or punishing each other for cause of conscience or religion."[18]

What frustrated Williams was his opponents' inability to see that orthodox religion—from a society or its leaders—is not necessary for civil society to flourish. Examples abound, he observed, of societies that maintain peace and order and allow citizens to live productive lives without the enforcement of proper Christianity. "So many stately kingdoms and governments in the world have long and long enjoyed civil peace and quiet, notwithstanding their religion is so corrupt as that there is not the very name of Jesus Christ amongst them. And this every historian, merchant, [and] traveler in Europe, Asia, Africa, and America can testify."[19] Especially powerful were his nods toward Catholic, Muslim, and Native American communities, given English Protestants' open suspicion of all three groups. Williams thought it obvious that Catholic and Muslim societies were capable of flourishing, even though the official religion in their realms was one English Protestants considered repugnant. So it was with Native American communities with which Williams engaged in New England, whom he thought outperformed English society on several moral markers, including their concern for one another and hospitality to strangers.[20] If whole communities of reprobates could create healthy societies, so Catholics, Muslims, Jews, and other citizens within England could be trusted to be "civil and courteous and peaceable."[21]

Williams's commitment to the separation of church and state was not based on an acceptance of, or even respect for, alternate visions of religious truth. Williams argued for religious liberty and moral respect for Catholics, Jews, Muslims, atheists, "pagans," and other groups despite

---

[18] *The Bloudy Tenent Yet More Bloudy*, ORL, 183.

[19] *The Bloudy Tenent*, ORL, 133.

[20] Roger Williams, *Key into the Language of America* (1643; Bedford, MA: Applewood, 1997), 7, 129.

[21] *The Bloudy Tenent Yet More Bloudy*, ORL, 190.

believing they were all going to hell. (To be fair, Williams believed most English Protestants were headed there too.) His commitment to religious liberty did not depend on theological ambivalence but on his deeply held religious commitments. As a good Calvinist, Williams believed God endowed all human beings with a natural capacity for creating moral community: "It is most true that godliness is profitable for all things, all estates, all relations. Yet there is a civil faithfulness, obedience, honesty, [and] chastity even amongst such as own not God nor Christ."[22] A natural capacity for moral and civil leadership could equip a person to be a just and caring ruler, regardless of whether that leader subscribed to Christianity. In fact, he thought it a waste for a society like England to limit leadership opportunities to professing Christians: "There is a moral virtue, a moral fidelity, ability, and honesty which other men (besides church members) are, by good nature and education, by good laws and good examples, nourished and trained up in—[so] that civil places of trust and credit need not be monopolized into the hands of church members (who sometimes are not fitted for them), and all others deprived and despoiled of their natural and civil rights and liberties."[23] Williams knew that examples abounded of societies in which citizens and their leaders outperformed the English in moral and civic duty, despite "on whose souls he has not yet pleased to shine in the face of Jesus Christ."[24] He believed their success was due to a common grace God gave all human beings, whether or not they acknowledged the God in Christ as its source. As a result, "many thousands of cities and states in the world have and

---

[22] *The Bloudy Tenent Yet More Bloudy*, ORL, 194. For more on this natural capacity for civic virtue and how Williams's understanding of it was rooted in a Puritan conception of natural law, see James Calvin Davis, *The Moral Theology of Roger Williams: Christian Conviction and Public Ethics* (Louisville: Westminster John Knox, 2004), especially chapters 3 and 5.

[23] *The Bloudy Tenent Yet More Bloudy*, ORL, 206–7.

[24] *The Bloudy Tenent*, ORL, 144. See also *The Bloudy Tenent Yet More Bloudy*, ORL, 201.

do flourish, for many generations and ages of men, wherein (whatever Caesar gets) God cannot get one penny of his due in any bare permission or toleration of his religion and worship."[25]

Ultimately, Williams believed the realms of the civil and the spiritual were best kept as separate as possible. The civil magistrate's responsibility was to the "bodies and goods" of the state, not the religious subscription of their spirits.[26] The church did not require civil protection to survive and flourish, and the state did not require the establishment of Christianity to assure peace, order, or moral health. To give the state jurisdiction over ensuring the health of the church puts Christianity at risk, by threatening to dissolve piety into nothing more than civil religion: "When Constantine . . . drew the sword of civil power in the suppressing of other consciences for the establishing of the Christian, then began the great mystery of the church's sleep, the gardens of Christ's churches turned into the wilderness of national religion."[27] Over a century before Thomas Jefferson penned a similar phrase, Williams argued that God intended a "hedge or wall of separation between the Garden of the church and the wilderness of the world" and that Christians "opened a gap" in that wall to the detriment of both church and state.[28]

---

[25] *The Bloudy Tenent Yet More Bloudy, ORL*, 197.

[26] *The Bloudy Tenent, ORL*, 87.

[27] *The Bloudy Tenent Yet More Bloudy, ORL*, 217.

[28] *Mr. Cotton's Letter, ORL*, 70. Although they used the same metaphor, Williams and Jefferson understood the importance of this "wall of separation" between church and state in different ways. For the anticlerical Jefferson, the separation was primarily important to protect the state from overreaching religious establishment; the fact that he used the metaphor in a letter to Connecticut Baptists was more an indication of Jefferson's need for political allies than his deep concern for minority religious communities. For Williams, the "wall of separation" was meant to protect the integrity of the church, religious Dissenters, and the state itself. In other words, Williams had both theological and political concerns in mind when he imagined a sharp distinction between religious and civil institutional power.

Controversies

As much as he advocated a separation of civil and spiritual concerns, however, Williams recognized that it is impossible to define their separation *absolutely*. In reality, the two realms of church and state occasionally will intersect, particularly around the *acts* and *practices* of minority religious communities. Sometimes convictions will commend an action that runs afoul of civil law, and other times religious beliefs will require an adherent to abstain from an action civil society generally requires. It is the sphere of action, not thought or even necessarily speech, where appeals to religious freedom run up hardest against social obligations. Williams recognized this potential for conflict, and he had to navigate it in several episodes of his leadership in Rhode Island.

Unsurprisingly, none of Williams's texts arguing for religious liberty was published—or even allowed—in New England, and several of them were burned by factions in the mother country. The only text Williams ever wrote that was published in Boston was the transcript of his debates with Quaker insurgents in Rhode Island in August 1672. Most of *George Fox Digged Out of His Burrowes* is a point-by-point rebuttal of the theological beliefs of three Quaker emissaries, the account of which delighted the Quaker-hating Massachusetts leadership. Periodically, though, *George Fox* reflects Williams's objections to the way the Quakers behaved toward him and others, as well as his willingness to invoke civil penalties for that behavior. He resented the Quakers' penchant for interrupting him and shouting him down, and he called out their disregard for honorific titles and disruption of religious and civil ceremonies. Williams argued that the Quakers were not just being rude in a trivial way, but they acted in a manner that communicated disrespect for their fellow citizens and civil order. He considered these public affronts to be violations of civility or a society's norms for public moral conduct. Violations of civility were a challenge to social expectations, and they threatened the stability and authorities of civil society. Their actions were civilly dangerous and, thus, subject to restrictions and penalties, even if they were offered in the name of religious freedom. As he wrote in *George Fox*, "I have therefore publicly declared that a due and moderate restraint and punishing of these incivilities (though pretending conscience) is as far from persecution (properly so called) as that it is a duty and command of God to all mankind, first in families, and then in all [human] societies."[29]

Williams regarded some of the Quakers' public behavior so disruptive to standards of decency, order, and authority that he was willing to entertain penalties for some of their practices. He also argued that religiously inspired *abstentions* from actions considered social obligations could be met with civil penalty. In 1665 Providence voted to form a militia to protect itself both from Native American tribes and efforts of the other colonies to encroach on their territory. Some residents of the town, including Williams's own brother, refused to serve in the militia, and they invoked a conscientious objection to violence as the reason. Williams's response was direct and clear: religious liberty is not a blank check to do (or avoid doing) whatever you want. "That ever I should speak or write a tittle that tends to such an infinite liberty of conscience is a mistake," he assured them, "and [one] which I have ever disclaimed and abhorred."[30] He compared the civic compact to a ship at sea: if every sailor had the right to invoke conscientious objection to avoid doing his duty, the ship would not reach its destination and the entire crew would perish. The common good obliges us to certain responsibilities, and sometimes those responsibilities override our right to practice our convictions. In this case, Williams believed a citizen's obligation to the collective defense necessarily overrode a principled objection to violence.[31]

---

[29] *George Fox*, *ORL*, 263. See also *The Hireling Ministry*, *ORL*, 258.

[30] *A Letter to the Town of Providence* (1655), *ORL*, 278.

[31] Williams employed this nautical metaphor several times in his writings, sometimes to illustrate the irrelevance of Christian piety to public leadership and sometimes (as here) to make the point about the importance of commitment to the common good. In *The Examiner Defended*, he introduced the image and then argued "not to endeavor the common good, and to exempt ourselves from the sense

With both the Quaker agitators and the militia Dissenters, Williams acknowledged that sometimes individual convictions urge actions (or abstentions) that conflict with social duty. In those moments, we must do the hard work of navigating that conflict, and we must recognize that sometimes the result of that negotiation will be our considered judgment that social duty trumps conscience-driven practice. Williams was clear, however, that restrictions on religious practice should be a last resort, to be employed reluctantly in the adjudication of conflict between rights and duties.

To some of Williams's critics, in his day and since, his willingness to entertain limits to religious liberty looks like a significant move away from the commitment to freedom of conscience that got him exiled from Massachusetts.[32] In reality, however, Williams simply acknowledged the inevitability of conflict between liberty and the public good, something that would have been more immediately clear to him as a political leader in Rhode Island than a Dissenter in Massachusetts. Compared to the Massachusetts leadership, Williams's openness to restrictions on religious expression was much more cautious. His working default remained a robust protection of religious liberty that occasionally had limits, rather than a default commitment to religious conformity as a public good. Though the distinction may seem subtle, it is tremendously important, for it is the difference between a realistic commitment to individual freedom within the context of a common good and a persistent imposition upon freedom in the name of the public good.

Even if we grant that this balancing act is necessary, however, we must also acknowledge that it is difficult to discern the line between individual right and social obligation. Williams sometimes implied that the

---

of common evil is a treacherous baseness, a selfish monopoly, a kind of tyranny, and tends to the destruction both of cabin and ship, that is, of private and public safety." See *The Examiner Defended, ORL*, 238.

[32] For an example of this interpretation, see Edmund S. Morgan, *Roger Williams: The Church and the State* (New York: Harcourt, Brace, & World, 1967), 133–35.

distinction between benign and socially malignant religious practices was easier to delineate than it is. For instance, he thought it obvious that verbal incivility and immodest appearance were real harms to society that warranted restriction of religious practice, when most people today would contest his assumptions on either front. His concern about long hair and acceptable salutations similarly marks him as a man of his time. Even his historically myopic assumptions instruct us, however, because they remind us how hard it is to define the boundary between appropriate protections for religious freedom and necessary restriction on freedom in the name of the common good. In our day, concern with long hair and pronouns has been replaced by conscientious objections in the name of sexual and reproductive moral values, for instance, but the challenge is the same. When should we protect unpopular practices or the conscientious objection to certain civil requirements out of respect for religion, and when must we curtail religious freedom in the name of a collective good? This is the great challenge in appeals to freedom of conscience, but Williams offers us three cautions.

First, he reminds us we cannot avoid the challenge altogether, either by giving religion a categorical veto over social requirements or by restricting the protection of religious convictions to private belief or speech. Williams acknowledged that sometimes public good appropriately overrides appeals to conscience, but he also rejected a straightforward "private-public" distinction in figuring out when to do so.[33] He was unwilling to say categorically, as Locke and Jefferson did, that conscientious convictions were protected only when they remained private, that is, as long as they remained unintrusive in public life. Williams recognized that religious belief consists not just of

---

[33] Reading a strict "private-public" distinction into Williams's understanding of religious freedom is just one example of how scholars have insisted on interpreting Williams through Thomas Jefferson. See, for instance, Ellis M. West, "Roger Williams on the Limits of Religious Liberty," *Annual of the Society of Christian Ethics* 8 (1988): 139–40.

words and opinions, of course; it also mandates actions, and when religion manifests in public acts (or the rejection of civilly required acts), no easy private-public formula will do justice to the protection of religious freedom, at least as Williams understood it.[34]

Second, Williams reminds us that in those moments when we conclude that some curtailment of religious practice is justified in the name of the public good, we should never lose sight of the fact that we are engaging in coercion of conscience. It is not the case that there is no injury because the coercion is justified; rather, we determine the injury is justified when measured against the social cost of the conscientious objection. This distinction is important because it reminds us that moments of incursion on religious liberty in the name of public good still do harm to the dissenting religious citizen by requiring them to do (or not do) something their conscience tells them is wrong (or right). Consequently, even if our collective judgment is that the harm to religious freedom is necessary, such moments of encroachment ought to be engaged deliberately, thoughtfully, and conservatively.

Finally, in forcefully making the case for separation of church and state, Williams defiantly rejected the assumption that civic health depends on the protection of religion and vice versa. In arguing that "the flourishing of religion is the flourishing of the civil state, and decay of religion is the decay and ruin of the civil state," John Cotton simply echoed a presumption that many Christian thinkers before and after him have taken for granted.[35] In contrast, Williams insisted it was the *separation* of church from state, not mutual sponsorship, that ensures health for them both.

---

[34] For Williams's rejection of this simplistic private-public distinction, which he believed John Cotton ironically employed to justify his banishment, see *The Bloudy Tenent, ORL*, 120.

[35] John Cotton, *The Bloudy Tenent, Washed and Made White in the Blood of the Lamb* (1647) in Alan Heimert and Andrew Delbanco, ed., *The Puritans in America: A Narrative Anthology* (Cambridge: Harvard University, 2021) 205.

Legacies

While hardly celebrated in his time, and often eclipsed by First Amendment heroes like Thomas Jefferson and James Madison ever since, Roger Williams had a profound influence on American political history, in part because of his importance to an emergent Baptist political theology in the eighteenth century.[36] By the time of the Revolution, Baptists were a formidable religious presence in America and an important propellant for the new Republic's commitment to religious freedom. The chief spokesperson for Baptists in this struggle was Isaac Backus, and his resistance to religious establishment in Massachusetts made direct appeal to Williams.[37] Baptists were such an influence in the debates over religious freedom that it was to an association of Baptists in Danbury, Connecticut, that Jefferson penned his own understanding of the "wall of separation" between church and state, signaling his commitment to the protection of minority religion. Without the political alliance between Baptists and Enlightenment spokespersons, the First Amendment may never have happened, and that Baptist commitment was directly inspired by Williams's efforts a century before.[38]

More broadly, Williams's legacy lies in his reminder that the commitment to religious freedom is not just a secular Enlightenment dictum, borne from an ambivalence to religion as a personal experience. Religious

---

[36] For more on Williams's limited legacy in the generation immediately after his death, see Gaustad, *Liberty of Conscience*, 199–201.

[37] For a discussion of Isaac Backus's indebtedness to Williams, see Edwin S. Gaustad, *Roger Williams (Lives and Legacies)* (New York: Oxford University, 2005), 122–24. Williams's importance to the new Republic through the activism of the Baptists is lost even on some historians who appreciate Williams's contributions to an American doctrine of religious liberty. For instance, see Perry Miller, *Roger Williams: His Contributions to the American Tradition* (New York: Atheneum, 1974), 254.

[38] See William Lee Miller, *The First Liberty: America's Foundation in Religious Freedom* (Washington, DC: Georgetown University Press, 2003), 175–80, on the importance of this Baptist-Enlightenment alliance for securing "the first liberty" of religious freedom—and Williams's importance to the leaders of the Baptist caucus.

freedom is also a bequest of religious thinkers and communities, especially those minority Christian traditions like the Baptists who struggled against majoritarianism in the earliest days of the United States. The Christian contribution to an American doctrine of religious freedom, especially as Williams understood it, offers nuance to an understanding of this right that philosophical perspectives and their commonly thin representations of religion may not. The contribution of theological perspectives like Williams's reminds us that deeply held religious conviction is not antithetical to a commitment to religious freedom for others. As we have seen, Williams believed that most of the people he encountered, English Christians and "pagan" Americans alike, were going to hell, yet he defended to great cost the human freedom to believe, profess, and practice religious convictions that were out of step with majority perspectives.

Williams also recognized that the most complicated claims on religious freedom were those pertaining to public speech and actions because it is in the public realm where religious convictions run into civic authorities' jurisdictional claims. At the same time, Williams's respect for practice as an important manifestation of conscientious conviction prevented him from invoking a simplistic public-private distinction, where religious freedom is guaranteed only in the private realm and is uncritically regulated once it dares to venture into public life. Williams recognized that religion, because it manifests in beliefs and actions, is necessarily a public as well as a private experience. This did not prevent him from imagining circumstances in which the public good could curtail freedom to engage in (or refrain from) public acts in the name of religion. But he understood that such restrictions on religion had to be justified more carefully than an artificially hard distinction between private and public realms.[39]

---

[39] See Timothy L. Hall, *Separating Church and State: Roger Williams and Religious Liberty* (Urbana: University of Illinois Press, 1998), 116–32, for more on Locke and Jefferson's assumption of a rigid distinction between private and public matters (rooted in an equally firm distinction between beliefs and acts) and the

Finally, because Williams understood the relationship between religious freedom and social obligation to be complicated, his teachings remind us that the navigation of this relationship requires nuance and subtlety. Figuring out how to balance freedom to profess and practice religion in the public realm (especially for minority communities) with the obligations that all citizens have to the civic good requires more thoughtfulness than bumper-sticker appeals to "First Amendment rights," the "separation of church and state," the concept of a "Christian nation," or even "the common good" can capture. The hardest cases involving religious freedoms are those where a sense of the public good appears to be pitted against the right to religious expression of a minority community. The difficulty in balancing these competing claims is precisely what makes the religion clauses of the First Amendment such a taxing protection to adjudicate.

Conclusion

In American lore around the First Amendment, Thomas Jefferson and James Madison occupy most of our historical attention, yet Roger Williams was just as consequential in the formation of our national commitment to religious freedom. He inspired Baptist communities and other Dissenting groups to push for a constitutional guarantee of their religious freedom in the early days of the American Republic. Since that time, he continues to serve as an essential historical resource for the cause of religious liberty by providing a distinctly *theological* justification for conscientious freedom as a religious and civic good. Williams modeled authentic Christian investment in religious freedom as a human right, an investment grounded in religious conviction as much as political vision.

---

oversimplification of conflict between religious rights and social duties that results from assuming religion is only a matter of private "opinion."

4

The Baptists and John Locke

By Malcolm Yarnell

John Locke's profound impact upon the modern Western mind is difficult to overstate. He is "considered by many to be the greatest British philosopher of all time."[1] Voltaire, the grand *philosophe* of the French Enlightenment, christened Locke "the Hercules of metaphysics" due to his portrait of the human mind.[2] Immanuel Kant, the leading philosopher of the German *Aufklärung*, synthesized Locke to construct his own philosophy of mind and approved Locke's social contract theory and separation of political powers.[3] Henry May listed Locke among the two philosophical giants who shaped America's foundational

---

[1] Philip Stokes, *Philosophy: 100 Essential Thinkers: The Ideas That Have Shaped Our World* (London: Arcturus, 2012), 143.

[2] Voltaire to Horace Walpole, 1768; cited in Hans Aarsleff, "Locke's Influence," in *The Cambridge Companion to Locke*, ed. Vere Chappell (New York: Cambridge University, 1994), 252.

[3] Roger Scruton, *Kant: A Very Short Introduction*, 2nd ed. (New York: Oxford University, 2001), 35, 115, 121.

cultural assumptions.[4] Jonathan Edwards, America's premier philosophical theologian, read Locke's most famous work, *An Essay Concerning Human Understanding*, with excitement and lasting effect.[5] Timothy Stanton thus concludes, "Most of us have become so accustomed to thinking on Lockean assumptions and pursuing Lockean styles of explanation that we rarely pause to consider alternatives."[6]

If Locke stands like a colossus over the Western Enlightenment, my fellow Oxonian has exercised scarcely less influence on Baptists in both Great Britain and America in ways both general and specific. Locke was intimate with the leading Particular Baptist (Kiffen) and sought to advance the cause of liberty of conscience for seventeenth-century Dissenters, including Baptists. In the eighteenth century, English Baptists and other Dissenters drank deeply from the well of Locke's writings. As the British colonies in North America developed, Locke's constitutionalism imprinted itself upon colonial Baptists' social, economic, and political virtues (and vices). Locke also contributed to Baptists the most well-known theological phrase in *The New Hampshire Confession of Faith* and *The Baptist Faith and Message*. Finally, denominational historians have claimed both more and less for the relationship between Locke and Baptists than they should have. After surveying the history of Locke with the Baptists, we will consider five Lockean lessons requiring recall today.

Locke and Seventeenth-Century Dissenters

John Locke's earliest recorded intellectual ruminations affirmed fidelity to the Church of England and the Crown. In late 1660, he queried "whether

---

[4] Henry F. May, *The Enlightenment in America* (New York: Oxford University, 1976), 5.

[5] Aarsleff, "Locke's Influence," 252.

[6] Timothy Stanton, "The Reception of Locke in England in the Early Eighteenth Century: Metaphysics, Religion, and the State," in *The Bloomsbury Companion to Locke*, ed. S.-J. Savonius-Wroth, Paul Schuurman, and Jonathan Walmsley (New York: Bloomsbury, 2014), 301.

the civil magistrate may lawfully impose and determine the use of indifferent things in reference to religious worship." Yes, he answered, magistrates may legislate in matters not addressed by God's law through nature or Scripture. Manifesting typical conformist fears, he reasoned universal freedom would "turn us loose to the tyranny of a religious rage." Liberty of conscience may be held privately, but public dissent from the magisterial church only incites social turmoil.[7]

However, during a 1665 embassy for the English Crown to Brandenburg, he observed a new phenomenon. In the divided city of Cleves, the Lutherans, Calvinists, and Catholics "quietly permit one another to choose their way to heaven."[8] By January 20, 1667, Locke had returned to London, where a sermon by a Nonconformist preacher helped initiate a radical shift in Locke's views. The Dissenter exposited Gal 5:6: "For in Jesus Christ neither circumcision availeth any thing, nor uncircumcision; but faith which worketh by love" (KJV). In his notes, Locke reported an anthropology granting the human being more capability, responsibility, and peaceability than he once allowed. The human being "is an active and rational creature endowed with a faculty of apprehending good and evil, and according to his apprehension, choosing and coveting the one, but refusing and turning from the other." An individual person's faculty of reason is, therefore, capable of perceiving moral truth. Personal reason informs the personal will to act. The human being may then move responsibly from merely internal assent to engage in "actions of piety and charity." Faith is not to be held as merely private, as he previously thought, but also public. "Faith worketh by love."[9]

---

[7] Roger Woolhouse, *Locke: A Biography* (New York: Cambridge University, 2007), 39–43.

[8] John Locke to Robert Boyle, December 22, 1665, in *The Correspondence of John Locke*, ed. E. S. de Beer, vol. 1 (Oxford: Clarendon, 1976), 228. Boyle, one of the leading scientists of the early Enlightenment, was a lifelong friend.

[9] Richard Ashcraft, *Revolutionary Politics and Locke's Two Treatises of Government* (Princeton: Princeton University, 1986), 92–93.

When faith works by love, it expresses "affection and general good will for men." Moreover, such affection must be extended to all. Faith working by love "makes every man a neighbor, and a neighbor a brother." However, there are also false faiths. Some "forget their fallible and imperfect nature" and hate "those who are not of our way, our sect, or party." These false Christians work "under a pretence of zealous contending fury" and exhibit both "bitterness of spirit" and "contention." Richard Ashcraft says it is difficult to tell whether Locke is merely recording the Dissenting preacher's viewpoint or advocating it. But Locke himself soon argued in his 1667 *Essay on Toleration* for a similar highly personalist faith that seeks to persuade others toward truth within an idealized context of universal religious toleration.[10] Locke's subsequent views of Christianity, society, and liberty of conscience coordinated well with his contemporaries in the Baptist churches.

Locke and the Early English Baptists

The most important Baptist connection the great philosopher had was with their most prominent pastor, William Kiffen. Kiffen, a self-identified "dissenter," was also declared such by the Crown.[11] This influential pastor and wealthy businessman was the leading figure within the Particular Baptist movement from the moment it came into public view in 1642 until his death in 1701. Theologically, Kiffen headlined the signatories in both the First London Confession of Faith (1644) and the Second London Confession (1689). Politically, he led the Baptists to navigate the tumultuous changes from the Civil War through the Restoration to the Glorious Revolution.

Kiffen ably represented Baptist interests during the Protectorate and after the Restoration of the monarchy. With regard to the Protectorate,

---

[10] Ashcraft, *Revolutionary Politics*, 94–97.

[11] William Orme, *Remarkable Passages in the Life of William Kiffin: Written by Himself and Edited from the Original Manuscript* (London: Burton and Smith, 1823), 50, 159.

Captain Kiffen's daughter married one of Cromwell's grandchildren.[12] With regard to the Court, he successfully procured from King Charles II the release of twelve General Baptists sentenced to death for assembling. Alas, however, he was unable to secure the release of two grandsons, who were executed by the Lord Chief Justice George Jeffreys for their role in the Monmouth Rebellion. Jeffreys told one boy that "his grandfather did as well deserve that death, which he was likely to suffer, as he did."[13] Later, Kiffen was surprisingly favored by King James II.

In 1670, Locke helped his patron, Lord Anthony Ashley Cooper, First Earl of Shaftesbury and leading Whig politician, craft the charter for the Bahama Islands. Approved by Charles II, it contained one of the earliest constitutions enshrining liberty of conscience for Dissenters like Kiffen.[14] Locke and Kiffen became business partners in 1672, investing together in the Bahama Adventurers Company, which also owned a slave transport ship. Even after selling their interests in 1677, the two remained in close touch. Having visited Kiffen's home, Locke mentioned Kiffen four times in his personal journal and several more times in his account book. During the late 1670s, when Locke was traveling extensively in France, the Baptist served as the philosopher's London financial agent.

Baptists had been arguing for universal religious liberty since Thomas Helwys returned to London and penned a personal note to King James I on the flyleaf of his prophetic 1612 work, *A Short Declaration of the Mystery of Iniquity.*[15] Edward Underhill's collection of earlier seventeenth-century

---

[12] Alfred W. Light, *Bunhill Fields: Written in Honour and to the Memory of the Many Saints of God Whose Bodies Rest in This Old London Cemetery*, 2nd ed., vol. 1 (1915; repr., Stoke-on-Trent: Tentmaker, 2003), 94–103.

[13] Orme, *Remarkable Passages*, 82.

[14] "William Kiffen, John Locke, and the Bahama Adventurers of 1672," in Larry J. Kreitzer, ed., *William Kiffen and His World (Part 1)*, vol. 1 (Oxford: Centre for Baptist History and Heritage, 2010), 363–410.

[15] Malcolm B. Yarnell III, "'We Believe with the Heart and with the Mouth Confess': The Engaged Piety of the Early General Baptists," *Baptist Quarterly*

religious liberty texts does not, however, contain the careful and thoughtful works of one of the most poignant Baptist defenders of liberty of conscience, Thomas Delaune. Delaune had coauthored a defense of believers-only baptism with Kiffen in 1675. He then coauthored a monumental volume on biblical metaphors with Benjamin Keach in 1682.[16] However, the most relevant writings of Delaune, regarding liberty of conscience, came during the period when both radical Whigs like Locke and Baptists like Kiffen and Delaune were suspected of fostering sedition and rebellion.

Kiffen successfully steered most Baptists away from involvement with the apocalyptic insurrection of the Fifth Monarchy movement in the 1650s. He rejected their conflation of crown and church for being akin to that of divine right Royalists. Both groups usurped the rule of Jesus over the separate institutions of religion and state.[17] However, Baptists and other Dissenters were nonetheless imprisoned by the thousands after the Restoration of the monarchy in 1660, which had led to Parliament's adoption of the harsh provisions of the Clarendon Code. Among the first arrested, Baptist pastor John James was sentenced to be hanged, drawn, and quartered. William Penn estimated 5,000 Dissenters died in prison during the persecutions.[18] Baptist pastor John Bunyan, author of *The Pilgrim's Progress*, spent twelve years in prison for his refusal to stop preaching and disband his congregation.[19]

After two decades of rolling persecution, it should be of little surprise that the Rye House Plot to assassinate Charles II in 1683 included

---

44 (2011): 55. See also Edward B. Underhill, *Tracts on Liberty of Conscience and Persecution, 1614–1661* (London: Haddon, 1846).

[16] Michael A. G. Haykin, "Delaune, Thomas (d. 1685)," *Oxford Dictionary of National Biography* (Oxford: Oxford University, 2004).

[17] Two prominent Fifth Monarchy leaders, Christopher Feake and Thomas Venner, were also Baptist pastors. Ian Birch, "Baptists, Fifth Monarchists, and the Reign of King Jesus," *Perichoresis* 16 (2018): 19–34.

[18] John Marshall, *John Locke, Toleration and Early Enlightenment Culture* (New York: Cambridge University, 2006), 95–96.

[19] Marshall, *John Locke*, 101.

numerous Baptists among the radical Whigs with whom Locke affiliated. After that plot's failure, "Most of the conspirators had managed to make their way, individually and in pairs, to Holland," Locke among them.[20] The Monmouth Rebellion, an attempt to overthrow James II in 1685, was similarly populated by both radical Whigs and Dissenters,[21] including three members of Kiffen's own family.[22] The Glorious Revolution of 1688, like the previous plots, was also led by radical Whigs supported by Dissenters. This time, however, absolutist Royalism was defeated, and Locke returned with Kiffen and his wife, Mary, to finish his days in England.

Locke and Delaune on Simple Christianity

Immediately before and during his Dutch exile, Locke penned his most famous works, including *A Letter Concerning Toleration* (composed 1685–1686), *Two Treatises of Government* (composed 1679–1682), and *An Essay Concerning Human Understanding* (completed 1687), but all three were published only upon his return to England in 1689. Locke's *The Reasonableness of Christianity As Delivered in the Scriptures* was published anonymously in 1695. Locke's faith has sometimes been ignored, even cast into doubt, by those who treat him as a philosopher detached from his personal and contextual history.[23] However, scholars such as John Dunn, Jeremy Waldron, and Greg Forster argue Locke's philosophy "rests firmly upon a religious

---

[20] Ashcraft, *Revolutionary Politics*, 406–7.

[21] For a sample of revolutionary Baptist figures during these years, like Nicholas Lock and Elizabeth Gaunt, begin with Ashcraft, *Revolutionary Politics*, 461, 470. John Marshall adds Thomas Walcott, Richard Rumbold, and Joseph Keeling. Marshall, *John Locke*, 447.

[22] Ashcraft believes Kiffen himself was likely involved in the plotting. Ashcraft, *Revolutionary Politics*, 369–70, n. 136, 428.

[23] The detached interpretation of Locke has been referred to as "tomb-robbing" while the contextual reading is likened to "serious archeology." Roger Woolhouse and Timothy Stanton, "Contemporary Locke Scholarship," in *The Bloomsbury Companion to Locke*, 314.

premise."[24] Locke cannot be properly understood apart from his theological convictions.[25]

In *The Reasonableness of Christianity*, Locke set out to disclose "the Doctrine of Salvation" in a biblicist mode over against the dissatisfying portrait of the gospel painted by most "Systems of Divinity."[26] He believed Scripture was "the Written Word of God" and "a Collection of Writings designed by God for the Instruction of the illiterate bulk of Mankind in the way to Salvation." The "plain direct meaning of the words and phrases," with reference to the original "Language of that Time and Country," must have precedence over any "learned, artificial, and forced senses of them."[27] This common method of Bible study, respected by all English Protestants but embraced thoroughly by Dissenters, led Locke to affirm knowledge of the way to righteousness is available through either the law of Moses or natural law to every person. However, because every person has committed sin, law ensures death.[28]

Thankfully, faith in the covenantal promise of the Messiah will "supply the defect of full Obedience."[29] Jesus proved he was Messiah through his

---

[24] John Dunn, *The Political Thought of John Locke: An Historical Account of the Argument of the 'Two Treatises of Government'* (New York: Cambridge University, 1969), xi. See also Jeremy Waldron, *God, Locke, and Equality: Christian Foundations of Locke's Political Thought* (New York: Cambridge University, 2002); Greg Forster, *Starting with Locke* (New York: Continuum, 2011).

[25] Early American Baptists like Asa Messer recognized the Christianity of Locke too: "Hume and Paine are infidels. Locke and Newton are Christians." Asa Messer, "A Discourse Delivered in the Chapel of Rhode Island College, to the Senior Class, on the Sunday Preceding Their Commencement, 1799," in *The Literary Remains of the Rev. Jonathan Maxcy*, ed. Romeo Elton (New York: A. V. Blake, 1844), 427.

[26] John Locke, *The Reasonableness of Christianity* (1695), in *Writings on Religion*, ed. Victor Nuovo (New York: Oxford University, 2002), 89. "Biblicist" is used here in its original, positive, early modern sense of simple dependence upon Scripture.

[27] Locke, *The Reasonableness of Christianity*, 91.

[28] Locke, 96–98.

[29] Locke, 100–101.

resurrection. Human salvation or damnation thus depends upon how each person responds to "this single Truth," "this one Proposition."[30] Relying upon the apostles, Locke refused to make anything beyond this simple evangelical claim necessary for salvation: "I mean, This was all the Doctrine they proposed to be believed."[31] The remainder of the Christian faith develops from "this Fundamental article."[32] Those churchmen who make their own theological and moral inferences fundamental for salvation are guilty of "Priest-craft," an undue grasping after authority.[33] Locke believed "the simplicity of the Gospel" can save even the "poor," for it is "plain and intelligible" rather than "filled with speculations and niceties, obscure terms, and abstract notions."[34]

To demonstrate where early Baptists and John Locke coalesced in their religious and political beliefs, it may be helpful to compare the philosopher with one of the Baptists. Delaune displays a similar simplicity of faith, depth in learning, and ability to turn a phrase with Locke. However, where Locke alluded to contemporary events with studied reserve, the Baptist schoolmaster was more confrontational, though politely so. Delaune's political naivety, in contrast to Locke's savvy, ended with terrible results. In 1683, Delaune wrote *Compulsion of Conscience Condemned* to show how the Church of England's intolerance toward religious Dissenters was not only contrary to Scripture, but also to England's "Fundamental Laws" and natural standards of justice. Delaune used a biblical hermeneutic similar to Locke's, preferring that which is "plainly Demonstrated."[35] Like Locke, Delaune taught that "Love" is required of

---

[30] Locke, 108–9.

[31] Locke, 128.

[32] Locke, 132–34; cf. 208–9.

[33] Locke, 203.

[34] Locke, 210.

[35] Thomas Delaune, *Compulsion of Conscience Condemned* (London: John How, 1683), 34.

"all that profess his Name."[36] And like Locke in *The Reasonableness of Christianity*, Delaune described Scripture as "the Word of God" in which all God's children have "an Equal Interest."[37]

In a philosophical vein the author of *An Essay Concerning Human Understanding* would soon make famous, Delaune claimed human beings must exercise their reason vigorously rather than depend upon "blind assent," for reason is "the Essential part of Man."[38] Moreover, like Locke, Delaune believed God placed "the Light of Nature" before all human beings to require them to act morally. And, as with Locke, Delaune distinguished between that which is universally "clear in Scripture" and those peculiar inferences derived from various minds.[39] Like Locke, Delaune decried the systems of "School-Divinity," yet commended learning the biblical languages.[40] Like Locke, Delaune simplified his exposition of the fundamentals of salvation. The commands to love God and neighbor and to have "Faith in Christ Jesus" summarize the law and the gospel.[41] Finally, like Locke, Delaune believed God's law and the gospel of Jesus Christ were available to "any Reader of common Capacity."[42]

---

[36] Delaune, 5–7.

[37] Delaune, 8.

[38] Delaune, 9. See also John Locke, *An Essay Concerning Human Understanding*, ed. A. S. Pringle-Pattison and Diané Collinson (Ware, UK: Wordsworth Classics, 1998). "Understanding" is "the most elevated faculty of the soul." Moreover, "it is not worth while to be concerned what he say or thinks, who says or thinks only as he is directed by another." Locke, 3–4.

[39] Delaune, *Compulsion of Conscience*, 10.

[40] Delaune, 13, 19.

[41] Delaune quickly proceeds through the deity of Christ to the moral duties of the believer. Delaune, *Compulsion of Conscience*, 32. "It was enough for the Apostle to know nothing but Jesus Christ, and him Crucified, and 'tis most assuredly true, that whatsoever is necessary to Salvation, is so plainly laid down in the Scripture, that the meanest Capacity may (by the aid of Divine Grace) understand it." Delaune, 34.

[42] Delaune, 35.

Locke on Governance

Whereas John Locke wrote *The Reasonableness of Christianity* and *An Essay Concerning Human Understanding* as general pieces, he wrote *Two Treatises of Government* to counteract the Tories and Church of England clergy who were advocating Robert Filmer's religiopolitical system.[43] Locke published this basic text in the canon of modern political liberalism anonymously,[44] perhaps because England's final book burning, staged in Oxford University's Bodleian Quadrangle after the 1683 Rye House Plot, was fresh on his mind.[45] Locke grounded his opposition to Filmer, described by his modern editor as "an uncompromising absolutist,"[46] upon his own egalitarian theological exegesis of the book of Genesis.

Filmer, an enthusiastic patriarchist, argued that Adam as first father received rule over all humanity. Adam's right to rule was then passed through the patriarchs down to contemporary kings.[47] The fifth commandment, requiring obedience to the father, is thereby applicable to politics. The "natural power" of kings to rule thus derives from the divine right of Adam. The opposing "unnatural" idea that people have a right to rebellion against a tyrannical monarch is dismissed as the innovation of papist scholars and overzealous Genevan Protestants.[48]

Locke's theological exegesis answered Filmer's three questions about Adam. First, is Adam sovereign by creation? While Adam was certainly created by God, Locke believed the donative act of dominion occurred after creation and human governance was established after the fall.[49] The gift of

---

[43] Robert Filmer, *Patriarcha and Other Writings*, ed. Jóhann P. Sommerville (New York: Cambridge University, 1991).

[44] John Locke, *Two Treatises of Government*, ed. Peter Laslett (New York: Cambridge University, 1960), 135–43.

[45] Locke, 24; Ashcraft, *Revolutionary Politics*, 404–5.

[46] Filmer, *Patriarcha*, xi.

[47] Filmer, 6–7.

[48] Filmer, 2–3.

[49] Locke, *Two Treatises of Government*, 151–55.

dominion certainly grounds human ownership of earthly property, but it does not manifestly grant a man sovereignty over other humans.[50] Second, did Adam have dominion over Eve? Genesis 3:16 describes the difficult power relation between the first man and the first woman, which occurred because of the fall and not by creation. While the fallen woman was punished with struggle, the fallen man was not rewarded with monarchy but punished with servitude. Genesis 3:16 has to do with family relations, not state relations.[51] Third, did Adam have dominion over his children? *Jure divino* patriarchists believed fathers have the power of life and death because they supposedly gave life to their children. Locke responded that only God may give and take life.

Locke deconstructed the facile and self-serving hermeneutic of Filmer and his absolutist patriarchal-monarchical ilk. A man is not made sovereign over others simply because he is born a man, marries a wife, and/ or conceives children. God alone is the absolute, sovereign king![52] In his second treatise, Locke turned toward the more practical aspects of government. His ideas about personal rights were based on equality in the state of nature while diverse political orders were based on voluntary social contract. Government requires a separation of powers to preserve both individual human dignity and property rights.[53]

Locke and Delaune on Liberty of Conscience

Locke addressed the relation between religion and governance in *A Letter Concerning Toleration*. The Latin version and the English translation by

---

[50] Locke, 157.

[51] Locke, 171–74.

[52] Locke, 176–79.

[53] Locke, 267ff. For a relevant structural summary of Locke's general political philosophy, including his treatises on government, see Malcolm B. Yarnell III, *John Locke's 'Letters of Gold': Universal Priesthood and the English Dissenting Theologians, 1688–1789* (Oxford: Centre for Baptist History and Heritage, 2017), 4–15.

William Popple were published anonymously in 1689, but Locke was outed as the author.[54] Locke began by claiming "mutual toleration among Christians" as "the principal mark of the true church." Those engaged in forcing "orthodoxy" upon others exhibit to the contrary "signs of competition for power and dominion."[55] God grounds toleration in Christ's command to love. All who follow Christ may be deemed Christian, but persecutors are hypocrites who contradict Christ's call to discipleship.[56] "We must above all distinguish between political and religious matters, and properly define the boundary between church and commonwealth."[57] Commonwealths are established for the preservation of life, liberty, and property. Their purposes cannot include the salvation of souls for three reasons: each human being is directly responsible to God; true religion must be embraced internally by persuasion alone; and there is only one way of salvation, yet diverse opinions about that way exist in every commonwealth, so none may be privileged.[58]

Locke adopted both the religious psychology and congregationalism of the evangelical Dissenters. The definition of "church," according to Matt 18:20, is "a free and voluntary association. No one is born a member of any church."[59] The duties, therefore, of "mutual toleration" extend to four entities: individuals, churches, clerics, and rulers. First, all "human rights" and "civil rights" are grounded in the maintenance of a real respect for the

---

[54] Locke exchanged a series of letters with Jonas Proast, a defender of the *ancien régime* relation between state and church. The original letter and relevant excerpts from the exchange are gathered in Richard Vernon, ed., *Locke on Toleration*, Cambridge Texts in the History of Philosophy, trans. Michael Silverthorne (New York: Cambridge University, 2010).

[55] Vernon, *Locke on Toleration*, 3.

[56] Vernon, 4–5. Persecutors also fail to perceive the differences between what Scripture defines as "necessary and fundamental beliefs" and what are their own peculiar inferences. Vernon, 44–46.

[57] Vernon, 6.

[58] Vernon, 7–9.

[59] Vernon, 9–10.

inviolability of the religious conscience.[60] Second, the "pretext of religion" may not be used to attack the rights of other churches, for "every church is orthodox in its own eyes."[61] Third, each church's clergy have their authority "confined only within the bounds of [their] church." They cannot appeal for help to civil authority in swaying others.[62]

Fourth, the ruler must recognize that "each person then has a care for his own soul and must be allowed to exercise this care."[63] The Christian ruler's personal duties to the church do not include enforcing either ritual or doctrine, including indifferent matters.[64] Locke reminded rulers they must leave people to follow their religious conscience and warned that religious zeal covers a lust for power. Christians are not under Mosaic law but the gospel, and "under the Gospel there is absolutely no such thing as a Christian commonwealth."[65] Locke recognized four special cases when civil society is truly endangered and the ruler may take an interest in what goes on in religious assemblies.[66] Locke's advocacy of toleration, though advanced, was not as liberal as that of the Baptist Roger Williams.[67] Nevertheless, the philoso-

---

[60] Vernon, 13.

[61] Vernon, 14–15.

[62] Vernon, 15–17.

[63] Vernon, 17. "You can say all you like about your goodwill for another person, you can strive as you like for their salvation—a person cannot be forced to be saved. At the end of the day he must be left to himself and his own conscience. Vernon, 21.

[64] Vernon, 22–26.

[65] Vernon, 27–29.

[66] When a dangerous teaching is condemned by the whole human race, when Roman Catholicism undermines the state, when Muslims claim loyalty to another ruler, and when professing atheism, which is presumed to have no moral basis. Vernon, 35–37.

[67] Teresa Bejan demonstrates Locke's idea of toleration was limited in comparison to Roger Williams, the early American advocate of religious liberty who was also a Baptist for a short time. Williams taught not the "civil silence" of Thomas Hobbes, nor the "civil charity" of John Locke, but "mere civility." Bejan defines the latter as "minimal conformity to norms of respectful behavior and decorum expected of all members of a tolerant society as such." Williams thus required less

pher concluded, like the earlier Baptist Helwys, that religious liberty should be extended even to heretics, pagans, Muslims, and Jews, for Christianity is a "peace-loving religion."[68]

Thomas Delaune's *Compulsion of Conscience* had been written as a general piece to help Dissenters argue against persecution. However, his next book was written in direct response to the conformist Benjamin Calamy's lionized sermon of 1683, *A Discourse about a Scrupulous Conscience.* Calamy was the son and younger brother of two ministers ejected for nonconformity. His major patron was George Jeffreys, to whom he dedicated his famous work.[69] It will be remembered Jeffreys would soon prosecute the execution of Kiffen's grandsons. More recently, Jeffreys had sentenced a radical Whig, Stephen College, to death, and Locke personally coordinated the radical Whig's defense in Oxford.[70] Soon after, when Jeffreys also pursued the condemnation of Algernon Sidney, a fellow political philosopher in Shaftesbury's circle, Locke fled the country.[71] Locke was then deprived of his lifelong fellowship at Christ Church College in Oxford "for Whiggism" at the request of Charles II.[72] James II sought Locke's extradition from the Netherlands after coming to the throne, but Locke evaded capture.

Unlike Locke, the Baptist Delaune chose to remain vulnerable in England. Staying under royal sovereignty, Delaune defended the Radical Whig position publicly. Alas, however, Jeffreys, the judicial hammer of

---

conformity than Locke, and Locke required less than Hobbes, but there is a difference between the three approaches. Teresa M. Bejan, *Mere Civility: Disagreement and the Limits of Toleration* (Cambridge: Harvard University, 2017), 9–13.

[68] Vernon, *Locke on Toleration*, 41.

[69] Benjamin Calamy, *A Discourse about a Scrupulous Conscience* (London: Rowland Reynolds, 1683), "The Epistle Dedicatory." Jeffreys had procured Calamy's first curacy for him, granting to the conformist son that place from which his nonconformist father had been ejected. "Calamy, Benjamin," *Oxford Dictionary of National Biography*, vol. 8 (Oxford; Oxford University, 1886).

[70] Ashcraft, *Revolutionary Politics*, 345–47.

[71] Ashcraft, 404–6, 422.

[72] Woolhouse, *Locke*, 207–11.

the monarch, took a prejudiced interest in the Calamy-Delaune debate. Judge Jeffreys instructed the jury at Delaune's trial to consider his recent book a formal breach of the law against "force and arms," which deserved the judgment of sedition.[73] The accusation that Baptists, Quakers, and other Dissenters were "Seditious Sectaries" was a common trope justifying such persecution.[74] The debate between Delaune and Calamy discloses the ideas that were in debate between Royalists like Filmer and Calamy, on the one side, and Radical Whigs like Locke and Dissenters like Delaune, on the other.

Calamy argued that a "scrupulous" conscience was not an acceptable reason for disobeying the royal will for the church, even in indifferent matters. The scrupulous conscience is only concerned with indifferent things, in which it may err.[75] Moreover, scrupulosity is "a sign of Hypocrisie" and a pretence to superiority.[76] Calamy said the Dissenters' appeal to the "royal priesthood" of all believers wrongly undercuts the authorized priesthood of the national clergy.[77] He labeled the Dissenters' regulative principle a "superstition." The people should merely submit to the publicly authorized clergy rather than elevate their private opinions.

Calamy's overarching rule for the proper governance of conscience is stated succinctly as "not wilfully to omit any thing that God hath commanded, to avoid to the utmost of our Power what God hath forbid; and what ever else we have no particular divine law about, to guide our selves by the general rules of Scripture, the commands of our Superiours, and by the measures of Prudence, Peace, and Charity."[78] The back cover of

---

[73] *A Narrative of the Sufferings of Thomas Delaune* ([n.p.]: [n.pub.], 1684), 15.

[74] Richard L. Greaves, "Seditious Sectaries or 'Sober and Useful Inhabitants'? Changing Conceptions of the Quakers in Early Modern Britain," *Albion* 33 (2001): 24–50; Marshall, *John Locke*, 440–44.

[75] Calamy, *A Discourse about a Scrupulous Conscience*, 4–5.

[76] Calamy, 10–11.

[77] Calamy, 11–12.

[78] Calamy, 31.

Calamy's book listed "Anabaptists," who notoriously appealed to liberty of conscience, first in the slippery slope to atheism.

Speaking for the proponents of religious liberty, Delaune responded to Calamy in 1684 with *A Plea for the Non-Conformists*. Evincing a deep knowledge of both church history and English law, Delaune constructed a three-way comparison between Roman Catholic persecution, the Church of England's unreasonable demands for conformity, and the Nonconformist understanding of biblical Christianity and liberty of conscience. Delaune answered five major objections that both Calamy and Edward Stillingfleet, one of Locke's primary opponents, made against the Dissenters' case for religious liberty.[79]

First, Conformists argue they are not demanding anything forbidden by Scripture. The Nonconformists replied with the regulative principle: they may obey only what Scripture commands.[80] Second, Conformists argue there is no cause for separation, because the disputed matters were "small indifferent things." But the Nonconformists pointed to the hypocrisy of the state "imposing" these same things as if they were "absolutely necessary."[81] Third, Conformists argue the indifferent matters they require predated the pretensions of Roman Catholicism. Delaune responded with a lengthy series of examples demonstrating this was not always the case. Ultimately, for Delaune, if any practice lacks biblical sanction, it must not be required.[82]

The fourth and fifth objections revolved around the Conformist concern that Dissenters are seditious by virtue of religious nonconformity.

---

[79] Neil Fairlamb, "Edward Stillingfleet (1635–99)," in *The Bloomsbury Companion to Locke*, 113–16.

[80] Thomas Delaune, *A Plea for the Non-Conformists, Giving the True State of the Dissenters Case* (London: [n.pub.], 1684), 3–8. For a three-way comparison between paganism, papacy, and true Christianity, see Thomas Delaune, Εἰκων του θηριου. *Or, the Image of the Beast* (n.p.: 1684). Available on Google Books.

[81] Delaune, *A Plea*, 9–14.

[82] Delaune, 14–66.

Delaune agreed that Nonconformists must obey the magistrate for the sake of "conscience." However, just as the midwives disobeyed Pharaoh in order to obey God, so the Nonconformists should obey only "in all lawful things." Moreover, if any Dissenters were actually engaged in physical treason and sedition, rather than religious nonconformity, they should be prosecuted.[83] Reflecting Locke's parallel concerns for both liberty and property, Delaune appealed to the generally "peaceable and profitable" nature of the Dissenters.[84]

While he addressed the opponents of the Radical Whigs and the Dissenters in his discourses favoring religious tolerance, Delaune's reasoning closely tracks that of Locke.[85] Sadly, however, Delaune died in the horrific confines of Newgate Prison, despite repeated appeals to Calamy for assistance. Delaune's impoverished wife and their two small children perished with him in the gaol by February 1685.[86] Thomas Delaune and his family must be counted among the most pitiful Baptist martyrs for liberty of conscience. The triumph of the Glorious Revolution, which was supported by Radical Whigs like John Locke and Baptist Dissenters like William Kiffen, helped ensure Delaune was among the last of the Baptist martyrs.

---

[83] Delaune, 66–73.

[84] Delaune, 80. For the philosophical basis of contemporary capitalism, see C. B. Macpherson, *The Political Theory of Possessive Individualism: Hobbes to Locke* (New York: Oxford University, 1962).

[85] Delaune concluded his last work with Locke's central argument in *A Letter Concerning Toleration*: the true Christian church is characterized by "No forcible Imposition of Christ's Service, no Persecution, corporal mulects, and punishments, upon Dissenters, or gainsayers, but the exercise of all Love, Patience, and long suffering, with Gentleness toward them." Delaune, Εἰχων του θηριου. Or, *the Image of the Beast*, 6.

[86] Per note in a contemporary hand on the title page to the copy of *A Narrative of the Sufferings of Thomas Delaune* held by the Burke Library of Union Theological Seminary.

Locke and the American Political Economy

As demonstrated elsewhere, John Locke was revered among eighteenth-century English Dissenters, including Baptists. Isaac Watts believed Locke's writings were composed of "Letters of Gold."[87] Across the Atlantic, Locke's new paradigm for a political economy centered upon individual religious liberty and property rights was also instrumental in shaping American political expectations. His works had a prominent place in the libraries of many of the Founding Fathers of the United States and were used by Congress during the construction of the nation's Constitution.[88] The tradition of American political rights looks back to Locke and to British Nonconformists for such things as a "bill of rights," "religious freedom," and the rights of "petition," "assembly," "speech," and "press" as well as various judicial rights. Indeed, the evolving recognition of further rights through the centuries is an outgrowth of "freedom of conscience."[89]

The Lockean legacy arguably made its greatest impact upon the Southern colonies. At Shaftesbury's behest, Locke wrote *The Fundamental Constitutions of Carolina* in 1669. The Church of England's official status was maintained in an article included against the advice of Locke.[90] However, Dissenters were granted religious toleration and, in an important revision in 1682, fully exempted from taxation to support the Church of England parishes.[91] *The Fundamental Constitutions of Carolina* shaped

---

[87] Yarnell, *John Locke's 'Letters of Gold.'*

[88] Richard L. Greaves, "Radicals, Rights, and Revolution: British Nonconformity and Roots of the American Experience," *Church History* 61 (1992): 151–52.

[89] Greaves, 158, 162–68.

[90] Article 96, "The Fundamental Constitutions of Carolina, March 1, 1669," in *The Works of John Locke, A New Edition, Corrected*, vol. 10 (London: Thomas Tegg, 1823), 194n.

[91] See Malcolm B. Yarnell III, "Early American Political Theology," in *First Freedom: The Beginning and End of Religious Liberty*, ed. Jason G. Duesing, Thomas White, and Malcolm B. Yarnell III, 2nd ed. (Nashville: B&H Academic, 2016), 54–55.

Southern culture and Southern evangelicalism. But the Lockean legacy for Southerners is a checkered one in two important respects.

First, while Locke's principles of human rights, religious liberty, and self-governance suffuse the document, he nevertheless helped create a class of landed nobility, the Landgraves, and expressed suspicion of democracy.[92] Numerous prominent Dissenters, including Baptists, benefited from this early class system. The pastors of the First Baptist Church of Charleston, South Carolina, thus taught their people both the necessity of constitutional government and of submitting to the established order.[93] Other Dissenters, like the Quakers, refused to recognize the Carolinian "etiquette of power" or to integrate with its "culture of power."[94]

Second, while Locke thoroughly excoriated "slavery" in *Two Treatises of Government*, he allowed for it in Carolina and worked with it in his role at the Board of Trade.[95] Locke's ambiguity regarding slavery still puzzles commentators. Locke expressed disdain for slavery in the context of his polemic against absolute monarchy.[96] However, Locke countenanced the slavery of those who were conquered in a just war, but with one important limit. Deeming slavery unnatural and an ongoing act of war, he denied it could be applied to subsequent generations. Glausser notes pithily that, according to one theory, "Locke the opponent of slavery" could not suppress the greed and classism of "Locke the Landgrave."[97] *The Fundamental*

---

[92] "The Fundamental Constitutions of Carolina," preface and articles 1–22.

[93] Thomas J. Little, "The Origins of Southern Evangelicalism in South Carolina, 1700–1740," *Church History* 75 (2006): 786; Yarnell, "Early American Political Theology," 54–67.

[94] Charles H. Lippy, "Chastized by Scorpions: Christianity and Culture in Colonial South Carolina, 1669–1740," *Church History* 79 (2010): 266.

[95] Locke, *Two Treatises of Government*, 137, 157–58; Wayne Glausser, *Locke and Blake: A Conversation across the Eighteenth Century* (Gainesville: University Press of Florida, 1998), 66–67.

[96] Ashcraft, *Revolutionary Politics*, 398–99.

[97] Glausser, *Locke and Blake*, 68–75.

Constitutions of Carolina allowed slaves to join whatever church they chose, for they retained some basic human rights, but church membership did not automatically free them from their masters.[98] A prominent historian of Western political theory recently concluded, "Slavery is the original sin of liberalism."[99]

The contrast between reverence for religious liberty, human rights, and property rights, on the one hand, and aristocratic pretensions coupled with a proslavery form of capitalism, on the other, characterizes the political legacy of John Locke. The same contrast also characterizes Southern political culture in the United States of America. Sadly, following the "Carolina way," and "without the ancient tradition of class reciprocity or the Enlightenment philosophy of human equality," slaveholders created a barbaric system of race-based chattel slavery. Southern evangelicals helped propagate this oppressive political culture, which stretched from Virginia to Louisiana.[100] Clerical apologists for African slavery argued that Christian liberty, though real and applicable to African believers, was "entirely spiritual" and does not bring physical freedom in this world.[101]

---

[98] "Since charity obliges us to wish well to the souls of all men, and religion ought to alter nothing in any man's civil estate or right, it shall be lawful for slaves, as well as others, to enter themselves, and be of what church or profession any of them shall think best, and, therefore, be as fully members as any freeman. But yet no slave shall hereby be exempted from that civil dominion his master hath over him, but be in all things in the same state and condition he was in before." See *The Fundamental Constitutions of Carolina*, article 107.

[99] Mark Goldie, professor emeritus of intellectual history at the University of Cambridge, made this the opening line of his sixth Carlyle Lecture. Mark Goldie, "Africans, Native Americans, Slavery, and Christian Evangelism," John Locke and Empire (lecture, Oxford University, February 23, 2021). Goldie also argued Locke did not countenance race-based chattel slavery.

[100] Thomas D. Wilson, *The Ashley Cooper Plan: The Founding of Carolina and the Origins of Southern Political Culture* (Chapel Hill: University of North Carolina, 2016), chap. 4.

[101] William Fleetwood, *A Sermon Preached Before the Society for the Propagation of the Gospel* (London: Joseph Downing, 1711), 203–7.

Soon after the Denmark Vesey Rebellion of 1822, Richard Furman, the leading Baptist in the South, started defending slavery as an institution, although beforehand he had considered it "undoubtedly an evil." Baptists across the slaveholding region were driven by fear to make the same transition.[102] The Southern Baptist Convention began as a separate denomination in 1845 with intentional approval of the American system of slavery. In recent decades, the denomination has officially repented of its complicity in the systemic evil of slavery and its racism, but we continue to struggle with the horrific impact of our own tradition's "original sin."[103]

Locke and Later American Baptists

The influence of Locke was not confined to the South. In the late eighteenth century, one New England Baptist elder, Ebenezer Smith, incorporated Locke's natural rights theory into his poetic plea for religious equality,[104] while another, Isaac Backus, used Locke's arguments for private property in his battle against universalism.[105] Locke's opinions on the colonization of native lands also influenced Baptist political discourse.[106] In the early nineteenth century, one of Locke's private letters shaped Baptist confessional identity in a profound way. In 1833 John Newton Brown incorporated

---

[102] Yarnell, "Early American Political Theology," 67–75. The so-called slave rebellion, which prompted Furman's shift, was in fact the product of a judicial sham. Michael P. Johnson, "Denmark Vesey's Church," *Journal of Southern History* 86 (2020): 805–48.

[103] Malcolm B. Yarnell III, *The Formation of Christian Doctrine* (Nashville: B&H Academic, 2007), 199–203.

[104] William G. McLoughlin, "Ebenezer Smith's Ballad of the Ashfield Baptists, 1772," *New England Quarterly* 47 (1874), 99.

[105] Isaac Backus, *Isaac Backus on Church, State, and Calvinism: Pamphlets, 1754–1789*, ed. William G. McLoughlin (Cambridge: Harvard University, 1968), 16–17, 40–42.

[106] Obbie Tyler Todd, *Let Men Be Free: Baptist Politics in the Early United States, 1776–1835* (Eugene, OR: Pickwick, 2022), 130–32.

Locke's affirmation that Scripture "has God for its author, salvation for its end and truth, without any mixture of error, for its matter" into the *New Hampshire Confession of Faith*.

According to Myron Noonkester, Brown may have seen Locke's statement in Richard Watson's popular *An Apology for Christianity*, first published in the United States in 1794.[107] Richard King, Locke's nephew, had asked in 1703, "What is the shortest and surest way for a young Gentleman to attain a true Knowledg [*sic*] of the Christian religion, in the full and just Extent of it?" Locke replied, "Let him study the Holy Scripture, especially the New Testament. Therein are contain'd the Words of Eternal Life. It has god for Its Author; Salvation for its End; and Truth, without any mixture of Error, for its Matter." Locke expressed amazement that anyone might think there is any other book "wherein it is all contain'd, pure and entire." In particular, all our questions regarding morality are answered there perfectly. He recommended other works for the gentleman, but for "an ordinary Man," knowledge of Scripture and of his vocation is sufficient.[108] Locke's advice has long been deemed a helpful representation of the Baptist view of Scripture, for his language was retained in the 1925, 1963, and 2000 editions of *The Baptist Faith and Message*.

Baptists also used Locke, sometimes inaccurately, to buttress their own standing in the history of religious liberty. During the 1936 meeting of the Southern Baptist Convention in St. Louis, Augustus Hopkins Strong was cited as saying, "As John Locke said more than two hundred

---

[107] Myron C. Noonkester, "'God for Its Author': John Locke as a Possible Source for the New Hampshire Confession," *New England Quarterly* 66 (1993): 448–50; Richard Watson, *An Apology for Christianity: In a Series of Letters, Addressed to Edward Gibbon* (Providence: Carter and Wilkinson, 1794), 155.

[108] John Locke to Richard King, August 25, 1703, in *The Correspondence of John Locke*, 8:56–59. Richard King responded that he appreciated both how Locke was resolved "into the Study of the Scriptures alone" although he was continually reading other helpful theological texts. Richard King to John Locke, September 13, 1703, in *The Correspondence of John Locke*, 8:63–64.

years ago: 'The Baptists were the first and only propounders of absolute liberty, just and true liberty, equal and impartial liberty.'"[109] But, embarrassingly enough, these were not Locke's own words. A church historian at Rochester Theological Seminary, the liberal author of *How Jesus Became God*,[110] moreover, excoriated the idea that Locke might have ever held such a positive view of Baptists. Conrad Henry Moehlman traced the genesis of Strong's claim through various Baptist historians, including Henry Melville King, John T. Christian, and George B. Taylor as well as Thomas Armitage, George C. Lorimer, and John Newton Brown.[111] Moehlman offered several corrections to this Baptist historiographical tradition.

First, Moehlman demonstrated that Edward B. Underhill was the faultless originator of the tradition. In 1851, Underhill indicated the quoted material from Locke began with "absolute liberty," but later historians moved the quotation mark to begin with "the Baptists." I agree with Moehlman that both Underhill and Locke were thereby mischaracterized. However, Moehlman's first correction must be modified. Moehlman believed Underhill's citation belonged to Locke, but Moehlman himself was not entirely adept with original texts. The truncated statement should never have been ascribed to Locke either by the errant historians or by Moehlman. The famous phrase "absolute liberty . . . impartial liberty" actually comes from William Popple, who composed the short preface to Locke's *A Letter Concerning Toleration*.[112] The internal evidence in the preface alone prompts reservation. The preface refers to Locke's letter as "this discourse, which

---

[109] *Annual of the Southern Baptist Convention* (1936), 113.

[110] Conrad Henry Moehlman, *How Jesus Became God: An Historical Study of the Life of Jesus to the Age of Constantine* (New York: Philosophical Library, 1960).

[111] Conrad Henry Moehlman, "The Baptists Revise John Locke," *Journal of Religion* 18 (1938): 174–77.

[112] John Locke, *The Works of John Locke in Nine Volumes*, 12th ed., vol. 5 (London: Rivington et al., 1824), 4; Woolhouse, *Locke*, 274; Caroline Robbins, "Absolute Liberty: The Life and Thought of William Popple, 1638–1708," *William and Mary Quarterly* 24 (1967): 190. The preface was written enthusiastically, contrary to the taciturn disposition of John Locke.

treats of that subject, however briefly, yet more exactly than any we have yet seen." The author of the preface thereby clearly distanced himself from the author of the letter.

Moehlman's second correction to the Baptist tradition must also be modified. While it is certainly true that Locke did not make Strong's positive statement about Baptists, Moehlman overstated his case by arguing that Locke "indirectly severely criticized" the Baptists.[113] Moehlman dismisses the idea that Baptists were advocates of religious liberty, demonstrating his own unfamiliarity with the contents of Underhill's work and with the Baptist witness in the seventeenth century. Moreover, as we have already seen, while Locke typically spoke in general terms when addressing contemporaries, he advocated many Baptist ideas. Moehlman properly corrected the misquotation by the Baptist historians, but he mischaracterized the substance of the Baptist tradition, even while hypocritically claiming the mantle of a critical historian.[114] Locke was never an outspoken proponent of the Baptist movement, but he certainly understood that Baptists, like other Dissenters, were advocates of religious liberty. Both liberal and conservative Baptist historians would do well to step back continuously from their favored historiographies and reexamine the original artifacts.

Locke among the Twenty-First Century Baptists

John Locke can help Baptists face at least five critical challenges today by prompting us to reclaim our identity. First, Locke and earlier Baptists clearly emphasized liberty of conscience. If Baptists do not retain our fundamental belief that every human being is personally responsible before God, we may find ourselves captivated by inferior religious psychologies with devastating

---

[113] Moehlman, "The Baptists Revise," 179.

[114] "Only a person utterly ignorant of sixteenth- and seventeenth-century European and English history could even conceive so rash a sentiment, to say nothing of committing it to paper." See Moehlman, "The Baptists Revise," 179.

consequences. Second, Locke and the early Baptists recognized diversity of opinion, religious liberty, and voluntary communities are inextricably bound with all human and civil rights. Locke and his Baptist contemporaries have much to offer those who wish to advance universal human dignity and human flourishing. Third, the lessons we can learn from the failures of Locke and the Baptists are also germane. The original sin of both Western liberalism and Southern evangelicalism, privileging the powerful and subjugating the weak, culminated *inter alia* in the anthropological heresy of racism. Such evil continually demands our heartfelt and thorough repentance whenever and wherever that sin raises its hoary head. Fourth, the recent advocacy of Christian nationalism by amateur historians and religious enthusiasts can be corrected by recalling how Locke and the Baptists taught that Jesus alone is king of his church and that his lordship requires the separation of church and state.[115] Locke wisely reminds us, "But under the Gospel there is absolutely no such thing as a Christian commonwealth."[116] Finally, both Locke and the Baptists excelled when they submitted themselves thoroughly to the authority of the Word of God and gave priority to the simple proclamation of personal faith in Jesus Christ. Baptists would be wise to recover the same biblical and Christological priorities.

---

[115] Andrew L. Whitehead and Samuel L. Perry, *Taking America Back for God: Christian Nationalism in the United States* (New York: Oxford University, 2020).

[116] Vernon, *Locke on Toleration*, 29.

5

Baptists and the American Revolution

By Kristina Benham and Thomas S. Kidd

The era of the American Revolution and the founding of the United States carried great significance for churches and denominations, including Baptists in America. One of the most important changes was the disestablishment of state churches, such as the Anglican Church in Virginia, and the somewhat less successful effort to disestablish the Congregationalist Church in New England. Disestablishment came about largely through the struggles against state-church mandates by new congregations emerging from the First Great Awakening, many of which were Baptist. In the period of the American Revolution, many Baptists—especially those coming from the radical evangelical movement—went from having an uneasy relationship with American political authorities to having a strongly positive, providential view of the American nation.

Baptist Beginnings

Baptist churches had existed since the early period of colonial history, but their more widespread growth came from the First Great Awakening in New England and the political conflicts with the colonial governments that resulted. The series of spiritual revivals that became known as the Great Awakening first spread in New England in the 1730s and 1740s, pitting itinerant revival preachers against many established church ministers. During the revivals people shared their experiences of truly meeting Christ, or feeling conviction from the Holy Spirit, and realizing they had never been born again. In the founding years of New England, Puritans set up a religious establishment to create a pure church and a godly society, but to maintain religious order they eventually compromised, allowing unconverted parents to have their children baptized, an arrangement now known as the "Halfway Covenant." By the mid-eighteenth century, revivalists saw the Halfway Covenant as a compromise that allowed the established Congregationalist churches to be filled with nominal, unconverted adherents. Moreover, some itinerants went so far as to question the salvation of state-supported ministers. Radical Evangelicals formed "Separate" churches that met without the required legal authority. Although many new evangelicals, like their traditional counterparts, practiced infant baptism, many of these Separate churches revisited the biblical mode of baptism and became Baptist congregations. Like their Puritan forebears, they attempted to purify churches, but they did so by limiting membership to those who testified to a conversion experience and received baptism as believers.[1]

The New England revivals and the expansion of Baptist churches turned toward missionary work in the 1750s. In the eighteenth century, New England was the most heavily churched region of the British colonies,

---

[1] Thomas S. Kidd, *God of Liberty: A Religious History of the American Revolution* (New York: Basic Books, 2010), 4, 24, 41, 47.

but the Anglican establishment in the South provided only a modicum of religious participation outside of cities such as Williamsburg, Virginia, and Savannah, Georgia. Northern Baptists took their preaching into the unchurched South. For example, Shubal Stearns, a convert of the revivals in the 1740s, started his pastoral career as a leader of a Separate church in Tolland, Connecticut, and became a Baptist preacher by the 1750s. Stearns quickly turned to missionary labors, seeing need in the South for conversion of the lost and adherence to believer's baptism. He moved his family to Sandy Creek, North Carolina, in 1755 to start a new church and network of Baptist churches. Stearns's Sandy Creek network planted forty-two congregations within seventeen years across the Carolinas and Virginia. Stearns died in 1771, so he did not get to see the American Revolution unfold, but by then he and other Separate Baptists had begun to transform the backcountry South into an early version of the Bible Belt.[2]

Baptists and Religious Freedom in Revolutionary America

In many colonies, Separate evangelicals and Baptists had a difficult relationship with colonial authorities and the established churches (Congregationalist in New England and Anglican in the South). Generally, pastors were not legally allowed to preach wherever they wanted, nor could revivalist Christians simply plant new churches without permission, especially in the colonies with the heaviest burden of establishment. Colonial governments' dislike of Separates and other Radical Evangelicals generated a wave of new laws and regulations against itinerancy and other features of the evangelicals' free market of religion. Appealing to sources including the Bible and John Locke for inspiration, the new Evangelicals coming out of the Great Awakening argued that governments should tolerate the work of

---

[2] Kidd, 49.

the revivalists and that authorities should permit what came to be called the "free exercise" of religion. Locke had developed his theory of toleration in the context of the Glorious Revolution in England in the 1680s and '90s (see chapter 4), and now the Radical Evangelicals and Baptists applied his theories to the colonies. Colonial authorities in church and state tended to see unregulated evangelical activity as subversive of godly order and potentially destabilizing for good government if large numbers of people rejected the state-backed congregations and pastors.

Earlier figures, such as the theologically peripatetic and erstwhile Baptist Roger Williams, had argued against state establishments of religion too (see chapter 3), but the Separate Baptist movement generated the most sustained challenge to establishments to date in American history. Probably the most influential such challenge came through the preaching and writing of Isaac Backus. Backus had experienced conversion amidst the Great Awakening in Connecticut, joined a Separate congregation, and finally came to Baptist convictions in the early 1750s. He received believer's baptism himself and ultimately founded a Baptist church in Massachusetts in 1756. Backus knew well the grave difficulties Separatists and Baptists faced from the established churches as relatives of his, including his mother, spent time in jail in the 1750s for refusing to pay taxes to support the establishment (see chapter 7). Other Baptists suffered beatings and public humiliations or had their property seized because of their failure to meet the expectations of the official churches and their state backers.

By the 1760s, the combination of persecution and the unfolding imperial crisis helped to turn Backus and other Separatists and Baptists toward a full-blown Christian defense of separation of church and state. From colonial villages to the imperial stage, the talk of the time was about government tyranny and the liberty of the virtuous individual against arbitrary coercion, whether spiritual, economic, or political. In a 1768 pamphlet arguing against the established ministers, Backus noted that Separatists and Baptists were "often represented as rebels." Backus made a clear distinction between the obedience commanded by civil rulers and by gospel ministers, however. The former rightly claimed a coercive authority to promote peace, good order, and morality in the civil sphere. But gospel ministers should never coerce anyone, Backus cautioned, because "force tends to shut the eyes rather than open them" to spiritual truths. He lambasted the established ministers, who "profess to be Christ's ambassadors and yet . . . if they once can get footing in a town or parish, let people dislike them ever so much," they would never relinquish control because they had the state's backing and salary. Gospel ministers should preach the gospel freely, and hearers should receive it freely.[3]

State establishments of religion enjoyed support from formidable figures in the Patriot movement, including Massachusetts's John Adams. The defenders of established religion assumed a republic needed virtuous people to thrive and most people derived virtue from their religious commitments and divine precepts, such as the Ten Commandments and the Beatitudes. Thus, it made sense for a traditional Christian denomination to receive official support. Backus, however, believed the fractious Christian diversity emerging from the Great Awakening rendered the traditional justification for establishments moot. Yes, republics needed virtuous people, but giving preference to one denomination over others necessitated galling coercion for Dissenters, however devout they might be. Baptists, in particular, were always out of favor with any given established denomination because virtually all Christians at the time practiced pedobaptism. Defenders of establishment argued that civil rulers were to be "nursing fathers" (Isa 49:23) to the churches. Backus asked what kind of parent would ever "rob one child of his food or cast him into a dungeon to uphold another in grandeur!" Although Baptists would engage in theological combat with rivals as

---

[3] Isaac Backus, *A Fish Caught in His Own Net* (Boston, 1768), in *Isaac Backus on Church, State, and Calvinism: Pamphlets, 1754–1789*, ed. William G. McLoughlin (Cambridge: Harvard University, 1968), 190–92.

fiercely as any other Protestant, Backus was beginning to develop a vision for an American religious scene where multiple denominations competed in freedom, without direct government support, and none had exclusive title to all theological truth. Backus was no theological relativist, but he countenanced the possibility that God might have more than one denominational "child" in the gospel and that God would not play favorites among those children. Much less should the civil government choose favorites among denominations.[4]

Although established churches were a major source of controversy in many colonies (and new states), the most decisive battle between establishment and dissent took place in Virginia. Baptist preachers connected to Stearns's North Carolina network of churches moved into Virginia by the 1760s, replacing Presbyterians as the most prevalent Dissenting group in the colony. Methodists also made inroads, but their growth was delayed significantly by the outbreak of the Revolution and John Wesley's strident hostility toward the American Patriot movement. As in New England, Baptists in Virginia bristled at legal requirements like licenses to preach and taxes paid to the establishment. As a result, persecution of Baptists in Virginia in the 1760s and '70s included violent disruption of Baptist meetings and imprisonment of Baptist preachers.

Pastor John Waller's turbulent transition from an irreligious member of the Virginia gentry to a Baptist preacher highlights the dynamics of Virginia's battle over religious freedom. Waller initially despised the Baptists, who criticized the swearing, fighting, and gambling endemic to Virginia elite culture. As a lawyer, he first encountered the Baptists more closely while prosecuting the Baptist itinerant preacher Lewis Craig. In court, Waller was struck by Craig's serene endurance of persecution, and Waller began attending Baptist meetings out of curiosity. Within months he became convinced of his need for salvation and abandoned the official Anglicanism of his youth, and the life of a gentleman, for baptism. Soon he began itinerant

---

[4] Backus, *A Fish Caught*, 238.

preaching too. The persecutor now became the persecuted. In 1771 at an outdoor meeting in Caroline County, authorities cracked down on Waller's troublemaking ways. The local sheriff, the Anglican minister, and a posse of angry members of the community seized Waller in the middle of preaching a sermon and whipped him severely. Waller, who had already experienced previous arrests, cleaned himself up and immediately returned to preaching, finding joy in the privilege of being persecuted for the cause of Christ and for religious liberty.[5]

Key figures in the emerging revolution against Great Britain took special notice of the persecution of Baptists. Thomas Jefferson and James Madison, neither of them evangelicals, nevertheless saw persecution of Dissenters as a violation of the principles of liberty for which the American revolutionaries clamored. Baptists simultaneously began petitioning the Virginia government for repeal of laws that required support of the established church and regulation of Dissenters. In 1776, Virginia established its independent government, and Baptists immediately took the opportunity to petition for religious liberty as part of political liberty. Meanwhile, the new legislature crafted its Declaration of Rights. Madison urged fellow representatives to change drafted language concerning religious liberty from "toleration" of Dissenting churches to "free exercise of religion." But it would take years to secure any such drastic step of disestablishment. Jefferson, who penned the first draft of his Bill for Establishing Religious Freedom in 1777, testified to the influence of Dissenters, including many Baptists, in the emerging campaign for religious liberty. After asserting that most Virginians had become Dissenters who were forced to support a religious establishment in which they did not believe, he recounted the hope for relief brought on by the creation of the Revolutionary state government: "The first republican legislature which met in '76 was crowded with petitions to abolish this spiritual

---

[5] Rhys Isaac, *The Transformation of Virginia, 1740–1790* (Chapel Hill: University of North Carolina, 1982), 162–63; Kidd, *God of Liberty*, 37–38, 52.

tyranny. These brought on the severest contests in which I have ever been engaged," Jefferson recalled.[6]

Baptists, the War for Independence, and the American Nation

The partnership between elites of Revolutionary leadership and Dissenting groups, including Baptists, extended beyond religious liberty. War with Great Britain demanded widespread support for independent governments. New states enlisted Evangelical preachers to convince reluctant locals, especially in backcountry areas. For example, Baptist pastor Oliver Hart of Charleston took up the Patriot cause with Presbyterian Evangelical preacher William Tennent (and nephew of the more famous revivalist Gilbert Tennent) at the request of the South Carolina provincial assembly in 1775. The two men turned their itinerant skills toward convincing backcountry residents who held little trust in their provincial government. The task was to argue that rather than relying on imperial laws to shelter Dissenters, Americans should resist the increasing British threat of religious-political enslavement. Tennent and Hart convinced many, but division between Patriot and Loyalist sides in the Carolina backcountry quickly burst into localized civil war. As military leaders raided outposts and towns on opposing sides, continued Patriot religious leadership was key to convincing people in Loyalist strongholds. Richard Furman, who had recently become the Baptist minister at High Hills of Santee, South Carolina, joined Tennent and Hart in preaching for the Patriot cause. Growing resistance to British tax policies brought up biblical questions for all Christians. It was an age-old debate between the clear biblical commands in the New Testament to obey civil authorities and counterinterpretations against unquestioning submission. When Colonel Richard Richardson of High Hills of Santee led an attack

---

[6] Thomas Jefferson, "Autobiography," in *Thomas Jefferson: Writings*, ed. Merrill D. Peterson (New York: Library of America, 1984), 34; Kidd, *God of Liberty*, 52–54.

on a raiding group of Loyalists in late 1775, he used an open letter from Furman to help convince and not just defeat his enemies. Furman argued that when a God-ordained leader, like the king, abused his power and acted contrary to the British constitution, Christians were not obligated to obey.[7]

Similar conflicts occurred in New England, where the Congregationalist church held firmly to its established status. Massachusetts law before the Revolution, as with the Anglican Church in Southern colonies, required taxes to support Congregationalist churches and other regulations for Dissenting churches. Since their expansion following the Great Awakening, Massachusetts Baptists had fought against these laws. Before the Revolutionary War broke out, commonly shared colonial protests against British policies lightened the load for Dissenters because Patriot leaders needed as much support as they could get. Baptists used the arguments of the Patriot cause to push for religious freedom as well as civil freedom. In 1773, Backus argued in *An Appeal to the Public for Religious Liberty* that God would not assist their cause against England without lifting unfair tax burdens at home. Addressing the Patriot leaders, Backus wrote that they could not submit to British policies because they were "taxed where you are not represented. And is it not really so with us? . . . Have we not as good right to say you do the *same thing*?" Although his work was widely read, Baptists and other Dissenters in Massachusetts did not find immediate relief. In 1774, Backus appealed to the Continental Congress for redress, but it did little good with Massachusetts delegates John and Samuel Adams brushing the establishment question off as a minor issue.[8]

As the protests against England turned toward the prospect of war, some citizens of Massachusetts questioned the loyalty of Baptists. Although many New England Baptists supported the Revolutionary cause, their Dissenting position often looked suspicious to neighbors. In 1770, the town

---

[7] James A. Rogers, *Richard Furman: Life and Legacy* (Macon: Mercer University, 2001), 27–30; Kidd, *God of Liberty*, 84–85.

[8] Isaac Backus, *An Appeal to the Public for Religious Liberty* (Boston, 1773), in McLoughlin, ed., *Isaac Backus*, 338–39; Kidd, *God of Liberty*, 171.

of Ashfield, Massachusetts, seized the land of Baptist residents for refusing to pay taxes to the Congregationalist Church. Ashfield's Baptists appealed to the king of England to intervene, and King George III annulled the law that Massachusetts used to justify the confiscation.[9]

A more widespread crisis for Baptists occurred when Massachusetts attempted to draw up its new state constitution in 1778. The proposed new government still required public tax support for religion, which ultimately meant financial support for Congregationalist churches. In response Baptists generated over seven hundred signatures on a petition declaring that churches should be supported only by the authority of Christ, not the state. Although the constitution failed on a broader concern for rights, many in Massachusetts responded to Baptist protests with bitter attacks against their moral and social character and against their loyalty as Americans. During the debates, Congregationalist minister Phillips Payson preached a sermon before the Massachusetts assembly, warning against a collapse of public virtue without the establishment. He also derided evangelicals and Dissenters as low-class ruffians and fanatical mystics who should hold little standing in religion or government. Occasionally, more violent resistance to Baptists broke out. During the fallout from the constitutional debates, the town of Pepperell turned against local Baptists meeting for a baptismal service. A mob brandishing clubs descended on the scene and performed mock baptisms on a dog and on men using liquor. Then they accused the Baptists of siding with Tories and the devil and demanded they leave town. After another mob, this time carrying whips, drove the point home later that day, the town passed resolutions that any itinerant Baptist would be met with similar violence.[10]

---

[9] Isaac Backus, *A History of New England with Particular Reference to the Denomination of Christians Called Baptists*, vol. 2 (Newton: Backus Historical Society, 1871), 152–59.

[10] Thomas S. Kidd and Barry Hankins, *Baptists in America: A History* (New York: Oxford University, 2015), 65; Kidd, *God of Liberty*, 171–72.

Despite these attacks, Baptists continued to resist the establishment for decades. In 1780, when the state made another attempt at a new constitution, the Congregationalist establishment stayed in place, though indirectly. The state still required taxes to support churches with the exception that individuals could choose to pay toward whatever church they chose. Members of Dissenting churches, however, had to acquire certificates to redirect their taxes from the local Congregationalist church. Baptists found the registration requirements onerous and obnoxious, however, and some heavily Congregationalist towns proved resistant to granting exemptions even if Baptists (or other groups such as Quakers) pursued them.[11]

Baptists and Slavery during the Revolution

The ongoing struggles with state establishments of religion gave many white Baptists reasons to keep the colonial and new state governments at arm's length. African American Baptists had even better reasons to do so. The revivals of the Great Awakening had made small but significant inroads among the African American population, both free and enslaved, though first-generation enslaved people in America remained overwhelmingly non-Christian. Some African American evangelicals, such as Phillis Wheatley and Lemuel Haynes in New England, issued protests against slavery, but published African American voices of any kind remained exceedingly rare. Numerous Southern founders, including Patrick Henry and Thomas Jefferson, acknowledged that chattel slavery was morally problematic, but colonial governments in the South countenanced few restrictions on slavery. Although the Northern state governments effected immediate or gradual

---

[11] John Witte Jr. and Justin Latterell, "The Last American Establishment: Massachusetts, 1780–1833," in *Disestablishment and Religious Dissent: Church-State Relations in the New American States, 1776–1833*, ed. Carl H. Esbeck and Jonathan J. Den Hartog (Columbia: University of Missouri, 2019), 408–11; Kidd, *God of Liberty*, 172–73.

emancipation in the era of the Revolution, there was little hope of movement against slavery in the regions of America where it mattered most. Indeed, British authorities sometimes sought to drive a wedge between enslaved people and their white masters. Most controversially, the royal governor of Virginia, Lord Dunmore, in 1775 offered freedom to slaves who ran away from their masters and enlisted with the British armed forces.[12]

David George was one of the people caught in the cross-cutting tensions between slavery, the Revolution, and the Baptist faith. George had been born into slavery in Virginia, where he endured daily deprivations and brutal treatment. Growing up, he watched multiple family members, including his mother, suffer horrible beatings at the hands of slave drivers. He eventually ran away from his Virginia master but came into the possession of another master in Silver Bluff, South Carolina. At Silver Bluff, George began hearing from Baptist itinerants, including the great African American preacher George Liele, one of the most effective evangelists in spreading the gospel in the South and the Caribbean during the period. After George experienced conversion and received believer's baptism, Liele encouraged George to begin preaching himself. (Once named just "David," George also took George Liele's first name as his surname.) Soon George became the pastor at the Silver Bluff church, founded around 1773 as the first enduring African American–led church in America.[13]

Lord Dunmore's offer of freedom to slaves in 1775 signaled the descent of the American South into revolution and sometimes into civil war between Loyalists and Patriots. Slaves and formerly enslaved African Americans such as David George tended to side with the Loyalists and the British, seeing them as truer friends of liberty than the Southern Patriot defenders of African slavery. In 1779, George and his family took an opportunity to cross the Savannah River to British-occupied Savannah, Georgia. There, he

---

[12] Douglas R. Egerton, *Death or Liberty: African Americans and Revolutionary America* (New York: Oxford University, 2011).

[13] Maya Jasanoff, *Liberty's Exiles: American Loyalists in the Revolutionary World* (New York: Vintage Books, 2011), 46–47.

happily reunited for a time with his mentor George Liele. Liele stayed in Savannah until after the Battle of Yorktown and evacuated with the British to Jamaica in 1782. George and his family moved to British-occupied Charleston and then evacuated in 1782 to the British Canadian colony of Nova Scotia. (Later, David George would relocate again, this time to Sierra Leone.) These black Baptists were among tens of thousands of Loyalists who left America at the end of the Revolutionary War. Their commitment to liberty took them down a different path than that of white Patriot leaders, including white American Baptists, a path that historian Maya Jasanoff has described as a Loyalist "Spirit of 1783." Such people saw a more reliable future for liberty in the British Empire than in the new American nation.[14]

Back in Virginia, the new state constitution of 1776 guaranteed citizens the "free exercise of religion." Madison and the First Congress would employ that phrase again in the First Amendment to the Constitution fifteen years later, at the urging of Baptists such as John Leland, Madison and Jefferson's hard-and-fast ally. Dissenters also pressured Virginia for relief from licensing requirements, which they regarded as unnecessary state meddling in the church, and to appoint military chaplains from denominations besides the Anglican Church. Virginia suspended the taxes that had traditionally funded operations of the Anglican Church too, but whether this entailed a permanent change to the establishment was unclear. Some Virginians, such as Patrick Henry, pushed for a "general assessment" for religion, which would maintain religious taxes but allow the payee to designate the church to receive their tithes. Meanwhile, Jefferson introduced his Bill for Establishing Religious Freedom in 1779, but in the middle of the war, the time was not right for dramatic moves on disestablishment.[15]

Once the war's major engagements ended with the Battle of Yorktown in 1781, the ever-popular Patrick Henry advocated for the general

[14] Jasanoff, 71, 76–77.

[15] Carl H. Esbeck, "Disestablishment in Virginia, 1776–1802," in Hartog and Esbeck, eds., *Disestablishment and Religious Dissent*, 142–46.

assessment plan. He encountered fierce opposition from Baptists and from James Madison (by then Thomas Jefferson was out of the state and would soon begin serving as American minister to France). Madison penned his "Memorial and Remonstrance against Religious Assessments," striking many of the same themes as petitions drawn up by Baptists around the same time. One petition from Orange County signed by the oft-suffering John Waller warned that the general assessment would be "opening the door to religious tyranny." Popular pressure from Baptists and other Dissenters, and clever maneuvering by Madison against Henry, helped to secure the passage of the Bill for Establishing Religious Freedom in 1786. The law ensured that no one would be forced to attend or financially support any church and that people's religious beliefs would not affect their civil standing in the state. Baptist advocacy was not over, however, either on the state or national level. They protested the Episcopal (Anglican) Church's glebe lands, which it controlled as part of its established status, and they urged Madison to promote the no-establishment and free exercise clauses in the Constitution. Partly to ensure the Constitution's ratification in Virginia, Madison promised to advocate for the addition of these religious liberty clauses during the meetings of the First Congress, even though he initially thought a Bill of Rights was unnecessary.[16]

Especially outside of New England, states made progress toward disestablishment, but few made such a thoroughgoing change as did Virginia. Many kept a kind of religious test oath, under which officeholders had to profess belief in God or the Bible to be qualified to serve. Baptists were delighted that the Constitution in Article VI prohibited the use of any such test oath for national officeholders. They simply did not want the government to be involved with policing people's religious beliefs. The relative successes in the states and in the new Constitution warmed many Baptists to the idea of the American nation as a special home for liberty.

---

[16] "Protest against the bill establishing a provision for teachers of the Christian religion," November 17, 1785, Library of Virginia digital collections; Esbeck, "Disestablishment in Virginia," 162.

On the eve of the Revolution, of course, that nationalistic warmth had not been a settled sentiment among Baptists, who sometimes found the British crown more open to their appeals for liberty. African American Baptists, as we have seen, had their reasons to side with the British in the war too. White Baptists sometimes suffered persecution from the same officials who led the Patriot movement. Moreover, the Baptist movement in the early 1770s retained a powerful pacifist strain, leading some critics to class the Baptists with Quakers and other Dissenters whose temporal commitments seemed unreliable and unpatriotic. Of course, some Baptist leaders, such as Oliver Hart, Richard Furman, Samuel Stillman of First Baptist Boston, and John Allen of Second Baptist Boston, were enthusiastic supporters of the developing Patriot resistance. Allen wrote the enormously popular *An Oration upon the Beauties of Liberty* in 1773, which became one of the most influential Patriot pamphlets before Thomas Paine's *Common Sense*. But Allen was not exactly a mainstream figure among Baptists, as he had only recently immigrated from England, partly due to financial and legal problems he had there. In Allen's other writings he had been critical of the English Baptist pastor John Gill's views on the eternal generation of the Son (Allen preferred the idea that Christ had always been "independent, eternal, [and] self-existent"). Gill was a popular writer among Baptists in America, so Allen operated under something of an ethical and theological cloud among Baptists before his death in 1774. Still, many American colonists resonated with Allen's call for them to "stand fast in the Liberty wherein they were made free," citing Gal 5:1.[17]

Many Baptists were not pleased with the outbreak of war in 1775. Beyond the obvious concerns about violence and political disruptions, they worried the conflict would scuttle ongoing revivals in Baptist congregations.

---

[17] John Allen, *The Spirit of Liberty* (London, 1770), 88; John Allen, *An Oration upon the Beauties of Liberty* (Boston, 1773), v; John M. Bumsted and Charles E. Clark, "New England's Tom Paine: John Allen and the Spirit of Liberty," *William and Mary Quarterly* 3rd ser., 21, no. 4 (Oct. 1964): 565.

The Warren Association of Baptists in New England wrote in September 1775 that the Baptists of Providence, Rhode Island, had seen 110 baptized converts added to their congregation in the past year. This "to the praise of God's glorious grace, in this time of public calamity and distress," they said. "As the judgments of almighty God hang heavy and threatening over our land and nation," they recommended prayer and fasting "to beseech the Lord to remove those calamities, and to restore peace and tranquility to our colonies and to the nation [Britain] again, and to revive pure religion." A year later, Pastor James Manning of Providence was even more concerned about the effects of the war. Writing to the English Baptist John Ryland, Manning told him of the "glorious and gloomy days" he had seen in America in the past year. A powerful revival had transpired in Providence, but the beginning of the Revolutionary War at Lexington, Massachusetts, in 1775, "like an electric stroke put a stop to the progress of the work. . . . Oh horrid war! How contrary to the spirit of Jesus!" Ezra Stiles, the Congregationalist pastor and Patriot leader in Providence, suspected that Manning was really a Loyalist and "against his country in heart." "Though some few Baptists and Quakers are heartily with us," Stiles wrote, "too many are so much otherwise." Americans would lose their liberty if they had to depend on reluctant, otherworldly Christians like Manning, Stiles thought.[18]

Through the campaigns for disestablishment, or from serving as soldiers or chaplains in the war, numerous white Baptists came to take quite a different view of the Revolution and the American nation than the reluctant Manning took at the beginning of the war. Samuel Stillman, pastor of First Baptist Church in Boston, was selected to give the election day sermon in Boston in 1779, a signal of Stillman's revered status among

---

[18] Warren Association, *Minutes of the Proceedings of the Baptist Association at Warren* (Norwich, Conn., 1775), 7–8; James Manning to John Ryland, November 13, 1776, in Reuben Aldridge Guild, *Life, Times, and Correspondence of James Manning* (Boston: Brown University, 1864), 244; Franklin Bowditch Dexter, ed., *The Literary Diary of Ezra Stiles* (New York: C. Scribner's Sons, 1901), 1:491, 2:23.

Patriot leaders in the city. Stillman had spoken in favor of Americans' rights since he took the pulpit at First Baptist around the same time as the Stamp Act crisis in 1765–66. In 1779 he urged Massachusetts officials not to grow weary in their prosecution of the war against Britain or to "amuse" themselves with thoughts of an easy peace. "If we should, it may prove greatly injurious to the *freedom and glory of this* RISING EMPIRE," he told the assembly.[19]

Baptists had to contend for the right to appoint their own military chaplains, especially in states with traditional established churches. Once selected, Baptist chaplains often became among the most zealous defenders of the righteousness of the American cause. Hezekiah Smith, for example, was a Massachusetts Baptist minister and Continental Army chaplain who had served during episodes including the Battle of Saratoga in New York in 1777, one of the most important Patriot victories in the war. Smith believed the wondrous victory over the British at Saratoga was providential and reflected God's intent to establish America as a new, "rising empire," as Stillman put it. On the two-year anniversary of Saratoga, Smith addressed his troops from Isa 26:8: "Yea, in the way of thy judgments, O LORD, have we waited for thee; the desire of our soul is to thy name, and to the remembrance of thee" (KJV). Smith effusively marked the anniversary as a day that was "big with the fate of America, and which offers to view the grandest conquest ever gained since the creation of the world." The chaplain went so far as to compare Saratoga to Christ's victory over sin and death in his resurrection. Smith knew the comparison might seem excessive, but he did it with "utmost propriety" since Saratoga afforded "the happy prospect of earthly felicity, the other the most pleasing hope of celestial happiness." The surprising victory at Saratoga was, providentially, "a prelude of Britain falling before rising America." Saratoga was undoubtedly an essential victory for the Patriot army and perhaps the most strategically valuable of the

---

[19] Samuel Stillman, *A Sermon Preached before the Honorable Council* (Boston: T. and J. Fleet, 1779), 36.

whole war because it helped convince the French to enter an alliance with the United States in 1778. But Smith's effusive comparison of Saratoga to the resurrection illustrates the risks in political ideology of conflating the kingdom of God with one's contemporary nation. Despite Baptists' traditional wariness about such conflations, the experiences of war encouraged some Baptist leaders toward embracing extreme versions of the new American civil religion.[20]

Enthusiasm for the American nation was checked repeatedly, however, by ongoing struggles and notable failures in the campaigns against state establishments of religion. Nowhere was that struggle more difficult than in Massachusetts, which had maintained a form of establishment in its 1780 constitution, over the protests of Isaac Backus and others. Defenders of the new state constitution spread the (mostly unfounded) rumor that Baptists were saying that if they did not get full religious liberty, "they would help no more in the war." The American victory at Yorktown in 1781 largely took that imagined threat off the table. Indeed, the end of major actions in the war may have emboldened Baptist enemies in Massachusetts who did not depend quite as much on the Dissenters' wartime cooperation anymore. In 1782, Baptists in Attleboro had property confiscated, and one congregant, Elijah Balkcom, was put in jail for tax evasion. A Massachusetts court decided on behalf of Balkcom, however, making New England Baptists think the 1780 constitution might be rendered unenforceable. As Backus wrote hopefully in 1783, the power of the defenders of establishment "to enslave others is now greatly weakened. And a faithful improvement of our privileges will weaken it more and more till there shall be no more use for swords because there shall be none to hurt or destroy in all God's holy mountain," referencing Isa 11:9. Baptists like Backus believed that if America would consistently apply its ideals of

---

[20] Reuben A. Guild, *Chaplain Smith and the Baptists* (Philadelphia: American Baptist Publication Society, 1885), 227, 230; Kidd and Hankins, *Baptists in America*, 56–57.

liberty for all, it would lead to full religious freedom and perhaps herald Christ's millennial reign on earth.[21]

Backus and the Warren Association continued to register an anxious desire to see religious liberty manifested fully. In 1784, Backus, James Manning, and the other association ministers signed a circular letter prepared by Samuel Stillman of First Baptist Boston, who along with Hezekiah Smith was one of the most zealously patriotic Baptist pastors in New England. Stillman no doubt believed in the righteousness of the American cause. In a calculation made by religious and ethnic minorities of many types in American history, however, he also seems to have believed that untrammeled patriotism in time of war would help Baptists achieve more legal respect and mainstream status. "The American revolution," Stillman wrote, "hath been accomplished by many astonishing interpositions of Providence." He reckoned that American independence was "design'd by the Lord to advance the cause of Christ in the world; or as one important step towards bringing in the glory of the latter day . . . it ought to be considered by us as one capital blow at the kingdom of the beast."[22]

As we have seen, Manning registered much graver doubts than these about the war in 1776. Backus suggested the war and independence *could* have millennial significance, but American authorities were still obligated to grant full religious liberty to Baptists and other Dissenters if the Revolution was to manifest its full providential potential. Stillman tended to suggest, however, that it was inevitable that the Revolution would contribute, as part of God's plan, to the unfolding of the millennial reign of Christ. More than that, Stillman posited that America itself was possibly "reserved in the mind of JEHOVAH, to be the grand theatre on which the divine Redeemer will

---

[21] McLoughlin, ed., *Isaac Backus*, 408, 428–29; William G. McLoughlin, "The Balkcom Case (1782) and the Pietist Theory of Separation of Church and State," *William and Mary Quarterly* 3rd ser., no. 24 (1967): 267–83; Stanley J. Grenz, *Isaac Backus—Puritan and Baptist* (Macon: Mercer University, 1983), 168.

[22] Warren Association, *Minutes of the Warren Association* ([Boston: n.p., 1784]), 6.

accomplish glorious things. . . . If we observe the signs of the times, we shall find reason to think he is on his way."[23]

Baptists in America also tended to see electoral outcomes in favor of religious liberty through such providential lenses. Along with virtually all Americans who supported independence, Baptists took a positive view of George Washington, even though Washington had not necessarily supported Jefferson and Madison's campaign for complete religious freedom in Virginia. Washington had, as president, assiduously courted religious minorities, including Baptists, Catholics, and Jews, assuring them the American canopy of religious liberty would shelter them in the new nation. Baptists were less keen on Washington's successor, John Adams, because of Adams's support for ongoing establishment in Massachusetts and rumors that he intended to create a national established church, the First Amendment's prohibition of one notwithstanding.[24]

Thomas Jefferson, of course, enjoyed Baptist support that was warm and sometimes even eschatological. One Massachusetts Baptist, Elias Smith, asserted that Jefferson "is the angel who poured out his vial upon the river Euphrates" in the book of Revelation. Smith knew he would be called an enthusiast for this interpretation, and indeed, Smith's was hardly a mainstream view among Baptists or evangelicals generally. More common were the sentiments expressed by the Danbury (Conn.) Baptist Association, who wrote an adulatory note to President Jefferson in 1801. They hoped the president's sentiments on religious liberty would "shine & prevail through all these states and all the world till hierarchy and tyranny be destroyed from the Earth." Again, political success for religious liberty might, in their estimation, be a step toward the millennium. "We have reason to believe

---

[23] *Minutes of the Warren Association*, 7; P. J. Marshall, "Transatlantic Protestantism and American Independence," in *Ambiguities of Empire: Essays in Honour of Andrew Porter*, ed. Robert Holland and Sarah Stockwell (New York: Routledge, 2009), 11.

[24] Vincent Phillip Muñoz, "George Washington on Religious Liberty," *Review of Politics* 65, no. 1 (Winter 2003): 24–27.

that America's God has raised you up to fill the chair of state," they declared. Although Jefferson's skeptical views about Christian doctrine were well known by 1801, they prayed God would bring him "at last to his Heavenly Kingdom through Jesus Christ our Glorious Mediator." This letter set the stage for Jefferson's public reply, the "wall of separation" letter on church and state, written on New Year's Day of 1802.[25]

John Leland also marked that first weekend of 1802 by delivering to the new president, on behalf of New England's Baptists, the gift of a four-foot-wide, 1,200-pound "mammoth cheese" (see chapter 6). On January 3, Leland spoke before the president and members of Congress on Matt 12:42: "Behold, a greater [one] than Solomon is here" (KJV). This was a not-so-subtle allusion to Jefferson. Anti-Jefferson critics found the "cheesen" events of the weekend ludicrous and nearly blasphemous. By 1808, Leland had become more circumspect in his praise of Madison, Jefferson's successor. The Jeffersonian movement had been damaged by political controversies in Jefferson's second term, and the novelty of a full-blown defender of religious liberty becoming president had perhaps lost some of its providential gloss. Nevertheless, Leland reminded Baptists in Vermont that Madison was the author of the "Memorial and Remonstrance" against Virginia's general assessment for religion back in 1785. That was "one of the best state papers ever written," Leland averred. Madison's morals were "pure and conspicuous." (This was perhaps a cloaked reference to allegations about Jefferson's moral problems, including rumors about his long-term affair with Sally Hemings, news of which had broken during Jefferson's first term.) Although Madison had never "joined any religious society, yet [he] contends for the rights of all of them," Leland noted. Vermont had embraced full religious liberty in

---

[25] Elias Smith, *The Whole World Governed by a Jew* (Exeter, N.H., 1805), 77; "Letter from Danbury Baptist Association to Thomas Jefferson," (Oct. 7, 1801), in *The Sacred Rights of Conscience*, ed. Daniel L. Dreisbach and Mark David Hall (Indianapolis: Liberty Fund, 2009), 526; Kidd, *God of Liberty*, 239–40. On the wall of separation debate generally, see Daniel L. Dreisbach, *Thomas Jefferson and the Wall of Separation Between Church and State* (New York: New York University, 2002).

1807, but Baptists still had to wait years for Connecticut and Massachusetts to abandon the remaining remnants of their establishments.[26]

Conclusion

After the Great Awakening, Separatists and Separate Baptists went through a season of rapid expansion, especially in New England, that also led to major Baptist growth in the South, starting in the 1750s. Their aggressive proselytization led to an anti-Baptist backlash among colonial American officials, especially in Virginia and Massachusetts. This backlash gave many Baptists pause about supporting the Patriot movement, although other Baptists such as Samuel Stillman of Boston were early adopters of Patriot zeal. The experience of fighting in the American Revolution turned some, such as Chaplain Hezekiah Smith, into ardent Patriots, while African American Baptists such as David George often regarded the British as more consistent defenders of liberty for all. The experience of the war, and progress (albeit inconsistent) toward religious freedom, eventually convinced most of the politically active white Baptists that "America's God" was doing something special through the Revolution and the nation's great defenders of religious liberty, especially Thomas Jefferson.

---

[26] John Leland, *An Oration, Delivered at Bennington* (Bennington, VT, August 16, 1808), 18.

6

John Leland

By Casey Hough

Truth disdains the aid of law for its defense—it will stand upon its own
merit. . . . It is error, and error alone, that needs human support; and
whenever men fly to the law or sword to protect their system of religion,
and force it upon others, it is evident that they have something in their
system that will not bear the light, and stand upon the basis of truth.

—*THE RIGHTS OF CONSCIENCE INALIENABLE, 1791*

Introduction

From his conversion until a few days before his death, John Leland was a
preacher. The gospel that converted him also compelled him to preach to
others. In his mind, no greater priority existed than preaching the gospel.
Although he is often remembered as one of the fathers of religious liberty
in the United States, his advocacy for America's "first freedom" must be
understood in the context of his commitment to the gospel. Leland was not

looking for special aid or treatment from the government for Christians. He simply believed that in a free public square, the gospel would triumph. The story of his life and work is the story of one man's confidence in the life-changing freedom offered to all sinners in Jesus Christ.

Contexts

In 1723, Captain James Leland Sr. moved his family from Sherburne, Massachusetts, to an unsettled region on the Blackstone River in the south-west corner of the township of Hassanamisco, which lies roughly forty miles west of Boston. King Philip's War had left the once "promising settlement entirely broken up."[1] The old, abandoned cornfields of the Nipmuc Indians were still discernible when the Leland family settled the land, which was incorporated in 1735 as the town of Grafton.[2]

At the time of the move, Captain Leland's son, James Jr., was roughly three years old. Like his father, James Jr. would grow up farming the family land. As a religious family, they were Congregationalist, but James Jr., as a young man, expressed reservations about infant baptism due to reading his Bible.[3] "When he broke his mind to his mother, she gave him an alarm-

---

[1] Frederick Clifton Pierce, *History of Grafton, Worcester County, Massachusetts: From Its Early Settlement by the Indians in 1647 to the Present Time* (Worcester: Chas. Hamilton, 1879), 34.

[2] "When Captain Leland settled here the marks of the old Indian cornfields were plainly to be seen." Pierce, 27.

[3] Regarding his father's struggle with the proper subject and mode of baptism, Leland wrote, "After *my father* was married, and had a son born unto him, he presented his child for baptism: but after the rite was performed, his mind was solemnly arrested with the text, 'Who hath required this at your hands?' that it was with difficulty he held his son from falling out of his arms; nor did he get over the shock until he had six more children born. He then got his scruples so far removed, that he invited the minister of the town to come to his house on a certain Sunday, after public service was over, and baptize all of them. At this time I was something more

ing warning against heresy; and as there were no preachers thereabout but pedobaptists, he sunk from his conviction, and concluded that his mother and his ministers were right."[4] On June 21, 1744, James Jr. wed Lucy Warren of Weston, Massachusetts, and over the course of roughly eighteen years of marriage, they welcomed nine children into their home: two sons and seven daughters.[5] All of Leland's children were born in Grafton and eventually baptized into the Congregationalist church. Of their nine children, it was their sixth child, John, who left an indelible mark on Baptist political theology.

John Leland was born on Tuesday, May 14, 1754. By Leland's own account, he "had a thirst for learning." He spent his early years with his father, who could not afford to give his son an education beyond the schools in his town. By age five, Leland could read the Bible and demonstrated an ever-expanding interest in other common topics of the day. Fortunately, Leland's love for the written word was not stifled by his father's lack of a library.[6] However, for whatever thirst for learning he possessed, Leland

---

than three years old. When I found out what the object of the meeting was, I was greatly terrified, and betook myself to flight. As I was running fast down a little hill, I fell upon my nose, which made the blood flow freely. The flight was in vain; I was pursued, overtaken, picked up and the blood scrubbed off my face, and so was prepared for the baptismal water." John Leland, *The Writings of the Late Elder John Leland, Including Some Events in His Life, Written by Himself,* ed. L. F. Greene (New York: G. W. Wood, 1845), 9–10. Henceforth in this chapter, this resource will be known as *The Writings.*

[4] Leland, *The Writings,* 2.

[5] Sherman Leland, *The Leland Magazine: Or, a Genealogical Record of Henry Leland, and His Descendants . . . Embracing Nearly Every Person of the Name of Leland in America, From 1653 to 1850* (Boston: Wier & White, 1850).

[6] "When he was twenty-one years of age, the only books in his father's house, and that he had ever read, were the Bible, Bunyan's *Pilgrim's Progress,* and Doddridge's *Rise and Progress of Religion in the Soul." George N, Brigg's Recollections of Leland,* printed in William B. Sprague, *Annals of the American Pulpit,* vol. 6 (New York: Robert Carter & Brothers, 1860), 178.

lacked social decorum.[7] As one schoolmaster recounted, "John has more knowledge than good manners."[8]

Everyone in Grafton seemed to have a plan for Leland's vocation. The local minister wanted him to go to college while the doctor planned to make him a physician, but his father desired John to remain with him "to support his declining years." Leland wanted to be a lawyer, but providence proved otherwise. During the summer of 1772, when Leland was eighteen years old, God began working in his life. Leland wrote, "When I was returning from my frolics or evening diversions, the following words would sound from the skies, 'You are not about the work which you have got to do.' The last time I heard these sounds, I stood amazed; and turning my eyes up to heaven, it seemed that there was a work of more weight than a mountain, which I had yet to perform."[9] It is doubtless that the supernatural work of grace Leland experienced in his conversion influenced his views of church-state relations.

After this event in Leland's life, he noted a change in his affections, wherein "the charms of those youthful diversions, which had been sweeter to me than the honeycomb, lost all their sweetness, nor could I conceive how there could be any pleasure in them."[10] Leland's acquaintances perceived a change in him due to his newly acquired interest in speaking of religion. God was at work in the young Leland's life, yet the assurance of salvation still evaded him.

Toward the end of the summer in 1772, a young revivalist named Elhanan Winchester was preaching in Grafton.[11] As Winchester ministered

---

[7] Eric C. Smith, in his biography on Leland, noted that "it was Lucy Leland's dynamic, Spirit-filled, intensely individualistic faith that took deepest root" in John. Lucy's influence on her son likely pushed him to "embrace the role of a nonconformist in Grafton's conservative society." Smith, *John Leland: A Jeffersonian Baptist in Early America* (Oxford: Oxford University, 2022), 17.

[8] Leland, *The Writings*, 10.

[9] Leland, 10.

[10] Leland, 11.

[11] Winchester was ordained as a Baptist preacher in 1771, but eventually converted to Universalism later in his life. Leland's association with Winchester would

in the area, several people were converted. Still, the conversion of a woman named Priscilla, an acquaintance of Leland's, shook John to his core. He wrote, "When I heard the report, it greatly affected me, for I had been at many dances with her. The result with me was, now the waters are troubled, and it is time for me to step in."[12] Within a few weeks, Winchester returned to Grafton, and Leland went to hear him preach. Leland recounted that "while he was preaching, something kept answering in my breast, yes, yes, yes, it is so." As Leland observed the baptismal service at the end of the preaching, he "made his vows to God to forsake all sinful courses and seek the Lord, if he would direct me how."[13]

Over the next two years, Leland wrestled with the genuineness of his conversion, writing, "Strange to relate, one hour I would entertain a comfortable hope that my sins were pardoned; the next hour, nearly give up all hope; fearing that all my exercises were self-learned, and that I had not been taught of God; the third hour, be impelled that I must preach or perish. This conflict wore off my flesh, and made me irresolved about anything."[14] In the mercy of God, however, Leland did not languish in unresolved assurance. On June 1, 1774, at the age of twenty, Elder Noah Alden of Bellingham came to Northbridge and baptized Leland alongside seven others. After his baptism, Leland described himself as strengthened. Hardly nineteen days after his baptism, in a meeting at Grafton, Leland began what would become a lifelong ministry of preaching the gospel of Jesus Christ.

As Leland detailed his conversion and call to ministry, he often borrowed language steeped in the Scriptures, especially the Old Testament prophets.[15] Though fully aware of his weaknesses, Leland did not deny

---

provoke suspicion about Leland among some Baptists early in his ministry. Sprague, *Annals of the American Pulpit*, 175.

[12] Leland, *The Writings*, 11.

[13] Leland, 11.

[14] Leland, 16.

[15] "On Sunday, the 20th of June, I went to meeting at Grafton, where there was no preacher. My mind was greatly embarrassed about preaching, and my prayer

God's call upon his life. In the autumn of 1774, he was licensed to preach at the Bellingham church, a Separate Baptist congregation, by Elder Noah Alden.[16]

In between his licensing and ordination to ministry, Leland married Sally Devine on September 30, 1776. Together, they welcomed nine children into their family throughout their marriage, which lasted until Sally's death on October 5, 1837. During her life, Sally was described as the consummate "helpmate" to Elder Leland, spending many years raising their children as Leland traveled the region, preaching the gospel and advocating

---

was, that I might know my duty. The words of the Prophet occurred to my mind, 'There is none to guide her of all the sons she has brought forth.' Having the Bible in my pocket, I drew it out, and, without design, opened to Mal. 9." Leland, *The Writings*, 17.

[16] The Bellingham church identified with the Separate Baptists, which "had arisen from the revivalism of the Great Awakening among Congregational churches in New England. Those Congregationalists who were supportive of the revival movement were called New Lights. These eventually separated from the Congregational churches because of their concern over the regenerate nature of the congregations. The Separate Congregationalists moved toward Baptist views; Baptists had been sympathetic to their movement and the two groups had some affinity of position. Both groups advocated a regenerate church membership, rejected the Half-way Covenant, disliked government interference with churches, were wary of strong inter-church control, and both favored democratic ideals. Both groups represented the discontented element in society. They held almost identical views regarding ministry and ordination. Most importantly, they both had a common opponent: the established church. The Baptists frequently pointed out to the Separates their similarity in desire for regenerate church members and that 'the surest safeguard of the pure or regenerate church concept was the practice of believers baptism.' This alone, Baptists argued, would keep the church 'distinct from the world. Infant baptism looked forward hopefully to a divine election, while believer's baptism testified to a salvation already secured.' Separate Congregationalists did not rush to leave their churches, even after they adopted anti-pedobaptist views. Inevitably, the differences of the members regarding baptism became irreconcilable and the anti-pedobaptist members left to form new churches or to join existing Baptist churches." Martha Eleam Boland, *Render unto Caesar: Sources of the Political Thought of John Leland* (PhD diss., New Orleans Baptist Seminary, 1998), 92.

for religious liberty. Leland would not have accomplished everything he did without Sally's support.[17]

At this point, it is interesting to note that in Leland's personal account of his life between 1776 and 1777, he made no direct comments about the Revolution. Furthermore, we possess no extant writings from this period. With that said, Leland did indirectly reveal his sentiments about the Revolution in a pamphlet titled "Free Thoughts on War." Leland published the pamphlet in 1816, denouncing war as evil but also making a case for defensive measures by both individuals and nations when "the natural right of life, liberty, and property" are threatened by an aggressor. Without explicitly mentioning the Revolution, Leland implied that America was justified to defend itself "out of love to right" instead of a "spirit of hatred."[18]

In August 1777, after moving to Culpeper, Virginia, and joining the church at Mount Poney, Leland was ordained "by the choice of the church, without the imposition of the hands of a Presbytery."[19] By his testimony, Leland "undertook to preach among them half the Sundays."[20] When he was not serving at the congregation in Culpeper, Leland was "going and preaching to a large congregation; traveling as far south as Pedee River, in South Carolina." While the congregation in Culpeper initially took no issue

---

[17] Admittedly, Leland spoke sparingly of his wife in his writings, but Samuel Harriss recounted Leland's personal testimony regarding Sally's character in his "Further Sketches of the Life of John Leland," which is preserved by editor L. F. Greene in Leland, *The Writings*, 41–54.

[18] Leland, *The Writings*, 467.

[19] Leland, 19. Leland would go on to receive "a regular ordination by the imposition of the hands of the presbytery" on June 24, 1787. On details of this second ordination, see L. H. Butterfield, "Elder John Leland, Jeffersonian Itinerant," *The American Antiquarian Society* (October 1952): 167. By Leland's own admission, "By this [his ordination] not only was a union effect between me and others, it was a small link in the chain of events which produced a union among all the Baptists of Virginia not long afterwards." J. T. Smith, "Life and Times of the Rev. John Leland," *Baptist Quarterly* (April 1871): 237.

[20] Leland, *The Writings*, 19.

with Leland's itinerant ministry, their patience wore thin by early 1778 as Leland recalled, "My stay [there] was not a blessing to the people. I was too young and roving to be looked up to as a pastor. Difficulties arose, the church split, and I just obtained a dismission and recommendation."[21]

The dismissal served to stir Leland's heart for itinerant ministry, yet it was not without its difficulties. He wrote, "Having moved to Orange, I commenced my labors with ardor. Twelve and fourteen times a week I frequently preached. But, notwithstanding the constancy of my preaching, and the multitudes that attended, there was but small appearance of the work of God's spirit. I said before, I knew my heart did not burn with the holy fire as it ought to."[22] Leland struggled to reconcile his call to ministry with an internal sense of apathy toward the sinners' plight. In October 1779, however, the apathy lifted, and Leland recorded, "My mind was graciously impressed with eternal realities. Souls appeared very precious to me, and my heart was drawn out in prayer for their salvation. Now, for the first time, I knew what it was to travail in birth for the conversion of sinners."[23]

Leland's fourteen years of ministry in Virginia bore fruit, but not without deep struggles.[24] Leland's description of his ministry as "travailing in birth" seems fitting.[25] While God indeed blessed his efforts, Leland openly wrote how his "mind was greatly depressed" during times of sickness and that "the spirit of prayer left [him]."[26] At one point, Leland said, "My hope for heaven was shaken to the centre. The truth of what I had been preaching was doubted. The fear that I had been governed by an ambitious spirit,

---

[21] Leland, 19.

[22] Leland, 19.

[23] Leland, 20.

[24] On the struggle in Virginia, Leland wrote, "The love of my God, and the worth of immortal souls, has stimulated my heart and borne me up under all the pressure of the mobs, tumults, reproaches, and contentions; and having obtained help of God, I remain until this very day." Leland, 172.

[25] Leland, 501.

[26] Leland, 22.

like Jehu, was great. In short, I was a poor, forlorn, sick worm of the dust."[27]
God, however, was pleased to use this "poor, forlorn, sick worm of dust" as
a "prominent instrument in the most extensive and powerful works of grace
in Virginia in the latter part of the century."[28]

As the gospel advanced through the evangelistic efforts of Virginia
Baptists, the established church grew weary and began systematically persecuting ministers who would not submit to state licensure.[29] Intending to
address the "political grievances of the whole Baptist society in Virginia,"
various Baptist associations united in 1784 to form a general committee
with delegates from each association to address.[30] Leland served as a delegate
and played an essential role in the repeal of the Incorporation Act, which
had granted the state jurisdiction to regulate church associations and which
opponents believed presaged the establishment of the Episcopal Church.[31]
In their argument against the Incorporation Act, Leland, along with Reuben
Ford, stated:

New Testament Churches, we humbly conceive, are, or should be,
established by the Legislature of Heaven, and not earthly power;

---

[27] Leland, 22.

[28] Smith, "Life and Times of the Rev. John Leland," 237.

[29] "As Baptists in Virginia became stronger, the established Anglican church
found it more difficult simply to ignore their activity. Baptists refused to purchase
required licenses qualifying dissenting ministers to preach in specified places, thus
flouting statutes set forth in the 1689 Act of Toleration. They considered accepting
licenses from the civil power to preach God's word as idolatry. A more systematic
persecution of Baptists began. Baptist ministers were regularly jailed and fined."
Boland, *Render unto Caesar,* 95.

[30] Robert B. Semple, *A History of the Rise and Progress of the Baptists in Virginia*
(Richmond: Pitt and Dickenson, 1894), 95.

[31] The Incorporation Act (which passed in 1784) established a Protestant
Episcopal church in Virginia in place of the Church of England. The act pro-
vided land and other benefits to the Episcopal church as a state-established society.
According to Butterfield, the petition brought by Leland and Ford had the "ring of
Leland's style and . . . is one of the most forceful expressions of principles that the
long controversy in Virginia produced." Butterfield, "Elder John Leland," 177–78.

by the Law of God and not the Law of the State; by the acts of the
Apostles, and not by the Acts of an Assembly. The Incorporating
Act then, in the first place appears to cast great contempt upon
the divine Author of our Religion, whose Kingdom is not of this
world, and Secondly, to give all the property of the State established
church to one Society, not more virtuous, nor deserving than other
Societies in the Commonwealth, appears contrary to justice, and
the express words of the IV Art: of the Bill of Rights, which prohibits rewards or emoluments to any Man, or set of men, except
for services rendered the State; and what services that Church has
rendered the State, either by her Clergy or Laity, more than other
Churches have done, we no [*sic*] not. [32]

Thus, Leland and Ford made a legal argument (the Incorporation Act violated the fourth article of Virginia's Bill of Rights) and a theological argument (God, not governments, establishes the church) for religious liberty
and disestablishment in Virginia.

In addition to securing religious liberty in Virginia through his work as
a delegate with the Baptist General Committee, Leland was instrumental
in ratifying the Constitution by Virginia.[33] Before writing approvingly of
the Federal Constitution, Leland harbored significant reservations and concerns about the work. Quoting the work of Robert Semple, Martha Boland
noted, "The General Committee voted unanimously in their 1788 meeting that the proposed Federal Constitution did not make sufficient provision for the secure enjoyment of religious liberty."[34] Leland articulated ten
problems with the proposed Federal Constitution at the request of Thomas
Barbour. Leland expressed concern about the lack of a Bill of Rights and no

---

[32] H. J. Eckenrode, *Separation of Church and State in Virginia: A Study in the Development of the Revolution* (Richmond: Davis Bottom, 1910), 119.

[33] I am thoroughly indebted to the work of Boland, *Render unto Caesar*, in this paragraph.

[34] Boland, 96.

assurance of the freedom of the press being noted in the Constitution, but he saved his most significant concern for the end, stating:

> What is clearest of all—Religious Liberty, is not sufficiently secured, No Religious test is Required as a qualification to fill any office under the United States, but if a Majority of Congress with the President favor one System more than another, they may oblige all others to pay to the support of their System as much as they please, and if Oppression does not ensue, it will be owing to the Mildness of Administration and not to any Constitutional defense, and if the Manners of People are so far Corrupted, that they cannot live by Republican principles, it is Very Dangerous leaving Religious Liberty at their Mercy. [35]

Whether or not Leland and Madison ever met in person to discuss Leland's objections, one cannot doubt the influence the Virginian itinerant Baptist minister had in shaping religious liberty in the new and expanding nation.[36]

After fourteen fruitful years of work in Virginia, Leland moved to Massachusetts in 1791. Leland's ministry and influence continued after he settled in Massachusetts.[37] While his most significant impact upon the American legal landscape was his role in shaping the precedent for the First Amendment while in Virginia, Leland made another unique contribution to political history on New Year's Day 1802, delivering a "mammoth cheese" to President Thomas Jefferson.[38] Historian Daniel Dreisbach recounted the

---

[35] Butterfield, "Elder John Leland," 187–88.

[36] Mark Scarberry, "John Leland and James Madison: Religious Influence on the Ratification of the Constitution and on the Proposal of the Bill of Rights," *Penn State Law Review* 113:3 (2009): 733–800.

[37] "In Massachusetts, as in Virginia, Leland interspersed his ministerial exhortations with pleas for the complete emancipation of religion from politics." C. A. Browne, "Elder John Leland and the Mammoth Cheshire Cheese," *Agricultural History* 18, no. 4 (1944): 146.

[38] Daniel Dreisbach noted that on the same day Jefferson welcomed Leland to the White House to receive the mammoth cheese, he also wrote his consequential

significance of the event: "The colossal cheese was made under Leland's direction by the predominantly Baptist and staunchly Republican citizens of Cheshire, a small farming community in the Berkshire Hills of western Massachusetts," he wrote. "It symbolized political support among New England's religious dissenters for Jeffersonian Republicans, the new administration in Washington, and the president's celebrated defense of religious liberty."[39] The fact that the idea for the cheese was announced from the pulpit reveals that Leland had few qualms about speaking favorably (even promoting) a particular political figure over another.[40] His concern for religious liberty was more with the government not interfering or influencing religion in America. By principle and example, Leland demonstrated that religious communities, so long as they were not seeking support from the government, were free to petition and influence the government for the sake of the common good.[41]

In the years following his delivery of the mammoth cheese to Jefferson, Leland described himself as "living several years in great barrenness of soul, *having* but little, if any success."[42] From 1802 to 1811, Leland underwent what, in modern terms, could only be described as depression. As he

---

letter to the Baptist Association of Danbury, Connecticut. In that letter, Jefferson used the (in)famous metaphor of a "wall of separation" between church and state. For a thorough examination of the phrase, see Dreisbach, *Thomas Jefferson and the Wall of Separation.*

[39] Daniel L. Dreisbach, "Mr. Jefferson, a Mammoth Cheese, and the 'Wall of Separation Between Church and State': a Bicentennial Commemoration," *Journal of Church and State* 43, no. 4 (Autumn 2001): 726.

[40] "He ardently supported Jefferson and Madison, with whom he had worked for religious liberty in Virginia, and, not averse to preaching politics, he celebrated Jefferson's 1801 inauguration with a sermon on religious liberty." Philip Hamburger, *Separation of Church and State* (Cambridge: Harvard University, 2002), 165–66.

[41] On this point, it is important to note that Leland did not believe all political grievances should be handled by petitioning Congress. See Leland's example later in this chapter, in the section titled "The Virginia Chronicle (1790)—Slavery," regarding an approach to the matter of slavery and government intervention.

[42] Leland, *The Writings*, 32.

witnessed the success of other ministers, Leland grappled with his own seeming ineffectiveness: "My fears were, that I did not preach right, which was the cause why I was so barren in myself and useless to others."[43]

In God's mercy, "a time of refreshing came" to Leland in 1811 while he was in Cheshire.[44] For the next thirty years, Leland continued to serve as an itinerant minister. He preached the gospel until a few days before he died. Over those thirty years, he recognized his health had declined and took solace in the gospel that he had preached to so many. As he neared the end of his race, Leland wrote,

> I am now in the decline of life, having lived nearly two-thirds of a century. When Jacob had lived twice as long, his days had been few and evil. I have spent my years like a tale that is told. Looking over the foregoing narrative, there is proof enough of imperfection; and yet what I have written is the best part of my life. A history seven times as large might be written of my error in judgment, incorrectness of behavior, and baseness of heart. My only hope of acceptance with God, is in the blood and righteousness of Jesus Christ. And when I come to Christ for pardon, I come as an old grey-headed sinner; in the language of the publican, "God be merciful to me a sinner." How long I have to stay on earth I know not. What labors or suffering I have yet to sustain below, I cannot tell. O, that the God of all grace would keep me in his holy care, and never suffer me to make shipwreck of faith and a good conscience, but make me faithful unto death, that I might finish my course with joy and receive a crown at last.[45]

By the end of his life and by his own account, Leland preached roughly 8,000 sermons, baptized 1,524 people, and personally knew 962 pastors. He

---

[43] Leland, 33.
[44] Leland, 33.
[45] Leland, 35.

died on January 14, 1841 and was buried beside a grave marker that read: "Here lies the body of Rev. John Leland, of Cheshire, who labored 67 years to promote piety and vindicate the civil and religious rights of all men."

Texts, Tenets, and Controversies

A fair amount of Leland's extant preaching addressed "political grievances." Still, it would be a mistake to assume Leland was more concerned with these things than with the gospel.[46] Whatever political engagement marked Leland's life, the engagement aimed to facilitate the free exercise of religion. For Leland, that meant the freedom to be Baptist following his convictions regarding the Scriptures. It is noteworthy that in Leland's account of his life, he rarely mentioned his involvement in politics.[47] Leland's essential character was that of a gospel preacher. Even when Leland addressed the "civil and religious rights of all men," it was in service of the ministry of the gospel. Thus, as we consider the most significant political writings of Leland's life, it is important to remember that being a faithful Baptist minister of the gospel was what compelled him to engage in politics. To that end, in this section, we will consider four topics related to political engagement that regularly appeared in the writings of John Leland: religious liberty, slavery, the separation of church and state, and the role of government.[48]

---

[46] Some have argued that the shift in emphasis in his writings and addresses on political matters toward the end of his life signaled a change in Leland. To be sure, the writings and addresses recorded (and remaining) do have a more pronounced political bent; but the fact that Leland continued to preach until his final years of life and, by his own account, give greater attention to his gospel ministry should give readers pause in suggesting that Leland drifted. Instead, I believe we ought to understand Leland's political activity as serving the preaching of the gospel.

[47] While *The Writings* contains many texts that address political matters, the opening sketch of Leland's life, which he penned, focuses far more on his work as an itinerant minister than on any specific political engagement.

[48] As with many aspects of this chapter, I am indebted to Boland's work, *Render unto Caesar*. In this case, I am appropriating the four categories that Boland

The Rights of Conscience Inalienable *(1791)—Religious Liberty*

Leland wrote a pamphlet outlining and vindicating the doctrine of religious liberty shortly after he departed from Virginia.[49] It is regarded among scholars as his most important writing on religious liberty.[50] In the pamphlet, Leland posed the question "Are the rights of conscience alienable, or inalienable?" Leland argued persuasively for the inalienable rights of the consciences of all people, noting that "every man must give an account of himself to God, and therefore every man ought to be at liberty to serve God in that way that he can best reconcile it to his conscience." Furthermore, Leland stated that "it would be sinful for a man to surrender that to man which is to be kept sacred for God." In other words, the conscience of man belongs to God, not the government. As a third point, Leland granted that even if a person were able to bind their own conscience, it would be immoral to bind the conscience of others. Finally, Leland appealed to the nature of religion as a "matter between God and individuals, the religious opinions of men not being the objects of civil government, nor in any way under its control." In restating his argument, Leland made one of his most well-known statements about religious liberty, stating:

---

employed in her work to organize Leland's political writings. While I will not be attempting to cover each writing as thoroughly as Boland, I will rely on the categories and identifications in her work as foundational to this section in my chapter.

[49] "This writing, *The Rights of Conscience Inalienable* (1791), was a sermon published in Connecticut just after Leland visited there in 1790. In it, he relies heavily on Thomas Jefferson's *Notes on the State of Virginia*, echoing his arguments that established religions were a violation of the laws of God." Matthew L. Harris and Thomas S. Kidd, eds., *The Founding Fathers and the Debate over Religion in Revolutionary America: A History in Documents* (Oxford: Oxford University, 2012), 140. Other works in which Leland addressed religious liberty are *The Yankee Spy, A Blow at the Root, The Government of Christ a Christocracy, Von Trump Lowering His Peak with a Broadside,* and *Speech Delivered in the House of Representatives.* All are contained in *The Writings.*

[50] Michael J. Hostetler, "Liberty in Baptist Thought: Three Primary Texts, 1614–1856," *American Baptist Quarterly* 15 (1996): 242–56.

Government has no more to do with the religious opinions of men than it has with the principles of mathematics. Let every man speak freely without fear, maintain the principles that he believes, worship according to his own faith, either one God, three Gods, no God, or twenty Gods; and let government protect him in so doing, i.e., see that he meets with no personal abuse, or loss of property, for his religious opinions. Instead of discouraging him with proscriptions, fines, confiscations, or death, let him be encouraged, as a free man, to bring forth his arguments and maintain his points with all boldness; then if his doctrine is false, it will be confuted, and if it is true (though ever so novel) let others credit it.[51]

Given the historical climate of established religion in various states, Leland's clarity on the matter of religious liberty was viewed by some as radical. People were skeptical that such freedom would lead to flourishing. To combat such thinking, Leland pointed to how states with greater religious liberty were experiencing greater revival, which, in his mind, was at least one way the principle of religious freedom was validated as blessed by God.[52]

The Virginia Chronicle *(1790)—Slavery*

Before his move to Massachusetts, Leland wrote a historical account of Baptist life in Virginia with discussions of the different groups of people in the region. Leland addressed slavery, religious liberty, and some of his general views about government. In particular, he argued for liberty of conscience

---

[51] Leland made a similar statement in his pamphlet *Yankee Spy.*

[52] "Baptist Antifederalists lauded the lack of religious tests and hardly believed that the lack of an establishment or a religious test would foster immorality or skepticism. Virginia's John Leland noted that the southern states, where disestablishment proceeded most quickly, had seen the greatest religious revivals in the late 1780s." Thomas S. Kidd, *God of Liberty: A Religious History of the American Revolution* (New York: Basic Books, 2010), 221.

among slaves, writing, "Liberty of conscience, in matters of religion, is the right of slaves beyond contradiction; and yet, many masters and overseers will whip and torture the poor creatures for going to meeting, even at night, when the labor of the day is over."[53] Furthermore, Leland lamented the unjust treatment of black people under Virginia law.[54] On the evil of slavery, Leland contended:

> The whole scene of slavery is pregnant with enormous evils. On the master's side, pride, haughtiness, domination, cruelty, deceit, and indolence; and on the side of the slave, ignorance, servility, fraud, perfidy, and despair. If these, and many other evils, attend it, why not liberate them at once? Would to Heaven this were done! The sweets of rural and social life will never be well enjoyed, until it is case. But the voice of reason, (or perhaps the voice of covetousness,) says, it is not the work of a day; time is necessary to accomplish the important work: a political evil requires political measures to reform. Insurmountable difficulties arise to prevent their freedom. Can government free them? The laws have declared them property; as such, men have bought and enjoyed them. Is it not unconstitutional for government to take away the property of individuals? Can government ransom them? . . . If they are not brought out of bondage, in mercy, with the consent of their masters, I think that they will be, by judgment, against their consent. [55]

Given Leland's strident opposition to slavery in his earliest writings, some scholars have been puzzled by his statement on August 16, 1839, regarding "the futility of petitioning Congress to free the slaves."[56] In his "Address Delivered at Bennington," Leland stated:

---

[53] Leland, *The Writings*, 95.
[54] Leland, 96.
[55] Leland, 98.
[56] Boland, *Render unto Caesar*, 121.

Congress does not possess an individual slave. The slave-holders
have never alienated them to government. How preposterous is it,
then, to burden Congress with cart-loads of petitions to do that
which they have neither the right nor power to do? The slaveholders are to be addressed: the power lies in them alone. It is not
an article to be settled by legislation among us. It belongs to the
moral and *religious* department, and not to the *legislative*. Three
parties are concerned in the question, viz: God—the master—and
the slave.[57]

A shift in Leland's thinking is fairly undeniable, though the reasoning for
the change is harder to pinpoint.[58] In charting his evolution on the issue of
slavery, Bruce Gourley described Leland's timeline as follows: the Strident
Anti-Slavery Leland (1789–1802), the Silent Leland (1803–1830), the
Ambivalent Leland (1831–1836), and the Anti-Abolitionist Leland
(1839).[59] Gourley concurred in part with Brad Creed's explanation regarding the reason for Leland's shift on slavery in his later years, noting that
while Leland never changed his position on slavery per se, he disagreed
with the approach of the abolitionists of his day.[60] Another important factor at play was the individualism promoted by Leland. As a man who lived
through government tyranny and fought for religious liberty, Leland was
skeptical of government intervention, especially if the matter could be

---

[57] Leland, *The Writings*, 697–98, emphasis in original.

[58] "Despite Leland's antislavery sympathies, he never again pressured a legislature for emancipation. In fact, as the nineteenth century progressed, Leland's
antipathy for slavery was replaced by an antipathy for New England abolitionists.
Leland held fast to a commitment to conversionist antislavery, trusting in a millennial emancipatory moment and doubting the political nature of abolitionism."
Benjamin G. Wright, *Gospel of Liberty: Antislavery and American Salvation* (PhD
diss., Rice University, 2014), 50–52.

[59] Bruce T. Gourley, "John Leland: Evolving Views of Slavery, 1789–1839,"
Baptist History and Heritage 40, no. 1 (2005): 104–16.

[60] Brad Creed, *John Leland, American Prophet of Religious Individualism* (PhD
diss., Southwestern Baptist Theological Seminary, 1986), 94–105.

considered an issue of conscience. To be sure, Leland denounced slavery as evil until his death, but his view of the need for government intervention weakened over time. [61]

Given his willingness and enthusiasm for the government to intervene to promote religious liberty in the young Republic, Leland's opposition to government-enforced emancipation appeared to lack consistency.[62] It would not be wrong to infer that, based upon Leland's legal fight for religious liberty, he viewed freedom of conscience as fundamentally more important than the immediate, unconditional manumission of slaves that was being proposed by abolitionists during his day.[63] However, this was not because Leland was indifferent to the plight of enslaved people. Leland also proposed a plan that, while different from the abolitionists, ultimately aimed at the freedom and flourishing of slaves.[64] On this plan, Martha Boland wrote, "Leland recognized that in order for the slaves to be truly free, they must have access to all the opportunities that white citizens have. To free them without any provision for these necessities would be almost as cruel as keeping them enslaved. . . . Leland proposed a gradual plan for the freeing of slaves, one that would be fair to the slaves and not overtax the system in trying to care properly for them. This plan would also give masters time to restructure their systems so as not to be dependent upon slave labor."[65] Thus, while it is fair to say that Leland's approach to addressing slavery changed over time and that he appeared to demonstrate a degree of

---

[61] W. Harrison Daniel, "Virginia Baptists and the Negro in the Early Republic," *Virginia Magazine of History and Biography* 80, no. 1 (1972): 68.

[62] Creed, *John Leland*, 102.

[63] On the various beliefs and practices of the abolitionist, see Daniel J. McInerney, "'A Faith for Freedom': The Political Gospel of Abolition," *Journal of the Early Republic* 11, no. 3 (1991): 371–93.

[64] For a thorough account of Leland's work alongside the General Committee to address slavery, see Andrew L. Feight, *The Good and the Just: Slavery and the Development of Evangelical Protestantism in the American South, 1700–1830* (PhD diss., University of Kentucky, 2001): 177–203.

[65] Boland, *Render unto Caesar*, 121.

inconsistency when it came to how and when the government should intervene to address various societal evils, Leland remained personally opposed
to slavery as an evil to be eradicated and believed that conversion, not legislation, was the best means of destroying the violent institution.

In summary, Leland did not wrestle with whether slaves should be set
free; his mind was settled on that issue. Instead, he wrestled with what
means of manumission would result in the best long-term prosperity and
protection of his fellow image-bearers.[66] Leland ultimately decided the
conversion of slaveholders through the preaching of the gospel was a better solution than legislating emancipation. Leland's position on this point
is thus consistent with his advocacy of religious freedom as the highest
priority. For if religion could be practiced without interference from the
state, then truth would prevail, and slaveholders would come to embrace
the gospel and obey Christ by setting their slaves free. Such an approach
to the issue, while admittedly inadequate and representative of a naive
conversionism on Leland's part,[67] was consistent with his strict separatism and belief that the transformation of a society ultimately rests in the
preaching of the gospel, which was the same work to which Leland committed his life.

On Sabbatical Laws (1816)—The Separation of Church and State

Leland's opposition to Sabbath legislation is a prime example of his commitment to the separation of church and state. He believed there were
no grounds for legislating holy days.[68] The issue of legislated holy days
and the relationship between the church and state came to a head in

---

[66] For other writings by Leland that address the issue of slavery, see *Letter of
Valediction on Leaving Virginia, in 1791, Address Delivered at North Adams, on the
4th of March, 1831, Free Thoughts on Times and Things*, and *Address Delivered at
Bennington, August 16, 1839,* all of which appear in *The Writings*.

[67] See note 92, later in the chapter, for an explanation of conversionism.

[68] Boland, *Render unto Caesar*, 122.

1810 when the US Congress passed "An Act Regulating the Post Office Establishment," keeping the post office open every day of the week, including Sunday, which was regarded by many as the Christian Sabbath.[69] In his pamphlet *On Sabbatical Laws*, Leland argued the legislature was obligated "to make laws for the security of life, liberty, and property, and leave religion to the consciences of individuals."[70] If, however, legislature attempted to coerce a particular obedience to God by legal force, this would violate its God-given role. Leland wrote, "Legal force is not the armor with which the Captain of our salvation clothes the soldiers of the cross. An honest appeal to the reasons and judgments of men, is all the force that Christians should use to induce others to believe in and worship God as they themselves do."[71] In his characteristic form, Leland used the controversy regarding Sabbath legislation to highlight once again the distinction between a religious practice coerced by the state and a religious practice compelled by the Spirit of God. He concluded his argument, stating, "However others may seek to regulate religious societies by law and by force, to me a man cannot give greater evidence that he is ignorant of the precepts and destitute of the spirit of Christianity, than by calling the aid of the civil arm to legalize religious days and modes, and punish those who will not submit."[72] Leland believed that legislating particular religious opinions would harm religious communities in America.[73] Some suggest it was Leland's commitment to enlightenment individualism in a similar vein to that of Jefferson and Madison (who were both deeply influenced by

---

[69] Brad Creed, "John Leland and Sunday Mail Delivery: Religious Liberty, Evangelical Piety, and the Problem of a 'Christian Nation,'" *Fides et Historia* 33, no. 2 (Summer/Fall 2001): 1.

[70] Leland, *The Writings*, 441.

[71] Leland, 443.

[72] Leland, 445.

[73] Edwin Scott Gaustad, "Religious Liberty: Baptists and Some Fine Distinctions," *American Baptist Quarterly* 6, no. 4 (December 1987): 215–25.

Locke) that caused him to oppose legal matters like Sabbath legislation.[74] Others, however, have noted that Leland was skeptical of anything that resembled the establishment of religion.[75] Thus, not only did Leland contend that the government must not dictate how or what people worship, but also the time when they worshipped was to be left to the conscience between God and man.[76] Leland was ruthlessly committed to the idea that religion could not be legislated.[77]

Of the other writings in which he addressed the matter of the relationship between church and state, Leland specifically enumerated Baptist reasons for dissent from the established church in *The Virginia Chronicle*.[78] Leland wrote:

1.   No national church, can, in its organization, be the Gospel Church.
     A national church takes in the whole nation, and no more; whereas,

---

[74] Andrew M. Manis, "Regionalism and a Baptist Perspective on Separation of Church and State," *American Baptist Quarterly* 2, no. 3 (September 1983): 213–27; William T. Reddinger, *Political Thought in Political Sermons of the American Founding Era* (PhD diss., Northern Illinois University, 2010), 61. Also, see Reddinger's article, "'Virtue' and 'True Virtue': Competing Ethical Philosophies in the American Founding Era," *Journal of Church and State* 59, no. 1 (February 2017): 23–42.

[75] Joe Coker, "Sweet Harmony vs. Strict Separation: Recognizing the Distinctions between Isaac Backus and John Leland," *American Baptist Quarterly* 16 (Spring 1997): 241–50.

[76] "The Baptist minister Leland explained that 'the legitimate powers of government, extend only to punish men for working ill to their neighbours, and no ways effect the rights of conscience.' Elsewhere, Leland insisted that government had no right to restrict free exercise in 'time, place or manner.' This notion was a long-standing part of Baptist and dissenter doctrine." John A. Ragosta, *Wellspring of Liberty: How Virginia's Religious Dissenters Helped Win the American Revolution and Secured Religious Liberty* (Oxford: Oxford University, 2010), 155.

[77] Rosalie Beck, "John Leland: The Consistent Separatist," *Baptist History and Heritage* 47, no. 3 (September 2012): 65–75.

[78] For other writings in which Leland addressed the separation of church and state (with particular interest in Sabbath legislation), see *Leland Again*, *Transportation of the Mail*, and *Extract of a Letter to Col. R. M. Johnson*.

the Gospel Church, takes in no nation, but those who fear God, and work righteousness in every nation. The notion of a Christian commonwealth should be exploded forever, without there was a commonwealth of real Christians.

2. The Church of England in Virginia has no discipline but the civil law . . . but a Gospel Church has nothing to do with corporeal punishments. If a member commits a sin, the church is to exclude him, which is as far as church power extends. If the crime is cognizable by law, the culprit must bear what the law inflicts. In the church of England, ecclesiastical and civil matters are so blended together, that I know not who can be blamed for dissenting from her.

3. Religion is a matter entirely between God and individuals. No man has a right to force another to join a church; nor do the legitimate powers of civil government extend so far as to disable, incapacitate, proscribe, or in any way distress, in person, property, liberty or life, any man who cannot believe and practice in the common road. A church of Christ, according to the gospel, is a congregation of faithful persons, called out of the world by divine grace, who mutually agree to live together, and execute gospel discipline among them; which government, is not national, parochial, or presbyterial, but congregational.[79]

At this point, it is important to note that Leland's emphasis on the individual and on personal accountability to God, which were foundational to his view of the separation of church and state, was nonetheless harmful to Baptists in Virginia and Massachusetts in significant ways. In his dissertation, "How High the 'Wall'? A Comparison of the Church-State Separation Positions of Thomas Jefferson and John Leland," Richard Huff noted, "Leland lost sight of the imperative of corporate obligations by an over enamoredness with individualism, bucking both political and religious

---

[79] Leland, *The Writings,* 107–9.

leaders of his day by the extent to which he set personal concerns over those of society as a whole."[80] Others have noted a "decline in doctrinal standards" among "Massachusetts Baptists after Leland's death partly due to his influence in misguidedly taking individual liberty to such an extreme that confessions of faith were opposed."[81] Among other unique features of Leland's individualism was his apathy toward the observation of the Lord's Supper and skepticism of associations and missionary societies.[82] Sadly, Leland's concern for individual freedom often provoked him to be skeptical of even good institutions.[83]

Short Essays on Government *(1820)—The Role of Government*

Leland held that "civil government is certainly a curse to mankind; but it is a necessary curse, in this fallen state, to prevent greater evil."[84] In defining the institution of government, Leland wrote,

> Government is the formation of an association of individuals; by mutual agreement, for mutual defense and advantage, to be governed by specific rules. And, when rightly formed, it embraces Pagans, Jews, Mahometans and Christians, within its fostering arms—prescribes no creed of faith for either of them—proscribes

---

[80] Richard Curry Huff, "How High the 'Wall'? A Comparison of the Church-State Separation Positions of Thomas Jefferson and John Leland" (PhD diss., Westminster Theological Seminary, 2003), 383.

[81] Huff, 385.

[82] Albert W. Wardin Jr., "Contrasting Views of Church and State: A Study of John Leland and Isaac Backus," *Baptist History and Heritage* 33, no. 1 (1998): 12–20.

[83] On the matter of missionary societies, Huff noted that Leland "was apprehensive that the organization of institutional Christianity to this degree might lead it to 'call in the civil arm to enforce its dogmas and punish non-conformists.'" Huff, *How High the Wall?*, 388.

[84] Leland, *The Writings*, 103.

none of them for being heretics, promotes the man of talents and integrity, without inquiring after his religion—impartially protects all of them—punishes the man who works ill to his neighbor, let his faith and motives be what they may. Who, but tyrants, knaves and devils, can object to such government? [85]

As most aspects of Leland's worldview were informed by Scripture, it is not surprising to encounter him alluding to Romans 13 when considering the role of government. Government was limited to the role of defense and advantage for all citizens, regardless of their creed or lack thereof. Leland made an important distinction between criminal acts and moral sins as well. The role government should play in those matters is implicit in Jesus's own ministry. Speaking of the revelation of the nature of God's kingdom in Christ's ministry, Leland wrote, "When *Jesus* pardoned the sin of a criminal, and promised him admission into Paradise, he yet left him to bear the penalty of the law, which he had broken."[86] Thus, one can discern a clear though implicit differentiation between the spheres of responsibility between the church and state. While both the church and state may speak to and deal with a particular issue in society (e.g., murder), their respective roles remain distinct on account of being fundamentally grounded in different realms.[87]

In all four areas (religious liberty, slavery, separation of church and state, and the role of government), Leland made genuine contributions to Baptist political theology. The most enduring of those contributions rests in how he influenced religious liberty in the United States. As noted, Leland's

---

[85] Leland, 476.

[86] Leland, 4.

[87] "The kingdom of Christ is not of this world—all parts of it are unlike everything in state policy. He never interfered with Caesar's dues—would not act as civil judge in dividing the inheritance between two brethren, or in giving judgment on the adulterous woman. He claimed no civil prerogative, and had no civil promotion to bestow on his followers." Leland, *The Writings*, 475.

strong advocacy for individualism was a two-edged sword, promoting the separation of the church from the state while also impacting the theological identity of the Baptists in Virginia and Massachusetts. On this point, it is helpful to remember that Leland's individualism was not only influenced by the Enlightenment but also situated in his work as an itinerant preacher.[88] The primary work of the roving evangelists was to confront individual souls with the truths of the gospel. As a result, Leland cared for individuals and wanted to protect them from any perceived threat to their freedom to hear the true gospel.[89]

Leland's Legacy

Leland's life and ministry leave behind a positive legacy of radical confidence in the gospel of Jesus Christ.[90] Speaking of Leland, Thomas Kidd wrote, "The preacher had no doubt that the gospel of Christ would triumph in open competition with other religious beliefs."[91] In Leland's mind, the kingdom of Christ was not powerless, needing aid from the government to advance and flourish; it simply needed space. Where the gospel was given space, Leland saw lives and communities transformed. As contemporary

---

[88] Eric Smith has a helpful chapter, "A Bow Too Great for My Stiff Neck," in *John Leland: A Jeffersonian Baptist in Early America*, which considers Leland's relationship with the Baptist church. He notes that while Leland was a Baptist in theology, "the self-sufficient Leland simply did not share the Baptist reverence for the local church" (105).

[89] C. Douglas Weaver, "Baptist Ecclesiology from John Clarke to E. Y. Mullins: The Personal, the Communal, and the Eschatological," *Perspectives in Religious Studies* 41, no. 3 (2014): 277–95.

[90] Andrew T. Walker makes this same point regarding Leland: "Religious liberty is thus an expression of Christian confidence in the gospel." Walker, *Religious Liberty in Contemporary Evangelical Social Ethics: An Assessment and Framework for Socio-Political Challenges* (PhD diss., Southern Baptist Theological Seminary, 2018), 160.

[91] Kidd, *God of Liberty*, 177.

Baptists reflect upon political theology, we would do well to have our confidence in the gospel renewed by considering Leland's example. If the gospel truly is the power of God unto salvation, then the presence of competing truth claims in society pose no lasting threat to the church or her mission. Such confidence in the gospel should prompt Baptists to continue advocating for legislation that promotes and protects religious freedom in America and around the world. Religious liberty advocacy declares with Leland that "truth disdains the aid of law for its defence—it will stand upon its own merit."[92]

With Leland's celebrated legacy for the promotion of religious liberty noted, I want to conclude by suggesting there is also a cautionary lesson to be learned from Leland's narrow, individualistic approach to societal change.[93] Without denying the sufficiency or power of the gospel to transform society through preaching, I would also note that Leland's "conversionistic" approach to the emancipation of slaves in the later years of his life was naive and presumptuous.[94] Could the preaching of the gospel result in slaveholders willingly deciding to release their slaves? Yes. There should be no doubt that such a possibility existed. Yet where true evil existed in society, the government had a God-given responsibility to address the matter. Even where the gospel transformed the lives of individuals, a need for structural change at a governmental level still existed, and failure to initiate change reflects a defective understanding of repentance. Furthermore, contrary to Leland, the church of Jesus Christ should have (as many eventually did) petitioned Congress for change. Such political action does not demonstrate

---

[92] Leland, *The Writings*, 185.

[93] To be fair, given his postmillennial theology, Leland was no "transformationist." He trusted that such change would take place with the coming of the kingdom.

[94] "Conversionism refers to the ideology that looked to the millennial expansion of salvation as the most effective means of combating social injustice. This ideology had its core in evangelicalism, but conversionist expectation spilled out beyond evangelicals and seeped into the wider Protestant world as well." Wright, *Gospel of Liberty*, 4.

less confidence in the gospel but rather a more holistic approach to obeying Scripture and holding the government accountable according to God's intention for it.

In contemporary Baptist life, some fall victim to Leland's naive and narrow thinking regarding how the gospel transforms a society. As history has demonstrated, it is not simply by "just preaching the gospel" that society is changed and public moral reform takes place.[95] The gospel also forms the identity of believers in society to be engaged in the promotion of public good, which extends beyond the mere promotion of religious liberty. In addition to preaching the gospel, God also ordained the role of government, which, while not doing less, extends beyond the mere preservation of freedom.

Therefore, from Leland, we should learn to be confident in the gospel's power while recognizing that part of what it means to be confident in the gospel is being emboldened by its promises to love our neighbors and advocate for a common good that extends beyond advocacy for their religious liberty. While Leland got the power of the gospel and religious liberty right, he could have used the same political approach that resulted in the

---

[95] For the sake of clarity, it is important to note that I understand the phrase "just preach the gospel" as referring to an ideological conviction that assumes that all (or even the majority of) social issues can and should be addressed simply by means of evangelism. An example of such an ideology in action would be when a person claims the church should not address matters of injustice in society, such as abortion, racism, or poverty, through advocacy or political action but instead should solely focus on preaching the gospel because it is only through the gospel that a person can be saved and reconciled to God. The refrain "just preach the gospel" is a modern example of a myopic, conversionist political theology that does not do justice to the whole message of Scripture regarding the Christian's identity and ethic in light of the gospel. Finally, I would note that while Jesus prioritized the preaching of the gospel of the kingdom in his ministry, he was also inclined to address temporary issues of illness and confront aspects of injustice in society. The fact that an eschatological healing/renewal of all things is coming does not make Christians less obligated to demonstrate love for their neighbors. For more on "conversionism," see Wright, *Gospel of Liberty*.

shaping of the First Amendment to overturn the evil of slavery through leg-islation. Or, to put it another way, Leland's convictions regarding the gospel and the government, though good, were also shortsighted and narrow in certain places, leading to a needlessly deficient understanding of how the government can promote social good that corresponds to Christian truths and natural law without establishing a state religion. Despite this short-coming, Leland's legacy is worth remembering and learning from as a source of Baptist political theology that reflects great confidence in the gospel and a steadfast commitment to the truth of God's Word even in the face of hard-ship and opposition.

7

Isaac Backus

By Brandon J. O'Brien

Because he had an active ministry that spanned fifty critical years in American history—from the Great Awakening, through the Founding Era, and into the nineteenth century—it is virtually impossible not to view Isaac Backus as a liminal figure. One expects to find him oriented to the future rather than the past, celebrating the pluralism of religious (at least Christian) expression instead of Puritan tradition and championing Enlightenment common sense instead of Reformed orthodoxy. Historians and theologians concerned about the long arc of American religious history have tended to interpret Backus as something like an urtext of the commitments and habits of mind among later generations of American evangelicals.

Backus is best known as an early and tireless advocate for the separation of church and state in the American colonies and the new Republic. He is known for portraying the ideal relationship between church and state as a "sweet harmony" in which ecclesiastical and civil authorities operate in distinct but complementary domains, a *via media* between religious

175

establishment on the one hand and the "wall of separation" on the other. Describing his contribution in this way can give the impression that his goal was to articulate a moderating position between extremes.

It was not. Backus's overarching goal was to advance an accurate interpretation of both Scripture and the Christian tradition to position Baptists as the rightful heirs of the Reformation legacy in America. Fewer than 20 percent of Backus's written works were dedicated to the formal separation of church and state. The majority addressed theological and ecclesial issues, and his magnum opus was a multivolume church history of New England. He was not primarily—perhaps not at all—a political theorist. He was a pastor and self-taught theologian. His advocacy for religious liberty, as important as it was, is best understood as the outworking of broader and more theological goals.

Contexts

Norwich, Connecticut, was founded in 1660 when several dozen residents of nearby Saybrook, Connecticut, left over unwelcome developments in church governance. The Congregationalist church in Saybrook was gravitating toward a more presbyterian form of government that would ultimately reduce the autonomy of the local congregation and increase the authority of a collective body of ministers in the region. One power this body would hold was approving candidates for ministry in local churches. These developments eventually were formalized in the Saybrook Platform (1708). By then the founding settlers of Norwich were long gone. Among those settlers was Isaac Backus's great-grandfather.

By the time Isaac was born in Norwich, the Backuses were prominent residents in town. His father, Samuel, served in the General Assembly, and his grandfather had been a justice of the peace. In important ways, the whole trajectory of young Isaac's career in ministry lay in seed form in these events that involved his family before he was born.

Backus became born-again during the Great Awakening. Following conversion in 1741, he was hesitant to commune with the Congregationalist church in town because the pastor honored the Halfway Covenant, which Backus and others believed undervalued the personal experience of saving faith. After nearly a year's hesitation, he joined the church, hoping he and other born-again members could reform its membership practice. They did not. In 1745, Backus and his mother, along with several of the most prominent families in town, left the Norwich church and began holding Separate worship.

Two years later, Backus felt a call to preach and began itinerating in Separate churches in the region. In February 1748 he drew up a church covenant for "The Church of Christ in the Joining Borders of Bridgewater and Middleborough" and was ordained as its pastor. This Separate congregation was Congregationalist in theology, except that it would not admit Halfway members. It was around this time that Backus married Susanna Mason (November 29, 1749). Isaac and Susanna were married almost fifty-one years and raised nine children together.

When he started his church in 1748, Backus had not yet rejected pedobaptism. Finally in 1751, Backus concluded the Baptists were right. Just over a month later, he was baptized along with six members of his church.[1] This was ten years after his conversion. Backus's mind was now settled, but his decision put him at variance with many members of his own church. Years of dialogue and experiments in compromise followed until finally, in January 1756, Backus and six members of his church left the Separate church he founded and reorganized as a Baptist church in nearby Middleboro with Backus as pastor.[2]

---

[1] The full and moving account of Backus's journey to this conclusion is recorded in Alvah Hovey, *A Memoir of the Life and Times of the Rev. Isaac Backus* (Boston: Gould and Lincoln, 1858), 82–93.

[2] Hovey, 118–19.

This protracted summary of Backus's early ministry is important to illustrate a central motivating impulse of his. Backus did not conceive of himself as forward-thinking or iconoclastic. He was conservative by nature, always careful to situate his new experiences and growing convictions within his interpretation of both the Scriptures and the broader story of God's work in New England. His progression from New Light to Separate to Baptist took a decade because of his slowness to break with his inherited convictions.[3] Even so, once he was convinced, he was convinced. He spent the last fifty years of his life a principled and unwavering Baptist, an identity he came to view as entirely consistent with Scripture, the spirit of the Backus ancestors, and the intentions of New England's spiritual "founding fathers."

While Backus viewed his theological commitments as entirely consistent with the New England religious tradition, his fellow New Englanders did not. Separate Baptists faced a unique situation. Quakers and Baptists had been exempted from compulsory religious taxes since 1728. But Separate Baptists were neither Quaker nor recognized as Baptists by the region's older Baptist churches. In the eyes of the Congregationalist Church and the law, Backus's congregation and others like it were Separates who refused to baptize their children and had broken both Christian fellowship without sufficient cause and the law by refusing to pay taxes to support the local clergy. Thus, for the first twenty years of his ministry, Backus attended locally to meet the spiritual and social needs of his own flock and regionally to support and encourage Separate Baptist congregations and others. "Between 1756 and 1767, he traveled nearly 15,000 miles within the region, visiting Old Baptist churches, open-communion congregations, and new groups which sought his help in the task of organizing as churches."[4]

---

[3] The term "New Light" can refer to someone who was supportive of the revivalism of the Great Awakening. Some New Lights remained in their churches even if the pastor disapproved of the revival (i.e., was an "Old Light").

[4] Stanley J. Grenz, "Isaac Backus," in *Baptist Theologians*, ed. David S. Dockery and Timothy George (Nashville: Broadman, 1990), 106.

Twice, he petitioned local governments to repeal laws requiring compulsory religious taxation to support the Standing Order.[5] But his concerns were exclusively local until 1769, when the Warren Baptist Association appointed a grievance committee to gather accounts of religious persecution against Baptists and, under Backus's direction, draft a formal petition to the Massachusetts legislature. Representing the Warren Association forced Backus to sharpen his argument for the separation of church and state, situating it within the larger context of the American Revolution. In published appeals to the public, a presentation before the Continental Congress, and a proposed bill of rights for the Massachusetts state constitution, Backus tried to leverage the new nation's revolutionary zeal to advance the cause of religious liberty. He remained pastor of Middleboro's Baptist church until his death in 1806.

Intellectual Influences

Backus received no formal education. He inherited from his family an instinctive conservatism about the religious vision of New England's founders. He believed his great-grandfather left Saybrook and founded Norwich to preserve this vision. He regarded his own decisions to separate from the Congregationalist Church and later to become Baptist as efforts to return to this founding vision. To make sense of his own experiences, and justify his convictions to others, two intellectual influences stand out as most significant.

One is John Robinson, "the first pastor of the Church that came first to New England, and settled in Plymouth."[6] Robinson's *A Justification of*

---

[5] The term "Standing Order" referred, in New England, to Congregationalist clergy whose ministries were supported by taxation of the general population.

[6] Isaac Backus, *A Discourse Showing the Nature and Necessity of an Internal Call to Preach the Everlasting Gospel* in *Isaac Backus on Church, State, and Calvinism: Pamphlets, 1754–1789*, ed. William G. McLoughlin (Cambridge: Belknap of Harvard University, 1968), 107.

Separation from the Church of England (1610) gave Backus the historical and mental framework for organizing his key convictions: the principles of separation, credobaptism, requirements for ordination, church membership, and the separate jurisdictions of civil and ecclesiastical government. These are the issues about which Backus wrote for all his writing career. Robinson helped Backus conceive of Baptist convictions on these matters as fundamentally consistent with the Plymouth tradition over against Standing Order critics, who viewed Baptist convictions as theological and ecclesiastical innovations.

A second key influence was Jonathan Edwards. Backus self-identified as among the "friends of Edwards's writings"[7] and cited from a variety of Edwards's treatises and sermons. But to call Backus an admirer of Edwards would understate the case. Backus cited, debated, and employed Edwards on every major issue he addressed in print: his work on religious liberty, his defense of Calvinism, and his historiography of New England. If Robinson identified the core convictions central to authentic biblical Christianity, the theology of Edwards provided Backus the means of articulating how those core convictions held together, even if Edwards himself never explicitly connected them.[8]

Backus was particularly interested in Edwards's rejection of the Halfway Covenant and his support of the Great Awakening. In Backus's mind, Baptist views on these issues and others were "triumphantly asserted by Jonathan Edwards."[9] Before the Great Awakening, New England had been in a "sad declension," but Edwards reversed this trend by publicizing

---

[7] Isaac Backus, *A Church History of New-England. Volume 2. Extending from 1690 to 1784* (Providence: John Carter, 1784), 252.

[8] For more on the role of Edwards's theology in Backus's work, see Brandon J. O'Brien, "The Edwardsean Isaac Backus: The Significance of Jonathan Edwards in Backus's Theology, History, and Defense of Religious Liberty," (PhD diss., Trinity Evangelical Divinity School, 2013).

[9] Hovey, *Memoir*, 45.

the New England awakenings and defending orthodox Calvinism. Backus credited Edwards with restoring the value of church membership and the proper observance of the Lord's Supper by opposing the Halfway Covenant endorsed by Edwards's grandfather, Solomon Stoddard. Backus's most famous treatise, *An Appeal to the Public for Religious Liberty* (1773), depends for its logic on Edwards's *Freedom of the Will*. Backus saw in Edwards a kindred spirit who was working within the established church to return it to its founding principles.

Scholars debate the degree to which Backus was influenced by the political theories and epistemology of John Locke. Backus quoted "the great Mr. Locke" occasionally in his public tracts, and his defense of liberty of conscience harmonized significantly with Locke's.[10] Nevertheless, as will be clarified, the fundamental elements of Backus's positions on human understanding, liberty of conscience, and the separation of church and state were firmly in place when he wrote his first tract in 1754, before he read Locke. It appears Backus found Locke helpful for articulating his position but not essential for forming it. A passage from his single-volume *A History of New England* illustrates the point. After praising Roger Williams and John Clarke as exemplary defenders "for equal liberty of conscience," he noted that "Mr. Locke's letters upon that subject," while excellent, "were written near forty years afterward."[11] Locke was right. But the essential ideas preceded him by a generation, and Backus regarded those earlier sources as the greater influences.

Thus, Backus viewed himself not as an innovator but as committed to continuing the spiritual experiment of the Plymouth founders and the religious revival that began with Edwards.

---

[10] Isaac Backus, "Government and Liberty Described," in McLoughlin, ed., *Isaac Backus on Church, State, and Calvinism*, 357.

[11] Isaac Backus, *An Abridgment of the Church History of New-England from 1602 to 1804* (Boston: E. Lincoln, 1804), 216.

Texts and Tenets

Backus began publishing tracts in 1754, shortly after becoming Baptist and largely to defend that decision. His last published work appeared in 1805, just a year before his death. In that short half-century, he published thirty-seven tracts and pamphlets, a three-volume church history of New England and a later abridgment, as well as numerous newspaper articles. Among his unpublished works are numerous sermon manuscripts, decades of detailed diary entries, and other short works on miscellaneous topics. Although he is best known for his advocacy of religious liberty, the bulk of Backus's public writing was dedicated to defending Baptist beliefs (specifically) and Calvinism (more broadly), both on exegetical and historical grounds. His writing about religious liberty is best understood as a social-political application of that broader ecclesiastical agenda.

It is helpful to think of Backus's work in two major phases: (1) from 1754 to 1770, during which time Backus wrote almost exclusively for local ecclesiastical audiences and (2) from 1771 to 1805, during which time his work took on more public and sometimes national dimensions. His opinions did not vary in these periods. His arguments became sharper over time, as different audiences called for different emphases.

1754–1770

A common charge critics leveled against Baptists was that they erred both in their interpretation of Scripture and in their disregard for Christian tradition. This second charge especially saddled them with a reputation for trusting their own opinions over the consensus of spiritual forefathers. When writing for these critics, Backus primarily addressed issues of exegesis, Christian history, and liberty of conscience. He primarily appealed to the authority of Scripture, John Robinson, and Jonathan Edwards.

Backus's first pamphlet was titled *A Discourse Showing the Nature and Necessity of an Internal Call to Preach the Everlasting Gospel* (1754). The goal of this text was to establish historical precedent for rejecting formal ordination by a council of local pastors and relying, instead, on the "internal call" of the Holy Spirit confirmed by members of one's local congregation. To make his argument, Backus cited both Robinson and Edwards, albeit obliquely. In this way the contours of Backus's future writing were visible already in *An Internal Call* and run like this: (1) Baptist convictions had precedent in the Protestant Reformation; (2) Robinson and his Plymouth coreligionists—not the Puritans of Massachusetts Bay—were the archetypal New England Christians and, for this reason, their example was of utmost significance; and (3) Edwards affirmed important Baptist convictions, whether he realized it or not. His arguments became sharper and clearer over time. But that Backus remained committed to the general thrust of the argument in this pamphlet is evidenced by his publishing a revised edition of *An Internal Call* in 1792.

His second book, *A Short Description of the Difference between the Bond-Woman and the Free* (1756; revised edition 1770), gave more careful attention to biblical evidence for believer's baptism, which included a lengthy reflection on the relationship between the Old and New Testaments and how that relationship should influence biblical interpretation. Critical to Backus's mature argument for the separation of church and state was insisting that ecclesiastical and civil powers, while both ordained by God, have separate domains of authority. For the nation of Israel, civil and ecclesiastical powers were more closely aligned, as illustrated by the facts that Israel's worship was supported through general taxation and religious violations could be punished by civil power. But for Christ's church in the New Testament—and in America—the two authorities were strictly separate. Backus's *Bond-Woman* challenged this hermeneutical assumption.

While Backus was writing about theological issues, he and his fellow Baptists were experiencing social and political injustices at the hands of Standing Order ministers. His own mother, Elizabeth, was briefly imprisoned for refusing to pay taxes to support the Congregationalist minister in her town.[12] Consequently, a theological justification for liberty of conscience took greater prominence in Backus's writings. *A Seasonable Plea for Liberty of Conscience* (1770) illustrates the challenge Backus aimed to address in these works.

Backus had baptized Abraham and Elizabeth Lord, who were members of the Congregationalist Church in another town. The Lords wanted to separate and join a Baptist church because the Congregationalist Church admitted members without testimony of personal conversion. They wrote their pastor to request a formal withdrawal of membership. Their pastor refused. He could not let them leave the church, he said, because to do so would violate his conscience. He could not knowingly allow them to persist in error.

Backus wrote the minister on the couple's behalf. He argued that staying in a church that had departed from the Scriptures would violate the couple's conscience. And that for the church to presume to determine which matters were weighty enough to justify separation is to permanently bind the consciences of its members to error—in this case, the errors of pedobaptism and unconverted membership. He beseeched the minister to allow them the same liberty of conscience that he enjoyed. Baptists faced an uphill battle in their effort to worship according to their conscience because the region's ministers believed they already valued and protected liberty of conscience. Thus, in this period Backus was not primarily aiming to change laws but to change hearts. He appealed to local clergy to willingly release their Dissenting members from fellowship and exempt them from taxation, with little success.

1771–1805

In 1771 Backus's reading audience broadened. Increasingly, he wrote to members of the Massachusetts assembly, other legislators, and the general

---

[12] Hovey, *Memoir*, 29–30.

public. In 1773 he was asked by the Warren Baptist Association to represent their cause before the Massachusetts legislature. Rather than marking a change of opinion, 1773 marks a change in audience, occasion, and objective for writing. If before 1773 Backus had written as a pastor to pastors and with the goal of persuading the Standing Order to voluntarily allow Baptists liberty of conscience, beginning in 1773 Backus began writing as a representative of Baptists broadly, to an audience of legislators and the non-Baptist general public, with the goal of securing religious liberty, the legal protection from the state against secular coercion in religious affairs. In some of these writings, Backus quoted John Locke and leveraged the language of the Revolution. His use of revolutionary language, like his quotation of Locke, was more opportunistic than principled. As late as 1774, the Grievance Committee, of which Backus served as chair, was considering a position of neutrality concerning the war, as they believed they might need to appeal to the English Parliament to secure the liberty they sought.[13] Whatever else one makes of Backus's personal ambivalence about the war, in print he compared compulsory religious taxation to taxation without representation: "You do not deny the right of the British parliament to impose taxes within their own realm, only complain that she extends her taxing power beyond her proper limits, and have we [Baptists] not as good right to say you do the same thing?"[14]

An Appeal to the Public for Religious Liberty (1773) is Backus's best-known work from this period. The pamphlet was one prong of Backus's strategy as representative of the Warren Association. Another prong included a campaign of civil disobedience. By patiently enduring the inevitable persecution that would come when they refused en masse to support the Standing Order clergy or make use of the certificate exemption, the Baptists hoped to sway

---

[13] William G. McLoughlin, *Isaac Backus and the American Pietistic Tradition* (Boston: Little, Brown, and Company, 1967), 133–34.

[14] Isaac Backus, *An Appeal to the Public for Religious Liberty*, in McLoughlin, ed., *Isaac Backus on Church, State, and Calvinism*, 339.

the religious establishment and win the favor of the public. *Appeal to the Public* was the manifesto for this endeavor and was distributed to members of the Continental Congress in 1774.

The contents of this pamphlet are worth summarizing, as they form the foundation for Backus's argument for religious liberty. Backus maintained that true liberty is found in submitting to God-ordained governance. God mediates his rule through two early entities: the state and the church. The state is tasked with preserving the safety of the body. It prevents people from killing or robbing one another and punishes wrongdoers for such crimes. The church, by contrast, is tasked with preserving the soul. Put another way, the church is concerned with the First Table (the first three commandments) while the state is concerned with the Second Table (the last seven commandments) of the Mosaic law. The roles of church and state are thus complementary but distinct.

Church and state had been conflated in Massachusetts, as evidenced by (1) legislation that mandated "a pedobaptist worship" in every commonwealth, (2) a state-determined requirement for clergy selection, and (3) the maintenance of Congregationalist clergy by general taxation. These issues formed the heart of Backus's objection to state-organized religious expression. It was through infant baptism, performed by state-approved clergy who were supported by taxation of all citizens, including Dissenters, that the Standing Order maintained its influence over Massachusetts and throughout New England. If Dissenters refused to pay taxes, they could be coerced by the power of the state. The system of establishment incentivized the Standing Order to perpetuate its own hegemony over spiritual matters.

This was an immensely practical problem with a distinctly theological origin. Following Edwards, Backus believed that "all men have a power within them to act in every case as then seems best to them."[15] He quoted Edwards's definition of liberty: "the power, opportunity, or advantage that

---

[15] Isaac Backus, *Truth Is Great and Will Prevail* in McLoughlin, ed., *Isaac Backus on Church, State, and Calvinism*, 404.

any one has to do as he pleases or to conduct in any respect according to his pleasure."[16] In New England, only the Standing Order had this liberty. Thus, the human tendency toward self-interest becomes systemic injustice when laws protect the interests of one group at the expense of the rights of others. A few years later, Backus put the matter more succinctly: "In our dispute about religious liberty, we must take into consideration, that it is against the interest of the people we apply to, to grant us any remedy."[17]

Because the Standing Order refused to grant liberty of conscience, such liberty had to be protected through the formal separation of church and state. Far from being an abstract theory about religious liberty, this position was a political application of Backus's Calvinist doctrine. This focus explains Backus's apparent ambivalence about policies such as religious oaths for officeholders, Sunday mail delivery, and state-funded chaplains in the military. His attention was focused entirely on the root and not at all on the fruit or branches.

Published over the course of twenty years, a three-volume ecclesiastical history of New England was Backus's magnum opus (vol. 1, 1777; vol. 2, 1784; vol. 3, 1796). The single-volume abridgment, *Church History of New England from 1620–1804*, was Backus's final major work. All the themes in his other works appear in their mature and synthesized form in *Church History*. It was his most forceful effort to advance his two-blow offensive against religious establishment: he maintained with one hand that the Standing Order churches did not stand on Scripture; he maintained with the other that they did not stand on tradition. What was left? The Standing Order churches stood on the illegitimate use of coercive civil power. In Backus's telling, in addition to being champions of religious liberty, the Baptists had recovered the purity of gospel ministry from more than a century of compromise and decline.

---

[16] Jonathan Edwards, *The Works of Jonathan Edwards, Vol. 1: Freedom of the Will*, ed. Paul Ramsey (New Haven: Yale University, 1957), 453–54.

[17] Backus in Hovey, *Memoir*, 223.

Contributions

Backus was not a protean thinker who left behind a trove of theories about political theology. Instead, he carefully and thoughtfully remythologized what it meant to be Baptist in America in the final years of the eighteenth century. For Backus, to be Baptist meant to be rightful heir of the Protestant Reformation and, therefore, rightful heir of the first Christian congregation in New England. In some ways, what Backus left Baptists was not simply a way to think about religious liberty but a way to think about themselves in the great sweep of God's redemptive work. This was, at least, his primary aim.

In creating this mythology, Backus also constructed a thoroughly theological defense of religious liberty that did not rely on republican rhetoric or democratic logic, though he was not afraid to use either. Instead, he applied Scripture and the Reformation tradition, along with Edwards's Calvinistic understanding of human sin and volition, to the most pressing social issue facing his fellow Baptists: their inability to worship according to their conscience without fear of civil reprisal. He was able to share his theological vision in language that resonated with his countrymen, by leveraging John Locke and the rhetoric of the American Revolution, and to accompany argument with direct action, in the form of civil disobedience, to soften the hearts of the public.

Controversies

On the one hand, Backus was embroiled in controversy for his entire adult life. As a New Light, then a Separate, and finally as a Baptist, Backus held a minority opinion most of the time, and he advocated for others who shared his minority position in every case. On the other hand, Backus was temperamentally patient and conciliatory and, thus, appears altogether to have avoided schism and scandal among his fellow Baptists. After he became convinced of the merits of believer's baptism, he went so far as to experiment with a hybrid form of worship to accommodate both pedobaptists and credobaptists so his congregation did not have to break fellowship. It did not work. But the effort reveals a commitment to Christian unity so far as it depended upon him.

The most challenging aspect of his work in his own lifetime was trying to convince people with the authority to effect change that the problem he and his fellow Baptists faced warranted a change at all. His critics insisted that they too considered liberty of conscience a "darling point" and, therefore, dismissed Baptist concerns. *If it is liberty of conscience you want*, they seemed to say, *you have already got it*. The framers of the Constitution responded similarly. When Backus argued his case before the Constitutional Convention, some appealed to existing certificate laws and concluded that religious liberty was already protected by law and whatever local aberrations there might be here and there were not significant enough to warrant formal language ensuring religious liberty in the Constitution. Samuel Adams and John Adams both made speeches in which they acknowledged that Massachusetts had an established church, but only "a very slender one, hardly to be called an establishment."[18] So Backus labored to popularize a minority opinion among a majority who failed to see the problem.

It is also the case that in the two centuries since his death, Backus's work has received less scholarly attention than one might expect. His value in the Baptist struggle for religious liberty is never questioned, but it has more often been treated as axiomatic instead of carefully researched. The first biography of Isaac Backus appeared in 1858, half a century after his death. Backus does not appear to be a fixture in Baptist historiography until well into the twentieth century.[19] There has never been a season of

---

[18] Hovey, *Memoir*, 211.

[19] He does not appear at all, for example, in H. C. Vedder's *Short History of the Baptists* (Philadelphia: American Baptist Publication Society, 1907), even though Vedder maintains that Baptists "can honestly claim to have added another principle [to the Christian tradition], namely, that the union of Church and State is contrary

sustained debate among scholars about how to interpret Backus's work. Rather, there have been stages in which Backus has been leveraged as an exemplar of some broader cultural trend. We can roughly categorize these stages as (1) Backus as Quintessential Baptist; (2) Backus as Prototypical American Pietist; (3) Backus as Early Evangelical Modernist; and (4) Backus as Theologian-Activist.

Backus as Quintessential Baptist

For the hundred years between Alvah Hovey's biography and the mid-twentieth century, interpreters tended to construe Backus as a linchpin figure in the unbroken chain of Baptist advocacy for religious liberty. Older Baptist historiography tended to present the separation of church and state as a conviction passed down in unbroken succession from Thomas Helwys to Thomas Jefferson. Introduced by Helwys in *The Mystery of Iniquity* (1612), it was radicalized by Roger Williams in *The Bloudy Tenent of Persecution* (1644), popularized by Isaac Backus in *Appeal to the Public for Religious Liberty* (1774), and communicated from John Leland to James Madison and Jefferson, who put it into law. Indeed, since the early nineteenth century, both Baptist and non-Baptist interpreters have tended to construe early Baptists, especially Roger Williams, as proto-Jeffersonian secularists motivated by a philosophical commitment to religious liberty. In his 1837 *History of the United States*, for example, George Bancroft declared, "Freedom of conscience, unlimited freedom of mind, was, from the first, the trophy of the Baptists."[20] For many scholars, Baptists and non-Baptists alike, religious liberty and freedom of conscience have long been considered constitutive, fundamental Baptist principles, which Baptists bequeathed to

---

to the word of God, contrary to natural justice, and destructive to both parties to the union" (415).

[20] George Bancroft, *History of the United States, from the Discovery of the American Continent*, vol. 2 (Boston: Charles Bowen, 1837), 66–67.

the American spirit in general. In this interpretation, Backus is regarded not as an original thinker but as a popularizer of Williams's view of church and state. According to Joseph Martin Dawson,

> Governmental establishment of democracy, church-state separation and freedom of the soul, as first advocated by Roger Williams and later enunciated by Thomas Jefferson, required the conversion of the churches. For this essential evangelization a mighty man was required. His name was Isaac Backus.[21]

In this way, Backus's work is construed primarily as a key turning point in an ongoing and coordinated effort to secure legal protection of religious liberty. The chief motivation was the democratic spirit of the age. Edwin Gaustad argued, for example, that Backus and his coreligionist John Leland were "perceptively alert to the slogans and moods of their contemporaries" to such a degree that "it would be difficult to find persons more willing to accept and believe in their own culture."[22] His primary emphasis was not on where Backus had been but on where he was headed. He presents Backus as a cautious but zealous advocate for the separation of church and state, whose eyes were fixed on the future, not the past, and whose concerns were predominantly practical and not theological.

Backus as Prototypical American Pietist

The first major interpreter of Isaac Backus was William McLoughlin, whose contribution began with the publication of his 1967 biography, *Isaac Backus and the American Pietistic Tradition*, and was followed by the first published collection of selected writings by Backus and a three-volume

---

[21] Joseph Martin Dawson, *Baptists and the American Republic* (Nashville: Broadman, 1956), 46.

[22] Edwin S. Gaustad, "The Backus-Leland Tradition," *Foundations* 2, no. 2 (April 1959): 131.

set of his diaries.[23] McLoughlin continued to read Backus forward into Revolutionary America rather than backward into Puritan New England. In his estimation, "few men expressed so well in thought and action that vigorous, fervent, conscientious, experimental pietism which constituted the fundamental spirit of the new nation and which made its experiment in freedom unique."[24] For McLoughlin, Backus was not just a quintessential Baptist but something like the paradigmatic American whose religious convictions emphasized "experience as the primary source of knowledge rather than social rank or education; a direct experiential relationship between God and the individual superceding [*sic*] all institutional means; individual accountability to God alone, and, above all, equality among the brethren and between the brethren and their pastor."[25] According to McLoughlin, Backus so emphasized intuition and personal inspiration that "[h]is reliance on revelation [i.e., Scripture] was secondary to his direct personal perception of the truth."[26]

McLoughlin failed to take seriously Backus's self-conscious identification with "previous Puritan and separatistic movements in England and New England."[27] He portrayed Backus and his confreres as if they were merely products of their time who accepted contemporary habits of mind uncritically. Additionally, McLoughlin failed to recognize how Backus's

---

[23] McLoughlin's biography remains authoritative, if for no other reason than because there has not been another comprehensive work on Backus written since. It is, however, a frustrating resource for academic research as it contains no footnotes and no bibliography. Milton Vaughn Backman's unpublished doctoral dissertation, "Isaac Backus: Pioneer Champion of Religious Liberty," from 1959 is more helpful but less influential.

[24] McLoughlin, *Isaac Backus and the American Pietistic Tradition*, 230.

[25] McLoughlin, "Introduction," McLoughlin, ed., *Isaac Backus on Church, State, and Calvinism*, 30.

[26] McLoughlin, 28.

[27] Stanley J. Grenz, *Isaac Backus—Puritan and Baptist* (Macon: Mercer University, 1983), 5, n. 9. Grenz notes a couple of other deficiencies as well, which are less important to the current project.

view of church and state was integrated with his general theological perspective. In fact, he considered Backus's view of religious liberty and his Calvinist doctrine inherently incompatible, such that one would ultimately be sacrificed to the other. "The great irony of Backus' career was that the more successful he was in overthrowing the Puritan establishment, the more unsuccessful he was bound to be in defending the Calvinistic doctrines on which it was based."[28] The portrait of Backus that McLoughlin offers has its eyes set to the future, but tentatively. He finds in Backus the spirit of American pietism in its nascent form, forward-looking but fragmented and inconsistent.

Backus as Early Evangelical Modernist

In the 1980s, in his doctoral dissertation and a handful of articles, Stanley Grenz addressed Backus as a man of his times, but one self-consciously connected to the Puritan tradition. Grenz drew a line of continuity backward from Backus and primarily through the English Baptist tradition. He was also the first theologian (rather than historian) to study Backus's writing in great depth. Consequently, he was concerned with demonstrating that Backus's argument for religious disestablishment was the logical outworking of his systematic theology, which Grenz pieced together from Backus's occasional writings.

Even so Grenz viewed Backus as an example—if not patient zero—of the contamination of Evangelical theology by Enlightenment philosophical presuppositions. Specifically, Grenz identifies Backus as a devotee of John Locke rather than Jonathan Edwards. While he acknowledges that Backus "borrows part of his psychology from Edwards," he maintains that Backus's view of human understanding—including the operation of the will, his ecclesiology, and his understanding of the twofold source of truth—all

---

[28] Grenz, 53.

derive from Locke.[29] For Grenz, Backus's commitment to Lockean philosophy is what ultimately led him astray: "The defects in Backus's system are largely the result of his acceptance of the Enlightenment concept of the two-fold source of truth."[30]

Backus as Theologian-Activist

The most nuanced interpretations of Backus in recent years have come from historians of American law. John Witte Jr. has written extensively on the significance of theological influences upon the establishment of religious liberty in America in general and on the First Amendment in particular. Witte identifies four streams of influence that contributed to America's experiment in religious liberty: the Puritan, Evangelical, Enlightenment, and Republican.[31] Witte considers Backus a prime example of the Evangelical stream, which "sought to protect the liberty of conscience of every individual and the freedom of association of every religious group."[32] He likewise recognized that the "chief concern of the Evangelicals was theological, not political."[33]

Nicholas Miller gives greater attention to Backus in his larger-picture effort to establish the Protestant theological origins of American religious liberty. Miller correctly identifies the issues at the core of Backus's justification for religious liberty: "biblical revelation and its teaching regarding the fallen nature of man and the proper roles of civil and ecclesiastical rulers."[34] Miller

---

[29] Stanley J. Grenz, "Church and State: The Legacy of Isaac Backus," *Center Journal* 2 (1983): 75–84.

[30] Grenz, 87.

[31] John Witte Jr., *Religion and the American Constitutional Experiment* (Boulder: Westview, 2005), xxi.

[32] Witte, 27.

[33] Witte, 29.

[34] Nicholas P. Miller, *The Religious Roots of the First Amendment: Dissenting Protestants and the Separation of Church and State* (New York: Oxford University, 2012), 103–04.

helpfully puts Backus's use of Locke in its appropriate perspective, demonstrating that what motivated Backus was not Enlightenment philosophy but Reformed theology. "Locke and Backus agreed in embracing the heritage of dissenting Protestant theology regarding the relationship between civil and church powers," Miller asserts. "Backus rejected, however, what he viewed as Locke's efforts to place that heritage on different philosophical foundations, such as an enlightened human nature, rather than the biblical foundations that Luther or Roger Williams or the English Baptists had used."[35]

It should not surprise that McLoughlin and Grenz saw in Backus a progenitor for enduring characteristics of American Evangelicalism. Before he gave his scholarly attention to Backus, McLoughlin wrote biographies about revivalists Billy Sunday, Charles Finney, and Billy Graham. He found in Backus the beginning of a family line that ran through the nineteenth and twentieth centuries. Grenz, for his part, spent much of his career trying to move Evangelical theology beyond what he considered its lamentable reliance on Modernist categories and commitments. He found in Backus the beginning of Evangelicalism's fatal alliance with the Enlightenment. Thus, the most significant controversies surrounding Backus through the years have had to do with how to retrieve and assess his contribution to American Evangelicalism broadly and Baptist history more narrowly.

One might expect controversy related to Backus's opinions about slavery and indigenous peoples. The evidence is scant and can be given an overview here. In diary entries, Backus made passing mention of Samson Occom, a member of the Mohegan nation and a Presbyterian minister, with whom he had a relationship.[36] This author is aware of no public comments about Native Americans made by Backus.

Only slightly more clues exist for discerning Backus's opinions about slavery. Throughout his ministry, Backus preached in the homes of slaves,

---

[35] Miller, 105.

[36] Isaac Backus, *The Diary of Isaac Backus*, ed. William G. McLoughlin, vol. 2 (Providence: Brown University, 1979), 987.

baptized them, preached their funerals, and even admitted them to church membership. He offered no commentary about the institution of slavery, either publicly or privately, before the Revolution. A diary entry from June 26, 1757, is typical. On that day Backus baptized a man named Coffey, whom he identified as "a Negro man belonging to Mr. Ebenezer Lincoln of Taunton."[37] He appears to have taken Coffey's status as a slave as a matter of course. Backus's only public comments about slavery were made in 1788, when Backus represented Middleboro at a meeting to ratify the new US Constitution. He made an extemporaneous speech in which he dedicated a few words to advocate for abolition. "No man abhors that wicked practice [slavery] more than I do," he said, and he regarded the nation's founding as the perfect opportunity to "hinder the importation of slaves into any of these states." Even so, Backus did not think abolition needed to be written into the Constitution. Instead, he believed "each state is at liberty now to abolish slavery as soon as they please."[38] Perhaps he believed, as others did, that the trend of gradual abolition would continue in the North and eventually extend into Southern states.

Legacies

When Backus died in 1806, his work to secure religious liberty for New England Baptists remained unfinished. Massachusetts maintained an established church until 1833. He did not leave behind a school of thought or a cadre of disciples to carry on his project. Although he was part of the founding of the College of Rhode Island (Brown University), he did not leave behind an institution that bore his fingerprints or extended his shadow. For these reasons, his legacy is difficult to measure. As this survey shows, interpreters have measured his legacy in divergent ways. Often, they have found what they went looking to find.

---

[37] Backus, *The Diary of Isaac Backus*, 1:454.
[38] Backus, *The Diary of Isaac Backus*, 3:1220.

Taking his work as a whole, one might say he gave Baptists a narrative of the work of God in New England in which Baptists emerge as the heirs both of the Protestant Reformation and America's spiritual founding fathers in Plymouth. They are not simply one of many religious innovations resulting from the fervor of the Awakening, a mere sign of the democratization of American Christianity, but careful recoverers of biblical teaching and Christian heritage obscured by human sin.

Based on this narrative, Backus contributes a robustly biblical and theological case—not simply a secularist or opportunistic case—for religious liberty. Liberty of conscience was necessary so that the church could keep reforming. Reforming work had been interrupted by New England's conflated spiritual and civil power. This conflation had a theological explanation too: self-interest buttressed by an unregenerate will. Self-interest would necessarily prevent liberty of conscience, where granting it undermined the power of both church and state. So, the two must function separately. Finally, Backus modeled a multifaceted approach to advocacy that seems relevant even today. In his activism he worked to change the hearts of his fellow Americans and the ruling clergy as well as legislation at the highest levels.

Isaac Backus was not a political theorist. Given the option, he would no doubt prefer to be remembered as a pastor-theologian who championed orthodoxy and corrected misperceptions about America's early religious heritage. He stands as a reminder that being a champion for the truth and an advocate for one's community of faith can have surprising and lasting social implications.

8

Baptist Theology and Politics in the Early Nineteenth Century

By Tom J. Nettles

This essay will explore the political ideas and involvement of two Baptists: Richard Furman (1755–1825), who was a product of the American Revolution, and Francis Wayland (1796–1865), who lived in the immediate post-revolutionary generation. They shared a love of the US Constitution and the dominant ideals of the Declaration of Independence. Both were products of, as well as contributors to, what Mark Noll called the "surprising intellectual synthesis" that came to "prevail throughout the United States" in the first half of the nineteenth century. It consisted of "evangelical Protestant religion, republican political ideology, and commonsense moral reasoning."[1] They differed in one monumental issue: the present and future place of slavery in America.

---

[1] Mark A. Noll, *America's God: From Jonathan Edwards to Abraham Lincoln* (Oxford: Oxford University, 2002), 9.

Richard Furman (1755–1825): A Revolutionary Force

Richard Furman, though born in New York, became, as an infant, a South Carolinian. Precocious intellectually and irrepressible in motivation, he learned to read the Bible early in life, memorized the first book of the *Iliad*, and could read and write in Latin, Greek, and Hebrew.

He was converted in the High Hills Baptist Church in Santee, South Carolina, at sixteen years of age and began serving as its pastor at nineteen. His preaching disarmed even the most prejudiced establishmentarians, and he became a major force in removing discrimination against Dissenters. His zealous advocacy of the Revolutionary efforts of the colonies made him a marked man: General Cornwallis placed a £1,000 bounty on his head. For safety, he escaped for a while to Virginia, where Patrick Henry frequently attended his ministry.[2]

After the war, Furman returned to High Hills and in 1787 became pastor of First Baptist Church in Charleston, staying until his death thirty-seven years later. His conversion and life's ministry demonstrated the transforming power of experiential Edwardsean Calvinism. He advocated for denominational unity and benevolent activity, insistent on providing education for Baptist ministers of the gospel. As a member of the committee to develop a constitution for South Carolina, he fought against the exclusion of ministers from holding certain public offices. He served as the first president of the General Missionary (Triennial) Convention (1814), and his profound advocacy of ministerial education inspired the establishment of Furman University, Mercer University, and eventually, after his death, the Southern Baptist Theological Seminary. His own oratorical expressions of the ideas of the Revolution are a valuable primary source on the hopes and dangers of the experiment of government "by the people and for the people."

---

[2] Information about Furman and the citations from primary sources are taken from Richard Furman, *Life and Works of Dr. Richard Furman, D. D.*, ed. G. William Foster Jr. (Harrisonburg: Sprinkle, 2004).

Furman did not think his office as a minister of the gospel rendered him unable to state his political viewpoints. Although Richard Carwardine does not mention Richard Furman, he perfectly describes the impact of Furman's emphasis on virtue as fundamental to civil government: "The impact of evangelical Christianity might be assessed not just statistically . . . but by its more intangible effects on the mental attitudes, social relationships, and public discourse of the American people."[3] Evangelicals of Furman's stripe helped shape American attitudes about all the ideas pertinent to the developing sense of nationalism in the new nation, but in particular "about the political responsibilities of the moral individual in a democracy and a republic."[4]

Since George Washington's resignation from the presidency in 1796, American politics had been developing bitter factions involving party disputes about both domestic and foreign policies. Turmoil with France and Spain; nervousness about immigration that resulted in the Alien and Sedition Acts (1798); the strengthening and then quick recession of the Federalist Party; increasing attention to issues concerning slavery, fugitive slaves, and slave rebellions; and expanding territory all contributed to volatile growing pains of the new nation. The Louisiana Purchase (1803) brought a greatly expanded territory and dangerously inflamed political jealousies. Conflict between Alexander Hamilton and Aaron Burr produced a duel and Hamilton's death.

Richard Furman was intimately familiar with these developments. He celebrated the courage, vision, and spirit of the patriots who had given the colonies a place among the nations, poised to give such freedoms as had never been experienced in a body politic. At the same time, he knew that rivalries, party spirit, and personal ambition could bring a dissolution of the promise of America through corruption of virtue.

---

[3] Richard Carwardine, *Evangelicals and Politics in Antebellum America* (New Haven, CT: Yale University, 1993), 48.

[4] Carwardine, 48.

Theology and Politics

Eternal Vigilance

In preaching before the Charleston Association in 1800, Furman reminded the "Beloved Brethren" of the "greatness of the blessings we as a nation enjoy; by the continuance of peace, of civil and religious liberty, and by the prosperity of agriculture, commerce, arts and sciences among us." Also, he urged these Baptists to accept the duty of "firm attachment to the constitution, laws and government of our country." These are the "honored means, employed by heaven, to secure and diffuse so much happiness among our citizens, as we at this time enjoy."[5]

Christians, under God, had opportunity to encourage effective government by a proper stance toward the governing officials. Furman urged the "promotion of the public welfare is not to be effected by indulging the turbulent spirit of party, by extreme jealousy exercised over the conduct of the responsible magistrates and officers who are invested with public trusts, or by heated declamation." The party division surrounding Thomas Jefferson, Alexander Hamilton, and John Adams prompted Furman to ask for dispassionate "listening to the dictates of truth and wisdom," along with "firm adherence to the principles of rational liberty." He encouraged "subjection to the laws," in the spirit of "tender, patriotic concern for the good of the whole nation." He reminded the auditory of the "sage counsels" and "affectionate heart" of George Washington, "under God, the principal guardian of the liberties and happiness of his country" as essential to national interests.[6]

---

[5] Furman, "On Religious and Civil Duties," in Furman, *Life and Works of Dr. Richard Furman*, 547.

[6] Furman, 547–48.

For the Good of the Slave

Controversy, both political and religious, stirred over the presence of slavery in the country that had been founded on the assumption of human equality and the unalienable right to "life, liberty, and the pursuit of happiness." Scripture, however, in the view of Furman, regulated the slave-master relationship in a way consistent with that declaration. He assured his listeners, "As these truths are clearly stated in the word of God, so they appear, in the present state of things among us, and at all times, to be best adapted to promote the general good, not only of the community at large, but of that body of persons who are in a state of servitude."[7]

He distilled the relative duties of servants and masters from several scriptural passages. Speaking of servants, he said, "It requires of them faithfulness, submission, quietude and obedience; in respect of the wise and sovereign order of God's providence, which has placed them in that situation; and it directs them to perform their duty on conscientious principles, 'As to the Lord and not to men.'" Should they be faithful to their providentially ordered station in this way, they would "meet with the peculiar approbation and gracious reward of Heaven." If they conducted themselves otherwise, they would provoke divine displeasure.[8]

Masters also had "high and awful sanctions" given them from the "sacred oracles." Their duty was to "rule their servants with justice and moderation; to afford them a reasonable portion of the comforts, as well as necessaries of life." One South Carolinian in an elaborate defense of slavery as practiced in South Carolina explained that their allowance of food is "infinitely preferable to the *oatmeal of Scotland*, and the *potatoes of Ireland*." "Our negroes," he contended, "could not work if fed on the Irish potato."[9]

---

[7] Furman, 549.

[8] Furman, 549.

[9] A South Carolinian, *An Appeal to the People of the Northern and Eastern States: On the Subject of Negro Slavery* (New York: n.p., 1834), 17.

Most seriously, according to Furman, they are to regard their "religious interests, as of persons who are placed by the divine government under their care and direction." Furman knew of other opinions circulating on the issue and stated, "Rather, therefore, than advocate the speculative, abstract opinions, or attempt the innovations in practice which on this subject have been advanced and planned by others; let us adhere to these scriptural principles, and perform these duties, so clearly laid down in the volume of inspiration. On these we may and ought to insist."[10] Furman believed the principles of abolitionism were built on innovative philosophical ideas and, thus, relativized the plain text of Scripture.[11]

Furman's argument contributed to forming a highly traveled path by exegetical theologians of the South, a tradition that would continue with R. L. Dabney, J. H. Thornwell, Thornton Stringfellow, and others. Mark Noll points to three possible ways to relate the Bible to slavery: liberation versus the Bible, the Bible in defense of slavery, and a variety of mediating positions. Those of "mediating positions" who opposed slavery with a more delicately articulated exegesis of the plain texts "were compelled to perform an intellectual high-wire act by demonstrating why arguments against slavery should not be regarded as infidel attacks on the authority of the Bible

---

[10] Furman, "On Religious and Civil Duties," *Life and Works of Dr. Richard Furman*, 549.

[11] After an attempted slave insurrection in 1822, Furman explained more fully how he viewed the issue of slavery in the United States: "The right of holding slaves is clearly established in the Holy Scriptures, both by precept and example. . . . Then may the just and humane master who rules his slaves and provides for them, according to Christian principles, rest satisfied, that he is not in holding them, chargeable with moral evil, nor with acting, in this respect, contrary to the genius of Christianity." After arguing that, at present, "Negroes" are not qualified for freedom, he writes, "Should, however, a time arrive, when the Africans in our country might be found qualified to enjoy freedom; and when they might obtain it in a manner consistent with the interests and peace of the community at large, the Convention would be happy in seeing them free." See Richard Furman, *Exposition of the Views of the Baptists Relative to the Coloured Population of the United States*, 2nd ed. (Charleston: A. E. Miller, 1833), 6, 10.

itself."[12] Robert Dabney contended that abolitionists engaged in a hermeneutic governed by a "Jacobinical" theory of rights, and he asked Christians,
even in 1888, "Will you surrender the inspiration of the Scriptures to these
assaults of a social science so-called?"[13]

After a detailed study of how the issue developed throughout the first
half of the nineteenth century, Carwardine surmised that material interests
alone could not have launched the Civil War. Rather, he pointed to a more
recondite issue thoroughly consistent with Furman's concern for what he
believed was biblical fidelity and the moral character under God of servants
and masters alike. What was the moral meaning of being "Southern" or
"Northern" in relation to "the systems of free and slave labor each had developed"? Most potently, Evangelicalism provided "these divergent moral per-
ceptions of the appropriate social and economic direction of the Union."[14]
This judgment is pertinent when comparing Furman with Francis Wayland.

Lamentation for Washington

Furman's admiration for George Washington knew no bounds. He was
the "first of Americans" and a "friend of religion, of liberty, and of man."[15]

---

[12] Noll, *America's God*, 392.

[13] Robert Dabney, "Anti-Biblical Theories of Rights," in *Discussions of Robert Lewis Dabney*, vol. 3 (Edinburgh: Banner of Truth Trust, 1982), 27.

[14] Carwardine, *Evangelicals and Politics*, 323.

[15] Furman, "Humble Submission to Divine Sovereignty the Duty of a Bereaved Nation," in *Life and Works of Dr. Richard Furman*, 367. The admiration for Washington in the first half of the nineteenth century was unbounded. In 1833, Thomas Grimké stated, "Philosophy has nothing more admirable for symmetry, wisdom and virtue; poetry and eloquence have nothing more commanding and attractive than the life of Washington. . . . [That life] teaches you to believe the moral government of God in the world, his empire over nations, and his special providence in favor of our country." See Grimké, *Oration on the Principal Duties of Americans* (Charleston: William Estill, 1833), 19–20. More than three decades after Furman, his views still were reflected in such statements about Washington's virtue, providence, and destiny.

Precocious wisdom and right judgment in military strategy increased throughout his career, Furman believed, by which, as one observer noted, "We were raised from colonial vassalage to sovereign power."[16] No greater demonstration could be advanced than the victory and renown of an "eight years war, against the superior force of British and auxiliary veterans, headed by their ablest generals."[17]

Washington did not indulge personal ease or fame. Both his service in and resignation from the presidency of the country combined with a subsequent appointment as commander of American armed forces demonstrate his selfless and wise patriotism. Furman presented Washington as a "man endowed with superior gifts of nature"—his military strategy and courage in its execution, his statesmanship, his justice as a magistrate, his patriotism, and preeminently, his manifestation of "exalted virtues, and religion."[18] Virtue, necessary for the existence of a republic, found the epitome of its expression in Washington. His policies and instructions helped seal the true theory of a federal government, and his remonstrations with the military preserved the independence of the legislature.[19] Overall, Furman observed, "His modesty cast a softening shade over all his other virtues."[20]

The present volatility of both domestic and foreign relations yet called for a Washington, but he had been taken. Only gross impiety would refuse to acknowledge the "unerring wisdom, united with justice and goodness" in God's providence. It is enough that America "has had a Washington" in the genesis of the nation's pilgrimage. As both Moses and Joshua, he was worthy of love and respect from his indebted country. Humbly, he commended "the interests of our dearest country to the protection of Almighty God, and

---

[16] William Drayton, "The Farewell Address of the Hon. William Drayton to the Washington Society," in Grimké, 33.

[17] Furman, "Humble Submission," 372.

[18] Furman, 372.

[19] Furman, 374.

[20] Furman, 375.

those who have the superintendency of them to his holy keeping."[21] Most eminent in those "interests," in Furman's view, were the moral purposes of God in granting "genuine and enlarged liberty, both civil and religious, brought about by the revolution, and in connexion [*sic*] with law and justice, constitutionally established in these United States."[22]

The citizens, therefore, must continue in that spirit and manifest those divinely given virtues so prominent in Washington. As long as "we acknowledge the interposition of the Deity, supplicate his throne, fear his judgments, render thanks for his mercies, and honor religion by temper and conduct correspondent to its principles . . . America will remain the object of divine care and favor."[23] In short, we must "cultivate the masculine, as well as the mild virtues, and all that dignifies the man." For certain, "the foundation of every truly great character is laid in personal virtue, and a sincere regard to religion."[24]

Justifying the Revolution

On July 4, 1802, at the twenty-sixth anniversary of the Declaration of Independence, Richard Furman preached before formally organized patriotic societies on "America's Deliverance and Duty." The liberty won by a special agency from God brought into view certain obligations. Embracing the Reformed principles of the special circumstances that justify a right to revolt, Furman developed his argument: the cause was demonstrably just and would alleviate an encroaching and increasing evil, and governing authorities immediately connected with the colonies themselves were united in their opinion that the advance of tyranny must be halted.[25]

---

[21] Furman, 377.
[22] Furman, 379.
[23] Furman, 379–80.
[24] Furman, 383.
[25] Furman, "America's Deliverance and Duty," *Life and Works of Dr. Richard Furman*, 389–408.

The dictates of reason, conscience, and revelation must all be brought to play in examining how the wisdom of God's providence established American independence. Furman appealed first to the "justice of our cause." This he defended by claiming that the constitutional rights of the colonies had been violated in pursuit of an autocratic claim of a "right to bind the colonies, in all cases whatsoever." Had the colonies yielded, "every principle of liberty, every right, civil and religious, would have been placed in a state of the most abject prostration." The cause of honor and of God forbade compliance, for there was no reciprocity of protection and submission. Without the former, the latter is impossible to yield.[26]

Second, Furman discussed "the manner in which our citizens entered on and supported the contest." Far from the destructive theories of the French Revolution, Americans were influenced by orthodox Evangelical Christianity in its doctrine of providence, sin, the necessity of salvation, the revelational status of Scripture, and the reality of a final judgment. They embraced those doctrines that "rectify the heart, control the passions, and inspire the soul with sentiments of justice, benevolence, generosity, and peace." They would enter such a conflict, therefore, only after reaching the most serious conviction of its rectitude.[27] Political authorities and clergy alike recognized the need for prayer and dependence on the divine blessing.[28]

Third, Furman found evidence of the "interposition of Providence in favor of the revolution" in the united and rather prosperous state of the colonies at that time. Also, British mistakes as well as the strengthening effects of the most sobering American disasters proved to be providential intervention. The detection of Benedict Arnold, the entrance of France, and the preservation of George Washington manifest the benevolent working of providence.[29]

---

[26] Furman, 394.
[27] Furman, 395–96.
[28] Furman, 397.
[29] Furman, 397–98.

Fourth, Furman looked to the "happy termination of the war" and its immediate consequences. Suffering for liberty taught the citizens its beauty and cost and expanded their understanding of the meaning of "religion and the rights of conscience." Also, respect for the rights of others and determination to protect their own attached them to a "republican form of government" as most consistent "with the rational character of man, and with the happiness of an enlightened, free, and virtuous people." The providential superintendence in the formation of a federal constitution set up a "barrier against war and contention among ourselves," adding, with a hint of calamitous developments, "which nothing but the extreme of folly and madness will ever remove." The Second Great Awakening was extending "the influence of vital religion," creating a period "when the belief of gospel-truth, a just attention to the most important, eternal interests of men, and to the honor of God, were more general on this continent, than at the present moment."[30]

The fifth evidence of providential determination in the success of the revolution was an assumption about the "original destination of this country." America was to be "an asylum for religion and liberty," where the excellency of both would be exhibited. Flight from tyranny and persecution led to the first settlements from "civilized nations." In respect to religion, the first truly free government was developed since Christianity began its progress. So truly unified were virtue and hope in the leaders of the War for Independence and so fully realized in the Constitution, that a day will come when "America will be the praise of the whole earth," fulfilling the biblical prophecies of millennial peace and prosperity.[31]

---

[30] Furman, "America's Deliverance," 399. See Furman's comments on the Awakening in "A Letter from Dr. Furman of Charleston, to Dr Rippon of London" (1802), *Life and Works*, 413–17. Also, for contrast see Furman, "On the Languishing State of Religion in the Southern United States" (1799), *Life and Works of Dr. Richard Furman*, 533–43.

[31] Furman, "America's Deliverance," 400.

Duties

This obvious interposition of providence yields clear and certain duties. First and preeminently compelling is gratitude to God for the sparing of persons, lands, families, cultural and civil stability, and coveted freedoms that would have been destroyed if the outcome had been defeat. Such gratitude does not diminish the role of courage, self-sacrifice, wisdom, and determination on the part of the nation but engenders a worshipful recognition of having acted in the cause of God.[32]

Preservation of this nation, therefore, demands, as another duty, "strict attention to religion." With strong emphasis, Furman stated he had no reference to "a national religion, by civil authority," but the careful attention to the importance of this as befits "a rational, immortal creature, accountable for his actions, and under infinite obligations to his Creator." This personal interest also would serve the well-being of the Republic, for "without virtue there can be no real happiness, either to individuals or the body politic; and without religion there can be no genuine, stable virtue."[33] Furman urged, "Let us not rest satisfied with the establishment of republicanism alone," for "virtue must be added to make us truly respectable and happy."[34]

Even so, each has the duty of strict adherence to the Constitution for its principles to have "full and free operation." Party spirit will discourage due respect for those who are invested with authority by the Constitution. Care must be taken to avoid anything that would create unreasonable jealousies to obstruct measures "for the general interest."[35] For real abuses of power, ample provision for detecting and punishing has been made in the Constitution. Coveters of power can corrupt a system that depends on "truth, candor and the spirit of benevolence." In particular, the nation's legislative, executive, and judicial branches should know they are "invested with a dignity, and

---

[32] Furman, 402.
[33] Furman, 403.
[34] Furman, 405.
[35] Furman, 405.

entrusted with sacred interests which must suffer, whenever they even notice this subject, in any other manner than to prevent the evil, or heal the wounds it has occasioned."[36] Republican government is best for "an enlightened, virtuous people," so "the virtuous and wise, alone, should be chosen."[37]

Ministers of the gospel must prize this ideal and maintain distance from the "low arts, and abusive language of party."[38] Furman demonstrated this commitment when, in 1808, he urged South Carolinians to vote for Charles Cotesworth Pinckney despite his Federalist affiliation. Furman's opinion of Pinckney was formed through many years of common cause. Although James Madison, the other candidate, "*may* be a good and great man," Furman submitted, "we *know* that Gen Pinckney is so" (emphasis added). They should, therefore, overcome a "party spirit," recognize that Madison "has no claim to their confidence and regard," and avoid any "violence to their friendship and their feelings as well as justice and propriety" by voting for Pinckney, a man "most worthy of them."[39] For Furman, "party" was not more to be considered than the convictions and character of the man.

Can we suppose a person will be faithful to his country who is not faithful to God? Furman's intent was a clear recommendation of orthodox Evangelical Christianity. "We have seen," he reiterated, "what powerful, effective influence it had on the American revolution." Not only was Christian redemption the only preparation for eternity, but the gospel provides "the proper preventive" of destructive evils for civil society.[40]

Furman is a pristine example of what Martin Marty called "the evangelical empire-builders in the early nineteenth century." The Declaration of Independence called upon "Nature's God," the "Creator," the "Supreme Judge of the World," and rested in the determinations of "Divine

---

[36] Furman, 406–7.
[37] Furman, 405.
[38] Furman, 405–6.
[39] Furman, *Life and Works of Dr. Richard Furman,* 136–37.
[40] Furman, "America's Deliverance," 402–4.

Providence." Although its authors did not have the same expansive and reve-lational meaning that conversionist evangelicals like Furman did, "these Protestants could easily translate to their own satisfaction."[41]

Lamentation for Hamilton

At the tragic death by duel of Alexander Hamilton (1757–1804), patriotic societies again called for Furman to preach a memorial sermon. He warned about the suddenness of death and the immediacy of judgment from Heb 9:27: "It is appointed unto men once to die, but after this the judgment" (KJV). He expressed hope, based on the testimony of those who observed Hamilton's death, that "his soul had experienced a gracious change, and was in a state of reconciliation with his God."[42]

---

[41] Martin E. Marty, *Righteous Empire: The Protestant Experience in America* (New York: Dial, 1970), 43–44. The overall impact of Furman's view of the place of religious conviction as a shaper of politics fits perfectly with what J. Earl Thompson called "the religion of the Republic." Thompson wrote, "The God this religion reveres is an austere, righteous deity who sits in judgment upon the deformation and wickedness of the nation. [H]e expects them to order and conduct themselves in a virtuous, just manner and will reward them with prosperity, wealth and happiness only if they do." Sustaining the order calls for progress in virtue as they are a "chosen people with a divinely ordained destiny." Particularly precious is the "protection of the inalienable freedoms, especially the freedom of worship and religious belief secured by the separation of church and state." See J. Earl Thompson Jr., "The Reform of the Racist Religion of the Republic," in *The Religion of the Republic*, ed. Elwyn A. Smith (Philadelphia: Fortress, 1971), 268–70. Using Thomas Jefferson and Lyman Beecher as premier examples, Thompson viewed slavery and subsequent racial tension and oppression as the great failure of this religion, accumulating conglomerate guilt for those who are white: "Plagued by a swollen conception of the supremacy of the white race black studies can open whites to the ugly truth about themselves as haughty oppressors . . . to perceive the enormity of their crimes . . . to guide whites to the altar of repentance of their personal and corporate sin against blacks represent the great black hope for the religion of the Republic." Thompson, 284–85.

[42] Furman, "Death's Dominion," in Furman, *Life and Works of Dr. Richard Furman*, 243.

Less important than eternal well-being, but of remarkable importance for the nation, was Hamilton's political genius and genuine patriotism. These combined led to the calling of the Constitutional Convention. Along with James Madison and John Jay, Hamilton was a major contributor to the *Federalist Papers,* a critical epistolary discussion about the merits of the newly written Constitution. Furman noted, "His learned comments on it afterwards, and masterly reasoning in its support, are known to have contributed more toward its adoption, than the labors of any other man."[43] As a member of Washington's cabinet, Hamilton produced the policy that "restored the credit of these United States, and gave flow to that tide of prosperity with which they have since been favored."[44] His conflicts with other political powerhouses led to the formation of two political parties, Federalist and Democratic-Republican. Furman often warned against "party spirit and strife." He summarized his observations about Hamilton by calling him "a man of transcendent genius . . . an eloquent, powerful orator; a profound civilian; a heroic soldier; a great statesman; and . . . a sincere patriot."[45]

In this tribute, Furman argued forcefully against the practice of dueling. After a deeply pathetic description of the immediate effects of a duel on both victim and victor, Furman pointed to "its moral turpitude, and pernicious consequences as they affect man's chief duty, and everlasting interests." Murder and revenge, forbidden by God, are glorified in the practice.[46] While imminent danger justifies immediate self-defense at the expense of the aggressor, in an issue of civil society, "the whole of our personal interests should, according to the ordinance of God, be committed to the guardianship of the laws."[47] Furman pled for clear and forceful laws that would eliminate reasons for dueling. For the practice to remain lawful is a disgrace to

---

[43] Furman, 240.
[44] Furman, 240.
[45] Furman, 241.
[46] Furman, 245.
[47] Furman, 246.

government. He lamented, however, that this outrage would go uncorrected "unless the public sentiment and taste are corrected."[48] Virtue gives rise to just laws.

Francis Wayland (1796–1865): A Christian Instructor of Civic Duty

Born twenty years after the Declaration of Independence, Francis Wayland lived through the first two-thirds of the nineteenth century. He reflected deeply on the freedoms embedded in the Constitution of the new nation, their relation to individual freedoms, and how Christians and churches should respond to this experiment. His parents had come from England, and his father served as a Baptist pastor at several places in New York. Wayland was a graduate of Union College in Albany, New York, and Andover Theological Seminary. He served as pastor of First Baptist in Boston from 1821 to 1826. From 1827 until his death, he served as president at Brown University.

In 1824, Wayland published *The Moral Dignity of the Missionary Enterprise*. In 1825, he presented two sermons based on Matt 22:21 on the subject "The Duties of an American Citizen" at the First Baptist Church of Boston.[49] He dealt with the subject again in a series of three sermons in 1847 titled "The Duty of Obedience to the Civil Magistrate."[50] In 1835, he wrote and published *The Elements of Moral Science*, which he expanded later that year and then again thirty years later, shortly before his death in 1865.[51] This book included a section on "Duties to Man, as a Member of Civil Society." Other works that addressed governmental and political issues

---

[48] Furman, 247.

[49] Francis Wayland, *The Duties of an American Citizen*, 2nd ed. (Boston: James Loring, 1825).

[50] Francis Wayland, *The Duty of Obedience to the Civil Magistrate: Three Sermons* (Boston: Charles C. Little and James Brown, 1847).

[51] Francis Wayland, *The Elements of Moral Science* (Boston: Gould & Lincoln, 1872).

were *The Elements of Intellectual Philosophy* and *The Elements of Political Economy*.[52] Mark Noll observed, "He published popular textbooks on mental science and political economy where he aimed to fit the rising generation of young collegiates for the task of maintaining a virtuous republic," but recognized that sometimes Wayland was resistant to "commonsense republican reasoning."[53]

Principles to Discern Duty

Fundamental to all of Wayland's discussions is the axiom "Every man has a right to himself." On this basis, he set forth the physical liberty, intellectual liberty, and religious liberty of all individuals. This was his driving argument in his opposition to domestic slavery.[54] "Over my own faculties," he wrote, "and the means of happiness which they present, I am supreme; beyond these I have no right whatsoever."[55] Again, he contended, "Provided the individual interfere not with the rights of others, he has a right to use his own body and mind as he thinks will best promote his own happiness; that is, as he will."[56] This principle has application in every relationship of life and functions consistently but in distinct ways in relation to neighbor, family government, voluntary societies, and civil society.

Civil society arises from the natural instincts of men to protect their rights and property. Physical power alone produces a contest that has little propensity to produce a just outcome, devolving into "interminable wrong and unappeasable malice." Thus, individual rights within the context of others who claim, and surely have, the same right to self produces

---

[52] Francis Wayland, *The Elements of Intellectual Philosophy* (New York: Sheldon, 1854; a second edition was published in 1865); Francis Wayland, *The Elements of Political Economy* (Boston: Gould, Kendall, & Lincoln, 1843).

[53] Noll, *America's God*, 250, 252.

[54] Wayland, *The Elements of Moral Science*, 344, 203–8.

[55] Wayland, 344.

[56] Wayland, 206.

civil society. "Every man is so created as instinctively to commit to the community of his fellow-men the protection of his rights and the redress of his wrongs; and his fellow-men, on the other hand, instinctively assume this authority."[57]

Christianity has nothing to do with establishing forms of human government. Its directives were given in the face of absolute, and wicked, monarchy. Its tendency, however, is to create free institutions. Wayland fully approved of the system of government established by the Constitution. Drawing from phrases in the Declaration of Independence, Wayland affirmed, "The great object for which civil government is established among men, I suppose to be, to protect every man in the enjoyment of those rights which have been conferred upon him by his Creator." Indeed, every person "has a perfect right to the natural results arising from the labor of his body, in what manner soever that labor may have been employed."[58]

Governments, however, may unlawfully encroach on the rights of an entire people. While individuals must in themselves submit even to tyranny, refusing to do wrong, they may, as a corporate entity, seek to throw off such a government and establish one that is more consistent with unalienable liberties. In this manner, unjust civil societies may be resisted. He believed that Great Britain was guilty of grievous wrong in her treatment of her colonies unless the rationale given in the Declaration of Independence is a falsity.

Form and Function of Government

Because men tend toward encroachment on the rights of others, that government is best that most successfully protects these freedoms. This purpose gives rise to the various departments of civil magistracy. The legislature enacts the laws concerning individual rights and penalties for infractions. The judiciary ascertains whether a law has been violated and sentences the

---

[57] Wayland, 345.
[58] Wayland, *Duties of an American,* 8.

legal penalty. Also, that branch decides on "the constitutionality of a law" before enforcing it.[59] The executive carries into effect the decision of the judiciary. Civil government ends its authority here. "This is," Wayland opined, "the view of the subject entertained by the authors of the Declaration of Independence." To secure the rights of "life, liberty, and the pursuit of happiness," unalienable rights granted by the Creator, this form of government was established.[60]

Virtue and Duty

Wayland discussed a variety of forms of government and then set forth this general principle, which would determine the character and perpetuity of any form of government. The blessing of freedom is "inseparable from moral restraint in the individual." It is vain to expect freedom unless a people "are first willing to be virtuous." The "permanence of the present form of government of the United States" turns on that reality. This form of government makes necessary "a given amount of virtue in the people." If they possess or can attain to it, "the government will stand; if not it will fall." No political or social organization has self-sustaining power. That exists only "in individual virtue." A government's form will "adjust itself to the moral condition of a people."[61]

In light of the necessity of civil society and voluntary submission to its protective purpose, Wayland assumed people have a general instinct to submit to the rulings of "the power of the whole community." Moreover, "the Christian religion imposes upon us subjection to the civil power, as a matter of moral duty."[62] Particular duties extend from this principle. Voting

---

[59] Wayland, *The Elements of Moral Science*, 361.

[60] Wayland, *Duties of an American*, 10. See an extended discussion of Wayland's view in *The Elements of Moral Science,* 352–62.

[61] Wayland, *The Elements of Moral Science*, 356.

[62] Wayland, 346.

is politically and morally necessary to give effect to the executive and legislative departments. Payment of taxes is morally obligatory to support those in service of the body politic and necessary public services they provide.[63] Citizens willingly serve on juries to affect a portion of the judicial branch. In pursuit of a just cause, they serve in the military.

Provisions of Government

Revenue is procured for the purpose of providing several necessary advantages to civil society. In its right of the sword (Romans 13), the civil authority must protect from injury each member of a society from others. A legitimate extension of that purpose is the function of protecting its citizenry from injury by the member of another society. Its use of force is right when it is "directed toward the injurious person alone, and when employed to no greater extent than the accomplishment of the purpose renders necessary."[64] Internal law enforcement and protection from external aggressors constitute a legitimate use of revenue.

The support of each branch of government is necessary. Such payment should be given that will draw the ability, character, and talent each office requires so that those thus elected or employed would serve to the advantage of the society.[65] Mediocre pay, mediocre governance.

---

[63] Wayland, *The Elements of Political Economy,* 395–97. For example, "The necessaries of life, if taxed at all, should be taxed at the lowest rates. . . . Taxation should be heaviest upon articles of luxury and ostentation; not for the sake of interfering with those modes of pursuing happiness, but because those who are able to expend in this manner, are able to bear, with the least inconvenience, the expenses of government." Surplus from taxation is corrupting, for it tends to be used "for party purposes" and removes capital from the hands of the citizens, where it is most useful, and puts it in hands where it is likely to be spent "uselessly, if not viciously." The world has not seen a government so pure, Wayland asserted, that it would not become corrupt if a surplus revenue were permanently placed at its disposal.

[64] Wayland, *Duties of an American,* 11.

[65] Wayland, *The Elements of Political Economy,* 398–99.

Provision of education in a representative government is peculiarly necessary. Both common and scientific education can lay claim to the support of the society. For common education, smaller districts have the greatest propensity to value the well-being of their own and thus will be most efficient in both selection and payment of teachers. The need of training teachers, moreover, for each district to maintain currency with the advance of science and other forms of knowledge and for uniformity in skill and the system of instruction, requires that "seminaries" be provided, in light of the public good, by the public. To diffuse and add to knowledge must both be the functions of scientific education. Since the instruments for this kind of education are so expensive, it must be borne by the public or only the rich will have access to it.[66] Wayland also insisted that salaries be commensurate with the public value of the subject and the skill of the instructor. Special provisions for the indigent should be made without reducing the tuition for the whole.[67]

Two other matters for public support with taxation are the needs of constant improvement of infrastructure and aid for paupers. Infrastructure may be public in some instances and private in others. Wayland provided brief principles for determining at whose expense these things should be undertaken. Three sources cooperate in the relief of pauperism. Since Scripture sets this forth as a particular obligation, religious organizations must engage. In some cases, public funds must be employed. In many cases, all that is needed is a means for suitable labor in profitable occupation. This relieves the public and provides satisfaction to those who can make good use of time and strength in supporting themselves.[68]

Although some countries support religion from the public coffers, neither true religion nor the United States Constitution give legitimacy to such a use of public funds.

---

[66] Wayland, 400–01.
[67] Wayland, 402–3.
[68] Wayland, 404–5.

The Error and Evil of Slavery

Unlike Furman, Wayland argued that the maintenance of slavery cannot be justified—it violates the principle of liberty espoused in the Declaration of Independence and implied in the Constitution. Courts that act to uphold it act in violation of unalienable personal liberty.

Wayland believed domestic slavery had no support either from natural law or from Scripture.[69] After an energetic and emotionally laden engagement with arguments, both natural and biblical, that supported slavery, Wayland stated in general, "By the inculcation of true moral principles, slavery would fall of itself, with harm to no one, while both parties would be rendered essentially better."[70] His careful engagement with the precise language of instructions to slaves and masters combined with general principles of right conduct in the face of both just and unjust relations brought him to a conclusion based on several rhetorical conditional statements:

> [I]f the principles of conduct which the gospel inculcates are directly at variance with the existence of slavery; if the relations which it establishes, and the obligations which it enforces, are inconsistent with its existence; if the manner in which it treats it is the only manner which could lead to its universal extermination; and if it inculcates the duty of slaves on principles which have no connection with the question of the right of the masters over them,—I think it must be conceded that the precepts of the gospel in no manner countenance, but are entirely opposed to, the institution of domestic slavery.[71]

Considering all that is involved in that institution and the indefensibility of every argument to sustain it, Wayland asked, "Have we publicly borne

---

[69] Wayland, *The Elements of Moral Science*, 202–28.
[70] Wayland, 223.
[71] Wayland, 225.

testimony against this wrong, and done all in our power to change the legislation under the protection of which the wrong has been perpetrated? Until we have done all this, we cannot, surely be innocent of the guilt of slavery."[72] Each person considering with candor and proper fear the divine sanctions that accompany God's moral law must be convinced "of the imperative obligation resting upon him to remove it without delay."[73]

Limitations of Authority

Limitations exist to the obligations of citizens to governmental authority.[74] As Christian citizens, "we are to determine precisely what belongs to the civil government," and then "we are under moral obligation to render it." What belongs to God, however, cannot belong to any government, and "we may be confident that in obeying him, we shall never violate any duty which we owe to the magistracy."[75] A government that would command disobedience to God has transcended its authority. It is only when the objects of a government are right and its means are innocent that it can demand, on the principles of the gospel, the aid and cooperation of the disciples of Christ. Should the magistrate command one to do wrong, Wayland expressed his personal conviction in no uncertain terms: "I will regard it as I do any other command to do wrong, I will not obey it. I will look the magistracy calmly and respectfully in the face, and declare to it that in this matter I owe it no allegiance." He vowed to have nothing to do with the government's wrongdoing but would separate himself "as far as

---

[72] Wayland, 227.

[73] Wayland, 227. For an insightful discussion of Wayland's journey to this statement of immediatism, see James Paul Eckman, *Political Expediency over Individual Conscience: The Changing Antislavery Thought of Francis Wayland* (master's thesis, Dallas Theological Seminary, 1983).

[74] Wayland, *Duties of an American*, 3.

[75] Wayland, 5.

possible from the act and its consequences, whether they be prosperous or adverse. It is wickedness; it has the curse of God inwrought into it, and I will have nothing to do with it."[76]

Not only should the citizen refuse to do wrong personally, even if it means suffering to defy government order, he must oppose government policy and actions when he sees that "the government transgresses the limit within which its action is, by reason and revelation restricted." He should, in fact, "determine concerning every one of its actions whether it be right or wrong." While the Christian must honor government officials "with sincerity in all the legitimate functions to which they have been assigned," such officers can "claim no immunity from scrutiny on account of the dignity of his station if he uses the power committed to him for any other purpose than that for which it was committed."[77]

Wayland mentioned several issues that constituted transgression of legitimate, virtuous functioning. Like Furman, Wayland believed the party spirit to be detrimental to the well-being of the nation and a selfish violation of assignment. If an official prostitute his public influence "to pander to the wishes of a political party" to gain the emoluments of office, "I can look upon him henceforth with no other feeling than those of pity and disgust."[78] He should never seek to build up "one political party or crush another."[79]

A selfish and rapacious use of war should be opposed. National force should never be employed "except for the sake of protecting the citizen from injury" and then only to the degree for the accomplishment of its just end. He also believed the government was "guilty of grievous wrong in its treatment of many of the tribes of Indians on our western frontier, and especially

---

[76] Wayland, 17.

[77] Wayland, 16.

[78] Wayland, *Duties of an American,* 17.

[79] Wayland, *The Elements of Moral Science,* 362.

in the removal by force of the Cherokee nation from their ancient homes and the burial-places of their fathers."[80]

If we refuse all innocent means to oppose and correct these wrongs, we partake of the wrong. In seeking the right from those whom we elect, our actions can "be swayed neither by the terrors of power, nor by the allurements of affection; neither by the frown of a tyrant nor the frenzy of a mob."[81]

If a Christian rendered passive obedience in such a case, this would be "manifestly wrong," for we have no authority to obey an unrighteous law.[82] He may resist by force, but such an action by a single individual "would be absurd." This could succeed only by combining all the aggrieved against the aggressor, a civil war. This is uncertain, dissolves the social fabric, never fails to demoralize and render men more wicked, and "of all evils which men inflict upon themselves, [is] the most horrible."[83] The only acceptable option is to suffer for the cause of right. "The cause of civil liberty has always gained more by martyrdom than by war."[84] He summarized the advantage of suffering in the cause of pursuing what is right:

> Suffering for the sake of right can only arise from a love of justice and a hatred of oppression. The real spirit of liberty can never exist in any remarkable degree in any nation where there is not this willingness to suffer in the cause of justice and liberty. Ever so little of the spirit of martyrdom is always a more favorable indication for civilization than ever so much dexterity of party management, or ever so turbulent protestation of immaculate patriotism.[85]

---

[80] Wayland, *Duties of an American,* 28.

[81] Wayland, 30.

[82] Wayland, *The Elements of Moral Science,* 366.

[83] Wayland, 366–67.

[84] Wayland, 367.

[85] Wayland, 368.

Postscript

Both Furman and Wayland loved the Declaration of Independence, the American Constitution, the freedoms it enunciates, the governmental arrangement that was adapted to protect those freedoms, and the courage and political foresight of those who gave form to the country. They differed on political and biblical grounds on the place of slavery in the Republic. Wayland despised the idea and the moral implications of civil war; Furman would have agreed, calling its possibility "extreme of folly and madness," but wanted slavery in the past tense as quickly as possible. Ironically, only by one despicable thing could the other despicable thing be eliminated. But Wayland's call for the spirit of martyrdom in pursuit of a great moral vision found scores of volunteers on both sides.

How did these two men, so firmly in agreement on theology, ecclesiology, and the most fundamental elements of American freedom and the constitutional system that undergirded it, come to such clear and principal disagreement on slavery? Their comparison must be reduced to a short statement on two issues: (1) the governing ethical principle that determines how one should live in respect to another, and (2) the meaning of the passages of Scripture that speak to slave-master relationships.

Furman saw in the Bible a general ethical principle that made a necessary accommodation for distinct relations in society, such as the master-slave relation.[86] The rules of exegesis did not allow for the extension of a principle of virtue—such as the virtue of equality—to supersede the text of Scripture. Furman believed that application of Christ's principle "do unto others," as a way to rule against the slave-master relationship, becomes absurd if allowed to imply absolute equality or freedom from duty or enforcement in every legitimate legal, regulated relationship of Scripture. Wayland, on the other hand, insisted that slavery violates the nature of personal liberty and the law of universal reciprocity. Scripturally, Wayland employed Matt 7:12 and

---

[86] Furman, *Exposition of the Views*, 1–19.

Luke 10:27–37 (the golden rule and the command to love one's neighbor as oneself) as a moral energy that would eliminate slavery. Both the duty of reciprocity and consequent benevolence as well as the scriptural principles of human relations enforce the idea that "every man has a right to himself."[87] For Wayland, this constituted an unalterable ethical principle egregiously violated by slavery.

On the scriptural admonitions to slaves and master, Furman reasoned that if a system of society that involved slavery was immoral, Christ and the apostles would have abolished it. It would have been given no quarter in the church at all. The apostles and early church fathers feared not to speak of sins in pagan society in the most vigorous terms when true moral evil was involved. Moral evil would not be tolerated for an instant in the body of the redeemed. Yet Furman saw the relationship of slave and master pressed into a godly, Christ-centered regulation along with other legitimate relationships—husband and wife, parent and child, workman and customer, governed and governors. If a relationship is immoral in itself, it cannot be regulated but must be destroyed.

Wayland, on the other hand, responded point by point. To the Old Testament regulations concerning slavery, after significant discussion, he concluded, "If the laws and precepts of Moses [concerning slavery] are of unchangeable obligation, the precepts of the New Testament must be surrendered, and the teachings of the Saviour of mankind become an absolute nullity."[88] His discussion of the New Testament's regulations of the relation of slave to master proposes that Christ and the apostles chose a method that would not bring immediate and prolonged war to a pagan culture but would give immediate reasons for sanctifying submission, growth of brotherly kindness, and eventual complete abolition. Duties enforced on slaves have no connection with the rights of masters over them, any more than turning the other cheek gives permission for abusive and violent behavior.

---

[87] Wayland, *The Elements of Moral Science,* 203, 344.
[88] Wayland, 221.

Slaves must be respectful to masters as all Christians must be to the emperor. But if wrongs are commanded, then both Christians in the empire and slaves in their household must choose to disobey and suffer. The New Testament regulations "looked not at the abolition of this form of evil for that age alone, but for its universal abolition."[89] Wayland believed "the precepts of the gospel in no manner countenance, but are entirely opposed to, the institution of domestic slavery."[90]

---

[89] Wayland, 223.
[90] Wayland, 225.

9

"They That Wait": Baptists, Slavery, and Segregation

By Eric M. Washington

"Always people have believed that their physical and spiritual strength can be renewed," uttered Gardner C. Taylor, pastor of Concord Baptist Church of Christ in Brooklyn, New York, on September 6, 1959. As Taylor worked through Isa 40:31 on that late summer day, Jim Crow blew his hot breath on African Americans, possibly knowing his days were numbered. But who really knew? This decade witnessed the monumental decision of *Brown v. Board of Education*, which overturned *Plessy v. Ferguson* in 1954; but the very next year segregationists in Mississippi extinguished the life of fourteen-year-old Emmett Till. In 1957, segregationists in Little Rock, Arkansas, fought ardently to keep Central High School lily-white, defying the Supreme Court's decision of 1954. These two episodes portended some of the worst days of the civil rights movement as scores of African American protestors, both young and old, would be physically assaulted in their efforts to supplant discriminatory and unjust laws in the South.[1]

Taylor, a son of the South, surmised that the civil rights movement was picking up steam to mount its righteous challenge to the monstrosity of American racism. As he approached the crescendo of his sermon, Taylor anticipated a rejoinder to his thesis of waiting on the Lord. "Someone young of years and hard of heart immediately cries out, 'This is exactly what I do not like about all this babbling of religion. I want to be doing things, not waiting.' Our land, burdened by the ugly weight of its discouraging discriminations, needs bold action from fearless people who will cut it loose from its old chains." For Taylor, waiting on God's promise of renewal was by no means a passive act, not in the face of the ugly enemy. For African Americans, the enemy's identity was clear, and renewal, constant renewal, was necessary.[2]

African American Baptist experiences reflect the general experiences of African Americans in slavery and into the period of segregation. African American Baptists struggled to "make a way out of no way." This is evident in the existence of independent churches during slavery and the establishment of district and state associations and then national conventions throughout segregation. From local churches and national conventions emerged key leaders among African Americans who pressed against social injustices in hopes of witnessing a beloved community. These African American Baptist experiences occurred in a context of white Baptists who were disunited on the question of slavery and segregation. White Baptists in the South were outright hostile to African American resistance against slavery and second-class citizenship. Some Northern white Baptists did contend against slavery

---

[1] Gardner C. Taylor, "The Promise of Renewal," in *The Words of Gardner Taylor, Volume 1: NBC Radio Sermons 1959–1970,* comp. Edward L. Taylor (Valley Forge: Judson, 1999), 41.

[2] Taylor, 44.

and for African American freedom, but the majority were complicit in the continuity of white supremacy in the United States.

Baptists and the Two "Worlds of Race"

Late historian John Hope Franklin, in his essay "The Worlds of Race: A Historical View," wrote, "From the time Africans were brought as indentured servants to the mainland of English America in 1619, the enormous task of rationalizing and justifying the forced labor of peoples on the basis of racial differences begun."[3] He asserted that more than a hundred years before the American Revolution, "the status of Negroes in the English colonies had become fixed at a low point that distinguished them from all other persons who had been held in temporary bondage."[4] Franklin referenced the South Carolina Slave Code of 1712, which intended to control the movement of enslaved Africans owing to what the state believed was their natural inclination toward rapacious and disorderly behavior, borrowing from the language of the code. Franklin wrote, "By the time that the colonists took up arms against their mother country in order to secure their independence, the world of Negro slavery had become deeply entrenched and the idea of Negro inferiority well established."[5] Based on this, Franklin saw the creation of two worlds in the British North American colonies, one white and one black, based on law.

Within this larger context of the intentional and purposeful creation of two racial worlds, enslaved and free Africans began to convert to Christianity. From the advent of the Atlantic slave trade, European powers justified African enslavement, asserting that Christianization was a moral good and worth their enslavement. In British North America, King Charles II

---

[3] John Hope Franklin, *Race and History: Selected Essays 1938–1988* (Baton Rouge: LSU, 1989), 132. This essay was originally published in *Daedalus* in 1965.

[4] Franklin, 132.

[5] *The Negro American* (n.p.: Houghton, Mifflin, 1966), 48.

implored English masters to seek the conversion of their enslaved during the 1660s. Even with the king's encouragement, the conversion of enslaved Africans was slow. The major impediment was the slaveowners themselves, who failed to see the moral good of the Christianization of their human chattel. Enslaved Africans were in the colonies to labor. Slaveowners also feared that enslaved Africans who became Christians would resort to being "saucy" or haughty, believing themselves the equal of their European masters. A larger concern for masters was the belief that baptism meant freedom to the enslaved. In fact, baptized and enslaved Africans pressed for their freedom. In 1664, the Maryland colonial legislature responded to this by enacting a measure that declared baptism did nothing to change the social condition of an enslaved African. They would remain enslaved for life. Virginia followed suit in 1667. These laws were to settle the consternation of masters while allowing them to pursue the conversion of their African property. At the end of the seventeenth century, the number of enslaved Africans who were members of churches in British North American colonies was moderate at best.[6]

In 1636, Roger Williams founded the colony of Rhode Island and Providence Plantations after protesting some of the teachings of the Congregationalist Church in Massachusetts Bay Colony. The significance of Williams in Baptist history is critical. African American Baptist pastor and historian Leroy Fitts states, "The tremendous influence of Roger Williams in the birth of Baptists in America is a matter of great significance to the subsequent development of the sociopolitical thought among black Baptists."[7] Shortly after founding the colony, Williams became a Baptist and helped to found the first Baptist church in America. Along with founding

---

[6] Albert J. Raboteau, *Slave Religion: The "Invisible Institution" in the Antebellum South* (New York: Oxford University, 1977), 98–99; Paul Harvey, *Through the Storm, Through the Night: A History of African American Christianity* (Lanham, MD: Rowman & Littlefield, 2011), 19.

[7] LeRoy Fitts, *A History of Black Baptists* (Nashville: Broadman, 1985), 22.

the first Baptist church in America, Williams was the first political leader in the British North American colonies to offer religious freedom to colonists. This social and political tenet has also been part and parcel with Baptist social and political doctrine. Williams had company, though, in helping to establish Baptist churches in colonial America.[8]

The Great Awakening that launched in the 1730s in New England and then traveled south in subsequent decades was the watershed moment in the history of African American Christianity during the colonial period. During this time, British American Baptist preachers preached more fervently and attracted large numbers. There is consensus among historians of the African American church in general and the African American Baptist tradition in particular that the Great Awakening was "the dawn of a new day" for enslaved Africans and Creoles as well as those free persons of color as they joined Protestant churches. Raboteau and Campbell, for example, hold that the Great Awakening in the 1740s fostered the growth of African American converts to Christianity, especially in the South.[9] Not discounting that this era witnessed the first period of African American conversion, Gomez adds to this that some slave masters freed their enslaved persons, owing their adherence to Revolutionary principles. He concludes that both antislavery preaching and the revivals attracted African Americans to Christianity.[10] Frey and Wood accurately describe that African Americans were active in their own religious transformations and that the Great Awakening was a period of transformation within European-American Protestantism.[11]

---

[8] Fitts, 22.

[9] James T. Campbell, *Songs of Zion: The African Methodist Episcopal Church in the United States and South Africa* (Chapel Hill: University of North Carolina Press, 1998), 4–5.

[10] Michael A. Gomez, *Exchanging Our Country Marks: The Transformation of African Identities in the Colonial and Antebellum South* (Chapel Hill: University of North Carolina, 1998), 251–52.

[11] Sylvia R. Frey and Betty Wood, *Come Shouting to Zion: African American Protestantism in the American South and British Caribbean to 1830* (Chapel Hill: University of North Carolina, 1998), xii.

Adding clarity to Frey and Wood's assertion, Gomez remarks that African converts could respond to preaching in their own way, which meant they responded according to their cultural personality.[12]

From this context, it is no surprise that African American converts during this period joined Methodist and Baptist churches in large numbers. Luther Jackson argued that Baptists and Methodists preached everyone—man, woman, European, African—was equally sinful and in need of salvation. This spiritual egalitarianism drew African Americans into its ranks.[13] In New England, where the movement began, Jonathan Edwards reported that "many of the poor negroes" had experienced a great change "wrought upon" them by the preaching of the gospel and the Holy Spirit. By 1740, when the movement launched, there was a discernible African American presence at revival meetings. Chief revival preachers like George Whitefield and Gilbert Tennent noted the presence of African Americans within the crowds that came to hear this preaching. Whitefield reported that on one occasion in Philadelphia, "near fifty negroes came to give me thanks for what God had done to their souls." This was in 1740. Tennent, in a letter to Whitefield, stated that the preaching in Charlestown, Massachusetts, greatly affected the Africans and African Americans present.[14]

What drew Africans and Creole Africans to Baptist churches, in particular, were their style and culture. Lawrence Neale Jones states that the "spontaneity and informality of worship" in Baptist churches was a

---

[12] Gomez, *Exchanging Our Country Marks*, 252.

[13] Luther P. Jackson, "The Religious Development of the Negro in Virginia from 1760–1860," *Journal of Negro History* 16, no. 2 (April 1931): 172.

[14] See Jonathan Edwards, "Thoughts on the Revival of Religion in New England, 1740," in *The Works of Jonathan Edwards*, vol. 1 (Peabody: Hendrickson, 2005), 375; Raboteau, *Slave Religion*, 128–29; James T. Campbell, *Songs of Zion: The African Methodist Episcopal Church in the United States and South Africa* (Chapel Hill: University of North Carolina, 1998), 4. See also Carter G. Woodson, *The History of the Negro Church* (Washington, DC: Associate, 1921), ch. 2.

point of attraction to African Americans.[15] There is evidence of African Americans being members of Baptist churches in New England before the eighteenth century, however. According to former Baptist pastor and writer William Banks, an enslaved man by the name of Jack is considered the first African Baptist. He received baptism into the Baptist church in Providence, Rhode Island, in 1652. In 1685, an unknown African woman received baptism in a church in Connecticut. In the same year, an African American woman named Peggy Arnold was a member of the Newport Seventh Day Baptist Church in Rhode Island. Theologian and African American church historian Henry Mitchell wrote that in 1743, an enslaved man named Quassey was a member of the Baptist church in Newton, Rhode Island. Mitchell added that in 1762 First Baptist in Providence, Rhode Island, baptized eighteen Africans into its membership. In 1771, the First Baptist Church in Boston began to admit Africans into the church. In 1772, Robert Stevens and eighteen other African Americans held membership at First Baptist Church of Providence, Rhode Island. In the same year, First Baptist Church of Boston received African American members. Moving south to South Carolina by 1796, First Baptist Church of Charleston, South Carolina, had 248 members with the majority being enslaved African Americans. According to Baptist historian H. Leon McBeth, First Baptist of Charleston was the leading church in South Carolina. Under the ministry of Richard Furman, who began his long pastorate in 1787, First Baptist became the leading Baptist church in the entire South.[16]

---

[15] Lawrence Neale Jones, *African Americans and the Christian Churches 1619–1860* (Cleveland: Pilgrim, 2007), 128. By "Creole African," I refer to persons of African descent born in the Americas.

[16] Fitts, *A History of Black Baptists*, 24–25; H. Leon McBeth, *The Baptist Heritage: Four Centuries of Baptist Witness* (Nashville: Broadman, 1987), 217, 220; Henry Mitchell, *Black Church Beginnings: The Long-Hidden Realities of the First Years* (Grand Rapids: Eerdmans, 2004), 27; William L. Banks, *A History of Black Baptists* (West Conshohocken: Infinity, 2005), 10.

As the Baptist movement expanded southward, different attitudes emerged regarding African American membership and the evangelization of enslaved persons. Late in the eighteenth century, some Kentucky Baptists questioned the propriety of African Americans (enslaved or free) holding a seat in the Kentucky Baptist Association. The association responded in favor of African Americans holding a seat in associational business meetings provided they have been sent by their home churches. In 1795, the Lick Creek Church in Kentucky split over the issue of slavery, and the Rolling Fork Church also endured turmoil regarding slavery.[17]

Even though there was ambivalence on the part of white Baptists in the South concerning the legitimacy of enslaved African-descended persons as a Christian prerogative, Woodson argued that African Americans joined Baptist churches owing to their antislavery sentiments. But he asserted they failed to have a great concerted effort, owing to their decentralized church polity. Surprisingly, in slaveholding Virginia there arose a group of Calvinistic Baptists calling themselves "Emancipating Baptists" or "Anti-Slavery Baptists," who, like many of their Methodist counterparts, refused to admit slaveholders into their fellowships and sought to preach against slavery.[18]

By the late eighteenth century, African Americans were organizing and leading their own churches. According to Woodson, religious freedom in America is inextricably linked with the carving of space for and by African Americans in Protestant churches. He also asserted that the revolutionary sentiment was conducive to the rise of African American independent churches. Woodson suggested this type of spirit was present with the rise of African American Baptist churches in the South during this period. This phenomenon was the result of expediency, not divisiveness. According to Fitts, the African American independent church movement among Baptists resulted primarily from plantation missions. Before the advent of independent churches, African American men preached on their plantations

---

[17] Fitts, *A History of Black Baptists*, 24–25.
[18] Woodson, *History of the Negro Church*, 29, 31–33.

with their masters' permission. During this period, slave codes prohibited enslaved African Americans from organizing their own churches. It was the practice of enslaved African Americans to worship in the white churches at times designated by plantation owners.[19]

These African American preachers could lead other African American Christians informally. They would escape to wooded areas or secluded cabins for preaching and prayer services. Fitts states that these informal meetings were precursors to the formal establishment of independent churches late in the century. The number of African American preachers who preached on plantations and led informal meetings is lost to the historical record. Some slave masters saw the gift these enslaved men possessed and ignored the slave codes that disallowed them to preach publicly. White Baptist churches allowed these men to exercise their gifts, and eventually these churches allowed their enslaved and free African American congregants to form their own churches.[20]

Discernible African American Baptist churches have been in existence since the end of the Revolutionary period in American history. Writing on the beginning of African American Baptist congregations, late pastor and writer Walter Brooks noted, "The freedom and local democracy of the Baptist Church enabled the Negroes to participate in the affairs thereof much earlier than they were so indulged in the other denominations."[21] According to Jordan, the first African American Baptist church began in Aiken County, South Carolina, before 1776;[22] this is the Silver Bluff Baptist Church. There is a lack of scholarly consensus regarding the founding date of the Silver Bluff Baptist Church. Yet David George, a formerly enslaved

---

[19] Woodson, 40–41; Fitts, *A History of Black Baptists*, 24, 31.

[20] Fitts, 32.

[21] Walter H. Brooks, "The Evolution of the Negro Baptist Church," *The Journal of Negro History* 7, no. 1 (January 1922): 11–22.

[22] Lewis G. Jordan, *Negro Baptist History U.S.A. 1750–1930*, rev. ed., vol. 2 (Nashville: Townsend Press, 1995), 21.

person turned Baptist elder, wrote a firsthand account of the founding of this church.[23]

Drawing from George's account, Silver Bluff Church began as a plantation mission circa 1774. According to the text, George Liele, a formerly enslaved preacher living in South Carolina at the time, preached there on at least two occasions. But George indicated that a white New Light Baptist preacher, Wait Palmer, organized the church upon hearing the testimony of eight enslaved persons on the plantation of George Galphin. On the confession of their faith, Palmer baptized these enslaved persons into the church.[24]

There is dispute on who was the first pastor of this church. George credits Palmer with founding the Silver Bluff Church, but Pugh argues that both Liele and Palmer founded the church.[25] Additionally, the late National Baptist Foreign Mission secretary and writer William Harvey asserted that Liele was the first pastor of the Silver Bluff Church. In attempting to gain clarity in this dispute, there is some evidence to weigh. First, Liele was only a licensed preacher at the time and unqualified to administer the sacraments of Baptism and the Lord's Supper. Palmer, according to George, was a pastor of a church, and this is why he baptized his wife, Jesse Peters, and five other enslaved persons. Since Liele had preached there before, he would have been interested in the organization of persons he had preached to and probably helped to bring them to Christianity. This would have made him the first pastor. Soon after George's baptism and at the behest of the church and Palmer, George became the elder of the congregation. He remained pastor of the church until the British captured the city of Savannah in 1778.

---

[23] David George, *An Account of the Life of Mr. David George, from Sierra Leone in Africa; Given by Himself in a Conversation with Brother Rippon of London, and Brother Pearce in Birmingham* (1793), in *"Face Zion Forward" First Writers of the Black Atlantic, 1785–1798*, ed. Joanna Brooks and John Saillant (Boston: Northeastern University, 2002), 180–89.

[24] George, *Account of the Life,* 180–81.

[25] Alfred Lane Pugh, *Pioneer Preachers in Paradise* (Lauderhill, FL: Paradise, 2003), 12.

In analyzing this evidence regarding the first pastor of this church, African American Baptist writers stressed the recognition of an African American man as the first pastor.[26]

Another historic African American Baptist church founded during this period was First African Baptist Church of Savannah. According to Charles Elmore, who has written the most recent history of this church, it is now known as First Bryan Baptist Church, or "Old Bryan," even though a church in Savannah still bears the name "First African Baptist." The story of how this came to be is beyond the scope of this work. Elmore clearly links the founding of this church in 1788 with the Silver Bluff Baptist Church. Both began as plantation missions, and it was the ministry of Liele that produced the first Christians who formed this church. According to Jordan and Fitts, the year 1778 is the founding year of this venerable, old church. Andrew Bryan formally organized and constituted the church on January 20, 1788. Andrew Bryan was an enslaved man owned by Jonathan Bryan, who encouraged him to preach on the plantation. Later, Jonathan Bryan allowed his enslaved persons, including Andrew Bryan, to build a meeting place on his property in Yamacraw. Late church historian James Melvin Washington stated that Jonathan Bryan was a New Light Presbyterian. Two white Baptists helped in constituting First African and in formally ordaining Andrew Bryan. These men were Reverend Thomas Burton and Reverend Abraham Marshall; both of whom were Separate Baptists. Washington added that Jesse Galphin (also known as Jesse Peters and the second pastor of Silver Bluff) helped Andrew Bryan and his fellow African Baptists form a connection with the Separate Baptists.[27]

---

[26] George, *Account of the Life*, 180–81; Pugh, *Pioneer Preachers in Paradise*, 12; William J. Harvey, *Bridges of Faith Across the Seas: The Story of the Foreign Mission Board National Baptist Convention, USA, Inc.* (Philadelphia: Foreign Mission Board National Baptist Convention, 1989), 13.

[27] Jordan, *Negro Baptist History U.S.A.*, 22; Fitts, *A History of Black Baptists*, 33, 36–38; James Melvin Washington, *Frustrated Fellowship: The Black Baptist Quest for Social Power* (Macon: Mercer University, 2004), 10–11; Mechal Sobel, *Trabelin' On:*

After experiencing initial growth and success, the church disbanded due to the British occupation of Savannah. The church reorganized with the help of Abraham Marshall. First African suffered from white interference after its founding. Its independence was limited, and members of the church suffered persecution such as imprisonment and floggings. Andrew Bryan and Sampson Bryan twice received floggings, and about 50 members received whippings from whites as well. Fitts states, "With few exceptions, members of Bryan's entire congregation were persecuted for their faith and practices." Savannah officials charged the entire congregation with plotting an insurrection and imprisoned them. They lost their building circa 1790, but magistrates exonerated the church of these unfounded charges in the Inferior Court of Chatham County. In the aftermath of this trying incident, Jonathan Bryan allowed the church to meet in his home or barn. Also, in 1790 First African joined the Georgia Baptist Association, becoming the first African American church to do so. It remained the only African American church in the association for years. Even when the association divided into two districts, First African remained a member. By 1800, First African had 800 members, and it founded two other churches: Second Baptist in 1802 and Ogeechee Baptist in 1805.[28]

Although the first independent African Baptist churches began as plantation missions along the South Carolina–Georgia border, other independent African Baptist churches sprouted in Virginia. The independent church movement in Virginia occurred simultaneously with the movement further south in South Carolina and Georgia. Washington noted something special about the formation of the African Baptist churches in Virginia. He

---

The Slave Journey to an Afro-Baptist Faith (Princeton: Princeton University, 1988), 107; Charles Elmore, *First Bryan 1788–2001: The Oldest Continuous Black Baptist Church in America* (Savannah: First Bryan Baptist Church, 2002), 1–2.

[28] Jordan, *Negro Baptist History*, 22; Fitts, *A History of Black Baptists*, 33, 36–38; Washington, *Frustrated Fellowship*, 10–11; Elmore, *First Bryan*, 1–2.

contended that the free African American population had a greater influence on the formation of these churches than in Georgia. This was because there were more free African Americans in Virginia than in Georgia during this period. The pattern of organization, however, was similar, as African American converts began to meet and then form into congregations with the support of white Baptist associations. According to Woodson, the first African Baptist church founded in Virginia was the First Baptist Church on Harrison Street in Petersburg, Virginia, in 1776 (though the cover of its original constitution dates its organization in 1774[29]). According to Washington, free African Americans and slaves founded the Harrison Street church circa 1788. Woodson also noted that the second African Baptist church founded in Virginia was in Williamsburg in 1785. Washington, however, asserts that Reverend Gowan Pamphlet, a free African American minister, organized the African Baptist Church at Williamsburg in 1781, but the church had met informally since 1776. In 1791 (or by this year), the church became a member of the predominately white Dover Baptist Association. Fitts states there were two churches founded in Petersburg; in addition to Harrison Street, there was Gillfield Baptist Church. Washington provided more detail on the founding of Gillfield, stating that in 1788 African Americans founded this church "as a racially mixed congregation." When the congregation moved to Petersburg by 1809, the African American portion of the church separated and formed the Sandy Beach Baptist Church, which became a member of the Portsmouth Baptist Association in 1810. Another church founded in the late eighteenth century in Virginia worth mentioning is the First Baptist Church of Richmond. At its founding, it was a biracial church consisting of African Americans (mostly slaves) and whites. The importance of this

---

[29] See "Constitution of the First Baptist Church, Harrison Street, Petersburg, Virginia," Encyclopedia Virginia website, accessed November 16, 2022, https://encyclopediavirginia.org/4553-3b5712d12383440/,

church, however, is that it became an all–African American church in 1841 with a membership of more than 1,700.[30]

Moving west from the vast state of Virginia, African Americans organized their first Baptist church in the state of Kentucky in 1790 according to Fitts. An enslaved man named Old Captain, or Brother Captain, began this work. Brother Captain was the enslaved person of Lewis Craig, one of the Baptist pioneer preachers in Virginia who suffered persecution owing to his Baptist beliefs. Craig sent Brother Captain to Kentucky to grow a crop in 1780, but the crop suffered destruction and Captain had to return to Virginia. In 1790, Captain returned to Kentucky in Lexington and, from his cabin, preached the gospel to fellow African Americans for a period of seven years. The founding of this church was like that of others founded in the slave South during this period. This church could possibly qualify as a plantation church, but it began as a "cabin church" by a slave who loved Christ, the gospel of Christ, and his own people.[31]

Early in the nineteenth century, racially integrated Baptist churches in the South placed limitations on the activity of enslaved members. This is evident from an 1802 report from the Dover Baptist Association in Virginia. The report addressed a problem within the association regarding the practice of some churches to allow enslaved men, who were rightful members of the church, to vote in church business meetings. The report reflected a conventional opinion regarding African American inferiority. Fitts asserts such thinking on the part of this association contradicted Baptist principles.[32]

---

[30] Woodson, *History of the Negro Church*, 85; Fitts, *A History of Black Baptists*, 45; Washington, *Frustrated Fellowship*, 14–15; Luther P. Jackson, "The Religious Development of the Negro in Virginia from 1760–1860," *Journal of Negro History* 16, no. 2 (April 1931): 189–90; Jones, *African Americans and the Christian Churches*, 133–35. Jackson and Jones concurred with Washington regarding the date of the first African Baptist church in Virginia founded by Gowan Pamphlet.

[31] Fitts, *A History of Black Baptists*, 50–51.

[32] Fitts, 25.

White-led district associations were prone to respond in unjust ways toward African American members of local churches. In 1809, for example, a majority African American Baptist church in Virginia experienced violence at the hands of whites. These belligerent whites displayed utter disrespect for African American Christians as they whipped an African American minister, Reverend Moses, for preaching in a service. The church's association placed a ban, in effect prohibiting any African American man, whether enslaved or free, from preaching. This prohibition carried the threat of ex-communication from the association. According to Fitts, such actions reveal that the institution of slavery in the South placed whites under great stress. To clarify this statement, Fitts intimates that during this period, Southern whites were fearful of African Americans, both enslaved and free, meeting in independent churches. This persisted into the antebellum period.[33]

From the Revolutionary era onward, Southern slaveholders defended their practice of owning Africans in bondage. The invention of the cotton gin spurred the expansion of slavery from the Upper South to what was "the Southwest," into Alabama, Mississippi, and Louisiana, during the first three decades of the nineteenth century. As cotton fueled the Southern economy, slaveholders, Christians among them, crafted defenses for slavery. Christians among these slaveholders argued that slavery offered a great opportunity to teach their bondspersons the most holy faith. They connected this aspect of the slavery apologetic to their attempt to introduce the "benighted" Africans to Western civilization. It is interesting that slaveholding Baptists in the South employed the use of catechisms among enslaved persons. For much of the antebellum period, Southern states forbade slave education. It is paradoxical that in Southern Baptist slaveholding circles, there was a movement to catechize enslaved persons, which meant these enslaved persons received a modicum of education. Southern Baptists such as John L. Dagg embraced the Providential Design argument, which expressed that it was the will of

---

[33] Fitts, 26.

God that Africans be enslaved and brought to America so that, once freed, they would return to Africa to preach the gospel.[34]

Resistance and Contentions Against Slavery

During this time, a key antislavery event threatened the slavocracy and those Baptists within it. In 1822 in Charleston, South Carolina, Denmark Vesey, a formerly enslaved man, organized a plot to free the enslaved in Charleston and its environs. Before the plot could ensue, authorities received word of it. Vesey, who had been a Presbyterian but by 1822 was a member of the African church in Charleston, had "turned his back on the Christian passivity commonly taught by white ministers and free black preachers in favor of an Old Testament activism forged of wrath and justice," according to historian Douglas Egerton.[35] It was Vesey's vision to lead enslaved persons out of slavery in South Carolina to freedom in Haiti. He had planned to stage the revolt on the second Sunday of July, but word had dribbled out. Vesey then moved up the day of revolt to the second Sunday in June, but authorities had arrested coconspirators who lived outside of Charleston. After a cursory trial, authorities executed Vesey and forty-six others involved in the plot.[36]

In the immediate aftermath of the thwarted Vesey plot, the state of South Carolina passed specific legislation to oppress further the entirety of their African American population. The measure was to ban the African Methodist Episcopal Church in the state. Authorities believed this independent African church served to mediate African American resistance

---

[34] Tom J. Nettles, *Teaching Truth, Training Hearts: The Study of Catechisms in Baptist Life* (Amityville: Calvary), 19–23, 127.

[35] Douglas R. Egerton, *He Shall Go Out Free: The Lives of Denmark Vesey* (Madison: Madison House, 1999), xv, 110.

[36] Egerton, xv. See also John Hope Franklin and Evelyn Brooks Higginbotham, *From Slavery to Freedom: A History of African Americans,* 9th ed. (New York: McGraw-Hill, 2011), 156–57.

to the established racial order. No evidence connected any church leader to the plot. One other measure passed, which strengthened the Negro Act of 1740 that forbade enslaved persons from learning to read and write; the new measure prohibited any type of education for African Americans. Free blacks had to place themselves under white custodians to ensure their proper behavior. These measures in the wake of the Denmark Vesey conspiracy reflected the legalities of white supremacy and fear with implicit white Baptist support.[37]

During late summer and into fall of 1822, white South Carolinians breathed a deep sigh of relief, believing God had spared them from the voracious revenge of the enslaved and free blacks. As the state considered when to observe a day of Thanksgiving, Richard Furman, president of the Baptist Convention of South Carolina and pastor of First Baptist in Charleston, addressed the South Carolina Legislature. Representing the State Convention, Furman gave an official Baptist defense of slavery. He argued that Holy Scripture provided the right for people to own others in bondage. Furman stated, "In the Old Testament, the Israelites were directed to purchase their bond-men and bond-maids of the Heathen nations."[38] When he turned to the New Testament, Furman relied on what he termed "Gospel History" to assert that slavery was an institution in the Roman world and that enslaved persons were members of local churches "under the ministry of the inspired Apostles."[39] In the aftermath of a foiled plot by free blacks and enslaved blacks to free themselves, the leading Baptist of South Carolina stood flat-footed and boomed a definitive biblical apology for perpetual African enslavement in the United States.

---

[37] Albert J. Raboteau, *A Fire in the Bones: Reflections on African-American Religious History* (Boston: Beacon, 1995), 93; White et al., *Freedom on My Mind*, 212.

[38] Richard Furman, "Exposition of the Views of the Baptists Relative to the Coloured Population of the United States in a Communication to the Governor of South Carolina, Charleston, 24th December 1822," in *A Sourcebook for Baptist Heritage*, ed. H. Leon McBeth (Nashville: Broadman, 1990), 253.

[39] Furman, "Exposition," 253.

The year 1845 was a pivotal one in the history of American Baptists. As the country was on the eve of the Mexican War, a war that would expand slavery's footprint, Baptists found themselves embroiled in a controversy over slavery that would drive an enduring regional wedge among them. This was also a time of growing abolitionist and antislavery sentiment in the North. Leading abolitionist William Lloyd Garrison was on the circuit in Northern locales, arguing against slavery and using the Holy Scriptures as his primary support. Garrison and other abolitionists, such as Theodore Weld and the Tappan brothers, gained support of some Baptists in the North, but it would be a stretch to assert that Northern Baptists had become abolitionists. More ministers took up a moderate stance on the issue to preserve the unity of Baptists. Nevertheless, this abolitionist and antislavery advocacy was present enough for some Northern Baptists to voice their concerns over the propriety of slaveholders on the foreign mission field. Their protestations drove the debate regarding the issue of slaveholders on the mission field.[40]

Most Baptists believed unity was more important than the slavery issue. On this point they underestimated the power of the slavery debate among Baptists in which they were one segment of a broader national debate. Two prominent Baptists, one from the South and one from the North, attempted to keep unity amidst the disagreement on slavery, slaveholders, and missions. Richard Fuller, a South Carolina slaveholder and vice president of the General Convention's Board of Managers, contended that the New Testament protected slavery wherever it existed. Francis Wayland, a Northerner, agreed with Fuller's position; yet he believed the New Testament articulated principles that would lead to slavery's end. Even with that stance, Wayland urged his fellow Baptists to disallow slavery to rend them apart.[41]

---

[40] On the general climate of Baptists and antislavery in the North during the 1830s and '40s see Robert G. Torbet, *A History of the Baptists* (Valley Forge, PA: Judson, 2000), 286–87.

[41] Torbet, 290; Bill J. Leonard, *Baptist Ways: A History* (Valley Forge: Judson, 2003), 187.

An important turning point occurred in 1840 when the American Baptist Antislavery Convention met in New York City. This meeting of abolitionist Northern Baptists and international missionaries who found it untenable to remain united with slaveholders in the mission field began the five-year path to disunion among Baptists. Key highlights led to disunion in the aftermath of the American Baptist Antislavery meeting. First, Alabama Baptists in November 1840 sent a resolution to the Triennial Convention, asserting they would discontinue funding foreign missions unless they could be assured the convention was by no means supporting abolitionism. Second, the Triennial Convention meeting in 1841 in Baltimore forged a compromise that urged for calm and for there to be no statements condemning or promoting slavery. This so-called Baltimore Compromise displeased the growing abolitionist faction as well as the slavery faction. It was clear neutrality on the issue of slavery was no longer an option.[42]

In 1843, a small but vocal contingent of Northern Baptists threw down the gauntlet on the slavery issue, which brought the Triennial Convention to the breaking point. Northern Baptist abolitionists founded the American Baptist Free Mission Society, which pledged to support only non-slaveholders in the mission field. The Foreign Mission Board ruled that such a society had no authority in missionary matters. It was clear the organizing of the Free Mission Society was a political jab thrown at Southerners. This action by a sparse number of Northern Baptists posed a great threat to Southern Baptists. In November 1844, Alabama Baptists issued a set of resolutions to counter the stance of the American Baptist Free Mission Society. The so-called Alabama Resolutions were unequivocal in demanding that slaveholders should be given the equal right to serve as missionaries. One resolution posited that the Triennial Convention give "explicit avowal that slaveholders are eligible, and entitled, equally with non-slaveholders, to all privileges and immunities of their several unions; and especially to receive any agency, mission, or other appointment, which may run within

---

[42] Torbet, *A History of the Baptists*, 288–89; Leonard, *Baptist Ways*, 187–88.

the scope of their operations or duties."[43] Upon receiving these resolutions, the Foreign Mission Board responded in December by reiterating the position of the convention of equality of slaveholders and non-slaveholders regarding "all privileges and immunities."[44] The Board wrote further that in the thirty years of its existence, a slaveholder had never applied to be a missionary. Then, they asserted a new policy never articulated before:

> [A]s we send out no domestics, or servants, such an event as a missionary taking slaves with him, were it morally right, could not, in accordance with all our past arrangements or present plans, possibly occur. If, however, any one should offer himself as a missionary, having slaves, and should insist on retaining them as his property, we could not appoint him. One thing is certain, we can never be a party to any arrangement which would imply approbation of slavery.[45]

This statement by the Foreign Mission Board spelled the end of unity of American Baptists. By deciding not to support slavery, the board and the convention gave its support against slavery. The decision demonstrated how powerful the antislavery influence had become in the Northern faction of the convention. On May 8, 1845, Southern Baptists organized the Southern Baptist Convention.[46]

Now a new convention of Southern Baptist ministers put forward efforts to catechize the enslaved. One such minister was James Petigru Boyce, who catechized enslaved persons during his tenure as pastor of First Baptist Church, Columbia, South Carolina. Robert Ryland, who served as pastor of First African Baptist Church in Richmond, Virginia, catechized

---

[43] "The Alabama Resolutions," in McBeth, ed., *A Sourcebook for Baptist Heritage*, 258.

[44] "Reply of the Foreign Mission Board to the Alabama Convention," in McBeth, ed., *A Sourcebook for Baptist Heritage*, 259.

[45] "Reply of the Foreign Mission Board," 259.

[46] Torbet, *A History of the Baptists*, 289, 291; Leonard, *Baptist Ways*, 188–89.

enslaved persons as well. In fact, Ryland wrote a catechism in 1848 titled "A Scripture Catechism for the Instruction of Children and Servants." This catechism served to immerse enslaved persons in Christian doctrine and practice and was by no indication watered-down.[47]

Baptists and the Long Civil Rights Movement

As the Civil War ended and freedom became a reality for approximately four million enslaved persons, a new era of church planting and denominational building occurred for African American Baptists in the South. During the 1860s, African American Baptists founded independent churches and commenced to organize district associations and state conventions. Historian William Montgomery writes, "Of all the ways the former slaves displayed their newly acquired freedom, leaving the white-controlled churches and forming their own religious organizations was perhaps the easiest and most gratifying."[48] Echoing this, historians Hine, Hine, and Harrold assert, "In the years after slavery, the church again became the most important institution among African Americans other than the family."[49] From the numerous district associations formed in the 1860s and 1870s came state conventions. It was within a few important state conventions that a national movement was prompted among African American Baptists to organize for African missions, namely the 1880 founding of the Baptist Foreign Mission Convention (BFMC). The BFMC would serve as the founding convention of the later National Baptist Convention (NBC) of 1895. Twenty years later the National Baptist Convention of America (NBCA) would emerge from the NBC,

---

[47] Nettles, *Teaching Truth*, 131–32.

[48] William E. Montgomery, *Under Their Own Vine and Fig Tree: The African-American Church in the South 1865–1900* (Baton Rouge: Louisiana State University, 1993), 55.

[49] Darlene Clark Hine, William C. Hine, and Stanley C. Harrold, *The African-American Odyssey* (Saddle River: Prentice Hall, 2000), 257.

owing to an ugly struggle over the ownership of the National Baptist Publishing Board. Although African American Baptists proved to be fractious, their growth into the twentieth century was unquestioned. National Baptist pastors would soon emerge as key spokespersons for African American rights.[50]

African American Baptist ministers were some of the most vocal and forthright leaders of the civil rights movement during the 1950s and 1960s. Other than Martin Luther King Jr., who was only twenty-six years old when he assumed the ostensive leadership of the Montgomery bus protest in late 1955, there were pastors Fred Shuttlesworth, Ralph Abernathy, and T. J. Jemison. Adam Clayton Powell Jr., pastor of Abyssinian Baptist Church in Harlem, New York, served as a member in the House of Representatives, effecting legislation for African American rights. Countless men and women were courageous protestors, organizers, and cooks for the protestors and organizers, and all were members of Baptist churches.[51]

Important African American Baptist thinkers attacked white supremacist ideology poignantly and eloquently. One such was Howard Thurman. As an undergraduate student at Morehouse College in the early 1920s and a Baptist pastor and thinker (though later he became a Unitarian/Universalist) who was dean of the chapel at Boston University beginning in 1953, Thurman concerned himself with how African American faith in Jesus of Nazareth was the chief means of enduring under the harsh realities of slavery and segregation.[52] While at Boston University,

---

[50] Numerous writings exist on the early years of the National Baptist Convention and subsequent split that founded the National Baptist Convention of America. Helpful here are Jordan, *Negro Baptist History*; Fitts, *A History of Black Baptists*; and Owen D. Pelt and Ralph Lee Smith, *The Story of the National Baptists* (New York: Vantage, 1960).

[51] For a summary of Powell's work in the House, see Fitts, *A History of Black Baptists*, 271–80; Leonard, *Baptist Ways*, 280.

[52] Vincent Harding, "Foreword," in Howard Thurman, *Jesus and the Disinherited* (Boston: Beacon, 1996), xiii–ix.

he served as a mentor to Martin Luther King Jr. In Thurman's most well-read work, *Jesus and the Disinherited*, published in 1949, he levied moralistic blows against segregation.[53] Rumor has it that Martin Luther King Jr. carried a copy of *Jesus and the Disinherited* with him constantly, thereby maintaining this link between the prophetic words of Thurman to the prophetic actions of King.[54]

In the American context that upheld the status quo of white supremacy (in which the white American church, especially the white American Protestant church, was interwoven), Thurman argued that Jesus was a marginal person in his context—a Jew under Roman colonialism, a poor person, and a person who belonged to an ethnic minority group. Far from representing the position of white Americans in general, the life and experiences of Jesus mirrored African Americans. With candor, Thurman wrote:

> I belong to a generation that finds very little that is meaningful or intelligent in the teachings of the Church concerning Jesus Christ. It is a generation largely in revolt because of the general impression that Christianity is essentially an other-worldly religion, having as its motto: "Take all the world, but give me Jesus." The desperate opposition to Christianity rests in the fact that it seems, in the last analysis, to be a betrayal of the Negro into the hands of his enemies by focusing his attention on heaven, forgiveness, love, and the like. It is true that this emphasis is germane to the religion of Jesus, but it has to be put into a context that will show its strength and vitality rather than its weakness and failure.[55]

In another astonishing statement, Thurman wrote: "The striking similarity between the social position of Jesus in Palestine and that of the vast majority of American Negroes is obvious to anyone who tarries long over the

---

[53] Thurman, *Jesus and the Disinherited*.
[54] Harding, "Foreword," xii. See also Harvey, *Through the Storm*, 111.
[55] Thurman, *Jesus and the Disinherited*, 19.

facts. . . . It is the similarity of a social climate at the point of a denial of full citizenship which creates the problem for creative survival."[56]

Thurman's thoughts on the fear that segregation produced among African Americans is clear and perceptive. He wrote:

> The threat of violence within a framework of well-nigh limitless power is a weapon by which the weak are held in check. Artificial limitations are placed upon them, restricting freedom of movement, of employment, and of participation in the common life. These limitations are given formal or informal expression in general or specific policies of separateness or segregation. These policies tend to freeze the social status of the insecure. The threat of violence may be implemented not only by constitutional authority but also by anyone acting in behalf of the established order.[57]

These are sentiments from a person who knew what it meant to live under the violence of Jim Crow and believed in the nonviolent philosophy he learned from Gandhi. What this passage assumes is that the powerless and the insecure are just that; they have no other recourse but to struggle without violence against the powerful. In the American context, the powerful were the white population in general. Nothing had changed from slavery. This was reflected even in the Fugitive Slave Act of 1850 in which every white person could be deputized as a slave catcher.[58]

When surveying the life and thought of Martin Luther King Jr., Thurman's influence is clear. Yet King's own social context, especially being a lifelong member of an African American Baptist Church, served to give King's thought and activism a different flavor. He would eventually become the most significant Baptist of the civil rights era.

---

[56] Thurman, 23.
[57] Thurman, 31.
[58] See "Preface," in Thurman, *Jesus and the Disinherited*, x–xi.

Martin Luther King Jr. was born January 15, 1929, in the Auburn Avenue neighborhood of Atlanta, Georgia, to Reverend Martin Luther King Sr. and Alberta Williams King. King described himself as a precocious young person who performed well in school. At the age of fifteen, King enrolled at Morehouse College. While there, he received mentoring from the president of the college, Dr. Benjamin E. Mays, a Baptist minister as well. During his senior year at Morehouse, King became a gospel minister. It was King's Christian sensibilities and convictions along with his liberal arts education and his father's influence that intersected and prompted his decision to adhere to the ministerial call. Upon graduating from Morehouse at the age of nineteen, King decided to gain further training at Crozer Theological Seminary and then at Boston University, where he earned his doctorate in systematic theology in 1955.[59]

During his time at Crozer, King joined his experiences of living under the injustice of Jim Crow with a theology concerned about social justice. King stated that the theology of Walter Rauschenbusch, also a Baptist, gave him the theological vocabulary to struggle against injustice. After reading Rauschenbusch's work, King had become convinced that a religion that claims to be concerned about souls but that is not just as concerned about those individuals' economic and social conditions is at death's door.[60] During his time at both Crozer and Boston University, King developed his nonviolent position. This came through learning the teachings of Gandhi, careful and critical reading of Reinhold Niebuhr's critique of pacifism, and continued training in philosophy and theology in his PhD studies.[61]

When King finished his course work at Boston in 1954, he sought work either in academia or in the pastorate. Dexter Avenue Baptist Church in

---

[59] Martin Luther King Jr., *The Autobiography of Martin Luther King, Jr.*, ed. Clayborne Carson (New York: Warner Books, 1998), 1–17.

[60] See King, 18.

[61] King, 23–24; 26–27; 31–32.

Montgomery, Alabama, was without a pastor at this time and heard about the young King from the elder King. This interest by a church in the South lured King back to his homeland.[62] It was in this position that the civil rights struggle in real time met King. It would be inaccurate to argue that King created an activist climate at Dexter Avenue. When he arrived in Montgomery, African American women, two of whom were members of Dexter Avenue, had organized to fight against segregation as mentioned below.

From 1955 to 1965, King contributed to the movement not only by his personal, visible activism but also by his sharp writings, clarifying Christianity's opposition to the scourge of racism manifested in terrible and inhumane acts of violence. In addition, King's thought elucidated Christianity's support of a radical love ethic to endure suffering to achieve shalom. All during this time though, some white Southern Baptists issued public statements in opposition to the civil rights movement and, in some cases, in defense of segregation with Scripture. One such Baptist was Carey L. Daniel, pastor of First Baptist Church in West Dallas, Texas, who argued that Jesus Christ was the "original segregationist."[63] Prominent white Baptist pastor W. A. Criswell of First Baptist in Dallas, Texas, was a vocal proponent of the system of segregation as evinced in a public address before the South Carolina State Legislature in 1956.[64] By 1970, Criswell seemed to have repudiated his former stance, stating, "To separate by coercion the body of Christ on the basis of skin pigmentation was unthinkable, unchristian and unacceptable to God."[65] Even in this statement, Criswell gave Christians the space to separate by their own free will. In this context, no piece of writing by King explained his defense of a Christianity that opposed injustice of any sort more than "Letter from Birmingham Jail" published in 1963. This

---

[62] King, 41–44.

[63] Jemar Tisby, *The Color of Compromise: The Truth about the American Church's Complicity in Racism* (Grand Rapids: Zondervan, 2019), 134.

[64] Leonard, *Baptist Ways*, 413.

[65] Quoted in Leonard, 413.

work can be considered the manifesto of the King-led civil rights movement as well as a paragon of intellectual Christian social engagement.

It was during the Birmingham Campaign in the spring of 1963 that King found himself arrested and placed in solitary confinement. White ministers had written an open letter criticizing King and his tactics of non-violent civil disobedience. One of the signatories of the "Law and Order Statement" of these white "moderate" clergy was Earl Stallings, pastor of First Baptist Church in Birmingham. Stallings and his colleagues wrote their statement as a sort of middle way of approaching the civil rights struggle in Birmingham. They issued their statement to "urge our Negro community to withdraw support from these demonstrations, and to unite locally in working peacefully for a better Birmingham." They labeled these King-led protests as "extreme" and "unwise and untimely." The statement recognized the struggle that African Americans waged against racial and social injustice, but these clergy called for addressing those concerns in the courts and through "honest and open negotiation." Someone "slipped" King the newspaper that printed the letter. He then wrote his letter in response.[66]

In the letter, King supported his method of civil disobedience, basing it on the Western Christian tradition and Western philosophy. He brought tenets of the ancient faith to bear on racial injustice in the United States. King's critics argued that the proclivity of African American protestors to break laws troubled them. He explained to his naysayers that people have a moral obligation to defy laws that are unjust, basing this on Augustine of Hippo, who claimed that an "unjust law is no law at all."[67]

---

[66] "Statement by Alabama Clergymen," April 12, 1963, https://kinginstitute .stanford.edu/sites/mlk/files/lesson-activities/clergybirmingham1963.pdf; King, *Autobiography*, 187.

[67] Martin Luther King Jr., "Letter from Birmingham Jail," in *Martin Luther King, Jr., Malcolm X, and the Civil Rights Struggle of the 1950s and 1960s: A Brief History with Documents*, ed. David Howard-Pitney (Boston: Bedford/St. Martin's, 2004), 79.

King proclaimed that every person had the unquestioned obligation to abide by just laws. What did King mean when he asserted one was morally responsible to defy an unfair and unreasonable law? King felt that unjust laws were discordant with the moral law.[68] Like he drew from Augustine, King also culled from Thomas Aquinas in giving authority to his definition of an unjust law. In applying this to segregation, King contended that segregation is damaging to both soul and personality and makes the one enforcing segregation falsely superior and the victim falsely inferior. Therefore, any segregation law of any kind is unjust.[69] This poignant tone brought clarity that undergirded why segregation and white supremacy had to be dismantled and replaced with just laws, and this had to be done immediately.

This was another key theme King addressed in his letter: the urgency of the protest. Following King's line of thinking that unjust laws must be disobeyed, he argued that mere disobedience means nothing without an urgent call to create just laws that uphold the human soul and personality.[70] King's detractors urged him to wait, to go slow. They believed his method was dangerous and "extreme." King responded in so many words that the oppressed will not remain oppressed because the desire for freedom will ultimately bring them to action, just as it was doing within the black community.[71] Freedom, he argued, *can* be achieved. He drew inspiration from independence struggles in Asia and Africa and connected the struggle of African Americans to the larger context of oppressed and colonized people gaining their freedom.[72] Owing to this, King asserted that he would rather be an extremist like Jesus himself, a radical who fought for love, for truth, for goodness, in spite of the evil and hate around him.[73] With that point,

---

[68] See King, "Letter from a Birmingham Jail."

[69] See King, 80.

[70] King, 80–81.

[71] See King, 84.

[72] King, 84.

[73] See King, 84.

King lifted his theologizing beyond the situation of African Americans, planting it in eternal truth to be applied in any and every case of struggle for freedom.

This brief summation of King's letter indicates that his theologizing emerged from a certain Christian tradition. More than merely Baptist, or even liberal, King's thought was part of an Afro-Baptist faith tradition forged and tempered by years of oppression yet hoping for a better day. A mere liberal Christian theology was unable to give voice to a freedom movement and grant hope to an oppressed people. Although grounded in the Scriptures and the Western Christian tradition, King's theology of justice in his letter spilled from the collective experience of an oppressed people, an oppressed people of which he was part. The African American Baptist Church nurtured King, and it was in and through the African American Baptist Church that King thought and fought. Thus, King's theology and activism remain at the pinnacle of Christian engagement of unjust societal structures.[74]

The most documented tension was between Martin Luther King Jr. and J. H. Jackson within the National Baptist Convention, USA. Tensions led to the founding of the Progressive National Baptist Convention. King, Ralph Abernathy, L. Venchael Booth, and Gardner C. Taylor believed the NBC should adopt a strong stance on civil rights. Because of this, they formed a group to oppose the more conservative position of Jackson, who believed the convention should remain out of politics. He believed the fight was through the courts, not an activist convention. The King-Abernathy group failed to unseat the powerful Jackson and his supporters. As a result, King and others organized the Progressive National

---

[74] Mika Edmondson, *The Power of Unearned Suffering: The Roots and Implications of Martin Luther King, Jr.'s Theodicy* (Lanham: Lexington Books, 2017), 1–17. Edmondson advances the argument that one cannot understand King's theology and activism as a whole without grounding him in an African American cultural context of segregation and the Baptist church.

Baptist Convention in 1961, which took a bold position on civil rights and social justice.[75]

Jo Ann G. Robinson was a member of Dexter Avenue Baptist Church, which King pastored in Montgomery, Alabama, and a coleader of the Social and Political Action Committee.[76] She taught English at Alabama State University and was at the center of organizing the Montgomery bus protest of 1955–1956. She was leader of the Women's Political Council in Montgomery, described as a "black middle-class women's organization."[77] Founded in 1946 by Dr. Mary Fair Burks, also a professor in the English department at Alabama State and a member of Dexter Avenue, its mission was to uplift African Americans educationally, politically, and socially.[78] She was the person who mapped out how African American taxi cab drivers would give rides to workers on a daily basis.[79]

Another prominent (arguably more so than Robinson) African American Baptist woman in the civil rights struggle was Ella Baker. Martin Luther King Jr. was among other African American Baptist ministers to form the Southern Christian Leadership Conference (SCLC). Although the executive board consisted of men, Baker became the executive director. Her style clashed with the men on the board; she favored an approach that placed power in the hands of grassroots members rather than a top-down approach. Though Baker was an organizer in the National Association for the Advancement of Colored People (NAACP) before her work in the SCLC, Baker's method of organizing resulted from her rearing in a Baptist church in Littleton, North Carolina, where her mother was active

---

[75] Eddie S. Glaude Jr., *African American Religion: A Very Short Introduction* (Oxford: Oxford University, 2014), 75.

[76] King, *Autobiography*, 47–48.

[77] White et al., *Freedom on My Mind*, 491.

[78] Glaude, *African American Religion*, 72.

[79] Paul Harvey, *Through the Storm, Through the Night: A History of African American Christianity* (Lanham, MD: Rowan & Littlefield, 2011), 113. More on Burks see https://www.umes.edu/125/Content/Stories/Mary-Fair-Burks/.

in the Women's Convention of the state convention. It reflected the gender dynamics of Baptist churches in which the men in the pulpit were the visible leaders, but the women in the pews performed the necessary tasks to advance the churches.[80] Baker may be best known for her work and support of the Student Nonviolent Coordinating Committee (SNCC), which was the student arm of the SCLC.[81]

When Baptists split in 1845 over the issue of slavery, it was evident that an abolitionist sentiment was growing among Northern Baptists, and this was intolerable for their Southern brethren. Before the split, there were Southern Baptists who articulated clear racist justification of the institution while there were Northern Baptists who were indifferent or in agreement with race-based chattel slavery. The record is mixed, but lines began to be drawn during the 1820s onward. Although African American Baptists disagreed on the pace and tools of resistance within the civil rights movement, no leader disparaged the movement.

Still Two Racial Worlds?

As of 2021, Baptists fail to speak with one voice pertaining to racial justice. Early in 2021, the Anti-Racism Task Force of the American Baptist Convention of the United States of America (ABCUSA) issued a fresh statement that contextualized its formation. The context was the protests during the summer of 2020 in the wake of George Floyd's murder by former Minneapolis police officer Derek Chauvin. A portion of the Task Force's statement reads:

> Throughout the summer, many groups gathered, talked, wrote lofty statements, and prayed. And on August 5, the American Baptist Churches USA held a Call to Prayer. Following the Call to

---

[80] Glaude, *African American Religion*, 73–74.
[81] Glaude, 74–75; White et al., *Freedom on My Mind*, 530.

Prayer, the Anti-Racism Task Force was formed. The Anti-Racism Task Force represents American Baptists clergy and lay people from across the nation committed to live into our call to be the hands and feet of Christ in the world. Our initial goal is to provide anti-racism resources, exercises, and other materials to be used in our personal, congregational, and institutional work and to host a denominational wide anti-racism symposium.[82]

What is key in the work of this Task Force is its use of legal scholar and critical race theorist Kimberlé Crenshaw's definition of anti-racism: "the active dismantling of systems, privileges, and everyday practices that reinforce and normalize the contemporary dimensions of white dominance."[83] This Task Force identifies anti-racism as the work of the entire denomination.

As the ABCUSA responded to the George Floyd murder by organizing an anti-racism task force, in November 2020 the Southern Baptist Convention and the presidents of their seminaries disavowed critical race theory and failed to offer any type of statement regarding any formal committee or organization that is anti-racist. Then SBC president J. D. Greear's statement reveals: "While we lament the painful legacy that racism and discrimination have left in our country and remain committed to fighting it in every form, we also declare that ideological frameworks like Critical Race Theory are incompatible with the BFM. The Gospel gives a better answer."[84] The presidents' joint statement was even more pointed: "In light of current conversations in the Southern Baptist Convention, we stand together on historic Southern Baptist condemnations of racism in any form and

---

[82] "The ABCUSA Anti-Racism Task Force: A Call to Just Action," https://www.abc-usa.org/2021/02/the-abcusa-anti-racism-task-force-a-call-to-just-action/.

[83] "The ABCUSA Anti-Racism Task Force."

[84] Quoted in George Schroeder, "Seminary presidents reaffirm BFM, declare CRT incompatible," Baptist Press, November 30, 2020, https://www.baptistpress.com/resource-library/news/seminary-presidents-reaffirm-bfm-declare-crt-incompatible/.

we also declare that affirmation of Critical Race Theory, Intersectionality, and any version of Critical Theory is incompatible with the Baptist Faith & Message."[85] Even on what many called a "national reckoning on race," Baptists are halted betwixt two opinions.

On January 5, 2021, the Georgia electorate made history. On that night, Georgia voters chose to send an African American man to represent them in the United States Senate. This man, Raphael Warnock, serves as pastor of the historic Ebenezer Baptist Church in Atlanta, the same church where Martin Luther King Jr. co-pastored with his father, M. L. King Sr. This speaks of the continuity of African American Baptist faith and civil rights activism. This is an enduring legacy that stretches all the way back to colonial history, where enslaved Africans and African Americans found spiritual freedom in their plantation congregations and independent churches, appropriating the faith of their oppressors but for a far different reason. African American Baptist history fits within the larger narrative of African American history, which is a narrative of the struggle and fight for freedom. The struggle has continued, in part, owing to white Baptists who have stood against civil rights and, more recently, to those who have soft-pedaled racial issues. African American Baptists sought more than spiritual freedom though. Every generation dreamed of physical freedom from the shackles of slavery. Even when freedom came in 1865, African American Baptists remained vigilant in struggling for full citizenship rights in the country of their birth. From Liele to Warnock and all in between, African American Baptists live by the words of the prophet of old: "They that wait on the Lord shall renew their strength" (cf. Isa 40:31 KJV).

---

[85] Quoted in Schroeder, "Seminary presidents."

10

Baptists and the Civil War

By Gregory A. Wills

American politics centered inextricably on matters related to slavery beginning in the mid-1840s. Slavery dominated the platforms of the political parties, even the Know Nothing party's efforts to pursue a principled silence regarding slavery. Secession and the Civil War further polarized the political parties.

In 1860 Baptists were deeply divided in their political views, and their divisions reflected those of the nation generally. Disagreements concerning slavery fueled those passions. For thirty years, issue after issue arose in courts, legislatures, foreign and domestic policy, and elections, in which the contested interests of slaveholding determined the boundaries of the debate. John Brown's insurrection at Harpers Ferry in late 1859 elevated the distrust and fear of Southern whites. Some Northern whites condemned the insurrection in the mildest way. Others celebrated it. Southern whites interpreted this limited repudiation of Brown as Northerners' refusal to safeguard the lives and property of Southerners.

The election of 1860 kindled deep passions. Political parties splintered along sectional lines, leaving four major tickets for the presidency, each distinguished chiefly by its proposed approach to the nation's divisions relating to slavery. Lincoln won the presidency without any electors from the South. Since Lincoln was committed to preventing the spread of slavery into any new states or territories and since he seemed unlikely to insist that Northern states uphold the Fugitive Slave Act, Southerners concluded that he was effectively an abolitionist and would spread abolitionism by his presidential powers. Southerners in eleven slave states voted to secede from the United States and formed the Confederate States of America. The bloody Civil War ensued from 1861 to 1865.

The war polarized political opinions further for Baptists, no less than the general population. For all involved, blacks and whites in the North and South, patriotism and religion commingled easily. Patriotism called upon all the convictions and commitments of piety to uphold the national interest of the one nation or the other. Baptists on both sides assured themselves they stood upon God's truth and righteousness in advancing their patriotic duties.

Key Baptist Figures

Most of the key Baptist figures in the politics of the Civil War era were clergy. Clergy have always had significant political influence. Politics necessarily touch upon matters of moral and religious concern. Politicians instinctively recognize the power of religious convictions and communities for many voters and seek ways to adapt their message and platform to woo religious votes. Since those on all sides of the slavery issue appealed to the Bible, the clergy's interpretations of the Bible regarding slavery had great political significance. Baptist clergy North and South helped shape distinctive Northern and Southern versions of Christian nationalism.

Debates over slavery helped redefine American nationalism. For American Christians, the interpretation of the Bible was central to defining American nationalism vis-à-vis slaveholding. The clergy, therefore, played a central role, not just in light of their views regarding slavery but also in their construction of appropriate nationalism.

Leonard Grimes

Leonard Grimes (1815–1873) was an effective and courageous conductor of fugitive slaves. Born free in Virginia, Grimes operated a carriage service in Washington, DC, in the 1830s and advised, aided, and transported slaves who dared to abscond. In 1838 he was arrested and imprisoned for rendering this good service. Released in 1840, he was called to the gospel ministry and served churches in the North. He was pastor of Boston's Twelfth Baptist Church from 1848 to 1873. In this role he aided hundreds of fugitive slaves, including by raising money to purchase the freedom of those who were caught in the net of the Fugitive Slave Act.

The Fugitive Slave Act polarized sectional politics. Along with the conflict over slavery in Kansas from 1854 to 1859 and the response to John Brown's 1859 insurrection effort at Harpers Ferry, the issue of fugitive slaves raised the passions of whites in the North and South. Congress passed the Fugitive Slave Act as part of the Compromise of 1850, which forestalled the secession of slave states at that time. Large numbers of slaves absconded because they had encouragement and help from blacks and whites in the border states and in the North.

Grimes played a central role in gaining the freedom of fugitive slave Anthony Burns in 1854. After a controversial trial, the court ordered the rendition of Burns to his Richmond, Virginia, owner, who sold him secretly to a slaveholder in Rocky Mount, North Carolina. When his location was later discovered, Grimes raised $1,300 and negotiated the purchase of Burns's freedom. The entire affair galvanized the Massachusetts public and led to the passage of laws that effectively prevented the enforcement of the Fugitive Slave Act.[1]

---

[1] See William Wells Brown, *The Black Man: His Antecedents, His Genius, and His Achievements* (New York: Thomas Hamilton, 1863), 217–20; William J. Simmons, *Men of Mark: Eminent, Progressive, and Rising* (Cleveland: George M. Rewell, 1887), 662–65.

Grimes helped publicize the immorality of American slavery by his activity in protecting and aiding fugitive slaves. He helped shape the conscience of Massachusetts and the North against the federal Fugitive Slave Act. The Anthony Burns trial was the last time the law was enforced in Massachusetts. Vermont and Wisconsin joined Massachusetts in effectively nullifying the law by preventing its enforcement. (It was an uncomfortable assertion of the priority of state sovereignty that forced Southerners just as uncomfortably to assert federal sovereignty.)

Grimes played a leading role in the affairs concerning Black Bostonians, including the enlistment of Blacks as frontline soldiers and the effort to assure them equal pay. Before, during, and after the Civil War, Grimes's Twelfth Baptist Church welcomed and hosted a wide variety of organizations and movements and permitted them to use the church's facilities, all to serve the purposes of opposing slavery and racial injustice.[2]

Francis Wayland

Francis Wayland (1796–1865), president of Brown University (1827–55), exercised wide influence in American higher education, philosophy, economics, and ethics. He was the most respected scholar among Baptists. His 1835 *Elements of Moral Science* was widely adopted by American colleges and went through many editions. In it, Wayland argued that slavery was immoral, but slaveholding was not intrinsically immoral, depending on the circumstances. Slavery should be abolished, but immediate abolition might do more harm than good.

Wayland argued that slavery was not just a personal and moral issue, but also a legal, political, and social issue. He believed that when whole societies exonerated something immoral—when the entire social conscience

---

[2] See Stephen Kantrowitz, *More Than Freedom: Fighting for Black Citizenship in a White Republic, 1829–1889* (New York: Penguin, 2013) 289–94, *passim*; Kenneth L. Kusmer, ed., *Black Communities and Urban Development in America, 1720–1990: Antebellum America*, vol. 2 (Madison: University of Wisconsin, 1991), 235–43.

is misled—individual Christians may walk in real piety and at the same time practice the immorality that all society has exonerated. The gospel over time would reform the conscience of societies as well as individuals. In this, the gospel would lead the United States to abolish slavery over time.

Because of Wayland's position and influence, his antislavery arguments became well known, and his arguments in *The Elements of Moral Science* were widely attacked. Georgia Baptist leader Patrick H. Mell defended slavery against them in his 1844 *Slavery: A Treatise, Showing That Slavery Is neither a Moral, Political, nor Social Evil*. William H. Brisbane, a South Carolina plantation owner, established and edited the *Southern Baptist and General Intelligencer* largely to defend slavery against abolitionist agitation. Brisbane judged that Wayland's arguments against slavery possessed more plausibility than others he had encountered. Brisbane studied Wayland's arguments carefully so he could refute them thoroughly, but finally became convinced that Wayland's views were scriptural. Brisbane's new antislavery views rendered him a danger to society, and he relocated to the North.

Wayland defended his antislavery views against the proslavery arguments of his fellow Baptist leader, Richard Fuller. Published in book form in 1845, Wayland argued narrowly that although slavery should be abolished, that did not mean immediate abolition of slavery was demanded. Whether slavery is wrong is one question; how to remedy the evil was a different question. In the meantime, Wayland said, slaveholders should not be expelled from church fellowship, since the apostolic churches did not expel them.

Abolitionists opposed Wayland also. His complex and nuanced analysis angered and perplexed abolitionists. It was a compromise. They thought Wayland contradicted himself when he condemned slavery but exonerated slaveholding.

Basil Manly

Basil Manly Sr. (1798–1868) was among the most influential Southern Baptist leaders. He was pastor of the influential Charleston, South Carolina,

First Baptist Church (1826–37), president of the University of Alabama (1837–55), and chairman of the board of trustees of the Southern Baptist Theological Seminary (1858–68).

Manly played a central role in persuading Baptists in the South to separate from their Northern brethren and form the Southern Baptist Convention when he drafted a set of resolutions in 1844 challenging the Foreign Mission Board to endorse openly the equal rights of slaveholders to serve as missionaries. Manly's resolutions were adopted by the Tuscaloosa Baptist Association and the Alabama Baptist State Convention. When the board refused, Manly and others endorsed the call for the Southern Baptist Convention.

Manly defended slaveholding. He argued that providence demonstrated that God appointed Africans to serve as slaves in perpetuity and that, therefore, they had no natural rights of liberty. He also argued that slavery was a beneficent institution and that it benefitted everyone—masters, slaves, and all society. Slavery was part of the natural social order. Southern slaves, Manly said, were better clothed, fed, and cared for than the laboring classes of Europe or the North.[3]

Manly strongly advocated secession. The Alabama Baptist Convention gathered in Tuskegee just three days after the presidential election. Manly offered a pro-secession resolution that the body adopted unanimously and prayerfully. They solemnly declared their conviction that the United States "has failed" to fulfill its original purposes to protect the property of all. "We can no longer hope for justice, protection, or safety" from the federal government, "especially with reference to our peculiar property recognized by the Constitution"—that is, property in persons, African slaves. They, therefore, declared themselves prepared to submit "to the call of proper authority in defense of the sovereignty and independence of

---

[3] See *Report on Slavery and Racism in the History of the Southern Baptist Theological Seminary* (Louisville: Southern Baptist Theological Seminary, 2018), 13–15.

the State of Alabama and of her right, as a sovereignty, to withdraw from this Union."[4]

His supporters in Tuscaloosa ran him as a pro-secession candidate for election to the Alabama secession convention. Although he lost the election, the secession convention elected him as their chaplain, and he offered the opening prayer on January 7, 1861. When the Confederate government organized its provisional congress, they appointed Manly congressional chaplain. Manly owned several plantations and held at least thirty-eight slaves on one Alabama plantation.[5]

Richard Fuller

Richard Fuller (1804–1876) was among the most respected Southern Baptist clergy of the era. After his conversion in the 1820s, he was called to the pastorate of the Baptist Church of Beaufort, South Carolina, his birthplace. From 1846 until his death, he preached weekly to a large congregation in Baltimore, Maryland.

Fuller sought to prevent the division of the Baptist mission boards over slavery. At the 1841 meeting of the boards, delegates adopted his resolution, pledging to put aside their differences over slaveholding for the sake of unity. This unity was too fragile to last, however. In 1845 he joined his fellow Southern Baptists in organizing the Southern Baptist Convention.

Fuller defended the morality of slaveholding in an extensive literary debate with Francis Wayland, their letters published as a book in 1845. Fuller's defense of slaveholding was narrow. He aimed to demonstrate that slaveholding was not intrinsically immoral. He defended slavery in the

---

[4] Alabama Baptist State Convention, *Proceedings of the Thirty-Eighth Annual Session of the Alabama Baptist State Convention* (Tuskegee: South Western Baptist, 1860), 11.

[5] For the most detailed account of Manly's life and beliefs, see A. James Fuller, *Chaplain to the Confederacy: Basil Manly and Baptist Life in the Old South* (Baton Rouge: Louisiana State University, 2000).

abstract, as a principle. He advocated the morality of slaveholding as it ought to be, in his view, not as it was in fact.

Fuller was held in high regard by his fellow clergy, who elected him president of the Southern Baptist Convention in 1859 and 1861. Although many Southern Baptists believed his arguments were not sufficiently pro-slavery, his public defense of slaveholding was no doubt an important source of his popularity. Even in May 1861, after the start of the Civil War, most delegates at the annual meeting of the Southern Baptist Convention in Savannah, Georgia, voted to elect him as president of the convention.[6]

Joseph E. Brown

Joseph E. Brown (1821–1894), one of the most successful politicians in Georgia's history, was governor of Georgia (1857–65) and United States Senator (1880–90). He artfully managed the secession movement. On election day in 1860, before anyone knew who had won the election, he requested the legislature to appropriate one million dollars for military preparations and to appoint a day to elect delegates to a secession convention. When Lincoln's victory was announced, Brown immediately published arguments for Georgia's immediate secession from the Union. He ordered the seizure of Fort Pulaski even before the secession convention convened.

Brown was also an active Southern Baptist layman. At the 1863 meeting of the Southern Baptist Convention, Brown gave a speech defending the adoption of resolutions in support of the righteousness of the Confederate cause in the war: "All must admit that the institution of slavery is one of the prime causes of the war, and that its perpetuation depends upon the success of our arms. . . . In planting it here our Heavenly Father had a great purpose in view for the promotion of his kingdom on earth. I believe, sir,

---

[6] Fuller received 79 of the 118 votes cast. P. H. Mell polled second with 35 votes. Southern Baptist Convention, *Proceedings of the Southern Baptist Convention* (Richmond: MacFarlane and Fergusson, 1861), 9.

that it is an institution of God, and that we have revealed to us in the Holy Bible clear and overwhelming evidence of its establishment by Him and of his intention to perpetuate it."[7] Brown's speech swept away all reservations. The resolutions passed unanimously.

He participated in denominational meetings and served on the Southern Baptist Theological Seminary board of trustees for nearly twenty years, including eleven years as board chairman. He gave $50,000 to Southern Baptist Theological Seminary in 1880, which saved the school from collapse.

Brown had always been astute in business, whether buying and selling land and mineral rights or leasing out his slaves for regular income. In 1873 he formed the Dade Coal Company and began leasing convicts from the state penal system to supply the labor for the coal mines. Many states in the postwar era established convict-lease programs in which businesses paid the state for the labor of its convicts. The system flourished primarily in the South as a means of supplying cheap labor for businesses, a large revenue stream for state and local governments, and a new means of social control of Blacks. Legislators, law enforcement, and judges had financial inducements to entrap mostly young Black men in the system. Many were entrapped. Many died under the harsh labor conditions and the cruel punishments.

Dade Coal Company was the core of a conglomerate of related businesses that flourished through the convict-lease system and produced a fortune for Brown.[8]

Jabez L. M. Curry

Jabez L. M. Curry (1825–1903), an influential Alabama Democrat, played an important role in the politics of the era and helped shape the

---

[7] Joseph E. Brown, "Speech of Governor Brown in the Baptist Biennial Convention," *Christian Index*, May 25, 1863, 2.

[8] See *Report on Slavery*, 33–37.

political legacy of Southern Baptist involvement in slavery, secession, and the Civil War.

Curry studied law at Harvard University and was admitted to the bar in Alabama in 1846. He was elected three times to the Alabama state legislature, and in 1857 he was elected to the United States House of Representatives. He represented Alabama in the Congress of the Confederate States (1861–64).[9]

Curry secured his status as a reliable defender of slaveholding in his speech on December 10, 1859, on the floor of the House of Representatives. Curry made his speech as Southern whites grew increasingly alarmed and resentful toward Northern leaders who supported John Brown's antislavery insurrection at Harpers Ferry or refused to condemn the violence as a treasonous act.

Curry's views were not new. Strict constructionist or constitutional union Democrats made similar arguments frequently since the debates over the Wilmot Proviso, slavery in the territories, and the admission of new slave states. He repeated the same line of arguments with more passionate oratory in his speech in Talladega, Alabama, just before Alabamans were to vote on delegates to the secession convention. He urged them to act without delay to preserve Southern rights to hold slaves.

In early 1864 Curry composed the *Address of Congress to the People of the Confederate States*, which was adopted as a joint resolution by the Confederate Congress to boost lagging morale. Curry blamed secession and its consequent war on Northern opposition to slavery. The fundamental aim of the Republican party was to destroy slavery, and since the United States Constitution and the doctrine of state sovereignty blocked them, they determined to engage in war in order to overturn the Constitution and abolish both slavery and state sovereignty.[10]

---

[9] For the most detailed account of Curry's life, see Edwin Anderson Alderman and Armistead Churchill Gordon, *J. L. M. Curry: A Biography* (New York: Macmillan, 1911).

[10] Jabez L. M. Curry, *Address of Congress to the People of the Confederate States* (Richmond: n.p., 1864).

He was president of Alabama Baptists' Howard College (now Samford University) from 1865–68 and taught philosophy at Virginia Baptists' Richmond College from 1868–81. He was a trustee of the Southern Baptist Theological Seminary, a chairman of the denomination's Foreign Mission Board, and elected president of the 1872 Baptist General Association of Virginia. He served as the United States Ambassador to Spain from 1885 to 1888.

Curry, like most white Democrats, maintained white supremacist views. He published numerous books defending the righteousness of white Southerners' in holding slaves and establishing a separate slaveholding nation. Curry's main work, however, was to spread support for establishing universal education for all children, Black and white, especially in rural areas and in poor communities. From 1881 until his death in 1903, Curry labored chiefly at this task. The two most effective educational foundations of the era, the Peabody Education Fund and the Slater Fund, elected him as their agent. He used these large funds to establish schools and extend universal education, especially to Blacks and poor whites in the South.

Curry's statue stood at the United States Capitol from 1908 to 2009, when Alabama replaced it with a statue honoring Helen Keller.

Baptist Debates

Baptists disagreed substantially on most of the political issues facing the nation. They disagreed on the issue that, since the mid-1840s, had dominated American politics: slavery. In 1845 Baptists divided over the issue when Baptist churches in the slave states formed the Southern Baptist Convention. Baptists, like Americans generally, held divergent views across the spectrum from abolitionism to proslavery. Black Baptists were abolitionists. By 1860 a significant minority of white Baptists in the North were abolitionists, but most held gradualist emancipation views like those of Francis Wayland. White Baptists in the South were rather evenly divided between those who held thoroughgoing proslavery views, similar to Basil

Manly's, and those who held a qualified proslavery position that looked toward eventual emancipation, similar to Richard Fuller's. The following section explains these different positions.

Slavery

Black Baptists were uniformly antislavery. A few supported the colonization society, mostly because they judged that whites would never protect the freedom of free Blacks. Some others supported colonization in order to serve as missionaries to colonists and to indigenous Africans. But most Black Baptists were abolitionists and opposed to colonization efforts. Among white New England Baptists in 1860, abolitionists may have been the majority. They advocated immediate abolition of slavery and refusal of fellowship to slaveholders. They formed Baptist antislavery societies. They adopted antislavery resolutions in some of their association meetings. Among Baptists in other parts of the North, abolitionists were in the minority.

Some Northern Baptists in 1860 were proslavery, especially around New York City and in New Jersey. Most white Baptists in the North in 1860, however, were emancipationists. They held that slaveholding was immoral in principle and produced great evils in practice, and therefore, it should be extinguished as soon as a practical remedy could be found. Until a practical remedy could be determined, however, they argued for retaining fellowship with slaveholders who were otherwise pious. They concluded that Southern Christians and Southern states should be tolerated in ecclesiastical and political relations while they worked to improve Southern society through the spread of the gospel and Christian principles. They generally abhorred abolitionism as impractical, dangerous, and fanatical, for it would incite slaves to rebel against their masters and assault or murder them, and it would alienate the South from the good influences of fellowship with the North.

Most white Baptists in the South were proslavery. Two distinct forms of proslavery thought existed. In the Upper South, most white Baptists held a limited, qualified proslavery view. They held that slavery was morally permissible in principle but destructive of morals in practice. They argued that Christianity would leaven society sufficiently over time to emancipate all slaves. But they held that they must retain slavery until they found a good and workable solution to the problems emancipation would entail. This was the old Southern Evangelical view of slavery. It was the view of John Leland and many other early American Baptist preachers. It was also the view held by Thomas Jefferson and other Revolutionary War–era leaders. Richard Fuller's defense of slavery follows this approach.

The second form of proslavery was sometimes called "ultra proslavery." It was the belief that slavery was intrinsically good. It was good both in principle and practice. It was a moral, social, and political good for all persons in society, including slaves. Furthermore, it taught that the Federal Constitution protected the right to possess African slaves as legal property and prohibited any restrictions on slaveholding that did not apply to other forms of property. This position grew rapidly beginning in the 1830s and seems to be the common view in the Lower South by 1860. Patrick H. Mell's defense of slavery follows this approach.

Ultra proslavery adherents sometimes accused qualified proslavery Baptists of being abolitionists. The editor of *The South*, a Democratic party newspaper in Richmond, Virginia, accused Robert Ryland, the president of Virginia Baptists' Richmond College, of being an abolitionist in 1858. Ryland allegedly sowed the seed of abolitionism and sought to overthrow slavery by teaching its principles in the college, "implanting a spirit of northern fanaticism." Trustees of the college, students, and Baptist leaders vehemently denied the charges. Ryland frequently preached to large congregations of Blacks and, after the war, served two years as pastor for the African Baptist Church in Richmond, one of the largest Black churches in the nation. It was his preaching to slaves and free Blacks that rendered him odious to non-Evangelical proslavery leaders.[11]

---

[11] See James R. Graves, "The Richmond College Attacked," *Tennessee Baptist*, March 27, 1858, 2.

James M. Pendleton, a prominent Tennessee Baptist preacher who taught theology at Union University near Memphis, was similarly vilified as an abolitionist because he held the qualified proslavery view. In 1849 Pendleton advocated a gradual emancipation plan for Kentucky. He also supported the American Colonization Society, as many Northern and Southern Whigs did.

John Dawson, fellow Southern Baptist and editor of the *Southwestern Baptist* in Alabama, accused Pendleton of being an abolitionist in early 1860. Some political newspapers repeated the charge. Pendleton explained that he thought slavery should ultimately wither away and vanish, but he nevertheless had been a slaveholder and thought it likely that in the future he would be again. He did not believe slaveholding was intrinsically evil: "I never had a serious thought about emancipation in any state except Kentucky. I know of no practicable plan of emancipation for a state in which there is a large slave population. . . . I certainly have never believed slavery a sin, per se. . . . No man is further from being an abolitionist than I am. I would consider the abolitionist policy, if adopted, ruinous to the country. The best Christians I know are slaveholders, and my own mother is among the number. At her death I shall probably become a slaveholder."[12]

Pendleton held the same views as Richard Fuller, but Fuller's outraged many proslavery Baptists. "Before Dr. Fuller can expect his voice to be regarded by Southern Baptists on the slavery question," wrote Florida Baptist Maria Baker Taylor in 1860, "he must go back and retract his temporizing arguments."[13] For many white Southerners, including many Baptists, to fall short of the full orthodoxy of ultra proslavery was effectively to be an abolitionist.

---

[12] James M. Pendleton, "The Junior Editor," *Tennessee Baptist*, April 28, 1860, 2.

[13] Maria Baker Taylor, quoted in Kathryn Carlisle Schwartz, *Baptist Faith in Action: The Private Writings of Maria Baker Taylor, 1813–1895* (Columbia: University of South Carolina, 2003), 106.

Secession

Baptists disagreed about the cause of secession and the purpose of the war. Most Northern Baptists supported the war to preserve the union of the states and to punish rebellion. As the war progressed, more and more became convinced that the abolition of slavery was necessary. Francis Wayland came to this conclusion during the war. For Southern Baptists, the cause of sectional conflict, the secession, and the Civil War was first and foremost slavery. They appealed to the doctrine of state sovereignty as the mechanism guaranteeing the rights of individual states against such unconstitutional acts as restricting slavery. Secession was legal and necessary in order to protect the constitutional right to hold African slaves as property. Abolishing slavery would violate the Constitution by depriving owners of their property without the legal protections of due process. Secession was necessary to preserve slavery.

Jabez L. M. Curry urged Alabamans to vote in favor of secession on November 26, 1860, in Talladega. Southern whites were in grave peril, for the new Republican government would move quickly to abolish slavery everywhere. The real source of this peril, however, was not Abraham Lincoln or William Seward but the Northern people generally, whose fanatical anti-slavery beliefs resulted in Northern majorities polling for Lincoln. The "vox populi," Curry said, will require "the destruction of African slavery." Non-slaveholding Southern whites had as deep an interest in preserving slavery as slaveholders, Curry said. Slavery resolved the problems of class warfare between capitalists and the laboring class. Furthermore, if the slaves gained their liberty, a "war of extermination between the races" would likely ensue. "It is suicidal to defer action," Curry concluded. "The Republican party is a standing menace. Its success is a declaration of war against our property and the supremacy of the white race."[14]

---

[14] Jabez L. M. Curry, *Perils and Duty of the South: Substance of a Speech Delivered by Jabez L. M. Curry, in Talladega, Alabama, November 26, 1860* (Washington: L. Towers, 1860).

After Lincoln issued the Emancipation Proclamation in 1863, Samuel Boykin, a Georgia Baptist leader, viewed it as a vindication of the Southern argument from the beginning. Since the time of the election, Southerners justified secession on the claim that Lincoln would work to abolish slavery. "If there had ever, during this war, been any doubt as to the true issue between the North and South," Boykin said, "that doubt has been dispelled by the late message and proclamation of President Lincoln. Slavery is the only issue. The United States is fighting against the Confederate States for slavery. . . . If slavery be not of God, then we are fighting against Him, and our cause will fail; if it be of God, then our enemies are fighting against Him and we for Him and Truth."[15]

The Charleston Baptist Association met ten days after the election and affirmed the secession movement. They adopted five resolutions in order to express Baptist support for "our beloved Commonwealth," South Carolina. The first four resolutions addressed slavery. The first resolution affirmed their belief that "the institution of slavery, as existing among us, is sanctioned by the Sacred Scriptures." The second resolution affirmed the duty of Christians to separate from Christian abolitionists. The fourth resolution affirmed their duty of "resisting the encroachments of the enemies of our domestic institution"—that is, the enemies of slavery. Less than two weeks after the election, Charleston Baptists affirmed that the Bible sanctioned Southern slavery, that Christians had a duty to withdraw fellowship from professed Christians whose abolitionist agitation had divided the nation, and that it was their Christian and patriotic duty to resist "the encroachments of the enemies" of slavery.[16] James C. Furman, president of South Carolina Baptists' Furman University, gave stump speeches

---

[15] Samuel Boykin, "Slavery," *Christian Index*, December 25, 1863, 1.

[16] Charleston Baptist Association, *Minutes*, 1860, 4. Hard copies and microfilm facsimiles of these minutes are held by many libraries, including the Southern Baptist Historical Library and Archives and the Boyce Centennial Library of the Southern Baptist Theological Seminary.

supporting secession and won election overwhelmingly as a delegate to the state Secession Convention.[17]

Many white Baptists in the North opposed secession but sympathized with their Southern brethren. Likewise, many Southern Baptists opposed secession. Sam Houston, James Boyce, James Pendleton, and many others opposed secession not because they opposed slavery, but because they believed negotiations would preserve both the union and slavery. Boyce believed secession would result in a destructive war and the loss of slavery.

Virginia Baptist editor Jeremiah B. Jeter insisted that the North cease its "incessant agitation of the slavery question," but hoped for peaceful resolution. "I cling with great tenacity to the Union." Revolution was a perilous course. "It is easier to pull down than to build up. . . . When the spirit of discord is once fully aroused, who can slay it?"[18]

War, Patriotism, and Politics

After secession and the formation of the Confederate States of America, Baptist leaders enthusiastically aligned their faith and their patriotism. Southern Baptists called upon the faithful to support the Confederate cause. Northern Baptists called upon the faithful to support the Union cause.

By the time of the annual meeting of the Southern Baptist Convention in May 1861, nine slaveholding states had voted to secede from the United States of America and had established the Confederate States of America. In response to the loss of Fort Sumter and other federal forts and armories, Lincoln ordered the formation of a great army to put down the rebellion in the South, and Confederate president Jefferson Davis called for 400,000 soldiers to defend the South's independence. The gathered Southern Baptist leaders adopted a lengthy set of resolutions in support of the new nation.

---

[17] "Election Returns," *Southern Enterprise* (Greenville), December 13, 1860, 2.

[18] Jeremiah B. Jeter, *Jeremiah B. Jeter to John A. Broadus, December 11, 1860*, letter, from Southern Baptist Theological Seminary, *A. T. Robertson Papers*.

In view of the "lawless reign of terror at the North," the delegates said, "we most cordially approve of the formation of the Government of the Confederate States of America."[19]

The delegates recognized that misery and ruin would accompany their internecine war and that victory depended upon God's mercy. They urged Christians to humble themselves before God in fasting and prayer in order that "He may avert any calamities due to our sins as a people, and may look with mercy and favor upon us." They believed nevertheless that they stood upon truth and justice and, therefore, agreed to "pledge our fortunes and lives in the good work of repelling an invasion designed to destroy whatever is dear in our heroic traditions."[20]

Baptist preachers and editors throughout the South proclaimed the same message as the editors of Georgia Baptists' *Christian Index*: "Let the entire South, as one man, rise up and prepare for the conflict, assured that the victory shall be ours, for RIGHT and JUSTICE are with us, and where these are, there the God of battles presides and bestows his favors . . . for when right and liberty are assailed, religion tells us to take up the sword to defend heaven-bestowed privileges, and never, never, never to lay down our arms, while ruthless assailants and freedom-disregarding hosts pollute our soil or taint our atmosphere."[21]

Politics in wartime placed constraints on dissent. Criticism of leaders and policies could demoralize citizens and harm support of the war effort. Newspapers had to be careful how they addressed the serious problems facing the Confederate war effort. When Baptists mentioned problems publicly, they always did so with a morale-boosting statement of complete confidence in the South's ultimate victory.

---

[19] Southern Baptist Convention, *Minutes*, 1861, 63–64. The 1861 Annual of the Southern Baptist Convention is available at the Southern Baptist Historical Library and Archives at http://media2.sbhla.org.s3.amazonaws.com/annuals/SBC _Annual_1861.pdf.

[20] Southern Baptist Convention, 63–64.

[21] Samuel Boykin and C. M. Irwin, "War," *Christian Index*, May 15, 1861, 2.

The problems were legion. State governors pursued their own policies. The Confederate constitution gave the Confederate government little power in deference to the independent authority of each state. Governors opposed, delayed, altered, and rejected the requisitions imposed by the general government. The Confederate government requested more money and soldiers to prosecute the war but had little leverage to pressure governors to comply. Southern Baptist governor of Georgia, Joseph Brown, distrusted Confederate leadership and refused compliance with various Confederate directives on the plea that his state could not send the requested money and soldiers because the state's militia needed them.

Confederate fiscal policy was ineffective since it depended on persuading the state legislatures to support it. James P. Boyce devised a plan of raising the needed funds by issuing state bonds for the Confederate cause and persuaded the South Carolina legislature to adopt the measure. The Confederate government commissioned Boyce to accomplish the same feat in the other twelve state legislatures. The other states demurred.

Baptists denounced hoarders and war profiteers among the citizenry along with corruption and incompetence in the government and military. The chaplains found more drunkenness, gambling, and prostitution than revival in army camps.[22] The former matters disheartened the people, so Baptist leaders reported on preaching the gospel, spiritual interest, and conversions and baptisms. Baptist leaders, in public at least, were unwavering patriots of the Confederate cause to the bitter end.

God's Judgment or Blessing

Baptists disagreed on the extent to which they proclaimed the righteousness of their cause. Some Baptists in the South recognized the war was divine judgment for their sins. Seven weeks before the bombardment of Fort

---

[22] See James L. Reynolds, "National Declension," *Confederate Baptist*, June 17, 1863, 2; James L. Reynolds, "Secular News," *Confederate Baptist*, July 22, 1863, 3.

Sumter, Basil Manly Jr. lamented that the imprudence of many in the South rendered open warfare unavoidable. He was a slaveholder and a secessionist, but he believed God appeared to be preparing to pour out his wrath upon the South. "It may be a cup of wrath for our sins, in which he has mingled these elements of confusion and misery."[23]

White Southern Baptist clergy often viewed the war and the suffering it entailed as God's judgment upon the South for its sins. Texas Baptists in 1861 reported the churches were in a "cold and apparently lifeless condition." Church members seemed to lack "brotherly affection, a love to God and delight in his worship, and an ardent and self-sacrificing spirit for the glory of Christ and the salvation of souls." Secession, war, and their entailments, "our national calamities, instead of driving us nearer to God, seem rather to distract and draw the public mind away from His house and worship." The people of God were not humbling themselves before God.[24]

Texas Baptists in 1862 were confident God was judging the South for not providing for the spiritual needs of slaves. "It must be clear to every Christian mind that God is angry with us as a people for some great and general sin or sins, and as it cannot be wrong to own slaves, may it not be that much of our present deep affliction is a manifestation of God's displeasure against us for our neglect to furnish the slaves that are among us the means of gospel grace, by which their souls may be saved?"[25]

Other Baptist leaders saw no need for humility and confession. They were confident the South would prevail because Southerners were innocent in matters of the national political compact and because the South would fight for honor. Robert B. C. Howell, the highly respected pastor

---

[23] Basil Manly Jr., *Basil Manly Jr. to Parents [Sarah Manly and Basil Manly Sr.], February 23, 1861*, letter, from Southern Historical Collection (UNC), *Basil Manly Papers*.

[24] Baptist State Convention of Texas, *Minutes*, 1861 (Houston: Texas Printing House, 1863), 8.

[25] Baptist State Convention of Texas, *Minutes*, 1862 (Houston: Texas Printing House, 1863), 6.

of the First Baptist Church of Nashville, Tennessee, told his church that Southern soldiers were motivated by their religion as well as their patriotism and would therefore die before permitting the enemy to invade Southern homes. "Fail! No, never. Our armies conquered! Our country subjected! Our land overrun and desolate! You have determined not to survive such a dishonor." Howell called on "every man, woman, and child" to imitate the ancient Romans, who preferred to die for their country than to submit. With such resolve, the South might be overrun, but Southerners would never yield. "We cannot be conquered."[26] Within two months the Union Army had overrun the two great forts protecting Nashville, captured 12,000 Confederate soldiers, and occupied the city.

Baptists and Their Critics

White and Black abolitionists criticized white Baptists for supporting slavery. William Lloyd Garrison, for example, criticized all denominations and frequently covered the various ways in which Baptists defended slavery. Garrison was especially critical of Baptists in free states who nevertheless defended slavery or refused to condemn it, or else condemned it but refused to withdraw fellowship from slaveholding Christians. Black Baptist preachers criticized their white counterparts for their proslavery and white supremacist views.

At the same time, many Southern whites considered Baptists untrustworthy regarding slavery. Baptists' evangelical religion drove them to preach to slaves, baptize Black converts, and welcome them into their churches as spiritual equals of the white members. Many whites held that such regard for the souls of slaves contributed to discontent among slaves. Baptists instructed and ordained Black preachers, who exercised great influence over the Black membership of the church. They favored teaching Black preachers

---

[26] Rufus B. Spain, "R. B. C. Howell: Nashville Baptist Leader in the Civil War Period," *Tennessee Historical Quarterly* 14, no. 4 (1955): 333–34.

to read. But slaves who could read were susceptible to abolitionist fanaticism. Black preachers were generally found at the forefront of slave insurrections. The slave insurrection in Jamaica, for that reason, became known there as the "Baptist War." And some white Baptist preachers in the nation's early decades had denounced slavery.

Southern whites generally thought Baptists held slaves in too high a regard. Baptists argued that slaveholders needed to do more to evangelize their slaves and care for their eternal souls and that the Bible required slaveholders to treat slaves with humanity and justice. Such exhortations, however, suggested that many slaveholders did not care for the souls or the bodies of their slaves. It gave abolitionists "evidence" of the ill treatment of slaves in the South. When the accomplished Charlottesville preacher John A. Broadus gave a lecture in Richmond on the duty of benevolent treatment of slaves, the editor of the Richmond *Dispatch* refused to advertise the talk or report on it.[27]

When Baptists complained that the failure to evangelize slaves was one of the reasons God in his providence brought "this war of punishment" upon the South, other Southern whites held that the propagation of Christianity among the slaves endangered lives and jeopardized the entire social order. The Blacks who had planned or led rebellions often appealed to the Scriptures and employed biblical imagery and language. Although Southern evangelicals characterized abolitionism as intrinsically atheistic and anti-Christian, English and Northern abolitionists included large numbers of evangelicals. William Lloyd Garrison criticized the churches for their complicity in slavery but at the same time employed biblical imagery and language in the very masthead of his newspaper, *The Liberator*. Black abolitionists likewise generally appealed to the Scriptures to support abolition.

Small wonder then that many Southern whites suspected that propagating Christianity and knowledge of the Bible among slaves was dangerous. It

---

[27] Jeremiah B. Jeter, *Jeremiah B. Jeter to John A. Broadus, February 21, 1859*, letter, from Southern Baptist Theological Seminary, *A. T. Robertson Papers*.

would tend, they believed, to make slaves discontent with their condition and more liable to rebel. In many places, therefore, whites in large numbers supported legislation that restricted freedom of religion among Blacks. Most white Baptists during the Civil War opposed all such restrictions. Samuel Boykin, editor of Georgia Baptists' newspaper, criticized "the Georgia Code, which prohibits slaves from preaching or exhorting." It is a violation of the sacred right of religious liberty, for it was an "assumption of power, by the civil over the ecclesiastical, to which it would be vain to expect submission on the part of Southern Christians."[28]

The Baptist Legacy

One Baptist legacy of the Civil War was the consolidation of the Southern identity of the border states. Baptist churches in Missouri, Kentucky, and Maryland opted to identify with the Southern Baptist Convention rather than the Northern Baptists. Methodists and Presbyterians in these states followed the same pattern. One of the factors was surely the harshness of military governments in these states. Pro-secession churches were confiscated, and pro-secession newspapers were suppressed. Pastors who did not fly the Stars and Stripes in their churches or did not pray publicly for Union leaders were held in suspicion and at times arrested.

Another Baptist legacy from the Civil War period was the establishment of party identifications. The overwhelming majority of Black Baptists throughout the nation identified with the Republican party, although they often criticized the party's modest response to their concerns. They sometimes cooperated in forming "fusion" tickets in which white Republicans and splinter Democrats cooperated.

---

[28] Samuel Boykin, "Repeal of an Unjust Law," *Christian Index*, April 6, 1863, 2. See also Visitor, "Fast Day Exercises in Milledgeville, Georgia," *Christian Index*, April 6, 1863, 1.

White Baptists in the North probably were divided in party identification. There is no obvious reason to expect them to have differed from the Northern white populace generally. Class was probably a more important predictor of party affiliation than religious identity. Yet white Baptists in the South aligned strongly with the Democrats. Baptists, like Southern whites generally, advocated white supremacy and supported the efforts of Democrats to control and discourage Black voting until they could pass state legislation to suppress it wholesale. White Baptist clergy opposed the gross violence and hatred that often accompanied white supremacy campaigns, but they acquiesced outwardly even if disquieted inwardly.

The experience of secession and the war seems to have boosted Baptists' sense of Christian nationalism. The effect is hard to measure since Christian nationalism was already an important part of the religious identity of most Baptists. For Northern Baptists, the ultimate victory over slavery and the preservation of the Republic seemed to confirm their belief that God had established the United States to advance Christian civilization along with the Christian faith, liberty and democracy, education, and free trade.

Black Baptists experienced repeated disillusionment with American nationalism. The ideals of human equality expressed in the Declaration of Independence and the guarantees of equality enshrined in the thirteenth, fourteenth, and fifteenth amendments nurtured hope of progress toward actual political and social equality. Within a few short years of the Union victory and emancipation, most American whites, however, advocated or accepted various forms of discrimination against Blacks. Some Black Baptists developed forms of Black nationalism. Most, however, advocated a Christian nationalism that retained hope in the nation's founding ideals and emphasized the awakening of the social conscience of the nation.

White Baptists in the South developed a form of Christian nationalism that emphasized the central role of the South in redeeming the nation. In God's mysterious providence, he brought the South through the crucible of military defeat and economic privation in order to purify it of slaveholding and worldliness and to preserve it from the errors that were undermining the church in Europe and in the North. God had chosen the Southern church to redeem the nation and America to redeem the world.

The Southern version of Christian nationalism was predicated substantially on the Myth of the Lost Cause, which asserts that the Confederates never had a chance of winning the war. This is perhaps the substantial political and cultural legacy of the Civil War. Lost Cause mythology was not confined to the South, but it became popular among whites throughout the nation from the late nineteenth century and endures to the present. Southern Baptist clergy played an important role in developing and popularizing the Lost Cause.

Jabez Curry wrote several popular books advancing the Lost Cause. Curry and other Baptist advocates of the Lost Cause aimed to restore the honor of the South. They advanced the following assertions: White Southerners were patriots, not rebels. They, not the radical Republicans, were the true defenders of the federal Constitution. Slavery was not immoral and treated its laborers better than other systems of labor. The signers of the Declaration of Independence had never intended to include Africans in its declaration of equal rights. The Constitution required the protection of slave property in all territories and states, and the Fugitive Slave Act was a constitutional protection of Southern property rights.

At the same time, Curry argued that "the introduction and continuance of African slavery" was "the greatest curse that ever afflicted the South." White Southerners were slaveholders not by choice but by imposition. Slavery was not the cause of secession and the Civil War: "Slavery was rather the occasion." Since the war, Southern whites dealt justly and generously with Blacks and placed no obstacles in the way of Black advancement. But the radical Republicans did grave injury to Blacks by imposing voting rights on Blacks and urging them to exercise authority over whites.[29]

---

[29] Jabez L. M. Curry, *The Southern States of the American Union* (Richmond: B. F. Johnson, 1895), 4, 209–48.

J. William Jones, who spent most of the Civil War employed as a Southern Baptist missionary preacher among the Confederate armies in Virginia, was a veritable "apostle of the Lost Cause." He wrote popular biographies of Robert E. Lee, Jefferson Davis, and Stonewall Jackson and spearheaded an effort to vindicate the South by writing history from the perspective of its righteous cause in seceding from the Union, its honorable and glorious prosecution of war, and its noble and righteous suffering during Reconstruction.[30]

The most successful promoter of the Lost Cause was Thomas Dixon Jr., whose popular novels *The Leopard's Spots* (1902) and *The Clansman* (1905), became the basis of the blockbuster movie, *The Birth of a Nation* (1915). Dixon began his career as a Southern Baptist preacher.

From the perspective of the leaders of this Southern Baptist nationalism, the United States alone could save the world by spreading true Christian civilization. The South alone could save the United States. And Southern Baptists were best adapted by God to save the South.

---

[30] Christopher C. Moore, *Apostle of the Lost Cause: J. William Jones, Baptists, and the Development of Confederate Memory* (Knoxville: University of Tennessee, 2019).

11

Progressive Baptists: The Activist Faith of Walter Rauschenbusch, Henlee Barnette, and James Dunn

By Aaron Douglas Weaver

For more than 100 years, a progressive wing has existed within the American Baptist tradition. This progressivism has taken different shapes and forms over the decades with diverse theological and political commitments. While lacking a cohesive identity in many respects, these progressive Baptists have been united through a shared belief in the Social Gospel and the conviction that Christianity must be an activist faith lived daily in the world on behalf of others.

In *A Genealogy of Dissent: Southern Baptist Protest in the Twentieth Century* (1999), historian David Stricklin describes and gives voice to an important group of progressive Baptists. He uncovers a "progressive, reformist tradition" within Southern Baptist life composed of Social Gospel proponents.

These progressive Baptists were varied in their interests—included among them were civil rights advocates, labor organizers, peace activists, and champions of women's equality in church and society.[1] This subversive tribe of progressive dissenters featured well-known Southern Baptists like Clarence Jordan and Carlyle Marney alongside lesser-known pastors and laity. They were often viewed as irritants to establishment leaders like Foy Valentine, executive director of the Southern Baptist Convention (SBC) Christian Life Commission from 1960–1987. Their impact was limited due, in part, to their denominational outsider status, often chafing at traditional SBC structures and institutions.[2]

Progressives in Southern Baptist life were not only outsiders. There were indeed notable progressive Baptists who chose to participate and exert their influence within SBC structures and institutions, seeking to reform and shape the future of their denominational home. With an insider status, these progressive Baptists pushed pastors and lay leaders to address social concerns with the same enthusiasm and level of support they had for evangelism and matters of traditional morality. They desired to see their Southern denomination live into scriptural expressions of justice, love, and freedom.

This chapter explores the political theology of two key progressive Baptists during this period: Henlee Barnette, a trailblazing ethicist from the 1950s until his "retirement" in the late 1970s, and James Dunn, the denomination's chief religious liberty watchdog and church-state separation defender during the pivotal 1980s. The ministries of both men were not immune from theological and political controversies. Barnette and Dunn were neither conservative inerrantists nor liberal modernists in their theologies. Rather, both advanced an ethic rooted in scriptural arguments

---

[1] David Stricklin, *A Genealogy of Dissent: Southern Baptist Protest in the Twentieth Century* (Lexington: University of Kentucky, 1999), 6–7.

[2] Stricklin, 74–77. Stricklin argues that Valentine, after serving as the "conscience" of Southern Baptists on racial equality issues during the 1960s, became in the 1970s and 1980s a "symbol of mainstream Southern Baptists, that of a denominational bureaucrat."

that put Jesus Christ as the foundation and final word on matters of faith and practice.

Additionally, this chapter overviews and assesses the political theology and contributions of Walter Rauschenbusch, regarded as the father of the Social Gospel movement and certainly its most successful advocate. As a Northern Baptist, his writings and witness helped to inspire and form the progressive Baptist tradition and had an obvious impact on the ethical thinking of both Barnette, who wrote his doctoral dissertation on Rauschenbusch, and Dunn, who closely studied and frequently cited the Social Gospel leader throughout his ministry. Rauschenbusch and his political theology are a necessary lens through which to fully understand progressive Baptists.

Walter Rauschenbusch (1861–1918)

Walter Rauschenbusch was the most visible and effective proponent of the Social Gospel during the late nineteenth and early twentieth centuries. Equipped with a theology centered on the ethical teachings of Jesus Christ, he championed the transformation of the American economic system in order to realize the kingdom of God on earth. Capitalism—based on selfishness and greed in his view—was responsible for the poverty and immense suffering of destitute immigrant workers in New York City and other major cities. Churches had failed to address these social sins and were theologically incapable of doing so due to an incomplete theology of salvation that emphasized only the individual and ignored the necessity of social redemption. This is the message that made Rauschenbusch, a Baptist pastor turned public theologian, one of the most significant and influential religious thinkers of his day.

Born in Rochester, New York, on October 4, 1861, at the outset of the Civil War, Rauschenbusch was the son of a pietist Lutheran pastor. August Rauschenbusch was a German immigrant who moved to the Midwest to do mission work among other immigrants with the American Tract Society before becoming a Baptist and pastoring a German Baptist church. Walter grew up in Rochester, where August had relocated the family in 1858 to teach at Baptist-affiliated Rochester Theological Seminary. Following high school, he studied four years in Germany, then returned to the US to begin his studies at the University of Rochester as well as the seminary where he was exposed to the liberal intellectual developments of the late nineteenth century, including evolutionary theories, the scientific method, and historical-critical methods of biblical studies and church history.[3] These developments shaped Rauschenbusch's theology as he embraced historical criticism and the New Theology, which criticized traditional Protestant doctrines like the substitutionary view of atonement and placed a heightened and simplified emphasis on ethical teachings of Jesus—love for God and neighbor.[4]

While in seminary, Rauschenbusch spent two summers as pastor of a German Baptist congregation in Louisville, Kentucky, and after graduation he accepted a call to Second German Baptist Church in New York City. His church was in Hell's Kitchen, a neighborhood in Manhattan noted for gangs, prostitution, and gambling and surrounded by overcrowded tenements and factories rife with dangerous working conditions. The characteristics of this urban context included high unemployment, malnutrition and hunger, alcohol abuse, crime, deadly diseases like tuberculosis, and staggering economic inequality and exploitation of the working class—an environment that shaped Rauschenbusch's view of society.[5]

---

[3] Paul Lewis, "Walter Rauschenbusch: Pioneer of Baptist Social Ethics," in *Twentieth-Century Shapers of Baptist Social Ethics*, ed. Larry L. McSwain (Macon: Mercer University, 2008), 4. Over the last thirty years, two major biographies have been published on Rauschenbusch. See Paul M. Minus, *Walter Rauschenbusch: American Reformer* (New York: Macmillan, 1988), and Christopher Evans, *The Kingdom Is Always but Coming: A Life of Walter Rauschenbusch* (Grand Rapids: Eerdmans, 2004).

[4] William L. Pitts Jr., *The Reception of Rauschenbusch: The Responses of His Earliest Readers* (Macon: Mercer University, 2018), 18–22, 27–28.

[5] Lewis, "Walter Rauschenbusch," 5. See also Pitts, *The Reception*, 29–30. Scholars have noted that he was especially shaken by the task of preaching funerals for young children who passed away from poverty-related illnesses.

To better equip himself to meet the needs of his congregation and city, Rauschenbusch began an extensive study of the writings of the leading sociologists, Social Gospelers such as Washington Gladden and Josiah Strong, and economists like Richard Ely. He came to gain an appreciation for the Christian Socialist movement in Europe. Aware of the fears and stigma associated with the "Socialist" label in the US and its association with atheism, Rauschenbusch chose not to join the Socialist party. Rather, he identified with many of its goals and, according to historian William Pitts, "took a middle path between radicalism and capitalism as practiced in the United States" as he believed both Socialism and Christianity "stood for caring for other people."[6]

In 1891, Rauschenbusch's church granted him a sabbatical in Germany, where he drafted his first book, *Christianity Revolutionary*. While not published until decades after his death, this writing gives a glimpse of Rauschenbusch's early views on social Christianity: that Jesus had come to establish the kingdom of God on earth. Embracing the optimism of the era that was reflected in postmillennialism, he urged Christians to work for the kingdom through social reconstruction, but acknowledged the kingdom is never fully realized.[7] Following his return to the US, Rauschenbusch met and married Pauline Rother and the couple had five children together. After an eleven-year pastoral ministry, Rauschenbusch joined the faculty of his alma mater Rochester Theological Seminary in 1897, initially in the German department and, in 1902, the church history department. He was a popular professor who was regarded as accessible to his students and known as an activist in the local politics of Rochester, even as he gained national acclaim for his Social Gospel writings.[8]

---

[6] Pitts, *The Reception*, 44–45.

[7] Walter Rauschenbusch, "The New Evangelism," in *Walter Rauschenbusch: Selected Writings*, ed. Winthrop Hudson (Mahwah: Paulist, 1984), 138.

[8] Lewis, "Walter Rauschenbusch," 6–7.

In 1907, Rauschenbusch's *Christianity and the Social Crisis* was published and quickly received critical acclaim, becoming a bestseller and the top religious book in America for three years with multiple reprints and translations. Scholars have heralded the book as the chief manifesto of the Social Gospel and its most powerful expression, and it was published as the Progressive movement was gaining power in American politics.[9] According to ethicist Gary Dorrien, *Christianity and the Social Crisis* convinced thousands of pastors, academics, activists, and even religious institutions like the Federal Council of Churches to embrace the Social Gospel.[10]

In *Christianity and the Social Crisis,* Rauschenbusch advocated for a return to what he described as the essence of Christianity—an understanding of Jesus situated in his cultural and religious context and focused on Jesus's central teaching of the kingdom of God. To recover this "original Christianity," Rauschenbusch found biblical support in the Old Testament prophets who "demanded right moral conduct as the sole test and fruit of religion, and that the morality which they had in mind was not the private morality of detached pious souls but the social morality of the nation."[11] The prophets stood with the poor and against the injustices perpetuated by the powerful, he argued, noting they "have the satisfaction of knowing that the world must come their way whether it will or not, because they are on the way to justice, and justice is on the way to God."[12]

Recovering Jesus's message of the kingdom of God was the heart of Rauschenbusch's political theology. The process to get Christians to embrace the "social aims" of Christ, to shift from an individualistic to a social understanding of the Christian faith, was a project that would span decades, but the revolutionary social movement was no less significant than the Protestant

---

[9] Pitts, *The Reception*, 75.

[10] Gary Dorrien, *Soul in Society: The Making and Renewal of Social Christianity* (Minneapolis: Fortress, 1995), 41.

[11] Walter Rauschenbusch, *Christianity and the Social* Crisis (Louisville: Westminster/John Knox, 1991), 11.

[12] Rauschenbusch, 40–41.

Reformation of the sixteenth century, he contended.[13] "The fundamental purpose of Jesus was the establishment of the Kingdom of God, which involved a thorough regeneration and reconstitution of social life. Primitive Christianity cherished an ardent hope of a radically new era, and within its limits sought to realize a social life on a new moral basis," he noted. It was the duty of the church to "change the world-as-it-is into the world-as-it-ought-to-be."[14] He argued that the early church had pledged to do just this, but its revolutionary beginnings were sidetracked due to apocalyptic expectations, state persecution, and pursuit of ascetic ideals. Eventually, this central teaching of Jesus—the kingdom of God—was obscured and receded as a focal point for the church.[15]

While Rauschenbusch did focus most of his attention on the social dimensions of Christianity in contrast to the traditional emphasis on individual salvation, he also affirmed the necessity of personal conversion. His vision called for both the redemption of individuals and the redemption of society shared by individuals, which were both necessary to be faithful to Jesus's message of the kingdom of God. Pitts notes that "[Rauschenbusch's] strategy was not to deny the importance of individual salvation, but to affirm it and build on it—to bring to consciousness the mandate to transform society. It was a noble ideal but it was not so readily followed."[16]

Rauschenbusch followed this bestseller with a second major work titled *Christianizing the Social Order* (1912), which offers a sociological analysis of the problems the country faced and specific proposals on how to better align all sectors and institutions of the US with his understanding of Christianity. What Rauschenbusch proposed was to make the US more Christian—not as a theocracy, which would have been opposed to his Baptist views on religious freedom. Rather than a separation of religion and politics, he desired

---

[13] Rauschenbusch, 46.
[14] Rauschenbusch, 143.
[15] Rauschenbusch, 143.
[16] Pitts, *The Reception*, 75.

a social order that was "[brought] into harmony with the ethical convictions which we identify with Christianity."[17] He explained that "an unchristian social order can be known by the fact that it makes good men do bad things" and "a Christian social order makes bad men do good things."[18]

Rauschenbusch's primary aim was to redeem the American economy, which was characterized by an aggressive capitalism and wealthy elite called "robber barons," who exploited immigrant workers, children included, with dangerous working conditions, low wages, excessive hours, and unhealthy, cramped living quarters. While the new rich class celebrated their abundance with lavish homes and parties, dubbed "conspicuous consumption," the urban centers of America's major cities like New York City were rife with widespread poverty.[19] He emphasized that while the political system was governed through a system of checks and balances, the economic system was essentially unregulated to the detriment of humankind. Materialism had become the highest value of society, he argued. "When we try to keep both [Christ and Mammon] enthroned at the same time in different sectors of our life, we do what Christ says cannot be done," he wrote.[20] Rauschenbusch envisioned a cooperative economic system based on justice, collective property rights, democracy, and human equality that would eventually replace the corporate capitalism of the day.[21]

In 1916, Rauschenbusch's *The Social Principles of Jesus* was published. Designed as a pocket-sized textbook for college students, the volume featured twelve short chapters—each with a Bible reading, commentary, and discussion questions. As the title suggests, this accessible volume was focused on social concerns and the practical application of Jesus's principles to achieve

[17] Walter Rauschenbusch, *Christianizing the Social Order* (New York: Macmillan, 1912), 125.

[18] Rauschenbusch, 127.

[19] Pitts, *The Reception*, 31–33.

[20] Pitts, 315.

[21] Pitts, 435.

a more Christian society in pursuit of the kingdom of God.[22] His last major work, *A Theology for the Social Gospel* (1917), outlined a systematic theology to sustain the Social Gospel. He reiterated his earlier theme that the traditional focus on individual salvation was important but not complete. Christian theology needed an "adjustment" to also affirm a social conception of salvation. Additionally, the doctrine of sin was the other essential doctrine that needed an adjustment in modern society. Sin is selfishness in relation to others, and thus, the nature of sin is social, he argued. "Sin is lodged in customs and institutions . . . [and] runs down the generations," he wrote.[23] He employed the phrase "kingdom of evil" to capture this social character of sin. The Social Gospel sought the "eradication of sin and the fulfillment of the mission of redemption," according to Rauschenbusch.[24]

Following the publication of *Christianity and the Social Crisis* in 1907 until his death in 1918, Rauschenbusch was viewed as one of the most important Protestant leaders in America. He had become a public theologian whom national political leaders sought for counsel, including Theodore Roosevelt, Woodrow Wilson, and Eugene Debs and social reformers like Jacob Riis. Rauschenbusch published widely in popular periodicals, was quoted in secular and denominational newspapers, and spoke frequently in the northeastern United States.[25]

Although Rauschenbusch achieved national recognition as an influential Protestant voice, he also articulated and embraced his identity as a Baptist. He was an advocate for the Baptist tradition by participating in the local Baptist Ministers' Conference (New York City), attending the Baptist Congress (a gathering of progressive Baptists), and in 1911

---

[22] Walter Rauschenbusch, *The Social Principles of Jesus* (London: International Committee of Young Men's Christian Association, 1916).

[23] Walter Rauschenbusch, *A Theology for the Social Gospel* (Louisville: Westminster/John Knox, 1997), 60–61.

[24] Rauschenbusch, 31.

[25] Pitts, *The Reception*, 189–92.

addressing the quinquennium meeting of the Baptist World Alliance.[26] From 1905–1906, he wrote a series of articles titled "Why I Am a Baptist," which lauded Baptist principles of church freedom ("Christian democracies"), church-state separation, and a rejection of creeds. "I am a Baptist, then, because in our church life we have a minimum emphasis on ritual and creed, and a maximum of emphasis on spiritual experience," he wrote.[27]

Rauschenbusch's reach extended well beyond his lifetime and impacted future generations, including leading progressive Baptists during the second half of the twentieth century such as pioneer ethicist Henlee Barnette and religious liberty advocate James Dunn. Baylor University historian William Pitts recently traced the influence of Rauschenbusch in *The Reception of Rauschenbusch: The Responses of His Earliest Readers.* Indeed, Rauschenbusch's books are still read today and studied in seminary classrooms and graduate seminars throughout the US. While his Social Gospel vision was woefully incomplete for its failure to address the inequalities women endured and the rampant injustices African Americans faced, its inability to take hold in future generations, and its excessive optimism, Rauschenbusch's message still resonated deeply with Black scholars like Dr. Benjamin Mays, president of Morehouse College, who published an anthology of Rauschenbusch's works, and Mays's student Dr. Martin Luther King Jr., who wrote that *Christianity and the Social Crisis* had a profound influence on his faith and practice.[28]

---

[26] Pitts, 132–33, 151–53.

[27] Walter Rauschenbusch, "Why I Am a Baptist" (originally published in *Rochester Baptist Monthly*, 1905–1906), accessed February 13, 2021, https://trippfuller.com/2007/01/23/rauschenbusch-why-i-am-a-baptist/.

[28] See Martin Luther King Jr., "Pilgrimage to Nonviolence," *Christian Century*, April 13, 1960, https://www.christiancentury.org/article/pilgrimage-nonviolence. See also Pitts, *The Reception*, 326. Rauschenbusch condemned slavery and present-day lynchings. He knew of African American suffering but lacked solutions. He was exclusively focused on his context of the suffering of immigrant workers.

Henlee Barnette (1911–2004)

Henlee Barnette was a pioneer Baptist ethicist whose teaching ministry, spanning four decades, had an immeasurable influence on the ethical formation of multiple generations of Southern Baptist pastors and professors. His more than a dozen books spanned diverse subjects, ranging from the environment to drug addiction to bioethics to communism; he also wrote hundreds of popular columns in denominational publications that reached millions. First and foremost, he was an activist for racial equality amid the Jim Crow South. With an ethic focused on agape love, Barnette's ministry also led him to advocate for women's equality, peace, the rights of conscientious objectors, and environmental stewardship.

Born August 14, 1911, in a one-room cabin in Taylorsville, North Carolina, Barnette dropped out of school in the sixth grade and began working long hours at a textile mill in Kannapolis. His mother and older sister were committed churchgoers; Barnette and his father were not. As a nineteen–year-old, Barnette attended a revival service with his father, and both made professions of faith. Less than a year after being baptized, Barnette was licensed to preach and later was nicknamed the "Bible Preacher" for his extensive quotation of Scripture from the pulpit. He returned to complete high school in 1933 at age twenty-two, and at the age of twenty-six, enrolled at Wake Forest College, while continuing to pastor local Baptist churches.[29]

The next stop on his educational journey was the Southern Baptist Theological Seminary (SBTS) in Louisville, Kentucky, where he was mentored by Olin T. Binkley, a former student of renowned ethicist H. Richard Niebuhr. Binkley introduced Barnette to the Christian realism of Niebuhr and the Social Gospel theology of Rauschenbusch—the eventual subject of his dissertation. The influence and tension between the realism of Niebuhr and the idealism of Rauschenbusch would shape Barnette's approach to

---

[29] Henlee Hulix Barnette, *A Pilgrimage of Faith: My Story* (Macon: Mercer University, 2004), 25–29.

ethics. As a seminarian, inspired by progressive Baptist social reformer Clarence Jordan, Barnette made an intentional effort to live out what he learned in the classroom as a minister in Louisville's large slum area known as the "Haymarket." This ministry experience was significant in forming his activist-oriented ethic.[30]

In 1946, Barnette began his teaching ministry at Baptist-affiliated Howard College (now Samford University) in Birmingham, Alabama. After just one year, he left Howard to teach sociology at another Baptist school, Stetson College in DeLand, Florida. Barnette returned to Louisville four years later to join his mentor, Binkley, as a professor of Christian ethics at SBTS. During his tenure at the seminary from 1951–1977, Barnette earned a reputation as the denomination's leading ethicist alongside T. B. Maston of Southwestern Baptist Theological Seminary in Fort Worth, Texas. Following his "retirement" from SBTS, Barnette taught medical ethics for an additional fifteen years as a professor at the University of Louisville from 1977 to 1992. He passed away in 2004 at the age of 93.[31]

Barnette was an activist in an era when activism was frowned upon and uncommon in Southern Baptist life. He believed Jesus offered fundamental principles that should inform the political engagement of Christians. Barnette preached, wrote, and taught that Christians, as individuals and congregations, had a biblical responsibility to cooperate with the state in promoting human welfare and justice in society, and he encouraged his students to be actively involved in the political process at all levels. He also called on churches to urge their members to do the same.

---

[30] Ronald D. Sisk, "Henlee Hulix Barnette: Principalist in the Southern Seminary Tradition," in *Twentieth Century Shapers of Baptist Social Ethics*, ed. Larry McSwain (Macon: Mercer University, 2008), 82–85. Barnette was inspired to begin working in Louisville's "Haymarket" district after hearing a chapel sermon by Baptist gadfly Clarence Jordan, founder of Koinonia Farm. See Henlee Barnette, *Clarence Jordan: Turning Dreams into Deeds* (Macon: Smyth and Helwys, 1992).

[31] David Winfrey, "Pioneer Baptist Ethicist Henlee Barnette Dies at 93," *Associated Baptist Press*, October 22, 2004.

With all the social issues he confronted, Barnette rooted his ethical method in the teachings of Jesus Christ about love. He affirmed agape love as the ultimate authority for moral concern and action. "Love (*agape*) is the central motif of the Christian faith," Barnette wrote in his widely read *Crucial Problems in Christian Perspective*, defining "agape" as "spontaneous good will which seeks the highest good of every man."[32] This agape principle was his guide to decision-making. In contrast to Joseph Fletcher's situational love ethic, Barnette contended that the primary principles of biblical ethics—love and justice—were "inseparable." "Justice is love in action in all areas of human existence," he wrote.[33]

The mission of the church, in Barnette's understanding, is to represent Christ's society-transforming agape ethic to the world, demonstrating the gospel to be personal as well as social. "Personal regeneration and public reconstruction are the goals of the gospel," he wrote. "We must work at both of these simultaneously. It is unrealistic to try to transform the world into the Kingdom of God without transformed people."[34] Barnette emphasized the power of the Holy Spirit to bring individuals to a "new life in Christ" and experience the same type of transformation he had as a nineteen-year-old mill worker.

He sought to apply this agape ethic in the public square through activism at the local, state, and national levels, marching against segregation and voting restrictions and emerging as a significant shaper of the attitudes of some Southern Baptists toward support for racial equality. While a professor in Birmingham in 1946, Barnette helped establish an interracial organization for Baptist pastors, and the group's first gathering was headlined by Benjamin Mays, noted civil rights advocate and president of Morehouse

---

[32] Henlee Barnette, *Crucial Problems in Christian Perspective* (Philadelphia: Westminster, 1970), 59, 133.

[33] Barnette, 18.

[34] Henlee H. Barnette, "The Glorious Gospel," *Southwestern Journal of Theology* 34, no. 3 (Summer 1992): 5.

College. The presence of white and Black pastors and laymen under one roof was a historic occasion—and an act of civil disobedience under Alabama law. This was a pivotal step into a ministry of activism for Barnette.[35]

Back in Louisville in 1951 at SBTS, Barnette's advocacy for racial equality and justice became more visible. He introduced new courses on race relations and formed friendships with Black churches in the area. Before the Supreme Court issued its landmark *Brown v. Board of Education* ruling in 1954, mandating the desegregation of public schools, he was forcefully urging the integration of Southern Baptist colleges and seminaries. Barnette even called for the excommunication of unrepentant racist congregations.[36]

Undoubtedly, his boldest and certainly most controversial action was to bring Martin Luther King Jr. to SBTS to give the Julius B. Gay lectures in 1961. King's visit came at a tumultuous time as the city of Louisville was in the middle of a civil rights struggle with protestors demonstrating to integrate public facilities and Black students engaging in sit-ins at whites-only restaurants. The racial tension in the community was palpable. Not surprisingly, King's visit attracted extensive media coverage and prompted a severe reaction across the denomination.[37] While the seminary's faculty, staff, and students welcomed King, many SBC leaders and pastors expressed their anger, and churches threatened to withhold financial support of the school—at least six congregations in Alabama made good on their threat.[38]

-----

[35] S. Jonathan Bass, *Blessed Are the Peacemakers* (Baton Rouge: Louisiana State University, 2001), 15.

[36] Frank Stagg, "Henlee Hulix Barnette: An Activist," *Christian Ethics Today*, no. 12 (1997): 15–16. See also Henlee Barnette, "Negro Students in Southern Baptist Seminaries," *Review and Expositor* 53, no. 2 (April 1956): 210.

[37] Henlee Barnette, "The Southern Baptist Theological Seminary and the Civil Rights Movement: The Visit of Martin Luther King, Jr., Part Two," *Review and Expositor* 93 (Winter 1996): 79.

[38] Barnette, 77–126.

Despite the intense backlash, Barnette was not deterred. He went on to serve as a founding member of the Kentucky Christian Leadership Conference, a state affiliate of King's civil rights organization, the Southern Christian Leadership Conference. He also coauthored the KCLC's constitution with King's brother and Louisville pastor, A. D. Williams King. A participant in freedom marches, Barnette linked up with King again, three years after his seminary address, at the state capitol in Frankfort at a march for desegregated housing. The following year, Barnette took part in "Operation Selma" at Louisville's Broadway Temple AME Zion Church, where he spoke and helped raise funds for the now historic voting rights march in 1965 in Alabama from Selma to Montgomery.[39]

This was certainly not the last time Barnette was a target of conservative pastors within the denomination. Throughout the 1980s, he was labeled as a "liberal" by the SBC's new leadership over his criticism of the doctrine of inerrancy. Barnette rejected inerrancy on theological grounds and viewed it as "a political tool in the takeover." He caught the ire of Adrian Rogers, who had been elected SBC president at the outset of the "Conservative Resurgence," over an article Barnette wrote lambasting Rogers for appointing only "fundamentalists" to the denomination's powerful Committee on Committees. In personal correspondence with Rogers, Barnette urged "moving beyond the divisive arguments about inerrancy to the demands of the kingdom of God in terms of evangelism, religious education and missions." Although Barnette was cited as an example of a "liberal" professor, he had retired from Southern Seminary in 1982 and transitioned to his next chapter as a bioethics professor at the University of Louisville when the resurgence was reaching its crescendo in the mid-1980s.[40]

As an advocate for Niebuhrian realism in the 1940s, Barnette supported America's involvement in World War II against the Nazis and backed the

---

[39] Stagg, "Henlee Hulix Barnette: An Activist," 15–16.
[40] Barnette, *A Pilgrimage of Faith*, 145–52.

war effort in Korea. A shift in his thinking occurred in the 1950s as he began to emphasize the biblical theme of peacemaking.[41] In testimony before a subcommittee of the US Congress during the summer of 1954, Barnette urged the strengthening of the United Nations to prevent another world war, and in his 1961 book, *Introducing Christian Ethics*, he questioned the classic Christian philosophy of just war.[42] He wrote that the idea of a just war is no longer realistic because "no atomic war can be just in either intention or conduct." Barnette sought to elevate the importance of peacemaking within the SBC, helping to form a Southern Baptist Convention Peace Committee and participating in peacemaking promotion activities on the campus of Southern Seminary.[43]

He began to publicly oppose the Vietnam War starting in 1968.[44] This war was deeply personal for Barnette. His son Wayne was a draft resister who left for Sweden, and his oldest son, John, was a fighter pilot flying missions in North Vietnam. Barnette became an ardent advocate of conscientious objectors—citing his Baptist convictions affirming freedom of conscience—and called for Congress to grant amnesty to the thousands of young Americans who refused to aid the war effort. He even took aim at his own denomination, which had failed to offer support to its own Southern Baptist conscientious objectors in the Vietnam War as well as during previous military campaigns.[45]

During his academic career, Barnette was recognized as the SBC's leading expert on environmental issues.[46] As the modern environmental move-

---

[41] Sisk, "Henlee Hulix Barnette," 88. See Henlee H. Barnette, "Paths to Peace," *Florida Baptist Witness* 62 (December 28, 1950): 1.

[42] Barnette, *A Pilgrimage of Faith*, 208–11. See also Henlee H. Barnette, *Introducing Christian Ethics* (Nashville: Broadman, 2007), 171.

[43] Barnette, *A Pilgrimage of Faith*, 201.

[44] Henlee Barnette, "Some Proposals for an American Exodus," *Western Recorder*, August 15, 1968, 10.

[45] Sisk, "Henlee Hulix Barnette," 89–90.

[46] See editorial comment accompanying Henlee Barnette, "Ecocide! Are We Committing Ecological Suicide?" *World Mission Journal* 45 (January 2017): 1–7.

ment launched in the early 1970s, Barnette devoted most of his scholarship and advocacy to this pressing concern in American society. He helped a group of seminary students form an "Ecoclub" and organized his ethics students to participate in the first-ever Earth Day on April 22, 1970.[47] Barnette also taught a course on the ecological crisis in 1970 focused on pollution and consumerism, the first of its kind at any SBC seminary.[48]

In 1972, Barnette penned *The Church and the Ecological Crisis* with evangelical William B. Eerdmans Publishing Company. This book came just two years following the first Earth Day celebration on April 22, 1970, which historians consider the formal launch of the modern environmental movement. While environmental theologians were writing primarily for other theologians, Barnette offered an accessible and concise ecological theology and call to action for his fellow Christians. This groundbreaking book, another first in SBC life, was one of the early books on environmental issues written by a Christian author. Barnette situated himself between doomsdayers like Paul Ehrlich and those on the right who denied the need for environmental action.[49] His ecotheology rested on the foundational belief that God is the creator and sustainer of the universe. Barnette believed God to be immanent in his creation and revealed most fully in the incarnate Christ. Because humans enjoy a covenant relationship with God, according to Barnette, and since this covenant extends to the rest of God's creation, environmental abuse is sin.[50] He understood the biblical view of man as caretaker or "steward" of the earth. The first requirement of stewardship, per Barnette, is faithfulness to God's command to responsibly exercise dominion over God's creation.[51]

---

[47] Barnette, *A Pilgrimage of Faith*, 60, 161–62.

[48] Henlee Barnette, *CE 597: Social Ethics Seminar, Fall 1970*, syllabus, from Z. Smith Reynolds Library (Wake Forest University), *Henlee Barnette Collection*.

[49] Henlee Barnette, *The Church and the Ecological Crisis* (Grand Rapids: William B. Eerdmans, 1972), 14, 17.

[50] Barnette, 66–69, 72.

[51] Barnette, 81.

Environmental action was a central component of Barnette's ethic. He championed "personal ecotactics," such as recycling, carpooling, using biodegradable products, and participating in other lifestyle choices that limit waste and pollution. "Collective social ecotactics" are of critical importance, he contended. "For all the value in individual ecotactics, political action is necessary if the ecological problem is ever to be solved," according to Barnette. He called on Christians to lobby elected officials to exercise greater government oversight of air and water pollution among industries, businesses, and even the military.[52]

Government and individuals were not alone in their responsibility toward protecting the environment—churches have a vital role to play too. Barnette wrote that confronting environmental issues must be a priority of local congregations. To that end, he encouraged churches to begin educational programs, host seminars, participate in environmental organizations, and take part in community cleanup projects.[53] In addition to taking environmental action, Barnette pressed churches to redefine their theology to "see love in terms of willing the welfare of all God's creatures and things" and embrace an understanding of stewardship that "transcends giving a tithe faithfully and sees a responsibility to the whole earth."[54]

From his fight for racial equality in the Jim Crow South to his efforts to promote peace and encourage environmental stewardship, Henlee Barnette modeled Christian activism for his fellow Southern Baptists. And he did so equipped with a message assuming biblical authority, an emphasis on the work of the Holy Spirit, and a foundation rooted in the agape love ethic of Jesus Christ. His influence on multiple generations of moderate and progressive Southern Baptists is considerable.

---

[52] Barnette, 53–56.
[53] Barnette, 82–89.
[54] Barnette, 83.

James Dunn (1932–2015)

Throughout much of the second half of the twentieth century in the US, James Dunn was the most aggressive Baptist proponent for religious liberty, church-state separation, and political engagement in his roles leading the Texas Baptist Christian Life Commission (1966–1980) and the Baptist Joint Committee on Public Affairs (1981–1999). From his days as pastor in the mid-1950s until his death in 2015, Dunn was a visible and vocal advocate and activist for soul freedom: the freedom, ability, and responsibility of each individual to respond to God for herself or himself.

James Milton Dunn was born on June 17, 1932, in Fort Worth, Texas, during the depths of the Great Depression. The Dunns were a Baptist family, and as a child and teenager, he was raised in the faith at Evans Avenue Baptist Church near the campus of Southwestern Baptist Theological Seminary (SWBTS). Baptized at age twelve, Dunn was first exposed to Southern Baptist theology as a sixteen-year-old through a study of E. Y. Mullins's landmark book, *The Axioms of Religion* (1908). Mullins's intense focus on a voluntary, uncoerced, personal relationship with Jesus Christ and an unfettered conscience before God would stick with Dunn the rest of his life. [55]

In 1952, a year before his graduation from Texas Wesleyan College, Dunn accepted a "call to vocational ministry," which led him to SWBTS, where he earned his divinity degree and pursued a doctorate under the mentorship of renowned Southern Baptist ethicist T. B. Maston. With his emphasis on "applied Christianity," Maston, often hailed alongside Barnette as the preeminent shaper of Christian ethics in the SBC, had a tremendous impact on Dunn both personally and professionally. As Maston's student, Dunn came to understand that evangelism and social concern went hand in hand—a novel idea at the time for many Southern Baptists. [56]

---

[55] James M. Dunn in an interview with the author, December 10, 2009. For a biography of Dunn, see Aaron Douglas Weaver, *James M. Dunn and Soul Freedom* (Macon: Smyth and Helwys, 2011), 1–18.

[56] Dunn with author.

A turning point in Dunn's ministry came in 1966 with his appointment as associate director of the Christian Life Commission, the ethics agency of the Baptist General Convention of Texas (BGCT) formed in 1950 under the leadership of Maston.[57] Two years later, Dunn was elevated to the role of director, and for more than a dozen years, he led the CLC to put a great emphasis on public policy advocacy. He urged Texas Baptists to embrace their responsibility to participate in the political process as Christian citizens. Promoting an ethic of political engagement motivated by the Great Commandment (see Matt 22:36–40), Dunn urged his fellow Baptists to be "Christian lobbyists" and succeeded in establishing the CLC as one of the most influential organizations at the Texas capitol in Austin.[58]

As director, Dunn continued the Texas Baptist tradition of fighting all legislative efforts to legalize gambling and further the interests of the alcohol industry. He also became a respected advocate in Austin for a wide range of social concerns from juvenile justice reform to immigration reform to ensuring equal rights for women and minorities. Like Barnette, Dunn expressed opposition to the Vietnam War in the late 1960s as public protests mounted. Also in the late 1960s, as the environmental movement took shape, the BGCT became one of the first Christian groups in the nation to support strict environmental regulations under his leadership. A supporter for public education, Dunn combatted efforts to divert tax money from public schools to benefit private religious education.[59]

In 1981, at the age of forty-eight, Dunn left the CLC to head the Baptist Joint Committee on Public Affairs (BJC), an organization founded in 1936 and then representing eight Baptist bodies (comprising 28 million members) in the nation's capital in support of religious liberty and in defense of

---

[57] Weaver, *James M. Dunn*, 21–55.

[58] Dunn, "Southern Baptists and Christian Ethics" in *A Baptist Vision of Religious Liberty and Free and Faithful Politics: The Words and Writings of James M. Dunn*, ed. Aaron Douglas Weaver (Macon: Smyth and Helwys, 2018), 213–14.

[59] Weaver, *James M. Dunn*, 21–55.

church-state separation. He took the reins of the BJC as controversy was beginning to erupt within the SBC, quickly establishing himself as a vocal opponent of the "Conservative Resurgence" and its emerging leadership— whom he viewed as Fundamentalists. With an aggressive approach, Dunn spoke out against the threat of the "Religious Right" as represented by Jerry Falwell's Moral Majority and warned against a "marriage" between conservative Christians and the Republican party. According to Dunn, such an intimate and uncritical relationship threatened to make religion "the handmaiden of a particular ideology."[60]

Leaders of the Conservative Resurgence took aim at Dunn over his sharp criticisms of President Ronald Reagan's proposed prayer amendment to the US Constitution in 1982—which sought to place decision-making power about prayer in public school classrooms in the hands of state legislatures and local school districts. With blunt flair, Dunn exclaimed, "It is despicable demagoguery for the President to play petty politics with prayer. He knows that the Supreme Court never banned prayer in schools. It can't. Real prayer is always free."[61] Dunn questioned whether, in an increasingly pluralistic society, any citizens—conservative Christians included—would really want to turn the regulation of religious exercises over to any government.

Conservative Resurgence leaders were offended by Dunn's vituperative language directed at President Reagan, as well as his rebuke of the president's social agenda more broadly, specifically his proposed constitutional amendment to ban abortion. While his predecessor at the BJC, James Wood, had backed abortion rights in the early 1970s, Dunn refocused the BJC exclusively on religious liberty issues. This decision frustrated conservative leaders, who demanded that Dunn repudiate Wood and take an antiabortion position. In response to Reagan, Dunn bemoaned that "the complex issue

---

[60] James M. Dunn, "Reflections," *Report from the Capital* 37, no. 4 (April 1982): 15.

[61] Herbert H. Denton and Marjorie Hyer, "Reagan to Ask Hill for Prayer Amendment," *Washington Post*, May 7, 1982, A1.

of abortion is reduced to the simple cry of 'infanticide' by Mr. Reagan, who would redress 'a great national wrong' in the name of civil religion, making it virtually impossible for mothers to make their own decisions in this very private, very religious matter." Dunn's critique and reference to mothers making their own choices—his only public comments on abortion—sounded like a pro-choice position to conservatives.[62]

Despite the disagreements with Reagan, Dunn did align with SBC conservatives in support of the Equal Access Act in 1983 to ensure the rights of religious student groups at public schools and gave voice to SBC conservatives' opposition to the Reagan administration's appointment of an ambassador to the Vatican. Yet this common ground was insufficient to preserve a relationship between the SBC and the BJC, and in 1984 the denomination's top conservative leaders, Paige Patterson and Paul Pressler, launched their first big push to withdraw financial support from the BJC. This task took eight years to achieve fully, and ties were completely severed in 1991.[63]

Conservative Resurgence leaders asserted that Dunn was unresponsive to the obvious concerns of rank-and-file Southern Baptists. While the BJC represented multiple Baptist bodies, it was Southern Baptists who carried the financial weight of the organization, and these leaders demanded more accountability for their political concerns. Meanwhile, Dunn believed the denomination's new leadership was attempting to drastically alter the existing relationship between the institutions of church and state through state-sponsored prayer and legislative efforts to provide federal money to religious groups.[64]

During the SBC controversy, Dunn rooted his rhetoric in appeals to the ideas of soul liberty and soul competency, trumpeted frequently in Baptist history. He positioned himself as the public heir of E. Y. Mullins,

---

[62] Weaver, *James M. Dunn*, 117–18.

[63] For a comprehensive discussion of Dunn's relationship with the SBC and the defunding of the Baptist Joint Committee, see Weaver, *James M. Dunn*, 87–143.

[64] Weaver, 87–143.

insisting "soul freedom" was the key distinctive of Baptists. It was their greatest contribution to understanding the Christian faith. He passionately argued that soul freedom was based on a biblical view of persons. In the creation account of Adam and Eve (Gen 1:26–27), God called the first humans *imago Dei*, which presupposed freedom. This classic doctrine reveals that persons, made by God, can respond to their Creator. "All true freedom is in a real sense religious freedom. It is that which replicates the Divine in all of us that makes us *response-able*, responsible and free," according to Dunn.[65]

Freedom and responsibility are indissoluble, and without responsibility, he said, freedom is "directionless anarchy" without accountability.[66] Soul freedom is not a government invention or product of a social contract. Rather, human dignity comes from God as revealed in Scripture.[67] Dunn refuted critics who claimed soul freedom led to a hyper-individualistic, lone-ranger Christianity. "Without individual autonomy, there can be no authentic community," he said, emphasizing that Christian experience is always under the authority of Jesus Christ as revealed in the Bible.[68] "Real Baptists still test scripture by Jesus Christ" was his popular refrain.[69]

Dunn's view of soul freedom is far-reaching and extends well beyond personal morality and faith. As the ultimate source of all modern concepts of human rights, soul freedom is the cornerstone that precedes and demands religious liberty for all persons in the political arena. It is the biblical and theological starting point from which religious liberty naturally follows. "If

---

[65] Grady C. Cothen and James M. Dunn, *Soul Freedom: Baptist Battle Cry* (Macon: Smyth and Helwys, 2000), 7.

[66] James M. Dunn, "The Christian and the State: A Constructive Task," *Perspectives in Religious Studies* 12, no. 4 (Winter 1985): 23.

[67] Cothen and Dunn, *Soul Freedom*, 1.

[68] James M. Dunn, "Yes, I Am a Baptist," in *Why I Am a Baptist: Reflections on Being Baptist in the 21st Century*, ed. Cecil P. Staton Jr. (Macon: Smyth and Helwys, 1999), 44.

[69] Cothen and Dunn, *Soul Freedom*, 120.

we all, in some serious way, replicate God, religious liberty is a moral and social inevitability," he wrote.[70]

For Dunn, the separation of church and state was the logical theological and political consequence of soul freedom. Biblical principles, theological presuppositions, and historical examples lay firm the foundation that demands church-state separation, according to Dunn, who would frequently appeal to the witness of Baptist leaders such as Roger Williams, John Clarke, and John Leland.[71] While emphasizing that support for church-state separation does not define Baptist theology, it is "a logical, inextricable, inevitable corollary of religious liberty . . . it is the plug which if pulled out of our machine, the motor dies [and] we go no more," Dunn said. He often stressed that "it is hard to believe that one could be a Baptist and not cling tenaciously to that baptistic doctrine."[72]

This Baptist separationism was not a "strict separation" that is often accused of anti-clericalism, anti-Catholicism, and hostility toward religion. Instead, Dunn's separationist perspective called for a robust reading of the First Amendment's Free Exercise Clause and an interpretation of the Establishment Clause that required government to be strictly neutral toward religion. As a "no-aid separationist," he rejected all legislative efforts to fund religious organizations. "Persons of conscience of all religious and non-religious hues insist that it is impossible to attain an idyllic state of governmental fairness with aid and benefits for all religions," he wrote, observing that "when the government claims to aid all religions, it never fails to play favorites."[73]

---

[70] James M. Dunn, "The Baptist Vision of Religious Liberty," in *Proclaiming the Baptist Vision: Religious Liberty*, ed. Walter B. Shurden (Macon: Smyth and Helwys, 1993), 33.

[71] Cothen and Dunn, *Soul Freedom*, 44–45.

[72] Cothen and Dunn, 46.

[73] James M. Dunn, "Neutrality and the Establishment Clause," in *Equal Separation: Understanding the Religion Clauses of the First Amendment*, ed. Paul J. Weber (New York: Greenwood, 1990), 55–63.

Dunn forcefully argued that the separation of church and state should not be equated with the separation of religion from politics. Political engagement was a natural outcome of a commitment to soul freedom, in his view. Dunn often declared that "mixing politics and religion is inevitable but merging church and state is inexcusable." While noting that no simple plan exists for the right mix of politics and religion, "separation of church and state means at least that church and state have different reasons for being, diverse functions, separate sources of funding, distinctive methods and strategies and identities."[74]

The 1990s were a new era for Dunn and the BJC. In this post-SBC period, Dunn focused his energy on numerous church-state battles, including successful efforts to expand religious freedom (Religious Liberty and Charitable Donation Protection Act of 1998, International Religious Freedom Act, and the Parsonage Tax Exemption Act) as well as oppose school prayer and voucher legislation and proposals to provide funding to faith-based organizations.[75] Most notably, Dunn and the BJC helped form and lead a diverse coalition of religious and civil rights groups to restore the "compelling interest test" to decide religious freedom cases following the Supreme Court's controversial opinion in *Oregon Employment Division v.*

---

[74] James M. Dunn, "Religion and Politics: A Proper Mix," *Perspectives in Religious Studies* 13, no. 2 (Spring 1986): 155–56.

[75] Weaver, *James M. Dunn*, 145–78. In 1970, Dunn edited and contributed two chapters to a book titled *Politics: A Guidebook for Christians*. This guidebook contained chapters on various issues relating to Christian citizenship. His chapter titled "How to Get the Church into Politics" stressed that the church can respond to moral issues at the local and national levels unlike any other institution in society. Dunn offered specific ways in which churches could become involved in the political process. He suggested churches form groups to study problems facing society, take field trips to jails and impoverished neighborhoods as a means to motivate political action, and distribute educational resources dealing with pressing social concerns. Dunn was a firm believer in voter registration drives and nonpartisan get-out-the-vote campaigns, which he viewed as two of the best ways a church can begin an active citizenship program.

Smith in 1990.[76] The final result of the BJC-led coalition's efforts was the adoption of the Religious Freedom Restoration Act in 1993.[77]

In 1999, Dunn retired from his position as executive director of the BJC after nearly twenty years of service. This was more of a transition than an actual retirement, however, as he became a visiting professor at the new Wake Forest University School of Divinity. From 2000 until his death on July 4, 2015, Dunn taught students about issues at the intersection of Christianity, ethics, and public policy.[78]

Throughout his ministry spanning seven decades, Dunn developed and displayed a distinctly Baptist approach to advocacy—a vision of religious liberty and political engagement focused on the *imago Dei* and an ethic that prioritized an unfettered conscience, an uncoerced faith, and a loving concern for others. "It is our commitment to persons made in the image of God that fuels our passion for social justice, for Christian ministry, for evangelism, for ethical behavior," he preached.[79] The significant influence of Dunn on several generations of moderate and progressive Baptists cannot be understated.

Conclusion

Without a doubt, Walter Rauschenbusch and his brand of Social Gospel theology had a profound impact on American Protestantism broadly and the Baptist tradition specifically, especially his own denomination, the

---

[76] James M. Dunn, "Reflections," *Report from the Capital* 47, no. 1 (January 1992): 15. See also James M. Dunn, "Reflections," *Report from the Capital* 48, no. 2 (February 1993): 15.

[77] Ron Fournier, "Clinton Signs Freedom of Worship Law," Associated Press, November 16, 1993.

[78] Robert Dilday, "James Dunn, Robust Advocate for Religious Liberty, Dies July 4," *Baptist News Global,* July 5, 2015, https://baptistnews.com/article/james -dunn-robust-advocate-for-religious-liberty-dies-july-4/#.YCNJHOhKhPY.

[79] James Dunn, "The Word Was Made Flesh," in Weaver, ed., *A Baptist Vision of Religious Liberty*, 327–28.

Northern Baptist Convention (now known as American Baptist Churches USA). Amid poverty and suffering, congregations and individuals recognized a need for a more activist faith to address inequality and injustices in society—what Rauschenbusch described as "social sins." The need to recover Jesus's message of the kingdom of God and shift away from an individualistic to a more balanced, holistic understanding of the Christian faith was and has been compelling to his millions of readers.

Rauschenbusch's reach also extended below the Mason-Dixon Line to some Southern Baptists who had come to see evangelism and social concerns as inseparable, viewing sin also as structural and working for the redemption of economic structures and social institutions. During the second half of the twentieth century, Henlee Barnette and, later, James Dunn emerged as vocal, visible, and aggressive advocates for a progressive Baptist political theology. With Rauschenbusch's Social Gospel theology as an obvious influence, Barnette pressed his denomination to embrace racial equality and integrate its churches and seminaries. He did so from an insider position as an ethics professor at the SBC's flagship seminary. Dunn followed this same path as the executive of the social concerns agency of the SBC's largest state convention and then as head of a national organization responsible for representing the denomination on religious liberty issues.

Through their writings, sermons, and advocacy, Barnette and Dunn urged Southern Baptists to be politically engaged, rejecting a separation of religion and politics and modeling an activist faith in the public square. Whereas Rauschenbusch was exclusively focused on the economic plight of millions of European immigrants, Barnette and Dunn recognized that the Social Gospel vision had to be broadened to include other oppressed groups and confront social sins beyond the economic realm. To this end, they invested their energies in addressing discrimination of African Americans and women, environmental degradation, and never-ending war. All affirmed the importance of an unfettered conscience and uncoerced faith as the cornerstone theological commitments of an authentic Baptist identity. However, Dunn's particular context compelled him to put a much greater emphasis on championing soul freedom, which he viewed as under a pernicious attack from the denomination's new conservative leadership.

Rauschenbusch, Barnette, and Dunn were certainly not in lockstep on all aspects of their theology. Rauschenbusch was shaped by the intellectual trends of his era. Yet, with his own conversion experience and belief in individual salvation as well as the necessity of evangelism, Rauschenbusch was distinct from the theological liberals of the early twentieth century who reduced faith to experience alone. He was obsessed with Scripture, rooting his Social Gospel vision deeply in the teachings of Jesus Christ and the Old Testament prophets.

Like Rauschenbusch, Barnette and Dunn were devoted to citing and applying Scripture in their writings, speeches, and sermons. Barnette grounded his ethic in Jesus's agape love, and Dunn gained popularity for his folksy articulation of a Christocentric ethic: "If we have anything remotely resembling a creed, it is the Baptist oral tradition that insists, 'Ain't nobody but Jesus gonna tell me what to believe.'"[80] This intense focus on Jesus Christ as revealed in Scripture comes as no surprise as all three men began their ministries in the pulpit as pastors of local Baptist churches, where they proclaimed Jesus as Lord and came to see that personal faith necessitated a social faith. Together, these Baptist leaders with their activist faith have helped significantly shape and define the political theology of the progressive Baptist tradition in America.

---

[80] James M. Dunn, "Yes, I Am a Baptist," 44.

12

The African American Baptist Tradition

By Kenneth Reid

The African American Baptist tradition has a unique history compared to other ecclesiastical traditions.[1] Unlike other denominations, which usually form due to one or more theological issues, this tradition resulted from the enslavement of the African people. The existence of this denomination testifies to the presence of white supremacy in the society in which it was born and the unwelcoming posture that churches displayed toward enslaved and free Africans and those of African descent. It also illustrates how the enslaved would navigate their new land and their newfound faith: Black Christians would eventually establish their own churches.

---

[1] I am indebted to the research of Wayne E. Croft, *A History of the Black Baptist Church: I Don't Feel No Ways Tired* (Valley Forge: Judson, 2020).

The essay will summarize the history of the African American Baptist tradition.[2] It will briefly examine the formation of the Black Baptist church in the colonies and the United States, present key African American Baptist figures, and explain key debates within this tradition. It will also consider the legacy of the African American Baptist tradition.

Period of American History

The African American Baptist tradition begins in the seventeenth century and extends into the twenty-first century. This tradition begins with the intersection of religious practices between enslaved Africans and white American Baptists in the colonies.[3] While the enslaved brought their religious practices with them, they also adopted the religion of their captors and integrated their religious practices with Christianity.[4] It was not until

---

[2] For variety, this paper will use the terms "African American Baptist" and "Black Baptist" interchangeably.

[3] This essay will not summarize the formation of Baptists in England. To read about that history, see other essays in this book, and see Anthony L. Chute et al., *The Baptist Story: From English Sect to Global Movement* (Nashville: B&H Academic, 2015), 11–54. For the formation of Baptists in the British colonies through the Revolutionary War, see Thomas S. Kidd and Barry G. Hankins, *Baptists in America: A History* (New York: Oxford University, 2015), 1–58. For a comprehensive history of Baptists, see H. Leon McBeth, *The Baptist Heritage: Four Centuries of Baptist Witness* (1987; Nashville: Broadman, 1989).

[4] For extended treatments of the religious and cultural practices the enslaved carried into the New World, see Henry H. Mitchell, *Black Church Beginnings: The Long-Hidden Realities of the First Years* (Grand Rapids: Wm. B. Eerdmans, 2004), 1–21; Albert J. Raboteau, *Canaan Land: A Religious History of African Americans* (Oxford: Oxford University, 2001). There was a debate regarding whether slaves lost their religious and cultural practices in their new land. E. Franklin Frazier argued this thesis in *The Negro Church in America/The Black Church Since Frazier* (New York: Schocken, 1974), 9–14. In his later work, Albert Raboteau, debunks this thesis. Much more research after Frazier's book indicates the enslaved Africans did bring their culture and religious practices with them. "Thousands of Africans from diverse cultures and religious traditions, forcibly transported to America as

the first Great Awakening that mass evangelism was directed to the enslaved Africans. Many Africans identified with the worship, emotional zeal, and preaching during this revival. As a result, many enslaved people were converted, and the first churches they attended appeared after 1750, although these churches were white congregations with white leadership and did not mark the beginning of a separate Black Baptist tradition.[5]

While the desire for African American church independence grew, this desire did not become a reality before 1800 because of the white-dominant power structure. Black churches were dependent on some type of "white denominational recognition" to secure titles or confer legitimacy on the church.[6] Many churches began as mixed congregations or were organized under white leadership.[7] But many African American churches eventually became independent.

The reason for the separation of Black and white churches rests on three Cs: class, culture, and control.[8] Economic class distinctions drove a wedge between those who were more affluent and the economically challenged. As many white churchgoers became economically successful, they desired separation and wished to distance themselves from Black members.[9] A second issue was culture. Many predominantly white churches and churchgoers rejected the emotional style of worship characteristic of Black worshippers. "What for blacks had been a worshipful affirmation of their ancient culture became for white Baptists and Methodists a brief interlude in a longer

---

slaves, retained many African customs even as they converted to Christianity." Raboteau, *Canaan Land*, ix, as quoted in Mitchell, *Black Church Beginnings*, 2. See also Mitchell, 2–3.

   [5] Mechal Sobel, *Trabelin' On: The Slave Journey to an Afro-Baptist Faith* (Princeton: Princeton University, 1988), 97–98.

   [6] Mitchell, *Black Church Beginnings*, 48.

   [7] LeRoy Fitts, *A History of Black Baptists*, 1st ed. (Nashville: Broadman, 1985), 44–45.

   [8] Mitchell, *Black Church Beginnings*, 51.

   [9] Mitchell, 52. Mitchell notes that Saint George's Methodist Church, which drove away Black members including Richard Allen, illustrates this dynamic.

Western history of a culture of formality in worship."[10] The third issue was control. Most Black churches were either sponsored by white churches or subject to discriminatory laws (e.g., Black churches could meet only for two hours on Sunday).[11] White churches and sponsors owned the land where Black churches met. In the view of society at large, white sponsors gave legal and denominational legitimacy to these churches. Thus, most white churches and organizations were hesitant to relinquish control of Black churches and their practices. Mitchell summarizes this dynamic, which continues to the present day:

> These same three major issues of class, culture, and control, and especially the latter two, confront and hinder every effort of different races to worship and work together, even now. From the outset, these two factors bore heavily on the terms of actual "independence" (or lack of it) prevailing in the very first African American churches in the South, and later in the North. . . . The crucial issue of control at times rendered bitter even the otherwise heroic educational efforts of white denominations in the South after the Civil War. . . . The ones who provide the financial resources tend to insist on control, but those who provide the participants want equality of vote, regardless of how much they can or cannot give.[12]

The church most considered to be the first Black Baptist church is the Silver Bluff Church in Aiken County, South Carolina.[13] The church was formed sometime between 1773 and 1775.[14] The second church considered to be the

---

[10] Mitchell, 52.

[11] Mitchell, 47–49.

[12] Mitchell, 52–53.

[13] For an argument that Silver Bluff is the oldest Black Baptist church, see Walter H. Brooks, "The Priority of the Silver Bluff Church and Its Promoters," *The Journal of Negro History* 7, no. 2 (April 1922): 172–96.

[14] Lincoln and Mamiya state the present church building claims a founding date in 1750. However, Mitchell states that further research indicates this cornerstone is

first Black Baptist church is the First African Baptist Church of Savannah, Georgia (originally named First Colored Baptist). This church claims to be the oldest continuously existing Black Baptist church, having been founded when George Liele led fifty members from Silver Bluff to Savannah in 1773 and began the church during the Revolutionary War. The third church that claims to be the first Black Baptist church is the First Baptist Church of Petersburg. This church originated from Bluestone Church, which was founded in 1758 in Lunenburg County, Virginia. White missionaries Philip Mulkey and William Murphy "started a predominantly slave congregation on the plantation of William Byrd III on the Bluestone River."[15]

Why Baptists?

Why were enslaved African Americans drawn to Baptists? Many reasons explain why the Baptist denomination was attractive to African Americans. William Banks in *A History of Black Baptists in the United States* presents a helpful list. The list may be grouped under four ideas: the gospel, equality and autonomy, cultural accommodation to the enslaved, and the historical influence of slavery and racism.[16]

Enslaved African Americans were drawn to the Baptists because of the preaching of the gospel. Of course, many denominations were preaching the gospel, but Baptists stood out because of the way they preached the gospel. The message of freedom provided in the gospel, which Baptists

---

not associated with Silver Bluff. See C. Eric Lincoln and Lawrence H. Mamiya, *The Black Church in the African American Experience*, 1st ed. (Durham: Duke University, 1990), 23, 428 n. 47. See also Mitchell, *Black Church Beginnings*, 58.

[15] Croft, *A History of the Black Baptist Church*, 44. For the story of the first African American Baptist churches in the North, see Croft, 47–55; Fitts, *A History of Black Baptists*, 47–51. For a list of the first African American Baptist churches nationwide, see Sobel, *Trabelin' On*, 251–55, appendix IA.

[16] Much of this section comes from William L. Banks, *A History of Black Baptists in the United States* (West Conshohocken: Infinity, 2013), 27–44.

emphasized more than others, appealed to slaves who were in bondage. In addition, evangelistic zeal and energy seemed more prominent during the Great Awakening from Baptists and Methodists. Their aggressive preaching and evangelistic efforts met "the deep emotional hunger" of the enslaved.[17] Moreover, the preaching seemed to come from the heart and was communicated in plain language that slaves understood without the formality of creeds and catechisms.[18] Baptists, then as now, came from and tended to attract those with less formal education, both among whites and Blacks. Finally, the emotional nature of Methodist and Baptist preaching coincided with enslaved Africans' felt emotional needs resulting from their bondage.

The enslaved were also drawn to the denomination because of Baptist autonomy. The self-ruling nature of Baptist churches enabled enslaved African Americans to partially avoid denominational rule, particularly under predominately white leadership. African American Baptists were able to construct their own churches. Sobel explains:

> In contrast [to other denominations], the Baptist associations were technically no more than mutual aid societies, with absolutely no formal control over the beliefs or practices of member churches. Each church was the body of Christ in itself, and each held to "the liberty wherein Christ has made you free" as the basic tenet of independent church life. In practice, group pressure might have a great deal of influence, but churches broke away from associations with impunity; division and divisiveness were part and parcel of Baptist life. No uniformity could be demanded.[19]

Banks adds, "For a people long experienced at being 'second class' citizens, it was heady stuff to be able to choose their own pastor, manage their own

---

[17] Banks, 28–29.
[18] Banks, 30.
[19] Sobel, *Trabelin' On*, 129.

affairs without 'outside' interference."[20] Before the Civil War, this decen-
tralization was an assent to both Black members and whites, who usually
housed these churches on their plantations before emancipation, allowing
them to maintain more control than their denomination might formally
allow. In addition, it was easier for Black men to become preachers. Baptists
did not have any central ordination or educational requirements. Unlike
Congregationalists, Presbyterians, and Episcopalians, Baptists were well
suited to allow leadership that was impoverished. Furthermore, they did not
need a formal license in order to preach and pastor.[21] Finally, white ministers
preached a gospel that appeared, despite reality, to treat Black and white
members equally.[22]

Cultural sensitivity was another reason Baptists appealed to enslaved
African Americans. Water baptism by immersion was of particular interest
to the enslaved. Banks notes that some scholars argue that "the distinctive
symbolism of water baptism drew the slaves, for they understood well the
representation of the drowning or dying of the old man, and the rising or
resurrection of the new man."[23] Whether or not this is the case, if baptism by
immersion coincided with features of African religion, it seems this sacrament
as practiced by Baptists appealed to the enslaved.[24] In addition, the ability for
enslaved Africans to integrate some of their traditions from Africa with their
worship was present among Baptists (as well as other Black denominations).

---

[20] Banks, *A History of Black Baptists*, 32.

[21] Banks, 33. Edward L. Wheeler, "Beyond One Man: A General Survey of
Black Baptist Church History," *Review & Expositor* 70, no. 3 (August 1973): 312.

[22] Banks, *A History of Black Baptists*, 33–35.

[23] Banks, 37.

[24] Banks, 37. Wheeler notes, in agreement with Melville J. Herskovits, that
baptism by immersion resembled "the West African rites associated with the worship
of the river gods who were among the most powerful West African deities." Wheeler
downplays any direct associations between the two rites but notes their resemblance
as an attractive feature toward Baptist worship and practice. See Wheeler, "Beyond
One Man," 311; and Melville J. Herskovits, *The Myth of the Negro Past* (New York:
Harper & Bros., 1941), 232–33.

For example, one tradition from Africa is the personal possession of sub-deities, which is characterized by shouting at the climax of the rite in which possession took place. This was transplanted into Christianity with shouting as a sign of possessing the Holy Spirit.[25] In addition, some of the spirituals and the call-and-response patterns in worship originated from West Africa.[26] Banks notes the complexity of Black Baptists in that they integrated their practices with the faith they received from their white masters. The result was a blend that became a new form of African American Baptist worship:

> They blended their African heritage with their American experience. . . . From the amalgamation was produced a unique religious style—Baptists, but black Baptists! Do not stretch the chain between West Africa and Afro-American folk religion in an attempt to account for the preference for the black denomination. . . . Yet it is wrong to attempt to trace all religious practices of the blacks to white Christians. The influence of the minority black slave population upon the majority white free population's culture was significant. It was not a one-way street. The blacks took much from the whites; the whites took much from the blacks. Africanisms and spiritual strivings remain, but they exist in a Euro-American context.[27]

The final factor that influenced the enslaved toward the Baptist denomination was the nature of racism and slavery itself. In addition, some slaves

---

[25] Mitchell, *Black Church Beginnings*, 14.

[26] Mitchell, 14. Other examples include the African rite of pouring libation as similar to Communion and the habit of addressing one another as "brother" and "sister" in the church (which is common in all ethnic groups). This habit points to the practice that "familial titles such as mother or brother were applied to everybody, and many Africans from small communities had no experience with any other way to address people" (15). Banks notes that other aspects of African culture that survived include a worldview that unifies the sacred with the secular, as well as "certain funeral rites, the congregational response, emotionalism, singing, and general temper." See Banks, *A History of Black Baptists*, 39.

[27] Banks, *A History of Black Baptists*, 40.

became Baptist because they attended church with their masters. Some slave owners were more comfortable allowing their slaves to practice the religion they themselves practiced. Thus, more white Baptist slaveholders naturally led to more Black Baptists—but those same slave owners were often uncomfortable with integrated churches.[28] The act of segregation itself within the churches created the need for and reality of Black Baptist churches. Without segregation, there would be few Black Baptist churches.

Key Baptist Figures

Many important people shaped the African American Baptist tradition.[29] This section summarizes the contributions of key people in the history of the African American Baptist tradition, including founders, missionaries, ministers, one who organized a public ministry, and leaders in the struggle for equality.

David George and George Liele

David George and George Liele were instrumental in the formation of the Silver Bluff Church, which many regard as the first African American Baptist church. Both were former slaves; both were called into ministry. Both engaged in missions and planted churches.

David George (1742–1810) was born on a plantation in Essex County, Virginia, to parents who were born in Africa known as Judith and John in 1742.[30] He was owned by Mr. Chapel, who was a cruel and brutal master. George escaped the plantation and, when traveling on his own, lived as a

---

[28] Banks, 42–44.

[29] Dr. Martin Luther King Jr. was a pivotal figure in the history of the African American Baptist tradition. However, since his story is addressed in another chapter in this volume, his life will not be summarized here.

[30] Sobel, *Trabelin' On*, 105.

chattel servant to the "Creek and 'Nautchee' Indian peoples."[31] He came
under the ownership of George Galphin, whom he regarded as a "'very
kind' man who owned a plantation and trading station at Silver Bluff,
South Carolina, some twelve miles from Augusta, Georgia."[32] After con-
verting around 1773, he was one of the original members of Silver Bluff
Church and served as its pastor.[33] His master allowed him to be a traveling
minister and serve on several plantations.[34] Under the preaching ministry
of Brother Palmer, George committed himself to preaching to his fellow
enslaved brothers and sisters.[35] During the Revolutionary War, his master
left the plantation, and the enslaved were left on their own. George and his
family fled to British-occupied Savannah, where he gained his freedom.[36]
On the verge of British defeat, George left the South and traveled with
the British military and Loyalists to Nova Scotia in 1782.[37] Sobel notes
that "in Canada, he was a highly successful missionary to both blacks and
whites, often working at great personal risk. In 1792, he decided to lead a
black hegira 'back' to Africa; over 1,000 joined him in his emigration to
Sierra Leone."[38] With English support, he was among those who established
a Particular Baptist presence in a colony called Freetown. The company
that supported the settlement envisioned establishing a Christian presence
with European culture in Sierra Leone with a desire to create an integrated
and equal community of Blacks and whites. Upon his death in 1810, the
Baptists did not grow. Chute, Finn, and Haykin note that "in the final two

---

[31] Sobel, 105.

[32] Sobel, 105.

[33] Tom Nettles, *The Baptists: Beginnings in America*, vol. 2, illust. ed. (Fearn:
Mentor, 2009), 336. For his testimony, see Sobel, *Trabelin' On*, 105–6.

[34] Nettles, *The Baptists*, 336.

[35] Sobel, *Trabelin' On*, 106. Sobel notes this person is most likely Reverend
Wait Palmer, considered a "Connecticut New Light preacher."

[36] Chute et al., *The Baptist Story*, 99.

[37] Chute et al., 99.

[38] Sobel, *Trabelin' On*, 106.

decades of the twentieth century, his spiritual descendants numbered only about 825 in eleven congregations."[39]

George Liele (1750–1820) was born to enslaved parents, Nancy and Liele. His father was regarded as one who knew the Lord.[40] While George dedicated his life to good works, it was not until 1774 that he came to Christ under the preaching of white Baptist minister, Reverend Matthew Moore.[41] George Liele planted a Black church outside Savannah in 1777, while preaching at plantation churches. His master, a Baptist deacon, freed him before the war, and he traveled to Jamaica with the English in 1782.[42] There, he "was the founding father of the Baptist faith in Jamaica, and, after years of severe trial, was very successful."[43] Despite enslavement, Liele was perhaps one of the first ordained African American preachers in the New World and one of the most prominent missionaries. The church he formed in Jamaica grew rapidly before his eighth year there, and he baptized 500 people.[44] Chute, Finn, and Haykin provide a helpful summary of Liele's legacy:

---

[39] Chute et al., *The Baptist Story*, 99.

[40] Sobel, *Trabelin' On*, 104.

[41] George Liele testifies, "[He] unfolded all my dark views, opened my best behavior and good works to me, which I thought I was to be saved by, and I was convinced that I was not in the way to heaven, but in the way to hell. This state I laboured under for the space of five or six months. The more I heard or read the more I [saw that I] was condemned as a sinner before God till at length I was brought to perceive that my life hung by a slender thread, and if it was the will of God to cut me off at that time, I was sure I should be found in hell, as sure as God was in heaven. I saw my condemnation in my own heart, and I found no way wherein I could escape the damnation of hell, only through the merits of my dying Lord and Saviour Jesus Christ; which caused me to make intercession with Christ, for the salvation of my poor immortal soul; and I full well recollect, I requested of my Lord and Master to give me a work, I did not care how mean it was, only to try and see how good I would do it." Sobel, 104–5.

[42] Sobel, 106.

[43] Sobel, 106.

[44] Joseph Early Jr., *Readings in Baptist History: Four Centuries of Selected Documents* (Nashville: B&H Academic, 2008), 55.

By the time William Carey and his family set sail for India in 1793, Liele had been laboring as a missionary for a decade. He should, therefore, probably be considered the first Baptist missionary, though some historians of mission would demur since a "missionary," by definition, is sent out by a church. Nevertheless, by 1814, Liele's ministry had produced a rich harvest, some 8,000 Baptists in numerous chapels throughout the island.[45]

Lott Carey

Lott Carey (1780–1828) was one of the founders of the African Baptist Missionary Society in Richmond, Virginia. He was born a slave around 1780 on the land of William A. Christian, south of Richmond, Virginia.[46] He was converted in 1807 and baptized. Like many of the enslaved, he learned to read and write from the Bible, and he loved the story of Jesus and Nicodemus. Nettles notes that "he began preaching to his fellow slaves with such positive impact that the church licensed him to preach and encouraged him to travel in the surrounding countryside for that purpose."[47] He purchased his freedom for $850 and the freedom of his two children in 1821. Carey was convinced that a move to Africa presented a great opportunity to spread the gospel in a place with little Christian influence and that he was more suited to minister in the climate than white missionaries.[48] Thus, he and his friend Colin Teague sailed to Africa from Norfolk, Virginia, in January 1821.[49] Banks notes,

> Carey was the first black missionary to Africa from America, representing a black missionary organization that operated outside the

---

[45] Chute et al., *The Baptist Story*, 98.

[46] Banks, *A History of Black Baptists*, 106.

[47] Nettles, *The Baptists*, 211.

[48] Chute et al., *The Baptist Story*, 127.

[49] Banks, *A History of Black Baptists*, 106.

continental United States. In Monrovia, Liberia, in 1822 he organized the First Baptist Church. Today the same church exists as the
Providence Baptist Church of Monrovia.[50]

Providence Baptist Church currently has over 2,700 members. Carey served
to bring stability and economic progress to the colony. He was the acting
governor at his death, yet he retained his evangelistic zeal for his people as
he worked to establish schools and Sunday schools.[51] He died in a "bizarre
accident when a candle fell into gunpowder setting off an entire room of
ammunition where he was busy filling cartridges in order to arm militia to
quell an uprising that threatened the colony. He lingered under injuries for
two days and died on November 10, 1828."[52] Organizers established the
Lott Carey Foreign Mission Convention (1897) and the Lott Carey Mission
School (1908) in tribute to his life and work.[53]

John Jasper

John Jasper (1812–1901) represents Black preaching from the antebellum
era into the Jim Crow era. Born on July 4, 1812, in Fluvanna County,
Virginia, he was converted at the age of twenty-seven.[54] While working for
his master, Samuel Hargrove, he lived a "riotous life" until his conversion.[55]
He was working in a tobacco warehouse at his conversion and possessed the

---

[50] Banks, 106–7. Liberia is named to commemorate the citizens' liberty.

[51] Nettles, *The Baptists*, 212.

[52] Nettles, 212. Nettles notes that the Southern Baptist Convention located his
grave in 1850 and set a marble monument inscribed on both sides with "Lott Carey's
self-denying, self-sacrificing labours, as a self-taught Physician, as a Missionary, and
Pastor of a Church, and finally as Governor of the Colony, have inscribed his name
indelibly on the page of history, not only as one of Nature's Noblemen, but as an
eminent Philanthropist and Missionary of Jesus Christ."

[53] Chute et al., *The Baptist Story*, 138.

[54] Banks, *A History of Black Baptists*, 57.

[55] Nettles, *The Baptists*, 338.

zeal to share his conversion experience with all those he encountered. He learned to read "with the aid of a New York speller and with the Bible, a book many slaves used to learn to read."[56]

Jasper was noted as an outstanding Bible-centered preacher with an excellent memory. His preaching became popular with both white and Black people. He was known for his commonsense approach, practical experiences, good grasp of the Bible, and "old time" preaching with emotion characteristic of Black preaching at that time.[57] His preaching was fit for his context and heavily influenced by the Baptist preachers in Virginia while combined with his own "thorough study of Scripture. He dealt with the issues of creation, sin, redemption, heaven, hell, the new birth, the holiness of God, and the glory of Christ in his person and work."[58] Two of his most famous sermons were "De Sun Do Move," a defense of Joshua's long day, which he preached about 250 times, and "Whar Sin Kum Frum," which was his apologetic to demonstrate that God is not the author of sin.[59] Jasper became known for his funeral preaching in the Richmond-Petersburg area. Sobel describes Jasper's funeral preaching approach in William Hatcher's quote:

> A negro funeral without an uproar, without shouts and groans, without fainting women and shouting men, without pictures of

---

[56] Banks, *A History of Black Baptists*, 57.

[57] Banks, 57–58. Banks notes that the less emotional or intellectual style of preaching was also present in Black churches during slavery.

[58] Nettles, *The Baptists*, 339.

[59] Nettles, 339. Henry Louis Gates quotes John Jasper's "De Sun Do Move" sermon (first delivered in 1878), where Jasper stated, "I take my stand by de Bible and rest my case on what it says. I take what de Lord says bout my sins, bout my Saviour, bout life, bout death, bout world to come and I take what de Lord say bout de sun and moon and I cares little what de haters of my God chooses to say." Gates quotes Reverend Martha Simmons' observation: "Everybody everywhere was talking about that sermon. . . . Even people who knew it didn't make sense scientifically were drawn to the way that John Jasper could paint a picture." Henry Louis Gates Jr., *The Black Church: This Is Our Story, This Is Our Song* (New York: Penguin, 2021), 86.

triumphant deathbeds and judgment day, and without the gates of heaven wide open and the subjects of the funeral dressed white and rejoicing around the throne of the Lamb, was no funeral at all. Jasper was a master from the outset at his work. . . . Before the torrent of his florid and spectacular eloquence the people were swept down to the ground, and sometimes for hours seemed to be in trances, not a few lying as if they were dead.[60]

After the Civil War, he planted the Sixth Mount Zion Baptist Church.[61] The church began in a deserted stable, then moved to an abandoned store, "then to an old Presbyterian church building that had to be enlarged and renovated twice. This church . . . became the premier place for preaching in all of Richmond while its membership grew to near two thousand."[62] Jasper pastored there until his death in 1901.[63]

Nannie Helen Burroughs

One hallmark of the African American Baptist church is the influence of women as members and leaders in various roles.[64] One woman who

---

[60] Sobel, *Trabelin' On*, 199–200. Sobel continues, "In the dying and travels, the believers often saw the dead: they visited mothers and fathers and other kin in Heaven, knew them to be well situated, and promised to join them when called to finish their journeys. Jasper helped them reach these states of excitement and gave them legitimation, and in return blacks elevated Jasper into one of the most important black preachers."

[61] Banks, *A History of Black Baptists*, 58.

[62] Nettles, *The Baptists*, 338–39.

[63] For biographies, see Richard Ellsworth Day, *Rhapsody in Black: The Life Story of John Jasper* (Philadelphia: Judson, 1953). See also William E. Hatcher, *John Jasper, the Unmatched Black Philosopher and Preacher* (1908; repr., Harrisonburg: Sprinkle, 1985).

[64] For a brief sketch of women who led in various roles, see Pamela A. Smoot, "African American Baptist Women: Making a Way out of No Way," *Baptist History and Heritage* 42, no. 3 (Winter 2007): 19–33. Bill J. Leonard, *Baptists in*

represents the determination, leadership, and strength of women among Black Baptists is Nannie Helen Burroughs (1879–1961).[65] Born to former slaves in Orange County, Virginia, in 1879, her mother, Jennie Burroughs, relocated to Washington, DC, out of a desire for better educational opportunities. Nannie graduated from M Street High School with honors in 1896. Though she prepared to teach, she was rejected. She dreamed of opening a school for women and began those efforts in 1900. Her speech at the National Baptist Convention (NBC) titled "How the Sisters Are Hindered from Helping" enabled momentum in establishing the Women's Conference at the convention.[66] Burroughs was one of the leaders of the Women's Conference in her lifetime. Taylor argues that her significance is connected to the establishment of the National Training School:

> Burroughs is worthy of our attention because with limited or no resources and fighting against sexism and racism, discrimination and despair, she provided a quality education for African American women and girls at a time and place where this was quite rare. Burroughs dedicated her life to training the women and girls who entered the gates of the National Training School to be highly qualified, independent workers. It was her faith in God that allowed her to find a way or make one, as she came to "specialize in the wholly impossible."[67]

America, Columbia Contemporary American Religion Series (New York: Columbia University, 2005), 222–24.

[65] Much of this section is a summary of Traki L. Taylor, "'Womanhood Glorified': Nannie Helen Burroughs and the National Training School for Women and Girls, Inc., 1906–1961," *The Journal of African American History* 87 (Autumn 2002): 390–402.

[66] Evelyn Brooks Higginbotham, *Righteous Discontent: The Women's Movement in the Black Baptist Church, 1880–1920*, rev. ed. (Cambridge: Harvard University, 1994), 150–51.

[67] Taylor, "Womanhood Glorified," 392.

Burroughs began her efforts by presenting her ideas to the women of the NBC in 1900 at the annual meeting in Richmond, Virginia. Over the next year, she encountered opposition and confusion regarding the school's funding and ownership. She did not want ownership but wanted decisions to reside with the NBC Woman's Auxiliary. Another complicating factor was that women at the time did not have a forum to address their concerns at the NBC. She faced doubts regarding whether she could raise the financial support needed from African Americans. Her vision was unique at the time as she wished to establish a single-sex school not dependent on white philanthropy. Some men opposed her school because she trained women to be self-sufficient, and some men claimed she was training women to be "breadwinners." However, she opened the school on October 19, 1909, in Washington, DC.

Her school offered a curriculum designed for domestic workers. While W. E. B. Du Bois envisioned the uplift of African Americans through the "talented tenth" and Burroughs agreed with his civil rights approach, she was more in line with Booker T. Washington's approach of empowering African Americans for trade. Thus, more affluent African Americans were unlikely to send their adolescent girls to her school. She required girls with high academic achievement, and entrance exams for math and English were required. She would not accept any girls with questionable character. They were not promoted unless they had a cumulative average of 75 in their vocational courses, and she had a curriculum that was intense for its training. Taylor notes that "her school offered both industrial education and academic courses to develop well-educated and well-rounded individuals."[68] Taylor continues:

---

[68] Taylor, 398. Isaiah Robertson also notes that "the women and girls who entered NTS were instructed in Old Testament Interpretation, Biblical Theology, Exegesis of the Epistles, and Christian Evidence." Robertson, *Black Church Empowered: Examining Our History, Securing Our Longevity*, ed. Tyran Laws (n.p.: BC Empowered, 2020), 158–59.

Burroughs nicknamed her institution "The School of the Three B's"—the Bible, the bathtub, and the broom. These three words represented Burroughs's standards for spiritual and physical cleanliness and industry. The students performed charitable and social service work. Burroughs rejected an educational philosophy that emphasized only intellectual development. She believed that if only academic training was offered, she would not succeed in achieving her aims and the students would be denied some important part of their education. She also believed in and worked towards the improvement of the economic status of African Americans in general. Training African American women to enter the labor market as skilled workers was one way she achieved this. Burroughs also sponsored workshops on self-help and self-improvement, and she gave numerous speeches on these topics.[69]

Those who went to the school became assets to their community. Burroughs died in 1961, and in 1964, the school was renamed the Nannie Helen Burroughs School, Incorporated.

Leaders of the Civil Rights Movement

The civil rights movement from the late 1940s into the 1970s and beyond was led by many Baptist ministers. No survey of key leaders among African American Baptists would be complete without looking at the civil rights legacy. Although Dr. Martin Luther King Jr. was the voice and leader of the movement, especially from 1954–1965, many came alongside him at certain junctures.

Adam Clayton Powell Jr. (1908–1972) was born in New Haven, Connecticut, on November 29, 1908.[70] After completing his education,

---

[69] Taylor, "Womanhood Glorified," 395.

[70] Biographical information for Powell is cited primarily from Davis W. Houck and David E. Dixon, eds., *Rhetoric, Religion, and the Civil Rights Movement, 1954– 1965: Volume 1* (Waco: Baylor University, 2006), 243.

Powell was ordained as a Baptist minister and assumed the pastorate after his father at Abyssinian Baptist Church in 1937.[71] In 1941, he was elected to the New York City Council and was elected to Congress in 1945. Powell, through his speeches and bills, advocated for African Americans as he confronted Southern racists.[72] He first turned his attention to advocating for equal treatment of African Americans in the armed forces. Although his bills and amendments did not pass, executive action provided some advancement in his cause. He also addressed violence against African Americans and voting rights by proposing a series of bills.[73] He introduced several civil rights bills throughout his congressional career. His career ended with a lot of controversy about his public morality, concerning the misuse of public funds. Although he was excluded from Congress in 1967, the Supreme Court reinstated him in 1969, and he had been reelected twice during his expulsion.[74] He lost his primary battle with Charles Rangel in 1970, and he died of cancer on April 4, 1972.

Ralph David Abernathy (1926–1990) was born in Linden, Alabama, on March 11, 1926.[75] He served in the armed forces during World War II and was ordained as a Baptist minister in 1948. He earned his BS in mathematics at Alabama State University and his MA in sociology from Atlanta University in 1951. After graduation he began pastoring First Baptist Church in Montgomery, Alabama, where he became friends with Dr. Martin Luther King Jr., and they collaborated in the Montgomery bus boycott. Houck and Dixon note, "For 13 years, where King went, so went Abernathy—including to jail. Perhaps the best 'warmup' act in the movement, Abernathy's

---

[71] He earned his degrees from Colgate (1930), Columbia (1932), and Shaw (1935).

[72] Fitts, *A History of Black Baptists*, 273.

[73] Fitts, 275–77.

[74] Fitts, 279–80.

[75] This biographical summary is adapted from Houck and Dixon, *Rhetoric, Religion, and the Civil Rights Movement*, 430–31.

rhetorical role typically involved getting a civil rights audience ready for Dr. King's eloquence."[76] With Dr. King, Abernathy was one of the founding leaders of the Southern Christian Leadership Conference (SCLC), a group that advocated for nonviolent social change. Upon King's return to Atlanta, Abernathy became pastor of West Hunter Street Baptist Church in 1961. He was present when Dr. King was shot in 1968 and held him in his arms as he died.[77] After Dr. King's death, Abernathy "took over the presidency of the Southern Christian Leadership Conference, preaching, teaching, protesting, and organizing until 1977."[78] Fitts explains Abernathy's legacy:

> The voice of Rev. Ralph David Abernathy was also heard aloud at the close of the decade of the 1970s, warning black Americans not to allow the gains of the revolution to be lost. He made many forceful attempts to remind black Americans of the civil rights struggles and urged them to continue in the struggle. It was Rev. Ralph David Abernathy and other black churchmen who helped make possible the election of President Jimmy Carter. They were highly impressed with Carter's stand on civil and human rights issues. Perhaps the linkage of black Baptists in the politics of "human rights" was the most significant achievement of the post revolutionary decade.[79]

After retiring from the movement, he continued pastoring at West Hunter. He died on April 17, 1990.

African American Baptist ministers had a profound effect on the civil rights movement and were involved in its leadership. Several leaders from within the movement and many more after the movement present a testimony to the legacy of this leadership. Fitts's summary is appropriate:

---

[76] Houck and Dixon, 430.

[77] Chute et al., *The Baptist Story*, 271.

[78] Houck and Dixon, *Rhetoric, Religion, and the Civil Rights Movement*, 430.

[79] Fitts, *A History of Black Baptists*, 291.

They were not afraid to criticize the political leadership of the nation and the failure of such leadership to live up to basic American idealism. The concepts of freedom, justice, and humanity are foremost in the thought of these great and talented black church leaders. From among them came some of America's great statesmen. Seen in this light, the black church has been far more than just another religious institution. It has never really shied away from politics. Born in the political and social institution of slavery, the black church responded to and participated actively in the great political and social issues affecting black Americans.[80]

Baptist Debates

The debates among African American Baptists were rarely theological in nature. Although there may have been some disagreements in areas of theology, these were not the driving forces for the schisms and the dynamics within African American Baptist conventions. Through the conventions, the main sources of conflict regarded issues of publishing, a schism over the direction of the convention during the civil rights era, and the ecclesial/theological tensions with the rise of the Full Gospel Baptist Church.

National Baptist Convention and Conflict

Until 1834, most Black churches were part of white Baptist associations.[81] The first three Black Baptist associations were the Providence Baptist Association (1834) of Ohio, the Association of Regular Baptists of Color (1836) in Ohio, and the Wood River Association (1839) of Illinois. Although many regional

---

[80] Fitts, 295.

[81] Black Baptist associations formed in order to advance racial progress. While many white associations were not hostile, progress was not their priority. See Croft, *A History of the Black Baptist Church*, 59.

African American Baptist associations, missionary societies, and conventions formed over the next fifty years, association goals necessitated a national convention.[82] On September 24, 1895, at Friendship Baptist Church in Atlanta, Georgia, the National Baptist Convention of the United States of America—the first and, still today, the largest African American national Baptist association—was organized and consolidated three associations: the Baptist Foreign Mission Convention, the National Baptist Educational Convention, and the American National Baptist Convention.[83] Fitts notes:

> The new consolidated convention was organized by black Baptist leaders of great genius. They were careful to lay the structure of a viable and durable Baptist organization. These leaders were also determined to structure the new convention broad enough in scope to facilitate a Tripartite Union. It was hoped that such an organization could withstand any devisable tendency on the part of the various regions of the nation.[84]

Elias C. Morris was elected as president and served for twenty-seven years. They selected three new boards: the Foreign Mission Board in Louisville, Kentucky; the Home Mission Board in Little Rock, Arkansas; and the Educational Board in Washington, DC. In December 1897, the Lott Carey Foreign Mission Society was formed, and because of women's efforts and Nannie Helen Burroughs's speech to the convention in 1900, the Women's Convention began.

---

[82] For a detailed account of the various African American Baptist associations, see Lincoln and Mamiya, *The Black Church in the African American Experience*, 23–28; John W. Kinney, "The National Baptist Convention of the United States of America: 'Give Us Free,'" *American Baptist Quarterly* (September 2000): 237–38; Croft, *A History of the Black Baptist Church*, 61–80.

[83] Croft, 80.

[84] Fitts, *A History of Black Baptists*, 79. Black Baptists attempted to consolidate this tripartite union in 1890 in a meeting in Washington, DC, but their efforts to form a convention were unsuccessful.

Schisms appeared throughout the history of the convention, the first involving the publishing needs for the convention. Through the years, Black Baptists had used material from the American Baptist Publication Society, which was also connected with the Southern Baptist Convention. This posed a problem for Black Baptists, as Croft notes:

> Literature published for religious education by whites but used by both Black and white people would continue to be written by whites only. No matter how educated Black people were, they would not be accepted as writers for literature to be read and studied by both races. Leaders among Southern Baptists vigorously protested using any literature prepared by Black Baptists. When the American Baptist Publication Society asked three Black Baptist authors to write for the publication, the white Southern Baptist Convention complained, and the editors rescinded the offer.[85]

The need for their own publishing branch became important, if not critical. However, there was internal conflict within the convention. In 1897 in Boston, leaders met to end their relationship with the American Baptist Publication Society, and they established the National Baptist Publishing House, which was placed under the authority of the Home Mission Board. Yet Richard Henry Boyd, an influential pastor in Texas, argued that the publishing house was not clearly provided for in the constitution of the convention. In essence, Boyd argued for the independence of the Publishing Board, while the convention argued they had control. In 1905, through a resolution, the connection between the Publishing Board and the Home Mission Board was broken, and Boyd ran the Publishing Board as an independent entity. After much controversy and many lawsuits, the Publishing Board was recognized as independent from the National Baptist Convention, USA.[86]

---

[85] Croft, *A History of the Black Baptist Church*, 82.

[86] "Under Boyd's leadership and on the basis of his personal credit the Publishing Board quickly became a successful business venture. New facilities were

The conflict over the Publishing Board became the basis for a new convention. After litigation in 1915, Boyd's followers scattered and eventually met at Salem Baptist Church in Chicago on September 9, 1915.[87] At this meeting, they organized the National Baptist Convention, Unincorporated, which would be named the National Baptist Convention of America. The relationship between the two conventions was distant for years. Croft notes, "This ongoing conflict was perhaps the greatest failure among Black Baptists and eventually led to a period of decline in both the Lott Carey Foreign Mission Convention and the National Baptist Convention of America."[88] It was not until 1920 that the Tennessee Supreme Court ruled in Boyd's favor. The board "became the nucleus of the National Baptist Convention of America."[89] The National Baptist Convention of America is still present as one of the largest Black Baptist conventions.

The Progressive National Baptist Convention

The National Baptist Convention remained strong and was a supporter of civil rights. Yet some tension existed within the convention as two issues bubbled under the surface. The first issue was the unlimited nature of

---

built on land owned by Boyd in Nashville, who had the agency incorporated in the state of Tennessee, and materials produced by the publishing house were copyrighted in his name. When in 1905 the Rev. Mr. Morris acted to separate the publishing house from the Home Mission Board, Boyd and the other members of the board revisited, and a decades-long controversy ensued centered around the question of ownership and control of the publishing interest. Ultimately the conflict was resolved in Boyd's favor by the courts of Tennessee. The convention itself was unincorporated and so unable to own property in its own name and although it had created the Publishing Board, it had neglected to make proper provisions for legal claim to it." Lincoln and Mamiya, *The Black Church in the African American Experience*, 34.

[87] Croft, *A History of the Black Baptist Church*, 92.

[88] Croft, 93.

[89] Croft, 93.

the presidential terms. Previous presidents had long terms;[90] due to the importance of the presidency of the convention and the status it held, some younger pastors craved the opportunity and were prevented from the office due to the seemingly indefinite length and limitless terms the president served.[91] Before Reverend Joseph H. Jackson's tenure, an amendment was proposed and passed in Chicago in 1952. "The proposal stated that the convention president could not be eligible for reelection after having served four consecutive terms until at least one year elapsed."[92] The debate continued, and after a loophole was discovered in the amendment process, Jackson was reelected to a fifth term at the convention in 1957.[93] The convention was divided over the election, and a court battle ensued over the results of the election. The plaintiffs, led by William Holmes Border, charged that

> Jackson's presence at the election was disruptive to the body and that their rights as members of the convention, had been suspended. Those who filed the claim also stated that when they tried to nominate someone to run against Jackson, they were denied access to the floor. Although petitions with hundreds of names had filed these charges against Jackson, a federal judge ruled in Jackson's favor.[94]

---

[90] E. C. Morris served from the convention's beginning until 1922. After W. G. Parks served one year, L. K. Williams served from 1924 to 1941. D. V. Jamison served from 1941 until 1952. J. H. Jackson became president in 1953 and served for twenty-nine years. See Lincoln and Mamiya, *The Black Church in the African American Experience*, 32.

[91] Wallace C. Smith, "Progressive National Baptist Convention: The Roots of the Black Church," *American Baptist Quarterly* (September 2000): 247–48.

[92] Croft, *A History of the Black Baptist Church*, 96.

[93] Wheeler notes, "The constitution in effect in 1952 stated that no amendments could be considered after the second day of the session. The amendment calling for the institution of a tenure plan had been passed on the third day of the 1952 session." Wheeler, "Beyond One Man," 316 n. 21.

[94] Croft, *A History of the Black Baptist Church*, 99.

A second important issue was the civil rights movement and the different views within the convention. Jackson was a supporter of Dr. Martin Luther King Jr., the National Association for the Advancement of Colored People (NAACP), and the Montgomery bus boycott.[95] However, a division between these men arose, which also represented a division among many African Americans. While Jackson supported civil rights, he did not support civil disobedience. He believed King's approach went too far, "violat[ing] those constitutional boundaries that permitted the right of assembly for the purpose of addressing government response to citizen's grievances," and he was wary of those who could bring more destruction from inside the movement by inciting further lawless behavior.[96] King, of course, disagreed with Jackson's methodology, opposed Jackson's view on tenure in the convention, and "also considered it a crushing blow to his stated goal of using the convention to bolster the civil rights movement."[97] This additional factor led to the election and the problems that would come to a head in 1961.[98]

The contest for the presidency of the NBC that year was between Jackson and Gardner Calvin Taylor, pastor of Concord Baptist Church of

---

[95] Croft notes, "In March 1956, he wrote a letter offering his support for King's 'heroic struggles,' enclosing two checks for a thousand dollars—one from the National Baptist Convention and one from his own Olivet congregation in Chicago. According to Martin Luther King, who had helped Jackson to secure the presidency a few years beforehand, he had even offered to buy a bus for the boycotters to assist with the car-pooling system." Croft cites *Jackson to King and the Montgomery Improvement Association, March 5, 1956*, letter, in *The Papers of Martin Luther King, Jr., Volume III: Birth of a New Age: December 1955–December 1956*, ed. Clayborne Carlson (Berkeley: University of California, 1997), 155. See Croft, *A History of the Black Baptist Church*, 98 n. 173.

[96] Leonard, *Baptists in America*, 199.

[97] Croft, *A History of the Black Baptist Church*, 99.

[98] For the dynamics of the 1960 presidential campaign and election that influenced and served as the background to this conflict, see Smith, "Progressive National Baptist Convention," 250–51.

Brooklyn, New York. Taylor's vision for civil rights differed from Jackson's and was more in line with King's. Wheeler summarizes:

> After the 1960 convention, the two sides moved further apart. Taylor supported the tactics of demonstrations, sit-ins, and kneel-ins as strategies for confronting and challenging racial discrimination, while Jackson was on record as opposed to such methods. After the 1961 conventions, Jackson implied in remarks to newsmen that M. L. King, Jr. was the inspiration behind the Taylor movement. This, however, was vehemently denied by the men involved with Taylor, and King probably was not involved. Indeed, he tried to remain outside the disputes, although he knew that an endorsement of his work would have been beneficial.[99]

The election was highly confrontational with physical violence on the convention floor that resulted in the death of Reverend A. G. Wright. When the count was finished, Jackson won with a vote of 2,721 to 1,519.[100] Jackson removed King from the office of vice president of the Sunday school board. Jackson also blamed King's support of Taylor's candidacy for Wright's death, which heightened the bitterness and destroyed any possibility of reconciliation.[101] At Taylor's defeat, the convention itself would not be a strong supporter of King's movement of nonviolent disobedience.

After the election, a group of pastors believed it was time to depart from the NBC and begin a new organization more committed to civil rights. Reverend L. Venchael Booth formed a committee to establish a new convention on November 14–15, 1961. This meeting had opposition from both sides, and Taylor, King, and others who followed Taylor did not support this convention split.[102] After the meeting of thirty-three delegates on

---

[99] Wheeler, "Beyond One Man," 318.
[100] Smith, "Progressive National Baptist Convention," 251.
[101] Smith, 251–52.
[102] Croft, *A History of the Black Baptist Church*, 105–6.

November 14, the Progressive National Baptist Convention formed with a seventeen to sixteen vote. Timothy Chambers became the first president, and a tenure plan was adopted so that after the first four years, officers would be limited to a maximum of two years.[103] Another principle of the convention was a commitment to civil rights according to Dr. King's vision.[104] Eventually Dr. King and his followers joined this convention.

The Full Gospel Baptist Church

A third debate occurred that was more theological in nature and challenged Baptist polity. Since the early twentieth century, Pentecostal and Charismatic denominations emphasized the continuing gifts of the Spirit. Paul S. Morton, in his address to the National Baptist Convention in September 1992, spoke about a "spiritual gifts" movement that favored the continuation of miraculous gifts from the Spirit, including and especially speaking in tongues.[105] Morton believed he was called by God to bridge the gap between the Baptist and Pentecostal/Charismatic traditions. His new movement became the Full Gospel Baptist Church Fellowship International. Croft describes the rationale for calling this a fellowship rather than a convention: "Morton was well aware of the historical schisms, divisions, and splits in the National Baptist Convention. Thus, he did not want to refer to this new movement as a convention, but rather a 'fellowship' designed to provide an opportunity for those who wanted to remain Baptist and yet exercise all the gifts of the Spirit, particularly speaking in tongues, without threatening or replacing mainline denominations."[106] This fellowship, formed in 1993, retained many of the distinctive Baptist elements and encouraged the practice of all spiritual gifts.

---

[103] Croft, 107.
[104] Smith, "Progressive National Baptist Convention," 254.
[105] Croft, *A History of the Black Baptist Church*, 113.
[106] Croft, 114.

One tension was the quasi-Episcopal nature of the Full Gospel fellowship. The fellowship did not participate in Baptist associations or conventions, and once churches chose to affiliate with the Full Gospel Baptist Church Fellowship, the National Baptist Convention requested these churches remove their membership. With the introduction of bishops, the autonomous nature of Baptist churches seemed to be discarded. Again, Morton emphasized each church's "right to choose" its theological approach.[107] Kenneth Ulmer mitigated this tension by sharing that the office of bishop is more of a mentoring designation of one pastor over a group of pastors so that all might be more effective in ministry.[108] Overall, the Full Gospel Baptist Fellowship presents an alternative approach for Baptist churches, and it is not designed to compete with the Baptist association and conventions, nor do they wish to cause any schism.

The African American Baptist Legacy

The legacy of the African American church is a powerful one. This section will survey three aspects of the African American Baptist legacy: the contributions of African American women, the social justice contribution of Black Baptists, and the enduring Christian testimony and theology within the African American Baptist tradition.

African American Women

Women have played a large role in the African American Baptist tradition. In many Baptist congregations, most members are women. Pamela Smoot notes that "as individuals, as members of church auxiliaries, and other types

---

[107] Croft, 117.
[108] Croft quotes Kenneth C. Ulmer, *A New Thing: A Theological Look and Personal Look at the Full Gospel Baptist Church* (Los Angeles: FaithWay, 1994), 56. Croft, *A History of the Black Baptist Church*, 117.

of organizations, and as missionaries, these Baptist women have been instrumental in the success of various church ministries, historic events as they pertain to African Americans, and major reform within African American communities."[109] Nora Antonio Gordon served as a missionary in the Congo in the late nineteenth century, and Shirley Russell served for twelve years in Haiti in the late twentieth century.[110] Several African American women were leaders in their communities. Maggie Lena Walker became the first female bank president, establishing Saint Luke Penny Savings Bank in 1903, and she opened a department store called Saint Luke Emporium in 1905.[111] Nannie Helen Burroughs established the National Training School in 1909.[112] Mary Fair Burks and Jo Ann Robinson, both English professors at Alabama State College in Montgomery, were critical in their leadership of the Montgomery bus boycott. They were critical in initiating the boycott and "shared in the planning and strategies to desegregate the bus system, managed the carpool system for domestic and other workers, and made demands on city officials."[113] Because of their success, the state removed them from their teaching positions. Diana Marshall, an ordained minister, founded the New Dawn Beginnings Outreach Ministries, which assists and empowers women in impoverished situations.[114] Evelyn Brooks Higginbotham tells the story of the women's movement in the Black Baptist church from 1880 to 1920. She connects the importance of the work of these women with the work of the Black church in civil rights and beyond.

---

[109] Smoot, "African American Baptist Women," 19.

[110] Smoot, 21–23. For Russell's story of survival and her ministry, see pages 22–23.

[111] Smoot, 23–25.

[112] See earlier section in this essay for an expanded account of Burroughs's story.

[113] Smoot, "African American Baptist Women," 28.

[114] Smoot, 29. Smoot states, "The purpose for the outreach ministry was to help those lost, left out, and ignored and to improve their situations. Unlike many ministries and some social service agencies, New Dawn Beginnings does not provide Band-Aids for bad situations, but rather teaches women how to stay fed and to stay dry."

Burroughs spoke of a new day dawning that would help discover the real American. Higginbotham comments:

> This vision of a "new day dawning" and a "real American" would inspire later leaders—a Rosa Parks and a Martin Luther King, a Fannie Lou Hamer and a Medgar Evers—and countless women and men who, in the sacred space of black churches, held rallies in support of boycotts, sit-ins, and protest marches and who transformed the songs of the church into the freedom songs of the Civil Rights Movement. The women's movement in the black Baptist church between 1880 and 1920 contributed to "foundation laying" and to "setting in motion" future forces that would escalate the assault on race and gender discrimination.[115]

Social Justice

A second legacy is social justice. The African American tradition formed out of struggle and oppression.[116] The fight for freedom and social equality has been a hallmark of the African American tradition, and it is seen in each stage of American history. Black Baptists were active in the abolitionist movement. For instance, Black Baptists organized the Union Anti-Slavery

---

[115] Higginbotham, *Righteous Discontent*, 229.

[116] Kidd and Hankins observe: "The major Black Baptist denominations formed for sociological rather than theological reasons. The slave experience often overshadowed theological differences over Calvinism that white Baptists inherited from the Protestant Reformation in Europe. Black Baptist cooperation emerged instead out of the struggle for freedom, a struggle often chronicled in black gospel music. Another way of putting this is that black Baptists were outsiders to the dominant white/European way of doing church. Instead, they forged a history of their own, and even their own distinct form of sacred music. In so doing, they turned their churches into institutions of African American identity within a society dominated by whites. Long after white Baptists became insider elites, especially in the South, black Baptists were still marked by the outsider/dissenter posture of early Baptist history." Kidd and Hankins, *Baptists in America*, 165.

Baptist Association in 1843, which was an exclusively Black organization, and Black women in 1837 organized the Roger Williams Baptist Anti-Slavery Society and an auxiliary organization.[117] The church was active during Reconstruction, maintaining independence for their congregations and emphasizing economic cooperation that would enable economic advancement among newly freed African Americans.[118] Black Baptists were active in the anti-lynching movement. One example is Reverend L. B. Brooks from Mount Ararat Baptist Church of Rutherford, New Jersey, who used his pulpit in the anti-lynching movement "to advance the cause for freedom and protection for Black Americans. His was also a very strong pen in the sociopolitical climate of the New England Baptist Convention. He was perhaps the first Black Baptist to lay the blame on the southern white clergy for the lynching."[119] Black Baptists were leaders in the civil rights movement in the mid-twentieth century through the leadership of Adam Clayton Powell Jr., Dr. Martin Luther King Jr., Ralph David Abernathy, and many Baptist ministers and laypersons. In the post–civil rights era, Jesse Jackson, a Baptist minister, continued to advocate for equal opportunities for African Americans in many aspects of life, including hiring practices, fair housing, fair wages, and many other human rights issues, as both a civil rights leader and in his Democratic presidential campaigns in 1984 and 1988. Today, Reverend Raphael Warnock continues in this same tradition of social action

---

[117] Fitts, *A History of Black Baptists*, 225.

[118] Fitts, 240, 242.

[119] Fitts, 254–55. Fitts quotes part of Reverend Brooks's sermon in 1922: "The white preachers of America can break up lynching, clean up the debauching evils of destructive prejudice, injustice and civil robbery in all parts of our land; if the true dispensation of the Gospel is preached and practiced! . . . But we find thousands of white preachers who hold the pulpits of the churches where lynchers are members, there men and women sit in the pews each Lord's Day who are members of State Legislature, where corrupt laws have been enacted, lawyers, judges of the courts, and jurors who are vile and unjust to men because of their color or race; and are too cowardly to raise their voices against these criminals in high places. God cannot use these preachers because they are slaves of wicked men."

in the Baptist church as the pastor of Ebenezer Baptist Church in Atlanta, Georgia, the same pulpit once held by Dr. Martin Luther King Jr., and as a newly elected US senator from the state of Georgia. At each stage of American history, Black Baptists are found advocating for social justice, and they exhibit a rich legacy of this work. William Brackney summarizes:

> A permanent feature of Black Baptist witness is social justice. Hardly a theological proposition or a denominational program, social justice (or lack thereof) is *felt* among Black Baptists. Being deprived of freedom and basic needs, living in a color-bound society, and being the targets of laws that codified segregation and discrimination, black Baptists have cried out from their pulpits with words of Scripture to identify God's role among the oppressed. They have marched on institutions and sat in jail cells on behalf of justice. [120]

Theological Emphasis

Finally, the legacy of the African American Baptist tradition, though it is an activist social tradition, is in continuity with the historic Christian tradition. The Black Baptist tradition affirms Christian orthodoxy through a Baptist lens. It retains its Baptistic elements: the independence of each church with a cooperative element through the associations and the conventions, the emphasis on believer's baptism by immersion, regenerate church membership, the symbolic nature of the Lord's Supper, the authority of the Scriptures, and the priesthood of all believers.[121] Yet some theological emphases are characteristic of the African American Baptist tradition and rightly form part of its legacy.[122]

---

[120] William H. Brackney, *Baptists in North America: An Historical Perspective* (Oxford: Wiley-Blackwell, 2006), 196.

[121] Banks, *A History of Black Baptists*, 113–15.

[122] The rest of this section is taken from Kinney, "The National Baptist Convention," 239–43. Although Kinney refers to the preachers and theology from

One theological contribution is the contextual nature of theology. The African American Baptist tradition was formed within cultural and personal experience. While the role of experience as a source of theology may be debated, the African American Baptist tradition is shaped in part by the experience of oppression within American culture. Kinney notes, "The Black Baptist tradition has recognized the contextually conditioned nature of theology. The fault is not in that theology is contextually conditioned, but in the failure to acknowledge the contextuality of one's own theology."[123] Recognizing the diversity of contexts and interacting with other traditions helps to create a more authentic community.

A second contribution is the hermeneutical method practiced by many African American Baptist ministers. This tradition pushes against an interpretive method that reinforced oppression. Most Black preaching is not limited to the results of a strict historical-critical method but is enabled by a more flexible (yet faithful to the text) hermeneutic that addresses relevant issues for their audience. Kinney explains:

> Through spiritual exegesis energized by sanctified imagination, contextual exposition, and application were rendered in a manner that exploded the reified reductions of an absolutist approach and revealed the message for the moment. . . . Black preaching ranges from the mystic whisperings of Howard Thurman, to the picturesque storytelling of Gardner Taylor, to the rhythmic philosophic inquiry of Martin Luther King, Jr., to the gravely groans of Cessar Clark, to the existential expositions of Miles Jones, to the melodious intonation of C. F. Franklin, to the reasoned rhapsodies of Wallace Smith. What is distinct is a hermeneutical principle that discerns the word behind, beneath, and beyond words. What is

---

the National Baptist Convention, he also states this is characteristic of much African American preaching.

[123] Kinney, 240.

offered with passion are not bible facts, but truth that sets free and a word that transforms.[124]

A third contribution is liturgical in nature. Most Western approaches downplayed the emotional aspects of worship in favor of worship that appealed to the intellect. Kinney notes that "emotion was linked with ignorance, and meaningful worship offered an appeal to the mind rather than an encounter with the Holy and an experience that gripped total being."[125] African American Baptists sought to integrate a robust worship that allowed for emotional expression authentic to the lived experience of its worshippers.

A fourth emphasis concerns the ecclesiological dimension. Kinney notes that true faith is not isolated from an embodied experience. True faith is incarnational, lived out in Christian community. He states:

> The true church was where believers did the right thing rather than focus on the right words. The evidence of faith was not in your creed but rather in the character and quality of your living. Blacks noted a clear difference in the Church of Jesus Christ and slaveholding piety and racist religiosity that was doctrinally pure but existentially corrupt. They made a distinction between what they called Churchianity and Christianity. Churchianity whipped, brutalized, and negated them while Christianity offered freedom. The test of faithfulness was in your being and not in the coherency of your philosophy and the correctness of your propositions. Long before scholars were employing the comparative terms of orthopraxis verses orthodoxy, Black Baptists were saying that the source of our separation was not our doctrine but rather the way we treated one another.

---

[124] Kinney, 240–41.
[125] Kinney, 241.

In other words, the exercise of our faith in community and in the public square is demonstrated by our treatment of one another. Black Baptist thought contrasts the theological sophistication of many white Baptists and reformed with their treatment of the enslaved and their oppression.

This point leads to a fifth contribution, which is the anthropology from Black Baptists. This anthropology, in light of the experiences of oppression, slavery, segregation, and dehumanization, emphasized the dignity and humanity of every person. Black people more than anyone understood the destructive nature of sin, in contrast to some of the "simplistic soft definitions of sin rendered by unbridled liberalism, but they nevertheless, continually called attention to the worth and dignity of humanity."[126] This respect for humanity was heightened by their emphasis on self-respect and an appreciation of Jesus's humanity "and offered a challenge to pervasive docetism."[127]

A final contribution is an eschatological framework. Black Baptists contributed to this with an emphasis on the next life. They were not otherworldly, but their faith in the future provided the stamina to endure the pains in the present age. Kinney states that "heaven was God's promise that usurped the authority of any present reality to define Black possibility and inspired and energized persons to continue to struggle."[128] He adds, "The focus on the promise does not lead to passive pining but it does provide power and purpose. We need to recover heaven, as a vision of God's possibility that tugs us into a meaningful future that is not limited to upward mobility in the present realm. Black Baptists still sing, 'there's a bright side somewhere and I won't rest until I find it.'"[129] The eschatological emphasis, along with these other theological approaches, is a gift that Black Baptists and the wider African American tradition have provided to the church in the United States and globally.

---

[126] Kinney, 242.

[127] Kinney, 242.

[128] Kinney, 242–43.

[129] Kinney, 243.

Conclusion

This essay has introduced the African American Baptist tradition. It has surveyed key persons in the history of the tradition, presented the relevant debates and schisms within the tradition, and discussed the legacy that has come from the tradition. As a final reflection, Reverend Dr. J. Alfred Smith Sr., in the afterword of Croft's book, poignantly states:

> As Black Baptists, we have a legacy of social justice bequeathed to us by our ancestors to stand in solidarity with the struggling and oppressed people of the world. And their salvation and commitment to Christ, the One who came to save, remains our cause. Croft's extensive historical exploration of Black Baptists should, in this time and in this space, allow us as Christ's disciples to hear with clarity the invitation of acclaimed theologian Howard Thurman to search for common ground and to follow the example of Martin Luther King, Jr., who lived and died for the coming of the beloved community.[130]

---

[130] Alfred Smith Sr., "Afterword," in Croft, *A History of the Black Baptist Church*, 126.

13

The Political Theology of Martin Luther King Jr.

By Daniel Lee Hill

Whatever might be said about Martin Luther King Jr. as an activist and civil rights leader, he was explicitly Christian and unashamedly Baptist, as were his father, his grandfather, and his great-grandfather before him.[1] As Charles Marsh observes about the civil rights movement as a whole, "particular ways of thinking about God, Jesus Christ, and the Church framed the basic purposes and goals of the movement, to be sure, purposes and goals, shifting in emphasis and meaning at different historical moments and in different political and social contexts. . . . But the spiritual energies of the movement were born of particular

---

[1] As Cornel West notes, "King was first and foremost a revolutionary Christian—a Black Baptist minister and pastor whose intellectual genius and rhetorical power was deployed in the name of the Gospel of Jesus Christ." West, "Introduction," in Martin Luther King Jr., *The Radical King*, ed. Cornel West (Boston: Beacon, 2015), xv.

forms of theological expression."[2] These energies are even more pronounced in the case of King. Because King was a member of the Southern Christian Leadership Conference (SCLC), a member of the National Baptist Convention, and an eventual founder of the Progressive National Baptist Convention, Baptistic threads were woven throughout King's life, work, and ministry. It is perhaps unsurprising that an avowedly Baptist preacher and vocational Christian minister such as Martin Luther King Jr. would tether his social activism to a Baptistic political theology.[3] This essay, then, is intended to introduce King's thought and work. Beginning with an overview of his context, background, and influences, it will proceed to discuss the main contributions he has made to the field of political theology, the controversies which surround him, and the legacy he has left behind.

Contexts

A Brief Personal Biography

On January 15, 1929, Martin Luther King Jr. was born to Michael and Alberta King in Atlanta, Georgia. The son and grandson of Baptist ministers in a South still firmly locked in the grip of Jim Crow, King became well acquainted with the power of preaching and the dynamics of the Christian

---

[2] Charles Marsh, "The Civil Rights Movement as Theological Drama: Interpretation and Application," *Modern Theology* 18, no. 2 (2002): 233.

[3] While King was indebted to Mahatma Gandhi's political activism, he continued to view the practice of nonviolence as principally Christian. He was critical of the more aggressive tactics of Black nationalists and the Nation of Islam, believing that the way of love and nonviolence was a more effective way of achieving social change. See Martin Luther King Jr., *Why We Can't Wait* (New York: Signet Classics, 2000), 100. This is, of course, not to deny the immense influence Gandhi's pacifism and social activism had on the life of King. However, as David J. Garrow makes clear, King viewed Gandhi's life as typifying Christian convictions and commitments. See Garrow, "The Intellectual Development of Martin Luther King, Jr: Influences and Commentaries," *Union Seminary Quarterly Review* 40, no. 4 (1986): 17.

community at an early age. King's family would have been numbered among the Black middle class in a heavily segregated South. His father was the president of a local chapter of the National Association for the Advancement of Colored People (NAACP). Accordingly, as a child, King was relatively sheltered from some of the harsher realities of American life.[4] While King does recall some instances of racial animus in his early years, what appears to stand out most is the Christian character of his parents, their commitment to civil rights, and their installation of a sense of self-worth.[5] Yet even in his adolescence, King was renowned for his public speaking and rhetorical skills, skills that surely served as a sign of things to come.

Eventually, King would follow in his father's footsteps and head to a local historically Black college, Morehouse College, where he joined the NAACP. He graduated at the age of nineteen with a bachelor of arts in sociology in 1948, the same year he was ordained as a Baptist minister. After completing his studies at Morehouse, King matriculated at Crozer Theological Seminary in Pennsylvania, where he was elected president of the student body before attending Boston University, where he received his PhD under the supervision of Edgar S. Brightman and Lotan Harold DeWolf.[6] While attending Boston University, King met his future wife, Coretta Scott. The two married and eventually had four children.

As he was completing his studies at Boston University, King sought a pastoral position where he could continue writing his dissertation while providing for his family. Although he had other opportunities available to him and he was initially torn between his desire for academia and pastoral ministry, King accepted a position in Montgomery, Alabama, in 1954 at Dexter Avenue Baptist Church and quickly became involved with the local

---

[4] John A. Kirk, *Martin Luther King Jr.*, Profiles in Power (London: Routledge, 2014), 15.

[5] Martin Luther King Jr., *The Autobiography of Martin Luther King, Jr.*, ed. Clayborne Carson, rep. ed. (New York: Warner Books, 2001), 2–9.

[6] Gary J. Dorrien, *Breaking White Supremacy: Martin Luther King Jr. and the Black Social Gospel* (New Haven: Yale University, 2018), 19–21.

chapter of the NAACP.[7] Soon, King would become involved in developing a protest movement in Montgomery alongside lifelong friend Ralph Abernathy. This would serve as the start of a career of community activism in which King found himself on the forefront of marches and civil rights demonstrations in places ranging from Selma to Chicago, from Birmingham to Washington, DC, a career that often put him in conflict with federal and local officials alike. King served as the final speaker in the famous "March on Washington" in 1963, an event his good friends A. Philip Randolph and Bayard Rustin organized, where he delivered his "I Have a Dream" speech. A year later, in recognition of his commitment to combatting racial injustice through nonviolent means, King received the Nobel Peace Prize in 1964. As King's public ministry progressed, he would continue to protest racial and economic injustice throughout his life, working alongside the SCLC to form the "Poor People's Campaign" until his assassination in 1968.

Social and Political Backgrounds

Throughout King's life, he viewed his pastoral role as intricately tied to public engagement. He adopted a critical disposition toward the United States for its involvement in the Vietnam War, its perpetuation and tolerance of Jim Crow, and its exploitative labor practices toward working-class peoples irrespective of their race.[8] Accordingly, these three points of emphasis provide a lens for understanding the social and political background of King's life and ministry.

King's name has become almost synonymous with the civil rights movement, a movement that sought to secure the rights of citizenship on

---

[7] Martin Luther King Jr., *Stride toward Freedom: The Montgomery Story* (Boston: Beacon, 2010), 4.

[8] Martin Luther King Jr., *"All Labor Has Dignity,"* ed. Michael K. Honey (Boston: Beacon, 2011), 58–59.

behalf of African Americans in the United States. After the abolition of slavery (1865) and the end of the Reconstruction era (1877), the United States Supreme Court argued that while the Fourteenth Amendment protected individuals from having their respective rights infringed upon by the actions of the state, individual citizens were not obliged to follow the same nondiscriminatory practices. As Joseph Luders notes, "Southern legislatures began adopting a set of laws designed to disenfranchise Blacks and erect the segregated racial order known as Jim Crow."[9] With the Supreme Court's decision in *Plessy v. Ferguson* to permit segregation, many aspects of American life became officially segregated under the logic of "separate but equal." The civil rights movement arose to address these institutional forms of racial oppression, as Blacks were prohibited from the goods of citizenship and denigrated to a second-class status. Institutions such as the Southern Christian Leadership Conference and the NAACP would play pivotal roles in organizing protests, advocating for voting rights, and mobilizing African American constituents in the pursuit of social change. King would play a pivotal role in both organizations.

Additionally, King's career as a political theologian is intertwined with US involvement in the Vietnam War, a conflict that helped expand his horizons for the role of Christianity in the public square. While the conflict had been growing for years, in 1965 President Lyndon B. Johnson dramatically escalated US involvement in the war. Since so many draftees came from low-income, Black neighborhoods, there appeared to be growing animus toward the war within the African American community, especially considering the unjust living conditions they faced at home.[10] Although he was initially

---

[9] Joseph E. Luders, *The Civil Rights Movement and the Logic of Social Change* (Cambridge: Cambridge University, 2010), 148.

[10] According to Kimberly Phillips Boehm, while the Selective Service Act in 1948 required young men to register for the draft, many of the deferments passed after the Korean War were not applicable to African American men (e.g., enrollment in college, possession of an essential civilian job). Additionally, as morale for the war waned, "many African Americans considered the use of troops in undeclared wars

reluctant to address it and faced significant opposition within the NAACP, American involvement in Vietnam was particularly troubling to King due to his commitment to nonviolence and his belief in the interconnectedness of humanity. As Lawrence Eldridge observes, King assumed "an overtly adversarial posture in dealing with . . . the Johnson administration."[11] King saw "fundamental solidarity between oppressed U.S. Blacks and the racially oppressed people of color in emerging countries around the world, including Vietnam. . . . In King's view, the United States was perpetuating the oppression of colonialism and stifling a local revolution under the guise of fighting communism."[12] King decried the war's violence and viewed it as compromising his moral vision of the beloved community. According to King, there was a clear connection between the fate of Blacks in the United States and what was happening in Vietnam. Seeing this connection caused King to view the war itself as a form of oppressing and antagonizing the poor.[13] This led King to adopt a more antagonistic disposition toward the Johnson administration and the federal government.

Lastly, King lived and worked during a time of economic and social turmoil, a topic he addressed with increasing frequency throughout the latter portion of his life. Throughout the 1960s, a series of urban revolts took place in major US cities, including but not limited to Los Angeles (1965), Detroit (1967), Philadelphia (1964), Harlem (1963), Cleveland (1966),

---

against a small nation of 'colored people' indefensible." Boehm, *War! What Is It Good For?: Black Freedom Struggles and the U.S. Military from World War II to Iraq*, John Hope Franklin Series in African American History and Culture (Chapel Hill: University of North Carolina, 2012), 197. In other words, many African Americans felt a degree of solidarity with those they were tasked to fight; that is, they perceived their station as ostracized citizens within the United States as parallel to the United States's treatment of the Vietcong.

[11] Lawrence Allen Eldridge, *Chronicles of a Two-Front War: Civil Rights and Vietnam in the African American Press* (Columbia: University of Missouri, 2011), 98.

[12] Eldridge, 98.

[13] See King, *The Radical King*, 203.

and Chicago (1966).[14] While many factors contributed to these riots, ranging from issues over segregation to a lack of economic opportunities, they
illustrate the volatility of King's time, a volatility that is not reducible along
racial lines. Toward the end of his life, King believed that economic factors provided the grounds for solidarity between poor, working-class people
irrespective of race.[15] Accordingly, King became increasingly involved with
labor movements and the pursuit of economic transformation.

Intellectual and Spiritual Influences

King's thought cannot be neatly labeled as either conservative or liberal as
he drew from a panoply of religious, spiritual, and philosophical resources,
ranging from Abraham Joshua Heschel to Paul Tillich.[16] However, for heu-
ristic purposes, it is possible to group King's influence into three stages,
according to his transition from his local church upbringing in Atlanta to
his seminary training and doctoral work through his life as a public advocate
for social reform. King's thought reflects all these disparate influences. He
was formed in the Black ecclesial tradition under the tutelage of his father
and Benjamin Mays before broadening his horizons to incorporate the theological and philosophical resources of Protestant liberalism and the political
activism of Mahatma Gandhi. We will look at each in turn.

---

[14] Boehm, *War!*, 201. For a discussion and analysis of the riots in Harlem
and Los Angeles in particular, see Janet L. Abu-Lughod, *Race, Space, and Riots in
Chicago, New York, and Los Angeles* (Oxford: Oxford University, 2007), 159–96;
197–226.

[15] See King, *"All Labor,"* 164.

[16] For his part, Cornel West identifies four key religious sources in King's
life and thought: (1) the Black church tradition of his upbringing; (2) the liberal
Christianity of his higher education; (3) the Gandhian commitment to nonviolence;
and (4) a prophetic approach to American civil religion. See West, "Prophetic
Christian as Organic Intellectual: Martin Luther King, Jr.," in *The Cornel West
Reader* (New York: Basic Civitas Books, 1999), 426.

The Black Baptist church served as one of the primary influences in King's life from an early age. For many people growing up within this tradition, the church bolstered an African American sense of self and solidified communal identity.[17] Moreover, many churches within this tradition, while still theologically conservative, were committed to addressing racial and social concerns.[18] As West points out, the prophetic nature of the Black church placed the problem of evil and the fundamentally tragic character of life at the center, refusing to accept either escapist or paradisical modes of being.[19] Spending his youth under the tutelage of his father before heading to Morehouse College where he met the infamous Benjamin Mays, King would have been well acquainted with the church's deep commitment to evangelical piety and its concern for social issues.[20] As Perkins observes, in King's appeal on behalf of the Montgomery bus boycott, "King tied the boycott to abolition, exile, and liberation. . . . King's appeal to the African American spiritual, the determination to press

---

[17] C. Eric Lincoln and Lawrence H. Mamiya, *The Black Church in the African American Experience* (Durham: Duke University, 1990), 96. Of course, it is important to note the locution "Black church" functions heuristically and pragmatically, as it obfuscates important distinctives of churches in differing geographic, economic, and ecclesial locations.

[18] For a discussion of the similarities and differences between Black and white churches on these grounds, see Daniel R. Bare, *Black Fundamentalists: Conservative Christianity and Racial Identity in the Segregation Era* (New York: New York University, 2019), 25–55.

[19] West, "Prophetic Christian as Organic Intellectual," 427. West, for his part, argues that the Black ecclesial tradition serves as the dominant schema in King's intellectual development, a schema into which other influences were incorporated (West, 430–31).

[20] As Gary Dorrien points out, King was "the product of a Black church family and congregation that espoused the social gospel in a broad sense of the category and prepared him for his singular role. King was nurtured in the piety and idioms of an urban, middle-class, Black Baptist family and congregation. He deeply absorbed the evangelical piety and social concerns preached by his father. He got a more intellectual version of both things when he studied at Morehouse College, a distinctly social gospel institution." See Dorrien, *Breaking White Supremacy*, 18.

on in the struggle to achieve freedom and his confidence in God as the source of hope when there is no way were . . . impossible apart from his formation within the Black church."[21] It was King's formation in the Black church that cultivated his concern for the manner in which the gospel itself addressed issues of social, economic, and racial import. More than that, his upbringing within the Black ecclesial context also inspired his reticence to adopt more violent approaches to participation in the public sphere, even in the face of gross injustice.[22]

Philosophically and theologically, King drew from diverse sources; however, three figures, Walter Rauschenbusch, Reinhold Niebuhr, and Josiah Royce, seem to be of particular importance for developing an understanding of King's life and thought. King appreciated Rauschenbusch's concept of the Social Gospel in that it recognized Christianity's horizontal implications and obligations, that is, the manner in which the gospel must address how sin warps and perverts human societies.[23] The gospel, if it is to be true to Jesus's own life and earthly mission, must address the concrete problems of our world, especially those that are economic and social in nature.[24] From Niebuhr, King developed an appreciation for the way in which sin affects human society as well as Niebuhr's criticism of Protestant liberalism's optimism regarding the human condition. King also appears to have inherited Royce's account of the "beloved community," an idea to which we

---

[21] Miriam Y. Perkins, "The Praxis of Prophetic Voice: Martin Luther King, Jr. and Strategies for Resistance," *Black Theology* 17, no. 3 (2019): 245.

[22] King wrote in criticism of Black nationalism's and the Nation of Islam's more aggressive tactics. See Martin Luther King Jr., *Why We Can't Wait* (New York: Signet Classics, 2000), 100.

[23] Martin Luther King Jr., *The Papers of Martin Luther King, Jr.,* Martin Luther King Papers, ed. Clayborne Carson et al. (Berkeley: University of California, 1992), 3:418. For a discussion of King's indebtedness to the Social Gospel movement, see Vanessa Cook, "Martin Luther King, Jr., and the Long Social Gospel Movement," *Religion and American Culture* 26, no. 1 (2016): 74–100.

[24] See King, *The Papers*, 3:450.

will return.[25] Of course, it is worth noting that King did not accept these figures uncritically, diverging from them at key points. For example, according to King, Rauschenbusch's account of the Social Gospel was too optimistic regarding humanity's potential for self-improvement. Similarly, King was dissatisfied with what he saw as a failure of Niebuhr's Christian realism to account for how divine grace influences and transforms the present.[26]

Additionally, later in King's life, he became deeply indebted to the social and political activism of Mahatma Gandhi. Gandhi's commitment to nonviolent resistance was especially influential on King's social praxis as it provided a vibrant example of how an oppressed, powerless group might meaningfully effect social change.[27] Through his participation in the Montgomery protests, King realized that Gandhi's approach to nonviolence was a means of avoiding both passivity and despair in the face of oppressive social conditions. As Garrow observes, "[King] came to view Gandhian nonviolence as precisely such a middle course—an active path of resistance that avoided the sins of passivity and despair in the face of injustice, but a form of resistance that also avoided the multiplication of evil."[28] King found in Gandhi an embodiment of "the love ethic of Jesus above mere interaction between individuals" that could serve as an instrument of social and collective transformation for oppressed peoples as they struggled to realize their freedom.[29]

---

[25] While a genealogy of King's intellectual development is beyond the scope of this paper, Royce's *The Problem of Christianity* was in the curriculum at Crozer Seminary, where King studied, and seems to have directly influenced some of the thinking of King's professors. Moreover, as Gary Herstein observes, King seems to have developed some of Royce's insights. For a discussion of the relationship between King and Royce's understandings of the beloved community, see Herstein, "The Roycean Roots of the Beloved Community," *The Pluralist* 4, no. 2 (2009): 105–6; Rufus Burrow Jr., "The Beloved Community: Martin Luther King Jr. and Josiah Royce," *Encounter* 73, no. 1 (2012): 37–64.

[26] King, *The Papers*, 4:479.

[27] King, *The Papers*, 5:505.

[28] Garrow, "The Intellectual Development," 13.

[29] King, *Stride toward Freedom*, 84–85.

If the "beloved community" is the goal toward which political activism is intended and nonviolence is the methodology that enables its realization, King viewed Christian, agape love as the tie that binds these disparate influences together. Here, we see that King's political theology entails a commitment to embodying the politics and example of Jesus Christ. King believed that Christian social activism and resistance should never succumb to the temptation to use violence. Instead, it must follow in the path of Christian love and nonviolence, a path that was demonstrated in the life of Jesus and the work of Mahatma Gandhi.[30] Christian love, for King, was the fuel that empowered Christian activism and provided the framework for his political theology. For King, it is the commitment to the universal implications of the life and ministry of Jesus Christ that fuels an approach to politics that is distinctly theological in shape.

Texts and Tenets

Bibliography

King was a prolific writer and public speaker, giving speeches and lectures throughout his lifetime. His first book, *Stride Toward Freedom*, was originally published in 1958 and then revised in 1986 and 2010. It recalls the story of the Montgomery bus boycott. Three other key texts in King's corpus, *Strength to Love* (1963), *Why We Can't Wait* (1964), and *Where Do We Go from Here* (1967), illustrate a progression in King's thought as he pursued long-term solutions to economic and racial inequalities persisting in American civic life. *The Autobiography of Martin Luther King Jr.*, edited by Clayborne Carson, was released in 1998 and then reprinted in 2001. While numerous anthologies of King's work and collections of his speeches exist, it is important to note that King benefitted from multiple research assistants and ghost writers throughout his lifetime. Accordingly, some scholars believe that a true

---

[30] See King, *The Papers*, 5:504.

understanding of King's contributions to political theory and theology must be gleaned from his complete, edited writings, which are being collected by the Martin Luther King, Jr., Research and Education Institute in a multi-volume work titled *The Papers of Martin Luther King, Jr.* (1992–present).

Main Contributions

A Passionate Commitment to Nonviolence

One of King's principal contributions to political theology was his adoption of nonviolence as a tool for cultivating social change on both an institutional and interpersonal level. On the one hand, King's commitment to nonviolence was pragmatic. He noted the strategic advantages of nonviolence in that it was better positioned to achieve the long-term goals of reconciliation, integration, and harmony than violent revolt. According to King, nonviolence can function as a unique kind of weapon when it comes to pursuing social change. Unlike more coercive and violent means, nonviolent resistance not only has the power to advance social causes, but it also possesses the power to heal and restore the social fabric.[31] Given the disproportionate institutional agency of the marginalized, nonviolence served as a means of effecting change in broader society through suffering presence. If integration is the *telos* of protesting segregation, nonviolence enables the possibility of a future harmonious coexistence by refusing to identify our neighbors as enemies. For King, nonviolent resistance is the primary means through which the church can advance society toward the realization of the beloved community.[32]

---

[31] See King, *Why We Can't Wait*, 16.

[32] Karuna Mantena writes, "In King's case, the end or goals of militant non-violence were associated, at the abstract level, with the founding of the beloved or redemptive community and, more concretely, with the demands of 'integration' in American democracy." See Mantena, "Showdown for Nonviolence: The Theory and Practice of Nonviolent Politics," in *To Shape a New World: Essays on the Political*

However, King's commitment to nonviolence was not only pragmatic, but was tethered to his desire to cultivate the communal goods of self-worth and friendship. First, King believed that nonviolence was a tool for developing dignity within the oppressed and marginalized. For King, the approach of nonviolence allows the oppressed to find within themselves new capacities for endurance and fortitude, capacities they most likely did not even know that they possessed. In drawing on these internal reserves of virtue, they would then be able to cultivate a sense of self-respect and dignity.[33] King frequently identifies the need for African Americans to develop a sense of "somebodyness," that is, the need to cultivate a positive sense of self in light of the depersonalizing effects of slavery and the Jim Crow South. According to King, unjust social systems pervert the souls of both the oppressor and the oppressed, working to internalize feelings of inferiority, inhumanity, and worthlessness.[34] This is problematic for both parties involved as it stunts the development of human personality. However, the pain is felt acutely in the souls of the oppressed because such a belittled self-perception limits the possibility of certain kinds of political action, actions that are intended to cultivate human freedom and flourishing. Social activism and engagement, for King, begins with a change in self-evaluation and in the acknowledgment of one's possession of dignity as an image bearer

---

Philosophy of Martin Luther King, Jr., ed. Tommie Shelby and Brandon M. Terry (Cambridge: Belknap, 2018), 88. See also Martin Luther King Jr., *The Trumpet of Conscience* (Boston: Beacon, 2010), 25; King, *Stride toward Freedom*, 86. As has been noted, King described his interaction with the politics of nonviolence as a progression and a gradual pilgrimage; he saw himself as indebted to both the Christian tradition and the political philosophy of Gandhi. See King, *Stride toward Freedom*, 72. For a larger discussion of how Gandhi influenced King's thought as well as the ways King developed it with unique inflections provided by his engagement with Scripture and his location within the church, see Garrow, "The Intellectual Development," 9–17.

[33] See Martin Luther King Jr., *Strength to Love* (Minneapolis: Fortress, 2010), 161.

[34] King, *The Papers*, 5:222; King, *"All Labor,"* 78.

and child of God.[35] "The tension which we are witnessing in race relations today can be explained in part by the revolutionary change in the Negroe's evaluation of his nature and destiny, and his determination to struggle and sacrifice until the walls of segregation have finally been crushed."[36]

Second, King believed nonviolence enables the possibility of friendship across racial, ethnic, cultural, and economic lines. He was adamant that the telos of nonviolence was not the destruction, defeat, or humiliation of one's oppressors. Nonviolent resistance was not a passive-aggressive attempt to attain retribution or vengeance. Rather, it sought justice for both the oppressed and their oppressor.[37] This again ties back to King's larger anthropology and philosophical personalism. In viewing the "other" through the lens of hate, we ossify an I-It relationship with them, one that transmutes our neighbor into a tool to be used in pursuit of our own flourishing. Instead, King argues that the struggle against oppression is not focused on individual villains but targets the overarching systems and social practices that incentivize wickedness. Nonviolence, then, is a means of offering the branch of friendship to those in positions of power or privilege through the medium of sacrificial love.

Love, Justice, and Politics

In addition to King's contribution of nonviolent protest and his understanding of its efficacy vis-à-vis social change, King's political theology provides a robust portrait of the role emotions can and must play in the public sphere. Some political theorists and theologians have argued that citizens must purge passions from public life if they are to engage in civic processes in pursuit of the common good. For example, Hannah Arendt argued that love is fundamentally antipolitical and unworldly, turning us

---

[35] King, *The Papers*, 4:170–71.
[36] King, *The Papers*, 5:222–23.
[37] See King, *The Papers*, 3:418.

inward, away from the needs of our neighbors and corrupting political processes.[38] However, for King, love is fundamental to political engagement, particularly a love modeled on the life and witness of Jesus Christ, because of how it orders us *to* our neighbors. King believed that love was far more than an interior feeling, a fleeting disposition, or pathos, but was concrete and realized in action that pursues the flourishing of the entire human family, an active disposition that is committed to reweaving the fabric of human community regardless the cost.[39] In other words, communities must be bound with their disinterested, agape love for one another. According to King, this is the difference the ethos of the kingdom calls us to; that is, we must love one another as Christ loved us. Here, agape love is a disinterested creative force that seeks the goodwill of humankind, a love which he contrasted with both erotic and philanthropic forms.[40] It is this disinterested, sacrificial love that serves as the foundation for forming a just society, or at the very least, it is the means through which we might address the presence of current social injustice. For King, the strength to love one's enemies is grounded in the very power of God in Christ.[41] King's call to reach out to the other with agape love is rooted in his belief that the other is loved by God.[42] Love then becomes the means through which imperfect justice is realized in the present and human freedom is actualized.

Eric Gregory believes that this is one of the key contributions King makes to the fields of political theology and political theory. He argues that

---

[38] Hannah Arendt, *The Human Condition*, 2nd ed. (Chicago: University of Chicago Press, 2018), 242. Arendt seems to be concerned with our capacity to be manipulated by our loves and ends up destroying human freedom, a destruction that is perhaps best typified in totalitarian regimes. She writes, "Because of its inherent wordlessness, love can only become false and perverted when it is used for political purposes" (Arendt, 51–52).

[39] See King, *The Radical King*, 52.

[40] King, *The Papers*, 5:417.

[41] See King, 4:321.

[42] King, 5:417.

for King, "Love . . . is neither private virtue nor materially cut off from justice and equity. It is a commanding, listening, and empowering presence that is necessary for a just society that is not focused solely on justice as fairness."[43] According to King, love places demands and responsibilities on citizens to seek the good of their neighbors.[44] More than that, love is imperative to the realization of a just society as it enables us to sacrifice our lives for the sake of our neighbors, to listen to their cries of pain, and to struggle to realize their freedom. It is the soil that enables the cultivation of a just society, of a human community.

The Beloved Community

Finally, King also developed and extended Royce's concept of the "beloved community" so as to avoid both a naive political optimism and a stagnating political pessimism. While King did not create the concept de novo, he advanced it in important ways and grounded it in a Christian vision of the world. According to King, the "beloved community" serves as a tangible and realizable goal that Christian social activism seeks to instantiate in the present.[45] The concept of the beloved community serves as a galvanizing force for political engagement as it puts forward a positive vision of our possible future social life.

According to King, because God is the Father of every human being, this fraternal relationship between members of the human community must

---

[43] Eric Gregory, *Politics and the Order of Love: An Augustinian Ethic of Democratic Citizenship* (Chicago: University of Chicago, 2010), 194.

[44] Gregory, 194.

[45] Lewis V. Baldwin identifies four components of King's understanding of the "beloved community": (1) God's impartiality toward humanity; (2) a sacramental account of the world; (3) a belief in the value and dignity of every human person; and (4) a commitment to communal solidarity with other members of the human community. Baldwin, *Toward the Beloved Community: Martin Luther King, Jr., and South Africa* (Cleveland: Pilgrim, 1995), 2.

ground our vision of a common life.[46] For King, you and I are "our brother's keeper" because each of us is our brother's sister or brother. What affects one person impacts everyone in one way or another.[47] It is precisely this interconnectedness of humanity, an interconnectedness rooted in the filial relationship in which we exist, that motivates our concern and care for one another. As Wills observes, "[King] fervently believed that this common tie to God could bridge benevolent relations between individuals, groups, and even nations."[48] The concept of the "beloved community" functions as a cipher for this vision of a possible future made viable by the reconciling work of God in Christ, one we must work to realize and attain.[49] Herstein posits that King's understanding of the beloved community contains two central characteristics: it is "an embodiment of agapic love" and it is "the embodiment of Moral Laws."[50] As a finite instantiation of the eschatological kingdom of God, the beloved community is characterized by harmony and peace between its members. It is a community where needs are met and the bonds of friendship are not constrained by the boundaries of race, ethnicity, or class.[51] Moreover, it is a community where the material, psychological, and spiritual needs of its members are met, and there is no lack so that Blacks and whites experience political, social, and economic equality.

---

[46] King, *The Papers*, 3:449.

[47] See Martin Luther King Jr., *Where Do We Go from Here: Chaos or Community?* (Boston: Beacon, 2010), 191.

[48] Richard W. Wills, *Martin Luther King, Jr. and the Image of God* (Oxford: Oxford University, 2009), 140.

[49] King, *The Papers*, 3:328. As Rufus Burrow Jr. observes, "Martin Luther King speaks and writes about the beloved community as if it was something that is not only partially achievable in history, but that which may, at some point, be fully achievable. . . . The beloved community concept was for King more than an operative or regulative ideal, although it was also this. He believed that as long as human beings put forth the effort we can more nearly approximate the requirements of such a community." Burrow, *Martin Luther King, Jr., and the Theology of Resistance* (Jefferson, NC: McFarland, 2015), 124–25.

[50] Herstein, "The Roycean Roots," 93–95.

[51] King, *Where Do We Go from Here*, 201.

Controversies

At this point, it is perhaps easy to see how King serves as a powerful example of a Christian political theology that moves beyond ecclesial spaces to effect transformation in the wider world in the pursuit of freedom. His legacy indeed is a powerful one. However, it is worth noting the many ways King failed to live up to the ideals he espoused. One of the more well-known blemishes on his résumé is that King committed acts of plagiarism and took credit for the work of others without acknowledging his indebtedness to them. While King benefitted from many assistants and speech writers throughout his career, numerous times he passed off someone else's work as his own. In 1991, an independent panel at Boston University confirmed that King plagiarized significant portions of his doctoral dissertation, *A Comparison of the Conceptions of God in the Thinking of Paul Tillich and Henry Nelson Wieman.*[52] Additional instances of plagiarism appear in some of King's seminar papers throughout graduate school.[53] Similarly, there are many undocumented citations in King's speeches and sermons, and many other instances throughout the major texts of King's corpus borrow multiple ideas and paragraphs without citation.[54] These examples are problematic primarily because of how they complicate King's claims regarding truthfulness, integrity, "somebodyness," and human dignity. Put bluntly, King's actions seem to deny many of these authors the same dignity and respect he believed was inherent to the human race.

Finally, while King's marital troubles and infidelity are well noted and documented,[55] a pattern of behavior that seems to have been endemic to the SCLC, what is more troubling is the way this complicates his ethical project

---

[52] King, *The Papers*, 3:25–26, 340.

[53] Ralph Luker, "Plagiarism and Perspective," *International Social Science Review* 68, no. 4 (1993): 152–55.

[54] For an overview of the sources of King's texts and the manner in which he borrowed from them, see Keith D. Miller, *Voice of Deliverance: The Language of Martin Luther King, Jr., and Its Sources* (Athens: University of Georgia, 1998).

[55] See David. J. Garrow, *Bearing the Cross: Martin Luther King, Jr., and the Southern Christian Leadership Conference*, rep. ed. (New York: Harper Collins,

as a whole, especially in light of King's personalism and critiques of power. As Traci West observes, "The subject of King's extramarital sexual relationships allow us to engage in a much-needed dialogue about the merits of separating private from public behavior when assessing community leaders. . . . [B]oundaries of appropriate conduct are necessary for leaders, especially ministers. Their power and authority are so centrally derived from the deep trust they are given without having to earn it."[56] In other words, King was not merely a minister, but a man in a position of incredible power and influence within the civil rights movement and the African American community. Any accounting of his political theology must deal with the women whose lives he left in his wake, especially given his emphasis on noncoercive, agape love. It is worth wondering, in a manner not dissimilar to the situations involving figures such as John Howard Yoder and Jean Vanier, the degree to which King saw his actions as consistent and compatible with his political, theological proposals and the implications for how we understand his project on a larger scale. However, what is more troubling still is the recent work conducted by David Garrow, which raises the possibility that King's extramarital activity was far more egregious than we realize, and more information will most certainly come to light when the King tapes are declassified in 2027.[57]

Legacies

Martin Luther King Jr. stands as one of the most memorable and influential figures in American political theology. As Cornel West proposes, "Martin Luther King, Jr., was the most significant and successful organic intellectual in American history. Never before in our past has a figure outside of

---

2004), 373–76; Stephen B. Oates, *Let the Trumpet Sound: A Life of Martin Luther King, Jr.* (New York: Harper and Row, 1982), 283.

[56] Traci C. West, "Gendered Legacies of Martin Luther King Jr.'s Leadership," *Theology Today* 65, no. 1 (2008): 49–50.

[57] David J. Garrow, "The Troubling Legacy of Martin Luther King," *Standpoint* (June 2019): 30–37.

elected public office linked the life of the mind to social change with such moral persuasiveness and political effectiveness."[58] While he borrowed from a host of sources, he consistently brought the logic of Christian theology to bear on the environment in which he lived. Moreover, King illustrates that political theology can be both critical and constructive. Without a doubt, King frequently criticized the United States government for its failure to extend the goods of human freedom to every member of its society. His hope was that in exposing the injustice of American life, he could motivate and mobilize its participants toward the formation of a more just society.[59] In so doing, he provides a positive vision of the fundamentally prophetic disposition of Christian political theology, a vision that refuses to accept the sinfulness of this world as inevitable.

Additionally, King was unwilling to stop merely at prophetic critique. Instead, he moved beyond criticism to put forth a positive and practical vision of what communal life could entail. It is a vision of economic opportunity, peaceable coexistence, and integrated communities. It is a positive vision of human flourishing, albeit flourishing within the confines of a fallen world. It is perhaps instructive that King is most fondly remembered, rightly or wrongly, for his exhortation to realize the beloved community. Avoiding a triumphalist approach to American life, King nevertheless believed that progress was possible through sacrificial love and suffering presence. He believed human agents in general and Christians in particular could serve as the means through which the love of God would be made manifest in the world for the sake of the world.

Conclusion

For Martin Luther King Jr., the church has a responsibility in public space and must adopt the tools indicative of its eschatological nature to move the

---

[58] West, "Prophetic Christian as Organic Intellectual," 426.
[59] King, *Where Do We Go from Here*, 166–67.

world in accordance with the will and law of God. The church has a ministry to the public and, yes, to the state. It must seek the advancement of human freedom and the cultivation of beloved communities. While King remained realistic about the frailty and sinfulness of the societies in which he lived, his life and work reflect a perception of the church's theological task as having a public and horizontal face: addressing the roots of social evil and cultivating the beloved community. The church is a community that bears witness to the dignity of humanity, mediates the sacrificial love of Christ, and actualizes a historical instantiation of the eschatological kingdom of God. In so doing, the church calls the state to change, to become a place where the people whom God loves can one day be free.

14

Carl F. H. Henry

By Jason G. Duesing and Jesse M. Payne

From 1948 to 1949, Carl F. H. Henry spent a series of evenings in Hollywood answering questions from college students. The conversations explored theology, philosophy, science, and even touched on relevant issues for the demographic including "How to Find a Wife." As seen in the compilation of the Q&A sessions, most of Henry's answers to the students' questions were substantive, but the striking short-ness and simplicity of one in particular is interesting:

[Question]: I don't think the Christian ought to have anything at all to do with politics, do you?

[Henry]: Why not found a monastery? I know a chap who wants to sell some real estate out near the desert.[1]

---

[1] Carl F. H. Henry, *Giving a Reason for Our Hope* (Boston: W. A. Wilde, 1949), 85.

Ironically, the terse answer both clarifies and muddies Henry's posture toward politics. On the one hand, the answer reveals his conviction that yes, Christians should participate in the political sphere. He "bewailed the attrition of evangelical influence in the public sector."[2] On the other, Henry's sarcasm might insinuate he had nothing more to say on the topic. It dims the fact that he spent his remaining decades building a theological case for this response. From his first bestseller, *The Uneasy Conscience of Modern Fundamentalism*, to his first article for *Christianity Today*, "The Fragility of Freedom in the West," to his final book, *Has Democracy Had Its Day?*, Henry argued that "serious reflection on the Christian philosophy of politics" is "an important aspect" of Christian thinking.[3]

This chapter will analyze Henry's understanding of faith and politics. It will demonstrate that his political vision emerged from the matrix of three theological concepts, each distinct but related: theology proper, anthropology, and the kingdom of God.[4] That is, Henry's political theology was constructed from the biblical portraits of God, man, and the reign of the God-man. While Henry's conception of political theology was not altogether unique in Baptist history, the cultural moment in which he operated provides a helpful lens through which to understand the intensity with which he applied Baptist principles to a changing world. Contemporary Baptists find in Henry a model thinker and guide as they navigate a shifting political and cultural landscape while remaining true to their Baptist beliefs.

---

[2] Paul Henry, "A First-Term Congressman Looks at Faith and Politics," *Christianity Today* (March 15, 1985): 41.

[3] Carl F. H. Henry, *Has Democracy Had Its Day?*, 2nd ed. (1996; Nashville: Leland House, 2019), 46.

[4] These categories are adapted from Jason G. Duesing, "Is There a Baptist Contribution to Political Theology?" (presentation, Ethics and Religious Liberty Research Institute Symposium, Dallas, Texas, October 10, 2018).

Contexts: The News, the New Birth, and the New Evangelicalism

Carl F. H. Henry (1913–2003) was born to German immigrants in Long Island, New York. His childhood was humble, and his religious experience nominal. He had one consuming passion throughout his teenage and young-adult years: journalism.

Henry quickly ascended Long Island's journalistic ranks after graduating high school, assembling an impressive résumé for a young writer. His work exposed him to the inner life and underbelly of politics at an early age. Reflecting on these days, he told an audience in 1990 that he was "quite early into politics."[5] In his autobiography Henry recalled, "I covered political rallies and civic meetings. . . . This inside glimpse of politics lent a certain tempting fascination to see it as a possible future career option."[6] This early context helps inform his later attraction to political theology. His journalistic experience extended into his next life as a theologian in that it gave him a "sensitivity" to the political climate of his day and contributed to his ability to make informed policy judgments.[7] Later, Henry's son, Paul, taught political science and served Michigan in the United States House of Representatives until his death from brain cancer in 1993. Paul was his father's closest political conversation partner, and they had monthly chats "about what it requires and does not require for a Christian to be faithful in political service."[8]

---

[5] Carl F. H. Henry, "If I Had to Do It Again," address to the West Suburban Evangelical Fellowship, May 7, 1990, from Rolfing Library (Trinity Evangelical Divinity School), *Carl F. H. Henry Papers*, 3.

[6] Carl F. H. Henry, *Confessions of a Theologian* (Waco: Word Books, 1986), 38.

[7] Mavis M. Leung, "With What Is Evangelicalism to Penetrate the World? A Study of Carl Henry's Envisioned Evangelicalism," *Trinity Journal* 27, no. 2 (Fall 2006): 231.

[8] Henry, "If I Had to Do It Again," 5.

Early in his newspaper days, Henry forged a relationship with his "white-haired, middle-aged" colleague Mrs. Mildred Christy, whom he affectionately referred to as "Mother Christy."[9] Through her prayers and consistent witness, Henry was put into contact with the man who would eventually lead him to Christ in 1933. Soon after, Henry devoted his life to Christian ministry.

After his conversion, Henry graduated from Wheaton College, Northern Baptist Theological Seminary, and Boston University. He was a central figure in the founding of numerous institutions, including the National Association of Evangelicals, Fuller Theological Seminary, and *Christianity Today*, and he functioned as the "theological architect" of mid-twentieth century evangelicalism.[10] His efforts helped catapult a new movement that was "determined to reject the quietism of yesteryear and engage culture at a variety of levels. . . . [Early leaders] referred to their movement as the 'new evangelicalism.' Historians would label it neo-evangelicalism."[11] Neo-evangelicalism encompassed a variety of conservative denominations, and Henry embodied this interdenominational inclination. Gregory Thornbury captures Henry's legacy well: "It would be fair to say that if Billy Graham was the heart of evangelicalism, Carl F. H. Henry was its head."[12]

Henry's Key Texts: The Manifesto, the Magazine, and the Magnum Opus

While he authored or edited over forty books and wrote reams of journal articles, Henry's career was bookended by his two most significant

---

[9] Henry, *Confessions of a Theologian*, 33–46.

[10] Peter Goodwin Heltzel, *Jesus and Justice: Evangelicals, Race, and American Politics* (New Haven: Yale University, 2009), 71.

[11] Miles S. Mullin, II, "Evangelicalism as Trojan Horse: The Failure of Neo-Evangelical Social Theology and the Decline of Denominationalism," *Criswell Theological Review* (Fall 2014): 51.

[12] Gregory Alan Thornbury, *Recovering Classic Evangelicalism: Applying the Wisdom and Vision of Carl F. H. Henry* (Wheaton, IL: Crossway, 2013), 22.

contributions, *The Uneasy Conscience of Modern Fundamentalism* (1947) and *God, Revelation and Authority* (1976–1983). Midway between these, Henry served as founding editor for *Christianity Today* (1956–1968).

The Uneasy Conscience of Modern Fundamentalism served as a spirited manifesto for Evangelical social action and has been deemed perhaps "the most important evangelical book of the twentieth century."[13] Henry thought fundamentalists had surrendered a comprehensive vision of cultural engagement and replaced it with a myopic focus on a limited range of individual vices. He saw mid-century fundamentalism as "the modern priest and Levite, by-passing suffering humanity" through their reluctance to sympathize with societal brokenness.[14] Despite the consideration Henry gave to political theology in the decades following the book's publication, David Weeks argues that "none of his political writings has had the reach and impact" of this slender volume (other than, perhaps, his work at *Christianity Today*).[15]

Henry was pivotal in the birth and blossoming of the fortnightly periodical *Christianity Today* (*CT*). With Henry at the helm, *Christianity Today* became "the magazine of record" for most evangelicals.[16] Despite unresolved tension that lingered throughout Henry's tenure, he was proud of the product and reminded his team (and himself) that not even Billy Graham could speak to as many Protestant ministers every two weeks as they did.[17] One of the first decisions between Billy Graham and L. Nelson Bell was that the

---

[13] Russell D. Moore, review of 2003 reprint of *The Uneasy Conscience of Modern Fundamentalism*, by Carl F. H. Henry, *Journal of the Evangelical Theological Society* 48, no. 1 (2005): 182–83.

[14] Carl F. H. Henry, *The Uneasy Conscience of Modern Fundamentalism* (1947; Grand Rapids: Eerdmans, 2003), 2.

[15] David L. Weeks, "Carl F. H. Henry's Moral Arguments for Evangelical Political Activism," *Journal of Church and State* 40, no. 1 (Winter 1998): 94.

[16] Thomas S. Kidd, *Who Is an Evangelical? The History of a Movement in Crisis* (New Haven, CT: Yale University, 2019), 87.

[17] Henry, *Confessions of a Theologian*, 174.

magazine would be based in Washington, DC.[18] They believed this would lend credibility to the start-up publication as well as provide physical and intellectual proximity to the nation's political hub. Henry's office overlooked the White House, which was a daily reminder "of Christianity's relevance for all facets of life, politics included, and also of the importance of church-state separation."[19]

The magazine frequently carried political content. Because "numerous articles and nearly 40 percent of the editorials were politically oriented," politics, once rebuffed by fundamentalists, became "common fare" for readers.[20] *Christianity Today*'s self-understanding was "primarily as a theological tool," challenging rigid fundamentalism and Protestant liberalism, but its "political import was acknowledged."[21] As David S. Dockery notes, Henry "used the pages of *CT* to become the leading voice" on Evangelical cultural engagement and social ethics.[22] In the early 1960s, Henry was proud that "at present an evangelical philosophy of politics is doubtless more frequently discussed in *Christianity Today* than in any other conservative religious journal."[23] Henry used both articles and editorials (some of which bear his name, many of which do not) to address how the Christian gospel and God's self-revelation in Scripture ought to bear upon human interaction and institutions in the public sphere. His editorial voice and oversight carried significant weight in how the magazine approached specific issues, leaving

---

[18] George Marsden, *Reforming Fundamentalism: Fuller Seminary and the New Evangelicalism* (Grand Rapids: Eerdmans, 1987), 158.

[19] Henry, *Confessions of a Theologian*, 149.

[20] Weeks, "Carl F. H. Henry's Moral Arguments," 96.

[21] Phyllis E. Alsdurf, "The Founding of *Christianity Today* Magazine and the Construction of An American Evangelical Identity," *Journal of Religious and Theological Information* 9 (2010): 31.

[22] David S. Dockery, introduction to *Architect of Evangelicalism: Essential Essays of Carl F. H. Henry*, by Carl F. H. Henry (Bellingham: Lexham, 2019), 5.

[23] Carl F. H. Henry, *Aspects of Christian Social Ethics* (1964; Grand Rapids: Baker, 1980), 129.

Henry as one of the chief shapers of how broad evangelicalism thought about political topics of the day.

Henry's capstone achievement was his monumental *God, Revelation and Authority* (*GRA*). Published in six volumes between 1976–1983, Henry's magnum opus "contains more than three thousand pages, and none of them is meant for light bedtime reading."[24] It is simultaneously about *one* thing and *everything*—how God's divine revelation informs and appraises all human thought and activity. *GRA* was the *telos* of Henry's career and demonstrates "an investment of energy commensurate with [his] lifelong conviction" that "authority and revelation are the commanding theological issues of the time."[25]

The most sustained treatment of political theology in *GRA* is found in volume 5 as part of Henry's discussion on justice and the kingdom of God. It represents decades of Henry's thinking and bears the classic marks of his hand: forceful argumentation; exchanges with his contemporaries; movement between history, philosophy, and exegesis; and, especially in this section, an appeal for the primacy of special revelation (rather than natural law) as the transcendent authority over all political considerations.[26]

While not his most read or remembered works, other volumes and articles help fill out Henry's political theology. Their spotlight on Christianity and politics sheds light on his political thought. In particular, Henry's final book, *Has Democracy Had Its Day?*, demonstrates that he "sides with a distinctly Baptistic vision for religion and politics, church and state."[27] His

---

[24] Timothy George, foreword to *Essential Evangelicalism: The Enduring Influence of Carl F. H. Henry*, ed. Matthew J. Hall and Owen Strachan (Wheaton, IL: Crossway, 2015), 11.

[25] Gabriel Fackre, "Carl F. H. Henry," in *A Handbook of Christian Theologians*, ed. Dean G. Peerman and Martin E. Marty, enlarged ed. (Nashville: Abingdon, 1984), 589.

[26] Carl F. H. Henry, *God, Revelation and Authority*, 6 vols. (Wheaton, IL: Crossway, 1999), 6:454. Hereafter, *GRA*.

[27] Andrew T. Walker, introduction to *Has Democracy Had Its Day?*, by Carl F. H. Henry, xi.

1964 *Aspects of Christian Social Ethics* is something of an extensive follow-up to *The Uneasy Conscience of Modern Fundamentalism*. These and others confirm where we began: Henry devoted himself to political themes more than is remembered, and by retrieving his thought, Baptists will find a valuable guide in challenging political times.

Henry's Key Tenets: Theology Proper, Anthropology, and the Kingdom

With Henry's key texts outlined, we can begin developing the chapter's thesis: Henry's political vision emerged from the matrix of three theological concepts, each distinct but related: theology proper, anthropology, and the kingdom of God. That is, Henry's political theology was constructed from the biblical portraits of God, man, and the reign of the God-man.

Henry's thought was anchored and controlled by Scripture, and while he traversed other fields throughout his argumentation, he always returned home to the Book as the full and final authority. One of Henry's contentions with certain self-professed "Christian" conceptions of political theology was that they viewed the Bible less as God's self-revelation and more as a collective proof text for their political ends. In his entry for "Political Theology" in *Baker's Dictionary of Christian Ethics*, Henry found these approaches to be theologically wanting, anthropocentric, and potentially sub-biblical concepts dressed "in Christian garb."[28] Henry aimed for a more expressly biblical and theological alternative.

We will also see that while Henry's political vision does not deviate from the Baptist tradition, the theological intentionality with which he wrote and the challenges he confronted provide today's readers with a thorough and thoughtful resource. He dedicated *Aspects of Christian Social Ethics* to "all

---

[28] Carl F. H. Henry, "Political Theology," in *Baker's Dictionary of Christian Ethics*, ed. Carl F. H. Henry (Grand Rapids: Baker, 1973), 513–14.

who share a passion for applying God's truth to these disjointed times."[29] Our disjointed days are not altogether different than his, and we will profit from leaning into what Henry has to share.

"The God of Justice and Justification": Theology Proper and Political Theology

Henry anchored his understanding of political theology in the Creator and Sustainer of the cosmos, the triune God as revealed in the Old and New Testaments. For Henry, "the concept of God is determinative for all other concepts."[30] Every topic Henry addressed was a spoke emanating from the hub of theology proper, including that of political theology. His emphasis on God's consuming relevance for all of life is clear in *Aspects of Christian Social Ethics*: "According to the Christian doctrine of the sovereignty of God, the ultimate principles of ethics are derived from the will of God; further, man's entire moral endeavor must be set within the purposes of God."[31] God's exhaustive sovereignty is one reason (among many) that Henry rejected totalitarianism—totalitarian leaders viewed their own prerogatives as decisive rather than yielding to the God who reigns. God is "the centre and circumference of all democracy," said Ishmael in Herman Melville's *Moby Dick*—a notion Henry could endorse.[32]

Thus, Henry's understanding of political theology can be traced back to the rule of God over his creation. God's dominion is imaged in

---

[29] Carl F. H. Henry, *Aspects of Christian Social Ethics* (Grand Rapids: Eerdmans, 1964), 5.

[30] Carl F. H. Henry, *Remaking the Modern Mind* (Grand Rapids: Eerdmans, 1948), 175. He also wrote, "The doctrine of God is unquestionably the most important tenet for comprehending biblical religion." See Henry, *GRA*, 5:18.

[31] Henry, *Aspects of Christian Social Ethics*, 87.

[32] Herman Melville, *Moby Dick; or, The Whale*, Great Books of the Western World, ed. Robert M. Hutchins and Mortimer J. Adler (London: Encyclopædia Britannica, 1952), 85.

his creation of man and woman, who are commanded to exercise God's will in God's world. After the fall, this command extended to how they organize and assemble themselves.[33] This political activity lay not outside of God's transcendent will but is a crucial aspect of it. Henry was convinced that politics is not an incidental aspect of society born out of expediency; rather, it is sanctioned by God's will and fused with divine interest and import.[34] There exists a "divine linking of God's will with civil government."[35] The fact that government "exists by the providential will of God" should shape the Christian's posture toward the political enterprise.[36]

One of Henry's favorite designations for God was "the God of Justice and Justification."[37] God is not just because he adheres to an external standard of righteousness but because "he in himself consistently affirms his nature and is unswervingly faithful to his own promises and his covenant."[38] The political process was one key way Christians could express something of the justice of God, which "is at home in eternity . . . but has an uneasy foothold in civil government."[39] Political power, as utilized by individuals or governments, is a "divine entrustment, accountable to the Deity for the preservation of justice and order."[40] Henry believed that the political process was a mechanism

---

[33] Henry saw civil government as a post-fall institution granted by God to help allay the ramifications of the curse: "Civil government has been introduced by God because of the fall of mankind into sin. Were it not for sin, we would know no government but the rule of God." See Carl F. H. Henry, "Christianity and the American Heritage," *Vital Speeches of the Day* (August 1953), 621.

[34] Carl F. H. Henry, *The Christian Mindset in a Secular Society* (Portland: Multnomah, 1984), 131.

[35] Henry, *GRA*, 6:446.

[36] Carl F. H. Henry, "Church and State: Why the Marriage Must Be Saved," *Christianity Today* (April 19, 1985): 12.

[37] Henry, *GRA*, 6:402.

[38] Henry, *GRA*, 6:425.

[39] Henry, *GRA*, 6:433.

[40] Henry, *Has Democracy Had Its Day?*, 4.

by which believers could explicate and expand upon the common good, which would serve to illuminate God's justice and curtail injustice in a fallen world.[41] He saw political activity as a form of "translation," wherein God's justice is formulated into concrete manifestations of his will:

> God's people should be a mighty voice for justice in the land— aware that biblical justice does not necessarily coincide with propagandistic perceptions of justice. Given a comprehensive vision and theology of politics illumined by scriptural principles, God's people have the task of translating these into policies and platforms and support for desirable programs and candidates.[42]

God's Image and God's Servants: Anthropology and Political Theology

Henry based his political theology not only on the authority and justice of God, but also on the unique dignity and creation of man in God's image. He believed "all members of the human community are simultaneously carriers of a created dignity and of divinely stipulated responsibilities and rights."[43] In other words, by implication of the *imago Dei*, all men have both a *right* to worship their Creator and a *responsibility* to participate in God's ordained means of civil organization.

The *Right* to Worship: Religion and Politics

Because all people of all times in all places are bearers of God's image, Henry believed "all human activity—political activity included—is religious,

---

[41] Henry, *GRA*, 6:432.

[42] Carl F. H. Henry, "The Concerns and Considerations of Carl F. H. Henry," *Christianity Today* (March 13, 1981): 22.

[43] Henry, *Has Democracy Had Its Day?*, 5.

involving the human service of either the true God or of false gods."[44] A value system is "implicit in all thought and action," including as related to civil government.[45] He summarized this well in one 1976 article: "[E]ven when a society is not explicitly religious it nonetheless is implicitly so. Mankind is by nature religious, even if some members of the human species devote themselves religiously to irreligion. . . . The issue touching civil religion is not *whether* we shall have it, but *what* sort of civil religion we do and ought to have."[46] As Henry saw it, embedded in human nature is an inescapable propensity to serve either the true God or false ones through every aspect of one's activity in the world.

This anthropological reality has significant ramifications for how one understands the political sphere. Because human beings are by nature children of worship, a Christian's right to worship God should be recognized and upheld by the subordinate authorities operating under the sovereign Lord and King. Henry always stressed "man's unique relationship to the Creator" as "the divine source and sanction of human rights."[47] He saw this relationship between biblical anthropology and politics as an indispensable emphasis to any "sound political theory."[48] This is another reason Henry rejected totalitarianism—it attempted to "obscure" and "cancel" the divinely stipulated rights possessed by all people.[49] Both rulers and ruled everywhere should respect these rights.[50]

---

[44] Henry, *The Christian Mindset in a Secular Society*, 131.

[45] Henry, *Has Democracy Had Its Day?*, 28.

[46] Carl F. H. Henry, "Theological Reflections on Bicentennial Concerns," *Religious Education* 71 (May–June 1976), 295.

[47] Henry, *Aspects of Christian Social Ethics*, 90.

[48] Henry, 90.

[49] Henry, *Has Democracy Had Its Day?*, 5.

[50] Carl F. H. Henry, "Human Rights in an Age of Tyranny," *Christianity Today* (February 4, 1957): 20.

The *Responsibility* to Participate: Service and Politics

Henry thought biblical anthropology not only grants a *right* to all people to worship freely (which implies boundaries to political authority), but also a *responsibility* to participate in the political structures available to them. Politics is not strictly a personal endeavor; it is "communal" in nature—in other words, it is one way love can be expressed in the public order.[51] Henry's prioritization of political participation was due to his belief that it was one of the most neglected opportunities to love one's neighbor. It was an opportunity to contribute to the relief of injustice and suffering in a fallen world. Because of the shared ecosystem of the human experience, believers should see themselves as their "brother's, sister's, and neighbor's keeper."[52]

Henry's estimation that conservative Protestants were not seeing themselves as such was the impetus behind his *The Uneasy Conscience of Modern Fundamentalism*. He sensed a "reluctance to come to grips with social evils" in the collective persona of fundamentalism, and he hoped to spark a greater sense of heavenly responsibility to address worldly ills.[53] Politics was not the leading edge of alleviation for these societal problems, but it was an instrument to be utilized.[54] He stressed the call for Christians to be politically active not as a substitute for love of God and neighbor, but as a consequence of it because "one desirable way of loving one's neighbor as one's self is to promote good public policy."[55] He believed Scripture speaks

---

[51] Henry, *Has Democracy Had Its Day?*, 5.

[52] Henry, *The Christian Mindset in a Secular Society*, 102.

[53] Henry, *The Uneasy Conscience of Modern Fundamentalism*, 4.

[54] Henry wrote, "The illusion that all the world's problems can be solved merely by political change is disastrous. But to neglect political imperatives can likewise be naturally devastating." See Henry, "The Concerns and Considerations of Carl F. H. Henry," 21.

[55] Carl F. H. Henry, "The Church in the World or the World in the Church? A Review Article," *Journal of the Evangelical Theological Society* 34 (September 1991): 383.

to general principles of justice rather than to the specifics of layered and complex policy, but he hoped the challenges of linking the Bible to modern politics would not discourage believers from striving to do so in a humble and prayerful manner.[56]

The Reign of the God-Man: The Kingdom and Political Theology

Henry's emphasis on the kingdom of God and the risen and reigning Christ remains his most important contribution to Evangelical political theology.

Henry gave attention to the kingdom of God in virtually every publication over his decades of work, whether explicitly or implicitly. Therefore, it seems fitting to let him summarize his understanding of the kingdom, as outlined in *GRA* near the end of his career. It is a rich and detailed paragraph, but every word contributes to his developed thought on the nature of the kingdom:

> The kingdom of God is decisive for present earthly history, even though its glory is now only transcendently present and must await future horizontal manifestation. While the authority-claims and transforming power of that kingdom presently call for voluntary commitment, its future manifestation will involve compulsory recognition and response. God's historical redemptive acts, scripturally attested, and supremely so in the sinless life, atoning death and bodily resurrection of the incarnate Logos, already manifest the powers of the kingdom. Christ comes at present by the Holy Spirit to renew and indwell the people of God and rules over the church as the new society; at the last he will come as eschatological

---

[56] Carl F. H. Henry, "Linking the Bible to Public Policy," in *Politics and Public Policy: A Christian Response—Crucial Considerations for Governing Life*, The Christian Response Series, ed. Timothy J. Demy and Gary P. Stewart (Grand Rapids: Kregel, 2000), 68.

God-man fully to actualize and to horizontally complete the king-dom's final reality.[57]

The first sentence of this paragraph captures what Henry introduced into Evangelical political thought, beginning with *The Uneasy Conscience of Modern Fundamentalism*.[58] While contemporary Evangelicals might assume the already/not yet schema for understanding the kingdom, in his day Henry felt caught between two unsatisfactory kingdom frameworks: either entirely *already* (Protestant liberalism and postmillennialism) or entirely *not yet* (fundamentalism and quietism). In contrast to both Protestant liberal-ism's over-realized eschatology (imminent utopianism) and fundamental-ism's under-realized eschatology (distant restoration), Henry argued for an inaugurated eschatology that is "essentially distinct from any of the now/then philosophies in that it accepts both now and then as proper kingdom orientations, simultaneously present and future."[59]

This view shaped Evangelical political theology. Russell Moore's *The Kingdom of Christ: The New Evangelical Perspective* remains the best articu-lation of the lasting significance of Henry's perspective on the kingdom, including its political implications.[60] According to Moore, Henry was chal-lenging multiple kingdom conceptions simultaneously. Not only did he cri-tique Protestant liberalism and the Social Gospel; he also questioned the intramural discussions between covenantal and dispensational views of the kingdom—and it was these later discussions that led directly to the "near

---

[57] Henry, *GRA*, 6:505. See also Carl F. H. Henry, "Reflections on the Kingdom of God," *Journal of the Evangelical Theological Society* 35, no. 1 (March 1992): 39–49.

[58] Henry returned to the interplay of eschatology, ethics, and the kingdom ten years later in *Christian Personal Ethics*, albeit with greater academic rigor than he undertook in *The Uneasy Conscience of Modern Fundamentalism*. See Carl F. H. Henry, *Christian Personal Ethics* (Grand Rapids: Wm. B. Eerdmans, 1957), 549–72.

[59] Thornbury, *Recovering Classic Evangelicalism*, 173.

[60] Russell D. Moore, *The Kingdom of Christ: The New Evangelical Perspective* (Wheaton, IL: Crossway, 2004).

consensus" of how evangelicals understand the kingdom in relation to the church and the world today.[61]

Henry realized that the disagreements between the covenantal view (which emphasized the in-breaking of the kingdom now) and the dispensational view (which emphasized the not-yet nature of restoration) were directly related to the sociopolitical task.[62] The theological cold war needed to end, and Henry's entrance into the fray allowed the strengths of both views to rise to the fore.[63] In doing so, he demonstrated that the kingdom has *already* broken into the world in the person and work of Christ, placing responsibilities upon citizens of the kingdom who call on Jesus as Lord in the here and now, including how they engage politically. He also recognized that the kingdom will be fully manifest only when Christ returns, tempering ultimate Christian hope from the political and redirecting it toward the gospel and the *not yet* of the eschatological remaking of all things. How Henry related the church to the world through the prism of the kingdom provides a helpful vantage point from which to understand how kingdom citizens should operate politically in light of the reigning and returning God-man. Moore's own evaluation springs from the logical consequences of Henry's thought: "American evangelicalism ought to become more *and* less political."[64]

What role did Henry see the church playing in this already/not yet kingdom framework? Here he used the language of the church "approximating" the kingdom today.[65] The church does not "externalize" the kingdom,[66] but through her life and teaching she bears witness to macro kingdom realities on a "miniature" scale.[67] The church is a "new society" and "a colony

---

[61] Moore, *The Kingdom of Christ*, 21–22, 131.

[62] Moore, 22.

[63] Moore, 22.

[64] Moore, 12. Italics added for emphasis.

[65] This was Henry's fourteenth thesis in *GRA*. See Henry, *GRA*, 4:542.

[66] Henry, "Reflections on the Kingdom of God," 45.

[67] Henry, *GRA*, 4:542.

of heaven" living in the world.[68] Because she gives ultimate allegiance to Christ as King and operates according to the governing documents of the Old and New Testaments, Henry saw the church as an "alternative political community."[69] This community was not in competition with other political parties or movements; it transcended the world's political structures and carried out a divine mission granted by Jesus himself.

Henry connected the already/not yet kingdom framework with political theology by seeing believers as existing simultaneously in two spheres: "Christianity also has discriminated between the religious and political spheres, yet without fully disjoining them. Both are indispensable aspects of faithful Christian calling, and each renders service to the other."[70] In operating as kingdom citizens, believers should proclaim the good news of Christ and live according to his Word. In operating as earthly citizens, they should seek justice in the name of Jesus through the various mechanisms available. But Henry's Baptist roots were obvious in his recognition that the church is never to co-opt the political to fulfill her divine mission—that is to misunderstand the spheres and incorrectly collapse them together. The church's chief responsibility in the world is to seek voluntary persuasion of the lost, not to impose ecclesiastical mandates.[71] The church's commission is to announce redemption through the cross and empty tomb, for this good news alone is the only true and lasting antidote to spiritual and sociopolitical brokenness. The crux of his political theology was regeneration, and his accent was always placed on the primacy of individual transformation by the Spirit. He stressed this in *The Uneasy Conscience of Modern Fundamentalism*:

> The divine order involves a super-natural principle, a creative force that enters society from outside its natural sources of uplift, and regenerates humanity. In that divine reversal of the self-defeating

---

[68] Henry, "The Church in the World or the World in the Church?," 381.
[69] Henry, 381.
[70] Henry, "Church and State," 9.
[71] Henry, *The Christian Mindset in a Secular Society*, 124.

sinfulness of man is the only real answer to our problems—of whatever political, economic, or sociological nature. Is there political unrest? Seek first, not a Republican victory, or a labor victory, but the kingdom of God and His righteousness. Then there will be added—not necessarily a Republican or labor victory, but—political rest.[72]

To tie these threads together: Henry's political vision emerged from the matrix of theology proper, anthropology, and the kingdom of God. These three concepts—God, man, and the reign of the God-man—led Henry to believe Christians should have a committed interest in the political sphere, but not ultimately so. Because all people bring their gods into the political arena,[73] Henry thought it only right for Christians to proclaim the God of justice and justification as kingdom citizens living as the new society with Jesus Christ as their Head.

Henry *the Baptist* Came Preaching: Henry and Baptist Political Theology

Was there anything distinctively *Baptist* about Henry's political thought? The answer is yes, and it is focused on the first freedom: religious liberty.

Carl F. H. Henry *was a Baptist*. That might seem like an unnecessary remark in a volume devoted to Baptist political theology, but with Henry it is a point worth making. During his time at Wheaton College, he was convinced of Baptistic views and would be affiliated with Baptist churches and institutions for the remainder of his life.[74] The Baptist understanding of church and state was one of the influences that drew him to Baptist

---

[72] Henry, *The Uneasy Conscience of Modern Fundamentalism*, 84–85.

[73] Jonathan Leeman, *How the Nations Rage: Rethinking Faith and Politics in a Divided Age* (Nashville: Thomas Nelson, 2018), 46–47.

[74] Carl F. H. Henry, "Twenty Years a Baptist," *Foundations* 1 (January 1958): 46–47.

distinctives.[75] But while he made no reservations about his Baptist identity, his "most critical involvements have been outside denominational life."[76] He is usually recalled as *an Evangelical* rather than *a Baptist* and for understandable reasons. He nearly always referred to the "evangelical church" in the singular, "not referring to any particular denomination but to all conservative Protestants committed to the formal and material principles of the Reformation."[77] This was undoubtedly due to his role as theologian-at-large for a conservative interdenominational evangelicalism.

But how did Henry *as a Baptist* think about politics? Henry adopted the Baptist understanding of religious liberty, and he articulated a distinctly Baptist version of the first freedom throughout his life.[78] This view originated from the Bible and was filtered through his kingdom framework, stressing the two spheres believers inhabit and concluding that the state ought not dictate to the church and the church ought not overrun the state. For Henry, the church should seek in good faith to evangelize her neighbors but should never "impose upon society at large her theological commitments."[79] However, because God "wills the state as an instrumentality for preserving justice and restraining disorder," Christians *should* engage in political affairs, vote faithfully and intelligently, and seek and hold public office.[80] The church should respect the authority granted to the state by God, but not as a fire wall against any prophetic proclamations. Further, religious liberty provides space for irreligion (though, as we have seen, Henry believed nobody is *truly* irreligious) as well as those

---

[75] Henry, 47.

[76] R. Albert Mohler Jr., "Carl F. H. Henry," in *Theologians of the Baptist Tradition*, ed. Timothy George and David S. Dockery (Nashville: B&H, 2001), 292.

[77] Timothy George, "Evangelicals and Others," *First Things* 160 (February 2006): 19.

[78] See Henry, *The Christian Mindset in a Secular Society*, 63–80.

[79] Carl F. H. Henry, *Christian Countermoves in a Decadent Culture* (Portland: Multnomah, 1986), 118.

[80] Henry, 118.

of other faiths. Henry believed evangelicals should "earnestly protect" the freedom of all people—"be they Christian, Jewish, Muslim, Buddhist, Hindu, Confucian, or whatever—even while we passionately proclaim to all the gospel of Christ."[81] While Henry's intellectual efforts were claimed by some among the Religious Right, this was a key place where he distanced himself from the movement. He criticized its tendency to elevate *Christian* freedom over and above *religious* freedom and to be less-than-interested in religious freedom "across the board" for people of various and differing faith traditions.[82]

Beyond Henry's view of religious liberty, other Baptist influences can be discerned in his thought, especially in the area of ecclesiology. While Henry has been critiqued for neglecting the locality of the church (due to his scant attention to polity and ordinances), he did appeal to the local church in the construction of his political theology.[83] Because Henry believed "public virtue depends on private character, and private character emerges from convictions about the ultimately real world," he began at the local level by emphasizing the church's ministry in the formation of believers who would conduct themselves politically in ways that honored transcendent realities.[84] For Henry, pulpits and pews were integral to Christian political theory—what flowed downstream into political activity, positive or negative, was contingent on ecclesiological faithfulness. As Jonathan Leeman states, "The church's political nature begins with its own life—with its preaching, evangelism, member oversight and

---

[81] Henry, *The Christian Mindset in a Secular Society*, 79.

[82] Carl F. H. Henry, "Lost Momentum: Carl F. H. Henry Looks at the Future of the Religious Right," *Christianity Today* (September 4, 1987): 31.

[83] See Russell D. Moore, "God, Revelation, and Community: Ecclesiology and Baptist Identity in the Thought of Carl F. H. Henry," *Southern Baptist Journal of Theology* 8, no. 4 (Winter 2004).

[84] Henry, *Has Democracy Had Its Day?*, 41.

discipline."[85] Henry recognized and appreciated this in his articulation of political theology. While Baptists are not alone in taking seriously the responsibilities of church membership, one can appreciate Henry the Baptist in how he related church discipline to civil life: "Through government of its own members, the Church indirectly promotes the welfare of society as a whole. . . . When the Church requires her membership to practice Christian principles in everyday life it unavoidably touches upon many areas of conduct subject also to civil legislation."[86] Henry connected the effectiveness of a proper Christian political vision with the spiritual vitality of the individual and, by extension, the formative role of the covenant community.

Peter Heltzel sees Henry as a "prophetic Baptist" because of Henry's radical reframing of Baptist cultural engagement.[87] Heltzel gives three reasons to justify this classification: While operating from the Baptist stream of theology, Henry championed the dignity of all people, demonstrated the best of the reformist and revivalist traditions, and rejected theocratic tendencies.[88] And while one wonders whether Henry was as much a "prophetic Baptist" as he was simply a consistent one, the point remains: his Baptist convictions informed his political theology, and Heltzel's emphasis reminds us of this.

Henry was a consistent Baptist, but he was not an altogether unique Baptist in his conception of political theology. Does he offer anything fresh to Baptists today beyond what has already been said? Certainly, the biblical and theological underpinnings of his political theology remain applicable.

---

[85] Jonathan Leeman, *Political Church: The Local Assembly as Embassy of Christ's Rule*, Studies in Christian Doctrine and Scripture (Downers Grove, IL: IVP Academic, 2016), 52.

[86] Henry, *Aspects of Christian Social Ethics*, 79.

[87] Heltzel, *Jesus and Justice*, 76.

[88] Heltzel, 76.

The theological intentionality that characterizes his work deserves continued emulation. His engagement with alternate views equips modern readers to understand other political options. But Henry offers more, and this is owing to his historical context.

Henry wrote amid "breathtaking changes in the human experience."[89] He witnessed massive upheaval in the shared societal assumptions of the nation. While every generation is forced to address new developments, the mid-twentieth century saw a titanic shift in how people thought about every aspect of life. From the discarding of traditional sexuality to secular encroachment in education to new forms of media and entertainment, these years marked a watershed in the life of the nation, and Henry addressed many of these changes through a theological lens and a Baptist emphasis on religious liberty.[90]

Baptists face similar challenges today. While Henry's articulation of Baptist political theology is not unique to him, the intensity with which he applied it was new, and it is here that modern Baptists can find an ally and guide as they navigate an era still grappling with these issues. Henry's work on political theology remains a valuable tool, especially because of the kinship between his cultural day and ours.

---

[89] George Marsden, *The Twilight of the American Enlightenment: The 1950s and the Crisis of Liberal Belief* (New York: Basic Books, 2014), xv.

[90] In addressing such issues, Henry's practice was to offer a prophetic "no" to issues clearly contrary to Scripture, but not a clear "yes" to specific policy proposals. This was likely due to his reticence to intertwine church and state and to one of the editorial principles that guided his work at *CT*: "The institutional church has no mandate, jurisdiction, or competence to endorse political legislation or military tactics or economic specifics in the name of Christ." See Richard J. Mouw, "Carl Henry Was Right," *Christianity Today* (January 2010): 32. This hesitancy to offer specific critique or endorsement of legislation became a point of contention for some of his contemporaries who wanted to see stronger engagement with direct policy matters from one of evangelicalism's chief thinkers. See Lewis B. Smedes, "The Evangelicals and the Social Question," *Reformed Journal* 16 (February 1966): 9–13.

Controversies and Criticisms:
Henry and His Challengers

Given Henry's massive output, criticisms and challenges were inevitable. Although numerous skirmishes throughout his career could be noted, three instances related to political theology stand out. First, Henry doggedly appealed to biblical revelation as necessary for healthy political theology and found any appeal to natural law suspect. Second, Henry has been challenged as to how *Christianity Today* handled racial injustice during his time as editor. Finally, Henry has faced criticism for wedding democracy and patriotism too closely with biblical Christianity.

Although Henry embraced the biblical concept of general revelation, he was never persuaded by advocates of natural law.[91] He thought a set of ethical norms stamped on the human conscience simply could not be proven given the demonstrable differences between peoples and cultures, and any "quasi-Christian" appeal to such would eventually result in subjective lawlessness.[92] Specific to politics, he thought: "The supposed fixed content of natural law is either too general and abstract to provide specific guidance or too specific to be truly universal. It is, in short, too ambiguous to be helpful in the difficult questions of public policy."[93]

Others have not been convinced by Henry's dismissal. Bryan McGraw, J. Budziszewski, and David Weeks all see positive uses of natural law and find Henry's evaluation and application of it lacking.[94] Near the end of his life, Henry himself seems to have recognized a weakness in preferring

---

[91] See Carl F. H. Henry, "Natural Law and Nihilistic Culture," *First Things* 49 (January 1995): 54–60.

[92] Henry, *GRA*, 6:454.

[93] Henry, *The Christian Mindset in a Secular Society*, 118.

[94] Bryan T. McGraw, "The Doctrine of Creation and the Possibilities of Evangelical Natural Law," in *Natural Law and Evangelical Political Thought*, ed. Jesse Covington, Bryan T. McGraw, and Micah Watson (Lanham: Lexington Books, 2013); J. Budziszewski, *Evangelicals in the Public Square: Four Formative Voices on Political Thought and Action* (Grand Rapids: Baker, 2006), 51–54; David

strictly special revelation and evangelism to a more general articulation of natural law in fashioning a political strategy.[95]

Second, Henry has been criticized for *Christianity Today*'s relative silence in addressing racism in the 1960s.[96] Gregory Thornbury, sympathetic to Henry, recognizes that he did push *CT* to address the issue (but lost to L. Nelson Bell), yet still thinks the magazine "lacked the prophetic edge it might have had during the Civil Rights era."[97] Although willing to expose racial injustice, Henry failed to overcome institutional voices that were leery of highlighting civil rights activity (from a fear of moving too quickly for their readership). Peter Heltzel argues that Henry's moderating position in response to these roadblocks was inadequate.[98] Henry rarely fashioned specific policy proposals on any issue, and he did not do so regarding legislation that perpetuated injustice toward African Americans (which could lead the magazine to appear inattentive or unresponsive to concrete situations). He could have taken more decisive action, either by forcing the issue at *CT* or using other avenues at his disposal. He did, however, defend the magazine's strategy on addressing civil rights,[99] and he led the *CT* editorial board to address racial inequality at multiple turns (Henry's insistence on spotlighting racial injustice beyond what his superiors were comfortable with likely contributed to his departure from the magazine a

---

L. Weeks, "Carl F. H. Henry on Civic Life," in Budziszewski, *Evangelicals in the Public Square*, 136–39.

[95] Carl F. H. Henry, *Twilight of a Great Civilization: The Drift Toward Neo-Paganism* (Wheaton, IL: Crossway, 1988), 166–67. See also Timothy W. Walker, "How Shall We Then Engage?: Assessing Alternatives to Natural Law in the Political Theologies of Carl F. H. Henry and Oliver O'Donovan" (PhD diss., New Orleans Baptist Theological Seminary, 2019), 113–14.

[96] See Curtis J. Evans, "White Evangelical Protestant Responses to the Civil Rights Movement," *Harvard Theological Review* 102, no. 2 (April 2009): 245–73.

[97] Thornbury, *Recovering Classic Evangelicalism*, 23.

[98] Heltzel, *Jesus and Justice*, 71–72, 83–88.

[99] Henry, *Confessions of a Theologian*, 158–59.

few years later).[100] Further, he was a public signatory to the 1973 Chicago Declaration of Evangelical Social Concern, which read in part: "We deplore the historic involvement of the church in America with racism and the conspicuous responsibility of the evangelical community for perpetuating the personal attitudes and institutional structures that have divided the body of Christ along color lines."

Finally, Henry has been criticized for wedding American democracy and biblical Christianity. Gregory Thornbury is representative when he writes, "[Henry] linked the United States and democracy too closely to godliness," though he recognizes that "during the Soviet era one could sympathize with that temptation."[101] Writing squarely within the Cold War, Henry thought Socialist governments rested upon a "perversion of basic biblical motifs," which ultimately polluted the entire system.[102] He found the Soviet government to be politically and militarily dangerous because it failed to recognize human dignity and the *imago Dei*. His opposition was not nationalistic or xenophobic but instead theological and humanitarian.[103] Beyond the specifics of the Cold War, Henry thought "Judeo-Christian revelation provides theological anchorage for patriotism."[104] He emphasized that healthy patriotism existed within "unqualified loyalty to God alone."[105] Still, in hailing patriotism as an appropriate and desirable way to express one's desire for a just and righteous nation, Henry often warned readers to keep from allowing patriotism to devolve into merely party loyalty.

---

[100] For example, see "The Church and the Race Problem," *Christianity Today* (March 18, 1957): 20–22; "Race Relations and Christian Duty," *Christianity Today* (September 30, 1957): 23; "Desegregation and Regeneration," *Christianity Today* (September 29, 1958): 20.

[101] Thornbury, *Recovering Classic Evangelicalism*, 23.

[102] Henry, *Christian Countermoves in a Decadent Culture*, 27.

[103] Timothy D. Padgett, "Carl F. H. Henry, the Principled Patriot?" *Trinity Journal* 35, no. 1 (2014): 97.

[104] Henry, "Theological Reflections on Bicentennial Concerns," 292.

[105] Henry, 292.

This criticism deserves attention, as any reading of Henry's political thought will eventually encounter his routine appeal to and interaction with America's founding documents. Henry leapt quickly from biblical argumentation about religious liberty to defending the concept using the Constitution. He bemoaned the fact that a series of national traumas (especially Watergate and Vietnam) led to a dilution of American patriotism among younger generations.[106] Whether he was concerned that a nation without patriotic spirit was at existential risk or because he had firsthand experience of the hope America can offer a family of immigrants like his own, he continually pressed Americans to reclaim the patriotic pride he saw fading from public view.

However, Henry opposed the idea that America plays a divine role in the unfolding story of salvation history. He defended democracy because he saw it as the closest embodiment of the biblical ideal of an interim earthly government, not because it was a flawless political arrangement. He chastised those for whom "God is an ever-living George Washington who serves invisibly as the father of our country."[107] As Timothy Padgett helpfully observes, Henry runs counter to the stereotypical impression many have of Evangelical foreign policy during the Cold War: "Rather than exhibiting an uncritical advocacy of the United States during the tense time of the Cold War, Henry manifested a complex view of global politics where America, though relatively better than its Russian rival, was itself deeply flawed. His support of the United States and openness to nuclear weapons was not the result of seeing the world through red, white, and blue-colored glasses."[108]

Certainly concerned with encroaching totalitarianism around the world, Henry returned his readers to their own preferred political heritage by reminding them of the uniqueness and brilliance of the American experiment. But to go beyond Thornbury's reasonable criticism and perceive

---

[106] Henry, 289.

[107] Henry, *Christian Countermoves in a Decadent Culture*, 32.

[108] Padgett, "Carl F. H. Henry, the Principled Patriot?" 96–97.

Henry as one who envisioned the Spirit as a bald eagle and embraced a type of "God and Country" patriotism with no theological nuance would be an overstatement. He loved his country, but it never eclipsed his love for the Lord. While he certainly believed "Christianity makes loyalty to government a kind of religious obligation," he also firmly recognized that "[w]hen exaggerated patriotism and uncritical loyalty to the state readily excuse its moral compromises and questionable power tactics, then a near-religious loyalty to one's government can, in fact, threaten loyalty to Jesus Christ. . . . When the state becomes one's object of ultimate loyalty, then authentic Christian patriotism yields to the religious cult of nationalism. And when faith results ultimately in the nation, the faith of citizens becomes essentially idolatrous."[109] Timothy Padgett captures Henry well: "To call him a patriot is undoubtedly fair, but, as this affection for his country was tempered by centuries-old Christian doctrines, we may best call him a principled patriot."[110]

Other disagreements could be mentioned. Some think he held a minimalistic understanding of justice.[111] Some think his lack of engagement with the Great Tradition was a liability in his argumentation.[112] Others question his regeneration-centric political strategy.[113] Still, Henry made an indelible imprint on Evangelical political thought, and he continues to be a deep well from which to draw. Even those who depart at points still appreciate his work. Lewis Smedes, a friendly critic of Henry's political theology, wrote him near the end of his life and said, "Our debt to you is great. I hope our gratitude will

---

[109] Carl F. H. Henry, "Has Democracy a Future?" *Christianity Today* (July 5, 1974), 26.

[110] Padgett, "Carl F. H. Henry, the Principled Patriot?" 93.

[111] David L. Weeks, "The Political Thought of Carl F. H. Henry" (PhD diss., Loyola University of Chicago, 1991), 312–16.

[112] Francis J. Beckwith, "Carl Henry's Quandary: Whose Bible, Which Anthropology?" *Journal of Christian Legal Thought* 5, no. 2 (Fall 2015): 21–24. This journal issue provides numerous articles that interact with Henry's political thought. See also Budziszewski, *Evangelicals in the Public Square*, 54.

[113] Budziszewski, 47–48.

grow and not diminish as we mature."[114] This is why J. Budziszewski, who is also critical of Henry at points, still writes in his dedication to *Evangelicals in the Public Square: Four Formative Voices on Political Thought and Action*, "In Memory of Carl F. H. Henry, 1913–2003, Pioneer."[115]

Conclusion: Returning to a New Release

Carl F. H. Henry's political vision emerged from the matrix of three theological concepts: theology proper, anthropology, and the kingdom of God. That is, Henry's political theology was constructed from the biblical portraits of God, man, and the reign of the God-man. Although not altogether unique in Baptist history, his conception of political theology is relevant in that he addressed early iterations of what modern Baptists continue to face.

We return to where we began: that lively auditorium in 1948, where Henry was answering questions among college students. And now, after expanding upon the original response, we can rephrase that conversation in hypothetical terms:

> [Question]: I don't think the Christian ought to have anything at all to do with politics, do you?

> [Henry]: Yes, indeed, as an act of Christian love and service. But politics is not king; Jesus is. So remember where your hope comes from, and share him with a disintegrating world. Treasure and uphold the freedom you have to do so . . .

> . . . and read my new release, *The Uneasy Conscience of Modern Fundamentalism*. You can find it for one dollar at the back table.

---

[114] Lewis Smedes, *Lewis Smedes to Carl F. H. Henry, December 28, 1997*, letter, from Rolfing Library (Trinity Evangelical Divinity School), *Carl F. H. Henry Papers*.

[115] Budziszewski, *Evangelicals in the Public Square*, 5.

15

Contemporary Baptist Political Theology: Billy Graham, Charles Colson, Richard Land, Albert Mohler, Russell Moore, and Jonathan Leeman

By Cory D. Higdon

The Baptist tradition is marked by political engagement and statecraft for the purposes of advancing the gospel of Jesus Christ. Indeed, to understand Baptists is to understand a chronicle of men and women who have devoted themselves to the preaching of the gospel and the promotion of societal flourishing. Those two goals often formed two sides of the same coin. From its earliest figures, Baptists like Thomas Helwys and John Murton articulated a capacious doctrine of religious liberty that encompassed not only trinitarian Protestants, but Catholics, Jews, Muslims, and atheists—ideas that were radical, indeed, seditious policy proposals in the early years of the seventeenth century. Roger Williams and John Clarke, moreover, founded that "livelie experiment" in Rhode Island, which established an American colony dedicated to soul freedom.[1] These figures in the 1600s dedicated their lives to the cause of religious freedom for two reasons: they believed disestablishment and freedom of conscience engendered civil flourishing, and they contended that religious liberty provided the necessary conditions for the true promulgation of the gospel and conversion.

Baptists have, by and large, remained committed to the tradition of political engagement for the purposes of human flourishing and evangelism, but it has rarely been a simple question as Baptists throughout the centuries confronted pressing and vital moral issues in the public square. The struggle of a Baptist political theology is no less arduous in the contemporary day. As a historian, I hesitate to label the challenges facing present-day Baptists—and all Christians for that matter—as "unprecedented." Yet, it would be foolish not to give due credence to a political, cultural, and social moment that has indeed spiraled into utter chaos and moral confusion. From issues of marriage, abortion, gender, sexuality, and religious freedom, modernity presents Baptists with an environment increasingly hostile to Christianity and the ontological truths of the Bible. As such, the social and even legal costs of holding fast to biblical orthodoxy continue to increase at an alarming rate.

Over the past several decades, Baptists continue to evince their resilience amid cultural pressures, revealing their unwavering steadfastness to contend both for human flourishing and for the centrality of the gospel. This is not to say that Baptists have an unvarnished and monolithic record when it comes to political engagement; indeed, enormous differences and

---

[1] "Charter of Rhode Island and Providence Plantations (1663)," in *The Sacred Rights of Conscience: Selected Readings on Religious Liberty and Church-State Relations in the American Founding*, ed. Daniel L. Dreisbach and Mark David Hall (Indianapolis: Liberty Fund, 2009), 115.

controversies instigated infighting amongst Baptists as they wrestled with complex questions amidst the quagmire and chaos of twenty-first century American democracy. This chapter, therefore, surveys the political theology of five key theologians and public intellectuals who have attempted to articulate a Baptist political theology—a theology of the Christian's and the church's responsibility in this world. While divergences exist among these men, one central idea unifies their political theologies, namely, that Christians *know* and *live* the truth in order to *proclaim* the truth of the gospel. In short, these men—Billy Graham, Charles Colson, Richard Land, Albert Mohler, Russell Moore, and Jonathan Leeman—contend for a political theology of Christian faithfulness and convictional living in a world lost to the ravages of sin. The ideas of these figures were not necessarily original—examples of their thought and political theology can be found throughout church history. They did, however, present their respective political theologies in an increasingly polarized and secularized political context.

Billy Graham: America's Pastor

Billy Graham (1918–2018) was one of the most remarkable American evangelists to have ever lived. No American religious figure since George Whitefield, the "divine dramatist" of the First Great Awakening, impacted the culture as Graham did. From his 1949 crusade in Los Angeles until his death on February 21, 2018, Billy Graham's simple message of the gospel of Jesus Christ was the essential element that gave coherence to his private life and his public ministry.

Much could be said, and has been said, about Graham's life. Grant Wacker, a historian at Duke Divinity School, wrote two biographical treatments of Graham—*America's Pastor: Billy Graham and the Shaping of a Nation* (Belknap, 2014) and *One Soul at a Time: The Story of Billy Graham* (Eerdmans, 2019). Like many public figures in American history, Graham was not an uncomplicated person. But unlike many public figures, there could never have been a question about whether Graham really believed what he preached in public. As Wacker described Graham, he was "duplicitous, rarely; evasive, often; sincere, always."[2]

Wacker estimates that Graham's sermons were heard by 215 million people in 185 countries via satellite, and 77 million over seventy countries heard and saw him in person during his sixty-year preaching career. From those audiences, over 3 million people came to faith in Jesus Christ as a result of his preaching. Those kinds of numbers are staggering for any public speaker and especially for a preacher bringing the gospel to an increasingly secular, or "post-Christian," population.[3]

One of the most striking features of Graham's personality was his earnest desire for humility. He loved people, and when he preached, he preached directly to individual persons. Many preachers speak to audiences. Their words are aimed at an abstraction—an audience of a nameless, faceless mass. And those words are often delivered as cold propositions presenting themselves to the mass of people for them to accept or reject. Other preachers make their sermons an extension of their personalities, and the force of their personalities carries their message; but the people hearing the message also appear to the preacher as a mass without individual identities. Not so with Billy Graham. He had the uncanny ability to connect with individuals, even when there were thousands, or tens of thousands, in the audience. Countless people have testified to the notion that the power of Graham's sermons was less in their content and more in their connection with them as persons standing in the presence of God and being ushered into saving faith. Graham could usher people into the presence of Jesus, introduce them to the Savior, and then let the Savior do His work of drawing them to faith.

Graham's personal style in public was also evident in private. One of the most intriguing features of Graham's public life was how he cultivated

---

[2] Grant Wacker, *One Soul at a Time: The Story of Billy Graham* (Grand Rapids: Eerdmans, 2019), 6.

[3] Wacker, *One Soul*, xv.

relationships with thirteen US presidents, from Truman to Trump. There is a compelling element in Graham's friendships with the presidents—although those friendships were in the public spotlight, many of them were intensely private. Graham appeared to the presidents the same man in the public eye as he was in private.

Graham was closer to some of the presidents than to others, but Graham's personal touch with the most public of all Americans was one of the reasons he had consistent access to the occupants of the White House from 1950 until 2018. Even the presidents valued the way Graham consistently treated them as people, not as the most powerful men on earth. In his remarks at Graham's memorial service, former President Bill Clinton told the story of how he first heard Graham preach when he was eleven years old. He met him personally for the first time while serving as governor and then grew to know him during the 1990s as he served his two terms. Whenever he thought of Graham, Clinton related, he was always that eleven-year-old boy who first heard him preach at a crusade in Little Rock.

Authors Nancy Gibbs and Michael Duffy, who cowrote *The Preacher and the Presidents* (Center Street, 2007), chronicled the history of Graham's relationships with the postwar presidents. When they met with him at his home in Montreat, they were struck by how Graham spoke of the presidents. He regarded them as ordinary friends, albeit with great responsibilities and unique stresses and hardships. To most Americans, the president of the United States is certainly a human, but there is something almost preternatural about a president. A president appears to the minds of most everyday people as an institution. But Graham saw the presidents in their humanity—the endearing elements of their humanity as well as their uglier parts too. For example, Graham was more personally drawn to Reagan than any other president because of his effervescent optimism. Richard Nixon was the president who gained Graham's trust, appeared to Graham as a decent and morally upright man, but it became obvious even to Graham that Nixon used him as a prop to convey the image of respectability. Graham felt deeply betrayed by Nixon because Nixon put forth the image of a Christian.

Conversely, Lyndon Johnson was every bit as crass and profane as Nixon but did not put on the veneer of Christian morality to manipulate Graham.[4]

Gibbs and Duffy were particularly struck by the fact that Graham knew many of the presidents long before they were elected. Graham met Reagan thirty years before he became president, and he became friends with the Bushes in the 1950s. He was personally closest to George H. W. Bush and pastorally closest to Lyndon Johnson. But he was not close to Jimmy Carter, even though Carter was a Southern Baptist. The reason the presidents trusted and befriended him was that he did not treat them as institutions. He disarmed them by his sincerity and his desire to see them be at peace with God, in the same way he desired every individual in his massive audiences to enjoy peace with God. But Graham was also in a position to identify with the presidents. As a public figure himself, he could understand the pressure the presidents felt continuously, the pressure of being under public scrutiny. For example, Graham appeared on Gallup's Ten Most Admired Men list sixty-one times between 1955 and 2017. The next most featured man on that list was Ronald Reagan—at thirty-one times. Being with Graham, someone who understood the pressures they were under, the presidents found it natural to seek spiritual counsel and cultivate a sort of spiritual companionship with him.[5]

The most difficult experience Graham had with the presidency was dealing with the revelation that Nixon had betrayed Graham. Graham had loved Nixon, defended him stalwartly for months during the Watergate crisis, and was one of the last of Nixon's allies to finally abandon him. When Graham heard the "smoking gun" tapes that finally and decisively implicated Nixon in the cover-up of the break-in at the Watergate Hotel, he

---

[4] Nancy Gibbs and Michael Duffy, "I Loved 'Em All: Inside Billy Graham's Powerful Relationship with U.S. Presidents," *Time*, February 21, 2018, https://time .com/5168589/billy-graham-president-relationships/.

[5] Nancy Gibbs, "Billy in the Oval Office: A Story of Faith, Friendship, and Temptation," interview by Timothy C. Morgan, *Christianity Today*, accessed February 16, 2022, https://www.christianitytoday.com/ct/2018/billy-graham/billy -graham-presidents-oval-office-confidante.html. Wacker, *One Soul*, 1.

was so shaken that he threw up. He knew he had become too enmeshed in politics and committed not to be drawn too deeply into partisanship again. He warned people like James Dobson and Pat Robertson in the early days of the Moral Majority against the allure of political power since he had learned powerful and unforgettable lessons the hard way.[6]

Still, Graham is one of the most unique personalities in American history and one of the most effective Christian preachers in the modern history of the church. His public life was devoted to evangelism—the leading of men, women, and children to faith in Jesus Christ, no matter how humble or lofty their circumstances. When Billy Graham died, he was one of only four civilians to be granted two days for his remains to lay "in honor" in the Capitol Rotunda, and the only religious leader to have been bestowed such a distinction. Presidents from both parties—possessing a variety of personalities and religious backgrounds, plagued with unique failures and blessed with salient gifts, and representing diverse political positions—knew that if they wanted success for their agendas, they had to be spiritually deferential to the man from Montreat. Graham's singular influence as an Evangelical was something akin to that of the pope for Catholics. But Graham was different than a pope in that he exuded the quality of being one of us. As Robert P. George, a Catholic, wrote of Graham: "We Catholics had the pope—but he was a distant and, to be blunt, foreign figure. Our Protestant neighbors had Billy Graham, the friend of presidents, business magnates and celebrities, who through the magic of television was a frequent, familiar guest in the homes of ordinary people; and he was as American as apple pie."[7] Graham would likely have smiled at George's description.

---

[6] Michael S. Hamilton, "How a Humble Evangelist Changed Christianity as We Know It," *Christianity Today*, accessed February 16, 2022, https://www .christianitytoday.com/ct/2018/billy-graham/how-humble-evangelist-billy-graham -changed-christianity.html.

[7] Robert P. George, "'America's Pastor,' About Billy Graham, By Grant Wacker," *The New York Times*, December 19, 2014, https://www.nytimes.com/2014/12/21 /books/review/americas-pastor-about-billy-graham-by-grant-wacker.html.

Charles Colson: An Enduring Revolution

For Christians, Charles "Chuck" Colson's life testifies to the profound grace and sovereignty of God. Born in 1931, Colson asserted himself into the political arena, ascending to the level of special counsel to President Richard Nixon. Known as Nixon's "hatchet man," Colson aided the White House's efforts in the Watergate scandal, eventually pleading no contest to the charge of obstruction of justice. In 1974, Colson was sentenced and served seven months in prison. During his arrest and imprisonment, Colson converted to Christianity; after his release, Colson became a Baptist and spent the rest of his life founding ministries, contending for the gospel of Jesus Christ. One of his ministries was Prison Fellowship, which endeavored to serve inmates and their families, especially ex-inmates who needed help reintegrating into society. He became a regular columnist for *Christianity Today*; founded the Colson Center for Christian Worldview; started a widely consumed radio program called *BreakPoint*; and authored, edited, or coauthored more than thirty books.

Colson devoted his post-prison years to the refinement and advocacy of a biblical political theology that accurately maintained the Christian commitment to the gospel as the primary foundation for political engagement. Indeed, in his acceptance speech for the Templeton Prize in 1993, Colson outlined a clear summation of his political theology: what he called the "enduring revolution." This revolution—a revolution promulgated by Christians—asserts that "freedom is found in submission to the moral law."[8] Western civilization, according to Colson, succumbed to the tyranny of four myths, namely, the goodness of man, a coming utopia, the relativizing of moral standards, and radical individualism. These "four horsemen" overran Western civilization and especially the United States. Left

---

[8] Charles Colson, "The Enduring Revolution" (The Templeton Address, University of Chicago, 1993), in *Chuck Colson Speaks* (Ulrichsville, OH: Promise Press, 2000), 20.

unchecked, society would eventually jettison transcendent moral authority, which is rooted in a Judeo-Christian worldview. The loss of that authority led, Colson believed, to the erosion of ordered liberty and, subsequently, human flourishing.

The antidote to this crisis of modernity was the enduring revolution. As Colson argued, "Christian conviction inspires public virtue, the moral impulse to *do* good. It has sent legions into battle against disease, oppression, and bigotry. It ended the slave trade, built hospitals and orphanages, tamed the brutality of mental wards and prisons."[9] In other words, Christianity provides both the positive and negative force to quell the effects of the four horsemen of the modern age. Positively, Christians introduce people to the God of the Bible when they evince the qualities and character of his kingdom. Negatively, when Christians engage the culture, they deter wickedness and the effects of sin, which assists in the preservation of a rightly ordered society that reflects a Judeo-Christian morality. Thus, when the church *acts* like the church and when Christians *faithfully* obey God, they inculcate in the culture a vision, albeit imperfect, of God's justice, mercy, and compassion. Indeed, Colson contended, "When Christians live out the biblical worldview, we become the source of renewal in a culture."[10]

Colson's context is key—he formulated his political theology in the midst of the Religious Right and the culture wars, both of which he found lacking.[11] As Owen Strachan argued, Colson was no culture warrior; nor, however, did Colson think Christians bore no responsibility when it came to political policy.[12] Colson was well aware of how Christians easily surrendered

---

[9] Colson, "The Enduring Revolution," 15.

[10] Charles W. Colson, *My Final Word: Holding Tight to the Issues That Matter Most* (Grand Rapids: Zondervan, 2015), 224.

[11] For a history of the Religious Right, see Neil J. Young, *We Gather Together: The Religious Right and the Problem of Interfaith Politics* (New York: Oxford University, 2015).

[12] Owen Strachan, *The Colson Way: Loving Your Neighbor and Living with Faith in a Hostile World* (Nashville: Thomas Nelson, 2015), 112.

key aspects of the gospel, which delineated the church's primary responsibility in the world. He argued, quite prophetically, that "Christian conservatives have become politicized, attempting to take dominion over culture through legislation and court decisions handed down by strict-constructionist judges."[13] The political activism and culture war precipitated by the Religious Right had ironically, in Colson's view, helped undermine Western civilization. The eclipse of Christian values had less to do with the rise of secularism than the capitulation of theology and conviction within the church.[14] When politics became the "ultimate goal," it suppressed true Christian "spirituality." Without vibrant spirituality and faithful obedience to the gospel, Christians had little to offer the public square, which primarily needed a resurgence of transcendent morality—of ontological moral first principles.[15]

When Christians adhered to the gospel, established healthy churches, and lived as Christ called them to live, they inevitably took into the public arena a Christian worldview and ethic that promoted human flourishing. Colson believed that "our cultural problems are not so much political as, in order, spiritual, intellectual, and moral in origin."[16] If the spiritual needs were to be met, then Christians must continually emphasize the Word of God, the gospel, and the flourishing only secured through an adherence to God's moral law. As Strachan surmised, "Colson wanted the church to be the church: a force for spiritual *and* social good."[17] Hence the need for the enduring revolution, which Colson framed as an effort to stem the tide against the harmful ideologies and ethical quagmires that descended from

---

[13] Charles Colson, *God and Government: An Insider's View on the Boundaries between Faith and Politics* (Grand Rapids: Zondervan, 2007), 50.

[14] Colson, 252.

[15] Colson, 267.

[16] Charles Colson, "The Common Cultural Task: The Culture War from a Protestant Perspective," in *Evangelicals and Catholics Together: Toward a Common Mission*, ed. Charles Colson and Richard John Neuhaus (Nashville: Thomas Nelson, 1995), 16.

[17] Strachan, *The Colson Way*, 114.

the moral chaos and confusion of modernity. For the Christian, love of neighbor necessitated engagement in the political arena—the goal of the enduring revolution was not electoral victory but the advocacy of God's gospel and the natural law.

Colson, however, included within the enduring revolution a capacious coalition between various denominations, specifically allying Evangelical Protestants with conservatives in the Roman Catholic Church. Indeed, Colson's career included two landmark moments, namely, "Evangelicals and Catholics Together" in 1994 and the Manhattan Declaration in 2009. "Evangelicals and Catholics Together" sought a social alliance between the two divergent theological traditions—while it did not attempt to minimize the real differences between the two groups on fundamental matters of doctrine, it endeavored to find common ground, especially on an array of moral issues. The document stated, "Together we contend for the truth that politics, law, and culture must be secured by moral truth." Following that statement, the signatories declared their common advocacy of religious freedom, pro-life policies, moral education, and parental choice in education, along with statements about a constellation of moral issues such as pornography, economics, marriage, sex, etc. The document was, above all, a summons for those who hold to a Judeo-Christian worldview to take that worldview into the public square in order to promote the common good.[18] Similarly, the Manhattan Declaration, signed now by well over

---

[18] The full statement, "Evangelicals and Catholics Together: The Christian Mission in the Third Millennium," can be found in the May 1994 edition of *First Things*. This statement, along with the Manhattan Declaration, received significant pushback from several leading evangelicals like John MacArthur and R. C. Sproul, both of whom refused to sign either statement. See John MacArthur, "Evangelicals and Catholics Together," Grace to You, accessed February 8, 2021, https://www.gty.org/library/articles/A149/. MacArthur argued, in a similar way to Sproul, that both statements failed to clarify what was meant by the "gospel." Both statements asserted that the primary goal of Christians in the culture is to share the gospel—but evangelicals and Catholics have fundamental disagreements over what constitutes the gospel, especially when it comes to questions over justification by faith.

500,000 people from a multitude of denominations, was drafted in direct response to three issues facing the United States: the erosion of religious freedom, the rise of abortion, and the erosion of the sanctity of marriage. The Manhattan Declaration asserted that, for Christians, nonengagement equated to unfaithfulness—soul freedom, human dignity, and the sanctity of marriage "are foundational principles of justice and the common good," and Christians "are compelled by our Christian faith to speak and act in their defense."[19]

Reasonable Christians will disagree over whether cobelligerency between evangelicals and Catholics is proper. Colson, however, contended for a political theology that he believed could encompass a broad range of denominations. The goal was a burgeoning coalition devoted to human flourishing and the reassertion of God's moral law in the political arena. The theological disagreements, significant though they were, in no way abrogated the broader commitment to contend for issues of justice and morality in a culture cascading into moral chaos. For Colson, declaring the moral truths of God's law represented a far more faithful political theology than merely attempting to alleviate wicked policies through the ballot box or the Supreme Court. Indeed, his political theology called all Christians to a more faithful obedience to Jesus Christ—to prize personal character and holiness above electoral victories. He wrote, rather presciently, "A nation that does not demand high standards of character in its leaders will end up being a nation of barbarians."[20] Corrupt and unholy ideologies, according to Colson, were besieging Western civilization; left unchallenged, the consequences would inflict unimaginable harm on subsequent generations. Colson's enduring revolution, therefore, was not a means to power

---

MacArthur and Sproul refused to sign the statements because they believed it sundered political engagement from a robust and orthodox articulation of the gospel.

[19] "Manhattan Declaration: A Call of Christian Conscience," November 20, 2009, https://www.manhattandeclaration.org/.

[20] Colson, *God and Government*, 273.

for Christians, but a channel through which to show the love of God to a lost and dying world—a way to exemplify Christ's command to love your neighbor as yourself.

Richard Land: American Exceptionalism Rightly Understood

For a quarter of a century, from 1988 to 2013, Richard Land served as the president of the Ethics and Religious Liberty Commission for the Southern Baptist Convention. Early in his tenure in 1995, Land played a leading role in the SBC's statement on racial reconciliation, which summoned Southern Baptists to reckon with and repent for the denomination's historical ties to race-based chattel slavery. Land traversed the tumultuous climate of post-9/11 America and the host of political issues that came in its wake, not least of which were issues of religious freedom for Muslims. He advanced a Baptist understanding of just war theory in an open letter to President George W. Bush as America prepared for war against Iraq and Saddam Hussein. His career, moreover, spanned profound shifts in American religious culture—as such, he endeavored for a political theology that was clear and rooted in timeless principles for a transient age.

Among the figures surveyed in this chapter, however, Land makes a particular contribution to Baptist political theology that demands careful attention. He contended, throughout his career, for a rightly understood doctrine of American exceptionalism. The topic of American exceptionalism raises important issues for Baptists to consider, especially as they contemplate their relationship to the United States and reflect upon God's providence among the nations. How one defines, for example, the hand of God upon a particular nation will necessarily exert enormous influence on that individual's political theology—that is no less true for how Land defined and applied American exceptionalism.

Land defined American exceptionalism as "a doctrine of obligations, responsibility, sacrifice, and service in the cause of freedom, not a doctrine of pride, privilege, and empire."[21] Land provided, as a biblical basis for his definition, Luke 12:48: "From everyone who has been given much, much will be required; and from the one who has been entrusted with much, even more will be expected." As citizens of heaven, Christians owed their allegiances first and foremost to Jesus Christ. That reality, however, did not diminish the obligations inherent in their American citizenship. On the contrary, Land's argument intensified the responsibility of Christians living in America—he intersected God's grace upon America with what he believed was a biblical application of the Christian's dual citizenship. Because God had uniquely blessed America with a degree of power and influence unmatched in the world, more was expected of this nation as a force for justice and righteousness in the world; and Christians living in this blessed nation bore a particular responsibility to maintain the moral and ethical integrity of the country. Land argued that "what God has to do with America starts with what Americans have to do with God."[22] Failure on the part of Christians to contend for a biblical worldview in the public square, according to Land, portended disaster for the nation, the removal of God's blessing, and the moral decay of the American people.

Land, however, attempted to carefully distinguish between a biblically understood notion of American exceptionalism and a malevolent Christian nationalism. Indeed, Land believed that Christian nationalism swung the pendulum too far toward idolatry by tethering the nation with God's providential and eschatological plan for the cosmos. While God had specially blessed the United States, Land continually chided against nationalism as a viable outlet for a Baptist political theology. Indeed, Christian nationalism, according to Land, threatened one of the core commitments of a Baptist political theology, namely, religious freedom. The goal for Christians, Land argued, was not to "impose Christianity on

---

[21] Richard Land, *The Divided States of America: What Liberals and Conservatives Get Wrong about Faith and Politics* (Nashville: Thomas Nelson, 2011), 30.

[22] Land, 11.

our society by government edict. God forbid that we should, and would, impose theocracy."[23] He dissuaded his readers from believing that moral change or the preservation of a biblical ethical framework in America could come through legislative or judicial fiat—what was required, on the part of Christians, was to proclaim the gospel of Jesus Christ. The "transformation of hearts and minds"—a transformation only possible through repentance and faith—represented the proper way Christians ought to engage others in the public square.[24]

This principle, moreover, demanded that, when appropriate, Christians must bring their underlying convictions and biblical worldview into the public square for issues of justice and the common good. Christians need not veil the gospel in their public witness. As Land argued, "A truly biblical vision opens our sight to the transforming power of the gospel in *all* of life."[25] Preserving the centrality of gospel proclamation was a core feature of Land's political theology, which, much like other figures in this chapter, protected Christians not only from the temptations of Christian nationalism, but also from the temptation to dampen the more offensive theological convictions of Baptists in the modern age. While the former temptation made an idol out of the nation, the latter made an idol out of the Constitution or out of moral and legal arguments sundered from a clear articulation of the Christian worldview.[26]

Land's emphasis on a biblically faithful conception of American exceptionalism is, perhaps, essential for contemporary Baptists as they consider their responsibility as citizens of both the kingdom of heaven and the United States of America. Land understood that belief in American exceptionalism might lead to the temptation of an idolatrous Christian nationalism. The

---

[23] Richard Land, *Imagine! A Blessed America: How It Could Happen and What It Would Look Like* (Nashville: B&H, 2005), 7.

[24] Land, *The Divided States of America*, 236.

[25] Land, *Imagine!*, 4, emphasis in original.

[26] Land, *The Divided States of America*, 9.

theological and moral quandaries facing Christians are enormous and complex, and the stakes could not be higher.

R. Albert Mohler Jr.: Secularism and the Christian Worldview[27]

R. Albert Mohler Jr., president of The Southern Baptist Theological Seminary, has long lent his prescient voice to the theological, cultural, political, and moral issues facing Christians and, to an extent, Western civilization. His historic career as president of the SBC's flagship institution precipitated a conservative resurgence at the seminary—an institution that Mohler, by the direction of the SBC and the Board of Trustees, has stewarded toward the training of theologically conservative, orthodox ministers of the gospel.[28] Mohler, moreover, has engaged the culture through his radio program, books, and especially his daily podcast *The Briefing*, which, as Mohler announces at the beginning of each episode, is "a daily analysis of news and events from a Christian worldview."

Because of his profile, the length of his career, and the sheer depth of his content, Mohler's importance for contemporary Baptist political theology carries enormous significance both within the SBC and in broader American evangelicalism. Indeed, contemporary Baptist political theology cannot be understood without the contributions of Mohler. He has devoted his career not only to the reassertion of orthodox theology within the SBC, but to the development of a robust Christian worldview that understands the complexities and challenges facing Christians in this contemporary moment. He has confronted rival and secular worldviews with the gospel

---

[27] At the time of this writing, the author serves as director of research for Dr. Mohler at The Southern Baptist Theological Seminary.

[28] For a history of the Conservative Resurgence in the SBC and Mohler's leadership at the institution, see Gregory A. Wills, *The Southern Baptist Theological Seminary, 1859–2009* (New York: Oxford University, 2009).

of Jesus Christ and with what he believes is a biblical ethic that will secure human flourishing—and he has sought to teach others to do the same.

His book *The Gathering Storm: Secularism, Culture, and the Church* contains his assessment of the challenges facing Western civilization and the church—yet this book also received critique in *Law and Liberty* from Greg Forster, who indicted Mohler as peddling an Evangelical Christian nationalism and as an advocate of a novel concept: Protestant integralism.[29] Mohler responded to this criticism in the same journal, contending that his distinctly Baptist political theology necessarily rejected any notions of Christian nationalism and integralism.[30] The exchange between Forster and Mohler may seem minor compared to other areas of Mohler's ministry; the debate, however, evinced crucial aspects of Mohler's political theology and draws Baptists into a profound consideration of the relationship between Christians and the state, between the gospel and matters of public policy.

First, Mohler argued in *The Gathering Storm* that without the "binding authority of Christian theism," Western civilization and the primacy of ordered liberty will crumble.[31] The impetus behind the loss of an ontological basis for society was, as Mohler contended, a process of secularization. The pillars of American democracy that emerged in the late eighteenth century were fundamentally rooted in a Christian worldview. This is not to say America was founded as a Christian nation but that the liberties

---

[29] Greg Forster, "A Protestant Integralism?," review of *The Gathering Storm: Secularism, Culture, and the Church,* by R. Albert Mohler Jr.," *Law and Liberty,* June 2, 2020, https://lawliberty.org/book-review/a-protestant-integralism/. See this source for all subsequent points drawn from Forster's argument.

[30] R. Albert Mohler Jr., "Secularism Cannot Sustain Liberty, a Response to Greg Forster," *Law and Liberty,* August 4, 2020, https://lawliberty.org/secularism-cannot-sustain-liberty/. See this source for all subsequent points drawn from Mohler's response to Forster.

[31] R. Albert Mohler Jr., *The Gathering Storm: Secularism, Culture, and the Church* (Nashville: Thomas Nelson, 2020), xiv.

enshrined in the Constitution originated within a Christian framework.[32] Secularization, and the forces of secularism, jettisoned that framework, supplanting what made ordered liberty thrive with a new subjective and amorphous ethical system that repudiated ontological moral first principles.

Mohler argued, furthermore, that this erosion of Western civilization and the American experiment of ordered liberty portended grave challenges for the church. *The Gathering Storm*, therefore, sought to confront Christians with the realities of what lay on the horizon, namely, a downgrade in liberty, justice, and morality.[33] He distilled in each chapter a sector of society ravaged by secularism and various worldviews antithetical to the Christian position. Yet it is in the knowledge of the challenges facing society that Mohler believed Christians could engage the culture more faithfully. By understanding the conflict of worldviews in the public square, Christians can better contend for the faith once delivered to the saints and give an answer for the hope within them. Christians, therefore, "bear the highest responsibility in this secular age," because Christians, equipped with the gospel, know *why* adherence to God's creational mandates represents the surest and safest channel for societal and human flourishing.[34] As Mohler argued, "Christians *do* have a political responsibility. . . . Governments matter. Laws matter. . . . But how are we to think about this responsibility?" To which Mohler answered, "love." In an Augustinian pattern, Mohler, on the one hand, vehemently protected the distinction between the city of God and the city of man while, on the other hand, ardently summoning

---

[32] For a helpful analysis of religion, the American founding, and the influence of religion on American life, see Mark David Hall, *Did America Have a Christian Founding?* (Nashville: Thomas Nelson, 2019); Thomas S. Kidd, *God of Liberty: A Religious History of the American Revolution* (New York: Basic Books, 2010); and John D. Wilsey, *One Nation Under God?: An Evangelical Critique of Christian America* (Eugene: Pickwick, 2011).

[33] Mohler, *The Gathering Storm*, xvi.

[34] Mohler, 190.

Christians to advocate for just laws, the unborn, religious freedom, and the good of our neighbors in all things.

Forster asserted, however, that Mohler's political theology sought the mobilization of Christians for culture war, which he believed was not only perilous for the gospel but coercive of liberalism and ordered liberty itself—especially the liberal commitment to religious freedom. In other words, Forster argued that Mohler's purported summons for a culture war inevitably required a society to adopt an "illiberal religious nationalism." The importance of Forster's critique cannot be overstated—if in fact Mohler advocates for an Evangelical Christian nationalism, then his political theology would shift the center of that theology away from the gospel and toward an Evangelical social activism that views politics as king, elections as of highest importance, and the United States as God's chosen nation. Secondarily, such a political theology would undermine the integrity of Evangelical witness, arousing suspicions within the broader culture that the Religious Right is a pawn for political opportunism. Forster, moreover, indicted Mohler for advancing Protestant integralism. Unlike its Roman Catholic variant, which makes the civil sphere subservient to the papacy and Roman magisterium, Protestant integralism asserts that all civil law must extend from biblical precepts and commands. Public policy must be rooted in both explicit and implicit biblical commands.[35] Forster, therefore, not only believes that Mohler's political theology spells disaster for the church and its witness, but also that it would eradicate the liberalism that protects some of the most important freedoms enshrined in the Constitution, namely, religious freedom.

Mohler, however, responded to Forster's accusation, arguing that *The Gathering Storm* highlights the unsustainability of American-ordered liberty without a "transcendent and objectively real basis for the declaration of human dignity, human rights, and human liberty."[36] Secularism, as an

---

[35] Forster, "A Protestant Integralism?"
[36] Mohler, "Secularism Cannot Sustain Liberty."

ideology, undermines the essential moral and ethical commitments necessary to sustain the Republic. Thus, Christians bear a responsibility to understand the conflict of worldviews at play in contemporary American society so they can better advocate for biblical notions of justice and human flourishing.

The debate between Forster and Mohler sheds crucial light on Mohler's political theology. Indeed, Mohler refuted the integralist accusation by unapologetically declaring his theological commitments as a Baptist—his Baptist beliefs nullified integralism as a possible political theology. To this point, Mohler cited the longstanding Baptist advocacy for religious freedom and the separation of church and state. For Baptists engaged in the public square, moreover, Mohler's argument may provide a middle way between the extremes of cultural capitulation or culture war. In an article for the magazine *First Things*, Mohler contended that at the heart of his identity as a Baptist (and subsequently, at the heart of his political theology) is the necessity of conversion. Much like Baptists throughout history, including figures like Helwys and Williams, Mohler situated the necessity of conversion as the core commitment of Baptist soteriology, which has enumerable implications for political theology and political involvement. In fact, Mohler rooted, as an example, the Baptist support for religious freedom in the centrality of conversionism. Holding conversion at the center of political theology, on the one hand, protects Baptists from surrendering the gospel for cultural credibility, while, on the other hand, dissuading Baptists from enlisting in an idolatrous culture war, thinking that the security and stability of the church is tethered to winning America back for God. Indeed, Mohler declared, "Put [Baptists] in jail, take away our earthly goods, do your worst—we will not ask permission from the powers that be. Whatever happens in the unfolding of history, we will still be preaching the gospel, plunging believers under water, telling people about Jesus, and singing the old, old story of Jesus and his love."[37] That is no summons to culture war or

---

[37] R. Albert Mohler Jr., "Why I Am a Baptist," *First Things*, accessed January 29, 2021, https://www.firstthings.com/article/2020/08/why-i-am-a-baptist.

a theological downgrade—it is, rather, a declaration that Baptists can meaningfully and faithfully engage the culture, contend for justice, and pursue human flourishing only when they keep before them the centrality of the gospel and the necessity of conversion.

Russell Moore and "Engaged Alienation"

Russell Moore is certainly no stranger to the American public square and the litany of issues facing Christians in America. He served as president of the Ethics and Religious Liberty Commission from 2013 to 2021, which witnessed massive shifts in American public life, not least of which was *Obergefell v. Hodges*, which legalized same-sex marriage in 2015. That same year, the Pew Research Center published "America's Changing Religious Landscape," which noted that from 2007 to 2014, Christianity in America fell from 78.4 percent to 70.6 percent. That study also revealed an exponential growth of the religiously unaffiliated, which jumped from 16.1 percent to 22.8 percent in the same seven-year time frame.[38] Moore, therefore, entered his role as head of the ERLC at a critical juncture in the American political landscape.

Indeed, in 2015, Moore sensed the volatility of the cultural climate and the impact it could have on Christians and the Southern Baptist Convention when he published his book *Onward: Engaging the Culture without Losing the Gospel.*[39] This book opened with three political theologies available—and at times deployed—by Christians in America. The first was a Christianity in capitulation to the culture. In this model, the church jettisons theological and doctrinal beliefs to conform to the prevailing mores

---

[38] Pew Research Center, "America's Changing Religious Landscape," Pew Research Center, May 12, 2015, https://www.pewforum.org/2015/05/12/americas-changing-religious-landscape/.

[39] Russell Moore, *Onward: Engaging the Culture without Losing the Gospel* (Nashville: B&H, 2015).

of the contemporary culture.[40] The second approach was Christianity sundered from the culture and political engagement. A Christianity walled off from the broader culture attempts to alleviate the clear tensions between a post-Christian America and the communities that hold fast to biblical orthodoxy.[41] Both approaches, however, fail to express, according to Moore, a right path for political theology and Christian engagement. He argued that both approaches represent a "Christianity that dies."[42]

Conversely, Moore offered a third approach to political theology: "engaged alienation," which he defined as "a Christianity that preserves the distinctiveness of our gospel while not retreating from our callings as neighbors and friends, and citizens."[43] Rooted and grounded in their gospel identity, Christians are, according to Moore, "free . . . to stand and to speak, not because we're a majority, moral or otherwise, but because we are an embassy of the future, addressing consciences designed to long for good news."[44] Moore directed his political theology toward cultural engagement due to a conviction that has long marked the Baptist tradition, namely, the goal of reconciliation. Baptists, emulating the gospel of Jesus Christ in their own lives and communities, confront the culture with the truth of the gospel and a system of biblical ethics that reflect God's creational design—a design

---

[40] Examples of this are too numerous to list. Mainline Protestantism represents the clearest expression of a Christianity in capitulation to the culture.

[41] Rod Dreher's book *The Benedict Option: A Strategy for Christians in a Post-Christian World* (New York: Penguin Random House, 2017) might come to mind as an example of a Christian withdrawal from culture. This would, however, be a false characterization of Dreher's thesis. He did not argue for a surrender to the culture or for Christians to retreat from the culture. Indeed, Moore and Dreher had a conversation about Dreher's book on Moore's podcast *Signposts*, wherein Moore and Dreher were on common ground about Dreher's argument. Dreher contended for a strategic retreat from the culture—Christians had, according to Dreher, neglected key commitments to the gospel and biblical ethics, without which there could be no faithful witnessing to a culture at odds with a biblical worldview.

[42] Moore, *Onward*, 8.

[43] Moore, 8.

[44] Moore, 9.

that when abided by not only inculcates human and societal flourishing but points to the glory of the eschaton.

Writing about political theology is one thing—it is another matter entirely to put that theology into practice, which Moore did in 2016–2017 when he led the ERLC to join an amicus brief that supported the construction of a mosque in New Jersey. The mosque had been denied the necessary permits in a manner that violated the First Amendment of the Constitution. Moore, however, received pushback from Southern Baptists who believed he unnecessarily and reprehensibly defended a religious faith they believed was bent on the destruction of Christians and the Christian gospel. How, the critique went, could the president of the ERLC contend for the religious expression, rights, and promulgation of a false god? His response to the disparagement and his stand for the Islamic Society of Basking Ridge, New Jersey, evinced not only his advocacy of religious freedom but the core of his Baptist political theology. Indeed, at the 2016 Southern Baptist Convention, Moore responded to a denunciation of his stance on the mosque by stating, "What it means to be a Baptist is to support soul freedom for everybody."[45] He declared that his stance on the mosque was not primarily motivated by self-interest but animated by his commitment to the gospel of Jesus Christ. Universal soul freedom simultaneously enables the proclamation of an unfettered gospel to souls not bound by state-enforced conformity to a socially mandated orthodoxy. Thus, Moore's role in the defense of Muslims building a mosque represented the outworking of his engaged alienation political theology. Contending for the religious freedom of all peoples not only nourishes human flourishing, but it fosters more favorable conditions for the gospel to be proclaimed and received.

---

[45] This quote comes from a video embedded in the following article: Paul Crookston, "Religious Freedom for Me but Not for Thee?," *National Review*, February 21, 2017, https://www.nationalreview.com/corner/russell-moore-muslim-mosques-religious-liberty-universal/.

Moore, therefore, sought the common good for the purpose of advancing the gospel. He espoused a Baptist political theology that advocated for justice, peace, biblical ethics, and a society patterned after God's creational mandate. That conviction, however, is indissolubly tethered to a surpassing allegiance to the King of kings and Lord of lords—an allegiance that, for Moore, frees Christians to fully engage with the culture without surrendering one millimeter of theological or doctrinal ground.

Moore's legacy as president of the Ethics and Religious Liberty Commission and his departure from the Southern Baptist Convention are certainly up for debate. Reasonable Christians will disagree over Moore's impact and influence in American evangelicalism. Still, Moore remains an important voice regarding Baptist political theology. Moreover, if anything he said was true, helpful, and in line with Christ's commands to his church, then they remain not only helpful but worthy of implementation.

Jonathan Leeman: Liberal Augustinianism

Jonathan Leeman has not been a right-hand man to a president of the United States; he has not, moreover, served as an entity head within the Southern Baptist Convention. He is, first and foremost, a man dedicated to the church and to espousing a biblically faithful ecclesiology—his leadership within the ministry 9Marks is evidence of that stewardship. It would, however, be a mistake to omit Leeman's place within this chapter on contemporary Baptist political theology. Indeed, Leeman makes a significant contribution toward political theology, especially as it is animated by his passion for ecclesiology and the vitality of the local church.

Leeman described his political theology as "liberal Augustinianism," which attempts to elucidate the obligations of Christians and the church within a political society.[46] Liberal Augustinianism has two primary goals:

---

[46] Jonathan Leeman, "Not an Augustinian Liberal, but a Liberal Augustinian," *Providence*, October 8, 2019, https://providencemag.com/2019/10/liberal-augustinian/.

First and foremost, Christians must recognize and keep perennially before them their true citizenship and identity in Christ. Christians belong to the city of God, not the city of Man. Indeed, Leeman borrowed from Augustine's *The City of God against the Pagans* as a foil for his political theology. Augustine began his tome, stating, "Most glorious is the City of God: whether in this passing age, where she dwells by faith as a pilgrim among the ungodly, or in the security of that eternal home which she now patiently awaits until 'righteousness shall return unto judgment.'"[47] This age, according to Augustine, also includes the earthly city, or the city of man, which is dominated by Satan and guided by a love for self.[48]

Christians, however, as citizens of the heavenly kingdom, await the blessings of eternal life and the fulfillment of God's promises in the age to come. Yet that eternal citizenship in no way negates the Christian's responsibility this side of eternity. Christians, animated by a gospel-rooted sacrificial love, engage the culture not as culture warriors but as ambassadors of a coming kingdom.[49] The line between ambassador and culture warrior fades when Christians permit corporeal political concerns to eclipse their incorporeal citizenship and inheritance. As Leeman wrote, "I want to help us be *less* American so that we might be *more* patriotic . . . to identify with Christ more so that we might love our fellow citizens more, no matter the name of our nation."[50]

If the first goal of liberal Augustinianism is to entrench Christians in their identity, the second goal seeks to provide a meaningful and biblically faithful method of engaging the culture *from* that identity. Leeman applied Augustine's two cities framework to his own political theology, arguing that the public square represents a clash of gods—a collision between disparate worldviews rooted in fundamentally divergent convictions, commitments,

---

[47] Augustine, *The City of God against the Pagans*, ed. and trans. R. W. Dyson (Cambridge: Cambridge University, 1998), 3.

[48] Augustine, 586.

[49] Jonathan Leeman, *How the Nations Rage: Rethinking Faith and Politics in a Divided Age* (Nashville: Thomas Nelson, 2018), 171.

[50] Leeman, 19.

and beliefs. He wrote that people enter the public square "on behalf of
their gods." A neutral public square wherein men and women can engage
in political debate from an agreed upon set of moral and ethical principles
does not, according to Leeman, exist.[51] He wrote that Christians ought not
think we can discover "some universal principle that will prove compelling
to all people. We who believe in the noetic effects of sin and the necessity of
regeneration should know better." There is no neutrality because the participants in the public square either enter with a love animated by the earthly
city (a self-love) or the city of God (sacrificial love).[52]

Given these realities, Leeman offered three erroneous approaches to
cultural engagement. If, as Leeman argued, the public square is a contest
of gods, then Christians might either disengage, capitulate, or mobilize
for a worldly political war. The love of God and love of neighbor nulli-
fies disengagement. Christian love nourishes a pursuit of biblical justice for
all people, which necessitates active involvement and contention for true
human flourishing. The Christian's citizenship in the city of God, however, curtails any notion of cultural capitulation. Theological and doctrinal
fidelity must always supersede any political aspirations in this world—this
means Christians must be prepared to go to jail and suffer for the cause of

---

[51] Jonathan Leeman, *Political Church: The Local Assembly as Embassy of Christ's
Rule* (Downers Grove, IL: InterVarsity, 2016), 81–82.

[52] Leeman, "Not an Augustinian Liberal." Leeman, therefore, disagrees with
the political theology asserted by John Rawls in *Political Liberalism* (New York:
Columbia University, 1993). Rawls contends for "public reason" as the method of
public discourse, wherein individuals in the public square must base moral, ethical,
and policy arguments on an agreed-upon system of ethical reasoning acceptable by
the broader population. Arguments rooted in religious convictions can be articulated, but only from the agreed-upon public reason. Leeman thinks this method is
impossible—there can be no agreed-upon consensus because each person enters the
public square as a citizen of two distinct and fundamentally divergent worldviews.
For a more philosophical alternative to Rawls, see Nicholas Wolterstorff's chapters
in *Religion in the Public Square: The Place of Religious Convictions in Political Debate*
(London: Rowman and Littlefield, 1997).

Christ. Faithful ambassadors of Christ, as Leeman argued, cannot jettison their allegiance to the King of kings and Lord of lords. Yet Christians must always be wary of the final erroneous political theology, which contorts political involvement into a worldly war. This final temptation often comes, according to Leeman, by falsely appropriating a providential status on one's nation, believing the United States, as an example, is God's chosen nation. Thus, disparate and idolatrous worldviews must be summarily destroyed through the ballot box and seats on the Supreme Court.[53]

Instead, Leeman asserted ambassadorship as the proper method for political engagement and a biblically faithful model for political theology. Christians and the church of Jesus Christ function as heralds of the coming kingdom, which grounds Christian political involvement in the centrality of the gospel. Yet, as ambassadors of Christ, the church engages the culture with a biblically rooted ethic—advocating for policies, participating in local communities, serving in places of need. The *telos* of this engagement is not political power but pointing pagans in the earthly city to the glory of the city of God; it is a political engagement that anticipates the eschaton.[54]

This political theology is similar to Moore's "engaged alienation." Leeman's distinct contribution, however, is how he articulated ambassadorship within what he called "liberal Augustinianism." The word "liberal," serving as a modifier, suggests that certain institutions associated with liberalism, such as democracy and American constitutionalism, must be viewed not as scriptural commands but wise pragmatism in a specific context. Certainly, liberal ideas like "religious tolerance, the separation of church and state, the equality of all people, and certain individual rights" must not be usurped— to do so, as Leeman argued, "is not just foolish, but sin."[55] Christians, therefore, even as citizens of the city of God, must remain vocal advocates of those political ideas rooted in a biblical conception of humanity and the

---

[53] Leeman, *How the Nations Rage*, 163–70.
[54] Leeman, 171–96.
[55] Leeman, "Not an Augustinian Liberal."

common good. Love of neighbor, inculcated by the power of the gospel, leaves the Christian no option but to engage the culture, ensuring that the church of Jesus Christ, as an embassy of Christ's kingdom, contends for biblical justice, peace, and human flourishing so as to point people to the gospel and the eternal kingdom to come.

Conclusion

Baptists face enormous moral and ethical questions in the twenty-first century. They live, as Leeman argued, in a public arena marked by a conflict of worldviews—a conflict between the earthly city and the city of God. When Baptists reflect on their biblical obligations and think through a scripturally faithful political theology, they are doing far more than developing a political strategy to enact a certain policy agenda. As has been seen in the figures surveyed in this chapter, a faithful political theology is integrally connected to one's devotion to the gospel. An orthodox political theology nourishes an orthopraxy for individual Christians as well as the Christian church. It protects God's people from surrender and retreat while also guarding them from making too much of a world that is passing away.

The pursuit of a faithful political theology could not be more paramount in this present age—an age marked by a culture increasingly hostile to ontological moral first principles and an age where evangelicals are still navigating the complexities of a post-Trump America. The issues at stake, which include policies like abortion and gender issues, are grave and deserving of careful, wise, and faithful thinking. Yet, as Graham, Colson, Land, Mohler, Moore, and Leeman show us, there is far *more* at stake than being right and morally true when it comes to policy proposals. Indeed, when Baptists adopt an erroneous political theology, they inevitably jettison what ought to be their unwavering, unyielding, and uncompromising conviction, namely, the centrality of the gospel of Jesus Christ.

16

The Christian Right: From Reagan to Trump

By Nathan A. Finn

Historical Overview

During the second half of the twentieth century, American conservatism came of age.[1] In the early postwar era, while conservatism was instinctual among some politicians in both major parties, the New Deal had helped forge a national consensus that conservatives considered to be center-left. That was changing by mid-century. A new conservative consensus was

---

[1] For more on the history of the modern conservative movement, see Lee Edwards, *The Conservative Revolution: The Movement That Remade America* (New York: Free Press, 1999); Jeffrey Hart, *The Making of the American Conservative Mind: National Review and Its Times* (Wilmington: Intercollegiate Studies Institute, 2005); George H. Nash, *The Conservative Intellectual Movement in America Since 1945*, 30th anniv. ed. (Wilmington: Intercollegiate Studies Institute, 2006).

being forged by thought leaders, periodicals, conferences, and organizations on the Right. By the 1960s, conservative intellectuals and policy experts—especially those in the orbit of William F. Buckley's *National Review*—were promoting a strategy of "fusionism" that brought traditionalist conservatives, economic libertarians, and anti-communists into a coherent (or at least strategic) conservative movement suitable to the Cold War era. Conservatism was resonating with some politicians, especially in Western states, such as Senator Barry Goldwater of Arizona, who ran unsuccessfully for president in 1964, and California governor and future president Ronald Reagan.

Beginning in the 1970s, a new ingredient was added to the recipe of modern conservatism: the Christian Right.[2] This new movement represented a synthesis of several features: a commitment to social conservatism on morally debatable issues; a religiously infused patriotism that could at times bleed over into Christian nationalism; and a conviction that government should take a friendly posture toward the Judeo-Christian tradition while protecting the religious liberty of people of all faiths (and no faith). The Christian Right was grounded in what Thomas Sowell calls a "constrained vision" of the universe wherein liberties must be ordered because of inherent self-interest, which traditional Jews and Christians attributed to the doctrine of universal human sinfulness.[3] The Christian Right shared many of the moral concerns of the traditionalist conservatives and was strongly committed to anti-communism. While the Christian Right was not

---

[2] For more on the Christian Right and its development, see William Martin, *With God on Our Side: The Rise of the Religious Right in America*, 2nd ed. (New York: Broadway, 2005); Daniel K. Williams, *God's Own Party: The Making of the Christian Right* (New York: Oxford University, 2012); Darren Dochuk, *From Bible Belt to Sunbelt: Plain-Folk Religion, Grassroots Politics, and the Rise of Evangelical Conservatism* (New York: Norton, 2012); Frances FitzGerald, *The Evangelicals: The Struggle to Shape America* (New York: Simon and Schuster, 2017). The remainder of my historical summary is informed by these works.

[3] For the distinction between constrained and unconstrained vision, see Thomas Sowell, *A Conflict of Visions: Ideological Origins of Political Struggles*, rev. ed. (New York: Basic Books, 2007), 9–35.

inherently committed to fiscal conservatism and indeed, at times, would resonate with government expansion in the pursuit of what came to be called "compassionate conservatism," for the most part the Christian Right had little trouble coexisting with other trajectories within the wider conservative movement.[4]

The believers who identified with the Christian Right were traditionally conservative in the sense that they were committed to voluntary associations and invested in mediating institutions within their communities.[5] As the consensus values of those local communities were undermined by progressive shifts, whether via general cultural trends or perceived government imposition, the disruptions led religious conservatives to mobilize politically on a larger scale. For the most part, those who mobilized were Evangelical in religion and Populist in political sensibilities. Early on, they hailed especially from the South and Midwest. They believed America had been shaped profoundly by the Judeo-Christian tradition, which was now under assault by secular humanism, and were supportive of the nation of Israel and her national interests in the Middle East. Many lamented that prayer and Bible reading in public schools had been ruled unconstitutional. Most resented that school textbooks taught Darwinian evolution as scientific fact. Many had been segregationists, especially in the South, and even as they gradually embraced integration, they continued to suspect that prominent civil rights

---

[4] Marvin Olasky coined the phrase "compassionate conservatism," which became an emphasis in George W. Bush's presidential campaign. See Olasky, *Compassionate Conservatism: What It Is, What It Does, and How It Can Transform America* (New York: Free Press, 2000).

[5] The classic work on the role of mediating institutions and local communities is Robert Nisbet, *The Quest for Community: A Study in the Ethics of Order and Freedom*, rep. ed. (Wilmington: Intercollegiate Studies Institute, 2010). Yuval Levin has argued for a renewed commitment to mediating institutions as the path to wider cultural and political renewal in *The Fractured Republic: Renewing America's Social Contract in the Age of Individualism* (New York: Basic Books, 2016) and *A Time to Build: From Family and Community to Congress and the Campus, How Recommitting to Our Institutions Can Revive the American Dream* (New York: Basic Books, 2020).

activists were Socialists and that enforced desegregation was a power-grab by liberal politicians. They rejected second-wave feminism and increased cultural acceptance of homosexuality. Finally, they scorned the legalization of abortion-on-demand and what came to be called the "culture of death" it represented.

In 1976, many who identified with the nascent Christian Right helped elect Governor Jimmy Carter of Georgia as president. Carter was a Southern Baptist who read his Bible and prayed daily, taught Sunday school, and did not hesitate to acknowledge he had been born again. But social conservatives were soon disillusioned with Carter. Many believed he was too supportive of feminism and not sufficiently oppositional toward abortion. Other conservatives were already critical of Carter because of his liberal economic policy and his commitment to a détente with the Soviet Union rather than containing or defeating global communism. With the 1980 election between Carter and Reagan, the Christian Right aligned with other conservatives in the Republican Party, as well as so-called Reagan Democrats who crossed parties, to elect the former film actor as president.

Over the following generation the Christian Right became a key constituency in the Republican Party. The movement found embodiment in many organizations, including Moral Majority (est. 1979), Family Research Council (est. 1983), and Christian Coalition (est. 1987), among others. These and similar groups advocated for their positions and mobilized evangelicals and others to vote for sympathetic candidates. The Christian Right helped elect Reagan in 1980 and 1984. While they were more lukewarm toward George H. W. Bush in 1988, by 1994 they had contributed to the GOP takeover of Congress and were among the most vocal critics of Bill Clinton's presidency (1993–2001), not least because of the latter's track record of marital infidelity. The Christian Right also became far more active in local and state politics during the 1990s, turning the GOP further to the right and contributing to the exodus of most of the remaining conservative Democrats from their party.

With the turn of the twenty-first century, the Christian Right played a key role in electing George W. Bush, an Evangelical Methodist, to the White House in 2000 and 2004. These "values voters" considered the younger Bush to be one of their own, partly because of his own testimony as an adult convert to Evangelical Christianity. He demonstrated personal sympathy for many of their convictions about social issues, and they resonated with his strong opposition to jihadist terrorism in the wake of the 9/11 terrorist attacks. For their part, the Christian Right were among the most avid of Bush's supporters, even as his approval ratings dropped during his second administration as the nation grew fatigued over the war in Iraq and the economy hurtled toward the Great Recession. The Christian Right suffered an electoral setback when mainline Protestant Barack Obama was elected to the presidency in 2008 and 2012. However, the results for the Christian Right were more hopeful at other levels of government (especially state and local).

With the 2016 election, the Christian Right faced a dilemma. The Democratic candidate, Hillary Clinton, had been objectionable to the movement since her tenure as first lady in the 1990s and continuing into her time in elected and appointed public office in the twenty-first century because of her strong commitment to abortion rights and because she was a symbol, for some, of nontraditional gender roles. The Republican candidate, Donald Trump, was a twice-divorced real estate magnate and reality television celebrity whose sexual ethics, public demeanor, ambivalence toward conservative political principles, and lack of a strong religious commitment was difficult to reconcile with the values of the Christian Right. Nevertheless, pollsters estimated that 81 percent of self-identified white evangelicals voted for Trump,[6] making them a key part of his base and pro-

---

[6] Katherine Stewart, "Eighty-One Percent of White Evangelicals Voted for Donald Trump. Why?," *The Nation*, November 17, 2016, https://www.thenation .com/article/archive/eighty-one-percent-of-white-evangelicals-voted-for-donald -trump-why/.

pelling him into the White House. Four years later, though the percentage was a bit lower, the Christian Right again gave their overwhelming support to President Trump's unsuccessful reelection bid. At present, there is little reason to think the Christian Right will break with the GOP anytime in the foreseeable future.

Key Baptist Figures

Many Baptists were involved in the Christian Right from its beginning. Independent Baptist pastor Tim LaHaye (1926–2016) and his wife, Beverly (b. 1929), were both ardent social conservatives and involved in founding Christian Right organizations. The former established the Council for National Policy in 1981 while the latter was a cofounder of Concerned Women for America in 1979. Southern Baptist evangelist James Robison (b. 1943) organized numerous major rallies in the late 1970s and early 1980s. Alongside Memphis Baptist layman Ed McAteer (1926–2004), Robison hosted the Religious Roundtable National Affairs Briefing in 1980 in Dallas, where presidential candidate Reagan "endorsed" his evangelical supporters. Other Baptists involved in the early days of the Christian Right include W. A. Criswell (1909–2002), Paul Pressler (b. 1930), Adrian Rogers (1931–2005), Charles Stanley (b. 1932), L. Paige Patterson (b. 1942), and Ed Dobson (1949–2015).

However, no Baptist, and arguably no individual, was more identified with the Christian Right than Jerry Falwell Sr. (1933–2007).[7] Falwell began his ministry as an Independent Baptist, part of the separatist Fundamentalist movement that positioned itself as a conservative rival of evangelicalism in postwar America. In 1956, Falwell graduated from Bible college and founded

---

[7] For more on Falwell, see Susan Friend Harding, *The Book of Jerry Falwell: Fundamentalist Language and Politics* (Princeton: Princeton University, 2000), and Matthew Avery Sutton, *Jerry Falwell and the Rise of the Religious Right: A Brief History with Documents* (New York: St. Martins, 2012).

Thomas Road Baptist Church in Lynchburg, Virginia. Soon thereafter he launched his television program, *The Old-Time Gospel Hour*, which when syndicated made Falwell one of the pioneers of the televangelism industry.[8] In 1971, Falwell established Liberty University, which is now the largest Christian university in the US and the institution with which his legacy is likely most identified.

Falwell was originally opposed to pastors engaging in political activism, criticizing Martin Luther King Jr. and other civil rights activists for promoting public demonstrations. However, in the mid-1970s Falwell became agitated with perceived governmental harassment of Bob Jones University (BJU) through the IRS because of the university's segregationist policy. Conservative Protestants, most of whom disagreed with BJU's segregationist stance, were convinced the government should not interfere with BJU's policy because of church-state separation.[9] More importantly, Falwell was concerned about the cluster of issues that became identified with Evangelical social conservatism. He abandoned his erstwhile separatism at the urging of popular apologist and antiabortion advocate Francis Schaeffer (1912–1984)

---

[8] For more on the influence of televangelism on the early Christian Right and the wider American culture, see Quentin J. Schultze, *Televangelism and American Culture: The Business of Popular Religion* (Grand Rapids: Baker, 1991).

[9] Historian Randall Balmer argues that the BJU case, as well as the racism inherent among conservative Evangelicals of the era, is the real issue that led to the formation of the Christian Right. See Balmer, *Thy Kingdom Come: How the Religious Right Distorts Faith and Threatens America* (New York: Basic Books, 2007), and Balmer, "The Real Origins of the Religious Right," *Politico Magazine*, May 27, 2014, https://www.politico.com/magazine/story/2014/05/religious-right-real-origins-107133. Historians are divided over whether Balmer overstates his case, though his thesis has become popular in recent works that seek to identify the Christian Right with white supremacy. What is clear is that in the 1960s, Christian conservatives were divided between segregationists and moderate integrationists. The New Christian Right that emerged in the 1970s and 1980s coalesced in part by sidestepping the issue of systemic racism, while increasingly rejecting interpersonal expressions of racism and focusing Evangelical political engagement on abortion and homosexuality.

and was coaxed into partisan Republican politics by GOP activist Paul Weyrich (1942–2008). In 1979, Falwell formed Moral Majority, which marked the symbolic beginning of the Christian Right.

Falwell outlined an agenda for the Religious Right in his 1980 book *Listen, America!*[10]

He divided the book into three sections, each of which represented a key facet of Evangelical social conservatism. The first section defended mainstream conservative principles such as ordered liberty, limited government, a strong national defense, and American exceptionalism, though these themes were synthesized with the idea that America was a distinctively Christian nation and a strong commitment to the modern state of Israel. Section two focused on public morality by defending the importance of nuclear families; advocating for traditional gender roles in opposition to feminism; renouncing abortion, homosexuality, and pornography; and criticizing the recreational use of drugs and alcohol. Falwell also took to task popular culture, especially television and music as well as public education, for reinforcing depraved values. The final section was a call to action. If America was to be rescued from the same civilizational collapse that fell upon ancient empires, believers were to pray for national revival and become politically mobilized on behalf of the social conservative cause. *Listen, America!* was not a scholarly treatise in Christian political theology, but a tract for the times for evangelicals and Fundamentalists concerned about the direction of American public life.

By 1988, the Moral Majority was dissolving as the Reagan administration was nearing its end. But the Christian Right was here to stay. Falwell had become a national figure through his television program, books, stump speeches, and appearances on cable news. He remained perhaps the most vocal advocate of social conservatism in the public square into the early twenty-first century. Falwell was close personally with Republican politicians and positioned Liberty University to be the preferred school of

---

[10] See Jerry Falwell, *Listen, America!* (New York: Doubleday, 1980).

many social conservatives. During the 1980s and 1990s, Falwell became less identified with separatist fundamentalism, and in 1996 he led Thomas Road into the Southern Baptist Convention. When Falwell died in 2017, his son Jerry Falwell Jr. (b. 1962) took over Liberty University. Although initially less politically active than his father, within a decade the younger Falwell became a standard-bearer for the Christian Right and a key supporter of Donald Trump's presidential campaign and subsequent administration before his own administration at Liberty ended in scandal in the fall of 2020.

A second key Baptist figure is Southern Baptist theologian Richard Land (b. 1946), who served as president of the Christian Life Commission (1988–1997) and its successor, the Ethics and Religious Liberty Commission (1997–2013).[11] Whereas Falwell was an entrepreneurial pastor and institution-builder, Land came to activism from a more academic route. A native of Houston, Land earned a bachelor of arts from Princeton University, a master of theology from New Orleans Baptist Theological Seminary, and a doctor of philosophy from Regent's Park College, Oxford University. Land served as professor and academic administrator at what is now Criswell College from 1975–1988, during which time he was active in the inerrancy controversy in the SBC. Following a sabbatical in the governor's office in Texas, Land took the reins of the SBC's public policy agency.

Land was a prolific author who wrote articles, chapters, and books for both scholarly and popular audiences. Between 2002 and 2011, Land wrote four books that put forward a post–9/11 vision for the Christian Right that focused on traditional family values, the need for national renewal, and

---

[11] For more on Land's role in promoting the Christian Right among Southern Baptists, see Jerry Sutton, *A Matter of Conviction: A History of Southern Baptist Engagement with the Culture* (Nashville: B&H, 2008), 271–420. See also Barry Hankins, *Uneasy in Babylon: Southern Baptist Conservatives and American Culture* (Tuscaloosa: University of Alabama, 2002), which discusses how Land and other SBC leaders embraced and promoted the agenda of the Christian Right as part of the wider Conservative Resurgence within the convention.

religious liberty for all.[12] From 1980 to 1988 and again from 1998 to 2013, Land hosted two syndicated radio programs focused on current events. Land was a frequent commentator on television and radio news outlets and in 2005 was named one of *Time* magazine's twenty-five most influential evangelicals in America.[13] While Land supported the full range of issues championed by the Christian Right, he was especially outspoken on matters of religious liberty, in part because of his role in the SBC. Land served five terms as a commissioner on the US Commission on International Religious Freedom. But Land was also willing to promote causes that were less identified with the Christian Right. He authored a 1995 Resolution on Racial Reconciliation that expressed repentance for the role racism played in the founding of the SBC and its subsequent history.[14] He also supported bipartisan efforts toward public education reform, immigration reform, and AIDS relief in Africa, and he criticized the Bush administration's use of waterboarding as torture.

In 2013, Land's quarter-century tenure as a Southern Baptist entity leader ended when he retired from the ERLC following controversial comments about slain Black teenager Trayvon Martin and accusations of plagiarism related to his radio program.[15] However, Land remained a leading

---

[12] See Richard D. Land and John Perry, *For Faith and Family: Changing America by Strengthening the Family* (Nashville: B&H, 2002); Richard D. Land, *Real Homeland Security: The America God Will Bless* (Nashville: B&H, 2004); Richard D. Land, *Imagine! A God Blessed America: What It Would Look Like and How It Could Happen* (Nashville: B&H, 2005); Richard Land, *The Divided States of America: What Liberals and Conservatives Get Wrong about Faith and Politics* (Nashville: B&H, 2011).

[13] TIME staff, "Richard Land," *Time*, February 7, 2005, http://content.time.com/time/specials/packages/article/0,28804,1993235_1993243_1993293,00.html.

[14] "Resolution on Racial Reconciliation on the 150th Anniversary of the Southern Baptist Convention," Southern Baptist Convention, June 1, 1995, https://www.sbc.net/resource-library/resolutions/resolution-on-racial-reconciliation-on-the-150th-anniversary-of-the-southern-baptist-convention/.

[15] Jeremy Weber, "Richard Land Announces Retirement from Southern Baptist Ethics Commission," *Christianity Today*, July 31, 2012, https://www

voice in the Christian Right from his new role as president of Southern Evangelical Seminary and executive editor of the *Christian Post*. He also maintained a relationship with the ERLC, serving as a research fellow. Along with many other Baptist leaders, Land served on President Donald Trump's evangelical advisory board, where he was arguably one of the more moderate participants.[16] While supportive of many of Trump's policies, Land was not an uncritical cheerleader for the president, nor did he suggest that Trump himself was an Evangelical like Trump's more enthusiastic supporters, whom historian John Fea has memorably termed the "court evangelicals."[17] Although Land no longer holds an official position in SBC life, he continues to represent the convictions of many Baptists who identify with the Christian Right and have maintained their support for the Republican party.

A final Baptist representative of the Christian Right is evangelist Franklin Graham (b. 1952). Graham is the son of famed Baptist evangelist Billy Graham (1918–2018), the founder of evangelical relief agency Samaritan's Purse, and since 2001 the president and CEO of the Billy Graham Evangelistic Association (BGEA). The elder Graham was a close confidant of many American presidents, though a too-close brush with political scandal during Richard Nixon's presidency persuaded Graham to tone down his political activity and keep his distance from the emerging

---

.christianitytoday.com/news/2012/july/richard-land-announces-retirement-from -southern-baptist.html.

[16] A Google search turns up numerous membership lists of the Evangelical advisory board. While none of the lists are identical, two features stand out. First, almost all the names are recurring, even if not all of them appear on every list. Second, on every list, half or more of the members are Baptists, with the bulk of the rest being Pentecostals.

[17] For more on the "court evangelicals" and their role in Donald Trump's election and subsequent administration, see John Fea, *Believe Me: The Evangelical Road to Donald Trump* (Grand Rapids: Eerdmans, 2018). It should be noted that Fea considers Land to be a "court evangelical" by virtue of the latter's participation in President Trump's Evangelical advisory board.

Christian Right.[18] For his part, the younger Graham developed a reputation for being far more politically partisan. During the George W. Bush administration, Graham became more closely tied to the Republican party. He was an outspoken supporter of the War on Terror, making negative comments about Islam after 9/11 that were widely criticized yet representative of what most conservative evangelicals likely believed.[19] Graham would continue to periodically make negative comments about Islam over the next two decades.

Following Barack Obama's election in 2008, Graham became a controversial critic of the liberal president. He questioned whether Obama's Christian faith was sincere and tied Obama to Islam by claiming he was born a Muslim.[20] These comments came at a time when many Americans, including Donald Trump, were embracing conspiracy theories that Obama was not really an American citizen and/or might be a closeted Muslim. In 2012, when Billy Graham endorsed Mitt Romney for president, many critics suggested the younger Graham had coerced his nonpartisan father into the move. Franklin and the BGEA also came under fire for removing references on the ministry's website to the cult status of Mormons at the very time when a Mormon was the GOP's presidential candidate.[21] Throughout this period, Franklin remained an outspoken critic of abortion

---

[18] See Steven P. Miller, *Billy Graham and the Rise of the Republican South* (Philadelphia: University of Pennsylvania, 2011).

[19] Todd Starnes, "Graham Stands by Statement Calling Islam 'Wicked, Violent,'" Baptist Press, November 19, 2001, https://www.baptistpress.com/resource-library /news/graham-stands-by-statement-calling-islam-wicked-violent/.

[20] Bradley Blackburn, "The Rev. Franklin Graham Says President Obama Was 'Born a Muslim,'" ABC News, August 20, 2010, https://abcnews.go.com/WN /franklin-graham-president-obama-born-muslim-pew-poll/story?id=11446462.

[21] Daniel Burke, "After Romney Meeting, Billy Graham Website Scrubs Mormon 'Cult' Reference," *The Washington Post*, October 17, 2012, https:// www.washingtonpost.com/national/on-faith/after-romney-meeting-billy-graham -website-scrubs-mormoncult-reference/2012/10/16/fa4ce826–17d1–11e2–a346 –f24efc680b8d_story.html.

and homosexuality and a vocal proponent of religious liberty, all of which proved controversial in the public square.

Beginning in 2016, Franklin Graham became one of Donald Trump's most prominent Evangelical boosters, especially on Twitter and in his public speaking ministry. Even in a book intended to reflect on his father's ministry, he took time to attribute Trump's election to the prayers of Christians, thank God that Trump had been elected, suggest this would mean a course correction for America, and recount his experience of reading Scripture at Trump's inauguration—all while noting that he had not technically endorsed Trump's candidacy.[22] Graham's enthusiastic support for Trump led to considerable consternation among scholars and pundits critical of Trump. Fea identifies Graham as one of the most vocal of Trump's "court evangelicals" and on his widely read personal blog. Fea has an entire "tag" dedicated to posts related to Graham's support for Trump.[23] A frequent complaint from progressive critics is the difference between Billy Graham's nonpartisan (and implicitly statesmanlike) posture and Franklin Graham's partisan (and implicitly hypocritical) backing of Trump.[24] While Graham's support for Trump is open to scrutiny, it is by no means unusual. If polls can be trusted—a debatable matter, to be sure—at least three-quarters of white evangelicals voted like Graham, even if they lack some of his enthusiasm in doing so.

---

[22] Franklin Graham and Donna Lee Toney, *Through My Father's Eyes* (Nashville: Thomas Nelson, 2018), 269–76.

[23] Fea, *Believe Me*, 26, 58, 102, 106; John Fea, The Way of Improvement Leads Home, accessed November 23, 2020, https://thewayofimprovement.com/category /franklin-graham/.

[24] For example, see Eliza Griswold, "Franklin Graham's Uneasy Alliance with Donald Trump," *The New Yorker,* September 11, 2018, https://www.newyorker.com /news/dispatch/franklin-grahams-uneasy-alliance-with-donald-trump, and Stephen Prothero, "Billy Graham Built a Movement. Now His Son Is Dismantling It." *Politico Magazine,* February 24, 2018, https://www.politico.com/magazine/story /2018/02/24/billy-graham-evangelical-decline-franklin-graham-217077.

For Baptists committed to the Religious Right, their political convictions outweighed their denominational loyalty. It is noteworthy that two of the US presidents who drew the ire of the Religious Right, Democrats Jimmy Carter (b. 1924) and Bill Clinton (b. 1946), were each Southern Baptists.[25] Although each of these men were frequent churchgoers who talked openly about their faith, the social policies they defended, particularly related to abortion and homosexuality, ran contrary to the Religious Right's agenda.[26] In addition, many believed Clinton's marital infidelity, especially his affair with a White House intern while in office, were at best problematic and at most disqualified him from public office.[27] For the Religious Right, political liberalism and especially progressive social views remained a perennial threat, even (perhaps especially) when promoted by politicians who were also committed Christians.

---

[25] The same was true of Al Gore (b. 1948), who served as Clinton's vice president and ran unsuccessfully as the Democratic candidate for president in 2000.

[26] Much has been written about Carter's faith. For the best introduction, see Randall Balmer, *Redeemer: The Life of Jimmy Carter* (New York: Basic, 2014). On Clinton's faith, see Gary Scott Smith, *Religion in the Oval Office: The Religious Lives of American Presidents* (New York: Oxford University, 2015), 329–66. In 2008, Carter and Clinton hosted a meeting called the New Baptist Covenant, which was intended to draw together centrist and progressive Baptist groups to offer a unified public witness in contrast to more conservative Baptist groups such as the SBC. See Erin Roach, "Carter and Clinton Call for 'New Baptist Covenant,'" Baptist Press, January 10, 2007, https://www.baptistpress.com/resource-library/news/carter -clinton-call-for-new-baptist-covenant/.

[27] In 1998, the Southern Baptist Convention adopted a resolution amid the scandal over Clinton's affair that called for government leaders to "live by the highest standards of morality both in their private actions and in their public duties, and thereby serve as models of moral excellence and character." See "Resolution on Moral Character of Public Officials," Southern Baptist Convention, June 1, 1998, https://www.sbc.net/resource-library/resolutions/resolution-on-moral-character-of -public-officials/. The SBC did not adopt a similar resolution during the presidency of Donald Trump, who was also an adulterer and was significantly less religious than Clinton. However, Trump's policies were more often amenable to the social conservatism of most Southern Baptists, his personal shortcomings notwithstanding.

Baptist Debates

Since the late 1970s, most theologically conservative Baptists have identified with the Christian Right. Progressive Baptists have pushed back on this alignment, though until the twenty-first century there was relatively little debate about abortion or homosexuality. Even progressive Baptists were, for the most part, socially conservative (or at least Center-Right) on those issues, with some notable exceptions.[28] Until recent years, the most controversial intra-Baptist debates were over the nature of church-state separation and whether America was, or ever had been, a Christian nation. In recent years, immigration and race have also emerged as hotly contested issues with the Christian Right—including among Baptists. The latter contributed to the controversy over whether conservative evangelicals, including Baptists, should support Trump's candidacy in 2016 and reelection bid in 2020. For the sake of space, I will focus on personalities and debates in the Southern Baptist orbit.

During the final quarter of the twentieth century, at least three general perspectives existed among Southern Baptists when it came to the question of America's Christian identity and how it relates to church-state separation. Some believed America was founded as an explicitly Christian nation as part of God's divine plan. This view was common within the wider Christian Right, as reflected in the 1977 book *The Light and the Glory*, Christian private school and homeschool history curricula, and the "soft reconstructionism" of David Barton's controversial WallBuilders organization.[29] Many Baptist laypeople and at least some pastors affirmed that America was, by

---

[28] For example, proabortion ethicist Paul Simmons taught on the faculty of Southern Baptist Theological Seminary from 1970 to 1993 and two churches in North Carolina were disfellowshipped from the SBC in 1992 for embracing a "welcoming and affirming" posture toward homosexuality.

[29] See John Fea, *Was America Founded as a Christian Nation? A Historical Introduction* (Louisville: Westminster-John Knox, 2011), 60–67; Julie J. Ingersoll, *Building God's Kingdom: Inside the World of Christian Reconstruction* (New York: Oxford University, 2015), 39, 79–118.

design, a Christian nation.[30] Sometimes proponents of this view rejected in principle church-state separation, identifying the concept with secular humanism more than the Baptist tradition. For example, longtime SBC leader W. A. Criswell memorably referred to the separation of church and state as "the figment of some infidel's imagination" during a 1984 television interview, putting Criswell at odds with many of the historic Baptist thinkers reviewed elsewhere in this volume.[31]

A second view of American history, more prominent among conservative SBC scholars, was that America was not founded as an explicitly Christian nation but that the Judeo-Christian tradition deeply influenced the nation's historic identity, and that fact should be acknowledged and celebrated. This perspective was common among SBC public theologians such as Richard Land and Albert Mohler.[32] Most Southern Baptists of this persuasion, as well as many who affirmed the Christian America thesis, embraced an "accommodationist" view of church and state.[33] They rejected the idea of a state-sponsored religion, but believed the government should adopt a generally friendly posture toward religion. As a rule, they emphasized the "free exercise" clause of the First Amendment more so than the establishment clause, though as Baptists they certainly opposed state-sponsored religion. America was not a Christian nation but a nation of Christians, and the Constitution guaranteed their (and others') religious liberty.

A third view argued that America has always been a secular nation, albeit one influenced significantly by Christians (especially Protestants) for much of its history. Sometimes this influence regrettably resembled a quasi-establishment that was inconsistent with the First Amendment and

---

[30] Texas pastor and former SBC president Jimmy Draper was the most noteworthy pastoral defender of this view. See James T. Draper and Forrest E. Watson, *If the Foundations Be Destroyed* (Nashville: Thomas Nelson, 1984).

[31] Cited in William Estep, *Revolution within the Revolution: The First Amendment in Historical Context, 1612–1789* (Grand Rapids: Eerdmans, 1990), 9.

[32] Hankins, *Uneasy in Babylon*, 63–64.

[33] Hankins, 139–64.

the best of the Baptist tradition. They leaned on earlier Baptist thinkers such as Roger Williams (1603–1683) and John Leland (1754–1841) as well as Thomas Jefferson's famous 1802 letter to the Danbury Baptists, wherein he coined the phrase "wall of separation" to advocate for a strict separation between church and state.[34] Later Baptist luminaries such as E. Y. Mullins and George Truett also represented this view.[35] While some theological conservatives affirmed a secular account of American identity, this view was more identified with progressives from the 1980s onward. Progressive Baptists sometimes allied themselves with secularist organizations such as the American Civil Liberties Union and Americans United for Separation of Church and State, seemed embarrassed about overt displays of patriotism, and were more generally supportive of progressive positions on social issues, especially the LGBTQ+ movement. This progressive trajectory became identified with the Baptist Joint Committee on Public Affairs (now the Baptist Joint Committee for Religious Liberty), which the SBC defunded in 1991 during the inerrancy controversy.

Most progressives disengaged from SBC life during the 1990s. Since the turn of the twenty-first century, the most important debates among Southern Baptists have been among those committed to theological and social conservatism. One major issue was immigration. During the years of the second Bush and Obama administrations, Southern Baptists affirmed a mediating position on immigration reform that called for securing borders, enforcing existing immigration laws, treating all foreigners in the US—including illegal immigrants—with compassion, and creating a pathway to citizenship. Both Richard Land and his successor as president of the Ethics

---

[34] Jefferson's letter is available at the Library of Congress website: Thomas Jefferson, "Jefferson's Letter to the Danbury Baptists," Library of Congress, January 1, 1802, https://www.loc.gov/loc/lcib/9806/danpre.html.

[35] See E. Y. Mullins, *The Axioms of Religion: A New Interpretation of the Baptist Faith* (Philadelphia: Griffith and Rowland, 1908), 185–200, and George W. Truett, "Baptists and Religious Liberty," The Reformed Reader, May 16, 1920, http://www.reformedreader.org/baptistsandreligiousliberty.htm.

and Religious Liberty Commission, Russell Moore, were advocates for immigration reform, participating in various bipartisan and faith-based initiatives. The SBC's mediating position was affirmed in resolutions in 2006 and 2011 as well as in numerous articles published for Baptist Press or the ERLC website.[36]

In 2016, Donald Trump campaigned on the promise of curtailing immigration and tightening border security, most notably by constructing a wall along the US–Mexico border for which the latter country would pay. He passed controversial executive orders limiting immigration and refugees from some majority Muslim nations. Tales of detention centers and families being separated at the border filled the news. While Moore continued to affirm the mediating position that had represented the SBC consensus during the previous decade, and the SBC reaffirmed that position in a 2018 resolution, it was clear many Southern Baptists appreciated President Trump's hard line on immigration and believed Moore and others like him were too progressive on the issue.[37] In 2020, Moore and the ERLC came under fire for its ties to the Evangelical Immigration Table (EIT), an organization also supported by other Southern Baptist leaders. When rumors circulated that progressive billionaire George Soros was secretly funding the EIT, Baptist Press was forced to publish an article explaining the work of EIT and rejecting the allegations linking Soros funding the organization.[38]

---

[36] See "On the Crisis of Illegal Immigration," Southern Baptist Convention, June 1, 2006, https://www.sbc.net/resource-library/resolutions/on-the-crisis-of -illegal-immigration/, and "On Immigration and the Gospel," June 1, 2011, https://www.sbc.net/resource-library/resolutions/on-immigration-and-the-gospel/. The search features at the websites for Baptist Press (www.baptistpress.com) and ERLC (www.erlc.com) result in dozens of articles related to illegal immigration and immigration reform.

[37] "On Immigration," Southern Baptist Convention, June 1, 2018, https:// www.sbc.net/resource-library/resolutions/on-immigration/.

[38] BP Explainer, "EXPLAINER: ERLC, George Soros and Evangelical Immigration Table," Baptist Press, January 9, 2020, https://www.baptistpress.com

On social media especially, conspiracy theories would persist that Moore and the ERLC had ties to Soros.

Race was another controversial issue among Southern Baptists, especially following Obama's election in 2008. Racism had played a central role in the founding of the SBC in 1845 and had characterized the denomination through much of its history. The aforementioned 1995 resolution on racial reconciliation signaled the change of heart that had occurred among Southern Baptists, and in 2012 Fred Luter became the first (and thus far only) African American to be elected SBC president. Nevertheless, racial tensions were reignited within the SBC (as elsewhere) by the debates over police brutality toward Blacks, how Christians should think about the Black Lives Matter movement (est. 2013), the resurgence of white supremacist views during the years of the Trump administration, and concerns about whether Christians should appropriate concepts from critical race theory (CRT) and intersectionality.

Chapter 9 of this volume is devoted to recent Southern Baptist tensions over race. For the sake of space, I will share snapshots that illustrate recent tensions. In 2017, the SBC adopted a resolution against the Alt-Right, a racist ideology that had allegedly influenced some within the Trump administration.[39] The resolution was originally rejected, though a combination of public advocacy and backroom politicking led to a revised version of the resolution being affirmed by messengers.[40] That same year, a collection of essays was published titled *Removing the Stain of Racism from the Southern*

/resource-library/news/explainer-erlc-george-soros-and-evangelical-immigration -table/.

[39] "On the Anti-Gospel of Alt-Right White Supremacy," Southern Baptist Convention, June 1, 2017, https://www.sbc.net/resource-library/resolutions/on-the -anti-gospel-of-alt-right-white-supremacy/.

[40] Adelle M. Banks, "In Dramatic Turnabout, Southern Baptists Condemn White Supremacy," Religious News Service, June 14, 2017, https://religionnews .com/2017/06/14/in-dramatic-turnabout-southern-baptists-condemn-white -supremacy/.

Baptist Convention.[41] The book received a number of positive endorsements from SBC leaders and scholars, though critics raised concerns that some of the essayists were influenced by CRT. In 2019, the SBC adopted a resolution stating that CRT and intersectionality should be rejected as worldviews, but that insights from these theories could be engaged to shed light on racism.[42]

The reaction against "Resolution 9" was fierce in some circles, leading to accusations that some Southern Baptist leaders were rejecting the sufficiency of Scripture and/or had been influenced by "cultural Marxism." Terms like *social justice* and *systemic racism* became flashpoints in SBC life. In 2020, the debate reached a fever pitch as several African Americans left the convention, a group called the Conservative Baptist Network formed to counter Resolution 9 within the denomination, and the six SBC seminary presidents published a statement denouncing CRT that only fanned the flames of the controversy.[43] The 2021 SBC adopted a resolution titled "On the Sufficiency of Scripture for Race and Racial Reconciliation."[44] Although the resolution was affirmed by an overwhelming majority of messengers, it did little to pacify the loudest critics because of the resolution's failure to

---

[41] Kevin Jones and Jarvis J. Williams, eds., *Removing the Stain of Racism from the Southern Baptist Convention: Diverse African American and White Perspectives* (Nashville: B&H Academic, 2017).

[42] "On Critical Race Theory and Intersectionality," Southern Baptist Convention, June 1, 2019, https://www.sbc.net/resource-library/resolutions/on -critical-race-theory-and-intersectionality/.

[43] For the statement from the seminary presidents, see George Schroeder, "Seminary Presidents Reaffirm BFM, Declare CRT Incompatible," Baptist Press, November 30, 2020, https://www.baptistpress.com/resource-library/news /seminary-presidents-reaffirm-bfm-declare-crt-incompatible/.

[44] "On the Sufficiency of Scripture for Race and Racial Reconciliation," Southern Baptist Convention, June 21, 2021, https://www.sbc.net/resource-library /resolutions/on-the-sufficiency-of-scripture-for-race-and-racial-reconciliation/. In the interest of full disclosure, the author served as vice chair of the 2021 Resolutions Committee.

call out CRT or intersectionality by name, instead focusing on rejecting any "theory or worldview" that falls short of a biblical perspective.

The recent debates over immigration and race cannot be divorced from the impact of Trump's presidency on Southern Baptist life. While the second Bush and Obama administrations were divisive in the wider culture, for the most part Southern Baptists enjoyed a consensus during this era, generally supporting the former and being suspicious of the latter. However, the 2016 election demonstrated an underlying rift in Southern Baptist political theology, despite the shared commitment to social conservatism and religious liberty. The center of the debate was how best to respond to Christian nationalism, an ideology that synthesizes elements of Christian identity with the resurgent nationalism among many Western nations that were growing increasingly hesitant about globalism in the 2010s.[45] Christian nationalism had always influenced the Religious Right, as evidenced in the aforementioned debates about the role of Christianity in American history. However, this understanding conflicts with the historic Baptist commitment to a free church in a free state and is at least in tension with a Baptist view of mission.

Christian nationalism enjoyed a resurgence that coincided with, and was reinforced by, the Trump administration. Some Christian thinkers, many of whom were Roman Catholics, advocated thoughtful versions of Christian nationalism.[46] However a more populist version influenced many evangelical

---

[45] The best introduction to Christian nationalism is Andrew L. Whitehead and Samuel L. Perry, *Taking America Back for God: Christian Nationalism in the United States* (New York: Oxford University, 2020). For a conservative and Baptistic critique of Christian nationalism, see Paul D. Miller, *The Religion of American Greatness: What's Wrong with Christian Nationalism* (Downers Grove, IL: IVP Academic, 2022).

[46] The journal *First Things*, under the leadership of editor R. R. Reno, became one of the most articulate defenders of Christian nationalism, publishing numerous editorials and essays on the topic beginning in 2017. The Edmund Burke Foundation, a think tank that promoted "national conservatism" as the best path to a revitalized conservative movement, closely overlapped with Christian nationalism.

pastors and laypeople, including Southern Baptists. Christian nationalists believe America is a Christian nation, or at least a nation with a special place in God's providential design. Historic American culture is closely identified with traditional white Protestant sensibilities, contributing to implicit racial assumptions among some Christian nationalists. Because of America's historically Christian identity, there is often a dotted line between civic virtues (patriotism) and Christian values (piety). Christian nationalists, as well as other nationalists, believe it is appropriate for government to use its power to reinforce patriotism and push back against perceived threats to traditional American identity, whether it comes in the form of immigrants from Muslim countries or revisionist historical initiatives that highlight systemic racism in American history. Although not particularly religious himself, Trump was believed by many Christian nationalists to be best positioned to protect conservative Christians—and all patriotic Americans—from progressive threats to American culture.

Christian conservatives who rejected Christian nationalism, and nationalism more generally, did so for a variety of reasons.[47] They believed Christian

---

See "National Conservatism," Edmund Burke Foundation, accessed September 11, 2021, https://nationalconservatism.org/about/.

[47] Arguably, the most prominent debate about Christian nationalism versus Christian support for traditional liberalism was represented in a 2019 dispute between columnists Sohrab Ahmari and David French. Ahmari, an atheist convert to Catholicism, criticized Christian efforts to accommodate liberal democracy as a failed experiment that would not advance the cause of social conservatism and natonal renewal. Ahmari identified Presbyterian lawyer and journalist French as a representative of that failure. See Sohrab Ahmari, "Against David French-Ism," *First Things*, May 29, 2019, https://www.firstthings.com/web-exclusives/2019/05/against-david-french-ism. French responded with "What Sohrab Ahmari Gets Wrong," *National Review*, May 30, 2019, https://www.nationalreview.com/2019/05/david-french-response-sohrab-ahmari/. What became known as the "Ahmari-French Dispute" resulted in many essays, blog posts, and at least two formal debates. Defenders of both men weighed in on the controversy. For a summary of the dispute and critique of each position, see Jonathan Leeman, "Conservatives Clash on the Goal of Government," *Providence,* September 6, 2019, https://providencemag

nationalism misunderstood American history and at times comingled church and state in problematic ways. They were concerned that Christian nationalism at least unintentionally downplayed or ignored minority experiences, sometimes giving cover to overtly racist white nationalism. They were troubled by the close identification of piety with patriotism, which can lead to idolatry. There were concerns that Christian nationalism, especially in its more strident forms, was incompatible with a classically liberal view of the American political order. This alternative conservative political theology was represented among many Southern Baptist scholars who were too young to have participated significantly in the first generation of the Christian Right and the inerrancy controversy during the final two decades of the twentieth century, but who remained deeply committed to both resurgent Baptist orthodoxy and social conservatism.[48]

Some prominent Southern Baptists who rejected Christian nationalism were identified with the "Never Trump" movement in 2016, most notably Russell Moore and seminary presidents Albert Mohler (who reversed his position and endorsed Trump in 2020) and Danny Akin. Other prominent leaders were vocally pro-Trump, most notably Franklin Graham, pastors Jack Graham and Robert Jeffress, executive committee president Ronnie Floyd, and Liberty University president Jerry Falwell Jr. The latter were influenced by Christian nationalism to varying degrees. When Trump carried white evangelicals by an overwhelming margin, Moore became a particular focus of criticism because of the accusation that he was out of step with most Southern Baptists. When the COVID-19 pandemic led the

---

.com/2019/09/conservatives-clash-goal-government-sohrab-ahmari-david-french
-debate/.

    [48] See Russell D. Moore, *Onward: Engaging the Culture without Losing the Gospel* (Nashville: B&H, 2015); Russell D. Moore and Andrew T. Walker, *The Gospel and Religious Liberty* (Nashville: B&H Academic, 2016); Jonathan Leeman, *How the Nations Rage: Rethinking Faith and Politics in a Divided Age* (Nashville: Thomas Nelson, 2018); Andrew T. Walker, *Liberty for All: Defending Everyone's Religious Freedom in a Pluralistic Age* (Grand Rapids: Brazos, 2021).

convention to cancel its 2020 annual meeting, leading to a third presidential term by default for North Carolina pastor J. D. Greear, the Conservative Baptist Network gave voice to Southern Baptists who lamented the influence of Never Trump leaders within the convention and believed Trump represented the best hope for the Christian Right's continued influence in American culture.[49]

Baptists and Their Critics

For Baptists who identified with the Christian Right, their critics were for the most part the same voices who criticized the Christian Right in general. Some critics were partisan, including Democrats and other political progressives who understood the Christian Right to represent a threat to progressive advance. This should come as no surprise and is not worth significant attention in this section. A second cluster of critics were found in the mainstream media, who with few exceptions were biased toward progressive views and critical of conservatism in general and the Christian Right in particular. Media bias against the Christian Right was especially pronounced during Trump's presidency, at least in part because the former was so closely identified with the latter. Again, this should be an uncontroversial assertion, so I will not reflect upon it further.[50]

---

[49] Greear was frequently identified with the Never Trump movement by his critics, though he never articulated that position. In fact, Greear argued on social media and his personal blog that Christians could in good conscience vote for and against Trump, advocating for Southern Baptists to remain united despite differing opinions over Trump. See J. D. Greear, "Who Should We Vote for This November?", J. D. Greear Ministries, October 11, 2016, https://jdgreear.com/who-should-we-vote-for-in-november/, and J. D. Greear, "Some Thoughts after the 2020 Election," J. D. Greear Ministries (blog), November 4, 2020, https://jdgreear.com/some-thoughts-after-the-2020-election/ (accessed September 6, 2021).

[50] Political scientist Tim Groseclose offers empirical evidence of progressive media bias, though his work predates the heightened anti-conservative bias of

Perhaps the most significant critics of the Christian Right in recent years, including socially conservative Baptists, were the historians, sociologists, and journalists who wrote on this topic. Not all of these authors were progressives; indeed, some attempted empathetic or relatively objective accounts of the Christian Right, such as the standard work by Clyde Wilcox and Carin Robinson.[51] Nevertheless, their works filtered into the thinking of the aforementioned partisan and media critics who frequently wore their biases on their sleeves. Scholarly and journalistic critiques can be divided into four categories.

Some critiqued religiously motivated social conservatism. Chris Hedges, Michelle Goldberg, and Ben Howe are representative journalistic critics while Seth Dowland and Marie Griffith are examples of scholars who wrote on this topic.[52] Others were critical of Christian nationalism, which they often simplistically conflated with movements such as theonomy or dominionism. Noteworthy examples include historian Julie Ingersoll, legal scholar Andrew Seidel, and journalist Katherine Stewart.[53] More recently,

---

the Trump years. See Groseclose, *Left Turn: How Liberal Media Bias Distorts the American Mind* (New York: St. Martin's, 2011).

[51] Clyde Wilcox and Carin Robinson, *Onward Christian Soldiers? The Religious Right in American Politics*, 4th ed. (New York: Routledge, 2010).

[52] Chris Hedges, *American Fascists: The Christian Right and the War on America* (New York: Free Press, 2007); Michelle Goldberg, *Kingdom Coming: The Rise of Christian Nationalism* (New York: Norton, 2006); Ben Howe, *The Immoral Majority: Why Evangelicals Chose Political Power over Christian Values* (New York: Broadside, 2019); Seth Dowland, *Family Values and the Rise of the Christian Right* (Philadelphia: University of Pennsylvania, 2015); R. Marie Griffith, *Moral Combat: How Sex Divided American Christians and Fractured American Politics* (New York: Basic, 2017).

[53] Ingersoll, *Building God's Kingdom*; Andrew L. Seidel, *The Founding Myth: Why Christian Nationalism Is Un-American* (New York: Sterling, 2019); Katherine Stewart, *The Power Worshippers: Inside the Dangerous Rise of Religious Nationalism* (New York: Bloomsbury, 2020). Whitehead and Perry offer a more nuanced account of Christian nationalism that refrains from disdain toward religious conservatives in *Taking America Back for God*.

a raft of scholars has narrowed their critiques to focus on white evangelicalism, in part because this group made up a high percentage of Trump's supporters. Prominent examples include the sociologist Robert Jones and historians Kristin Kobes Du Mez and Anthea Butler.[54] These critiques define white evangelicalism as an inherently and perhaps irreparably racist tradition. A final group of critics have focused their concerns more overtly upon Evangelical support for Trump. Examples include historian John Fea and journalists Angela Denker and Sarah Posner.[55]

The Baptist Legacy

The fortunes of theologically conservative Baptists and the Christian Right have been intricately connected since the latter movement came together in the late 1970s. For example, the so-called Conservative Resurgence in the Southern Baptist Convention ran parallel with the so-called Reagan Revolution in the Republican party. If we envision each of those movements as railroad ties moving from left to right (of course), the Christian Right is the crosstie that connects the two and creates a track. The intramural tensions that have plagued Southern Baptists since 2016 only demonstrate the degree to which conservative Baptists' self-understanding arguably is as influenced by political convictions as by doctrinal positions or ministry emphases. Moving forward, two questions will define how Southern

---

[54] Robert P. Jones, *The End of White Christian America* (New York: Simon and Schuster, 2016); Robert P. Jones, *White Too Long: The Legacy of White Supremacy in American Christianity* (New York: Simon and Schuster, 2020); Kristin Kobes Du Mez, *Jesus and John Wayne: How White Evangelicals Corrupted a Faith and Fractured a Nation* (New York: Liveright, 2020); Anthea Butler, *White Evangelical Racism: The Politics of Morality in America* (Chapel Hill: University of North Carolina, 2021).

[55] Fea, *Believe Me*; Angela Denker, *Red State Christians: Understanding the Voters Who Elected Donald Trump* (Minneapolis: Fortress, 2019); Sarah Posner, *Unholy: Why White Evangelicals Worship at the Altar of Donald Trump* (New York: Random House, 2020).

Baptists and other theologically conservative Baptists will continue to relate to the Christian Right.

Will Baptists continue to be at the center of the Christian Right? Beginning with Jerry Falwell Sr., many key leaders in the Christian Right have been Baptist ministers. This trend continued through Trump's presidency, though there was a noticeable shift toward greater Pentecostal (especially prosperity gospel) leadership during those years. Former megachurch pastor Paula White arguably became the public face of the Christian Right after being named special advisor to the Faith and Opportunity Initiative at the Office of Public Liaison in the Trump White House. However, as noted above, approximately half of Trump's Evangelical advisory board were Baptist ministers.[56] On social media, Baptist ministers (including some on the Evangelical advisory board) were vocal in their support of Trump's failed efforts to declare the 2020 presidential election invalid because of alleged voter fraud. At the time of writing, it looks as though Baptists will continue to occupy many of the most important seats at the Christian Right's table for the foreseeable future.

Will conservative dissent from the Christian Right be tolerated? While there have always been theologically conservative Baptists who were hesitant about aligning publicly with the Christian Right, this trend became pronounced beginning in 2016 because of the public platforms of some "Never Trump" Baptists. Differing postures toward the Christian Right have been especially pronounced among Southern Baptists, a denomination that remains strongly committed to social conservatism. However, several SBC agencies—most notably the ERLC—as well as many ministers under age fifty have raised concerns about Trumpism and pushed back against Christian nationalism.[57] Although fellow travelers with the Christian Right

---

[56] See footnote 15.

[57] In May 2020, Russell Moore announced his resignation from the presidency of the Ethics and Religious Liberty Commission to take a role as public theologian with *Christianity Today*. Moore subsequently moved his membership to a church

on most issues, they are not comfortable with identifying uncritically with the movement. This has led to backlash from Southern Baptists firmly committed to the Trump-era iteration of the Christian Right, most notably the Conservative Baptist Network. At the time of writing, the latter is mobilizing and making a similar argument as activist conservatives in the late 1970s, albeit one applied more to cultural (political) engagement than to particular doctrines: denominational elites are progressives who are out of touch with the grassroots conservative Baptists who pay their salaries. It remains to be seen whether this will be a passing denominational squabble or whether open dissent from the Christian Right will result in one being branded a neo-progressive in SBC life.

---

not affiliated with the SBC. Although Moore did not focus upon tensions over Trump as a key factor in his resignation, many commentators highlighted this topic in their reporting of Moore's departure. For example, see Ian Lovett, "Russell Moore, Southern Baptist Official Who Criticized Trump, Resigns," *Wall Street Journal*, May 11, 2021, https://www.wsj.com/articles/russell-moore-a-top-southern -baptist-convention-official-resigns-11621391912; and Kanishka Singh, "Southern Baptist Official and Trump Critic Russell Moore to Leave His Post," Reuters, May 19, 2021, https://www.reuters.com/world/us/southern-baptist-official-trump-critic -russell-moore-leave-his-post-2021-05-19/.

17

Baptist Witness in a Post-Christian Culture

By Karen Swallow Prior

Christians in twenty-first century America exist in a unique historical circumstance that has moved from a once-nominally Christian culture to a decidedly non-Christian one. While in doing so believers join the majority who, throughout the history of the Christian faith, have not lived and are not likely ever to live in a "Christian culture," this situation is different: American Christians are not merely moving into a non-Christian culture, but a post-Christian one. Those in this time and place are undergoing tremendous upheaval, change, and loss. To be post-Christian means that although the culture is no longer organized around Christian beliefs and principles, the remains linger. American Christians are living in what Flannery O'Connor famously termed a "Christ-haunted" culture.

In this chapter, "culture" will be approached as having both ethical and aesthetic components. In basic terms, ethics refers to *content* (what one believes or does), and aesthetics relates to the *form* those beliefs or actions take (how those beliefs are made manifest). In other words, culture—like witness—is embodied: it has form and content. Christians living in a post-Christian culture (who therefore share little, if any, common ethical ground with unbelieving neighbors) must move the culture to see, desire, and know the goodness and beauty of God's created order through the truth of their witness, a truth embodied in both word and deed.

Modernity, Technology, and Knowledge

To consider what it means to be on this cusp of a post-Christian age, it is helpful to understand what it means to be a "Christian culture" at all. The claim is often based on America having mostly enfranchised citizens who identify as Christian, but those numbers are now shifting significantly and quickly.[1] Some claim the nation was established in the name of certain religious and Christian ideals. Yet as we undergo a long (and long overdue) reckoning with the failures of Christian principles throughout the nation's history, that foundation seems less and less sure even as its walls crumble.

The waning of Christian influence on American culture is best understood within the broader context of the modern age and the late modernity in which we now find ourselves. While the central event of the modern age is the Enlightenment (along with all that immediately preceded and followed it), modernity began, by most accounts, with the printing press, which helped birth the Protestant Reformation. The Reformation, in emphasizing the role of the individual believer above the authority of the church or the priest, brought about the "turn to the subject," thus marking

---

[1] As of 2019, most Americans (65 percent) identified as Christian. However, this represents a 12 percent drop in a twelve-year period, a rate described by the surveyors as decline at a "rapid pace." See Pew Research Center, "In US, Decline of Christianity Continues at Rapid Pace," Pew Research Center, October 17, 2019, https://www.pewforum.org/2019/10/17/in-u-s-decline-of-christianity-continues-at-rapid-pace/.

the passage of premodernity into modernity. Subjectivity as the grounding of knowledge—whether in the form of Descartes's *"cogito, ergo sum"* or a conscious salvation experience or the search for "authenticity"[2]—is the defining characteristic of the so-called modern condition.

Baptists were made by the modern age. As detailed in *The Baptist Story: From English Sect to Global Movement,*[3] Baptist identity emerged in the century following the Protestant Reformation. Baptist doctrine and polity are, like those of other Protestant denominations, although in varying degrees, rooted in the Reformation's emphasis on the primacies of the individual and the Word—and of word over image, text over tradition, and a rationality rooted in the logic of the Logos of John 1:1. Baptists have always been a Word-centered people. Like Baptists, America was the product of a reading people.

But we now exist in a largely post-literate culture, which is defined as "the condition of semi-literacy, where most people can read and write to some extent, but where the literate sensibility no longer occupies a central position in culture, society, and politics. Post-literacy occurs when the ability to comprehend the written word decays."[4] Cultural critics such as Marshall McLuhan, Neil Postman, Sven Birkerts, and Nicholas Carr have documented how the shift from print culture to visual and digital cultures has given rise to this post-literacy as well as the effects this shift has on what and how people think.[5] Digital and social media cultivate so many streams of information that truth and facts can be as difficult to

---

[2] Charles Taylor, *The Ethics of Authenticity* (Cambridge: Harvard University, 1992).

[3] Anthony L. Chute, Nathan A. Finn, and Michael A. G. Haykin, *The Baptist Story: From English Sect to Global Movement* (Nashville: B&H Academic, 2015).

[4] B. W. Powe, *The Solitary Outlaw* (Toronto: Lester and Orpen Dennys, 1987), 15.

[5] See Sven Birkerts, *The Gutenberg Elegies: The Fate of Reading in an Electronic Age* (New York: Farrar, Straus, and Giroux, 2006); Nicholas Carr, *The Shallows: What the Internet Is Doing to Our Brains* (New York: W. W. Norton, 2020); Marshall McLuhan, *The Gutenberg Galaxy: The Making of Typographic Man* (University of

know today as they once were when information was scarce. This problem is further compounded by the additional influx of misinformation that deliberately distorts or misleads. Ironically, the technological and economic developments that brought about widespread literacy are the same forces that, a few centuries later, have returned society to a new kind of "dark age" wherein so much information (and misinformation) cultivates an ignorance similar to having too little. This post-literate condition has profound implications for a people of the Word living in such a culture as well as for the public sphere as a whole. The deterioration of literacy offers a twofold challenge to those with a Word-centered faith: they must maintain (perhaps even recover) a Word-centered identity within a culture that is post-literate, and they must learn how to offer effective testimony of a Word-centered faith in a culture alienated or even hostile to a Logos-based understanding.

As Charles Taylor notes, the public sphere itself is a product of modernity, consisting of a "common space" and "matters of common interest" that arise from not only personal conversation but also from various forms of media.[6] The public sphere is defined by and "depends upon manufactured, widely circulated, purchased words. Thus, it inevitably tends to commoditize language and human conversation."[7] As a "people of the Word," Christians, and Baptists in particular, should be particularly wise and careful stewards of language, even—especially—when it is being co-opted for political or market purposes. This stewardship applies not only to their own language but to that of others as well. In an age of communication that traffics in words, an essential part of Christian witness is the care with which words are treated, whether one's own or those of others. In his essay

---

Toronto Press, 1962); and Neil Postman, *Amusing Ourselves to Death* (New York: Penguin, 1985).

  [6] Charles Taylor, *A Secular Age* (Cambridge: Belknap, 2018), 185.

  [7] Jeffrey Bilbro, *Reading the Times: A Literary and Theological Inquiry into the News* (Downers Grove, IL: IVP Academic, 2021), 122.

"In Defense of Literacy," Wendell Berry shows how commodified language leads to post-literacy, which functions as a kind of illiteracy, and how and why we must resist such a condition:

> In our society, which exists in an atmosphere of prepared, public language—language that is either written or being read—illiteracy is both a personal and a public danger. Think how constantly "the average American" is surrounded by premeditated language, in newspapers and magazines, on signs and billboards, on TV and radio. He is forever being asked to buy or believe somebody else's line of goods. The line of goods is being sold, moreover, by men who are trained to make him buy it or believe it, whether or not he needs it or understands it or knows its value or wants it. . . . What is our defense against this sort of language—this language-as-weapon? There is only one. We must know a better language. We must speak, and teach our children to speak, a language precise and articulate and lively enough to tell the truth about the world as we know it.[8]

Not surprisingly, given the conditions of a post-literate culture that is overloaded with too much information, citizens are facing "a slowly evolving crisis of credibility for all of America's governing institutions," including government, the media, the economic system, and leaders, according to recent research from the Institute for Advanced Cultural Studies at the University of Virginia. "Without the legitimacy conferred to those who claim the authority to lead," the study's authors state, "the actions of leaders and their institutions can only be viewed as incompetent, ethically suspect, or perhaps even unprincipled, fraudulent, or corrupt." They continue, "This perception of American governing institutions—this legitimation

---

[8] Wendell Berry, "In Defense of Literacy," *Essays 1969–1990* (New York: Library of America, 2019), 204–5.

crisis—has been deepening for a long time."[9] More than six out of ten Americans (63 percent) see "disinformation," spread by "media distortions and fake news," "a very serious threat."[10] In response, many choose "fight or flight," polarization or apathy, the latter of which is the path of least resistance, leading to a "post-truth" culture.[11] While subjectivity and moral relativism are the oft-cited causes of the rejection of truth, the blame also owes to this increasingly unstable condition of legitimacy.

Baptists' witness as a Word-centered people within a culture no longer characterized by even the idea of objectively verifiable certainty has a dramatically different position in relation to the culture than in one in which certainty offers a stable ground even for disagreement. The crisis of faith for this post-Christian society is, in part, the result of post-literacy: it is a crisis of authority (the very concept of authority being rooted in the concept of authorship). In the hierarchical system of the premodern age, the masses were led by knowledgeable (even if often corrupt) authorities and institutions. Now, in a democratized system of late modernity, Americans find themselves having been led by a president famous for not reading books,[12] who was elected by a populace characterized by a steady decline in reading.[13] The more widespread college education has become, ironically, the more prone the population is to unfounded claims and conspiracy theories.[14]

---

[9] James Davison Hunter, Carl Desportes Bowman, and Kyle Puetz, *Democracy in Dark Times* (New York: Finstock and Tew, 2020), https://s3.amazonaws.com /iasc-prod/uploads/pdf/sapch.pdf.

[10] Hunter, Bowman, and Puetz, *Democracy in Dark Times*.

[11] "Post-truth" was chosen as word of the year by Oxford Dictionaries in 2016.

[12] David A. Graham, "The President Who Doesn't Read," *Atlantic*, January 5, 2018, https://www.theatlantic.com/politics/archive/2018/01/americas-first-post -text-president/549794/.

[13] Caleb Crain, "Why We Don't Read, Revisited," *New Yorker*, June 14, 2018, https://www.newyorker.com/culture/cultural-comment/why-we-dont-read-revisited.

[14] Osita Nwanevu, "The Democratic Party Has a Fatal Misunderstanding of the QAnon Phenomenon," *New Republic*, February 5, 2021, https://newrepublic .com/article/161266/qanon-classism-marjorie-taylor-greene.

A weakening ability to choose reliable authorities is a consequence of post-literacy.

This is also reflective of a crisis of community, specifically of interpretive communities—because reading and interpretation always occur in community, whether intentional or accidental, whether socially, geographically, or otherwise determined communities. This crisis of community feeds further into a crisis of trust, or what James Davison Hunter calls "a legitimation crisis," one rooted in the "sense that the American public has deep distrust of its governing institutions, a deep cynicism toward its political leadership and a sense of alienation from the powers that affect their lives on a day-to-day basis."[15] Who or what is the author of the beliefs and assumptions held by citizens? These crises are connected: the authorities trusted are those with whom citizens are in community, whether that community be healthy, good, or ill. The rise of the modern individual, which edged out the place of community and diminished circles of trust, and the abundance of competing and contradictory sources, have led to an inability to read the world.

The Ethical versus the Ideological

Baptist witness now must be not only about *what* they believe, but *how* and *why* they believe what they do—their sources and their reliability—and what *tangible* and *affective* differences those beliefs make. In a post-truth era, one in which people claim "their truth" may be different from "your truth," Baptists must not only proclaim there is truth, which is universal and unchanging, but also be reliable enough to be believed. When the words spoken are embedded in the lives they lead, not only individually but collectively, they earn the trust required by true authority, leading to true community.

---

[15] James Davison Hunter, interview by Peter Wehner and Josh Good, *Faith Angle Forum*, January 13, 2021. https://mailchi.mp/eppc/james-davison-hunter-against-the-post-modern-view-of-truth-is-an-incarnational-view-of-truth?e=28a5e0e824.

Baptist ethics are bound to Logos, the unchanging nature of the created order revealed in God's law and natural law, codified in human law and moral codes. God's law as revealed through the narrative of Scripture does not change. (This is, of course, separate from the fact that the church's emphasis and application over history has changed, even erring at times.) The essentials of the faith as worked out in the early centuries of the church and set forth in the church creed are also fixed. Baptists believe their doctrinal distinctives—while not infallible—represent their best understanding and application of biblical truth in both the life of the church and individual believer. In fact, these Baptist distinctives—especially soul liberty, autonomy of the local church, and religious liberty—offer, perhaps, the most robust and vibrant possibilities for believers living in a post-Christian culture.

However, in a secular age, one in which ideology replaces religion, it is necessary to distinguish an ethical or religious system from mere ideology to understand the necessity of objectivity and truth. While Christian beliefs derive from a transcendent authority and, accordingly, are oriented toward a transcendent end, ideology is a system of human origin, organization, and objectives. Moreover, ideology is a specifically *modern* phenomenon in being "a comprehensive science of ideas whereby the scientific method can be applied to gain understanding" (note the role of science, a specifically modern way of knowing).[16] While some ideologies can be mined for truth and fruitfully engaged, ideologies themselves "have a fundamentally distorted view of the world."[17] Not surprisingly, particularly within a post-Christian culture, some elements of Christianity, rather than judging ideologies with discernment, have given way to them, including Marxism, feminism, nationalism, progressivism, and white supremacism. Moreover, some have turned Christianity itself into an ideology rather

---

[16] David T. Koyzis, *Political Visions and Illusions: A Survey and Christian Critique of Contemporary Ideologies* (Downers Grove, IL: IVP Academic, 2003), 5.

[17] Koyzis, 15.

than a transcendently derived and applied ethos. Religion (including some approaches to Christianity both historical and contemporary) can, unfortunately, share in common with ideologies totalizing efforts "to eliminate different interests and to mold people in accordance with a single idea"[18] in order to "impose their own simplistic conception of a monolithic social order on the complexities of a real society."[19] Thus, the "essence of ideology," Celia Deane-Drummond explains, "is a failure to see tensions embedded in truths that are not necessarily resolvable," which is why John Henry Newman considered such "univocal thinking" to be heresy.[20]

But robust, orthodox Christianity rejects by its very nature any compulsory and totalizing ideology. For any ideology, as Koyzis argues, is a form of idolatry. The "nonidolatrous alternative" is "a kind of pluralism that spurns the reductive monisms of the ideologies."[21] The more ideological the culture becomes, the more intentional Baptists must be in resisting the temptation to cultivate a Christianity that operates merely as an alternative ideology. If they do not, Baptists risk narrowing a transcendent, universal Christian ethic into a material, hidebound formula.

Baptists in particular have a history that is helpful in resisting such totalizing efforts. Their history as a persecuted church (both in America and Europe) primes them toward vigorous defenses of pluralism and religious liberty—not only, they believe, for their own flourishing, but for the flourishing of their fellow citizens too. Historically, Baptists have shunned coercion, whether in matters of conscience or worship, whether through the church or government, yet they have been zealous in evangelism—a most modern form of persuasion, for evangelism is an appeal to individual subjectivity about ultimate truth.

---

[18] Koyzis, 8.

[19] Koyzis, 4.

[20] Celia Deane-Drummond, "The Amnesia of Modern Universities: An Argument for Theological Wisdom in the Academe," *Educating for Wisdom in the 21st Century,* ed. Darin H. Davis (South Bend, IN: St. Augustine's, 2019), 48–49.

[21] Koyzis, *Political Visions and Illusions*, 205.

Baptists' history began in a defensive posture against an oppressive state church; they had to contend vigorously for their freedom to worship as their consciences led by Holy Writ and the Holy Spirit dictated. Their defensive posture is, metaphorically speaking, in Baptist DNA. Today, in a religiously pluralistic context, they contend less for their own freedoms than for the flourishing of others. That reality necessarily alters their posture from defense to offense, from reactive to proactive. There is more freedom to *move*. Movement returns us to the aesthetic realm.

Ethics with Aesthetics

Baptists must also contend with the reality that the trajectory of the modern age has been that of subjective experience gradually eclipsing any sense of objective reality. This history is detailed by numerous thinkers, notably Charles Taylor, Alasdair MacIntyre, and, more recently, Carl Trueman. The sharpest turn occurred at the end of the eighteenth century as the Enlightenment gave way to Romanticism, and the emphasis on reason gave way to an emphasis on emotion. In other words, ethics gave way to aesthetics. Both terms name categories of value judgments: while ethics is tied to human action, which is external and objective, aesthetics is connected to sensory experience and perception, which is affective and, at least initially, subjective. The ethical entails acting toward some end, while aesthetics is something experienced. Both are ways of seeing.[22] Throughout the remainder of this essay, *ethics* will refer to beliefs and convictions (theological and political) that adhere through reason (or the Logos) and are oriented toward action or how one should live. *Aesthetics* is meant to suggest its root meaning of bodily sensation and movement (i.e., *emotion*, a moving out), sensory perception, the apprehension of appearances and beauty, as well as affective responses—how one experiences the world. While the earliest Romantics

---

[22] Diané Collinson, "Ethics and Aesthetics Are One" *British Journal of Aesthetics* 25, no. 3 (Summer 1985): 266.

held to an aesthetics infused with religious belief, as religious skepticism grew in the later nineteenth century, a secular aesthetics increasingly replaced religious experience. The sympathy, empathy, and compassion that form the basis of the polis, the common good, thus became, as Trueman put it, "functions of aesthetics rather than moral law," [23] and, consequently, sentiment became the foundation for ethics:

> Once aesthetics is detached from some universal understanding of what it means to be human, from some universally authoritative moral metanarrative, from some solid ground in a larger metaphysical reality, then aesthetics is king. Taste can drive what we think to be right and wrong. Ethically speaking, taste becomes truth. [24]

Yet it is important to remember that the turn to emotion and aesthetics was an overcorrection of the previous reign of reason. Ultimately, these two components of human experience—the ethical and the aesthetic—cannot be separated. Aesthetic experience is particular; it "enables us to see and know another person or object." The ethical is universal; it "enables us to see and know that each one of us belongs with the world as a whole."[25] Ethics is tied to truth; aesthetics to love.

History shows a tendency within different eras to emphasize one over the other, an imbalance that inevitably leads to error. The tyranny of reason at the expense of other aspects of humanity that characterized the Enlightenment is shown in the mechanistic, materialistic metaphors that populated the early modern social imaginary,[26] from the great chain of being to the "ghost

---

[23] Carl Trueman, *The Rise and Triumph of the Modern Self: Cultural Amnesia, Expressive Individualism, and the Road to Sexual Revolution* (Wheaton, IL: Crossway, 2020), 212.

[24] Trueman, 160–61.

[25] Collinson, "Ethics and Aesthetics Are One," 271.

[26] Charles Taylor defines the social imaginary as "the ways people imagine their social existence, how they fit together with others, how things go on between them and their fellows, the expectations which are normally met, and the deeper

in the machine"[27] to God as a watchmaker. The turn to aesthetics (over)corrected this error by privileging subjectivity—individual perception, taste, feeling, and agency—over objectivity, rationalism, and reason. In contrast to the physical metaphors that dominated the Enlightenment social imaginary (chain, machine, watch), the metaphors for a new set of values correspond to inner subjectivity: from following your heart or bliss to having a felt need to knowing your truth.

The social imaginary of our current, post-Christian culture is filled with images and ideas rooted in aesthetics-based epistemology and ontology. And Baptists are not immune from their influence. Where but from such a social imaginary did phrases such as "asking Jesus into your heart," "let go and let God," "faith over fear," and "sharing your heart" gain traction within Evangelical Christianity? If Baptists are to meet people where they are (as Jesus did) in order to lead them where they should go (as Jesus did), they cannot ignore the social imaginary of their times. (Indeed, they cannot ignore the social imaginary of their times if they are to move themselves where they should be.) They need not—and must not—repeat past errors of overcorrection. Indeed, to correct the course merely by attempting a nostalgic return to an earlier modern social imaginary—which is the root, more or less, of fundamentalism—is not only in vain but in error. As Jeffrey Bilbro

---

normative notions and images which underlie these expectations." Taylor, *Modern Social Imaginaries* (Durham: Duke University, 2003), 23. The social imaginary consists largely of unspoken, preconscious, unarticulated underlying assumptions. It is created by all the things that compose culture. Worldview, in contrast—whether biblical, Marxist, feminist, materialist, or other—is conscious and articulated. Competing and conflicting worldviews draw from the same social imaginary, which may be one explanation for why, anecdotally, many young people "trained" in a biblical worldview abandon it in pursuit of an unarticulated therapeutic deism, which is the product of the social imaginary of aestheticism they have been breathing in all along.

[27] The phrase used by Gilbert Ryle to characterize the error of Descartes's mind/body dualism in Ryle, *The Concept of Mind* (Chicago: University of Chicago, 2000), 15–16.

argues, "By imagining ourselves as rational beings, we become vulnerable to malformed affections and habits."[28] Those who desire, Bilbro continues, to revert to "an Enlightenment-style anthropology" will inevitably be "blinded to the social, intuitive dimensions of their own thinking."[29]

While modern use of the word *aesthetics* is usually related to matters of beauty or appearance, the word's origins in Greek denote sensory perception or emotions (the root meaning of emotion is *stirring*, *agitation*, or *movement*, which later came to mean *feelings*). At the most fundamental level, an aesthetic experience is an affective experience, one that moves people. While in the context of beauty one would be most inclined to understand the word *move* metaphorically (as in being *moved* by a song), the word should be understood literally as well: to be moved by something is to experience a bodily response, such as a quickened heartbeat, widened eyes, gathering tears, a gasp, a nod, or a smile.[30] People are moved by what they desire, and they desire what they love, as James K. A. Smith shows in his liturgical anthropology. One's loves and desires can be so shaped by ingrained habits that aesthetic response may not even be conscious. As Smith explains, "Over time, rituals and practices—often in tandem with aesthetic phenomena like pictures and stories—mold and shape our precognitive disposition to the world by training our desires."[31] Expressions of truth undistorted by human vehicles and that, therefore, manifest beauty are "aesthetic articulations of human flourishing."[32] Effective witness to the world, therefore, considers not only what is true, but how the beauty of truth will draw people toward it. As N. T. Wright writes in *Surprised by Hope*, beauty—both that of God's creation and that made by human hands—"is not simply the beauty it

---

[28] Bilbro, *Reading the Times*, 149.

[29] Bilbro, 150.

[30] Note that "inclined" is also a metaphor, one based on a meaning that is literal: to lie or lean down.

[31] James K. A. Smith, *You Are What You Love: The Spiritual Power of Habit* (Grand Rapids: Baker, 2016), 59.

[32] Smith, 58.

possesses in itself" but reflects the beauty of God's promise of what will be.[33] Although the essentials of our faith and the Word by which those essentials are revealed are unchanging, the desires or loves of those whose desires and loves one wishes to move do change. To move people in the right direction requires knowing not only the destination but also a person's or culture's current place and orientation—their starting point. "For things do not seem the same to those who love and those who hate," Aristotle says in *The Art of Rhetoric*, "nor to those who are angry and those who are calm, but either altogether different or different in magnitude."[34] After all, as Alan Jacobs argues, "Learning to *feel* as we should is enormously helpful for learning to *think* as we should."[35]

Because thinking relies on language, it is important to understand that while one expects the rhetoric of a well-crafted sermon or political speech or university lecture to move its listeners or readers, the casual language in which one is immersed every day wields the most power to move. Most of the words people encounter occur as they dialogue internally, with family members, coworkers, in the market or the public sphere (which includes information sources and social media). The entire advertising industry alone is built on the understanding of how language (although increasingly accompanied by images) *moves* people and cultivates desires. Therefore, Baptist believers in this current era are wise to employ this understanding of aesthetics and the power of words in order to be effective witnesses for the truth. In an age ruled by subjective sense rather than objective reality, people are more likely to be *moved* than *argued* toward truth. Truth needs to be shown as something embodied and lived, not merely thought:

---

[33] N. T. Wright, *Surprised by Hope: Rethinking Heaven, the Resurrection, and the Mission of the Church* (New York: HarperOne, 2008), 224.

[34] Aristotle, *The Art of Rhetoric*, trans. H. C. Lawson-Tancred (London: Penguin, 1991), 141.

[35] Alan Jacobs, *How to Think: A Survival Guide for a World at Odds* (New York: Currency, 2017), 87.

It is not a matter of learning how to repair cognitive deficiencies, but rather of how to live in the same world, share the same culture, face up to the same stakes, perceive a landscape that can be explored in concert. Here we find the habitual vice of epistemology, which consists in attributing to intellectual deficits something that is quite simply a deficit in shared practice.[36]

This idea of movement—or transport—is expressed in the traditional view of aesthetics as what draws the soul toward the ultimate source of all beauty, truth, and goodness. Living in and understanding the age as one primed by and toward aesthetic understanding brings the ethical and aesthetic back into proper balance as they should be. This demands a fully incarnational witness, one that celebrates and embodies both the ethics of the Logos and the aesthetic phenomenon of the *imago Dei*. As James Davison Hunter explains,

Against the argument the correspondence theory of truth, which is a kind of enlightenment view of truth, foundationalist view of truth, and against the post-modern view of truth, is an incarnational view of truth. That word and world—the words we speak, and the reality to which they are speaking come together not by fancy circumlocutions, not by fancy rhetoric, not by polemics, not even by great production values in our technology. It comes together when the words we speak are embedded in the lives that we lead. And not only individually but collectively. It's an incarnational view. It's the only context in which our words are going to be taken seriously.[37]

---

[36] Bruno Latour, *Down to Earth: Politics in the New Climatic Regime* (Cambridge: Polity, 2018), 25, quoted in Bilbro, *Reading the Times*, 150.

[37] Hunter, interview by Peter Wehner.

Such an incarnational view carries the understanding that to "bear witness is to tell the truth in such a way that new possibilities for human relationship, new possibilities for social arrangements come into view."[38]

This incarnational account, which embraces the inseparability of the ethical and aesthetic components of human understanding and being, is reflected in a principle of classical rhetoric. In this tradition, the ethical appeal of an argument is connected to the authority of the speaker, not only in terms of the speaker's expertise and knowledge, but also in the speaker's integrity in living in a way consistent with his argument—in other words, his moral authority. In this view, expertise and integrity—belief and the practice of that belief—form the very basis of ethics.[39] Likewise, effective public witness of Baptists in post-Christian America will begin with the conformity of their professed beliefs with their lived beliefs, with the integrity of their private lives and their communal church lives. This has, of course, always been true. But the necessity of integrity—and the absence of hypocrisy—for Baptist witness is even more crucial in a culture that does not share their worldview. They certainly cannot expect those who do not share their assumptions to give those assumptions credit when they fail to live by them themselves.

The Ethical and Aesthetic Aspects of Language

Like human experience itself, language is both ethical and aesthetic—it consists of both content (or ideas) and form (expression). A word corresponds to a thing that takes its meaning from the wider world of things. In its signifying function, language contains an idea. Words have semantic content or meaning. Using words in good faith and consistent with their

---

[38] Lee C. Camp, *Scandalous Witness: A Little Political Manifesto for Christians* (Grand Rapids: Eerdmans, 2020), 127.

[39] See Aristotle, *The Art of Rhetoric*, chapter 2.1 (1378a), where he says the character of the speaker is especially important within the context of political speech.

semantic content is an ethical act. But words also have histories, contexts, layers, hints, insinuations, implications, sounds, associations, suggestions— all sorts of expressive baggage. The power of language is in both its ability to signify an agreed-upon meaning and its ability to evoke more. Some words possess more one-to-one correspondence of name to thing, while others carry more multifaceted rhetorical layers and resonance. All language functions in a way that is more than the sum of its parts, and in the power it has to move, language is aesthetic.

The truth that language conveys "plus its artful presentation"—its aesthetic power—is called rhetoric.[40] Rhetoric, Richard Weaver argues in *The Ethics of Rhetoric,* is "something which creates an informed appetition for the good."[41] An "informed appetition" is another way of expressing the connection between reason (ethics) and affect (aesthetics). Part of living in a post-literate "new dark age" is the abundance of anti-rhetoric in the form of clickbait, hot takes, and viral takedowns—postmodern forms of the ancient art of sophistry—all of which help create an uninformed or malformed appetition for evil. Baptist witness in such an age must resist participation in anti-rhetoric.

The power of language to persuade, Weaver says, has its basis in what that person loves.[42] Persuasive speech is aesthetic in that it "can move us toward what is good; it can move us toward what is evil; or it can . . . fail to move us at all."[43] He explains:

> The soul's perception of goodness, justice, and divinity will depend upon its proper tendency, while at the same time contacts with these in discourse confirm and direct that tendency. The education of the soul is not a process of bringing it into correspondence with

---

[40] Richard M. Weaver, *The Ethics of Rhetoric* (Brattleboro: Echo Point Books and Media, 2015), 15.

[41] Weaver, 115.

[42] Weaver, 14.

[43] Weaver, 6.

a physical structure like the external world, but rather a process of rightly affecting its motion. By this conception, a soul that is rightly affected calls that good which is good; but a soul which is wrongly turned calls that good which is evil.[44]

Motion, according to the classical tradition, "is part of the soul's essence."[45] Correspondingly, Weaver says, "terms of tendency—goodness, justice, divinity, and the like—are terms of motion and therefore may be said to comport with the soul's essence."[46] Motion arises from dialogue, not monologue. A "base rhetorician" (who would use the power of language to move an audience away from good rather than toward it), Weaver says, fears "a true dialectic" because it leads to "intellectual independence": "What he does therefore is dress up one alternative in all the cheap finery of immediate hopes and fears, knowing that if he can thus prevent a masculine exercise of imagination and will, he can have his way. By discussing only one side of an issue, by mentioning cause without consequence or consequence without cause, acts without agents or agents without agency, he often successfully blocks definition and cause-and-effect reasoning."[47] The implications are that without allowing for the possibility of movement, which is aesthetic experience, that which moves reason is stilled, and the foundation of the ethical crumbles.

Weaver goes so far as to say that "a man's method of argument is a truer index in his beliefs than his explicit profession of principles."[48] In other words, the method of argument cannot be separated from the argument; the character of a person is revealed in how he or she witnesses. This is, again, the ethical appeal, an embodied, incarnational understanding of not only formal argument but effective witness that is effective because it is

---

[44] Weaver, 17.
[45] Weaver, 17.
[46] Weaver, 17.
[47] Weaver, 12.
[48] Weaver, 58.

being lived. Moreover, as Bilbro writes, "If we imagine ourselves as members of embodied communities, we will be better equipped to enter the public sphere redemptively while resisting its particular warping pressures."[49] The most effective witness to the world is also a witness to oneself. Baptists need to be the sort of citizens they wish to cultivate. Conceiving of Christianity as a citizen in a polis, Camp casts just such a vision:

> Christianity . . . shall be a citizen more faithful than all the pano-ply of patriots: it shall be a citizen who speaks the truth persis-tently in love because it knows that lies and deceit are an acid which destroys the bonds of community. One who welcomes the stranger and the foreigner, for hospitality is the very character of God and thus is the grain of the universe. One who welcomes the gifts of life and children and the challenges of keeping one's vows, for it is in giving that we receive and in loving that we know the beauty of living.[50]

To witness dialogically, in hopes of moving one's neighbor, is to partici-pate in the political; it is to be political. Thus, dialogue can be pursued and understood as the locus of personal, public, and political witness. The pursuit of religious liberty in a post-Christian culture requires an "ethic of humble truth seeking, and expecting deep disagreement," Andrew Walker argues. Such an ethic "places interrogation, debate, and liberty at the fore-front for settling disputes over religious, moral, and ideological difference" and "urges patience, *persuasion,* and a limited view of the state's power to play referee regarding religious truth claims."[51]

This necessity for a dialogical posture of believers toward an unbeliev-ing world is affirmed by Lesslie Newbigin. Even a confession (an ethic)

---

[49] Bilbro, *Reading the Times*, 154.

[50] Camp, *Scandalous Witness*, 54–55.

[51] Andrew T. Walker, *Liberty for All: Defending Everyone's Religious Freedom in a Pluralistic Age* (Grand Rapids: Brazos, 2021), 69–70, emphasis added.

is a kind of movement (aesthetic) in Newbigin's understanding: "There is no dichotomy between 'confession' and 'truth-seeking.'"[52] Such a dialogical approach, in fact, constitutes the Christian ethic because, he says, even Christians "do not possess the truth in an unassailable form."[53] Thus, in the very act of engaging in dialogue, particularly with those outside the faith, Christians make themselves vulnerable. Such vulnerability is both an ethic and an aesthetic. Newbigin writes:

> [O]bedient witness to Christ means that whenever we come with another person (Christian or not) into the presence of the cross, we are prepared to receive judgment and correction, to find that our Christianity hides within its appearance of obedience the reality of disobedience. Each meeting with a non-Christian partner in dialogue therefore puts my own Christianity at risk. . . . The purpose of dialogue for the Christian is obedient witness to Jesus Christ, who is not the property of the church but the Lord of the church and of all people and who is glorified as the living Holy Spirit that takes all that the Father has given to humankind—all people of every creed and culture—and declares it to the church as that which belongs to Christ as Lord. In this encounter the church is changed, the world is changed, and Christ is glorified.[54]

Politics and Public Witness

This understanding of witness-as-dialogue has direct implications for the body of faith and the body politic, two realms more integrated than often treated. Christianity itself is political, after all, as "an all-encompassing

---

[52] Lesslie Newbigin, *The Open Secret: An Introduction to the Theology of Mission*, rev. ed. (Grand Rapids: Eerdmans, 1995), 168.

[53] Newbigin, 184.

[54] Newbigin, 182–83.

manner of communal life that grapples with all the questions the classical art of politics has always asked" about how we live life together.[55] Christianity is a kind of dialogue, one in which believers wrestle together toward practicing a way of life distinct from the world, but also in the world. This was as true of the first-century church as in a post-Christian culture. The common life of the early Christians "was central to the claim that Jesus is Lord," as it should be today, and their very apologetic "was grounded in their new political way of being in the world."[56]

And politics, too, is a kind of dialogue. Politics is, Oliver O'Donovan says, actually "the name of a *discussion*, an exchange of speech."[57] While the idea of "the public" and the understanding of the political community as a "public possession" (*res publica*) developed from Roman republicanism, explains O'Donovan, it was Christianity that contributed the role of dialogue to the advancement of this form of the common life:

> It is from the Christianization of the Roman tradition that we have come to think of [a republic] as a discursive, rather than a material possession. Western civilization learned from the Christian gospel of community in the Word, a common life held together by a common truth, out of the infinite resources of which every member could speak. It learned to think of its secular institutions, as well as its sacred, in that light.
>
> Of course, there are public lands, public buildings, public roads, public institutions, and public revenue; but they depend on something more fundamental, a public *society* created by a public *discussion*.[58]

---

[55] Camp, *Scandalous Witness*, 4.

[56] Camp, 29.

[57] Oliver O'Donovan, "Politics and Political Service," *Breaking Ground*, January 8, 2021. https://breakingground.us/politics-and-political-service/.

[58] O'Donovan, "Politics and Political Service."

Like Newbigin, O'Donovan acknowledges the risk inherent in a discussion-based republic, warning that "the fabric of common speech that binds us together is vulnerable . . . to distrust."[59] As the research discussed shows, distrust runs deep in American culture, including within the church, as we enter this post-Christian age. But the Christian has reason for a hope not likely to be shared by fellow citizens who do not share their beliefs. That hope is expressed not in political wins and gains, but in the means that Christians embody as both faithful citizens and believers. When the results are left in God's hands (as they actually are), Bilbro argues, Christians are better able to preserve their "integrity and peace" as well as "the courage to do what is right regardless of the consequences."[60]

In contrast to a dialogical approach, a "culture war" model of the relationship of Christians, and Baptists in particular, to a hostile culture that sacrifices too much to partisan or short-term political gains, or sacrifices too little in being mere armchair soldiers, employs a logic that ultimately works against the "authentic religious freedom" that is the fruit of centuries of groundwork laid by the church's articulation and advancement of a moral and political theory based in natural law.[61] Certainly, that groundwork, which was centuries in the making, is being overtaken by a secularism that cannot sustain natural law (let alone God's law),[62] but even, as Charles Taylor and others show, that secularization has been at least as long in the making. And, as noted, the Protestant Reformation played a part in distinguishing and elevating the individual, individual rights, and individual conscience from and above ecclesiastical authority. If secularism is in part Baptists' own

---

[59] O'Donovan, "Politics and Political Service."

[60] Bilbro, *Reading the Times,* 53–54.

[61] Greg Forster, "A Protestant Integralism?", review of *The Gathering Storm: Secularism, Culture, and the Church,* by R. Albert Mohler Jr.," *Law and Liberty,* June 2, 2020, https://lawliberty.org/book-review/a-protestant-integralism/.

[62] R. Albert Mohler Jr., "Secularism Cannot Sustain Liberty: A Response to Greg Forster, *Law and Liberty,* August 2, 2020, https://lawliberty.org/secularism -cannot-sustain-liberty/.

doing, then identifying the enemy in a late modern religious culture war is tricky, to say the least. Baptists certainly are and must be at war with the culture. But the war must be engaged incarnationally. That is to say, it must be engaged not from the comfort of the armchair but a place of embodied participation, sacrifice, and knowledge. Indeed, the model of the armchair cultural warrior directly contradicts the incarnation of Christ, the Word that became flesh to be "with us," not against us (Isa 7:14). The "politics that operate on a simplistic them-and-us binary" is rooted, Trueman points out, in the same "pathologies" and "anti-culture" that marks secularism's emotivism. Yet Christians too often adopt such thinking and strategies: "Christians today are not opponents of the anticulture. Too often we are a symptom of it."[63] In an era dominated by fear, distrust, polarization, and power plays, a metanoic witness—one oriented toward changing the heart in an Augustinian sense—upends the "coercive control" that "dominates the agenda of modernity"[64] and has co-opted Christians into Nietzschean grasps for power.

"Historically," James Davison Hunter observes, "Christians have known what to do with a lot of power and they have known what to do when they have no power. They don't know what to do generally as a community when they have to share power."[65] But having to share power is exactly where Christians find themselves in a post-Christian culture.

Faithful Witness: Uniting Aesthetics and Ethics to Logos

People are moved by coercion or volition. The law is coercive. In a post-Christian culture, it will reflect less and less the will of Christian believers. Faced with seeking "a common good without a common god" without

---

[63] Trueman, *The Rise and Triumph of the Modern Self,* 388–89.

[64] Deane-Drummond, "The Amnesia of Modern Universities," 57.

[65] Hunter, interview by Peter Wehner.

declaring war on our neighbors or "rechristianizing civil law,"[66] as Forster characterizes it, we must rely ever more on persuasion. Indeed, if the last several decades of American evangelicalism have proven anything, it is that by assuming the posture of war, we lose. But, as Jeffrey Bilbro notes, "if we care less about whether our side is winning, we may be more able to bear faithful political witness."[67]

Faithful witness must begin with love. Not love of winning, or power, or access, or "influence" for the sake of influence—but genuine love for God and neighbor. It should go without saying, but it cannot. Love is clearly defined in the Bible: "Love is patient, love is kind. Love does not envy, is not boastful, is not arrogant, is not rude, is not self-seeking, is not irritable, and does not keep a record of wrongs. Love finds no joy in unrighteousness but rejoices in the truth. It bears all things, believes all things, hopes all things, endures all things. Love never ends."[68] "You can defeat things you hate," Forster argues, "but you can only change things you love. The deep structures of culture can only be changed by people who go out into their workplaces and communities every day on a mission to love their neighbors."[69] Love is an ethic, but it manifests in aesthetic ways. Love is an observable phenomenon. If Christians are not motivated by love, they must step down from the witness stand. And for the sake of the witness of the church, for the furtherance of the gospel, and for their love of Christ, believers must not countenance, curry favor with, or be yoked with those who fail to evidence love in actions taken or words spoken in the name of Christ.

Faithful witness also depends on truthfulness. The most obvious way Baptists have tended to think about standing for truth is through advancing the moral truths of God's law as reflected in divine revelation and natural law. That can never change, regardless of political or cultural context. But

---

[66] Forster, "A Protestant Integralism?"
[67] Bilbro, *Reading the Times*, 40.
[68] 1 Cor 13:4–8a.
[69] Forster, "A Protestant Integralism?"

where Baptists have been negligent in advancing and protecting truth is in subtler mishandlings and misrepresentations they make through careless language. For decades Christians warned of the dangers of postmodernism, which they feared would unleash a world of moral relativism. But they failed to wrestle with the underlying philosophy of postmodern theories, which are based in the view that language constructs reality—and, therefore, "truth." They failed to understand the elements of postmodern theories that were *descriptive,* not *prescriptive.* That negligence left them entirely unprepared to address the constructed "realities" and "truths" that have overtaken as many within the church as without. Because of the way language has created various and competing impressions, Christians have come to understand the world in vastly different—often entirely opposing—ways, depending on the discursive communities (news networks, social media sites, digital algorithms, etc.) they are immersed in. Their very understanding of the world—political, sociological, cultural—is constructed by the words they read and hear every day. This is the condition postmodern theorists warned about, and in neglecting to heed the warning, it has become the condition of the body of Christ. Christians must return to the right handling of truth—and the words by which truth is communicated. This begins with steps as small and simple as choosing words carefully to express not only truth but love. Like the bit of a horse's bridle, or the rudder of a ship, words set the direction of all that follows: "The tongue is a fire. The tongue, a world of unrighteousness, is placed among our members. It stains the whole body, sets the course of life on fire, and is itself set on fire by hell."[70] No less important than controlling words, truthfulness requires representing the words of others faithfully. If Christians lived in an agrarian society, stealing or harming a neighbor's sheep would be as harmful, perhaps, as the carelessness with which words are treated today. Christians must confront in love those among them who mistreat and mishandle the words of others no less than if they had run off with a neighbor's sheep.

---

[70] James 3:6.

Faithful witness must resist the anti-rhetoric described by Weaver. In recognition of the power language has to develop appetites for good (or evil), people of the Word, of all people, have the foundation and means for "artful presentation" of truth that moves others. In a post-Christian, digital age, Christians are faced with the responsibility of harnessing not only their words, but the technologies that serve to amplify, distort, and mislead. That power seems overwhelming to most living in the nascent stages of that power, but they can look upon a cloud of witnesses who similarly grappled with new possibilities, responsibilities, and challenges with something like the printing press.

Finally, faithful witness must originate in and embody humility. Love is not proud, so the truth spoken in love must be done with humility. As O'Donovan poignantly notes, "What recourse do we have when we face a breakdown in political discussion, when everyone speaks to themselves and nobody listens? Faith in God has something distinctive and important to say to this: we speak to one another *because we have first been spoken to.* We make laws and regulations because a law has first been given us."[71]

In considering the connection between feeling and thinking, the field of trauma studies offers helpful reminders of Christians' shared humanity—and shared humility under God. Research shows that emotions such as anger, fear, and anxiety (bodily, aesthetic experiences) impede the ability to reason (ethical judgments).[72] Further, one's sense of what is "real" begins with the visceral and kinesthetic sensations experienced in the body.[73] It is notable that while not every person has experienced trauma, strictly speaking, the term used to describe the human condition is "fallen." "The fall" is a term that denotes a dramatic, physical event; the traumatized body merely magnifies the way in which the mind and body always work in tandem.

---

[71] O'Donovan, "Politics and Political Service."

[72] Bessel van der Kolk, *The Body Keeps the Score: Brain, Mind, and Body in the Healing of Trauma* (New York: Penguin, 2015), 88.

[73] van der Kolk, 115.

Trauma studies, therefore, helps us to see the role aesthetic and kinesthetic sensations—bodily motions—play in understanding and responding to the external world and in being moved, emotionally and rationally. Notably, language is understood by trauma experts as playing a key role in overcoming visceral, precognitive triggers of bodily memories of trauma. In other words, language can move the body, then the mind. In countering the reductive Enlightenment concept of mind-body dualism, Mary Midgley argues for a complementary understanding of being. "Human beings are highly complex wholes," she explains. "We get the partial knowledge we do have of them in two ways: from the outside and the inside."[74] She continues, "Our inner experience is as real as stones or electrons and as ordinary an activity for a social mammal as digestion or the circulation of the blood."[75] In other words, she summarizes, "Subjectivity is an objective fact."[76]

Dialogue with another—whether between individuals or between a Christian people and a non-Christian people—is a recognition of the experience of others and of humility in the limitation of one's own. Only in that posture of humility can Baptists speak truth with a "love that moves."[77]

---

[74] Mary Midgley, *The Myths We Live By* (London: Routledge, 2011), 57–58.
[75] Midgley, 79.
[76] Midgley, 79.
[77] A phrase from the last line of Dante's *The Divine Comedy*.

PART TWO

18

Baptists in Babylon: On the Role of Politics in Modern Baptist Life

By Jonathan Leeman

Over the last two decades, many US Christians have arrived at the same conclusion: *This country does not feel very Christian anymore.* This is not to say America was ever a Christian nation, however that is defined. But this suggests that, in the post-*Obergefell* world, American Christians increasingly feel their defeat in the culture wars and their alien identity.[1] To borrow from Trevin Wax: if an older generation of American Christians was tempted to view the nation as Jerusalem, folks today count it as Babylon.[2]

---

[1] See Steven D. Smith, *Pagans and Christians in the City: Culture Wars from the Tiber to the Potomac* (Grand Rapids: Eerdmans, 2018), and Charles Taylor, *A Secular Age* (Cambridge: Belknap Press, 2007).

[2] Trevin Wax, "Five Observations about Younger Southern Baptists," May 5, 2014, blog, *The Gospel Coalition*, https://www.thegospelcoalition.org/blogs/trevin

As the sense of displacement and anxiety has grown, so have the conversations about political and public theology, whether in seminaries, Sunday school classrooms, or social media platforms. When people feel threatened, they often reassert control, like Peter picking up the sword in the garden of Gethsemane. Christians on the Right have begun exploring various forms of Protestant theonomy,[3] Protestant establishmentarianism, or Roman Catholic integralism, while the literary set of the Left has been flirting with the comparatively invasive programs of regulatory oversight involved with progressive social policy as well as with Socialist schemes for wealth redistribution and environmental control. But whether Left or Right, the common impulse animating such functional and formal public theologies is a belief in the power of government to bring change.

Furthermore, any conversation about public or political theology in America will inevitably be a conversation about liberalism and its discontents since liberalism has provided the major strands of America's DNA from the beginning. What the aforementioned theologies share, whether in their popular or academic forms, whether intentionally or unintentionally, is a growing rejection of this DNA. All argue that the nation should govern itself according to a more substantive or "thick" version of the good and the right and repudiates liberalism's long-standing attempt to build a nation on a "thin" version of justice.

-wax/5-observations-about-younger-southern-baptists/. See also Trevin Wax, *This Is Our Time: Everyday Myths in Light of the Gospel* (Nashville: B&H, 2017), 122–23.

[3] Since I am attempting to cover so much territory so quickly, I am not going to attempt to map out the differences between a full-blown "Christian reconstructionism" theonomy and the far-less developed "general equity" theonomy, a phrase that has grown in popularity among some groups of pastors in recent years, or anything in between. It is possible that some so-called general equity theonomists mean only to assert what I assert in this essay. For my purposes here, I am using the phrase "theonomy" to refer to any perspective that would view the civil law under Moses as directly applicable to governments today. By establishmentarian, I am referring to my self-identifying magisterial Protestant friends who would welcome some type of established church.

A "thin" theory of justice is called such because it requires agreeing only on a set of procedures, like shipwreck survivors on a deserted island agreeing that several rounds of rock paper scissors will decide who gets to rule the island without any larger philosophical conversations about truth and justice. [4] Liberalism drafts a social contract among these new islanders using consensus-building words like "consent," "rights," "freedom," and "equality," words that promise to leave each shipwreck survivor free to pursue the good life however he or she or they define it.

The challenge of liberalism, however, has always been who gets to define which rights, which freedoms, and which versions of equality remain protected? What about the right to an abortion? The freedom to define one's gender? Or marriage equality? The answer involves smuggling a thicker view of the good and the right through the back door. In the eighteenth and nineteenth centuries, the Protestant establishment and a Judeo-Christian worldview defined which rights were right and which freedoms were protected. In the twentieth and twenty-first centuries, the culture wars have awarded that job to the religions of expressive individualism and identity politics. Defenders of philosophical liberalism, faced with an increasingly skeptical Christian audience, rush to point out how the Founding Fathers affirmed God's justice, human dignity, and the fallenness requiring constraint. Natural law, too, "surely" provides a backstop to unconstrained views of freedom and rights.

Yet that is the smuggling project we are talking about, say the critics. To claim that every individual possesses "God-given dignity" or even just "dignity" represents a thick moral and theological viewpoint, which contradicts claims of neutrality or thin proceduralism. Nearly every critic of liberalism, whether Christian or secular, has called attention to this basic

---

[4] Many Liberals would plead otherwise. For instance, Jeffrey Stout argues that "the notion of state neutrality . . . should not be seen as [the democratic tradition's] defining mark. Rawlsian liberalism should not be seen as its official mouthpiece." See Stout, *Democracy and Tradition* (Princeton: Princeton University, 2004), 3.

self-contradiction: like all Enlightenment philosophy, liberalism places into the magic hat of philosophical discovery what it hopes to pull out (like individual dignity), while claiming to have put nothing into it.

Without a fixed and absolute basis for justice, human dignity becomes a malleable and pragmatic concept. Does it include African Americans, or does it allow for slavery or Jim Crow? A man's right to marry a man? A woman's right to choose an abortion? Death with dignity for the elderly? An anti-racist federal agency? It depends on who is on the court or which party has the most votes. Liberalism's Christian defenders argue that the nineteenth-century dehumanization of African Americans or the twentieth-century dehumanization of the unborn represents failures *to apply* the tenets of liberalism. Yet the assertion is question-begging. It presumes such populations *should* be humanized. Without an absolute or thick standard of justice and right, why that presumption?

To describe the smuggling project another way, liberalism is more like a mirror than the person standing in front of it, or more like the pipes than the water it carries. Such is a thin theory of justice. In a Judeo-Christian culture, the pipes of liberalism may in fact deliver Judeo-Christian water. In a Confucian or Buddhist or Hindu culture, the water will taste Confucian, Buddhist, or Hindu. And in an alternatively secular and pagan culture, like today's, so tastes liberalism's water, which brings us back to Babylon and our present moment. Liberalism, in the final analysis, becomes a fancy philosophical mechanism for transforming *is* into *ought,* or telling the majority that its desires are just. Minorities will be protected so long as they can prove they are not too great a threat to the majority's desires and worldview—which is precisely where Christians feel growing inhospitality—or that they are fully human.

Yet if liberalism's critics get the leg up by pointing to liberalism's conceptual contradictions, liberalism gets the better end of the argument when the conversation turns to institutional specificity, at least for twenty-first-century sensibilities. Liberalism's critics typically grow vague when it comes to those institutional specifics. They do not quite *say* the nation should abandon free speech, or religious freedom, or the separation of church and state, or the Bill of Rights, or the division between the three branches of government, or democratic elections. A few theonomist and magisterial Protestants might admit they are not opposed to an established church. A fringe Roman Catholic document might say that only Roman Catholics should hold office. And there have always been a few people who would be happy to write Jesus's name into the US Constitution. Yet what is lacking, so far as I am aware, is any major developed proposal from established voices for what a non-liberal constitution might look like in the twenty-first century.

The argument John Locke employed in his *First Treatise of Government* continues to beleaguer all of liberalism's critics: even if it is determined there is a divine right of kings, how do we decide who is king? Or more germane to our day, who gets to play the divine?[5] Suppose the theonomists, establishmentarians, and integralists manage to facilitate a new constitutional convention for the United States, one that promises to establish a thick view of justice and the common good. What hopes would they have of securing a Christian sovereign and not a pagan one?

The primary institutional advantage of liberalism and its "thin" version of justice, ironically, is impermanence and low expectations. You might lose today's round of rock paper scissors. But if there is the promise of another round in two years, you can live with it. Such liberalism, furthermore, is rightly anti-utopian. It will not give you all your dreams of justice in this world, but it will minimize the bad. Meanwhile, it encourages Christians and citizens generally to attend to their families, churches, and all the associations that compose a civil society's "third sector"—its non-governmental

---

[5] See John Locke, *First Treatise of Government* on the Natural Law, Natural Rights, and American Constitutionalism (NLNRAC) website, from Locke, *Of Government: Book 1*, in *Economic Writings and Two Treatises of Government* (1691), vol. 4 of *The Works of John Locke in Nine Volumes* (London: Rivington. 1824), at https://www.nlnrac.org/earlymodern/locke/documents/first-treatise-of-government.

and non-business associations, the very things that shape a society's reigning worldview over time.

To summarize the present moment: people are experiencing a public theology dilemma that appears, to Americans at least, as a binary choice between liberalism and something anti-liberal, between a thin and thick view of justice. Either we argue the nation's laws and principles of governance should aspire to stay neutral between its citizens' moralities and religions, or we do not.

A Baptist Third Way?

It is at this moment, on the horns of the public theology dilemma, that a Baptist political theology can walk up and offer something of a third way.[6] It agrees with the theonomists, establishmentarians, integralists, and advocates of a thick justice generally that requires both a substantive moral basis and substantive moral clarity—the ability to say, "These rights are rights and those rights are wrong." Yet it also agrees with philosophical liberalism's anti-utopianism and its call for institutional constraints. It is comparatively modest in the expectations it places on law and, therefore, the power of government. Instead, it focuses first on regenerate local churches as the beginning of a righteous and just political life, which is precisely what makes it a *Baptist* political theology. Correspondingly, it possesses a limited view of government's jurisdiction. It says governments possess authority over some rights and wrongs, not all. Like liberalism's critics, a Baptist political

---

[6] I refer to a Baptist political theology here in constructive, not historical, terms. In other words, I am not attempting to speak for all Baptist political theologies past and present. Rather, I am attempting to place the fundamentals of Baptist thought into an "updated" idiom that addresses today's conversations and animating concerns. If I might be so bold, I am saying to fellow Baptists, I think *this* is how we should talk about our political theology—not with unthinkingly borrowing the vocabulary of classical liberalism, as we so often have in the past, but with something a little more biblical.

theology bemoans living in Babylon. Like liberalism's defenders, it insists there is no Israel to return to other than the church.

From almost the beginning, Baptist political theology has been inter-twined with the language and categories of philosophical liberalism. Not that liberalism, at least in its Enlightenment form, came first. Before John Locke (1632–1704) was born, the first Baptists argued for religious lib-erty, the inviolability of the conscience, the noncoercive character of faith, and the virtue of republican institutions.[7] John Smyth (1554–1612) argued the magistrate was not permitted "to meddle with religion, or matters of conscience, to force and compel men to this or that form of religion, or doctrine."[8] To bind the conscience is to bind the soul, and "the king . . . hath no power over the immortal soules of his subjects," said Thomas Helwys (1575–1616).[9] Universal religious freedom is the natural conclu-sion: "Let them be heretics, Turks, Jews, or whatsoever, it appertains not to the earthly power to punish them."[10] Yet moving into the seventeenth and eighteenth centuries, Baptists discovered a natural alliance with America's founders, in large part because of the influence of Luther's two kingdoms theology on everyone from Locke to the Founding Fathers.[11] Baptist pastor

---

[7] Timothy George, "Between Pacifism and Coercion: The English Baptist Doctrine of Religious Toleration," in *The Mennonite Quarterly Review* 58 (January 1984): 39–43. See also Nicholas P. Miller, *The Religious Roots of the First Amendment: Dissenting Protestants and the Separation of Church and State* (New York: Oxford University, 2012).

[8] Quoted in George, "Between Pacifism and Coercion," 35.

[9] Quoted in George, 40.

[10] Helwys quoted in George, 40.

[11] James Madison drew the connection between Luther and liberalism when he referred in a personal letter to "the excellence of a system which, by a due distinc-tion, to which the genius and courage of Luther led the way, between what is due to Caesar and what is due to God, best promotes the discharge of both obligations. The experience of the United States is a happy disproof of the error so long rooted in unenlightened minds of well-meaning Christians, as well as in the corrupt hearts of persecuting usurpers, that without a legal incorporation of religious and civil pol-ity, neither could be supported. A mutual independence is found most friendly to

Isaac Backus publicly supported James Madison's First Amendment. The Danbury Baptist Association likewise supported Thomas Jefferson. It is not surprising, therefore, that historians have characterized the American experiment as a "consilience . . . between dissenting Protestant thought and Enlightenment thought."[12] Fast forwarding two hundred years, even the twentieth century stalwarts of an avowedly secular philosophical liberalism like John Rawls "thought that their move to neutrality was a generalization from the idea of freedom of religion."[13]

If liberalism's thin theory of justice is like a pipe through which water flows, or like a mirror that holds up a society's values, the "consilience" hammered out by Baptists and Enlightenment liberals through the first century or two of America's history is hardly surprising. Through those decades, most Americans, including non-Christians, arguably inhabited a Judeo-Christian worldview, especially the Founding Fathers. And insofar as that was the case, Baptists and Christians generally could rely on the mechanisms of liberalism to deliver results that broadly corresponded with their worldview.[14] Even

---

practical Religion, to social harmony, and to political prosperity." In James Madison, *Letters and Other Writings of James Madison,* vol. 3 (Philadelphia: J. B. Lippincott, 1865), 242–43. See also Jean Bethke Elshtain, *Sovereignty: God, State, and Self* (New York: Basic Books, 2008), 81; and Quentin Skinner, *The Foundations of Modern Political Thought: The Age of the Reformation,* vol. 2 (Cambridge: Cambridge University, 1978), 3–19.

[12] Nicholas P. Miller, *The Religious Roots of the First Amendment: Dissenting Protestants and the Separation of Church and State* (New York: Oxford University, 2012), 131. Similar views of a synthesis can be found in George M. Marsden, *The Twilight of the American Enlightenment: The 1950s and the Crisis of Liberal Belief* (New York: Basic Books, 2014), xxiii–iv; Stephen D. Smith, *The Rise and Decline of American Religious Freedom* (Cambridge: Harvard University, 2014), 7, 14–47, 105–8; Andrew Koppelman, *Defending American Religious Neutrality* (Cambridge: Harvard University, 2013), 56–64; Douglas Laycock, *Religious Liberty, Volume One: Overviews and History* (Grand Rapids: Eerdmans, 2012), 91.

[13] Koppelman, *Defending American Religious Neutrality,* 16.

[14] I am setting aside race-related issues for the moment. Historically, Baptists and Christians more broadly have divided over America's racial sins, with some

more to the point, they could count themselves *as* philosophical liberals, identifying it as *their* political philosophy.

Yet as the nation's worldviews have shifted and different water has begun to flow through liberal pipes, or as a different image has begun to appear in the liberal mirror, Christians have wondered whether they believe in liberalism after all. The experience has been similar to watching two people talk about "John," thinking they were discussing the same John, but then gradually realizing they were talking about different Johns. Baptists have long affirmed phrases like "religious liberty," "separation of church and state," and "natural rights." Yet the culture wars of the last century have demonstrated how contested those phrases are. It would appear different things are meant by those phrases. Baptists and Liberals are talking about different Johns.

Furthermore, as long as philosophically liberal American society has embraced a Judeo-Christian worldview, Baptists apparently have not felt the need to offer highly developed theories of government. Their works of theology and ethics have emphasized religious liberty: "We talked about it first!" But little more. Understandably, then, Roman Catholics and magisterial Protestants have sometimes criticized Baptists for their under-developed political theology. Yet now that cultural mores have shifted and most Christians have woken up to the fact that not only are they living in Babylon now, but they always have, Baptists are realizing they need to say more about political theology than just affirm religious freedom.

Yet here is where Baptists can offer a middle path between theonomy, establishmentarianism, or integralism and neutrality. Like liberalism, a Baptist political theology will affirm the crucial role of rights, equality, and freedom, especially religious freedom. It separates church and state in a particular way, and it limits the state's jurisdiction. It also acknowledges that, while democratic institutions may not be required by Scripture,

---

being complicit and some opposing it strenuously, e.g., Mark Noll, *The Civil War as Theological Crisis* (Chapel Hill: University of North Carolina Press, 2006).

they are typically wise. In all, this Baptist political theology, like liberalism, warns against utopianism and giving a misplaced trust to government. At the same time, it builds upon a much stronger foundation—not a pragmatic, malleable contract that sanctifies *is* as *ought*, but on the justice of God. It openly admits that it intends to bring justice as the God of the Bible defines it into the public square, and it tells everyone else to stop bluffing and admit they are bringing their gods too. It is impossible not to. The public square is a battleground of gods, and it is high time to stop pretending otherwise.

In short, a Baptist political theology is liberalism's much better looking and more honest fraternal twin. Or better, it is the real thing, not the generic knockoff. To that end, let me briefly propose the outlines of a Baptist political theology.[15]

A Baptist Political Theology Briefly Sketched

Baptists happily point to their Lutheran and Presbyterian and Reformed friends generally and thank them for the larger Protestant recovery of the gospel and the five solas of the Reformation. These things form the heart of their faith.

Yet the Baptist contribution to the Reformation and to Protestantism, at least from the Baptist's perspective, completed what these other Protestants began by drawing out the social and ecclesial implications of this gospel recovery. If Luther was right about the priesthood of all believers, said the

---

[15] I have attempted to build (Baptist) political theology from the ground up in *Political Church: The Local Assembly as Embassy of Christ's Rule* (Downers Grove, IL: IVP Academic, 2015). I then provide a practical and popular-level application of this in *How the Nations Rage: Rethinking Faith and Politics in a Divided Age* (Nashville: Thomas Nelson, 2020). Rather than repeatedly footnoting the rest of this chapter and pointing to those two books, I will simply remark here that most of the ideas in what follows are developed more fully in those two volumes.

Baptists to the magisterial Reformers,[16] the only people walking through the front door of baptism into church membership should be believers, not believers and their children.

Furthermore, magisterial Reformers may have believed the magistrate's jurisdiction "extends to both tables of the law" and to protecting true worship because "no government can be happily established unless piety is its first concern."[17] So, John Calvin argued by appealing to the Davidic kings. Yet not so fast, Baptists replied. Consider the new covenant. The new and better covenant was necessary, among other reasons, because the Law could not produce true righteousness and worship. For that purpose, believers must look to the church. Meanwhile, following Jesus's command to give even to a pagan king like Caesar what is Caesar's, civil governments were in for a big job demotion, at least relative to the king's work inside the Mosaic and Davidic covenants. Governments could keep the peace and adjudicate the rights and wrongs requisite for a basic, protectionist, life-preserving form of justice, one in keeping with what the Noahic covenant assigned to the governments of all nations (see Gen 9:5–6). But, please, no more Mosaic and Davidic talk about the government's work in upholding the first table of the law. The sword cannot do it. If the sword is to enforce the first commandment, it will kill literally everyone because everyone has broken it, even as God had to exile Israel. Such is the lesson of the old covenant (see Rom 3:23; 6:23). The most governments should do regarding the first table of the Law is enforce the second and create a space for people to worship God as *he* commands— that is, to respect religious freedom.

---

[16] For simplicity's sake and to remain within my allotted word count, I am skipping over the role of the Anabaptists. Most (though hardly all) Baptist scholars argue that Baptists developed their views independently of the Anabaptists.

[17] John Calvin, *Institutes of the Christian Religion*, ed. John T. McNeill, trans. Ford Lewis Battles, The Library of Christian Classics, vol. 21 (Philadelphia: Westminster, 1960), 4.20.9, p. 1495.

In other words, the Baptist's understanding of the Bible and covenantal history leans heavily into the newness of the new covenant. Their expectations of the state will be comparatively tempered and less likely to succumb to some version of utopianism. It will feel, in that regard, more like liberalism.[18] The following six planks of the Baptist's political platform follow this new covenant emphasis.

A Baptist Political Theology . . .

(1) Begins with the church and baptism. Like all Christians, Baptists believe the source of true justice and righteousness is the new covenant gospel. They affirm a faith that leads to obedience (see Rom 1:5; 16:26). Inside the membership of a regenerate local church, gospel obedience takes a social form as citizens of Christ's heavenly kingdom declare their shared allegiance to their covenant Lord, teach one another his law, and work to keep each other accountable to it. Together they work to exemplify, little by little, from one degree of glory to the next, a just body politic. God's new covenant people do not presently possess a permanent piece of geography since their Lord commands them to transgress the boundaries of every nation (see Matt 28:18). Yet their assemblies represent "a reall, not a metaphoricall Kingdome," in the words of Thomas Hobbes.[19] They are a holy nation, not just metaphorically but really (see 1 Pet 2:9). Gathered local churches, in that regard, are embassies of Christ's kingdom. Consecrated by the Lord

---

[18] In time, strains of pedobaptist thinking (perhaps influenced by Baptists?) would move outside the Constantinian settlement too, particularly under the influence of Luther's two kingdoms theology. These strains would more closely approximate both Baptist political theology and liberalism. Yet the error of two-kingdoms thinking, historically at least, has been the opposite error of the magisterial Reformers or theonomy generally—they can overly bifurcate the religious and political domains. In *Political Church*, I argue for a "two ages" perspective.

[19] Thomas Hobbes, *Leviathan*, Cambridge Texts in the History of Political Thought, ed. Richard Tuck (Cambridge: Cambridge University, 1991), chap. 35, par. 219.

Jesus himself, the gathering represents the temporary and proleptic geography of Christ's kingdom: "For where two or three are gathered together in my name, I am there among them" (Matt 18:20).[20] The church is where humanity will finally learn to love its enemies, to beat its swords into plowshares and spears into pruning hooks, and to turn the other cheek.

In other words, a Baptist program for political engagement begins with joining a church. Members must learn to live as a transformed nation before they try to transform the nation, a redeemed culture before they talk of redeeming the culture. These kingdom citizens must receive training to care about welfare policy as they give to the needy in their midst, to study tax policy as they consider a church budget and their own giving, to understand family policy by helping one another's marriages and education policy by caring for one another's children, to consider race politics as they struggle to repent of their own partialities, and so it goes. A church's kingdom politics should not remain in the gathering. It should spill outward and characterize a Christian's entire week. Yet if the pursuit of justice and righteousness as a way of life, individually and socially, does not begin inside the church, it possesses no integrity outside the church.

For a Baptist politics to begin with the new covenant, in other words, it must begin with the priesthood of all believers, regenerate church membership, and believer's baptism.

(2) Insists on separating religious and political authorities as well as national and church identity. A second implication of the new covenant is that religious and political authorities must remain separate. As Jesus said, "Give to Caesar the things that are Caesar's, and to God the things that are God's" (Mark 12:17). Among Western nations moving away from the Constantinian settlement, people make this point by referring to the separation of church and state. Yet the principle needs to be broadened to include

---

[20] I develop these ideas many places, most recently in chapter 1 of *One Assembly: Rethinking the Multisite and Multiservice Church Models* (Wheaton, IL: Crossway, 2020).

any religion-organizing authority, from Caesar enforcing the worship of Roman gods to the Iranian supreme leader's blend of religious and political authority. Here, I will simply speak about the separation of church and state as shorthand for the larger principle.

Casually considered, people often assume the principle of separation pertains to the content of laws or the source of a law, as if to say any laws from the Bible should not be imposed on people who do not believe in the Bible. It is this casual consideration that gets up the theonomist's dander. And he is right. What this casual consideration fails to reckon with is the question, can religious content be bracketed out of even the most basic laws, like the laws against murder or stealing? One political theorist says yes: the law can "be conceived of as issued by any number of commanders" and as possessing content with no necessary connection to those commanders.[21] The Bible might oppose murder because people are created in God's image; but Islam, Buddhism, Confucianism, utilitarianism, moralistic therapeutic deism, and secular humanism also oppose murder without that moral basis. Hence, the basic content ("do not murder") is not religious, but religiously neutral—so this theorist argues. The trouble is his argument turns the law against murder into something independent of all ethical systems and con- sciousnesses and moral bases—something issued from no one and for no reason but freely floating beyond all reckoning. In fact, murder is wrong only by virtue of someone's moral (and ultimately religious) basis. Therefore, it is better to say a law against murder represents a point of overlap between so many religions and gods. The law against murder is not religiously neutral. It is religiously popular. In the same way, no law is religiously neutral. Every law, even a law to drive on one side of the road rather than the other, pos- sesses a moral basis and relies on a moral judgment, which in turn relies on a set of anthropological and theological (or anti-theological) judgments. All that to say, the separation of church and state does not depend on whether a

---

[21] Jeremy Waldron, *God, Locke, and Equality: Christian Foundations in Locke's Political Thought* (New York: Cambridge University, 2002), 45–46.

law is religious (all are) or establishes religion (all do). Humans are religious creatures, which means their laws and governments are invariably religious. Their governments serve their gods. Invariably. It is an unbiblical and incoherent phenomenology that tries to divide politics and religion like this. When people enter the public square, they not only *do not* but *cannot* leave their "religion" behind. That is impossible. And a Christian should recognize he or she *must not*. We always represent one god or God or another.

To return, then, to Jesus's remark about rendering to Caesar what is Caesar's, it is worth noticing the context. Jesus asked his audience whose image was on the coin. "Caesar's," they replied. Yet his question would have called to mind for this Jewish audience an even deeper lesson: God's image was on Caesar, even as Caesar's image was on the coin. Caesar might own the coin, but God owns Caesar. Likewise, Jesus said to Pilate, "You would have no authority over me at all . . . if it hadn't been given you from above" (John 19:11). In other words, Jesus does not create separate circles: one labeled "Caesar's things" and one labeled "God's things." He creates one big circle labeled "God's things" and inside that is a smaller circle labeled "Caesar's things."

Yet he does give Caesar a circle, which is to say all politics may be religious, but Jesus still separates the political and religious authorities, or what are called church and state. Now we can sympathize with the philosophical liberals, at least as they *should* argue. From a biblical perspective, the separation of church and state instead pertains to (a) institutional authority and (b) identity or membership. Respectively, then, the separation is breached (a) when the state wields the authority God gave to the church or the church wields the authority given to the state or (b) when the members of a nation are held to the standards of the members of a church in matters beyond the state's jurisdiction. As an example of the first, one might think of Constantine's participation in a matter of doctrine at the Council of Nicaea or Calvin's participation in a matter of the sword with the execution of Michael Servetus. As an example of the second, one might think of Charlemagne forcing conversion by the sword or the Massachusetts state legislature taxing Baptists to support Congregationalist churches. Or, much more recently, in 2010, the separation was arguably breached on these latter grounds when the US Supreme Court decided by a 5–4 majority that Hastings (law school) at the University of California could require the campus chapter of the Christian Legal Society to comply with its non-discrimination policy covering religion and sexual orientation, thereby forcing membership and leadership positions in this Christian organization to be open to all (*Christian Legal Society v. Martinez,* 561 US 661).

Both pedobaptist and Baptist theology can, in principle, maintain the separation in both senses here. Yet Baptist theology *must* maintain that line in order to be consistent with itself while pedobaptist theology, whether Roman Catholic or Protestant, *can* blur it. After all, it has a mechanism for inducting every natural born citizen of a nation into the church—infant baptism—making membership in the nation and the church nearly coterminous. The result is "Anglican England," "Lutheran Germany," "Catholic Spain," "Christian Europe," or "Congregationalist Massachusetts"—*cujus regio, ejus religio,* as they put it in the sixteenth century. Within the Constantinian settlement, church and state formally remained separate authorities, adhering to the fifth-century Pope Gelasius's two swords doctrine. The pope was not the emperor, and the king was not the bishop. Yet the two authorities ruled jointly over one Christian nation or empire, which inevitably resulted in each involving himself in the jurisdiction of the other, again, as with Calvin's call for the magistrate to enforce the first table of the law.

Insofar as the new covenant identifies true religion only with Holy Spirit indwelt believers, new covenant religion—aka Christianity—cannot by definition belong to an entire nation or what a government is capable of imposing upon a nation. There is no such thing as a "Christian nation" in a Baptistic understanding since the membership borders of the nation and the church will not overlap. Christian Europe was never Christian, Baptists say, but a continent of people who got wet as babies, a handful of whom might have become sincere Christians along the way. Baptists will reserve the name "Christian" for members of churches who have repented and believed. The name must never belong to nations or political parties. Were a Baptist pastor somehow to become king, his Baptistic understanding of the new covenant, church membership, and baptism should prevent him from treating all his citizens like church members, as with enforcing the first table of the Ten Commandments.

In short, the Liberals are right: church and state must remain divided. Yet the theonomists and integralists are right: it all belongs to God. A Baptist political theology insists on both.

(3) Defines the state as a platform-builder and the church as a sign-maker. As said previously, the separation of church and state is breached when the members of a nation are held to the standards of the members of a church *in matters beyond the state's jurisdiction.* The question then is, what is beyond the state's jurisdiction?

To the state, God has given the power of the sword for the purpose of building the platforms on which humans can safely live and get on with all the dominion work and (for Christians) disciple-making work to which God calls everyone. To the church, he has given the power of the keys for the purpose of hanging signs that say, "Christian." The apostle Paul used the language of "the power of the sword" (Rom 13:4 CJB), but the original authorization occurred right after the flood. God said to Noah and all humanity: "And I will require a penalty for your lifeblood; I will require it from any animal and from any human; if someone murders a fellow human, I will require that person's life. Whoever sheds human blood, by humans his blood will be shed, for God made humans in his image" (Gen 9:5–6). God did not establish a particular form of government in these verses, whether monarchy, aristocracy, or democracy. Yet he handed human beings the basic ingredient necessary for forming governments in this fallen world: the ability to use morally legitimate coercive force for his purposes in justice. These verses might be counted as the "Great Commission" text for governments, just like Jesus's final words in Matthew's gospel operate that way for churches (see Matt 28:18–20).

Contrary to the claims of liberalism, therefore, this passage teaches that the government's authority comes from God. The US Declaration of Independence might say governments "[derive] their just powers from the consent of the governed." But three times God told Noah *he* would "require" these things. A government's just powers derive from him. A person might withdraw his or her consent, but that does not make a government's authority necessarily unjust or immoral, contrary to the Declaration. Paul would later say, "So then, the one who resists the authority is opposing God's command, and those who oppose it will bring judgment on themselves" (Rom 13:2).

What is crucial to recognize, furthermore, is why God authorized human beings to establish governments. Most immediately, he authorized them to prosecute crimes, to preserve life, and (by implication) to facilitate the flourishing necessary for their God-given dominion and rule (see the context of Gen 9:1–2, 7). Yet this immediate purpose serves a larger one: to provide a platform for God's work of redemption through his special people. The government's work is a prerequisite to the mission of the church and salvation, just as learning to read is a prerequisite to reading the Bible. Common-grace platforms are meant to serve special-grace purposes. Genesis 9 comes before Genesis 12 and the call of Abraham for a reason. Paul reaffirmed this point. In Acts 17, he said God established the boundaries of the nations so "that they might seek God, and perhaps they might reach out and find him" (v. 27). Likewise, in 1 Timothy 2, he said to pray for kings and authorities so as to live peaceful lives pleasing to God, "who wants everyone to be saved and to come to the knowledge of the truth" (v. 4). Governments exist, then, to serve the purposes of worship. People need to be able to walk to church without getting mauled by marauders. They cannot get saved if they are dead. The work of the government provides the platform.

If the state is a platform-builder, the church is a sign-maker. God has authorized gathered churches to hang signs on the *what* and the *who* of the Christian gospel—confessions and confessors. To this end, he has given churches the power of the keys of the kingdom. Jesus first gave the keys to Peter and, by extension, to all the apostles immediately after Peter confessed Jesus as the Christ, the Messiah. Jesus promised to build his church and then said, "I will give you the keys of the kingdom of heaven, and whatever you bind on earth will have been bound in heaven, and whatever you loose on earth will have been loosed in heaven" (Matt 16:19). Two chapters later, Jesus gave the keys to local churches for the purpose of removing someone from membership (Matt 18:18).

What does it mean for a church to "exercise the keys" by binding and loosing on earth what is bound and loosed in heaven? The short answer is churches render judgments on the *what* of the gospel (as Jesus did with Peter in Matthew 16) and the *who* of the gospel (as Jesus instructed the disciples in Matthew 18). Practically, churches do this through preaching and administrating the ordinances. Through preaching, a church says, "This is a right gospel confession." Through the ordinances, it declares, "This is a true gospel confessor." We gather in his name and baptize into his name (see Matt 18:20; 28:19). To put it programmatically, the keys allow churches to write statements of faith and to receive and remove members.[22]

The work of wielding the keys is a judicial activity, like the work of a judge in a courtroom. A judge does not make the law. He interprets it. Nor does he make a person guilty or innocent, yet he possesses the authority to declare it. He represents the legal system. Similarly, by virtue of the keys of the kingdom, churches do not "make" the gospel, nor do they "make" people Christians. But they possess an authority the individual Christian does not: to represent the kingdom of Christ by formally declaring, "this is a true gospel confession" and "here is a true gospel confessor." To put it another way, they hang signs on the *what* and the *who* of the gospel.

Placing the institutions of church and state side by side, what can be said about their relationship? Again, the two institutions should remain "separate," in the sense that neither should wield the authority God has given to the other. Pastors should not wield the sword. Presidents should not wield the keys. Churches, generally, should not delve in the intricacies of trade policy, while nobody wants Donald Trump or Joe Biden deciding

---

[22] See *One Assembly,* chap. 1, or my *Don't Fire Your Church Members: The Case for Congregationalism* (Nashville: B&H Academic, 2016), chap. 3 and 4.

on baptisms. Yet in the most ideal sense, church and state work not just separately but cooperatively toward the end of worship.

Still, how far does the state's jurisdiction extend? That leads to the next principle.

(4) Assigns the state a narrow, protectionist, nonutopian jurisdiction. Genesis 9:5–6 grants governments the ability to preserve lives and facilitate flourishing through a narrow form of justice that can be called "Noahic justice." What is justice? Biblically, it is the adjudication of right and wrong as God has defined it. Yet Noahic justice is not a maximalist, perfectionist form of justice, of the kind God required of old covenant Israel or to be declared by the new covenant church: "Be perfect, therefore, as your heavenly Father is perfect" (Matt 5:48). Government is not tasked with adjudicating the entirety of God's law. Rather, it is to pursue a narrowly defined preservative or protectionist form of justice. God intends *all* governments in *all* nations to establish this form of justice on their citizens, whether they acknowledge God or not. "By justice a king brings stability to a land" (Prov 29:4). Such justice ensures peace and order (see 1 Tim 2:2). Paul observed that God tasks governments with punishing the bad and rewarding the good (see Rom 13:3–4). Yet, clearly, he did not mean all conceivable bads and all conceivable goods. He meant those that fall within a Gen 9:5–6 jurisdiction.

To be clear, then, Christians entering the public square must not pursue some other form of justice or justice neutrally defined, even if the square is populated by those who deny God exists. Daniel never asked Nebuchadnezzar to define justice for him. If God indeed exists, any version of justice that is not God's justice is both unjust and idolatrous, which is where the instincts of the theonomists, establishmentarians, and integralists are correct. To pass laws is to legislate morality. It is to call something "sin" (if nothing else by virtue of its illegality) and something else "righteousness" (by virtue of its legality). The only question at stake is who gets to define sin and righteousness—the God of the Bible or some other god? The theonomists, establishmentarians, and integralists are correct, therefore, to say it must be the God of the Bible. Where those defending philosophical liberalism are correct, however, is to restrain such adjudication to only one part of God's law—the part that involves protecting life and taking steps conducive to human flourishing. The state should sheathe its sword everywhere else.

Everything a government does—every law it makes, every courtroom ruling it declares, every executive agency code it enforces—should be done for the purpose of protecting and affirming its citizens as God's image-bearers. Its work of establishing or upholding justice must always be measured by the standard of the *imago Dei.* The government should actively oppose anything that harms, hurts, oppresses, exploits, hinders, tramples upon, degrades, or threatens human beings as image-bearers. Furthermore, by implication, anything that aids, abets, promotes, or encourages a set of conditions that contributes to the ability of image-bearers to live their vocation of imaging God should be considered a candidate for possible governmental encouragement. Christians will disagree about what falls into that jurisdiction, which is fine, but that is the standard.

In short, a Baptist (or biblical) political theology offers government a narrow remit—protection, not perfection—like philosophical liberalism back when it carried the water of a Judeo-Christian worldview. The more liberalism carries the water of identity politics and expressive individualism, the more expansive it becomes. People place perfectionistic hopes on the state as if it could accomplish all righteousness. The new covenant, however, teaches Christians to invest their political hopes for real change and real justice in the gospel and the church, not in the next election or Supreme Court nomination. At best, the next election and Supreme Court nomination should serve to preserve life and facilitate flourishing. Beyond that, our expectations should remain low.

(5) Affirms religious freedom. One further jurisdictional matter should be clarified, and that is the limitation God places on government concerning organized religion. Bible scholars wading into the domain of political theology have sometimes denied that the Bible offers a doctrine of religious

freedom.[23] While it is true the Bible never explicitly enunciates the doctrine, it is clearly implied and rests on three pillars.

First, Gen 9:6 authorizes the use of force for crimes against "humans," and it insists on a concrete accounting for that crime—"shed[ding] human blood"—an early enunciation of due process. What the text does not do is authorize prosecuting crimes exclusively against God, like blasphemy or idolatry, nor does any other text in Scripture, save those within the confines of the Mosaic covenant given to ancient Israel. After all, how can a court measure crime against God? What blood is shed? And how in turn does the court recompense God? Instead, governments must tolerate false religions so long as no direct harm comes to human beings. But when this occurs, as with Christian Scientists who deny medical care to their children, such actions become actionable.

Second, the new covenant was necessary, as has already been considered, because the sword cannot produce true righteousness or worship. Only the Holy Spirit can. Civil governments are incapable of enforcing the first table of the Ten Commandments, as demonstrated in ancient Israel's life.

Third, God has assigned the institutional church, not the state, to formally distinguish true from false doctrine and true believers from unbelievers. The church alone has the authority to formally name the things of God, whether doctrines or people.

From the perspective of a Baptist political theology, the US Constitution's First Amendment's careful phrasing strikes a remarkably good balance. It does not carelessly say, "Congress shall not establish religion," since, again, every law essentially does; it says, "Congress shall make no law respecting *an establishment* of religion."[24] It does not get to wield the keys or organize the adherents of any particular religion, telling them who they are or what they must believe.

---

[23] Tremper Longman, *The Bible and the Ballot: Using Scripture in Political Decisions* (Grand Rapids: Eerdmans, 2020).

[24] Emphasis added.

(6) Encourages Christians to enter the public square as principled pragmatists with limited expectations. Points 1 through 5 offer the biblical blueprint of a Baptist political theology. They present job assignments for church and state in the ideal. In the ideal, church and state work separately but cooperatively for the greater end of worship. Churches should declare a perfectionist form of justice. Governments should enforce a protectionist form. Both should fulfill their duties according to God's law. There is the law of God and the law of other gods. Points of overlap exist. Neutrality does not. These are the principles that should instruct and animate every Christian entering the public square.

Yet at least two matters make a Christian's pursuit of justice in the public square difficult. First, the Bible does not script most judgments governors must make in pursuit of righteousness and justice. Even when biblical principles are at stake, as with the call to oppose abortion or racism, the precise strategies or tactics to use remain unspecified. The goal is always the same: justice. Yet the path toward that goal requires wisdom. So, Solomon was commended: "They stood in awe of the king because they saw that God's wisdom was in him to carry out justice" (1 Kgs 3:28). Wisdom personified declared the same thing in the book of Proverbs: "It is by me [Lady Wisdom] that kings reign and rulers enact just law; by me, princes lead, as do nobles and all righteous judges" (8:15–16). What is wisdom? It is the skill of knowing how to survey the landscape, determine what factors are relevant for decisions to be made, recall who God is and what fallen human beings are like, and then make correct judgments that lead to God's glory and human flourishing. Christians entering the public square need wisdom because every situation they will face is both unique and complicated.

Yet there is a second matter that makes the pursuit of justice difficult, particularly in a liberal or democratic setting: people do not share the same commitment to Scripture. One cannot merely appeal to biblical principles of justice. Liberalism offers its solution at this point by appealing to a procedural version of justice, which involves the smuggling project of hiding one's gods. A Baptist political theology recommends naming the public square for what it is:

a battleground of gods. Then, it encourages Christians to enter that square as principled pragmatists, employing whatever arguments win the case, the vote, the debate, the war. Pragmatism, after all, is just another word for wisdom.

Yet not only should Christians be pragmatic or wise in short-term considerations, like the next election, but they should pursue wise constitutional structures. What governing structures most wisely account for the fallenness of humanity? The separation of powers, both between branches and between federal and local levels, wisely serves to distribute power. A written constitution, a bill of rights, judicial review, and democratic elections all do the same. None of these are "biblical" or morally necessary. Yet all of them account for the fallen propensity to abuse power. Further, liberal democratic institutions, at least aspirationally, share with biblical Christianity the conviction that all people possess inherent dignity, equally possessing certain rights including the right to due process before the law. It is hardly surprising, therefore, that liberal democratic institutions have not proven perfect over the last few centuries, but better than any other form of government at both protecting life and facilitating human flourishing. For these reasons, I would urge a Baptist principled pragmatist to write a constitution that looks a lot like the American constitution, as amended. That is not a *biblical* recommendation, but a judgment of *prudence*. Operating within the framework of that constitution, Christians should openly and honestly pursue just and righteous laws as God has defined justice and righteousness.

Conclusion

It may feel like we are living in a Babylonian moment, where society's mores are increasingly turning against a Christian worldview. In fact, the world is Babylon and has been ever since Judah's Old Testament exile. Jesus's instructions to pay Caesar taxes affirmed that.

Yet it is worth recognizing that, even if the world is Babylon, Babylon has its better and worse moments. In one moment, Nebuchadnezzar seeks to devour God's people (Dan 3:8–23); in the next, he protects them

(3:29–30). So it is with the governments of this world. Some protect God's people, like Pharaoh at the time of Joseph. And some devour them, like Pharaoh at the time of Moses. It may be that, at this moment in American history, Christians are moving from a happy partnership with philosophical liberalism to a strained partnership. Whether or not that is the case, Christians need to beware their continual temptation as natively legalistic creatures, particularly in moments of cultural declension: the subtle utopianism of putting their hope in horses and chariots, governments and laws. In their thinking, they must not discard the importance of government altogether, but keep it in its proper place—clarifying the separation of church and state and religious freedom; reasserting what the church and state each are; entering the public square as principled pragmatists as occasion permits; and most of all seeking to live peaceful and quiet lives, not panicking even if the world turns against them, knowing that their political hopes rest in Christ and his church, whose victory is certain.

19

The Natural Law Tradition and Baptist Public Ethics

By Andrew T. Walker

As of 2021, six of the nine justices of the US Supreme Court were Roman Catholic. Whether Justice Neil Gorsuch is explicitly Protestant or Catholic is debated.[1] But there are no Baptists or evangelical justices. Considering the influence Protestant Christianity has had in shaping the United States' cultural firmament, the absence of a Protestant on the nation's highest court is both glaring and revealing. This observation is doubly noteworthy considering that since at least the mid-twentieth century, evangelical Protestants, particularly conservative Baptists, have invested tremendous political energy in cementing a conservative majority on the Supreme Court, believing the court the necessary mechanism to undo the cultural and legal wreckage of secular progressivism.

---

[1] Daniel Burke, "What Is Neil Gorsuch's Religion? It's Complicated," *CNN*, March 22, 2017, https://www.cnn.com/2017/03/18/politics/neil-gorsuch-religion/index.html.

That this newly minted conservative majority would arrive without a Protestant evangelical jurist speaks to a lacuna in Protestant evangelicalism's overall strategy for public engagement. This lacuna is especially pressing for conservative Baptists. For decades, evangelical Baptists have clamored for an opportunity to change the direction of American culture by changing the Supreme Court's makeup. When circumstances never seemed better, Baptists found themselves relying upon a religious tradition whose moral and legal tradition, namely, natural law, was more apt to change America's landscape in ways that Baptists can only hope to rival someday. There is something endemic to the theology and sociology of Roman Catholic social thought and its institutions that helped it develop a guild of thinkers united around a particular legal regime and moral tradition.

It is more than ironic that the Catholic tradition, with its long history of natural law thought, would establish the conservative majority so desired by evangelical Baptists, while Baptists, on the whole, have rejected the natural law tradition. There is no central natural law tradition in Baptist thought, and this neglect is to our loss.[2] Nevertheless, considering how Catholics' and Protestants' ethics often coincide or overlap, it would seem, then, that Baptists have unconsciously relied upon, borrowed, and benefited from a moral tradition they knowingly reject yet reap ethical outcomes aligned with their theology. Baptist public ethics appears to desire a specific outcome for public ethics while failing to appreciate the necessary foundation for those outcomes: namely, natural law, a tradition that helps give

---

[2] Paul Goodliff notes, "There has been no explicit Baptist theology of natural law." Rather, according to Goodliff, where there is Baptist acceptance of the natural law tradition, it has accorded less with the Baptist tradition outrightly and more with the Calvinistic underpinnings of Baptist thought. Goodliff, "Natural Law in the Baptist Tradition," in *Christianity and Natural Law: An Introduction*, ed. Norman Doe (Cambridge: Cambridge University, 2017), 140. For an additional Baptist perspective on the natural law, see Craig Mitchell, "Natural Law and Religious Liberty," in *First Freedom: The Baptist Perspective on Religious Liberty*, ed. Jason G. Duesing, Malcolm B. Yarnell, and Thomas White (Nashville: B&H Academic, 2007), 111–24.

centrifugal force to biblical ethics.[3] This conundrum raises a question: As America's Anglo-Protestant influence wanes, how will Baptists advance their moral arguments in a culture that no longer pretends to be even nominally Christian or appreciative of biblical morality? It also poses a challenge; that is developing a public ethic that can simultaneously affirm a common moral grammar necessary for public engagement while avoiding the pitfall of violating their convictions on church-state relations. The answer ought to be a vision of natural law grounded, ultimately, in Holy Scripture.

As this chapter will argue, the negative appraisals Protestants in general and evangelical Baptists in particular have rendered upon the natural law tradition are wrongheaded, unnecessary, and ultimately detrimental to the cause of formulating a Baptist public ethic. The rejection of natural law theory is one of the most unnecessary and tragic moves in Protestant ethics over the last seventy-five years. The lack of intellectual strategy Baptists have in confronting American culture's errors as it drifts further from its Protestant founding is the product of an ethic that has failed to appropriate the authority of general revelation. This doctrine examines what is knowable about God and morality apart from the "spectacles" of religion. It is general revelation, writes one scholar, that "provides the foundation of natural law thinking."[4] As the natural law tradition becomes better understood as the product of grace, not merely nature, Baptists should find resonance with a tradition that has a storied legacy in Christian moral theology.

There are three components to this chapter's argument. First, because the general Baptist demeanor to natural law is one of antipathy, it is important to articulate why Baptist thought has rejected the natural law tradition. Focusing

---

[3] For the Protestant roots of the American founding, see Thomas S. Engeman and Michael P. Zuckert, eds., *Protestantism and the American Founding* (South Bend: Notre Dame University, 2004); Lee J. Strang, *Originalism's Promise: A Natural Law Account of the American Constitution* (Cambridge: Cambridge University, 2019).

[4] Owen Anderson, "Natural Law and Philosophical Presuppositions," in *Christianity and Natural Law: An Introduction*, ed. Norman Doe (Cambridge: Cambridge University, 2017), 205.

on the work of Carl F. H. Henry, a Baptist figurehead known as an arch critic of natural law, I argue that Henry's objections—and in turn, Baptists' in general—are unpersuasive and, ultimately, confused in that Henry caricatures the natural law and, in fact, smuggles in a conceptual facsimile using his own terms. Second, biblical and theological arguments in favor of natural law will be advanced, and it will be described how Baptists have historical traces of natural law thought within their tradition. The final section will briefly highlight how Baptist distinctives could appropriate the natural law tradition. The goal in writing this chapter is to move Baptists from a rejection of natural law and toward a Baptist-appropriating embrace of natural law.

Any Baptist public ethic, even one that purports to be strictly biblical, will necessarily rely upon the lineaments of natural law for its coherence and application within the public square and civic arenas. Thus, Baptists should embrace the natural law tradition as a vehicle for public ethics. This is not borne from a lack of confidence in Scripture, but the belief that Scripture provides an account of the natural law that communicates the intelligibility of its ethics. As a biblical approach to natural law is taught and utilized, Baptists' understanding of God's Word and God's world will become strengthened and, in turn, more confident. Baptists have a biblical ethic in search of a public theology, and it is the natural law—understood through a biblical lens—that can better inform a Baptist approach to public ethics.

Baptist Antipathy to Natural Law

By now it is a truism that Protestant theology has largely rejected natural law ethics since the mid-twentieth century, if not earlier.[5] Ever since debates arose between Karl Barth and Emil Brunner on the shape and use of natural

---

[5] For a helpful resource reviewing Protestant antipathy to natural law, see Daniel R. Heimbach, "Natural Law in the Public Square," *Liberty University Law Review* 2, no. 3 (2008): 685–702. See also chapter 4 of J. Daryl Charles, *Retrieving the Natural Law: A Return to Moral First Things* (Grand Rapids: Eerdmans, 2008).

theology and Barth's famous reply, "Nein!," Protestant consensus—and by default, Baptist consensus—is that natural law's chief problem is its *supposed* anthropocentrism.[6] The objections take shape in a variety of formulations, but for our purposes, Protestant and Baptist critiques of natural law allege that natural law theory defers too sweepingly to human agents for the foundation and application of its ethics. In particular, Protestants dispute whether a universal moral grammar separate from Scripture can be normative for humans in a post-fall world.

What is not in dispute is the existence of natural law, but its apprehension by fallen agents. The debate fundamentally rests on epistemology, not so much ontology. Critics accuse natural law of *undervaluing* the noetic effects of sin, affecting human cognition and the volitional will and in turn *overvaluing* sinful agents' ability to grasp a system of morality apart from special revelation.[7] Hence, Protestants argue that only the transcendent norms of the Bible enable objective moral enlightenment. To contemporary Protestantism, Scripture is the basis for an objective ethic whose locus is outside the subjective moral agent. Protestant natural law scholar J. Daryl Charles notes that "at the heart of the rejection of natural law by Protestant social ethics is the erection of a false dichotomy between nature and grace."[8] Charles's categories bring focus to what is at stake concerning whether morality is the product of subjective speculation (nature) or objective endowment (grace).[9]

---

[6] For this debate, see Emil Brunner and Karl Barth, *Natural Theology* (1946; repr., Eugene: Wipf and Stock, 2002).

[7] On the problem of fallen epistemology for natural law theory, see Mark Liederbach, "Natural Law and the Problem of Postmodern Epistemology," *Liberty University Law Review* 2, no. 3 (2008): 781–96.

[8] J. Daryl Charles, "Protestants and Natural Law," *First Things* 168 (December 1, 2006): 37.

[9] For more on the false dichotomy, see J. Daryl Charles, "Burying the Wrong Corpse: Second Thoughts on the Protestant Prejudice toward Natural Law Thinking," in *Natural Law Today: The Present State of the Perennial Philosophy*, ed. Christopher Wolfe and Steven Brust (Lanham: Lexington Books, 2018), 87–109.

In this framework, natural law morality is elusive and unpersuasive, owing to its insufficient and flawed premises to provide a sufficient grounding for morality that can successfully combat human sinfulness. Rather than complementing Scripture, these criticisms redound to natural law, undermining the Reformation principle *sola Scriptura*. These criticisms are mistaken and the result of misreading the tradition and, at times, rely on uninformed caricature.

Carl F. H. Henry and the Natural Law

Evangelical theologian Carl F. H. Henry, in theological lore, is a fierce critic of natural law theory. A 1995 essay in the conservative journal *First Things* contains a summation of Henry's natural law criticisms.[10] Henry's negative appraisal of the natural law is representative of Protestantism's rejection of the natural law and will serve as a foil for this argument. Henry's criticisms of the natural law are what one scholar calls "messy ruminations."[11] His criticisms were mistaken and confused, yet his theology implied a functional and conceptual equivalent.[12]

---

[10] Carl F. H. Henry, "Natural Law and a Nihilistic Culture," *First Things* 49 (January 1995): 54–60.

[11] Bryan T. McGraw, "The Doctrine of Creation and the Possibilities of an Evangelical Natural Law," in *Natural Law and Evangelical Political Thought*, ed. Jesse Covington, Bryan T. McGraw, and Micah Watson (Lanham: Lexington Books, 2012), 62.

[12] As a convinced Henrician in my overall theology (and running an academic center in his honor at the institution where I teach), to critique an intellectual hero and giant such as Henry is no small matter. Nevertheless, in disagreeing with someone I find common cause with, virtually everything elsewhere creates an opportunity for scholarly exchange to flourish. One can positively adore the critical mass of someone's theological and ethical methodology without replicating them on *all* matters. Critiquing the thought of those one cherishes is a way of honoring the significance of his or her legacy.

Henry caricatured and misunderstood the natural law from the first sentence of his *First Things* essay. He defined natural law as a "body of ethical imperatives supposedly inherent in human beings and discovered by human reason. It therefore differs from statute law, from supernaturally revealed law, and even from so-called 'laws of nature.'"[13] The use of "supposedly inherent" belies the fact that the majority tradition of Christian interpretation has looked to Rom 2:15 ("the work of the law is written on their hearts") as a positive description of morality inscribed in human nature. The idea of *synderesis*, or innate moral capacity, is hardly controversial. It is a pillar of Christian moral thought.[14]

Henry wrote a few sentences later, "What it [natural law] excludes is a distillation of moral law from the transcendent supernatural, that is, from divine revelation. What it affirms is that all human beings share a set of ethical norms and imperatives that they commonly perceive without dependence on supernatural disclosure and illumination."[15] Natural law scholars would not recognize themselves in Henry's criticism. For one,

---

[13] Henry, "Natural Law and a Nihilistic Culture," 49. It is interesting from the outset how Henry pits natural law as distinct from supernatural law. While this is perhaps correct insofar as natural law speaks to moral norms discoverable by reason, to set it against supernatural revelation is incorrect. Self-professed natural lawyers do not see themselves working in opposition to divine revelation. In an interview with Robert P. George, I asked him whether natural law is opposed to revelation. He answered with "No. Nor do I know any other natural law theorist, past or present, who sees the project as one opposed to revelation." See "An Interview with Robert P. George and Andrew T. Walker on the Natural Law," *Eikon Journal*, 2, no. 2, https://cbmw.org/wp-content/uploads/2020/11/eikon_issue4_web.pdf.

[14] Matthew Levering, *Biblical Natural Law: A Theocentric and Teleological Approach* (Oxford: Oxford University, 2008), 23.

[15] Natural law advocates do not claim that they agree in full on the exhaustive details of natural law—that we have shared ethical norms (save one, the first principle of practical reason)—but only that the rightly formed intellect will rightly perceive natural law, which explains disagreement and variance about what the natural law is thought to be in different times and cultures.

no natural law literature I am aware of disputes the effects of sin on the known universality of the moral law or the ability to obey it. God's place in the natural law discussion is not about whether he exists, but at which point to bring God into the conversation.[16] Natural law simply affirms the contours of basic goods that reason, even fallen reason, can generally grasp as it perceives, reflects, and intuits. Natural law does not teach that *all* moral precepts are equally intuitive, but that objective morality exists because God has so ordered it, and humans can attune themselves to true and real moral insight by way of reason, wisdom, and conscience. The existence of the natural law reflects the divine order of God's decree. As Oliver O'Donovan writes, "The order of things that God has made is there. It is objective, and mankind has a place within it. Christian ethics, therefore, has an objective reference because it is concerned with man's life in accordance with this order."[17]

Henry is wrong to believe that natural law is distinct from supernatural revelation; it differs only according to the type of revelation, not the

---

[16] Very interestingly, a dialogue occurred between Robert P. George and Carl F. H. Henry on exactly this point at a conference hosted by the Ethics and Public Policy Center. The dialogue was transcribed. In the exchange, Henry disputes that a "shared" and "specific moral content" of the natural law survives the fall. George's reply is worth quoting in full: "Are they shared? Yes and no. Shared, yes, in the sense that in principle these reasons are available to all of us as possessors of a practical intellect that can grasp those reasons. But shared in that everyone knows all of them perfectly or that we all agree, or could in this vale of tears agree, on them? No, because reason and inference can miscarry in the practical sphere as they can in any other domain of inquiry, from mathematics to the sciences to historiography to logic itself. So it's true that we have broad differences over moral questions, and even over some practical questions that we wouldn't want to define as moral questions. But those differences themselves are no evidence at all for the proposition that no natural law exists." For this exchange, see Michael Cromartie, ed., *A Preserving Grace: Protestants, Catholics, and Natural Law* (Grand Rapids: Eerdmans, 1997), 44–45. See also part 3 of John Finnis, *Natural Law and Natural Rights*, 2nd ed. (Oxford: Oxford University, 2011).

[17] Oliver O'Donovan, *Resurrection and Moral Order: An Outline for Evangelical Ethics* (Grand Rapids: Eerdmans, 1994), 17.

category itself. Special revelation and general revelation, and philosophy and theology, are the two wings upon which the drama of God soars. It is a false dichotomy to set special revelation in opposition to natural law. General revelation precedes special revelation, but special revelation then allows for the proper interpretation of general revelation precepts. Nature is the product of grace, yet grace illuminates nature.[18] To quote Aquinas, natural law is "nothing else than the rational creature's participation" in the eternal law, which signifies that the existence of natural law emanates ultimately from grace, not autonomous nature.[19] Henry is correct to note that natural law believes in a moral law accessible through reason, but he separates, without warrant, natural law from statutory law and "nature." Contrary to Henry's formulation, natural law stands behind statutory law and assumes the existence of objective essences, or "nature," for its intelligibility. This is evident in Martin Luther King Jr.'s "Letter from Birmingham Jail." In it, King explicitly draws upon Aquinas, who draws upon Augustine for his understanding of just and unjust laws. According to King, the reason that laws elevating whites over blacks were wrong is that they did not accord with the natural law, and thus could not retain a true force of binding law. A law that does harm to people can never be true law. Laws that do harm are out of sync with the type of universe God has ordered.[20] Here, King spoke to how positive statutory law is only just and binding insofar as it accords with the natural law grounded in the eternal law.

Elsewhere in the essay, Henry mistakenly asserted that Calvin and Luther were "opponents" of the natural law. This historical claim is false, as church historian John T. McNeill famously asserted, "There is no real discontinuity

---

[18] Andrew T. Walker, "Grace in the Garden," *Christianity Today*, August 11, 2020, https://www.christianitytoday.com/ct/2020/august-web-only/grace-in-garden.html.

[19] Thomas Aquinas, *Summa Theologica*, part I-II, ques. 91.2.

[20] See Martin Luther King Jr., "Letter from a Birmingham Jail," April 16, 1963 (New York: HarperCollins, 1994).

between the teaching of the Reformers and that of their predecessors with respect to the natural law. Not one of the leaders of the Reformation assails the principle."[21] Henry seems to transpose post-Enlightenment rationalist antipathy to the natural law onto the Reformers.

Henry, insistent that no shared, universal body of moral law exists post-fall, was adamant on keeping revelation at the center of Christian ethics. "The integrity of Christian ethics," Henry declared, "requires an affirmation of God in His revelation, and not simply shared values in the public order and deeper stress on the common good."[22] This is doubtlessly true, but it raises an important question on the mode of God's revelation: Does God's general revelation and the cognizance of the moral order extend to those lacking supernatural enlightenment? To answer with anything other than yes is to render the whole project of ethics, let alone public ethics, meaningless. To deny that pagans can obtain moral ends, even if asserted from irrational grounds, is self-defeating. One need not be a Christian to understand the Holocaust was an evil tragedy. But if one answers yes, then it must be recognized that the moral intuition of non-Christians is a function of general revelation. The validity of a remnant post-fall morality works against the logic of Henry's theology. To say the unbelieving citizen lacks access to a universally shared morality, or is incapable of obtaining virtue, belies both history and lived experience. It is at this juncture where Henry must acknowledge the existence of an ongoing moral law. It is "fragmented" but "not nullified," he admitted, because of the *imago Dei*'s ongoing reality, the foundation that serves as the forum

---

[21] John T. McNeill, "Natural Law in the Teaching of the Reformers," *Journal of Religion* 26, no. 3 (1946): 168. One must consider whether evangelical resistance to natural law is born from scriptural deliberation or the residue of Catholic thought associated with natural law. A thought experiment worth considering is whether renaming natural law "creational law" would lead to a reconsideration of its basic arguments.

[22] Henry, "Natural Law and a Nihilistic Culture," 56.

for a post-fall remnant morality.[23] Whether Henry would consider it such, this is a massive concession to natural law theory. If the fall does not vitiate *all* moral knowledge, the question becomes the degree of knowledge, not its existence.

Here, then, is where Henry's doublespeak on natural law comes into focus. Henry had little appreciation for the role of general revelation when he posited something conceptually equivalent to natural law because, for Henry, natural law downplays the severity of sin's impact on reason and the will. Considering that natural law is more commonly associated with Catholic moral theory, one wonders whether Protestant and Catholic skirmishes undergirded Henry's rejection of natural law. However, once it is granted that a remnant post-fall morality survives, as Henry did indeed acknowledge, we find ourselves treading in natural law waters. Henry granted that "creation ethic doctrine holds that, prior to salvific knowledge of Jesus Christ, human beings universally have some knowledge of right and good through the divine law of creation addressed to reason and conscience. No less than natural law theory."[24] How Henry could propose to be such a vociferous critic of natural law while acknowledging this is befuddling. This seeming contradiction is also noted by Bryan T. McGraw, who alleges that Henry's "creation ethic" language serves as a "stand-in for much the same thing. . . . Does it work to help Henry smuggle the essential characteristics of natural law in through the back door while kicking its more obvious representations out the front?"[25]

What may account for this vacillation? Henry posited a distinction between Thomistic natural law theory, which is complex and highly rational, against a general revelation morality, which is textual and less theoretical. This false dichotomy does not hold up to scrutiny and is a distinction without a difference. In the *First Things* essay, Henry

---

[23] Henry, 59.

[24] Henry, 59.

[25] McGraw, "The Doctrine of Creation," 61.

criticized Lutheran theologian Carl Braaten, who argued for adapting natural law to "orders of creation." He wrote that "Braaten seeks to make the doctrine of natural law acceptable by redefining it."[26] The reverse is also true of Henry: he seeks to make the doctrine of natural law unacceptable by redefining it from its classical Christian—and most notably, scriptural—roots.

That, according to Henry, "Christianity offers no speculative theory of ethics that renders certain courses of action personally and socially obligatory" in no way complicates matters for Christian natural law theorists. As a message of divine redemption, one can expect the Bible to lack an explicit ethical or political theory. However, the lack of an explicit theory does not prevent reflecting—post hoc—on the pattern, coherence, and logic of morality inscribed in general revelation and developing theories of explanation afterward. Natural law is elaborate as a theory, but it reduces to something quite simple: a person acts on the basis of obtaining good ends, and good ends are intelligible by what is beneficial to human nature for its own sake.

What summarizes Henry and the natural law? Once Henry's ethical program of relying exclusively on special revelation is rejected by skeptics who reject Scripture's authority, the forcefulness of Christian ethics collapses. If what Christians believe to be true cannot be understood as intelligible apart from Scripture, Christian ethics runs the risk of sectarian ghettoization. That is the conundrum of Henry's ethic. On what basis can Henry engage in meaningful dialogue with non-Christians once the non-Christian rejects Scripture's authority? At that point, moral discourse necessarily defaults to natural law, which Henry denies as imminently useful for settling moral disputes. At best, Henry was confused and, worse, oscillating between denying natural law theory but relying upon and implicitly granting natural law morality.

---

[26] Henry, "Natural Law and a Nihilistic Culture," 57.

The Natural Law: Theological, Biblical, and Historical Evidence

Theological and Metaphysical Underpinnings

The previous discussion proceeded without offering a precise definition of the natural law. That was intentional. I wanted to clear out what natural law is *not* before putting forward a positive account. Before that, though, it is necessary to establish, conceptually, what a theory is that would designate natural law a theory. A theory of moral action should contain: (1) an explanation for the moral system's origins; (2) an account of its norming authority; and (3) a *telos* of its reason for action. A moral theory needs to explain where it came from, why it is obligatory, and the purposiveness of its directives. As will be argued below, natural law *as a theory* finds its origins in God and special revelation, bears witness to an innate moral law in human nature, and obtains the realization of human flourishing. At root, the vision for natural law in this chapter is theistic as natural law is nothing else than the sum and substance of humankind's moral nature and moral agency under the direction of God's providential ordering.[27]

What, then, is natural law? Natural law refers to the moral tradition in Christian thought that a divinely inscribed and self-evident moral order of basic norms and goods exists that human agents—though fallen—can still, in principle, grasp as a function of their nature as they reflect reasonably and conscientiously upon their choices and their reasons for action. These goods are transhistorical and transcultural and assume a static definition of human nature as a thing created by God. Behind natural law is a commitment to these *basic goods*—purposes, ends, or goods that are intelligible to order one's life around for their achievement. Among these goods are life,

---

[27] For more on the theistic foundations of natural law, see Steven A. Long, "God, Teleology, and the Natural Law," in *Natural Law Today: The Present State of the Perennial Philosophy*, ed. Christopher Wolfe and Steven Brust (Lanham, MD: Lexington Books, 2018), 3–18.

health, family, integrity, knowledge, friendship, play, skillfulness, aesthetic experience, authenticity, practical reasonableness, and religion.[28] The point of any moral act is that the action achieves an apparent or actual good. The decision to be truthful in one's utterances is understood as desirable because in living truthfully, one understands that living with integrity is desirable—though not always easy. Truthfulness is a prerequisite to trustful interactions. All of these goods contribute to human flourishing, which is the *telos* toward which natural law moves. When Scripture speaks of a pastor's qualification as "loving what is good" (Titus 1:8) or when the apostle Paul told us to pursue "whatever is true, whatever is honorable, whatever is just, whatever is pure, whatever is lovely" (Phil 4:8), the command to obtain these things only makes sense against a backdrop of the natural law speaking to ends worthy of our actions' conformity.

"The reality is that Christians who define Christianity in terms of historic Christian doctrine and moral teachings do not believe merely that these teachings are true," writes Baptist theologian Albert Mohler, "but that they point to the only truth that will produce real and lasting human happiness."[29] Mohler's statement implies the intelligibility of those norms to achieve the goods that facilitate happiness (or flourishing). To act as one ought implies an inclination to a knowledge of certain goods and an ultimate good, God, who made us in his image. Being created in God's image, according to Reformed theologian and ethicist David VanDrunen, "carried with it a moral purpose, a commission."[30] From the full sweep of Scripture, humans are to order their lives for the sake of God's glory (1 Cor 10:31). It

---

[28] For more on the basic goods of the natural law, see Robert P. George, *Making Men Moral: Civil Liberties and Public Morality* (Oxford: Oxford University, 1993); Finnis, *Natural Law and Natural Rights*; Alfonso Gómez-Lobo, *Morality and the Human Goods* (Washington, DC: Georgetown University, 2002).

[29] R. Albert Mohler, *The Gathering Storm: Secularism, Culture, and the Church* (Nashville: Nelson Books, 2020), 117.

[30] David VanDrunen, *A Biblical Case for Natural Law* (Grand Rapids: Acton Institute, 2006), 13.

is God's glory that then defines which actions are reasonable to pursue. This comprehension of the moral order and its basic goods defines and identifies which actions are reasonable and worth pursuing. Natural law relies on a realist metaphysic that posits universal constants concerning reality and human nature.[31]

VanDrunen defines natural law as the "idea that God makes known the basic substance of his moral law through the created order itself. Human beings therefore know this law simply by being human, even apart from access to Scripture or other forms of special revelation. They know it through their natural capacities as they live in this world."[32] The natural law is a common morality understood through the operations of conscience and reason given to humanity for its good. As Paul Helm writes, "the natural law, being given for mankind's good, is part of the practical reason, and so it is teleological in its operation."[33]

The natural law holds that moral goods can be known apart from an immediate appeal to special revelation as agents reflect on which actions are reasonable and worth pursuing. It is imminently teleological in that natural law serves to direct individuals to the goods consistent with the ends of their nature.[34] As individuals reflect on the goods and truths of their existence, they then act to bring about the fulfillment of those goods and truths.

---

[31] For more on these themes, see David S. Oderberg, "The Metaphysical Foundations of Natural Law," in *Natural Moral Law in Contemporary Society*, ed. Holger Zaborowski (Washington, DC: Catholic University of America, 2010), 44–75.

[32] David VanDrunen, *Politics After Christendom: Political Theology in a Fractured World* (Grand Rapids: Zondervan, 2020), 126.

[33] Paul Helm, *Human Nature from Calvin to Edwards* (Grand Rapids: Reformation Heritage Books, 2018), 79.

[34] This is a definition adapted from David VanDrunen, who writes that natural law is "the moral order that directs people to the proper human goals corresponding to the purposes for which God made them." VanDrunen, *Politics after Christendom*, 138.

There is a tacitness to natural law in that it is impossible to live an intelligible, sociable life apart from assuming necessary truths of its existence: "Good is to be done and pursued and evil is to be avoided." Aquinas went on to write how "all other precepts of the natural law are based upon this: so that whatever the practical reason naturally apprehends as man's good (or evil), belongs to the precepts of the natural law as something to be done or avoided."[35] Protestant Reformer Franciscus Junius says similarly, "Moreover, the end of that practical reason, which has been placed in both the just and the unjust, is one's own good, and for this reason it is the first and highest precept of the natural law. The good, as the end of nature, must be pursued and done; evil must be avoided."[36] Natural law assumes there must be indemonstrable, self-evident, and underived "oughts" that are unprovable. To quote C. S. Lewis: "If nothing is self-evident, nothing can be proved. If nothing is obligatory for its own sake, nothing is obligatory at all."[37] Practically speaking, there must be a true proposition that, were it not, no other proposition or truth-claim could be rendered intelligible or binding. Here is what self-evident must mean: an obviousness whose denial vitiates all other necessary truths.[38]

Natural law is God's moral law self-disclosed through general revelation within creation and ascertained by rightly formed practical reason. Natural law speaks to two domains: (1) the external moral order established by God in general revelation (creation) and (2) the practical reasonableness and justification for any worthwhile choice or action directed toward an intelligible good within the moral order. In other words, how does one grasp the

---

[35] Both quotations can be found in Aquinas, *Summa Theologica*, part I-II ques. 94.2, 2.

[36] Franciscus Junius, *The Mosaic Polity*, trans. Todd M. Rester (Grand Rapids: Christian's Library, 2015), 45.

[37] C. S. Lewis, *The Abolition of Man* (San Francisco: HarperOne, 2015), 41.

[38] For additional commentary on the first principle of practical reason, see Paul R. Dehart, "On the First Principles of Moral Reason," *Public Discourse*, July 6, 2020, https://www.thepublicdiscourse.com/2020/07/64302/.

binding intelligibility of morality? The first proposition, one of ontology, is met with virtually no resistance. The second proposition, one of epistemology, divides many Christians in their understanding of the natural law.

Biblical Arguments for Natural Law

Thus far, I have worked to offer a clear definition of natural law. The following offers a short survey of scriptural arguments in support of natural law.[39] It should be said at the forefront that if natural law can be proven biblical, then Baptists—a tradition noted for its strict adherence to biblical authority and fidelity—should have no problem adopting it as a moral framework. Baptists should put aside whatever intellectual prejudices they might harbor against natural law's association with Catholicism. To quote philosopher J. Budziszewski:

> There is a natural law, and it can be known and philosophically analyzed. But that which is beside the Scripture can be vindicated only with the help of Scripture; that which is revealed before the gospel can be secured against evasion only in light of the gospel. The doctrine of Natural Law is best grounded not in the study of nature independent of God's Word but in the Word of God itself.[40]

Budziszewski helpfully reframes natural law discussion: it is not a coldly, rationally, or autonomously grounded moral system. Natural law is, if

---

[39] Space prevents an exhaustive biblical survey. For additional evidence on the biblical grounds of natural law, see David Haines and Andrew A. Fulford, *Natural Law: A Brief Introduction and Biblical Defense* (Lincoln: The Davenant, 2017); David VanDrunen, *Divine Covenants and Moral Order: A Biblical Theology of Natural Law* (Grand Rapids: Eerdmans, 2014); VanDrunen, *A Biblical Case for Natural Law*; VanDrunen, *Politics After Christendom*; Charles, *Retrieving the Natural Law*; Levering, *Biblical Natural Law*.

[40] J. Budziszewski, *Written on the Heart: The Case for Natural Law* (Downers Grove, IL: InterVarsity, 1997), 184.

anything, a biblical concept rooted in the eternal law of God's being. To understand the biblical contours of natural law requires examination of texts and theological reflection on the logic of morality. Natural law is not afforded direct scriptural reference in such stark terms but is a concept that stands behind the story line of Scripture's moral arc. To make sense of a moral command requires examining the command's source and what good obtains or results through obedience. We neglect the natural law only to our detriment concerning how we understand God's moral law, our place within it, and our responsibility to proclaim it far and wide. Space prevents an exhaustive survey of texts witnessing to the natural law. Below are three passages that speak to essential lineaments of the natural law: (1) the metaphysics of order, (2) the existence of morality, (3) and the distribution of justice.

Order: Genesis 1–2

Although not often appealed to as an immediate pretext for natural law, the metaphysics of natural law is only intelligible against a backdrop where meaningful moral agency is possible. Moral action assumes a horizon where action is orderly, observable, and purposeful and assumes a natural order where identifiable goods can be discerned, safeguarded, and obtained. Genesis offers this by portraying creation as purposeful, not chaotic. The ontological backdrop of Genesis is what sets the stage for the natural law throughout the rest of Scripture.

Genesis 1–2 portrays both creation and Adam and Eve as teleological creatures in a teleological order. From the orderliness and stability of creation that makes life habitable to Adam and Eve's commission to multiply, implied in the creation narrative of Genesis 1–2 is an enchanted, teleological order directed by God's providence. God did not create a brute creation or animatronic agents. God created beings to act for certain ends perfective of their design and nature. As Matthew Levering observes, "God creates human beings so that they are naturally ordered to preserve the good of their human existence. Without the inclination to preserve this good, God's warning about the tree of the knowledge of good and evil would not be intelligible."[41] As two authors note about the relationship between creation and natural law:

> The very fact of divine creation seems to point towards what has been traditionally called *natural law*: the notion that there is, because of the divine intellect, a natural order within the created world by which each and every created being's goodness can be objectively judged, both on the level of being (ontological goodness), and, for human-beings specifically, on the level of human action (moral goodness). Ontological goodness is the foundation of moral goodness.[42]

Morality: Romans 2:14–16

Romans 2:14–16 is a *locus classicus* citation for natural law. These verses state:

So, when Gentiles, who do not by nature have the law, do what the law demands, they are a law to themselves even though they do not have the law. They show that the work of the law is written on their hearts. Their consciences confirm this. Their competing thoughts either accuse or even excuse them on the day when God judges what people have kept secret, according to my gospel through Christ Jesus.

In these verses, the apostle Paul spoke to the existence of a "law . . . written on their hearts." This law, known as the *synderesis* or "deep conscience,"[43] refers to the moral law's substance imprinted on our nature. As mentioned,

---

[41] Levering, *Biblical Natural Law*, 59.

[42] Haines and Fulford, *Natural Law*, 2.

[43] See Douglas Kries, "Deep Conscience," *Claremont Review of Books*, Fall 2015, https://claremontreviewofbooks.com/deep-conscience/.

it implies a body of moral knowledge we possess that our conscience testifies to as we either live in alignment with it or defy it. Although there is debate as to the identity of whom Paul was describing, the majority interpretive tradition argues that this refers to non-Christian Gentiles. In the flow of Paul's argument, it is because non-Christian Gentiles possess the natural law and at times are even obedient to it, despite not possessing the Mosaic law, that they are liable for judgment.

Even if one rejects this interpretation of Romans 2, Romans 1 itself testifies to the existence of natural law in holding that all persons are "without excuse" in their knowledge of suppressing and disobeying God (1:20), as the Old Testament prophets held the pagan nations to be without excuse when they condemned Babylon, Persia, and Egypt for oppression, tyranny, and wickedness despite not having special revelation. This is so because, for Paul, creation reflects the pattern of divine intelligence (see Ps 19:1–6). The grandeur of creation reflects God's majesty, and all persons have some irrepressible knowledge of this truth (see Rom 1:18). Natural law is thus a species of natural theology. To say that individuals are "without excuse" is to acknowledge the validity of their culpability. For Paul, rejecting creation and creaturely limits serves as a self-indictment against God's moral law (see Rom 1:24–28). Considering the catalog of sins humanity is indicted for in Romans 1 (sexual perversion, murder, covetousness, idolatry, parental disobedience, filthy speech, deceit), Romans 1–2 describes humanity's plight, not in its ignorance of God's moral law, but its defiance to it. This amplifies the existence of the natural law: post-fall image-bearers still retain a knowledge of the moral law holding them captive to future judgment if they do not repent.

Justice: Genesis 9:6; Matthew 7:12; Mark 12:31

The classical definition of justice is rendering to each what is his or her due. Justice is a state of affairs rightly ordered. Justice is present when any circumstance or action aligns with eternal law, natural law, and human law. Justice thus rejects and is thwarted by irrational actions, unfair procedures, biased standards, and exploitative circumstances. According to natural law, a just order distributes true rights and rectifies injustice. In this sense, justice is both reciprocal, retributive, and rectifying. The natural sense of justice reflects the Noahic foundations for natural law, which states, "And I will require a penalty for your lifeblood; I will require it from any animal and from any human; if someone murders a fellow human, I will require that person's life. 'Whoever sheds human blood, by humans his blood will be shed, for God made humans in his image'" (Gen 9:5–6). These verses reflect a fundamental principle of general equity to which all persons as partakers in creation are bound: justice intelligibly inheres within creation and is the backdrop for all interhuman dealings.[44] Natural law is an ethic whose universality is common to all persons as rational image-bearers. Just order desires the righting of all injustice. The desire for justice reflects a standard or measure of judgment from which to judge when something has gone wrong. When Nazis were on trial at Nuremberg, it was the universal sense that evil had been done and must be answered for that occasioned such trials.

When an offense has occurred, corrective measures should restore a breakdown in justice. How else can this be proven apart from the natural sense of justice that dwells deep within us? To get at this, observe Abraham and Abimelech's exchange in Genesis 20. In castigating Abraham for deceiving him, the pagan ruler Abimelech charged Abraham for doing to him "things . . . that should never be done" (Gen 20:9). How could a pagan ruler make such an accusation of moral wrongdoing apart from a natural sense of justice, that is, right and wrong? Where does such a moral code originate?[45] That this principle is located immediately in the context of a reconstituted social order speaks to the foundational role justice is to play in creation.

---

[44] For more on the Noahic covenant and natural law, see VanDrunen, *Politics After Christendom*, 124–49; VanDrunen, *Divine Covenants and Moral Order*, 95–132.

[45] For more on this exchange, see VanDrunen, *A Biblical Case for Natural Law*, 42–45.

Echoes of this principle reverberate behind Jesus's statements in Matt 7:12, "Whatever you want others to do for you, do also the same for them, for this is the Law and the Prophets," and Mark 12:31, "Love your neighbor as yourself." Verses as seemingly routine and uncontroversial as these, it turns out, reflect a tectonic aspect of natural law. Martin Luther noted how Matthew 7 points to the natural law: "Not an individual is there who does not realize, and who is not forced to confess, the justice and truth of the natural law outlined in the command, 'All things therefore whatsoever ye would that men should do unto you, even so do ye also unto them.'"[46] C. S. Lewis has shown how the golden rule has parallels around the world in different cultures and religions, including some predating Jesus, evidence of humanity's ability to grasp it without special revelation.[47] Markus Bockmuehl comments similarly on how "the uncomplicated assumption of a kind of natural reciprocity and commonality of human needs suggests the acceptance of a moral category that is general and self-evident, rather than positively revealed in the Torah."[48] Haines and Fulford also observe natural law reciprocity behind our Lord's words:

> Jesus teaches his disciples to take their own basic desires as ones that every human being has. Secondly, by telling them to satisfy those basic desires of others, he affirms those desiderata as good. The implication of these two premises is that Jesus teaches all people actually know what is good for them, on some level, since they have desires that ought to be met.[49]

---

[46] Martin Luther, *Sermon for the Fourth Sunday after Epiphany: Romans 13:8–10*, in *Luther's Epistle Sermons: Epiphany, Easter, and Pentecost*, ed. John Nicholas (Minneapolis: Lutheran, 1909), 73.

[47] Lewis, *The Abolition of Man*, appendix 1.

[48] Markus Bockmuehl, *Jewish Law in Gentile Churches: Halakhah and the Beginning of Christian Public Ethics* (Grand Rapids: Baker Academic, 2003), 118–19.

[49] Haines and Fulford, *Natural Law*, 82.

Behind the just treatment of our neighbors and those within society is a principle of reciprocity. Verses such as these stand behind interpersonal relationships and a commitment to the overarching common good of society. Humans are to act and live in ways consistent with their and society's mutual flourishing. Such an ethic underwrites the intelligibility of Christian social thought.

Baptist History and the Natural Law

Historically, there is not a distinctively "Baptist" natural law doctrine to highlight. This is true to the extent that Protestantism generally has not focused on developing intricate natural law paradigms. Even still, such a reality does not elide areas in Baptist thought and Baptist history that relied upon, or assumed, a doctrine of natural law. As there is no central Baptist natural law tradition, its existence is nonetheless present, though piecemeal.

The Second London Confession of 1689, regarded as one of the preeminent Baptist confessions born of Particular (Reformed) English Baptists, contains an article on Scripture that witnesses to the reality of general revelation:

> The Holy Scripture is the only sufficient, certain, and infallible rule
> of all saving knowledge, faith, and obedience, although the light of
> nature, and the works of creation and providence do so far manifest
> the goodness, wisdom, and power of God, as to leave men inexcus-
> able; yet they are not sufficient to give that knowledge of God and
> His will which is necessary unto salvation.[50]

Here, the confession drafters acknowledged that a "light of nature" exists despite sin's dominion. As in Paul's argument in Romans, this remnant

---

[50] The 1689 Confession of Faith, available at https://www.the1689confession .com. Provided by the podcast *Doctrine and Devotion* (http://www.doctrineanddevotion .com/).

morality is incapable of saving individuals; instead, the witness of general revelation holds individuals accountable for divine judgment.

It is the contention of this author that Baptist antipathy to natural law is more the result of the Enlightenment's overconfidence in rationalism and modernism's non-teleological conception of human nature, rather than biblical exegesis. Said differently, rejection of natural law, at least within the Reformed tradition, is an exception to the Reformed tradition's general acceptance of natural law categories. Present-day Baptist rejection of natural law has more to do with superficial connotative association with Roman Catholicism and Enlightenment philosophy than with theology proper. Even here, as noted in the introduction, Baptists display an inherent tension in their public theology as they search for a method of ethical engagement that is both faithful to Scripture while at the same time publicly accessible and conversant with secular society. Seen from this vantage point, the search for a moral tradition to communicate Christian moral norms requires retrieving a tradition already present at its beginnings. Understood as an entailment of general revelation, British Baptist theologian Paul Goodliff argues that Baptists should find alignment within the natural law tradition and retain it for themselves.[51]

As their history would unfold, Baptists would find themselves appropriating natural law most frequently and ardently in service to the principle of religious liberty.[52] According to Thomas Helwys, "Men's religion to God is between God and themselves. The king shall not answer for it. Neither may the king be judge between God and man. Let them be heretics, Turks, Jews, or whatsoever, it appertains not to the earthly power to punish them in the least measure."[53] According to the logic of Baptist thought, true faith

---

[51] Goodliff, "Natural Law in the Baptist Tradition," 147.

[52] For a contemporary Baptist natural law defense of religious liberty, see Andrew T. Walker, *Liberty for All: Defending Everyone's Religious Freedom in a Pluralistic Age* (Grand Rapids: Brazos, 2021).

[53] Thomas Helwys, *A Short Declaration of the Mystery of Iniquity*, ed. Richard Groves, Classics of Religious Liberty 1 (Macon, GA: Mercer University Press, 1998), 53.

is always voluntary, and the church consists only of those truly converted. The conversionary emphasis of Baptist theology is thus a significant segue to a Baptist natural law doctrine: individuals have a right (1) to come to voluntary conclusions about the object of faith; (2) to worship and express their faith unencumbered; (3) and to remain unmolested in their belief. Individuals have a right to allow their religious faculties to be undisturbed insofar as no threat to the common good occurs. Because the government has not been scripturally endowed with religious authority and is incapable of adjudicating true belief from false belief, individuals and churches remain independent and freely cooperating of their accord.

Rhode Island founder and Baptist iconoclast Roger Williams's thought was permeated with natural law concepts, which were formative to his overall project of ordering society not according to religious homogeneity but by the commonality and universality of moral norms born of conscience.[54] For his understanding of conscience, civility, and religious liberty, Williams relies on a natural law edifice. In a memorable quote, Williams personifies the operations of the natural law to explain its function:

> All light or truth—natural, civil, or divine—comes from without and is received by the internal faculty according to the capacity, nature, and measure of it. All truth or falsehood, light or darkness, is first espied by the watch or sentinel, or Comprehension. From thence it is conveyed to the Court of guard, where Captain Reason or his Lieutenant, Common Sense and Experience, take examination, and Memory keeps a record of proceedings which go on by degree to actions.[55]

---

[54] For a helpful volume on the natural law dimensions of Williams's thought, see the tremendously helpful James Calvin Davis, *The Moral Theology of Roger Williams: Christian Conviction and Public Ethics* (Louisville: Westminster John Knox, 2004).

[55] Roger Williams, *On Religious Liberty: Selections from the Works of Roger Williams*, ed. James Calvin Davis (Cambridge: Belknap, 2008), 269.

As one Williams scholar reflects on his natural law affinities, "Williams maintained that human beings' fallible awareness of the norms and values of natural law provided sufficient basis to make moral arguments, engage in moral conversation, and share cooperative ventures with persons of different religious and cultural backgrounds."[56]

The Baptist Faith and Message 2000's article XV, "The Christian and the Social Order," is unintelligible and cannot be operationalized apart from relying on universal moral norms for its authority to act socially. That Baptists are to bring society "under the sway of the principles of righteousness, truth, and brotherly love" implies that such ideals can be universally recognized and that it is desirable for society, even unregenerate segments of society, to live under its moral vision.[57]

A multitude of Southern Baptist Convention resolutions utilize natural law reasoning without expressly noting it.[58] For example, a 1978 "Declaration of Human Rights" from the Southern Baptist Convention annual meeting states that "Southern Baptists stand for the worth of the individual, the priesthood of the believer, freedom of conscience, and the sanctity of life. We hold that these human rights are the gift of God. We believe that they spring from the Bible's revelation that all persons are made in 'the likeness of God' (Jas 3:9 RSV)."[59] In the aftermath of the Supreme Court's *Obergefell* decision, the 2016 resolution "On Biblical Sexuality and the Freedom of Conscience," states that "marriage is between one man and one woman, ordered by God toward the union of the spouses, the means of procreation, formative of family, and foundational to the common good of

---

[56] Davis, *The Moral Theology of Roger Williams*, 64.

[57] "The Christian and the Social Order," *The Baptist Faith and Message 2000*, art. XV, https://bfm.sbc.net/bfm2000/#xv-the-christian-and-the-social-order.

[58] Others pertaining to homosexuality, transgender identity, and women in combat also contain overtures to natural law reasoning.

[59] "Declaration of Human Rights," Southern Baptist Convention, June 1, 1978, https://www.sbc.net/resource-library/resolutions/declaration-of-human-rights/.

society (Gen 1:28, 2:18–24)."[60] These are but a few examples of areas where Baptists have unconsciously relied upon natural law logic for their moral argumentation.

Reflections on a Baptist Natural Law Public Ethic

To end this chapter, it is appropriate to briefly survey areas where a new-found natural law concentration might interface in Baptist public ethics and how Baptist public ethics can incorporate natural law theory into its conceptual frameworks. Concerning the development of a Baptist natural law public ethic, natural law allows for Baptists (1) to make biblically faithful arguments in the public square that can (2) expose the irrationality of secular morality while (3) remaining consistent with long-held Baptist convictions about keeping church and state separate. There are four areas where these truths can be brought to bear in Baptist life.

Scripture and Hermeneutics

General revelation serves as a foundation and forerunner to special revelation. From appreciating beauty to gaining better foresight into humanity's elusive quest for self-fulfillment, behind both are questions that natural law serves to address. A better understanding of why people act, intuit, and desire the way they do will provide a rich opportunity to minister the Word's sufficiency to angst-ridden souls. Scripture should direct one's gaze outward to the way God has ordered His creation. The activity of reading, interpreting, and applying Scripture to one's life occurs through cognitive actions capable of grasping truths. Baptists should gain greater facility and

---

[60] "On Biblical Sexuality and the Freedom of Conscience," Southern Baptist Convention, June 1, 2016, https://www.sbc.net/resource-library/resolutions/on-biblical-sexuality-and-the-freedom-of-conscience/.

appreciation for how general revelation serves as a backdrop to cognitive and spiritual encounters with Scripture.

Chiefly, however, a Baptist public ethic would use natural law to seek common ground as a signpost to divert attention to the supernatural, revealed Word of God. The projects of general revelation and special revelation should not be seen as antitheses, for as Lutheran scholar Carl Braaten notes, "The choice between biblical revelation and natural law is a false one."[61] A Baptist public ethic can embrace natural law if only because we Baptists know the proper place of natural law in the economy of God's creation: as a prerequisite to supernatural encounter. When authority reduces to expressive individualism, the peculiarity of a supernatural and transcendent revelation may be the last recourse to awaken individuals to a voice outside of themselves.

The paradox of an evangelical doctrine of Scripture can simultaneously affirm that the fallenness of humankind will lead some to reject Scripture's authority while holding out the possibility for others to receive the same Scripture as good news by way of supernatural intervention.

Gospel

Baptist ethicist and theologian Russell Moore, although not known as a natural law proponent, grants that general revelation plays a pivotal role in the evangelistic process. He writes,

> General revelation informs our Great Commission activities when we understand that the universality of God's witness in the conscience means that *all* humans grapple with sin, guilt, and fear of death and judgment. We are able to speak in moral categories

---

[61] Carl E. Braaten, "Protestants and Natural Law," *First Things* 19 (January 1, 1992): 24.

and judicial categories precisely because we know that God has implanted these categories in the internal makeup of all humans.[62]

While it is undoubtedly the case that the natural law serves to decode and explain the mysteries of universal morality to a fallen race, the natural law reminds us we have been sentenced to death, though forgiveness and redemption await (see Rom 1:18–3:26). When sinners transgress the natural law, they are not rebelling against an abstract "force" or rule but against the God-man, Jesus Christ. Christ upholds the natural law, orders it, and is its terminal end (see John 1:3; Col. 1:15; Rom 10:4; Gal 3:24).[63] "That we might be given a supernatural and eternal perfection in Christ Jesus," wrote Junius, "we must also see that from God the author and leader, who is the way, the truth, and the life, we have the law of that way, truth, and life."[64] For Junius, the natural law begins and ends with Christ, revealing a Christotelic dimension to the natural law. An arresting passage from John Henry Newman reveals that the pangs of conscience remind us of our awaited fate unless we repent, and it is worth quoting in full:

> If, as is the case, we feel responsibility, are ashamed, are frightened, at transgressing the voice of conscience, this implies that there is One to whom we are responsible, before whom we are ashamed, whose claims upon us we fear. If, on doing wrong, we feel the same tearful, broken-hearted sorrow which overwhelms us in hurting a mother; if, on doing right, we enjoy the same sunny serenity of mind, the same soothing satisfactory delight which follows on our receiving praise from a father, we certainly have within us the image

---

[62] Russell Moore, "Natural Revelation," in *A Theology for the Church*, ed. Daniel L. Akin (Nashville: B&H Academic, 2007), 113.

[63] Andrew T. Walker, "The Gospel and the Natural Law," *First Things*, December 8, 2020, https://www.firstthings.com/web-exclusives/2020/12/the-gospel-and-the-natural-law.

[64] Junius, *The Mosaic Polity*, 48.

of some person, to whom our love and veneration look, in whose smile we find our happiness, for whom we yearn, towards whom we direct our pleadings, in whose anger we are troubled and waste away. These feelings in us are such as require for their exciting cause an intelligent being; we are not affectionate towards a stone, nor do we feel shame before a horse or a dog; we have no remorse or compunction on breaking mere human law: yet, so it is, conscience excites all these painful emotions, confusion, foreboding, self-condemnation; and on the other hand it sheds upon us a deep peace, a sense of security, a resignation, and a hope, which there is no sensible, no earthly object to elicit. "The wicked flees when no one pursueth;" then why does he flee? whence his terror? Who is it that he sees in solitude, in darkness, in the hidden chambers of his heart? If the cause of these emotions does not belong to this visible world, the Object towards which his perception is directed must be Supernatural and Divine; and thus the phenomena of conscience, as a dictate, avail to impress the imagination with the picture of a Supreme Governor, a Judge, holy, just, powerful, all-seeing, retributive, and is the creative principle of religion, as the Moral Sense is the principle of ethics.[65]

Baptists should rightly reject natural law if its use means jettisoning the name of Jesus in public debate. If, however, it can be a device that awakens people to their need for a Savior, ignorance of its possibilities to point individuals to Christ is only to our detriment.

The natural law also has drastic implications for the relationship between seeking justice and the gospel. The theism ultimately underwriting our natural law doctrine is what makes public ethics possible. The general

---

[65] John Henry Newman, *Grammar of Assent*, chap. 5, sec. 1, 101, quoted in Charles E. Rice, *Fifty Questions on the Natural Law: What It Is and Why We Need It*, 2nd ed. (San Francisco: Ignatius, 1999), 160–61.

contours of justice so many strive to see enacted, Christians proclaim, are shadows of an ultimate justice found in the kingdom of God. An eschatological reading of natural law would help us see it as a necessary ingredient to the gospel's proclamation of justice.[66]

Discipleship

Natural law is less a strategy to convince the hardened secularist to accept pro-life arguments (though it is never less than that) than a tool that helps bring a rational explanation to Christian ethics' coherence and logic. Familiarity with natural law will help Christians understand the normativity of biblical morality. Take, for example, the sixth commandment's prohibition on murder. Is the sixth commandment valuable *only* because of divine law and special revelation? Surely that cannot be the case, for divine laws of Old Testament Israel are no longer in force, even if they are inspired. Instead, natural law ethics helps bring focus and clarity to what the sixth commandment strives to advance: preserving life (a basic good). The safety and sustenance of life is a basic good since, by almost any accounting, it is better to be alive than dead. Thus, we are to order our actions so that the good of preserving and experiencing the blessings of life may continue. The moral intuition that murder is wrong is one precept of the natural law.

That persons reject the natural law says nothing about its intelligibility or forcefulness. That murderers exist does not vitiate the natural law. Indeed, it is in violating natural law that its moral goods are vindicated. Occasions of murder tell us of its violation, and it is the awareness of a violation that testifies to an enduring moral good. A murderer no more vitiates the natural law than a broken vehicle negates the medium of transportation. Rather, the existence of a lawbreaker ratifies the existence of the law, which exists as a standard to measure one's actions.

---

[66] Braaten, "Protestants and Natural Law," 25.

Mission, Natural Law, and Apologetical Ethics

I purposefully put the apologetical function of the natural law last. Why? Because far too often natural law discussion surrounds the issue of persuasiveness, as though the natural law is only valuable insofar as it is a tool for convincing others of the soundness of Baptist ethics. Do I deny this? Of course not. The question is one of triage. While natural law is a compelling and potent device, exposing the shallowness and illogicality of secular ethics, my belief in the power of human fallenness leads me to believe that natural law is not to be valued solely for its apologetical purposes.

To be clear, a massive implication of the natural law is the communication of universal moral norms (a subject we lack the space here to discuss).[67] Jettisoning the natural law means abandoning sound principles of morality that restrain injustice, decadence, misery, decay, and evil. These pathologies are incompatible with and hostile to the common good.[68] Same-sex marriage, abortion, pornography, human trafficking, artificial reproductive technology, parental rights, euthanasia, racial strife, transgenderism—the natural law implicates each. The call to a fully orbed Baptist public ethic is a call to defend, explain, and champion the goods and blessings necessary for human flourishing. The call to the natural law is the call to the public square—to prophetically declare the standards of righteousness and justice God has within the creation order. Baptists need to adopt the natural law as a public ethics framework to avoid the twin errors of theonomic enforcement and quietist withdrawal. The natural law thus offers a pathway for communicating moral truths that other humans, in principle, could grasp as true without relying on formal church-state establishments or evacuating the public square of Christian social responsibility for public justice.

---

[67] For discussion on how religion can function in public argument, see chapter 7 of Walker, *Liberty for All.*

[68] For a Baptist natural law understanding of the common good, see Andrew T. Walker and Casey Hough, "Toward a Baptist Natural Law Conception of the Common Good," *Southwestern Journal of Theology* 63, no. 1 (Fall 2020): 153–74.

Natural law is an idea that some Christians want to downplay or non-believers outrightly deny, but that all—including those who downplay or deny it—are incapable of living apart from if they hope to attain human decency, basic justice, and the common good.

Conclusion

A few years ago, I gave a set of lectures to a Christian high school in Florida on the transgender phenomenon. Much of my lecture was devoted to explaining how our bodily organization as males and females parallels with the scriptural account of males and females being ordered to reproductive acts so that they might "be fruitful, [and] multiply" (Gen 1:28). Before the next day's lectures, a teacher from the school approached me in the hall to thank me for my lectures. Her comments were unforgettable: "I never knew we had good reason to believe what we do about sex and gender." The comment could have been lost on me, but it was not. Here was a Christian teacher expressing gratitude not for teaching her the Bible but for explaining that what we believe as Christians comports with creation as we know it.

Explicitly or not, Baptist political and ethical thought has all along relied upon natural law categories to communicate its moral norms in society. In light of that, this chapter implies that Baptists ought not shy away from acknowledging a moral tradition we are already indebted to and should work to more fulsomely incorporate this theory into our broader tradition. We are, after all, to quote the apostle Paul, "without excuse."

20

Baptists and the Contemporary Challenge to Religious Liberty

By R. Albert Mohler Jr.

Baptists came to the affirmation of religious liberty driven by both theological logic and practical experience. Thus, from the beginning of the Baptist movement the impetus for religious freedom has included both an internal and external dimension.

The internal dimension, driven by theological convictions, has been consistently driven by ardent conversionism. Although other Nonconformists had shared a belief in the necessity of conversion, Baptists emerged as the most eager conversionists, and Baptist congregations included only those who gave testimony of conversion to Christ and had obeyed Christ in believer's baptism. Simply put, a commitment to conversionism is, at the very least, a commitment to the need for religious liberty—a liberty that includes the freedom to obey Christ, to form congregations of regenerate members, and to preach the gospel.

Baptists in the United Kingdom and United States

The external dimension, driven by historical events, can be traced to the fact that, from the first emergence of Baptists in seventeenth-century England, Baptists were marked as outsiders. The British Parliament's second Act of Uniformity (1662) made clear that Baptists could expect hostility from the state and from the state church, the Church of England. Nonconformists were considered outlaws of sorts, and their congregations were considered no church at all. Baptists quickly linked religious liberty with the freedom to preach the gospel, organize gospel churches, baptize believers, and maintain a Baptist ministry. For Baptists, the commitment to religious liberty has never been a matter of mere theologizing—it has been driven by both experience and doctrine.

Thus, religious freedom is a central feature of Baptist theology and heritage. From figures like Thomas Helwys (see chapter 2), John Murton, and Roger Williams (chapter 3) in the seventeenth century, or Isaac Backus (chapter 7) and John Leland (chapter 6) in the eighteenth century, to our present context, Baptists have embraced and advocated freedom of conscience. Baptists understand the importance of religious liberty as a requirement for human flourishing. Furthermore, the context of liberty creates more favorable circumstances for the free preaching and promulgation of the gospel.

Through the centuries of Baptist experience in Britain and America, the context that frames the concerns of religious liberty has changed multiple times. In Great Britain, official strictures against the Baptists and other Nonconformists had declined significantly by the late nineteenth century. It was not until the Universities Tests Act of 1871 that all Nonconformists were allowed to apply for admission at Oxford and Cambridge. By the end of the Victorian age, Nonconformists could attend universities and sit in Parliament.

But Britain remained a class-bound society in which Baptists appeared low in social rank and privilege. Legal discrimination had been reduced, but the Baptists were overwhelmingly drawn from the working classes and their great congregations, such as Charles Spurgeon's famed Metropolitan

Tabernacle, which were largely located across the Thames or on the periphery of London's seats of power.

The twentieth century, marked by two horrifying world wars and seemingly endless crises, advanced the process of secularization. By the end of the century, church attendance in Britain was marginal, and the processes of social and moral liberalization had created a climate of increasing intolerance of conservative or orthodox Christian belief.

In the United States, Baptists benefited from the energies of religious liberty that framed the constitutional order in the young republic. Baptist congregations proliferated on the frontier, and in many communities, establishment Baptist congregations, often styled "First Baptist Church," stood at the center of the community, or at least not far away. Baptists also drew energies from the Second Great Awakening and other waves of evangelism and church planting.

The historical context in the United States offered Baptists a very different experience from their brothers and sisters in Britain. Although their presence and prestige were concentrated in the American South and Southwest, Baptists now had the experience of arriving early and helping to establish communities, rather than emerging (as in England) in the context of an established church and its political and cultural dominance. But, more recently, the same "acids of modernity" about which Walter Lippman has warned have produced a similar pattern of more radical secularization. Amid a massive moral and cultural realignment in the United States, today's Baptists find themselves in a very different context.

Religious Freedom in Modernity

In decades past, a consensus in America had undergirded religious freedom—we knew what it meant, why it was important, and that it was rightly understood as America's first freedom. Now, however, we cannot take that consensus for granted. Modernity, the rise of secularism, and a radical progressivist agenda beholden to the sexual and gender revolutions has undermined the fundamental commitment to religious freedom in America. We can no longer assume that people understand what we mean by religious freedom, nor can we assume that everyone upholds this liberty as a right worthy of protecting. Consider, for example, the massive changes in the American political landscape from the overwhelming passage of the Religious Freedom Restoration Act of 1993 to our current cultural predicament.

Not only has understanding of religious freedom devolved over the past three decades, but the commitment to defending it has seemingly evaporated in many circles. Religious freedom is now often placed in scare quotes and is frequently labeled as a disguise for bigotry or discrimination. The cultural pressure today tends to replace religious freedom with the newly invented rights of the sexual revolution, with liberty of conscience and freedom of speech giving way to the demands of the LGBTQ movement. Indeed, religious freedom is now a liberty or set of liberties that can only manifest in the private confines of one's home or church—religious convictions, apparently, have no place in the public square. Time will tell whether even our private homes will remain safe havens for religious freedom.

We find ourselves, therefore, at a cultural crisis. If religious freedom dissipates, the consequences would be catastrophic for the American experiment in ordered liberty. Given the history and legacy of Baptists and their advocacy for religious freedom, it is incumbent upon us to reassert the need for this first freedom, what was meant by it, and why it is crucial to the flourishing not only of the religious, but all Americans.

Religious Freedom without the Bible?

In the aftermath of the Second World War, many nations came together to adopt the Universal Declaration of Human Rights.[1] This represented

---

[1] United Nations General Assembly, "Universal Declaration of Human Rights," United Nations, December 10, 1948, un.org/en/about-us/universal-declaration-of -human-rights.

the high watermark of twentieth-century internationalism, and the moral urgency was certainly understandable. The world had, in the span of forty years, undergone two unimaginable catastrophes. Zbigniew Brzezinski, national security advisor to President Jimmy Carter, described the twentieth century as the "century of megadeath."[2] Given the tragedies and atrocities the world faced after two World Wars, the Holocaust, and the realities emerging from the Soviet Union, the hope amongst the nations was to establish the primacy and fundamental nature of human rights—something that all nations, regardless of one's nationality, race, or religion, would recognize as inherently tethered to what it meant to be human. Eventually, more than 190 countries affirmed at least parts of the "Universal Declaration of Human Rights."

What seemed like a triumph turned out to be an empty moment. The declaration offered no rationale for human rights. It asserted that a species of rights exists, including rights eloquently prescribed in the American Declaration of Independence: life, liberty, and the pursuit of happiness. Without an ontological ballast to secure its conception of "human rights," however, the "Universal Declaration" included rights to economic security and lifelong employment. It became a mixture of claims classically defined as basic human rights along with newly invented and blatantly artificial rights. The failure of the declaration as a substantive document was eclipsed by the inability of the combined nations to enforce its tenets. Indeed, many nations that signed it, either in 1948 or in subsequent years, were great and eager violators of its precepts.

What the declaration did, however, was muddy the waters concerning what was understood as a human right. Suddenly, lifelong employment enjoyed the same status of a fundamental human right as freedom of religion or freedom of speech. The declaration confused the conception of a human right, which explains why, in our present context, a litany of new

---

[2] Zbigniew Brzezinski, *Out of Control: Global Turmoil on the Eve of the 21st Century* (New York: Simon & Schuster, 1995), especially 7–18.

"rights" has arisen with vigor. In many cases, these newly invented "rights" directly collide with classical freedoms like religious liberty. Indeed, Mary Ann Glendon, the Learned Hand Professor of Law at Harvard Law School, argued in her book *Rights Talk: The Impoverishment of Political Discourse* that the burgeoning quest to equalize newly invented individual "rights" with ideas like religious freedom actually undermined the cause of human rights altogether.[3] She concluded that "rights talk" had been severed from the concept of commensurate responsibility—that a freedom did not equate with individual license to do whatever one pleased but was connected to the broader social and cultural fabric of a community.[4] Thus, because rights increasingly became individualized, all rights, including religious freedom, were weakened.

Hence, there exists the present crisis facing many of the fundamental freedoms that have upheld Western civilization. The problems, however, are far deeper than Glendon realizes. She correctly diagnosed that rights talk gravitated around idolatrous individualism; but behind that was the loss of a metaphysical grounding for human rights. Moral assertions sundered from ontological reality cannot persist. If an assertion does not correspond to what is real, what is rooted in God's created order, then human flourishing is impossible. We are in trouble.

Three stages explain how we ended up in our present predicament. First, before modernity, intellectuals, and especially theologians, based rights supernaturally—this was the stage of *supernatural rights*. Thomas Aquinas, the great paragon of this argument, grounded what we call rights in human dignity, which was based upon the gift of the divine Creator. This conception recognized that God not only created human beings in his image, but also formed the world as the theater of his glory. Thus, any conception of

---

[3] Mary Ann Glendon, *Rights Talk: The Impoverishment of Political Discourse* (New York: The Free Press, 1991).

[4] For more on this argument, see especially chapter 4 of Glendon, *Rights Talk*, 76–108.

rights, in this stage, was inherently tethered to the Christian worldview. The existence of the God of the Bible, named or unnamed, secured human dignity and human rights.

The second stage was *natural rights*, which we can clearly see in the language of the Declaration of Independence, as it speaks of men endowed by their Creator with certain unalienable rights. The "Creator" was not named as the God of the Bible. This conception of natural rights arose from the Enlightenment, and for the American context, the English Enlightenment exerted the most significant influence on the American political and philosophical tradition.[5] Unlike more radical manifestations of the Enlightenment in France or Germany, the English Enlightenment was not necessarily anti-supernatural. But it was also not explicitly Christian.

Regardless, the vestiges of a Christian worldview still undergirded the conception of rights that took form in the early American republic.[6] That is to say, natural and supernatural rights synthesized into what became the American experiment in ordered liberty. The Bill of Rights, moreover, upheld the crucial idea that governments do not create rights. Indeed, because of nature and nature's God, certain rights were understood as pre-political, which meant they possessed an unassailable character deserving of the utmost protection and preservation.

The final drift was from natural rights to mere legal rights. The worldview that birthed the American Constitution disappeared, giving way to a regime of positive law—which is to say, whatever the law declares real *is* real. No longer supernatural or pre-political, rights became explicitly political, reduced to "positive" rights with no metaphysical foundation. In

---

[5] For the influence of the English Enlightenment during the American Revolution, see C. Bradley Thompson, *America's Revolutionary Mind: A Moral History of the American Revolution and the Declaration That Defined It* (New York: Encounter Books, 2019).

[6] For a survey of the Christian influence on America's founding, see Mark David Hall, *Did America Have a Christian Founding?* (Nashville: Thomas Nelson, 2019).

this new scheme, whatever the legislature and courts decree (or activists demand) is now the new system of rights and liberties. This means the "right" to identify as a gender different from the sex discovered at birth and to demand other people recognize one as such can eclipse the right to religious freedom or freedom of speech. Alasdair MacIntyre, for example, described the modern denial that natural rights exist at all: "There are no such things as rights and there are no such rights, and belief in them is one with belief in witches and in unicorns."[7] To be clear, MacIntyre was not against rights. He meant that metaphysical grounding for rights has disappeared in the larger culture. Now, believing in objective, ontological rights is just as fanciful as believing in a unicorn. Moreover, Leo Strauss declared, "Modern notions of human rights have undermined the classical notion of natural rights."[8] In other words, these newly invented rights do not merely join the classical rights on the landscape. Instead, they push them entirely aside.

Jeremy Bentham, the utilitarian philosopher, rejected the notion of human rights, calling them "nonsense upon stilts."[9] If human rights, including religious freedom, are nothing more than "nonsense upon stilts," then the entire human race is in a precarious state. Indeed, if Bentham's thesis, and the current vector of rights talk in modernity is sustained, then nothing can stop society from declaring that a human boy possesses the same dignity as a rat or a dog or a pig. That claim has already been made.[10]

---

[7] Alasdair MacIntyre, *After Virtue: A Study in Moral Theory* (Notre Dame, IN: University of Notre Dame, 2007), 69.

[8] Leo Strauss, *Natural Rights and History* (Chicago: University of Chicago, 1953), 128.

[9] Jeremy Bentham, *Rights, Representation, and Reform: Nonsense upon Stilts and Other Writings on the French Revolution*, ed. P. Schofield, C. Pease-Watkin, and C. Blamires (Oxford: Oxford University, 2002).

[10] Ingrid Newkirk, "A Rat Is a Pig Is a Dog Is a Boy," PETA, last modified March 6, 2015, https://www.peta.org/blog/rat-pig-dog-boy/.

Religious Freedom in the Bible

The Christian worldview, however, rejects the subjectivized rights talk that dominates present political discourse. The case we must make, especially in our present "rights crisis," is one of rights and freedoms rooted in ontological reality—rights rooted in creation, which extend from the one true God. We face a moral imperative, and Baptists, standing upon our rich tradition, must confront the moral and ideological temptations that would plunge society into an inescapable chaotic spiral. With this in mind, I want to posit five theses about human rights from a Baptist theology.

First, genuine rights are possessed by all human beings as the gift of the Creator. This represents a Christian assertion of rights grounded in a distinctly Christian understanding of human dignity. This means all human beings, even before they are born, bear this identity and enjoy its privileges. From the moment of fertilization until the time of natural death, human beings under every situation and condition, including those with or without consciousness, retain this dignity because of who they are in the image of God.

Second, genuine rights are defined by the commands of God and the order of creation. Rights, therefore, do not emerge from a vacuum. God defines them and has endowed men and women, by his grace, with the capacity to discover these rights in the order of creation.

Third, given the reality of God's created order and the dignity men and women have as image-bearers, all rights are pre-political. Religious freedom does not exist because the United States government declared it into existence. Religious freedom exists because God established it in his creation. Governments, therefore, exist to preserve and protect those pre-political rights. Indeed, in the case of religious freedom, consider Jesus's response to the Pharisees in Matthew 22 when they asked him about paying taxes to Caesar. Jesus declared, "Give, then, to Caesar the things that are Caesar's, and to God the things that are God's" (v. 21). This astounding answer indicated that *two* images were in focus—one being an image on a coin, but the other being the image of God. The coin belonged to Caesar; after all, his image was on it. But the soul belongs to God. It does not and cannot belong to Caesar because God did not grant any civil power dominion over the conscience or soul.

Fourth, rights that affirm the dignity of life as a divine gift and respect the conscience are the cornerstone of all the other rights. Preserving life, enhancing human flourishing, and respecting the operations of the conscience indicate a well-ordered society. Moreover, the lack of protection for human life as a gift and for the sacredness of the conscience erodes all other fundamental rights, making them less binding and inevitably destroying them.

Fifth, rights will survive only if they remain sufficiently acknowledged as gifts of the divine Creator. Rights that exist only as products of political negotiation and positive law are rights that are inherently fragile, even artificial.

Again, these theses have marked Baptist theology throughout the centuries. Additionally, religious freedom arose as the chief right articulated by Baptists, which they grounded in two vital doctrinal affirmations, namely, conversion and the believers' church. By lacing those two theological convictions together, Baptists reasoned the following: if the church is made up of only believers in Jesus Christ and if believers in Jesus Christ are those who have repented of their sins and, by faith, turned toward obedience to Christ, then what results is an ecclesiology that demands believers and believers *alone* are members of local churches. Thus, as Baptists believed, freedom of conscience preserved the purity of the church by ensuring that nobody, through coercion, hypocritically continued as members of Christ's church. Furthermore, religious freedom created the conditions where the conscience could operate as God created it—assenting to the truth of the gospel summons by its own volition, rather than through civil force.

The Baptist tradition reveals that Baptists have been the first-line defenders of religious liberty. That is a heritage we must preserve. Regrettably, I fear Baptists belie our distinct legacy. Presently, we are not contending for freedom of conscience and religious freedom like our forebears did; we are not critically assessing what is at stake and how to answer the rise of the secular rights now vying to displace religious freedom. We have taken for granted the freedoms guaranteed not only for our good but for the good of our neighbor, and we are watching religious freedom swiftly disappear before our eyes.

Indeed, we stand on the other side of a great revolution that includes the secularization of the culture around us. Secularization is, quite simply, the loss of the binding authority of theism. This does not mean religion disappears. It does, however, indicate that the binding authority of theism dissipates, giving way to a secular and necessarily subjective understanding of humanity. Consider recent examples in American politics. In the last year of the Trump administration, Secretary of State Mike Pompeo initiated a Commission on Unalienable Rights. It immediately created controversy because, according to the secular mind, the commission prioritized certain rights over others, creating a hierarchy at odds with a progressive agenda. Those on the Left demote religious freedom and freedom of speech, making them equal to, or in most cases lesser than, the newly invented sexual rights of the LGBTQ revolution.

Pompeo's commission produced an argument consistent with the American founding about the importance of unalienable rights and the need to define what those rights are. Consequently, the commission claimed other "rights" as synthetic; thus, a "right" to same-sex marriage is not pre-political like the right to religious freedom. The latter is rooted in the natural order while the former is a political creation. As can be guessed, Pompeo's successor, Antony Blinken, disbanded the commission, declaring, "Human rights are . . . co-equal; there is no hierarchy that makes some rights more important than others."[11]

---

[11] Quoted in Matthew Lee, "Blinken Ends Trump Rights Plan Promoting Conservative Agenda," *Associated Press*, March 30, 2021, https://apnews.com

Thus, the main collision right now is not merely between religious liberty and the newly contrived sexual liberties. The contest is one between liberty from the classical, and inherently theological, understanding of rights rooted in human dignity and an ideology purporting that there is no such thing as pre-political rights.

Contemporary Contest and the Baptist Response

Will America sacrifice religious freedom for the sake of subjective, secularized notions of rights? Will the fundamental rights that have shaped our society—rights rooted in human dignity and who we are as beings made in the image of God—give way to the radicalized, progressive agenda seeking to push freedom of conscience to the precipice? We will know the answer to that question in short order, and the prospects for preserving religious liberty hang in dangerous political balance.

Our present predicament can only be described as a moral revolution. Such a moral revolution is not merely an alteration in morality—a true moral revolution amounts to a capacious and fundamental transformation of the entire moral fabric of a society. Revolutions have happened before throughout human history, but the most recent example is the sexual revolution. Over the past half century, this revolution has swept the culture, transforming the entire landscape and mode of life, demanding a total redefinition of marriage, sexuality, what it means to be male and female, and consequently, our rights as citizens.

The erosion of liberal support for the liberties and freedoms enshrined in the Constitution comes down to this: the moral revolution is incompatible with theism. This revolution encompasses a constellation of issues—everything from abortion to LGBTQ issues to euthanasia to personal autonomy—all of which require the imposition of state power at the expense of liberty. If the

/article/antony-blinken-foreign-policy-mike-pompeo-85c3cbfb0bec09ed85fc8f
b6b6e5fd29.

entire moral fabric of a society is to be undone, the state will have to get involved. If a revolution is to be driven in the culture, the state will need to coerce. And the state is usually eager to coerce.

Theo Hobson, a British theologian and defender of the moral shift, defined a moral revolution this way: that which was repudiated must be celebrated. That which was celebrated must be repudiated. Those who will not celebrate must themselves be repudiated. He wrote:

> The public change in attitude towards homosexuality is not just the waning of a taboo. It is not just a case of practice losing its aura of immorality (as with premarital sex or illegitimacy). Instead, the case for homosexual equality takes the form of a moral crusade. Those who want to uphold the old attitude are not just dated moralists (as is the case with those who want to uphold the old attitude to premarital sex or illegitimacy). They are accused of moral deficiency. The old taboo surrounding this practice does not disappear but "bounces back" at those who seek to uphold it. Such a sharp turnaround is, I think, without parallel in moral history.[12]

In other words, homosexuality, once universally repudiated, is now celebrated. It must be celebrated. Marriage, as traditionally understood between one man and one woman, is now condemned as a vestige of a bygone, oppressive era. Finally, those who still uphold that traditional view of marriage and sexuality must be condemned with the utmost vitriol.

That formula captures what we can easily witness when it comes to the sexual revolution in Western civilization. Throughout *all* human history, anything associated with homosexuality or transgenderism (admittedly, a modern anachronism) was universally understood as contrary to nature and the moral law—indeed, for some of the letters in LGBTQ, there would not have even been an intellectual or moral category available.

---

[12] Theo Hobson, "A Pink Reformation," *Guardian* (UK), February 5, 2007, https://www.theguardian.com/commentisfree/2007/feb/05/apinkreformation.

That, however, has now changed. Following Hobson's definition, what was once universally condemned is now celebrated. Not only that, but what was once upheld as good and true is now condemned. This is a key element of a moral revolution. LGBTQ advocates are not merely concerned with toleration toward their ethical claims. Indeed, they are not even satisfied when their position enjoys celebration and affirmation. They demand that divergent moral systems and those who hold to them be condemned, repudiated, canceled, and castigated as outmoded relics of the past.

This leads to the third movement of a moral revolution, namely, the disavowal of those who refuse to assent to the new morality. All dissenters must be rejected and abrogated. They will either be coerced into submission or suffer the societal consequences for their failure to capitulate.

To accomplish legal changes, the sexual revolution has leaned upon the judicial system, seeking to advance its cause through judicial fiat rather than legislative deliberation. The LGBTQ movement has certainly achieved legal victories, such as the Supreme Court's ruling in *Obergefell v. Hodges* in 2015. They have, however, also met some level of resistance within the political system. Despite this, the LGBTQ revolution aims to secure success in the legislative realm—and the consequences could not be more significant.

Religious Freedom and the Equality Act

The Equality Act represents the greatest present threat to religious liberty in the United States. The House of Representatives passed the legislation twice—in 2019 and again in February 2021. The Democratic majority in that chamber has forwarded the bill to the Senate, and President Joe Biden campaigned on a promise to sign the bill. (Adding to this threat is the so-called Respect for Marriage Act [RMA], which Joe Biden signed into law in December 2022, mandating both federal and state recognition of same-sex marriages that took place in jurisdictions in which such "marriages" are considered legal. The RMA repeals the Defense of Marriage Act, which protected a state's right not to recognize a same-sex marriage that occurred in another jurisdiction. Space does not permit for a full discussion of this more-recent legislation, but suffice it to say that the RMA presents yet another challenge to religious liberty, with the Alliance Defending Freedom describing the legislation as having an "adverse impact on religious exercise and freedom of conscience."[13])

The Equality Act, however, is still pending legislation and is a defining issue for the entire nation, as it threatens the structure of our rights and liberties as Americans. It is the front line, so to speak, on that contest between natural rights and the merely political rights advocated by progressives. The act would amend the Civil Rights Act to add sex, sexual orientation, and gender identity to protected classes covered by the bill. The scope of the measure is vast, covering housing, employment, public accommodations, education, credit, and all programs receiving federal funding. No aspect of American public life would be unchanged, and the bill would invade the private sphere as well. The legislation would make the operation of a Christian college or philanthropy virtually impossible.

Beyond the direct legislative reach of the bill, the Equality Act would send a clear message throughout the culture with both national and international consequences. The forces pushing for the passage of the bill clearly intend those consequences. A moral message will be telegraphed throughout society, normalizing virtually everything comprehended within the ever-expanding categories of LGBTQ+ and condemning all individuals, churches, and institutions that would stand in its way.

The Equality Act, moreover, is not merely a communicative message. It is a draconian threat of legal, political, financial, and cultural coercion, and the coercive powers of the new moral order will be directly applied against any resistance. Make no mistake about it: that coercion will be brought against religious schools, ministries, nonprofits, and all religious

---

[13] Gregory S. Baylor, "What You Should Know about the Respect for Marriage Act," Alliance for Defending Freedom, last revised December 14, 2022, https://adflegal.org/article/what-you-should-know-about-respect-marriage-act.

institutions. The bill does not even acknowledge the sacred rights of religious congregations and denominations. The Equality Act, as it stands, contains no meaningful religious liberty exemptions or protections. That is intentional. Its advocates do not see the need for those protections, and the political left wing—the forces most eagerly behind the moral revolution—actively oppose those protections. Individual believers, too, will be coerced into compliance with the new moral regime, which is coming with a vengeance.

Yet, even if the Equality Act was amended to contain some religious liberty protections, those exemptions would, most likely, have extremely constrained boundaries. Those protections would almost assuredly be merely for churches, synagogues, mosques, and explicitly religious institutions serving a definable religious purpose. Exemptions like that would not encompass, for example, Christian colleges and universities—they would only cover aspects of those institutions that are specifically designated for the training of ministers; also, not covered here are Christians in the workplace and in the marketplace. Indeed, the wedding industry itself presents massive problems for Christian bakers, florists, and photographers who do not want to provide a service for something they believe is harmful, destructive, and a violation of their conscience. As it stands, the Equality Act would steamroll those claims of religious liberty.

Religious freedom cannot be reduced to a mere cultural affirmation. The Soviet Union claimed to respect religious liberty, even as millions disappeared into the gulags. Any subversion of religious liberty is a downgrade at odds with what is enshrined in the Constitution. It makes religious freedom a melting iceberg in a larger progressive ocean. That iceberg will eventually melt, until nothing is left.

During the oral arguments for the *Obergefell* case before the Supreme Court, Solicitor General Donald Verrilli, arguing for same-sex marriage, was asked by Justice Samuel Alito whether religious colleges and universities would eventually be forced to allow same-sex couples to live in student housing. Verrilli, without skipping a beat, responded, "It will be an issue."

You can bet it will be an issue. Student housing for married couples is but one in an apparently endless list of other accommodations the LGBTQ community now demands. But note that Justice Alito's question was pointedly defined regarding the coercion of a *religious* college or university. The solicitor general did not hesitate to affirm the threat against religious schools. As soon as the Supreme Court mandated the legalization of same-sex marriage in that case, the coercion of Christians and other citizens of religious conviction became an issue.

In clear-minded dissents to the *Obergefell v. Hodges* majority, Chief Justice John G. Roberts Jr., Justice Antonin Scalia, and Justice Clarence Thomas joined Alito in warning of the threat to religious liberty posed by the decision.

Then, five years later, the Supreme Court handed down its decision in *Bostock v. Clayton County*, extending federal employment nondiscrimination rights to citizens claiming LGBTQ identity. The decision turned mostly on sexual orientation and transgender issues, but the effects will cover the entire array of LGBTQ identity. Sadly, the majority opinion was written by Justice Neil Gorsuch, who went so far as to acknowledge that the decision would pose legal vulnerabilities for religious believers and that the questions would "merit careful consideration." In his dissent in this case, Justice Alito argued that the Court's majority had created a threat to the religious liberties of religious Americans and their religious institutions. He was clearly right.

The Equality Act would not only establish *Bostock* as federal law, but it would expand the reach of the law far beyond the text of the Court's decision. Put plainly, the legislation includes no acknowledgement of the right of Christian colleges and schools, for example, to hire teachers in accord with the school's stated religious convictions. The same would be extended to all other dimensions of operation covered by the bill—and almost nothing would escape that coverage. Individual believers and their private businesses would be covered, as would any institutional entity.

Furthermore, the text of the Equality Act specifically precludes any claims of religious liberty based on the Religious Freedom Restoration Act, which was adopted by Congress in 1993 with overwhelming bipartisan support. This bill would put Congress in the position of denying *in advance* defenses made on the basis of its own previous action. The audacity is breathtaking, and the threat to America's first liberty is all too real.

The lead sponsor of the Equality Act in the House of Representatives is an openly gay congressman who is confident of ultimate victory in the current Congress. When he was asked about the threat the act would present to religious institutions and their right to operate by their own religious convictions, David Cicilline, a Democrat from Rhode Island, offered these chilling words: "The determination would have to be made as to whether or not the decisions they are making are connected to their religious teachings and to their core functions as a religious organization," he explained, "or is it a pretext to discriminate?"[14]

The determination will have to be made. With those words, every religious congregation, denomination, and institution is put on notice: the government will determine whether your hiring and housing and student conduct and employee policies are truly "connected" to your religious teachings or you are merely using a claim of religious conviction as a "pretext to discriminate." These words mean the effective death of religious liberty, for the burden of proof will now fall to each religious institution to prove *to the government's satisfaction* that its convictions are authentic.

Furthermore, the United States government would be effectively transformed into an anti-theological state. Note carefully that the specific forms of religion targeted by the Equality Act share one major theological distinctive: each, in its own way, makes a claim to written revelation. Each of those religious texts defines sexuality, marriage, and gender in explicitly theological terms. The Torah, the Bible, the Quran, the Book of Mormon, and

---

[14] Quoted in Tom Gjelten, "Some Faith Leaders Call Equality Act Devastating; For Others, It's God's Will," *NPR*, March 10, 2021, https://www.npr.org/2021/03/10/974672313/some-faith-leaders-call-equality-act-devastating-for-others-its-gods-will.

other religious texts are recognized by American citizens as divinely inspired, and their religious bodies range, according to theological convictions, from Orthodox Judaism to Roman Catholicism to Evangelical Protestantism to Islam to Mormonism to the Seventh-day Adventist Church and more.

Evangelicals and Catholics, Orthodox Jews and Muslims, Seventh-day Adventists and Mormons all understand the radical theological differences that separate us. But the factor common to all is the claim of an authoritative Scripture. That is the central fact that explains the antipathy of the moral revolutionaries and their willingness to deploy the coercive powers of the state against believers. Those religious texts are incompatible with the normalization of LGBTQ identities, behaviors, relationships, and gender confusions.

The Equality Act, therefore, represents the threat of government coercion against a certain structure of theology, doctrine, and morality. This means the threat of the state against any claim of divine revelation that contradicts the new morality, the newly minted definition of marriage, and the newly constructed "rights" of the LGBTQ revolution.

Visible before our eyes is the rise of an anti-theological state and the end of authentic religious liberty in America. Do not take my word for it—just take Congressman Cicilline's. Indeed, the threats against religious liberty and religious conviction will soon challenge every institution that dares to live by its theology.

Conclusion

Given the trajectories of secularism, the shifts in rights from supernatural to natural to political, none of this should surprise us. On the contrary, why would any of us have concluded that secular people would think religious liberty is something particularly important for a society? The erosion of binding authority, the lack of ontological order, and the eradication of human dignity rightly understood not only threaten religious freedom, but every true human right codified in the US Constitution. This is where we are in our present moment.

This does not mean that, contrary to Jesus's promise to his disciples, the gates of hell *will* in fact prevail over his church. We know, no matter what happens in the United States or anywhere in the world, nothing will stop the God of the universe from accomplishing his purposes, protecting his church, and spreading the gospel to the ends of the earth.

The Baptist tradition reminds us of this humbling, sober reality. Thomas Helwys and John Murton preached the gospel and proclaimed Baptist theology. They advocated for religious freedom. They both were imprisoned for their beliefs, with Helwys dying in prison. They proclaimed the truth, regardless of the laws and statutes enforced to prevent them from spreading their message.

Today, this means Baptists must recognize that churches will survive without cultural affirmation. Churches will survive, and do survive even today, where there is no religious freedom. Put us in jail, take away our earthly goods, do your worst—we will not ask permission from the powers that be. Whatever happens in the unfolding of history, we will still preach the gospel, plunge believers under water, tell people about Jesus, and sing the old, old story of Jesus and his love.[15]

This does not, however, make religious liberty any less relevant. Indeed, remember Caesar's coin and Jesus's response to the Pharisees. The civil state has *no* claim over the conscience. That which belongs to God—our souls, our deepest religious convictions—belongs to God *alone*. As Thomas Helwys wrote:

> Hear O King, and diligently note the counsel of your poor, and let their complaints come before thee. The king is a mortal man, and not God, therefore hath no power over the immortal souls of his subjects, to make laws and ordinances for them, and to set spiritual Lords over them. If the king have authority to make spiritual Lords

---

[15] The bulk of this paragraph was adapted from R. Albert Mohler Jr., "Why I Am a Baptist," *First Things*, accessed January 29, 2021, https://www.firstthings.com/article/2020/08/why-i-am-a-baptist.

and laws, then he is an immortal God and not a mortal man. O king, be not seduced by deceivers to sin so against God whom thou oughtest to obey, nor against thy poor subjects who ought and will obey thee in all things with body life and goods, or else let their lives be taken from the earth. God save the king.[16]

That reminder to James I in 1612 is just as pertinent to the American political conversations in our present moment. No government has authority over souls; we are all mortal men and women, and anyone who dares to make the determination as to what is and what is not a sincerely held belief, and whether that belief deserves protection, is trying to play the role of God.

Furthermore, we recognize the disastrous consequences when any civil authority attempts to destroy that separation and usurp God's authority over the conscience. Out of love for our neighbor, we cannot passively watch as America's first freedom suffers blow after blow and moves closer toward complete eradication.

Much will be required of us as we contend for religious freedom. As argued at the beginning of this chapter, I believe we have taken for granted the freedom of conscience. As such, our apologetical defense of this liberty and its importance is now anemic. We must reinvigorate our understanding of rights, freedoms, and how they extend from God and his created order. We must declare, with boldness and intelligence, the central importance of religious freedom. This freedom is not only vital for the religious, but for all who wish to think freely and contemplate without fear of civil retribution the most important questions any human could ask.

Human flourishing, and our entire constitutional order, is at stake with every legal and legislative attempt to undermine religious liberty. It is incumbent upon us believers to reclaim our long tradition of advocating soul freedom.

---

[16] Thomas Helwys, *A Shorte Declaration of the Mistery of Iniquity* (Amsterdam: n.p., 1612). The quote does not have a page number because it is, in Helwys's own handwriting, a letter affixed to the beginning of the work before the title page.

21

Baptist Perspectives on Bioethics and Human Dignity

By C. Ben Mitchell

Human dignity has fallen on hard times. Philosopher and bio-ethicist Ruth Macklin of Albert Einstein College of Medicine dubbed human dignity a "useless concept."[1] In a now-famous article in the *New Republic,* Harvard cognitive psychologist and best-selling author Steven Pinker assailed the notion of dignity as "stupidity."[2] If these assessments are true, if appeals to human dignity are folly, what are the implications for the cluster of human goods we have sought to protect, such as human rights, human freedom, self-determination, and liberty of conscience? Can these basic human rights survive the assassination of human dignity?

---

[1] Ruth Macklin, "Dignity Is a Useless Concept," *British Medical Journal* 327, no. 7429 (December 2003): 327.

[2] Steven Pinker, "The Stupidity of Dignity," *New Republic*, May 27, 2008, https://newrepublic.com/article/64674/the-stupidity-dignity.

To add to the urgency of answering those questions, human dignity continues to possess significant currency not only in popular imagination but especially in bioethical and legal literature. Roberto Andorno, senior research fellow and lecturer at the Institute of Biomedical Ethics of the University of Zurich, maintains that the notion of human dignity is so ubiquitous in intergovernmental documents in biomedicine that "it is therefore not exaggerated to characterize it as the 'overarching principle' of international biolaw."[3] Writing in the *Bulletin of the World Health Organization* (WHO), Andorno further observes:

> Perhaps the two most distinctive features of international instruments relating to biomedicine are the very central role given to the notion of "human dignity" and the integration of the common standards that are adopted into a human rights framework. This is not surprising if we consider that human dignity is one of the few common values in our world of philosophical pluralism. Moreover, in our time, a widespread assumption is that the "inherent dignity . . . of all members of the human family" is the ground of human rights and democracy. It is indeed difficult, if not impossible, to provide a justification of human rights without making some reference, at least implicitly, to the idea of human dignity. This notion is usually associated with supreme importance, fundamental value and inviolability of the human person.[4]

In fact, all of the major international treaties and conventions that speak to bioethical issues invoke the notion of human dignity. For instance, following the Nazis' infamous atrocities and the subsequent Nuremberg Trials, one

---

[3] Roberto Andorno, "Human Dignity and Human Rights as a Common Ground for a Global Bioethics," *Journal of Medicine and Philosophy* 34, no. 3 (2009): 223–40.

[4] Roberto Andorno, "Biomedicine and International Human Rights Law: In Search of a Global Consensus," *Bulletin of the World Health Organization* 80, no. 12 (2002): 960. https://www.who.int/bulletin/archives/80(12)959.pdf

of the earliest and most formative affirmations of human dignity and human rights in the twentieth century is found in the United Nations' "Universal Declaration of Human Rights" (1948):

> Whereas recognition of the inherent dignity and of the equal and inalienable rights of all members of the human family is the foundation of freedom, justice and peace in the world. . . . All human beings are born free and equal in dignity and rights. They are endowed with reason and conscience and should act towards one another in a spirit of brotherhood. [5]

Note that the declaration points to "the inherent dignity" and "the equal and inalienable rights of all members of the human family." Human dignity and human rights are viewed as complementary concepts. This juxtaposition seems to commit the declaration's authors and signers to the view that human dignity is intrinsic to being human. That is, to be human is to possess inherent dignity independent from any capacity to exercise the rights that flow from it, simply by virtue of being a member of the species *Homo sapiens*. Every human being possesses human dignity; therefore, every human being has certain inalienable rights.

Interestingly, Jacques Maritain, one of the philosophers who consulted on the development of the declaration, said, "We agree about the rights but on condition that no one asks us why!"[6] What I take him to mean is the framers of the declaration understood that human rights are grounded in human dignity, but they could not offer a philosophically rich definition of human dignity. Framers of earlier documents defending human rights

---

[5] United Nations General Assembly, "Universal Declaration of Human Rights," United Nations, December 10, 1948, un.org/en/about-us/universal-declaration -of-human-rights. It is no accident that article 1, section 1 of the constitution of Germany, the Basic Law (1949), begins by affirming that "the dignity of man is inviolable."

[6] Quoted in Cass R. Sunstein, *The Second Bill of Rights: FDR's Unfinished Revolution and Why We Need It More Than Ever* (New York: Basic Books, 2004).

(e.g., the Magna Carta, the Declaration of the Rights of Man, and the Bill of Rights) seemed to know why, but their progeny had forgotten by the time of the UN declaration.

What Is Human Dignity?

How, then, are we to understand human dignity? What is it? What is its genesis? What does it mean? And, especially, what does it mean for bioethics? Can human dignity be at once both profound and indecipherable? What is its role in bioethics and biopolicy?

Alasdair Cochrane is lecturer in human rights at the Centre for the Study of Human Rights at the London School of Economics and Political Science. In an insightful review in the journal *Bioethics*, Cochrane explicates four conceptions of human dignity that are generally consistent with those found elsewhere in bioethics literature.[7] First, dignity may be construed as virtuous behavior. This notion is regularly invoked, says Cochrane, when praising individuals for their ethical behavior, self-control, or endurance in the face of suffering.

Second, human dignity may connote inherent moral worth. To be human is to possess dignity. Because one is a member of *Homo sapiens*, respect for one's person is required regardless of race, religion, gender, age, nationality, etc. Third, Kantian dignity points to a property or properties not necessarily inherent in every individual of the species, but in those with the capacities for Kantian personhood, that is, rational moral agency and autonomous free will. Kant famously argued that rational, autonomous persons are ends-in-themselves and may not, therefore, be used to serve someone else's ends. By extension, however, a Kantian anthropology would not recognize dignity for humans who have never possessed or who have lost rational capacity and free will.

---

[7] Alasdair Cochrane, "Undignified Bioethics," *Bioethics*, 24, no. 5 (June 2010): 234–41.

Finally, dignity may refer to species integrity; that is, to a form of flourishing. In this sense dignity is not a property but a way of functioning. So patients or family members sometimes say that a patient has lost her dignity if she loses control of her bodily functions. Or a person may describe losing their dignity through dehumanizing treatment such as torture or rape.

To add to the variety of ways the notion is elucidated, in their volume *Human Dignity in Bioethics and Biolaw*, Deryck Beyleveld and Roger Brownsword collapse their understanding of human dignity into two notions in tension with each other: human dignity as empowerment and human dignity as constraint. Human dignity as empowerment roughly corresponds to intrinsic human dignity: "the empowerment that comes with the right to respect for one's dignity as a human and the right to the conditions in which human dignity can flourish."[8] Autonomy, they assert, has priority in this case. Human dignity as constraint limits free choice "by virtue of being a collective good that represents each society's vision of the kind of society it wants to be."[9] Either paternalism or a defense of social goods tends to have priority where human dignity is seen as constraint.

Human Dignity As a Biblical Concept

Although there are other ways to explicate human dignity,[10] theologically speaking, human dignity is another way of describing what it means to be made in the image of God (*imago Dei*). According to the Bible, only human

---

[8] Deryck Beyleveld and Roger Brownsword, *Human Dignity in Bioethics and Biolaw* (Oxford: Oxford University, 2002), 11.

[9] Beyleveld and Brownsword, 11.

[10] See for instance, Michael D. Greaney, *In Defense of Human Dignity: Essays on the Just Third Way from a Natural Law Perspective* (Washington, DC: Economic Justice Media, 2008); George Kateb, *Human Dignity* (Cambridge: Harvard University, 2011); and the document produced by the President's Council on Bioethics, *Human Dignity and Bioethics: Essays Commissioned by the President's Council on Bioethics* (Washington, DC: US Independent Agencies and Commissions, 2008), https://bioethicsarchive.georgetown.edu/pcbe/reports/human_dignity/index.html.

beings are made in the image of God (Gen 1:27). The verb *bārā'* (to create) is used three times in Genesis 1 (vv. 1, 21, 27) to refer to the creation of humanity. Old Testament scholar Hans Walter Wolff has observed:

> [Adam] is created on the same day as the terrestrial animals (vv. 24–31), and fish and birds are also, through a blessing, given the right to multiply—a right otherwise reserved for man (cf. v. 22 with v. 28); and finally man and the land animals are assigned the same food (vv. 29f.). Yet man's special position is no less clearly brought out. The terrestrial animals, who are created immediately before man on the sixth day, proceed from the earth on the basis of a divine command to it; and God "makes them" (*'śh*) (vv. 24f.). But the man and woman in Gen. 1 do not emerge from the depths of the earth; they are completely and independently created, without the materials being provided beforehand and without the co-operation of the earth (this is characterized by the threefold *br'* in v. 27), by God's own personal decision. . . . The blessing given to man in v. 28 differs fundamentally from that conferred on the fish and the birds in v. 22, in that after they are empowered to multiply, men are entrusted with lordship over the earth and especially over all animals (v. 28b). This defines the decisive difference between man and beast, and it again derives from God's relationship to man.[11]

Genesis 2 says that God made the first man from the "dust from the ground," breathing "the breath of life into his nostrils" (Gen 2:7). God made Adam a "living being" (nepeš).[12] The material of Adam's body was absolutely earthy (cf. Pss 90:3; 103:14); the source of his life was absolutely divine.

---

[11] Hans Walter Wolff, *Anthropology of the Old Testament* (London: SCM, 1974), 95.

[12] The biblical creation account in Genesis 1 and 2 uses the Hebrew noun 'ādām to describe both "humankind" as a species and an individual person named "Adam." When 'ādām is used with the definite article, typically the text is referring

As God's creatures, human beings belong to God. The apostle Paul declared before the philosophers in Athens, "in [God] we live and move and have our being, as even some of your own poets have said, 'For we are also his offspring'" (Acts 17:28). Creatureliness both elevates human beings (in that they are not accidents of history) and humbles them (because God is sovereign over them).

In the beginning, everything God created conformed to his purpose and will and, thus, was "good," except one thing: it was not good for Adam to be alone (Gen 2:18). Adam's loneliness in the absence of a female partner indicates not merely the sexual, but the social character of human beings. So, for humanity's benefit, God graciously ordained that both human sexuality and sociability would find their fullest expression within the covenant of marriage, where one man and one woman would enter a "one flesh" relationship of deep unity for life (Gen 2:23–24).

Made in the Image of God

The "dean" of twentieth century evangelical theologians, Carl F. H. Henry, once said, "The importance of a proper understanding of the *imago Dei* can hardly be overstated. The answer given to the imago-inquiry soon becomes determinative for the entire gamut of doctrinal affirmation. The ramifications are not only theological, but [for] every phase of the . . . cultural enterprise as a whole."[13] Henry was right. As will be seen later, the *imago Dei* has profound implications for understanding what a truly human future might look like. Yet as University of Sheffield professor David J. A. Clines so keenly observes in his benchmark essay on the image of God in the *Tyndale Bulletin*,

---

to "humankind" (as in Gen 1:27). When the noun is used without the definite article, Adam, the man, is usually the object.

[13] Carl F. H. Henry, s.v. "Man," in *Baker's Dictionary of Theology*, ed. Everett F. Harrison (Grand Rapids: Baker, 1960).

The Old Testament references to the doctrine of the image of God in man are tantalizing in their brevity and scarcity; we find only the fundamental sentence in Genesis 1:26 'Let us make men in our image after our likeness', a further reference to man's creation 'in the likeness of God' in Genesis 5:22, and a final statement in Genesis 9:6: 'Whoever sheds the blood of man, by man shall his blood be shed; for God made man in his own image.' Yet we become aware, in reading these early chapters of Genesis and in studying the history of the interpretation of these passages that the importance of the doctrine is out of all proportion to the laconic treatment it receives in the Old Testament.[14]

In fact, there are no other direct statements about the image of God in humankind in the remainder of the Old Testament. Interestingly, however, the Apocrypha contains two very pregnant texts: "For God created man to be immortal, and made him to be an image of his own eternity" (Wis 2:23 KJVA) and "He [the Lord] endued them with strength by themselves, and made them according to his image, and put the fear of man upon all flesh, and gave him dominion over beasts and fowls" (Sir 17:3–4 KJVA). Although noncanonical, these verses may help to illuminate the Genesis account.

In the New Testament, two nouns are used for the image of God. First, *eikōn* ("image") is used in four Pauline letters with respect to the image of God in humankind: 1 Cor 11:7; 2 Cor 3:18; Rom 8:29; and Col 3:9–10. The other noun, *homoiōsis* ("likeness"), is found only in Jas 3:9. Among other things, these verses imply that the image of God was not lost through the fall and that redemption is the beginning of the rehabilitation of the image of God in those being transformed to be like Christ, who is himself the image of God.

---

[14] David J. A. Clines, "The Image of God in Man," *Tyndale Bulletin* 19, no. 1 (1968): 53.

Curiously, Scripture never tells us precisely of what the image of God consists. This indeterminacy has led biblical scholars to argue for a variety of perspectives. Baptist theologian James Leo Garrett Jr. has found at least eight views of the *imago Dei,* including: (1) humankind's erect bodily form, (2) human dominion over nature, (3) human reason, (4) human prelapsarian righteousness, (5) human capacities, (6) juxtaposition between man and woman, (7) responsible creaturehood and moral conformity to God, and (8) some composite view.[15] Another Baptist systematician, Millard J. Erickson, elucidates three general views of the *imago Dei*: substantive views, relational views, and functional views.[16]

Some scholars divide models for understanding the image of God in humankind into two: substantialism and relationalism. The substantialists typically identify that which makes us human as some immaterial aspect of our humanity. For instance, many of the early Fathers of the church, along with Augustine and Aquinas, believed that human rationality was the locus of our humanness. This view was doubtless greatly influenced by Aristotle and was arguably more indebted to Greek anthropology than distinctly Christian notions of human nature.

Relationalists include many in the Reformed tradition; Luther, Calvin, and Barth are notable examples. On this view, human beings are in a special relationship with God. That relationship constitutes what it means to be human. The emphasis is placed on the social aspects of the Trinity as a paradigm for the divine/human relationship. Stanley Rudman raises several cautions about this way of understanding relationality. He says, "The doctrine of the Trinity is not part of a campaign to improve human relationships."[17] That is, an understanding of trinitarian relationality should

---

[15] James Leo Garrett Jr., *Systematic Theology: Biblical, Historical, and Evangelical,* vol. 1 (Grand Rapids: Eerdmans, 1990), 394.

[16] Millard J. Erickson, *Christian Theology* (Grand Rapids: Baker, 1983), 457ff.

[17] Stanley Rudman, *Concepts of Persons and Christian Ethics* (Cambridge: Cambridge University Press, 1997), 172.

not be psychologized in order to explain humanity because (1) the fundamental differences between God as Creator and human beings as created
should not be blurred and (2) direct inferences between inter-trinitarian life
and human relationships are unwarranted because of the sui generis nature
of the Godhead.

Made As *the Image of God*

Does the multiplicity of perspectives on the meaning of the *imago Dei* confirm what detractors like Pinker have claimed? Not at all. Clines offers a
very persuasive argument that Gen 1:26 has been mistranslated. This mis-
translation, I think, is what has led to multiple views on the image of God.[18]

---

[18] The most natural meaning of the Hebrew phrase בצלם אלהים (in the
image of God), says Clines, "is, that God has an image, and that man is created in
conformity with this image." In this case, the prepositional prefix ב would be the
beth of norm. The word would be translated "according to the pattern, or model, of
our image." This interpretation raises a question, however. From the point of view
of ancient Near Eastern thought, Clines observes, such an image would either be
conceived of as (1) a physical form or (2) a spiritual quality or character. Despite the
numerous anthropomorphisms used to describe God and God's activity and despite
his appearances in theophanies in the Old Testament, Scripture seems to maintain
emphatically that, apart from Christ's incarnation, God is not a physical being.
According to Clines, the ב should not be taken as the *beth* of norm. This would
mean the image should be understood metaphorically, referring to some quality or
characteristic of the divine nature in the pattern of which humanity is made. There
are only two passages in which the word *tselem* (image) might be used in this way (Pss
39:6; 73:20). Yet in both cases, the idea of shape, form, or figure is still prominent.
Thus, says Clines, "No example remotely matches the meaning צלם would have in
Genesis 1:26 if it referred to God's spiritual qualities or character, according to the
pattern of which man has been made." A much more satisfying way of rendering
tselem with the *beth* here is the *beth* of essence, meaning "as" or "in the capacity of."
The classic example, according to Clines, is Exod 6:3, where God tells Moses: "I
appeared to Abraham, Isaac, and Jacob as God Almighty." That is, God appeared
in the capacity or nature as El Shaddai. Following a considerable engagement with
objections to taking Gen 1:26 as a *beth* of essence, Clines concludes that "Genesis
1:26 is to be translated 'Let us make man as our image' or 'to be our image', and

Following Clines, it seems more accurate to say that a human being does not *have* the image of God, nor is she made in the image of God, but she herself just *is* the image of God.[19] Clines's conclusion is especially helpful for its clarity:

> Man is created not *in* God's image, since God has no image of His own, but *as* God's image, or rather to be God's image, that is to deputize in the created world for the transcendent God who remains outside the world order. That man is God's image means that he is the visible corporeal representative of the invisible, bodiless God; he is representative rather than representation, since the idea of portrayal is secondary in the significance of the image. However, the term "likeness" is an assurance that man is an adequate and faithful representative of God on earth. The whole man is the image of God, without distinction of spirit and body. All mankind, without distinction, are the image of God. The image is to be understood not so much ontologically as existentially: it comes to expression not in the nature of man so much as in his activity and function. This function is to represent God's lordship to the lower orders of creation. The dominion of man over creation can hardly be excluded from the content of the image itself. Mankind, which means both the human race and individual men [and women], do not cease to be the image of God so long as they remain men [and women]; to be human and to be the image of God are not separable.[20]

Another way to put it is the image of God in humanity is neither a "value added" to the human animal, nor a set of functional capacities, but it

---

the other references to the image are to be interpreted similarly." See Clines, "The Image of God in Man."

[19] Adapted from Clines, "The Image of God in Man," 80.

[20] Clines, 101. Emphasis in original.

is an ontological status conferred on human beings as a species. Human beings are imagers of God. Because they are imagers of God, they enjoy a certain unique moral status, namely, human dignity. Human dignity, human exceptionalism, and human rights are inalienable because of God's investiture.

In a different context, Emory University legal scholar John Witte Jr. has argued that the dignity of the human person is a first principle, or "ur-principle," rooted in our species membership.[21] As the ground of human rights, it goes a long way toward an operational definition of what it means to be human that helps us make meaningful decisions about how we treat one another and what obligations we owe to whom. "[T]he current ubiquity of the principle of human dignity testifies to its universality. And the constant proliferation of human rights precepts speaks to their power to inspire new hope for many desperate persons and peoples around the world."[22]

Baptists, Human Dignity, and Bioethics

Southern Baptist churches speak into the culture in many ways. First, the local church may address beliefs and practices in the culture. Through their cooperation with one another, the SBC churches may also address beliefs and practices through the convention's doctrinal statement, *The Baptist Faith and Message 2000* (*BF&M 2000*). Apropos the subject of this chapter, human dignity, the *BF&M 2000* states in article III:

> Man is the special creation of God, made in His own image. He created them male and female as the crowning work of His creation. The gift of gender is thus part of the goodness of God's creation. . . . The sacredness of human personality is evident in that

---

[21] John Witte Jr., *God's Joust, God's Justice: Law and Religion in the Western Tradition* (Grand Rapids: Eerdmans, 2006), 44. The term "ur-principle" was borrowed from Louis Henkin et al., *Human Rights* (New York: Foundation, 1999), 80.

[22] Witte, 47.

God created man in His own image, and in that Christ died for man; therefore, every person of every race possesses full dignity and is worthy of respect and Christian love.[23]

Moreover, in article XV on "The Christian and the Social Order," the *BF&M 2000* maintains that it is the obligation of Christians to "speak on behalf of the unborn and contend for the sanctity of all human life from conception to natural death":

All Christians are under obligation to seek to make the will of Christ supreme in our own lives and in human society. Means and methods used for the improvement of society and the establishment of righteousness among men can be truly and permanently helpful only when they are rooted in the regeneration of the individual by the saving grace of God in Jesus Christ. In the spirit of Christ, Christians should oppose racism, every form of greed, selfishness, and vice, and all forms of sexual immorality, including adultery, homosexuality, and pornography. We should work to provide for the orphaned, the needy, the abused, the aged, the helpless, and the sick. We should speak on behalf of the unborn and contend for the sanctity of all human life from conception to natural death. Every Christian should seek to bring industry, government, and society as a whole under the sway of the principles of righteousness, truth, and brotherly love. In order to promote these ends Christians should be ready to work with all men of good will in any good cause, always being careful to act in the spirit of love without compromising their loyalty to Christ and His truth.[24]

---

[23] "Man," *The Baptist Faith and Message 2000*, art. III, https://bfm.sbc.net/bfm2000/#iii-man.

[24] "The Christian and the Social Order," *The Baptist Faith and Message 2000*, art. XV, https://bfm.sbc.net/bfm2000/#xv-the-christian-and-the-social-order.

Together, these two articles demonstrate that the doctrinal stance of the SBC decidedly attests to a thick notion of human dignity and the sanctity of every human life. In addition to its doctrinal statement, the messengers of the SBC in their annual meetings pass resolutions of many ethical and cultural issues. Interestingly, SBC churches have evolved concerning abortion. A survey of SBC resolutions on abortion reveals that the SBC passed its first resolution on abortion in 1971. As Baptist historian Timothy George has pointed out, "While this resolution included a perfunctory tribute to the 'sanctity of human life,' it was in essence a strong call for the liberalizing and legalizing of abortion in this country."[25] In fact, the final resolve states, "That we call upon Southern Baptists to work for legislation that will allow the possibility of abortion under such conditions as rape, incest, clear evidence of severe fetal deformity, and carefully ascertained evidence of the likelihood of damage to the emotional, mental, and physical health of the mother."[26]

We should note that the appeal to such a broad description of the "health of the mother" is consistent with the US Supreme Court decision in *Doe v. Bolton* (1973) that, together with *Roe v. Wade* (1973), gave America the most promiscuous abortion policy in the world.[27] It was not until the summer of 1974 that the SBC addressed abortion again in its annual resolutions process, reaffirming the 1971 resolution by claiming:

> WHEREAS, That resolution reflected a middle ground between the extreme of abortion on demand and the opposite extreme of all abortion as murder, and

---

[25] Timothy George, "Southern Baptist Heritage of Life," in *Life at Risk: The Crises in Medical Ethics*, ed. Richard D. Land and Louis A. Moore (Nashville: Broadman and Holman, 1995), 83.

[26] "Resolution on Abortion," Southern Baptist Convention, June 1, 1971, https://www.sbc.net/resource-library/resolutions/resolution-on-abortion-2/.

[27] See Mary Ann Glendon, *Abortion and Divorce in Western Law: American Failures, European Challenges* (Cambridge: Harvard, 1989).

WHEREAS, That resolution dealt responsibly from a Christian perspective with complexities of abortion problems in contemporary society . . .[28]

By 1976, Southern Baptist attitudes toward abortion had begun to change. In its annual meeting the SBC messengers passed the following resolution:

WHEREAS, Southern Baptists have historically held a biblical view of the sanctity of human life, and

WHEREAS, Abortion is a very serious moral and spiritual problem of continuing concern to the American people, and

WHEREAS, Christians have a responsibility to deal with all moral and spiritual issues which affect society, including the problems of abortion, and

WHEREAS, The practice of abortion for selfish non-therapeutic reasons want only destroys fetal life, dulls our society's moral sensitivity, and leads to a cheapening of all human life, and

WHEREAS, Every decision for an abortion, for whatever reason must necessarily involve the decision to terminate the life of an innocent human being.

Therefore be it RESOLVED, that the messengers to the Southern Baptist Convention meeting in Norfolk in June 1976 reaffirm the biblical sacredness and dignity of all human life, including fetal life, and

Be it further RESOLVED, that we call on Southern Baptists and all citizens of the nation to work to change those attitudes and

---

[28] "Resolution on Abortion and Sanctity of Human Life," Southern Baptist Convention, June 1, 1974, https://www.sbc.net/resource-library/resolutions/resolution-on-abortion-and-sanctity-of-human-life/

conditions which encourage many people to turn to abortion as a means of birth control, and

Be it further RESOLVED, that in the best interest of our society, we reject any indiscriminate attitude toward abortion, as contrary to the biblical view, and

Be it further RESOLVED, that we also affirm our conviction about the limited role of government in dealing with matters relating to abortion, and support the right of expectant mothers to the full range of medical services and personal counseling for the preservation of life and health.[29]

What changed? How were the consciences and, therefore, resolutions of the SBC reshaped and reframed over time? Although there is not space in this chapter to chronicle it all, historians have dealt with what transpired during the tumultuous days of the so-called Conservative Resurgence in the SBC. In summary, through grassroots efforts of individual Southern Baptists and their churches, changes were made not only in policies and resolutions, but in those who held important formative leadership in convention agencies, educational institutions, and, notably, the Christian Life Commission (now the Ethics and Religious Liberty Commission of the SBC).[30] That same survey of SBC resolutions will find that the convention has made a complete about-face. Resolution after resolution since 1976—including

---

[29] "Resolution on Abortion," Southern Baptist Convention, June 1, 1976, https://www.sbc.net/resource-library/resolutions/resolution-on-abortion-3/.

[30] On the abortion issue per se, see Timothy George, "Southern Baptist Heritage of Life," in *Life at Risk*. On the larger denomination reformation, see Thomas S. Kidd and Barry Hankins, "Schism in Zion: The Southern Baptist Controversy," in *Baptists in America: A History* (New York: Oxford University, 2015), 228–46 and Barry Hankins, *Uneasy in Babylon: Southern Baptist Conservatives and American Culture* (Tuscaloosa: University of Alabama, 1973). For a detailed insider conservative perspective, see James C. Hefley's six-volume work, *The Truth in Crisis*, published by Hannibal Books from 1986–1990.

the 1977 reaffirmation of the 1976 resolution—right up to the present has expressed commitment to the belief in "the biblical sacredness and dignity of all human life, including fetal life." In addition, resolutions treating other bioethical issues have also appealed either to "the sanctity of human life" or "human dignity," including resolutions on abortion (1980); the Freedom of Choice Act, Hyde Amendment (1993); health care reform (1994); gene patenting (1995); assisted suicide (1996); human embryonic stem cell research (1999); human fetal tissue trafficking (2000); human species-altering technologies (2006); the sanctity of human life (2015); Alzheimer's disease, dementia, and caregiving (2016); and the relatively comprehensive resolution titled "On Reaffirming the Full Dignity of Every Human Being" (2018), which states:

> The messengers to the Southern Baptist Convention meeting in Dallas, Texas, June 12–13, 2018, reaffirm the sacredness and full dignity and worthiness of respect and Christian love for every single human being, without any reservation whatsoever; and be it further
>
> RESOLVED, That we affirm the full dignity of every unborn child and denounce every act of abortion except to save the mother's physical life; and be it further
>
> RESOLVED, That we affirm the full dignity of every human being, whether or not any political, legal, or medical authority considers a human being possessive of "viable" life regardless of cognitive or physical disability, and denounce every act that would wrongly limit the life of any human at any stage or state of life.[31]

Another vehicle Southern Baptists use to express their views on moral, social, and religious liberty issues is the Ethics and Religious Liberty

---

[31] "On Reaffirming the Full Dignity of Every Human Being," Southern Baptist Convention, June 1, 2018, https://www.sbc.net/resource-library/resolutions/on -reaffirming-the-full-dignity-of-every-human-being/.

Commission (ERLC). The ERLC has a long history, although both its name and assignment have changed over the years. What began in 1908 as the Standing Committee on Temperance became the Christian Life Commission in 1953 and the Ethics and Religious Liberty Commission in 1997. The ERLC is governed by trustees elected by the convention who represent the geographical diversity of the denomination. According to its mission statement, "The Ethics & Religious Liberty Commission exists to assist the churches by helping them understand the moral demands of the gospel, apply Christian principles to moral and social problems and questions of public policy, and to promote religious liberty in cooperation with the churches and other Southern Baptist entities."[32]

According to historians Thomas S. Kidd and Barry Hankins, "Throughout the 1970s, largely as a result of the leadership of Foy Valentine and the CLC, the moderate SBC passed a series of resolutions that rejected abortion on demand while advocating that abortion remain an option wherever continuation of the pregnancy might result in the 'likelihood of damage to the emotional, mental, and physical health of the mother.'"[33] In 1988, trustees of the then Christian Life Commission elected Richard D. Land as executive director of the agency.[34] Land had a long history of advocacy for the pro-life position on abortion and other bioethical issues. He had also worked as an administrative assistant to the honorable William P. Clements Jr., governor of Texas. Land served as senior advisor on church-state issues and areas relating to traditional family values as well as anti-drug, anti-pornography, and anti-abortion legislation. He also had senior staff responsibility in the areas of public higher education, mental health and retardation, the physically

---

[32] "About the ERLC," ERLC, https://erlc.com/about/.

[33] Kidd and Hankins, *Baptists in America*, 241.

[34] In the interest of full disclosure, I was a trustee of the Christian Life Commission when Land was elected. In addition, I was hired in 1989 as the first director of bioethical and life issues with an early assignment to organize the CLC's inaugural conference on bioethics in 1993 in Nashville, from which resulted the volume *Life at Risk: The Crises in Medical Ethics*.

handicapped, and AIDS. Largely following the support of the convention and his own convictions, Land led what became the ERLC until 2013, when Russell D. Moore became president of the agency. Like Land, Moore was both pro-life and had significant public policy experience having served as an aide to US Representative Gene Taylor of Mississippi, a Democrat who later switched to the Republican Party in 2014. Well-known for his defense of adoption, cultural engagement, racial reconciliation, and pro-life advocacy, Moore is coeditor with Andrew Walker of the Gospel for Life series that puts human dignity front and center on a host of issues, including abortion, marriage, pornography, racial reconciliation, parenting, work, same-sex marriage, and religious liberty.

Since 1988, then, the ERLC has ardently supported human dignity, the sanctity of life, and human exceptionalism on those matters touching bioethics. More recently, the ERLC sponsored "Artificial Intelligence: An Evangelical Statement of Principles" (2019). Signed by a wide range of evangelicals, the statement invokes the doctrine of human dignity in article 1:

> We affirm that God created each human being in His image with intrinsic and equal worth, dignity, and moral agency, distinct from all creation, and that humanity's creativity is intended to reflect God's creative pattern.

> We deny that any part of creation, including any form of technology, should ever be used to usurp or subvert the dominion and stewardship which has been entrusted solely to humanity by God; nor should technology be assigned a level of human identity, worth, dignity, or moral agency.[35]

Although some grassroots Southern Baptists remain somewhat parochial, the leaders of its institutions have been willing to partner with other

---

[35] "Artificial Intelligence: An Evangelical Statement of Principles," ERLC, April 11, 2019, https://erlc.com/resource-library/statements/artificial-intelligence-an-evangelical-statement-of-principles/.

denominations, especially Roman Catholics, on public policy related to human life and human dignity. In his volume *Has Democracy Had Its Day?*, Carl F. H. Henry called for "co-belligerency" between Protestants and Catholics and even between Christians and non-Christians on the ethical and cultural issues of the day.[36] Southern Baptists have learned much from their Catholic friends about both the importance and defense of human dignity and are likely to fly wing-to-wing and row oar-to-oar in the foreseeable future.

Conclusion

Although under assault in certain quarters, the notion of human dignity is alive and well. There is every reason to believe Southern Baptists will continue to affirm a thick view of human dignity, advocating for its acknowledgement and the protection of those made in God's image. Likewise, there is every reason to believe bioethical issues will grow increasingly complex and potentially contentious. CRISPR technology, artificial intelligence in medical care, gender reassignment surgery, transhumanism, and a raft of other issues loom. Just as in the past, the doctrine of human dignity grounded in the *imago Dei* helped rescue and protect human beings from horrific abuse, so it shall in the future when appropriately recognized and applied.

---

[36] Carl F. H. Henry, *Has Democracy Had Its Day?* (Nashville: Leland House, 1996).

22

Sexuality and Gender in Baptist Perspective

By J. Alan Branch

In the summer of 1967, as many as 100,000 people converged on the Haight-Ashbury neighborhood of San Francisco for the "Summer of Love." The mood of people converging on the Bay Area was captured in John Phillips's song, "San Francisco," recorded by Scott McKenzie and released on May 13, 1967. The song promises a summertime "love-in" and encounters with "gentle" folks for all who go to San Francisco.[1] The purportedly gentle people of Phillips's song celebrated sexual hedonism fueled by rampant drug use, including sexual intercourse on public sidewalks and experiments in polyamorous relationships. The "Summer of Love" was an outlandish display of the sexual revolution, a broad cultural shift during the 1960s and early 1970s that abandoned

---

[1] See John Phillips, "San Francisco," Universal MCA Music Publishing, 1967, http://www.songlyrics.com/john-phillips/san-francisco-be-sure-to-wear-some-flowers-in-your-hair-lyrics. The term "love-in" is a play on the term "sit-in."

Judeo-Christian sexual ethics in favor of unrestrained promiscuity. Building on opposition to the Vietnam War, the youth counterculture of the 1960s made sexual liberation central to its political goals.

The political effects of the sexual revolution have been seen in subsequent years when abortion was legalized in January 1973 and when, in December of the same year, the American Psychiatric Association voted to remove homosexuality as a mental illness from the *Diagnostic and Statistical Manual of Mental Disorders (DSM-II)*. The Supreme Court struck down laws prohibiting same-sex conduct in 2003, legalized gay marriage in 2015, and applied the Civil Rights Act's nondiscrimination provisions to transgenderism in 2020. All these changes occurred within the context of widespread availability of hormonal contraception. Now, a host of identities across the LGBTQ spectrum have been mainstreamed. These goals of the sexual revolution have been accomplished while stigmatizing traditional Christian ethics as antiquated, hateful, and harmful to mental health.

Baptists now minister in an era of post-Christian sexual ethics. The Baptist view of gender and sexuality is countercultural and seems foreign to our neighbors. The contrast between the sexual ethics of the sexual revolution and of the Baptist tradition reflects the difference between competing visions regarding sexuality and gender, which can be described as the battle between an unrestrained versus a restrained vision of sexual ethics.

The Baptist perspective of sexuality and gender is profoundly shaped by a presuppositional commitment to the inerrancy and authority of Scripture.[2] Sexuality and gender are gifts from God to be celebrated within a restrained ethical vision with clear moral parameters, as opposed to the unrestrained

---

[2] By "Baptist perspective," I intend Baptists who are in the great tradition that has affirmed plenary and verbal inspiration of Scripture. Of course, many people have self-identified as Baptists who have rejected biblical authority, but theological liberalism is not just a variant form of Christianity; it is quite another religion altogether. See L. Russ Bush and Tom Nettles, *Baptists and the Bible,* rev. ed. (Nashville: B&H Academic, 1999); J. Gresham Machen, *Christianity and Liberalism* (New York: MacMillan, 1923), 2.

vision that rejects moral restraint and predominates in today's culture. To describe the restrained ethical vision of Baptists, I first define the issues of sexuality and gender. Next, I address the theological context with special emphasis on human nature and sexual ethics. I then offer a perspective on political and cultural developments. Finally, I review the state of the debate about gender and sexuality along with implications for Baptists ministering in a post-Christian culture.

I. Defining the Issue: Sexuality and Gender

Defining terms related to sexual ethics can be very challenging in the modern context. Moral autonomy, theories of literary deconstruction, and hedonism have been intermixed, leading to unpredictable changes in sexual and gender vocabulary. Proponents of the sexual revolution freely redefine terms on an ad hoc basis to suit the needs of the moment, usually to justify the pursuit of new areas of sexual indulgence or gender expansiveness. Much as a missionary must learn the language of a people he or she hopes to reach, sharing the gospel in modern cultures requires an understanding of the words used. The focus here will be on the terms *gender* and *sexuality.*

For the unrestrained vision of sexual ethics, a basic premise is that *sex* and *gender* are separate, identifiable concepts. *Sex* is used in reference to objective, biological, and anatomical traits, starting with the presence of the XY chromosome in males or the XX chromosome in females, which leads to the organic development of obvious differences in genitalia,[3] bone structure, hormones, and internal reproductive anatomy. In contrast, *gender* refers to one's subjective sense of identity and is used to describe what secularists see as purely socially constructed roles and behaviors, activities, and attributes that a given society considers appropriate for boys and men or girls and women. Defining gender as separate from biological sex leads to

---

[3] Cases of disorders of sexual development, such as androgen insensitivity syndrome, are the exception. It is not our point here to address these rare conditions.

the notion of gender identity. The American Psychological Association says, "*Gender identity* refers to a person's internal sense of being male, female, or even something else."[4] Notice that a person's internal sense of gender is bifurcated from the person's body. Separating the concepts of sex and gender is essential to the modern concept of transgenderism, which refers to the broad spectrum of individuals who transiently or persistently identify with a gender different from the one typically associated with the person's sex.[5] Bifurcating sex and gender is the intellectual precedent that allows for discussions of someone being born with a male sex but having a female gender or being born with a female sex while having a male gender or even being gender-neutral with no clear identification as either male or female.

The unrestrained vision is going even further, and at the extreme it seems to deny the very existence of a biological gender binary. This denial is seen most obviously in modern sports, where women worked for decades to create vibrant, well-funded athletic programs exclusively for women. But now biological males are allowed to compete as *women* and celebrate defeating biological females in athletic contests in the name of inclusion and tolerance. This shows that advocates of the unrestrained vision support an incoherent and absurd moral stance that simultaneously says, "We want to free women from the oppressive structures of Christianity" while at the same time saying, "We want biological men to compete with women while pretending they are females."

Sexuality has even broader connotations than gender. *Sexuality* includes one's sexual feelings, the concept of sexual orientation, or a person's specific sexual activities. The World Health Organization gives an expansive definition and says, "Sexuality is a central aspect of being human throughout

---

[4] American Psychological Association, "Answers to Your Questions about Transgender People, Gender Identity, and Gender Expression," 2014, 1, https://www.apa.org/topics/lgbt/transgender.pdf.

[5] Slightly modified from the American Psychiatric Association, "What Is Gender Dysphoria?," February 2016, https://www.psychiatry.org/patients-families/gender-dysphoria/what-is-gender-dysphoria.

life and encompasses sex, gender identities and roles, sexual orientation, eroticism, pleasure, intimacy and reproduction. Sexuality is experienced and expressed in thoughts, fantasies, desires, beliefs, attitudes, values, behaviors, practices, roles and relationships."[6] For the unrestrained vision of sexual ethics, sexuality is very fluid–the person or type of person to whom one is attracted today may not be the same tomorrow.

The unrestrained vision has only two ethical boundaries: the canons of consent and (usually) adulthood. For modern culture, sexual ethics has devolved into determining when and under what circumstances sex is consensual between adults. For the unrestrained vision, neither monogamy nor heterosexuality are considered normative. Instead, morality is defined only by the pleasure associated with consensual sex.

In the post–sexual revolution context, Baptists advocate the restrained ethical vision and define the terms gender and sexuality far more narrowly. For Baptists, the terms *sex* and *gender* are usually considered near synonyms and not separate conceptual notions, and many Baptists contend the culture has introduced artificial distinctions not present in Scripture. We can recognize there is some individual variation within people's experience or expression of their sex/gender—that is, masculine and feminine interests exist along a spectrum and do not have a single or narrow phenomenology—without divorcing sex from gender altogether or treating gender as wholly socially constructed.[7] To say one is born male or female means there are expected gender roles inseparably welded to either sex, that one's biological

---

[6] World Health Organization, "Defining Sexual Health: Report of a Technical Consultation on Sexual Health 28–31 January 2002, Geneva," Sexual Health Document Series (Geneva: World Health Organization, 2006), 5, https://www.cesas.lu/perch/resources/whodefiningsexualhealth.pdf.

[7] For example, Baptists can agree that to say "hunting and fishing are activities of male interest only" or "cooking is an activity for females only" are both unhealthy, narrow distinctions not mandated by Scripture: one can be thoroughly masculine and enjoy cooking, and one can be thoroughly feminine and enjoy hunting or fishing.

sex anchors gender and puts constraints on how fluid or malleable the latter can be. Likewise, for Baptists, *sexuality* certainly includes the idea of one's sexual attraction and feelings, which should be expressed within guidelines provided by God. Sexual ethics and sexual behavior are not infinitely fluid and expansive, but are restrained with sex designed to be enjoyed within heterosexual and monogamous marriage. The striking countercultural sexual ethics of Baptists emerges from deeper differences between Baptists and the current culture regarding beliefs about human nature and sexual ethics.

II. Theological Reflection

The restrained vision of gender and sexual ethics embraces limits imposed by Scripture and is readily distinguished from the culture's unrestrained view in which sexual ethics are released from virtually all limitations. Christian sexual morality assumes God exists and, in the Bible, has made known definite boundaries for appropriate sexual expression. God designed sex, and as its designer He knows its proper use and the correct parameters for sexual expression. Circumventing God's guidelines ultimately leads to pain, heartache, destruction, and God's judgment.

Regarding the relationship between human nature, gender, and sexuality, no scriptural teaching is more formative for the Baptist perspective than the image of God. Genesis 1:26 proclaims the inherent value of every human being, and says, "Let us make man in our image, according to our likeness. They will rule the fish of the sea, the birds of the sky, the livestock, the whole earth, and the creatures that crawl on the earth."[8] Humans are not mere brutes, nor are they the accidental result of a purposeless process:

---

[8] Carl F. H. Henry defines the image of God as "a cohesive unity of interrelated components that interact and condition each other, [which] includes rational, moral and spiritual aspects of both a formal and material nature. . . . But in contemplating the divine image in man, it should be clear that the rational or cognitive aspect has logical priority." Carl F. H. Henry, *God, Revelation and Authority: God Who Speaks and Shows*, vol. 2 (1976; Wheaton: Crossway Books, 1999), 125.

humans are made by God to reflect his power and glory. Baptist ethicist C. Ben Mitchell adds, "The *imago Dei* is not a 'function' human beings perform so much as it is a 'status' they enjoy. The *imago Dei* is not what humans *do* but who humans are."[9] From the perspective of the restrained vision, every human has an inestimable value attached to his or her life *prior to* and *separate from* the person's sexual availability. This is in stark contrast to the culture's crude and depressing insistence that one's value is defined by his or her sexual attractiveness and availability or the idea that we find meaning and worth in unrestrained sexual expression and sexual autonomy.

The gift of the biological sexual binary is inseparable from being made in the image of God. Genesis 1:27 says, "God created man in his own image; he created him in the image of God; he created them male and female." Like the broader Christian tradition, this verse shapes Baptists' restrained vision of sex and gender in two ways. First, both men and women share equally in the image of God and, thus, have an ontological equality—men are not better than women nor are women better than men. Second, one's biological sex is not an accident nor is one's gender something to be chosen. The biological sexual binary is normative and constrains the extent of permissible individual expression that surrounds gender. In other words, there may be different enculturated ways of living out biblical manhood and womanhood, but men cannot be women and women cannot be men. *The Baptist Faith and Message 2000* says, "[God] created them male and female as the crowning work of His creation. The gift of gender is thus part of the goodness of God's creation."[10] This premise is core to Baptist resistance to the idea that sex and gender can ever be completely distinguished into different ontological categories. Instead, one's anatomical sex determines the manner in which one expresses his or her gender.

---

[9] C. Ben Mitchell and D. Joy Riley, *Christian Bioethics: A Guide for Pastors, Health Care Professionals, and Families* (Nashville: B&H Academic, 2014), 55.

[10] "Man," *The Baptist Faith and Message 2000*, art. III, https://bfm.sbc.net /bfm2000/#iii-man.

Not only is gender directly tied to the image of God, but human sexuality is as well. In Gen 1:28, the goodness of the gender binary is tied to God's purposes for sex, which are procreation and marital unity: "God blessed them, and God said to them, "Be fruitful, multiply, fill the earth, and subdue it." Genesis 2:24b adds, "and they become one flesh," meaning sex strengthens the relational unity of a marriage by enabling a husband and wife to experience a shameless intimacy and joyful sexual pleasure (Song 4:1–16). These two purposes—procreation and unity—bring to light that sex does not exist for its own sake, but serves a greater purpose for a culture. The Colorado Statement on Biblical Sexual Morality stresses this point and says sex "fosters human nurturing, both through the union of husband and wife and also through the enrichment of society through the building of families and communities."[11] Sex was never designed by God as something to be indulged in for pleasure in any manner one chooses, in or out of marriage. Sex was intended to strengthen marriage and, by helping to build strong marriages, to build a strong society. Societies that abandon responsibility in sexual matters are doomed to implode from the weight of disintegrated families.

Not only are humans created in the image of God, but also they suffer the effects of the fall recorded in Genesis 3. Because of the fall, humans now inherit a nature and environment inclined toward sin. The entrance of sin means sexual desires are disordered, and humans frequently wish for sexual pleasures God has forbidden. Sexual passions pull heavily on the soul and, when indulged outside of God's moral parameters, lead to destruction and pain. Understanding both gender and sexuality correctly requires taking both the image of God and the fall into consideration. Emphasizing the image of God while neglecting the fall can lead to unbridled celebration of every sexual desire as if all are inherently good. Emphasizing the fall while

---

[11] Council on Biblical Sexual Ethics, "Colorado Statement on Biblical Sexual Morality (Full Statement)," in Daniel Heimbach, *True Sexual Morality* (Wheaton, IL: Crossway Books, 2004), 363.

neglecting the image of God can lead to a relentlessly severe and gloomy vision of gender and sexuality that contains no positive instruction at all.

Balancing the two concepts of the image of God and the fall is crucial, but the doctrine of human sinfulness differentiates the restrained and unrestrained visions. Many advocates of the unrestrained vision will grant the existence of God and that God has some role in shaping gender or sexuality, but what they reject is man's fallen nature. Romans 1:18–32 details the sinful nature of humanity, and distorted sexual desires are placed squarely at the center of rebellion and idolatry. Sexual ethics need restraint because humans' natural desires have been disfigured by sin. Sin so pervades the intellect and emotions that even the most unholy acts are sometimes affirmed as natural and good. But Scripture never denies that sexual temptation can feel natural: what Scripture denies is that all natural, sexual desires are inherently good. When sin prevails, thoughts about both gender and sexuality can be twisted and distorted; as such, moral boundaries are needed to safeguard human behavior.

The good news is God has provided for redemption from sin via the death, burial, and resurrection of Jesus Christ (1 Cor 15:1–11). The meaning of life is found in fulfilling God's purposes through believing in his Son and being conformed to the image of Christ, not in indulging every whim of lustful desire. The difference between the restrained and unrestrained visions of sexual ethics is this: the unrestrained vision believes sexual desires should be indulged while the restrained vision believes they must be *redeemed. Grace is necessary to redeem and complete nature.*

The meaning of redeemed sexual ethics is clearly articulated in 1 Cor 6:12–20. Here, Paul rejected the unrestrained vision and identified both moral autonomy and sexual hedonism as two wrong starting points for sexual ethics. In 1 Cor 6:12–13, he cited two slogans that, apparently, had become popular among believers in Corinth: "everything is permissible for me" and "food is for the stomach and the stomach for food." Paul cited these Corinthian slogans in order to refute them and contrasted these wrong starting points with true sexual morality.

The Corinthian slogan "everything is permissible for me" (1 Cor 6:12) was bandied about to justify an indiscriminate use of Christian liberty to participate in sexual immorality. The Greek word translated "permissible" incorporates the idea of a "right," implying the Corinthians claimed to have the moral autonomy to exercise sexual freedom, a striking foreshadowing of the ethic of the sexual revolution (and proof that there is nothing new under the sun). The New Living Translation captures the radical moral reasoning of this maxim, translating it as "I am allowed to do anything." The Corinthians demanded a broad category of acceptable sexual behavior. Paul negated the moral autonomy of the first Corinthian slogan by saying, "But *not everything* is beneficial" (1 Cor 6:12a, emphasis added).[12] He reminded the Corinthians that sexual immorality is a sin against Christians' corporate identity in Christ. Paul refuted the unrestrained vision's idea of individuals making sexual choices based on their own autonomy. Instead, Paul insisted that Christians should consider the way their actions affect others, especially fellow believers.

Sexual moral autonomy paradoxically leads to a form of moral and emotional slavery. Paul repeated the Corinthian slogan and refuted it again: "'Everything is permissible for me,' but I will not be mastered by anything" (1 Cor 6:12b). Robertson and Plummer suggest there is wordplay in the Greek text that might be paraphrased in English as follows: "I can make free with all things, but I shall *not* let anything make free with me."[13] Thiselton adds, "It is a well-known paradox that if *everyone* claims unqualified autonomy, *no one* can be free, for everyone is threatened by the freedoms of the other."[14]

The unrestrained vision's abandonment of moral restraint may indeed feel exhilarating and liberating during the initial phases of exploring a "free

---

[12] See Anthony C. Thiselton, *The First Epistle to the Corinthians,* The New International Greek Testament Commentary (Grand Rapids: Eerdmans, 2000), 462.

[13] Archibald Robertson and Alfred Plummer, *The International Critical Commentary: The First Epistle of St. Paul to the Corinthians,* rep. ed. (Edinburgh: T&T Clark, 1994), 122.

[14] Thiselton, *The First Epistle to the Corinthians,* 461.

love" ethic. Sadly, the result is not freedom but slavery. Sexual sin leads to compulsive behavior that dominates every aspect of a person's life, leaving him or her devoid of beauty and goodness.[15]

The second Corinthian slogan uses a bit of double entendre to advocate sexual hedonism: "Food is for the stomach and the stomach for food" (1 Cor 6:13). Some of the Corinthians apparently argued along these lines: "God made the stomach so we can enjoy the pleasure of eating food. In the same way, our genitals have been designed so we can enjoy the pleasure of sex. It is wrong for us to inhibit either of these natural desires." They argued the moral value of sex can be defined in terms of pleasure. Perhaps some of Paul's audience engaged in a form of sexual gluttony and fed a voracious appetite for immorality.

But Paul rejected hedonism as a foundation for sexual ethics and said, "'Food is for the stomach and the stomach for food,' and God will do away with both of them. However, the body is not for sexual immorality but for the Lord, and the Lord for the body" (1 Cor 6:13). The word translated "sexual immorality" is *porneia*, a broad term encompassing various forms of unsanctioned and unlawful sexual intercourse.[16] *Porneia* can be defined as any sexual behavior that deviates from the clear standard that sex is designed

---

[15] Sexual promiscuity among teenagers is associated with drug and alcohol abuse and increased self-reporting of suicidal ideation. Sophie Dubé et al., "Psychological Well-Being as a Predictor of Casual Sex Relationships and Experiences among Adolescents: A Short-Term Prospective Study," *Archives of Sexual Behavior* 46, no. 6 (August 2017): 1807–18. Research indicates a correlation between risky sexual behaviors and depression, but it is not always clear which way the correlation is working: Does the risky sexual behavior cause depression, or does depression motivate people to try high-risk behaviors? For one example of research, see Matthew T. Tull and Kim L. Gratz, "Major Depression and Risky Sexual Behavior among Substance Dependent Patients: The Moderating Roles of Distress Tolerance and Gender," *Cognitive Therapy Research* 37, no. 3 (June 2013): 483–97.

[16] Walter Bauer, *A Greek-English Lexicon of the New Testament and Other Early Christian Literature,* ed. Frederick William Danker, 3rd ed. (Chicago: University of Chicago, 2000), 854.

to be shared between a husband and wife within heterosexual, monogamous marriage (Gen 2:24–25). And Paul said Christians are to "flee sexual immorality" (1 Cor 6:18). He insisted that the physical pleasure associated with sex is not intended in and of itself to serve as the moral basis for one's sexuality. Instead, the overarching Christian principle of sexual ethics is to abstain from sexual immorality.

Sexual hedonism inverts the biblical order and attempts to make sexual pleasure the starting point. When one's sexual ethics are driven solely by pursuit of physical pleasure at any cost, sensual hedonism becomes a cruel tyrant driving the person into an endless array of deteriorating sexual practices and countless encounters with other people ending only in deeper brokenness. The person's entire world orbits his or her libido, and other innocent people often get caught in the strong gravitational pull of the person's sexual immorality. Unrestrained hedonism leads to exploitation: another person exists only to satiate someone's desire for pleasure. This creates an unsafe culture because autonomy-driven hedonism knows no limits. Paradoxically, a culture that insists on "consent" as the primary moral rule for sex soon abandons the canon of consent itself. The unrestrained vision of sexuality and gender creates a dangerous environment composed of predators and victims.

Based on a robust understanding of human nature and God-given boundaries for sexuality, the Baptist perspective sees gender and sexuality through the lens of God's creative purposes, accepts moral restraint as a way of bringing glory to God and is in complete contrast to the culture's embrace of licentiousness. This contrast is clearly seen in light of current political and cultural developments.

III. Political and Cultural Developments

The sexual revolution initiated a wholesale transition of values regarding gender and sexuality. The triumph of the unrestrained vision is seen in several political and cultural developments beginning with ideas emanating from the 1800s and moved forward by the seminal work of both Alfred Kinsey and Harry Benjamin during the twentieth century. The unrestrained vision is also reflected in legal decisions of the US Supreme Court and is clearly visible in entertainment media. For the majority in American culture, the rules of Christian sexual ethics are rejected as oppressive social constructions with no foundation in anything transcendent.

Antecedents to the sexual revolution can be seen in the 1800s. Friedrich Nietzsche loathed Christian sexual ethics and asserted, "It was only Christianity, with ressentiment against life in its foundations, which made of sexuality something impure: it threw filth on the beginning, on the prerequisite of our life."[17] Similarly, in the *Manifesto of the Communist Party,* Marx and Engels gave a distasteful caricature of home life in order to dismiss the traditional family, saying, "Our bourgeois, not content with having the wives and daughters of their disposal, not to speak of common prostitutes, take the greatest pleasure in seducing each other's wives."[18] They claim all bourgeois families are merely facades of respectability but do not make mention of happy, faithful families marked by sincere love and sacrificial acts. Advocates of the unrestrained vision today often use critiques similar to Marx and Engels, claiming Christian sexual ethics are used by men to suppress and exploit women. During the sexual revolution, the conservative sexual morality of the 1950s was seen as an expression of capitalism, and moral self-restraint and hard work were perceived as tools of class domination. Achieving sexual freedom was connected to economic revolutionary outcomes; overthrowing sexual morals was seen as a tool for overthrowing capitalism.[19]

---

[17] Friedrich Nietzsche, *Twilight of the Idols,* in *Twilight of the Idols and The Anti-Christ,* trans. R. J. Hollingdale (London: Penguin Books, 1990), 121.

[18] Karl Marx and Frederick Engels, *Manifesto of the Communist Party,* trans. Samuel More (New York: New York Labor, 1908), 30.

[19] For example, see Herbert Marcuse, *Eros and Civilization: A Philosophical Inquiry into Freud* (Boston: Beacon, 1966), 191–94. Citing Heinrich von Kleist,

The opening salvo of the sexual revolution occurred in 1948 when a group of researchers from the University of Indiana led by Alfred Kinsey (1894–1956) published *Sexual Behavior in the Human Male,* followed in 1953 with *Sexual Behavior in the Human Female.* Both works contain sweeping assertions and often move quickly from tables full of data to moral speculation about the repressed sexual ethics of America. Kinsey's poor research design—including the non-random population sample and the resulting selection bias—were noted even in his day, yet were foundational to the report's false and misleading conclusions.[20] For example, *Sexual Behavior in the Human Male* says nearly 69 percent of males in the United States had sex with prostitutes and "it is probably safe to suggest that about half of all married males have intercourse with women other than their wives, at some time while they are married."[21] Most disturbingly, Kinsey tacitly approved of sexual exploitation of children.[22] But his data was wildly inaccurate, and by overstating the frequency of various deviant behaviors, Kinsey was attempting to normalize them, that is, to defend them as moral merely because they are common, arguments still used to defend the unrestrained vision today.

An acquaintance of Kinsey was Harry Benjamin (1885–1986), a New York endocrinologist who wrote the landmark book *The Transsexual Phenomenon* in 1966, the first major work to argue in favor of what is now called transgenderism. A native of Germany, Benjamin had early in his life been closely acquainted with Magnus Hirschfeld (1868–1935), a German physician and sexual radical who coined both the words *transvestite* and *transsexual.* Beginning in the late 1940s, Benjamin began prescribing female hormones for male-to-female transsexuals and helped them network with

---

Marcuse says, "We must eat from the tree of knowledge in order to fall back into the state of innocence" (198).

[20] See my discussion of these problems in *Born This Way? Homosexuality, Science, and the Scriptures* (Bellingham: Lexham, 2016), 16–30.

[21] Alfred C. Kinsey, Wardell B. Pomeroy, and Clyde E. Martin, *Sexual Behavior in the Human Male* (Philadelphia: W. B. Saunders, 1948), 597, 585.

[22] Kinsey, *Sexual Behavior in the Human Male,* 161, 176–78, 501.

physicians who would perform gender reassignment surgery. *The Transsexual Phenomenon* argued that the best plan for transsexuals is to make their bodies fit their desires as opposed to professional counseling to help their gender identity match their bodies.

The ensuing triumph of the unrestrained vision for sexual ethics advocated by Kinsey and Benjamin can be traced in a series of Supreme Court cases in the US. The Supreme Court carved out a highly controversial principle of "right to privacy" in *Griswold v. Connecticut* in 1965. This right to privacy soon morphed into a radical form of moral autonomy used to justify abortion in *Roe v. Wade* and *Doe v. Bolton* in 1973. Eventually, in *Planned Parenthood v. Casey* (1992), the Supreme Court shifted abortion rights from the right to privacy to the more explicit liberty interests of the Fourteenth Amendment and, in so doing, articulated a philosophical form of unrestrained moral autonomy that served as the precedent for *Lawrence v. Texas* in 2003, which struck down laws criminalizing homosexual behavior.

The pinnacle of the unrestrained vision in legal decisions so far is 2015's *Obergefell v. Hodges*, which legalized same-sex marriage throughout the United States. Justice Kennedy authored the majority's decision and said, "Many who deem same-sex marriage to be wrong reach that conclusion based on decent and honorable religious or philosophical premises, and neither they nor their beliefs are disparaged here."[23] But Kennedy's statement seems disingenuous because he spends a great deal of space in his decision arguing that to deny gays and lesbians the right to marriage demeans them. Of particular concern to Baptists opposing these changes is that Kennedy says nothing about the free exercise of religion regarding opposition to gay marriage, an ominous silence that is foreboding regarding religious liberty concerns. Kennedy advances the cause of the unrestrained vision of sexual ethics, and to that degree, the *Obergefell* decision is merely the legal outworking of the sexual revolution. The natural extension of *Obergefell* was seen in 2020's *Bostock v. Clayton County,*

---

[23] *Obergefell v. Hodges*, 576 US 19 (2015).

which extended the Civil Rights Act's prohibition against employment discrimination based on sex to include transgenderism. The decision is likely to have sweeping implications regarding both homosexuality and transgenderism in public policy.

The culture swims in a moral environment of pornographic swill. Exact financial data about porn profits is hard to estimate. On the low end, some estimate porn has about six billion dollars in annual revenue in the US; on the high end, some estimate it to be a $97 billion global industry.[24] While pornography is available in an endless number of formats, internet pornography is the most vexing type because it employs a dangerously high number of addictive hooks such as isolation, fantasy, objectification, anonymity, and sexual images. The culture has normalized porn use so that viewing it is no longer seen as bad, but as expected behavior: not to view porn is to be abnormal.[25] Porn is also implicated in the trafficking and objectification of women and girls. In late 2020, Pornhub.com, the largest pornography site in the world, deleted most of its own content because it could not verify the people involved were adults who consented to the sexual activity portrayed in the videos, nor that they consented to being filmed.

IV. State of Debate

In modern Western culture, the unrestrained vision for sexual ethics reigns virtually triumphant in politics, entertainment, education, and corporate policies. While the culture's leitmotif is sexual freedom, the brutal reality is that people become collateral damage in the sexual revolution. In response,

---

[24] "Things Are Looking Up in America's Porn Industry," NBC News, June 20, 2015, https://www.nbcnews.com/business/business-news/things-are-looking-americas-porn-industry-n289431; Ross Benes, "Porn Could Have a Bigger Economic Influence on the US than Netflix," Yahoo Finance, June 20, 2018, https://finance.yahoo.com/news/porn-could-bigger-economic-influence-121524565.html.

[25] William M. Struthers, *Wired for Intimacy: How Pornography Hijacks the Male Brain* (Downers Grove: IVP, 2009), 51–52.

the clear picture of the restrained vision shines brightly against the dark backdrop of sexual anarchy.

The most profound philosophical presentation of the unrestrained vision of sexual ethics is found in the work of Michel Foucault. Foucault himself was a sexually adventurous person, and it is difficult not to see his own lack of restraint in the background of his philosophical work. In *The History of Sexuality,* volume 1, he looked back with great nostalgia on what he called the *ars erotica* or erotic art from ancient civilizations such as Rome. He claimed such societies celebrated the pleasurable aspects of sex for the sake of pleasure itself, freedoms lost with the rise of Christianity. For Foucault, sexual ethics are not based on an "absolute law of the permitted and the forbidden" (the restrained vision), but instead sex should first be understood from the experience of pleasure "evaluated in terms of its intensity, its specific quality, its duration, its reverberations in the body and in the soul."[26] Essentially, he advocated what has been called the natural impulse view of sex. Heimbach says such a view "begins with the physical pleasure associated with sexual experience and proceeds to construct an entire framework of moral thinking based on it."[27] This approach says any natural impulse that produces pleasure is good and should be allowed free expression, with a requisite nod to the moral rule that all sex should be consensual and between adults.

An ethical vision similar to Foucault's now reigns supreme across the culture. Different organizations represent a loose confederation of sexual revolutionaries advocating the unrestrained vision including Planned Parenthood; the Sexuality Information and Education Council of the United States; the World Professional Association for Transgender Health; the Human Rights Campaign; Parents, Families, and Friends of Lesbians and Gays; the Williams Institute at UCLA Law; and the Gill Foundation

---

[26] Michel Foucault, *The History of Sexuality: An Introduction,* vol. 1, trans. Robert Hurley (New York: Vintage Books, 1990), 57.

[27] Heimbach, *True Sexual Morality,* 270.

and Gill Action Fund. These groups have successfully lobbied and cajoled major corporations to endorse same-sex marriage, celebrate June as Gay Pride month, and teach employees to accept all manner of behavior from coworkers, including the adoption of new gender identities. Employees who push back against the latest avant-garde sexual or gender agendas are either fired or shuffled to the back of the line without any hope of advancement. In education, the spectrum of LGBTQ identities has been mainstreamed.

In response, Christians have scrambled in the fifty years since the sexual revolution to produce cohesive statements addressing the Christian view of gender and sexuality. "The Danvers Statement on Biblical Manhood and Womanhood" may be the most fundamentally important. Developed in 1987 by various evangelical leaders, the "Danvers Statement" affirms biblical complementarianism, insisting that males and females share an ontological equality grounded in creation and that distinctions in roles between men and women were grounded in creation and not part of the fall. The statement insists both the Old and New Testaments affirm the principle of male headship in the family and the church. This contrasts notions that equality between males and females obliterates role distinctions and allows for broad interchangeability in roles. The "Danvers Statement" is vital because it addresses the crucial issues of gender that underlie current debates about LGBTQ identities. Other statements of importance include "The Colorado Statement on Biblical Sexual Morality" (2002) produced by Focus on the Family and "The Nashville Statement" addressing transgenderism (2017). For Baptists, the restrained vision of sexual ethics is clearly articulated in *The Baptist Faith and Message 2000*, which affirms heterosexual and monogamous marriage, biblical complementarianism regarding gender, sexual purity before marriage, and faithfulness within marriage.

What will be the long-term impact of the US Supreme Court's decision in *Dobbs v. Jackson Women's Health Organization* in which both *Roe* and *Casey* were overturned? The issue of abortion has been returned to the federal and state legislatures.[28] Some states, e.g., California and New York, will have very liberal abortion laws while other states, e.g., Mississippi and Missouri, will have very conservative laws. And the availability of the abortion pill via mail virtually ensures that people who live in states where abortion is prohibited will likely order the abortifacient from states where it is legal. *Dobbs* points to the importance of moral persuasion with one's neighbors, and in their argumentation, Baptists should remember that defending the sanctity of human life begins by defending the sanctity of sex.

Two visions stand in stark contrast: The unrestrained vision insists expansive notions of gender and sexuality as essential to a free society. The restrained vision argues these expansive notions do not lead to freedom but breed a new kind of slavery and produce an unsafe environment for everyone, especially for women and children. What are the implications for Baptists if they advocate a minority view regarding gender and sexuality, especially a view often caricatured by cultured elites as hateful and bigoted?

V. Implications

Regarding sexuality and gender, Baptists today are in the same situation as the early church. The first-century Roman Empire was a time of moral approval for the most irresponsible sexual acts.[29] The first *real* sexual revolution did not occur in the 1960s in San Francisco; the first sexual revolution occurred with the preaching of the gospel and its corresponding ethical implications across the Roman Empire.

Sexually erotic images were common in the first century, demonstrated by the pornographic images present throughout the ruins of

---

[28] *Dobbs v. Jackson Women's Health Organization*, 597 US 4 (2022).

[29] Some have tried to downplay the permissiveness of the Roman Empire. Of course, many people lived lives of virtue, but in the wealthy elite especially, immorality was common. For a biblical example, see the adulterous relationship of Herod Antipas and Herodias, Mark 6:14–29.

Pompeii and commonly found on vases and pottery. Ribald statues of the god Priapus were common throughout the Roman Empire. A famous example of the era's vulgarity is the Warren Cup, a silver cup dated from the first century that is decorated with depictions of homosexual acts between a master and his male slave.[30] Such a cup would have been used at public gatherings: guests could have been handed a cup with homosexual pornographic imagery.

Dinner parties in the first century often became drunken orgies, and no great shame or embarrassment was attached to these events. Such behavior was simply expected. The sexual use of dining couches is widely portrayed on stone and pottery in museums throughout Greece with many depictions showing food nearby on dining tables, perhaps indicating that eating and sexual intercourse were commonly combined at banquets.[31]

Within the Roman Empire, male homosexual behavior was common. In Roman culture, the male who played the dominant part in a homosexual encounter was not viewed negatively at all as he retained his masculinity. In contrast, the male who played the passive part in a homosexual encounter was scorned because he had played a feminine role. Furthermore, the sexual exploitation of both male and female slaves was common. Additionally, transgender-like behavior was seen in the cult of the goddess Cybele, in which men who became her priests castrated themselves and dressed like women.

While married women of the first century were expected to remain faithful, it was expected that married men would visit brothels, which explains Paul's strong warning to the Corinthians that Christians should not have sex with prostitutes (1 Cor 6:15). Overlooking the city of Corinth was a temple to Aphrodite, the goddess of love, sex, desire, and beauty. Apparently, prostitutes dedicated to her were scattered throughout the city with the

---

[30] Kyle Harper, *From Shame to Sin: The Christian Transformation of Sexual Morality in Late Antiquity* (Cambridge: Harvard University, 2013), 26.

[31] John McRay, *Archaeology and the New Testament* (Grand Rapids: Baker Academic, 1991), 317.

possibility they were owned by the temple itself.[32] Into this sexually charged atmosphere, Paul preached the foolishness of the cross and instructed new believers that their old life of sexual promiscuity was no longer their identity (1 Cor 6:11) and challenged them to flee sexual immorality (1 Cor 6:18).

Early Christians initiated a sexual revolution by teaching and living an approach to gender and sexuality completely at odds with a decadent culture. First Peter 4:3 critiques the sexual permissiveness of the era, saying, "For there has already been enough time spent in doing the will of the pagans: carrying on in unrestrained behavior, evil desires, drunkenness, orgies, carousing, and lawless idolatry." In response, the early Christians' pagan neighbors were shocked at Christian sexuality and surprised Christians did not "join them in the same flood of wild living—and they slander[ed]" them (1 Pet 4:4).

When one considers the ethical stance of the first-century Roman Empire, it becomes clear the sexual revolution is not something new, nor are today's Christians the first to find themselves advocating a much-despised minority opinion. Noted Catholic pediatrician Eugene F. Diamond said, "The 'modern sexual revolution' is neither 'modern' nor a revolution. It is difficult to find any human folly more ancient than the desire to have sex without rules."[33]

VI. Conclusion

Two irreconcilable visions of gender and sexuality exist today: The unrestrained vision rejects the idea that God has created gender and sexuality, promotes gender fluidity, and encourages sexual experimentation. The restrained vision insists both gender and sexuality require God-given parameters for appropriate expression for a society to remain cohesive. In the twenty-first

---

[32] McRay, *Archaeology and the New Testament*, 315.

[33] Eugene F. Diamond, "Casualties of the Sexual Revolution," *Linacre Quarterly* 74, no. 4 (2007): 356.

century, Baptists will be providing urgent care for casualties of the sexual revolution. If the local church is to be a hospital for sinners, then believers must
be ready to minister Christian first aid to people suffering the traumatic consequences of sexual sin and confused ideas about gender. The Baptist response
should include rigorous academic critique of intellectual arguments of the
unrestrained vision and structured discipleship addressing gender and sexuality.

Advocates of the unrestrained vision insist it will lead to greater freedom
and human flourishing. Does empirical evidence support this claim? The
answer is clearly no. For example, it is no coincidence that abortion was
legalized in the United States in 1973, immediately following the sexual
revolution. When contraceptives fail, abortion becomes a brutal coping
mechanism for sexual freedom. The more than 63 million abortions in the
US since 1973 testify that the unrestrained vision cheapens human life.[34]

The unrestrained vision not only cheapens children, but it dehumanizes
women as objects for male sexual gratification. Nearly one in five women
have experienced completed or attempted rape during their lifetime,[35] violent acts fueled by a culture that tells men a woman's value is based only
on her ability to provide sexual pleasure. The confused thinking of sexual
liberals is seen in the legalization of prostitution in many European countries, supposedly for the benevolent purposes of protecting "sex workers"
(prostitutes) from exploitation and sexually transmitted infections. But in
Germany, for example, a prostitute has to have sex with four men just to
pay her room's rent on a given day, and most of the women come from
Eastern Europe and many have been trafficked.[36] A Baptist response will

---

[34] See Sam Dorman and Kyle Morris, "Over 63 Million Abortions Have
Occurred in the US Since Roe v. Wade Decision in 1973," Fox News, May 4, 2022,
https://www.foxnews.com/politics/abortions-since-roe-v-wade.

[35] "Statistics." NSVRC (National Sexual Violence Resource Center) website,
accessed October 29, 2022, https://www.nsvrc.org/statistics.

[36] "Prostitution Is Legal in Countries across Europe, but It's Nothing Like
What You Think," *Business Insider,* March 13, 2019, https://www.businessinsider
.com/prostitution-is-legal-in-countries-across-europe-photos-2019-3.

persistently and aggressively challenge the unsubstantiated claims of the unrestrained vision.

It is impossible to break God's rules without suffering consequences, and a vigorous critique of the unrestrained vision demands Baptists continually state that while sexual liberation may sound good in theory, its results are disastrous. The ubiquitous nature of sexually transmitted infections (STIs) also illustrates the deadly outcomes of the unrestrained vision. Approximately 65 million people in the United States are currently infected with an STI. Estimates vary, but nearly 20 million new STIs occur each year in the US, and there is a pronounced increase of new cases among young people ages fifteen to twenty-four.[37]

The sexual revolution has contributed to the destruction of marriage and the nuclear family. The percentage of Americans getting married has steadily decreased. In 2011, the US Census Bureau reported that married couples represented only 48 percent of American households.[38] This is a significant threshold as less than half of households represent the nuclear family. The result is that a startlingly high percentage of children are born to homes without the presence of the biological father with one estimate being that one in five children are living with a single mom.[39] In a culture that sexually objectifies women and disregards marriage, it is hardly surprising that many men see children as the bothersome side effect of sex.

---

[37] "Reported STDs in the United States: 2013 National Data for Chlamydia, Gonorrhea, and Syphilis," CDC Fact Sheet, December 2014, https://stacks.cdc.gov /view/cdc/26427; C. L. Shannon and J. D. Klausner, "The Growing Epidemic of Sexually Transmitted Infections in Adolescents: A Neglected Population," *Current Opinion in Pediatrics* 30, no. 1 (February 2018): 137–43.

[38] Stephanie Hanes, "Singles Nation: Why So Many Americans Are Unmarried," *Christian Science Monitor*, June 14, 2015, http://www.csmonitor.com/USA/Society /2015/0614/Singles-nation-Why-so-many-Americans-are-unmarried.

[39] Gretchen Livingston, "The Changing Profile of Unmarried Parents," Pew Research Center, April 25, 2018, https://www.pewresearch.org/social-trends/2018 /04/25/the-changing-profile-of-unmarried-parents/.

Baptist discipleship must be more intentional in teaching the restrained vision. Teaching godly messages about gender and sexual boundaries at early ages helps inoculate children against deadly sexual worldviews they will encounter. New believers in Christ will bring with them many wrong ideas about sexual ethics. Baptists should develop an intentional and direct age-appropriate curriculum that explains the restrained vision of sexual ethics as the norm for Christian behavior. As awkward as teaching such things may be, the alternative is to leave children and new believers to suffer with the confused and godless sexual ethics of the world.

The purported "sexual emancipation" of American culture leads to a diabolical slavery. The unrestrained vision encourages people to sin, and Jesus Christ said, "Everyone who commits sin is a slave of sin" (John 8:34). True freedom is not found in indulging every sexual desire without any moral reflection; true freedom is found in godly moral restraint. Baptists stand in a long line of Christians, beginning with the early church, who are the real sexual revolutionaries, the revolutionary idea being "God's way is always right."

23

Stewardship and Environmentalism

By Andrew Spencer

The health of Earth's ecological systems is something that affects every creature on the planet and will continue to affect the well-being of future generations until the Lord comes again to restore the created order. As technological solutions abound for viruses, surgery, and mental illness, there is always a hope that, at some point, an easy answer to overuse of ecosystems, pollution, and the extinction of species will appear in a lab. However, while technology may provide partial solutions to ecological problems, orthodox Christians should recognize that ecological degradation is the result of individual sin and sinful systems they create, to which the proper solution is faithfulness to humanity's original calling as stewards of creation. One of the responsibilities of faithful Christians is to live redemptively in the world, both by proclaiming the gospel verbally and living lives of increasing conformity to the gospel, which includes caring for creation.

Even as Christians come to recognize their responsibility as stewards, they still must sort out the best way to resolve each of the problems disrupting the integrity of the created order. Every proposed solution has trade-offs, which makes navigating environmental questions challenging.[1] How do we best steward God's creation? Faithful Christians must answer this question from a distinctly theological perspective, which is framed by the orthodox theology of historic Christianity.

Finding solutions is difficult given that much of the public dialogue on creation care is divisive. Some environmentalists see preserving the ecological integrity of the world as a grim duty humanity must pursue with little hope of success.[2] Simultaneously, some theologically orthodox Christians see concern for the environment as something to battle against, rather than an opportunity to serve Christ in light of his final redemption of the cosmos.[3] But caring for creation properly should be a delight, especially for the Christian. Humans are fulfilling their earliest calling from God when they exercise proper stewardship within God's creation (Gen 1:28). Because of sin in the human heart, that dominion has often been turned into domination and abuse, which is the cause of so many environmental crises.

This chapter outlines a theological basis for stewardship of creation. Then it surveys some of the major movements that define the environmental movement, particularly as understood in the United States. Next it discusses the major contours of the debate among various streams of Christians with a special focus on Baptists. Finally, the essay summarizes key implications of environmental stewardships as an emphasis within the Baptist political witness.

---

[1] Noah Toly, *The Gardener's Dirty Hands: Environmental Politics and Christian Ethics* (New York: Oxford University, 2019).

[2] One example of this is the emotionally gripping volume by Dale Jamieson, *Reason in a Dark Time* (New York: Oxford University, 2014).

[3] For example, see James Wanliss, *Resisting the Green Dragon: Dominion, Not Death* (Burke: Cornwall Alliance for the Stewardship of Creation, 2010).

Theological Context

At the heart of environmentalism are four basic questions: (1) What is the authority for making ethical decisions? (2) What sort of value does creation have? (3) What place do humans have within the environment? (4) What is the final state of the environment? These questions apply to both religious and non-religious environmentalisms, but they translate into Christian theology under the doctrinal headings of revelation, creation, anthropology, and eschatology.

Revelation

According to the Protestant tradition, the Bible is the final authority for all matters of life and practice.[4] Yet decisions about the use of particular chemical pesticides or the expansion of a real estate development are not clearly delineated in Scripture. In some cases, the environmental decisions faced by contemporary Christians would have defied the imagination of the human authors of the Bible. However, although ethical decisions may have to be informed by extra-biblical data, the doctrine of the sufficiency of Scripture calls orthodox Christians to affirm that the principles available within the Bible provide enough information to avoid sin and pursue holiness.[5]

Current scientific knowledge often provides the data from which decisions are made; Scripture provides the moral framework by which decisions are evaluated.[6] Additionally, social and ecclesial traditions influence what issues are of concern and which scientific sources are considered valuable, while the personal experiences of moral agents also influence their

---

[4] David Dockery, "Special Revelation," in *A Theology for the Church*, ed. Daniel L. Akin, rev. ed. (Nashville: B&H Academic, 2014), 120.

[5] John Frame, *The Doctrine of the Word of God* (Phillipsburg, NJ: P&R, 2010), 220–38.

[6] Andrew J. Spencer, "Resurrection, Natural Revelation, and Christian Ethics," in *Luther Rice Journal for Christian Studies* 2 (Spring 2016): 21–41.

decisions. Experience, tradition, and science all shape environmental ethics, but Scripture alone should be the ultimate authority.

In some circles, however, there is an assumption of conflict between Scripture and scientific data with the belief that newer information has greater moral authority. Political scientist Robert Booth Fowler notes, "Whether this fact is acknowledged or not, science often appears to be the ultimate authority among some Protestant environmentalists. Its findings are used to substantiate the claim of a current crisis, to provide the basic outlines of nature (of the biological and physical worlds), and to model the good society."[7] The identification of the problem and description of the physical order of the universe is both a proper and helpful function for science. However, as a discipline, science is ill-equipped for the determination of the good society. To the degree that science has prescriptive force for the moral life, it has exceeded the capabilities of the discipline. This approach is closer to scientism than orthodox Christianity.[8]

Using scientific data to help guide decisions is warranted in light of common grace. Traditionally, Protestant Christians have affirmed the supreme authority of Scripture because it is a unique form of special revelation. However, the Reformation slogan *sola Scriptura* (Scripture alone) was never intended to mean Scripture *only*, as if no other data besides the sixty-six canonical books of the biblical canon were needed for every issue. Respecting the final authority of Scripture includes allowing general revelation—information from sources like science and history—to provide the information used for making a moral determination that is ultimately shaped by the content of Scripture.[9] For example, the Bible makes clear that humans have a responsibility to properly steward creation; however, little

---

[7] Robert Booth Fowler, *The Greening of Protestant Thought* (Chapel Hill: University of North Carolina, 1995), 5.

[8] For a definition and discussion of scientism, see J. P. Moreland, *Scientism and Secularism* (Wheaton, IL: Crossway, 2018), 29–30.

[9] Kirsten Birkett, "Science and Scripture" in *The Enduring Authority of the Christian Scriptures*, ed. D. A. Carson (Grand Rapids: Eerdmans, 2016), 984–86.

information is given in the canon of Scripture for how to best preserve bio-diversity, what balance of fuels generates energy most efficiently, or whether shifts in weather patterns are caused by human activity or natural cycles. Contemporary ethics requires being informed by scientific data but conformed to the Bible, especially through its teaching on the value of creation.[10]

Creation

In the first chapter of Genesis, God declared the goodness of creation six times, once after each creational day (Gen 1:4, 10, 12, 18, 21, 25). After the creation of humanity, both male and female, he surveyed all of creation and declared it very good (Gen 1:31). This was a statement of the value of the whole of creation, which included humanity. The repeated pattern in the declaration of goodness was that "God saw that it was good." However, the goodness of creation did not come because of God's declaration. Rather, God described creation as good after he observed its quality. The goodness came from God, who created all things from nothing, but the goodness was inherent to creation.

Some environmental ethicists describe the created order as having intrinsic value,[11] which is defined as goodness that is native to an object itself for its own sake.[12] Intrinsic value is often positioned as being directly opposed to instrumental value, which is goodness ascribed to an object because of its utility to a subject.[13] No one questions that all of creation has instrumental value; much of nature is useful to humans, even just by providing aesthetic delight. But if creation is reduced merely to its usefulness to humanity, that

---

[10] Francis A. Schaeffer, *Pollution and the Death of Man,* in *The Complete Works of Francis A. Schaeffer* (Wheaton, IL: Crossway, 1985), 47.

[11] For example, see Kevin J. O'Brien, *An Ethics of Biodiversity: Christianity, Ecology, and the Variety of Life* (Washington, DC: Georgetown University, 2010), 53.

[12] Clarence I. Lewis, *An Analysis of Knowledge and Valuation* (La Salle: Open Court, 1946), 382.

[13] Lewis, 391.

tends to enable abuse. Thus, there has been a shift among environmentalists to revalue creation by ascribing intrinsic goodness to nature.[14]

Under first inspection, assuming all nature has intrinsic value appears to be a baseline point for increasing ecological sensitivity. However, describing nature's value as intrinsic complicates decision-making because intrinsic value implies that every object is equally valuable, thus reducing decision-making to an evaluation of the instrumental good of intrinsically valuable objects.[15] What seems advantageous for environmentalism ends up creating an unworkable ethics.

A third value category—inherent value, which is due to qualities in the object's relationship to some external object—helps break the logjam between the idealism of intrinsic value and the pragmatism of instrumental value.[16] Since God created all things and retains ownership of all things (Ps 24:1), all human and nonhuman creation should be valued in light of their relationship to him. The question of cutting down a tree becomes a question of the balance of the tree's purpose in the created order against the goal of cutting it down. It may be that cutting down a diseased tree will enhance the health of a forest, enabling it to more accurately represent God's orderly design for creation. Or it may be that cutting down a healthy tree is necessary to make room for a needed hospital, a decision that can be made only if there are different degrees of value in play for the affected objects.

Some arguments for intrinsic value in creation are tied to attempts to repaganize Christianity. For example, while considering why many conservative Christians do not believe in anthropogenic climate change, two engineers argue that making Christianity more pantheistic is the best hope for the environment.[17] Those committed to Christian orthodoxy see adopting

---

[14] Sahotra Sarkar, *Biodiversity and Environmental Philosophy: An Introduction* (New York: Cambridge University, 2005), 58–68.

[15] Sarkar, 57.

[16] Lewis, *An Analysis of Knowledge and Valuation*, 391.

[17] Bernard Daley Zaleha and Andrew Szasz, "Why Conservative Christians Don't Believe in Climate Change," *Bulletin of the Atomic Scientists* 71, no. 5 (2015): 27–28.

pantheism or panentheism as an unnecessary and unacceptable degradation of Christianity.[18] There is little doubt that repeated arguments for revising Christianity for the sake of ecology have tended to increase resistance to environmentalism among orthodox Christians. Such revisions are, in fact, unnecessary because opposition to policy solutions to climate change or more general environmental concern is not dependent upon theological convictions, but typically on rejection of the political solutions proposed in the name of environmental problems. Of course, it does not help that some climate advocates openly argue for a revision to Christian doctrine as a necessary component for environmentalism, but this is driven more by a desire to lump a revision of sexual ethics and other culturally driven ideas into concern about the environment.[19] Nevertheless, the minimization of concern for the environment among some Christians is unfortunate because within a Christian orthodoxy there is room for a balanced, theocentric environmental ethics, especially through the idea of stewardship.

Anthropology

Stewardship reflects the understanding that humans have a role as vice-regents in tending the created order on God's behalf (Ps 8:4–6). The value of this metaphor has been disputed,[20] but it is arguably the most consistent with the language used in Scripture. Stewardship balances the equality of humans with nonhuman creation while recognizing the unique role given to humans within creation. Adam was formed from the dust of the earth, and Eve was formed from Adam, cementing the place of humanity within the ecosystem (Gen 2:5–22). At the same time, humans were also granted dominion over

---

[18] Rowan D. Williams, "'Good for Nothing'? Augustine on Creation," *Augustinian Studies* 25 (1994): 9–24.

[19] Naomi Klein, *On Fire* (New York: Simon and Schuster, 2019), 137–48.

[20] Richard Bauckham, *Living with Other Creatures: Green Exegesis and Theology* (Waco: Baylor University, 2011), 58–62.

creation with authority to fill and subdue the earth (Gen 1:26–30). The use of the term "dominion" has caused some Christians to reject this portion of Scripture because they see it as authorizing the wanton abuse of creation.[21]

Ultimately, the vision of Scripture is a move from an undeveloped garden (Gen 2:15) to a garden city (Rev 21:9–22:5) that honors the original integrity of creation. The so-called cultural mandate to "fill the earth, and subdue it" (Gen 1:28) is a duty given to humans—not to dominate creation, but to encourage its flourishing through redemptive activity. Although the cultural mandate was frustrated by human sin (Gen 3:17–18), the calling remains. However, the task is not to bring all of creation under development, but to care for the creation so that it brings glory to God. In an orthodox environmentalism, humanity's authority over creation (whatever it is called) must be subordinate to God's purposes for creation, which speaks to the purpose of God in creation that will be finally revealed in the new heavens and new earth.

Eschatology

Eschatology points Christians toward the hope of renewal of the original goodness of creation by the power of God at the end of this age (Rom 8:18–25).[22] When Adam originally sinned, part of God's response was to curse the created order as an ongoing witness to the distortion that sin brought into the world (Gen 3:17–19).[23] But the end result of God's creative work—however one accounts for the timing and sequence outlined in the Bible—is a renewed creation where the effects of sin are no longer evident (Rev 21:1–4).

---

[21] Earth Bible Team, "Guiding Ecojustice Principles," in *Readings from the Perspective of the Earth*, ed. Norman C. Habel (Cleveland: Pilgrim, 2000), 50–51.

[22] Matthew Y. Emerson, "The Destruction of the Cosmos in 2 Peter 3:11–13, Or, Does God Own a Death Star?" in *Southwestern Journal of Theology* 57, no. 2 (Spring 2015): 281–94.

[23] Cornelius Plantinga Jr., *Not the Way It's Supposed to Be* (Grand Rapids: Eerdmans, 1995).

The primary purpose of eschatology is to encourage right living as it points along the arc of God's work throughout history (2 Pet 3:11–13). As Christians look backward, they recognize that human sin caused the created order to be disordered (Gen 3:17–19). They see that humans retained both the authority and responsibility of stewardship after the fall (Gen 9:1–7). But when Christ interacted with creation in his incarnate sojourn on earth, his work was consistently redemptive as he miraculously pushed back the signs of the fall.[24] Eschatology looks forward to the renewal of the created order when the effects of sin will be purged (2 Pet 3:10) and a redeemed creation will become the home of the elect in Christ.

The ethical thrust of eschatology is to encourage wise stewardship, recognizing the true owner of all creation will return and judge those who have been poor managers (Luke 16:1–13). After all, if God will judge even the careless words of every human, how much more will negligence toward a primary responsibility of creational stewardship be judged (see Matt 12:36)? At the same time, the biblical witness to eschatology puts the final responsibility for full renewal of the created order on God's shoulders, leaving humans with a duty to act wisely but without the need to recover Edenic perfection. It is God's earth, and he will restore it.[25]

There are other questions pertinent to environmental ethics from a Christian perspective and certainly other doctrines that could be brought to bear on the topic,[26] but revelation, creation, anthropology, and eschatology form a beginning framework to consider the central questions of the discipline. Any discussion of the topic of creation care must begin by determining sources of authority, the concepts of creation value in play, a determination of the appropriate role of humanity within creation, and the

---

[24] David W. Jones and Andrew J. Spencer, "The Fate of Creation in the Eschaton," *Southeastern Theological Review* 9, no.1 (Spring 2018): 87–88.

[25] Albert M. Wolters, *Creation Regained: Biblical Basics for a Reformational Worldview,* 2nd ed. (Grand Rapids: Eerdmans, 2005), 69–73.

[26] For example, see Michael S. Northcott and Peter M. Scott, eds., *Systematic Theology and Climate Change* (New York: Routledge, 2014).

final destination of the created order. Variations in basic understandings of environmental ethics typically stem from different interpretations of these four doctrines, although confusion has been introduced to theological arguments where political categories have replaced doctrinal ones.

Political, Institutional, and Cultural Context

Several shifts have occurred in the shape and tone of environmentalism since the industrial revolution, especially in North America. While there are close ties between environmentalism and Christianity in North America, rifts have developed and widened between theological factions, which have been muddled by sometimes conflicting political divisions. Complicating the debate on environmentalism, there has been a shift from concrete concerns over specific, observable environmental degradation to predictions and hypothetical scenarios, which have made discontinuity between theology and praxis more palatable for some Christians.

Early Christian settlers in North America had a deep interest in preserving the quality of nature in very specific terms. Puritans designed their towns for usefulness for humans, but also with an interest in setting aside natural areas for their beauty and to allow space for wildlife to propagate and prevent hillside erosion. Local laws codified these early environmental regulations and were often tied to caring for creation. For example, towns in early New England were typically laid out with community and sustainability in mind for agriculture and industry. Citizens were encouraged to plant trees to reduce soil erosion with the local pastor often leading the way.[27] The first Baptist church in the American South was established because of environmental degradation, as early Baptists moved from New England to Charleston, South Carolina, in part because the timbers they relied upon for

---

[27] Mark R. Stoll, *Inherit the Holy Mountain: Religion and the Rise of American Environmentalism* (New York: Oxford University, 2015), 60–76.

their industry were becoming depleted.[28] Healthy ecosystems were a common concern, which led to significant impacts on lifestyles even before the industrial revolution.

Historian Mark Stoll argues that many of the most active environmentalists in the history of the United States have been one generation removed from Christianity. Many of the most active in environmentalism have shifted from their Christian roots to a generally pantheistic vision of creation.[29] Among these is John Muir, a naturalist, explorer, and cofounder of the Sierra Club and arguably the most famous American advocate for the environment. He was raised in the Disciples of Christ tradition. Muir used language that resonates with Christianity in his environmental writing.[30] However, the religion he espoused has little connection with orthodox Christianity. Instead, Muir argued that God could be experienced properly only through nature.

Muir's poetic appeals to preserve Yosemite National Park and stop the Hetch Hetchy reservoir are replete with arguments that equate the grand vistas of the Western United States with seeing God.[31] On the other side of the Hetch Hetchy reservoir debate, Presbyterian Gifford Pinchot argued for responsible human use of nature.[32] Pinchot and Muir engaged in public debates through writing and lobbying President Theodore Roosevelt, himself a Presbyterian, for the preservation or use of government-owned land. In the end, it was Pinchot's influence and the instrumental value of nature that

---

[28] Anthony L. Chute, Nathan A. Finn, and Michael A. G. Haykin, *The Baptist Story* (Nashville: B&H Academic, 2015), 55–56.

[29] Stoll, *Inherit the Holy Mountain*, 2–9.

[30] Jeffrey Bilbro, *Loving God's Wildness: The Christian Roots of Ecological Ethics in American Literature* (Tuscaloosa: University of Alabama, 2015), 63–98.

[31] John Pierce, "'Christianity and Mountainanity': The Restoration Movement's Influence on John Muir," *Religion and the Arts* 17, no. 1/2 (2013): 114–34.

[32] Gifford Pinchot, "The Birth of 'Conservation,'" in *American Environmentalism: Readings in Conservation History*, ed. Roderick F. Nash (New York: McGraw-Hill, 1990), 73–79.

won the day. But both sides of the debate over the fate of Yosemite used religious language in their appeals for environmental policies.[33] Muir referred to the Hetch Hetchy Valley as "one of Nature's rarest and most precious mountain temples" and accused those who supported damming the water there of being "temple destroyers" who failed to lift "their eyes to the God of the mountains."[34] Pinchot joined progressives of his day, arguing, "Among the first duties of every man is to help in bringing the Kingdom of God on earth," which was intended to include the development of nature.[35] The battle was primarily political, but with unmistakable religious overtones.

A second wave of environmentalism began, roughly speaking, after World War II. There was an industrial boom that led to rapid expansions of industry, the explosion of automobile usage, and widespread use of pesticides like DDT in agriculture. American prosperity led the middle class to see clean air and water as amenities they could purchase with their growing wealth.[36] The environmental goods they desired were real and tangible. The publication of Rachel Carson's landmark book, *Silent Spring*, in 1962 is often considered the beginning of the contemporary environmental movement.[37] Carson's book helped launch widespread interest in increasing environmental regulations, the possible connections between pollution and cancer,[38] and the negative effects of agricultural chemicals on the ecosystem.

Overtly Christian interest in the environment arose in parallel with Carson's secular movement. In 1961, Lutheran theologian Joseph Sittler

---

[33] Michael B. Smith, "The Value of a Tree: Public Debates of John Muir and Gifford Pinchot," *Historian* 60, no. 4 (Summer 1998): 757–78.

[34] John Muir, *The Yosemite* (New York: Century, 1912), 255–62.

[35] Gifford Pinchot, *The Fight for Conservation* (New York: Doubleday, 1910), 95.

[36] Benjamin Kline, *First Along the River: A Brief History of the US Environmental Movement* (New York: Rowman and Littlefield, 2011), 79–93.

[37] Charles T. Rubin, *The Green Crusade: Rethinking the Roots of Environmentalism* (Lanham: Rowan and Littlefield, 1998), 35.

[38] William Souder, *On a Farther Shore: The Life and Legacy of Rachel Carson* (New York: Crown, 2012), 306–9.

addressed the World Council of Churches, calling for Christians to show solidarity with all of creation because of the incarnation of Christ. He argued that because of the hope of cosmic redemption, earth-care is a Christian duty, even before a pragmatic, crisis-induced need begins.[39] Sittler's writings were instrumental in moving mainline Protestants toward environmentalism. Denominations involved in the World Council of Churches engaged in the ecological issues of their day.

In the 1960s the main concern of environmentalists was gross pollution. For example, absurd events like the burning of the Cuyahoga River in 1969 became a rallying cry for the environmental movement and were catalysts for the first Earth Day.[40] The signs of pollution were significant and obvious, which raised interest across political and denominational lines to combat significant environmental catastrophes. Attempts to enlist Christians on a broad scale have been somewhat limited by attacks on the faith from environmentalists and the conflict that has resulted.

One of the most influential essays for religious environmentalism is "The Historical Roots of Our Ecological Crisis" by Lynn White Jr.[41] This essay, originally published in *Science* magazine in 1967, blames Christianity for the environmental problems in the West. The essay has encouraged attempts to make Christianity more pantheistic to support environmental activism. It has also encouraged others to reject the environmental movement as anti-Christian. In his attempt to find Christianity at fault for environmental degradation, White failed to recognize that when Christians participate in the degradation of creation—which they undoubtedly have and do—it is in opposition to, rather than fulfillment

---

[39] Joseph Sittler, "Called to Unity," in *Evocations of Grace: The Writings of Joseph Sittler on Ecology, Theology, and Ethics,* ed. Steven Bouma-Prediger and Peter Bakken (Grand Rapids: Eerdmans, 2000), 38–50.

[40] Kline, *First Along the River*, 87–92.

[41] Lynn White Jr., "The Historical Roots of Our Ecological Crisis," in *Ecology and Life: Accepting Our Environmental Responsibility*, ed. Wesley Granberg-Michaelson (Waco: Word, 1974), 125–37.

of, the first principles of Christianity. Because of its accusations, White's article has led to a slow consensus among Christians on efforts to preserve the goodness of creation.[42]

Even though many of the environmental problems were tangible, one of the worst solutions proposed dealt with theoretical projections rather than observable damage. In the mid-1960s modern environmentalism shifted its focus to controlling the increase of world population. Scientists like Paul Ehrlich raised the alarm, arguing in his 1968 book, *Population Bomb*, that the ecosystem could not sustain the growing population and that dramatic efforts to curb the procreation of humans were warranted.[43] That movement has become only more extreme with the rise of the human extinction movement.[44] Progressive Southern Baptist sociologist Edgar Chasteen described population growth as a "cancer" and asserted that "the basic cause of pollution and waste is simple: too many people."[45] The emphasis on curbing population growth encouraged both political and theological divides over the question of environmental stewardship, especially in the United States, and eventually led to political splits that have since confused the theological landscape. It also does not help that despite the continued growth of the population, the dire predictions made by people like Ehrlich and Chasteen have largely been proved false.[46]

Political division has not always been central to environmental ethics. In 1970, environmentalism was still a bipartisan concern. The first Earth Day was cosponsored by Republicans and Democrats. Republican

---

[42] Sabrina Danielsen, "Fracturing over Creation Care? Shifting Environmental Beliefs among Evangelicals, 1984–2010," *Journal for the Scientific Study of Religion* 52, no. 1 (2013): 201–2.

[43] Paul R. Ehrlich, *The Population Bomb* (New York: Ballantine, 1968).

[44] For example, Patricia MacCormack, *The Ahuman Manifesto: Activism for the End of the Anthropocene* (New York: Bloomsbury, 2020).

[45] Edgar R. Chasteen, *The Case for Compulsory Birth Control* (New York: Prentice Hall, 1971), 15, 33.

[46] Paul Sabin, *The Bet: Paul Ehrlich, Julian Simon, and Our Gamble over Earth's Future* (New Haven: Yale University, 2013).

Richard Nixon's administration is considered one of the most environmentally positive administrations, marked especially by the formation of the Environmental Protection Agency (EPA).[47] Because of the broad concern for the environment, Nixon also authorized a commission to study the relationship between the rising population and American prosperity. The resultant report, *Population and the American Future*, published in 1972, made recommendations including opposition to "legal, social, and institutional pressures that historically have been mainly pronatalist in character" and "enabling individuals to avoid unwanted childbearing, thereby enhancing their ability to realize their preferences."[48] Practical recommendations for implementing the commission's lofty-sounding recommendations included open advocacy for the legalization of abortion, government-funded distribution of contraceptives, and even capping the number of children per family. Many Christians reacted negatively to these suggestions. The overt connections between support for abortion and advocacy for the environment converted an issue that was largely a prudential argument into a hotly disputed political and doctrinal battleground with more fundamental issues than land use and economics at stake. The proposed responses to measurable environmental concerns were increasingly tied to morally objectionable policies, which increasingly divided the political Left and Right in the United States. This division has only increased confusion of political and theological categories, as a properly biblical rejection of abortion seems to create tension with an appropriately orthodox affirmation of creation care.

In recent years, the most significant concern in the contemporary environmental debate is climate change. In developed nations outside of the US, there is a general, popular consensus that human activity—particularly

---

[47] Byron W. Daynes and Glen Sussman, *White House Politics and the Environment* (College Station: Texas A&M University, 2010), 66–83.

[48] US Commission on Population Growth, *Population and the American Future: The Report of the Commission on Population Growth and the American Future* (Washington, DC: US Government, 1972), 78.

the release of carbon dioxide from the burning of fossil fuels—is accelerating the warming effects of the globe. In the US, especially, there is a great deal more popular skepticism on the merits of the available evidence for climate change.[49] Perspectives on global warming are divided largely along political lines, although age, region of domicile, and level of science knowledge also appear to be factors, according to a 2020 Pew Research study.[50] However, resistance to rhetoric about climate change tends to be political rather than theological, even though attempts have been made to make theological arguments against the evidence for anthropogenic climate change.

The most common theological objection to creation care in general and climate change in particular relates to a view of eschatology that anticipates the destruction of creation at Christ's return. In fact, a seminary professor once wrote on one of my papers that environmentalism was "like shuffling deck chairs on the Titanic" with specific reference to 2 Pet 3:10. In the King James Version, that verse states, "the heavens shall pass away with a great noise, and the elements shall melt with fervent heat, the earth also and the works that are therein shall be burned up." This seems like a cut and dried case, except for three major considerations. First, an apparent textual issue exists in 2 Pet 3:10, which would shift the meaning from the earth being "burned up" to the works done on it being "exposed" or "revealed." The latter meaning is found in the earliest texts of the New Testament and is generally the accepted modern translation.[51] The second consideration

---

[49] Moira Fagan and Christine Huang, "A Look at How People Around the World View Climate Change," Pew Research Center, April 18, 2019, https://www.pewresearch.org/fact-tank/2019/04/18/a-look-at-how-people-around-the-world-view-climate-change/.

[50] Cary Funk and Brian Kennedy, "For Earth Day 2020, How Americans See Climate Change and the Environment in 7 Charts," Pew Research Center, April 21, 2020, https://www.pewresearch.org/fact-tank/2020/04/21/how-americans-see-climate-change-and-the-environment-in-7-charts/.

[51] Al Wolters, "Worldview and Textual Criticism in 2 Peter 3:10," *Westminster Theological Journal* 49, no. 2 (1987): 405–13.

that prevents using 2 Pet 3:10 as an anti-environmentalist proof text is that even if the earth is going to burn up, no human knows when (Matt 24:36). Third, although our bodies will eventually fail, we do not eschew physical fitness or personal hygiene entirely (1 Tim 4:8). If a Christian is confident humans cannot bring about final destruction, she should still seek to care for this world as well as she can in this life. There are many possible theological objections to policies proposed in the name of climate change, but few valid theological objections to the data itself.

There is room, however, for a healthy skepticism toward many proposals made in the name of climate change. For example, in the US there is a broad overlap between progressive proposals for expansion of government control and proposals directed toward mitigating climate change. For example, Jeremy Rifkin's book *The Green New Deal* argues that a centrally planned economy can improve both the well-being of the average citizen and the environment. Rifkin's ideas include "ubiquitous sensors [that] will provide surveillance, collecting data on activity taking place in the homes, the shops, and the streets, with the goal of helping speed efficiencies and conveniences in commerce, social life, and governance."[52] Such visions of state surveillance are what empower activists like Naomi Klein to argue, "Most fundamentally, any credible Green New Deal needs a concrete plan for ensuring that the salaries from all the good green jobs it creates aren't immediately poured into high-consumer lifestyles that inadvertently end up increasing emissions."[53] Klein and others have paired environmental advocacy with highly debatable economic and social policies, making them inseparable aspects of the same progressive vision.[54] The connection between environmentalism, socialism, and increased abortion has significantly

---

[52] Jeremy Rifkin, *The Green New Deal: Why the Fossil Fuel Civilization Will Collapse by 2028, and the Bold Economic Plan to Save Life on Earth* (New York: St. Martin's, 2019), 38.

[53] Naomi Klein, *On Fire: The (Burning) Case for a Green New Deal* (New York: Simon and Schuster, 2019), 264.

[54] See Klein, *On Fire*, 191–206.

increased evangelical resistance to otherwise legitimate concern for the environment in the US. However, theologically orthodox Christians should be careful not to allow the political instinct to resist some proposals to cause them to reject an appropriate care for creation.

State of the Debate

Although creation care has become a political issue, it should be more properly treated as a theological one. Among environmentally engaged Christians, there are stark differences in environmentalism based on theological perspective.[55] At the risk of oversimplification, within the range of self-identified Protestant Christians, there are four basic approaches to creation care.[56] The four categories discussed will include the ecotheological, liberal, evangelical, and fundamentalist perspectives on environmental ethics.[57]

Ecotheology was a term coined to signify theology focused on environmental questions.[58] It has become synonymous with a form of liberation theology that has freeing the earth from the oppression of human pollution as a central aim. Ecotheology interprets Scripture and Christian tradition through the controlling paradigm of the environment.[59] The core of eco-

---

[55] For a more thorough treatment of this topic, see Andrew J. Spencer, *Doctrine in Shades of Green* (Eugene: Wipf and Stock, 2022).

[56] Approaching this topic in theological categories runs the risk of committing the fallacy of reifying artificial categories. Carl Trueman, *Histories and Fallacies: Problems Faced in the Writing of History* (Wheaton, IL: Crossway, 2010), 42–46.

[57] An additional reason to focus on theological categories instead of denominations is that a great deal of the advocacy for environmental issues, especially among Evangelicals, is done by parachurch organizations. This is a theme that appears in Katharine K. Wilkinson, *Between God and Green: How Evangelicals Are Cultivating a Middle Ground on Climate Change* (New York: Oxford University, 2012).

[58] For example, Fowler uses the hyphenated term "eco-theology" to indicate a range of Christian considerations of the environment in his 1995 volume. Fowler, *The Greening of Protestant Thought*, 91–107.

[59] David G. Horrell, *The Bible and the Environment: Towards a Critical Ecological Biblical Theology* (London: Equinox, 2010), 13.

theology is a hermeneutics of suspicion that typically sees the Bible as a flawed, anthropocentric record that must be reinterpreted to accommodate a more ecologically friendly Christianity.[60] This leads to a valuation of creation that is typically described as "intrinsic" in most cases, with some claiming the goodness of creation is not dependent upon God but "a reality that God discovers."[61] The goal of anthropology in ecotheology is to erase distinction between human and nonhuman creation, but with humans having a special responsibility for caring for creation.[62] The eschatology of ecotheology tends to see cosmic redemption by God's work (see Rom 8:18–23), but sometimes eliminates any sense of personal eschatology. Significant voices within the ecotheology movement include Ernst Conradie,[63] David Horrell,[64] and Norman Habel.[65]

Among liberal or modernist theologians, there tends to be a greater openness to contemporary culture, especially modern science, as a source of authority for Christian theology. As Roger Olson argues, "Real liberal

---

[60] See David G. Horrell, "Introduction," in David G. Horrell et al., *Ecological Hermeneutics: Biblical, Historical and Theological Perspectives* (London: T&T Clark, 2010), 5, 7.

[61] Earth Bible Team, "Guiding Ecojustice Principles," in *Readings from the Perspective of the Earth,* 44.

[62] Earth Bible Team, 49.

[63] Ernst M. Conradie, "What Are Interpretive Strategies?" in *Scriptura* 78 (2001): 429–41; Conradie, "Towards an Ecological Biblical Hermeneutics: A Review Essay on the Earth Bible Project," in *Scriptura* 85 (2004): 123–35; Conradie, *An Ecological Christian Anthropology: At Home on Earth?* (Burlington: Ashgate, 2005); Conradie, "Towards an Ecological Reformulation of the Christian Doctrine of Sin," in *Journal of Theology for Southern Africa* 122 (2005): 4–22.

[64] Horrell, *The Bible and the Environment.* See also the coedited volume David G. Horrell, Cherryl Hunt, and Christopher Southgate, eds., *Greening Paul: Rereading the Apostle in a Time of Ecological Crisis* (Waco: Baylor University, 2010).

[65] Norman Habel, "The Earth Bible Project," in *Ecotheology* 5, no. 7 (1999): 123–24; Habel, "The Origins and Challenges of an Ecojustice Hermeneutic," in *Relating to the Text: Interdisciplinary and Form-Critical Insights on the Bible,* ed. Timothy J. Sandoval and Carleen Mandolfo (London: T&T Clark, 2003), 141–59.

theology aims at reconstructing Christian doctrines to balance contemporary cultural relevance with faithfulness to Christian sources. Usually . . . relevance to contemporary culture is given equal if not greater weight than faithfulness to Christian sources."[66] Theologically liberal Christians have consistently led the way on political issues related to the environment because they have been a major concern in society. The intrinsic value of creation, with its self-existent goodness, fuels a call for humanity "to serve and to protect its earthly home."[67] Some streams of liberal theology tend toward pantheism.[68] The future of the earth is a restored creation, which is used to inspire contemporary action toward realizing the kingdom of God on earth as much as possible in the present age. Key environmentalists that write as theological liberals include Joseph Sittler[69] and Paul Santmire.[70]

Evangelicals continue to have a mixed reaction to questions of the environment. In part, this is due to the mixture of political categories with theological categories. Evangelicals tend to endorse the inherent value of creation, though terminology varies.[71] A range of perspectives exists on the human role within the created order among evangelicals, with some tending

---

[66] Roger E. Olson, *The Journey of Modern Theology: From Reconstruction to Deconstruction* (Downers Grove, IL: IVP Academic, 2013), 128. See also H. Paul Santmire's definition of "revisionist theology" in *Nature Reborn: The Ecological and Cosmic Promise of Christian Theology*, Theology and the Sciences (Minneapolis: Fortress, 2000), 7–10.

[67] Santmire, *Nature Reborn*, 39.

[68] Roger Olson, *The Story of Christian Theology* (Downers Grove, IL: IVP Academic, 1999), 550.

[69] Joseph Sittler, *Evocations of Grace: The Writings of Joseph Sittler on Ecology, Theology, and Ethics* (Grand Rapids: Eerdmans, 2000); Sittler, *The Care of the Earth* (Minneapolis: Fortress, 2004).

[70] H. Paul Santmire, *The Travail of Nature: The Ambiguous Ecological Promise of Christian Theology* (Philadelphia: Fortress, 1985); Santmire, *Nature Reborn*.

[71] Francis Schaeffer uses the term "intrinsic" when writing of the value of creation, but his definition supports the meaning of "inherent" as defined in this essay. See Schaeffer, *Pollution and the Death of Man*, in *The Complete Works*, 34.

toward a dominion model[72] and others tending toward stewardship as a framing paradigm.[73] Evangelicals tend to emphasize the uniqueness of humanity, which entails unique responsibility in the care of creation. They tend to affirm the final state of creation as a perfected, physical existence for eternity in the presence of God. There are variations on the means God will use to create that state, but the goal is consistent. The most helpful voice on creation care from evangelicals remains Francis Schaeffer in *Pollution and the Death of Man*, who urged his readers to rely upon scientific data read through a redemptive lens to pursue substantial healing of creation.[74] Other helpful voices include Richard Bauckham and Douglas and Jonathan Moo.[75]

From a fundamentalist Christian perspective, very little has been written on environmental ethics. The most favorable interpretation of this lacuna is that there is a much greater focus on shoring up core doctrines than applying them in public. Additionally, open attacks on orthodox Christians by proponents of environmentalism tend to discourage engagement. When prominent Christian environmentalists like Roger Gottlieb write, "Religious environmentalism and fundamentalism will always be in opposition,"[76] Fundamentalists may be forgiven for believing him. However,

---

[72] E. Calvin Beisner, *Where Garden Meets Wilderness: Evangelical Entry into the Environmental Debate* (Grand Rapids: Eerdmans, 1997).

[73] Sandra L. Richter, *Steward of Eden: What Scripture Says about the Environment and Why It Matters* (Downers Grove, IL: IVP Academic, 2020).

[74] Schaeffer, *Pollution and the Death of Man*, in *The Complete Works*, 47–55.

[75] See Richard Bauckham, *The Bible and Ecology: Rediscovering the Community of Creation* (Waco: Baylor University, 2010); Bauckham, *Living with Other Creatures: Green Exegesis and Theology* (Waco: Baylor University, 2011); Bauckham, "Joining Creation's Praise of God," in *Ecotheology* 7, no 1 (2002): 45–49; and Douglas J. Moo and Jonathan A. Moo, *Creation Care: A Biblical Theology of the Natural World* (Grand Rapids: Zondervan Academic, 2018); Douglas Moo, "Creation and New Creation," in *Bulletin for Biblical Research* 20, no. 1 (2010): 39–60; Jonathan Moo and Robert S. White, *Let Creation Rejoice: Biblical Hope and Ecological Crisis* (Downers Grove, IL: IVP Academic, 2014).

[76] Roger S. Gottlieb, *A Greener Faith: Religious Environmentalism and Our Planet's Future* (New York: Oxford University, 2006), 223.

taking a theological perspective to environmental ethics, Fundamentalists share with evangelicals the content of the same four central doctrines that support creation care, so the difference in perspective has more to do with application than the doctrines themselves.[77]

Broad theological categories may be the most helpful way to discuss religious environmentalism, but denominations have also influenced the shape of the conversation. For example, Baptists have been engaged theologically and politically in environmentalism since the 1960s with the primary ecological issues among them being population growth and climate change. The range of Baptist engagement on these topics is illustrated by comparing American Baptists and the Southern Baptist Convention, two of the largest Baptist denominations in the US.[78]

American Baptists have remained consistent in their advocacy for both population control and mitigating anthropogenic climate change. The official policy statement on ecology from the American Baptists urges members to "learn of the environmental dangers facing the planet," "exert our influence in shaping public policy," and "become involved in organizations and actions to protect and restore the environment and the people in our communities."[79] Population growth and climate change are listed among the environmental dangers in the official American Baptist Policy. In a "Resolution on Environmental Concerns," American Baptists are called to "support strong legislative and administrative action, both state and federal, to clean up pollution of air, land and water; to establish strict controls to prevent pollution; and insist that adequate funding be provided and that

---

[77] Consider the thesis of Carl F. H. Henry, *The Uneasy Conscience of Modern Fundamentalism* (Grand Rapids: Eerdmans, 1947).

[78] Aaron Douglas Weaver, "Baptist Environmentalisms: A Comparison of American Baptist and Southern Baptist Attitudes, Actions and Approaches Toward Environmental Issues" (PhD diss., Baylor University, 2013).

[79] American Baptist Convention, "American Baptist Policy Statement on Ecology: An Ecological Situational Analysis," last modified September 2007, https://www.abc-usa.org/wp-content/uploads/2019/02/ecology.pdf.

action take place now."[80] Similar language in a statement on global warming encourages strong interventions at local, federal, and international levels.[81]

The trajectory of the Southern Baptist Convention on the environment closely mirrors the seismic theological shifts in the denomination. In the 1960s and 1970s, the SBC passed several resolutions that supported abortion to varying degrees, expressed support for population control, and called for increased government action to improve the environment.[82] In 1971, a professor of sociology at an SBC-affiliated college published *The Case for Compulsory Birth Control*.[83] Through the 1970s the public position of the SBC on environmental issues mapped very closely to popular environmentalism.

The 1979 election of Adrian Rogers as convention president was the first major success of the Conservative Resurgence.[84] The theological change was apparent in many areas, including the language used to discuss stewardship. In 1983, a progressive social activist and pastor proposed a resolution titled "On the Care of Our Environment."[85] The resolution passed, but

---

[80] American Baptist Convention, "American Baptist Resolution on Environmental Concerns," last modified March 1995, https://www.abc-usa.org/wp-content/uploads/2019/02/ENVIRONMENTAL-CONCERNS.pdf.

[81] American Baptist Convention, "American Baptist Resolution on Global Warming," last modified September 2007, https://www.abc-usa.org/wp-content/uploads/2019/02/globwarm.pdf.

[82] "Resolution on Population Explosion," Southern Baptist Convention, June 1, 1967, https://www.sbc.net/resource-library/resolutions/resolution-on-population-explosion/; "Resolution on Population Explosion," Southern Baptist Convention, June 1, 1974, https://www.sbc.net/resource-library/resolutions/resolution-on-population-explosion-2/; "Resolution on Abortion," Southern Baptist Convention, June 1, 1971, https://www.sbc.net/resource-library/resolutions/resolution-on-abortion-2/; "Resolution on Stewardship of Gods Creation," Southern Baptist Convention, June 1, 1974, https://www.sbc.net/resource-library/resolutions/resolution-on-stewardship-of-gods-creation/.

[83] Chasteen, *The Case for Compulsory Birth Control*.

[84] Chute et al., *The Baptist Story*, 287.

[85] "Resolution on the Care of Our Environment," Southern Baptist Convention, June 1, 1983, https://www.sbc.net/resource-library/resolutions/resolution-on-the-care-of-our-environment/.

the final document's proposal was changed from Southern Baptists "reverence" the earth to "regard" it, due to concerns about nature worship. Two paragraphs encouraging greater government regulation and entry into international environmental treaties were also deleted after debate.[86] In 1992, the Christian Life Commission of the SBC published a volume that affirmed care for creation as proper stewardship, but simultaneously warned of the excesses of some forms of environmentalism, especially those versions that tend toward neo-paganism.[87] A distinct shift in the approach to creation care occurred among Southern Baptists during the early decades after the Conservative Resurgence.

In 2007, the SBC messengers approved a statement on global warming, which called for positive stewardship of the earth while raising questions about the validity of human-caused climate change.[88] In 2008, there was an attempt to pass a new resolution that called for communal action to fight climate change, but that resolution did not pass.[89] Interest in creation care among Southern Baptists has remained limited, though there are hopeful signs. Two Southern Baptists, both now on the faculty of Southeastern Baptist Theological Seminary, published a volume focused on encouraging creation care with the denomination's publisher.[90] In 2014, the former head of the SBC's Ethics and Religious Liberty Commission, Russell Moore, published a straightforward view of human responsibility for the environment that is theologically orthodox and entirely consistent with the legacy

---

[86] Weaver, "Baptist Environmentalisms," 249–52.

[87] Richard D. Land and Louis A. Moore, eds., *The Earth Is the Lord's* (Nashville: Broadman, 1992).

[88] "On Global Warming," Southern Baptist Convention, June 1, 2007, https://www.sbc.net/resource-library/resolutions/on-global-warming/.

[89] Neela Banerjee, "Southern Baptists Back a Shift on Climate Change," *New York Times*, March 10, 2008, https://www.nytimes.com/2008/03/10/us/10baptist.html.

[90] Mark Liederbach and Seth Bible, *True North: Christ, the Gospel, and Creation Care* (Nashville: B&H Academic, 2012).

of figures like Francis Schaeffer.[91] Furthermore, there is a growing politically conservative interest in environmentalism, which may allow the orthopraxy of evangelical creation care to become less alien to social conservatives.[92] However, it is likely that theologically conservative entities like the SBC will continue to be wary of environmentalism because of its associations with population control, abortion, and socialism. As long as abandoning or revising basic Christian doctrines is assumed as a necessary part of engaging in creation care, some Christians will continue to have difficulty disentangling the valid cause of environmentalism from its political and cultural context.

Implications

Environmental stewardship should be a growing part of Baptist witness in the world. Part of demonstrating the plausibility of any system of belief, such as orthodox Christianity, must be explaining how that system of belief can effectively address pressing problems in the world. Baptists, with their traditional adherence to the sufficiency of Scripture, the goodness of creation, valuing input from general revelation, the limited but significant placement of humanity as stewards of the created order, and hope in the coming cosmic renewal in the new heavens and earth, are well-equipped to answer this question.

The primary reason for engaging in sound environmental stewardship is not apologetic, however, but it is a matter of obedience. With God as owner of all creation (Ps 24:1) and humanity having an original and continuing responsibility for the care and use of creation (Gen 2:15; 9:1–4; Ps 8:5–8), it is morally unacceptable for Baptists to neglect teaching and acting on the responsibility to care for creation. Christ's work on earth was redemptive,

---

[91] Russell D. Moore, "Heaven and Nature Sing: How Evangelical Theology Can Inform the Task of Environmental Protection (And Vice Versa)," in *Journal of the Evangelical Theological Society* 57, no. 3 (2014): 571–88.

[92] For example, see Rod Dreher, *Crunchy Cons* (New York: Crown Forum, 2006) and Roger Scruton, *How to Think Seriously about the Planet: The Case for an Environmental Conservatism* (New York: Oxford, 2012).

as he healed the sick and pushed back the effects of the fall. Christians are called to imitate Christ in their lives on this earth (1 Cor 11:1), which seems to encourage a redemptive focus through creation care as part of a broad pursuit of holiness.

A second reason for increasing attention to the environment is that engaging in responsible stewardship of creation is an avenue for demonstrating the power of the gospel for renewal. Richard Land was correct to argue in 1992, "We must help our young people and others by moving from ascertaining orthodoxy to advocating orthopraxy. We must move from principle to practice and from advice to application."[93] Building on an orthodox, theocentric foundation, positive environmental action, like taking resource conservation into account in lifestyle decisions, can be a powerful demonstration of the renewing power of the gospel and a testimony of the coming redemption of all of creation (see Rom 8:18–23).

Third, not only does a clear theological basis exist for creation care, but also a strong ethical element for a proper concern for environmental ethics. Christians are called to have a special interest in the well-being of the poor (Gal 2:10). Typically, the poor are more likely to be negatively affected by environmental degradation. Therefore, whether the concern is reducing obvious signs of pollution or seeking to mitigate the impact of climate change on the poor, concern for the environment is closely tied to concern for the well-being of the poor. At the same time, the poor are also the most likely to be economically impacted by regulations designed to limit environmental degradation, which contributes to the complexity of environmental action for the sake of the poor.

Conclusion

There is fertile ground for environmental stewardship among Baptists and theologically conservative Christians. Yet it may not consistently look like

---

[93] Land, "Overview: Beliefs and Behaviors," in *The Earth Is the Lord's*, 25.

other versions of environmentalism, because along with concern for the environment, Scripture calls for affirming the dignity of all humans, which includes aspiring to alleviate global poverty through economic development. Ultimately, the vision of Scripture is a move from an undeveloped garden (Gen 2:15) to a garden city (Rev 21:9–22:5), which honors the original integrity of creation. Many ethical demands exist in tension. Orthodox Christians, including Baptists, must pursue the goodness of creation; at the same time, Baptists must continue to resist evils like abortion, eugenics, and environmental policies that restrict freedom of conscience, harm the poor, or call for counterproductive or unworkable alterations to economic life. Biblical stewardship integrates concerns for all areas of life, including caring for creation.

The task for Baptists is to not grow weary in doing good (Gal 6:9), but to continue pursuing orthodoxy and orthopraxy with sincere vigor while holding out the hope of the gospel through verbal proclamation. Environmental ethics, like other issues of justice, can never be allowed to crowd out a focus on personal evangelism, but it can be a tool to point others to the hope Christians have in Christ of a coming redemption for all things (see 1 Pet 3:15). As such, a Baptist political theology cannot neglect a robust vision of environmental stewardship.

24

The Necessity of Humility in Determining the Connection between Political Economy and Neighbor Love: Reflections on Baptist Political Economy

By Hunter Baker

Political economy refers to the application of ideas and methods to govern the production, exchange, and distribution of goods and services. No matter how libertarian or laissez-faire one might be in outlook, the intersection of economy with politics is essentially inevitable at some level. There must be some way to deter and punish theft, enforce the rule of law, provide for the peaceful adjudication of disputes, ensure that contracts are honored, and take action against fraud. All of the above items require government action. Others argue for more extensive public responsibility over economic affairs, such as ensuring the equal distribution of opportunities, resources, or even outcomes.

As a result, the question contended in modern society is how extensive the interaction between law and economy must be. Is a minimum, umpire-and-referee type of government the one best adapted to regulate the economic affairs of human beings? Or might justice be better served by subjecting the economy to some collective notion of fairness? Or is the right answer somewhere in between? The empirical practice of nations tends to cluster around some band of arrangements in the center of the spectrum, but it is important to consider the matter thoughtfully rather than simply drift along because the stakes are high. As Friedrich Hayek observed, the economy is the means for many of our ends.[1]

The case for an economy with minimum political control has probably been best made by thinkers such as Milton Friedman, Friedrich Hayek, and Robert Nozick. Friedman acted as an evangelist for limited government and free markets during the twentieth century. He pointed out that economic freedom and political freedoms tend to travel together. For example, Friedman noted that during the Cold War an avid reader visiting a newsstand in Manhattan would have been able to choose between the highly capitalistic *Wall Street Journal*, the Socialist-inspired *Daily Worker*, or a variety of other options. The intellectually curious individual in Moscow would have only the choice of regime-created and approved publications. The simple point is that if the state drives the economy, it will also tend to monopolize all other political and cultural activity.[2] Contained within this critique of the Socialist/Communist models is the idea that human beings who are able to gather power unto themselves via the state's coercive capability will work

---

[1] Friedrich Hayek, *The Road to Serfdom: Texts and Documents*, The Collected Works of F. A. Hayek, ed. Bruce Caldwell (Chicago: University of Chicago, 2007), 127.

[2] Milton Friedman, *Capitalism and Freedom*, 40th anniv. ed. (Chicago: University of Chicago, 2002), 18.

the system to their own advantage and prevent competition.[3] Friedman also had great faith, in an Aristotelian sense, that the relevant merit would vindicate itself in market competition. So rather than having a law promoting affirmative action for members of minority groups, Friedman believed the market would use competition to reward those who rationally ascertained ability and punish those who made irrational and invidious distinctions. Generally, Friedman believed competition could remedy many social abuses and would result in better outcomes for the people through lower prices and more abundant goods and services.[4]

Friedrich Hayek contributed his seminal attack on the idea, attractive to many, that enlightened social planning from experts would lead to better living for human beings. He pointed out that while the notion of a plan is naturally appealing, the reality is that it is extremely difficult to achieve social consensus around any unified course of action because any plan aiming to order the affairs of a society will inherently be quite complex.[5] Frustration with the problem of consensus will lead to great power being delegated to ambitious (and often ruthless) political leaders, democratically unaccountable bureaucratic experts, or both.[6] In the end, the costs in terms of lost freedom are likely to far outweigh any benefits. According to Hayek, realization of the fact that there is no single scale of value around which activities can be organized should lead people to opt for greater freedom so they can maintain their ability to satisfy their own goals rather than delegate their accomplishment to authorities they may not be able to control.[7]

The political philosopher Robert Nozick added an extensive critique of economic and governmental control to the conversation as well. Broadly speaking, he argued that a robust concept of self-ownership should lead us

---

[3] Friedman, 137–60.
[4] Friedman, 108–18.
[5] Hayek, *The Road to Serfdom*, 100–112.
[6] Hayek, 157–70.
[7] Hayek, 101–2.

to embrace a minimal state.[8] We might choose one of his specific insights simply to add to what Friedman and Hayek have said. According to Nozick, once citizens commit to social equality in terms of material outcomes rather than opportunities, they are consenting to permanent and continuous active interference in their lives because equality of outcomes can be achieved in no other way. If freedom exists, differences will assert themselves and social striations will emerge.[9]

If we change lenses to focus less on freedom and more on equality, then we could consider Karl Marx, John Rawls, and John Kenneth Galbraith as representatives. Marx read history through the lens of class struggle and sought to break what he saw as an abusive and oppressive relationship between the rich and poor through revolution and the seizure of the means of production by the proletariat. From his perspective, labor provided most of the value yet received a relatively meager reward approximating subsistence. Once the people fully owned and operated the economic apparatus, the state would wither away as human beings entered an eschatological golden age.[10]

Employing his celebrated device of the veil of ignorance, Rawls encouraged people to discover justice by imagining the rules they would want to govern the world if they could not know what position they would occupy in it upon being born.[11] His conclusion was that everyone would insist upon two primary principles: nondiscrimination based on race, sex, religion, etc., and equal opportunity accompanied by the proviso that any social and economic inequality ultimately redounds to benefit the least-advantaged members of society.[12] This proviso about inequality that benefits the least

---

[8] Robert Nozick, *Anarchy, State, and Utopia* (New York: Basic Books, 1974).

[9] Nozick, 163.

[10] Karl Marx and Frederick Engels, *Manifesto of the Communist Party*, February 1848, https://www.marxists.org/archive/marx/works/1848/communist-manifesto/.

[11] John Rawls, *Justice as Fairness: A Restatement*, ed. Erin Kelly (Cambridge: Harvard University, 2001), 80–88.

[12] Rawls, 42–43.

advantaged substitutes for a purely equal distribution of resources in Rawls's thinking and presumably is designed to take account of the differences in actual performance of economic systems.

John Kenneth Galbraith was an economist of the Left who sought to build his prescriptions upon the recognition that human beings of the mid-twentieth century found themselves in a new situation. They had benefitted from a massive increase in well-being sufficient to upset the often dismal economic conventional wisdom.[13] For him, then, the answer was not to overturn the capitalist system, but to take advantage of vastly increased wealth so as to build up the public sector as a needed balance for the rich private one.[14] It is notable that Galbraith thought it would be wise to avoid the temptation of redistribution in favor of the broadest possible taxes to achieve the result, while avoiding class antagonism.[15]

Today, we live in a world where the Chinese Communist Party presides over a national economy featuring publicly traded massive corporations owned by Chinese and American investors alike. North Korea continues with a state-ownership model and finds itself on the other end of unflattering comparisons with its neighbor to the south, composed of the same people who enjoy a far higher standard of living and greater human rights. Most political economic arrangements in the modern world sit between metaphorical 35-yard lines, where a substantial amount of private property and capitalism is essentially assumed. Likewise, redistribution, welfare systems, and social safety nets are common features of modern societies. The debate is almost entirely about where the balance will be struck rather than fundamental changes of the types attempted in the twentieth century by totalitarians or dreamt of by acolytes of Ayn Rand and libertarians.

---

[13] John Kenneth Galbraith, *The Affluent Society* (Boston: Houghton Mifflin, 1998), 65.

[14] Galbraith, 186–99.

[15] Galbraith, 229.

Theological Context

While various voices argue for a particular biblical interpretation of political economy, it is extremely difficult to draw conclusions adequate to sustain a normative model applicable in all times and places. Looking carefully at the Old and New Testaments, readers can draw forth some broad principles that can inform their view of how law and economics should interact.

The first principle one can pull from the text is the relationship between human beings, work, and dominion over the creation. Work tends to be considered a consequence of the fall, but Genesis depicts Adam working in the garden before the fall.[16] Work is natural for human beings. The fall brought difficulty and frustration to work but did not bring work itself as a curse. Human beings satisfy something in their nature by working. Subduing creation and exercising dominion are also part of the mantle of Adam that falls upon succeeding generations. It would seem a natural conclusion that subduing creation and exercising dominion have to do with development, stewardship, and use of natural resources.

Genesis also teaches that humans are social creatures: because it was not good that Adam was alone, God gave him a companion.[17] From the original pair came the formation of families and the various types of communities that eventually filled the earth with villages, city-states, and nations. As social creatures develop and use resources, they also engage in exchange. From this combination of dominion and social nature, the growth of economies can be seen. Because of the gains to be had from specialization (something humans apprehend and act upon), substantial interdependencies develop.

From the biblical text, then, comes a vision of human beings relating to each other economically as well as in other ways because of their nature and the tasks God set before them. This alone, however, is not enough to

---

[16] Gen 2:15.
[17] Gen 2:18.

give us something like a biblical political economy. The question is whether additional consideration of the text provides a clearer vision.

The Ten Commandments contain instructions not to steal and not to covet the property of others.[18] These commandments appear to presuppose the validity of private property. However, it is possible that these commandments recognize private property as something almost inevitable in the sense that human beings in a wide variety of social contexts are likely to have property they largely control whether that be land or possessions. Even if a person lived in a collectivist setting, it would make sense for him to have a dwelling that is functionally his even though the state ultimately owns it. In this case, the moral force of the command would still make sense. The man living in unit 22 should not covet unit 25. Nor should he attempt to maneuver so as to push the current occupant out. The point is private property would not necessarily mean the "fee simple" possession aimed for in modern capitalist societies. Still, the reasoning here may add up to casuistry. The prohibitions of theft and covetousness are fundamental moral commandments. Private property appears to be biblically essential in some way.

If private property is somehow essential to a biblical vision of economics, that alone would not lead to the conclusion that laissez faire must then prevail. To the extent that the Bible contains admonitions to deal honestly and to use accurate weights and measures, it tracks with the more limited type of prohibition against fraud, which is another type of theft.[19] But as to the question of whether such rules constitute a floor or a ceiling remains open.

When we attempt to discern whether the Bible promotes capitalism and free markets or a redistributive socialism, the admonition that the person who will not work shall not eat often comes to the fore.[20] Likewise, Prov 18:9 observes that slack work is akin to destruction. The moral command taken from these passages is that each person is expected to labor.

---

[18] Exod 20:15, 17.

[19] For example, see Deut 25:13–16.

[20] 2 Thess 3:10.

That makes perfect sense as we rely on each other's work as we seek to both survive and thrive. Opponents of the welfare state might draw upon these verses to support free markets and limited interaction of government with the economy. However, the argument is not as strong as one may suppose. It is entirely possible to imagine a socialist society with strong laws forbidding idleness and/or punishing sloth in ways to resonate with the Christian principle apparent in the passage.

The experience of Israel with government coming directly from God offers stimulus for thinking about political economy as well. Leviticus 25 contains instructions preventing most land from being sold in perpetuity. Rather, the system described is one with a preference for keeping land in productive use while allowing debtors to recover their land even after they alienate it.[21] While the philosophy is not explicitly stated, the intent appears to be preventing debtors from falling further and further behind while the wealthy rise further and further above them. Land can be redeemed. Debts are regularly released. While we today do not understand the laws of Israel to govern us theocratically, these kinds of laws are moral in nature rather than ceremonial and, thus, are suggestive of just practice for the time and place in which they were in force, at a minimum. The text states this limitation on alienation of land is a recognition of the fact that God ultimately owns all land and is thus entitled to regulate its exchange.

Along similar lines, we can reflect on the instruction in Lev 19:9–10 to leave the corners of fields unharvested and not to gather fallen fruit in the vineyard so that the poor and needy will be able to collect that food for themselves. Again, the relevant verses communicate God's ultimate ownership of the land and his right to dictate how it may be used. Based on the instruction, God cares for the poor and needy and issues regulations to provide for their survival through the apportionment of some percentage of what belongs to those with greater means.

---

[21] Lev 25:23–24.

The biblical teaching repeatedly asserts God's lordship over economic matters. Whether it regards prohibitions on theft and fraud, limitations on the way land can be used, or the days appropriate for labor (note the instruction to rest from labor on the Sabbath in imitation of God's rest after his own creative work), it is clear from a biblical perspective that perceiving the economy or business as activities with their own self-contained logic to which superseding morality is extraneous is out of the question in the Old Testament.

To this point, I have primarily considered Old Testament texts regarding economic life. Before moving to the New Testament, it is important to acknowledge the presence of slavery in the life of Israel. The harsh, oppressive slavery practiced by the Egyptians on the Israelites is clearly condemned and defeated by God, but it is also clear that some forms of slavery were practiced within the Hebrew community. It is important to note that this slavery, though predating the type practiced in the Americas and Caribbean by thousands of years, does not appear to have had the savage features of race-based, chattel slavery. Instead, the slavery practiced by Israel seems to occupy a place on a spectrum between the African slavery of the period between the 1600s and 1800s and something more like indentured servitude and even hired work. Indeed, the Old Testament itself contemplates occasions for the movement of human beings between the status of slave and hired workman. Isaiah 58:6, more satisfyingly, may be read as a call for an end to oppression and the breaking of yokes.

We gain additional insight on the issue in the New Testament when the apostle Paul wrote to Philemon about the fate of Onesimus, an escaped slave who had become his young helper. Paul wrote in a way that acknowledged Philemon's legal right, while simultaneously stating that he could command the release of the slave through his spiritual authority.[22] It would seem, then, that Paul respected the existence of the law, but noted that it represented a sub-Christian ethic for followers of Christ. The correct status for Onesimus

---

[22] Phlm 1:8.

was brother rather than slave.[23] It does not seem a stretch to conclude that if one truly intends to submit to Christ's lordship, then one would abjure the holding of slaves. Nevertheless, the issue of human bondage did result in the split of the US Baptists because of a disagreement over whether a slaveholder could serve as a missionary.

What we primarily see regarding economics in the New Testament is a focus on how Christians should treat their own wealth. The possession of riches appears to represent a significant spiritual danger for at least two reasons. First, the money may have been obtained in an illicit or unjust manner. Second, the person who has compiled substantial wealth has to answer for his stewardship of it.

The passage that attracts the greatest interest among those seeking guidance regarding the political economy of the New Testament is Acts 4:32–37, which describes owners of lands and houses selling their holdings and turning the proceeds over to the church, which then distributed the money to those who had need. Through this renunciation of personal rights to wealth, privation appears to have been eliminated. The action of giving generously accords well with the warning against creating stores of wealth on earth because of their inevitable perishability.[24] It is unclear how applicable this passage is to political economy, however, as it describes voluntary charity within the church rather than compelled redistribution through a government.

But the New Testament does address taxation and governmental authority. The disciple Matthew had a bad reputation on account of his occupation as a tax collector.[25] Zacchaeus had used his position as a tax collector to overcharge and defraud people.[26] Pharisees questioned Jesus about paying

---

[23] Phlm 1:16.

[24] Matt 6:19.

[25] See Matt 9:9 identifying Matthew as a tax collector. See Mark 2:13–17 on how tax collectors were received by the Jews.

[26] Luke 19:1–10.

taxes to Caesar in an attempt to trap him. If Jesus said it was appropriate to pay taxes to Caesar, he would offend those who resented the yoke of Rome. But if he said it was wrong to pay the taxes, he would be in open rebellion. Jesus answered without fear that it was right to pay the tax because Caesar's image was on the coin. In other words, the monetary system has something to do with the government in power. The government has a rightful claim. However, it is also important to note that Jesus paired his "give to Caesar the things that are Caesar's" with a complementary instruction to give to God what is God's.[27] By going beyond the question of taxation, Jesus pointed to God's greater authority and claims. It is reasonable to argue that Jesus's teaching in this instance offers support for the idea of a limited government. In other words, Caesar has a sphere in which he must be respected, but it is not coextensive with God's comprehensive reign.

From all this, we can draw forth some different angles to consider in thinking about political economy for Christians (and especially for Baptists as rigorously Scripture-oriented people), but it is questionable whether any specific system for law and government asserts itself in the biblical text. As far as individuals go, wealth should clearly never be an idol and should be held loosely. In addition, those who have wealth should use it to aid the poor. It is also clear that those with wealth should not use their resources to oppress the poor nor to gain further wealth via lying and cheating. We can think of this as procedural justice of the type embraced by virtually everyone in terms of legal expectations.

The Old Testament laws relating to the sale, use, and disposition of products of land indicate a concern for some form of distributive justice so that the poor will have something and that those who become poor through bad management will not leave their families locked in permanent cycles of poverty. These regulations are more radical in the sense that they encroach substantially upon laissez faire, but they are part of the moral law and demand reflection and possibly should influence modern political economy

---

[27] Mark 12:13–17.

in terms of moderating the impact of competition and favoring those who suffer from generational, inherited disadvantages of poverty, disenfranchisement, or oppression.

Within the church, sharing resources appears to be part of the model available in the early body Christians often claim to want to emulate. Whether that sharing in the church should be equated to a politically coerced sharing and forced redistribution seems doubtful other than in an eschatological sense when the political kingdom mirrors the spiritual one and acknowledges the same Lord. Certainly, the church could model the Acts example *in the body* far more vigorously and effectively than it does.

Political, Institutional, and Cultural Context

It is important to note the dominant political system observed in the Bible is monarchy.[28] While a combination of scriptural Protestantism and, perhaps, natural law Catholicism has helped lead Christians in a different direction over time, the brute fact of monarchy's dominance in the biblical text remains. When Paul counseled his readers to submit to the government, he was doing so in a world full of kings. When early Christians resisted the government (explicitly for the purpose of preaching the gospel in the Scriptures), it was through disobeying and enduring consequences rather than organizing, making appeals to fundamental human rights, and voting for change. Empirically speaking, kings largely ruled as they wished and were able to do so to the extent that the results were neither so incompetent nor so harsh as to occasion revolution.

Before the industrial revolution, wealth was predominantly agricultural in nature. Kings and lesser aristocrats presided over large tracts of land that were often not subject to dynamic exchange. Rather, the feudal model

---

[28] See generally Robert P. Kraynak's argument in *Christian Faith and Modern Democracy: God and Politics in the Fallen World* (Notre Dame, IN: University of Notre Dame Press, 2001).

featured political and economic power wedded through the possession of estates preserved generationally through primogeniture. As a result, those families with power and money tended to stay that way. Those born to the laboring classes also tended to remain in their station. Societies ran on a paternalistic basis from top to bottom with royals and aristocrats seeing themselves as fathers and mothers of the people. The unflattering corollary was that the people were children. Ideally, this responsibility (seen as God-given) was discharged benevolently.

The Reformation did not have the immediate effect of upsetting monarchies. Rather, the displacement of the Catholic Church's international dominance in Europe in favor of several state churches with monarchs at the head strengthened kings and queens who no longer had to contend with popes. Over time, however, the development of the printing press, the translation of the Bible into vernacular languages, the Reformation project of teaching literacy so people could read the Scriptures themselves, and the rise of a middle class of urban, educated, moderately wealthy citizens contributed significantly to the development of republicanism and, eventually, liberal democracy in Europe and across the Atlantic in the English colonies that would become the United States.[29]

It is also true, however, that the Reformation led to a lengthy period of religious wars in Europe. Some thinkers responded to the breakup of an authoritative tradition by attempting to reconstitute society from the ground up. It was through social contract theory and probably John Locke, most of all, that the idea of government depending on the consent of the people grew in influence.[30] Today, most modern countries assume consent-based polities as a given.

---

[29] The growth of literacy combined with acknowledgement of a common, authoritative text (the Bible) equalized ordinary people and the elite to the degree that both had to acknowledge the Bible's commands regardless of their station. In this way, scriptural Protestantism aided the development of liberal democracy.

[30] John Locke, *Second Treatise of Government* (1689; Project Gutenberg, 2003), https://www.gutenberg.org/files/7370/7370-h/7370-h.htm

As consent-based constitutional democracy grew, so too did ideas regarding laissez-faire economics (Adam Smith's capitalist manifesto, *The Wealth of Nations*, appeared in 1776). Initially, the free market political economy offered a way to cut through hereditary hierarchies, medieval guilds, and mercantilist protection to clear the way for an aristocracy of merit.[31] The United States offers an excellent example with the rise in the nineteenth century of self-made men in both politics (Andrew Jackson and Abraham Lincoln, for example) and business (Andrew Carnegie and Thomas Edison, among many others). Political and economic freedom helped unleash tremendous dynamism in economies and brought about technological leaps that ultimately improved the standards of living for human beings all over the planet. However, despite a general rise in living standards, economic freedom has also tended to result in gigantic gaps in wealth and a sense that huge fortunes can enable the rich to control governments as well.

In the modern world, we observe three fundamental political approaches to running economic systems. At one pole, with a strong emphasis on liberty, is a call to leave markets free with the lowest taxes and regulation possible. The idea is that free markets offer the greatest respect to individuals as they pursue their life goals and that the laissez-faire approach leads to the most impressive growth of wealth and technological progress due to ideal conditions for economic efficiency. The free market ideal, then, proposes a happy marriage of principle and prudence. However, it is also the case that a truly free market society effectively does not exist. In other words, it is a unicorn. At the other pole, with a strong emphasis on equality, are efforts to bring all economic production under the full control of the political process to achieve a unified experience of life. Regimes on the equality pole are not unicorns and have been attempted. Of course, ambitious attempts at this other type of society have invariably been totalitarian in nature with

---

[31] Thomas G. West, *The Political Theory of the American Founding* (Cambridge: Cambridge University, 2017), 74.

extraordinary costs to freedoms outside the economic process. The fact that such regimes are hostile to religious liberty is especially important for Baptists who emphasize the importance of voluntariness in matters of faith. At least prudentially speaking, modesty in visions of political economy bodes better for religious freedom than grandiose ones.

Between the two poles of liberty and equality are the intermediate systems that dominate most governments of the world today. The other systems depend on the existence of private property and free market capitalism at some level. What varies is the degree of state control and redistribution. The United States represents an intermediate form with a more restrained government and less redistribution. Some European countries have a more energetic government and more redistribution. China has developed a form closer to state control, combining state-directed capitalism with a highly powerful, autocratic state unrestrained by democratic accountability.

In the democracies of the world, the debate turns continually upon the question of how to manage liberty, equality, and prosperity in such a way as to maximize economic output, equality, and human flourishing. Running in the background of that discussion is the realization that prioritizing equality too highly may result in diminished standards of living and increased scarcity of goods. At the same time, prioritizing liberty and autonomy too highly may lead to generationally fixed, highly striated classes of winners and losers with the losers living marginal existences and threatening revolution.

The major factors influencing the shape of political economy are taxation, redistribution, regulation, and trade policy. Debate surrounds whether governments should interfere with economic efficiency by taxing at progressively steeper rates as income rises so as to redistribute resources from the wealthy to the poor and whether they should restrict the flow of international trade in an attempt to protect workers and industries inside a nation. There are also questions regarding the degree to which competition should be regulated within the nation's borders. For example, is it preferable to allow as many airlines to compete as are capable of purchasing aircraft, hiring workers, and renting terminal space, or would it be better to permit only a few competitors who will be expected to adhere to a regulatory price schedule, wages agreed to by a government board, and flying only approved routes?

To state the matter somewhat crudely, political economy grapples with reconciling liberty, equality, and social harmony while endeavoring not to kill the goose who lays the golden eggs. The strategies for managing political economy that have tilted too far in the direction of equality and the use of coercive state power to achieve that equality could result in terminal diagnoses for such wealth-producing metaphorical fowl. Anyone, whether citizen, statesman, or polis, must grapple with balancing equality with prosperity and human flourishing.

State of the Debate: Baptists and Outsiders

Baptists do not have a particular view of political economy to which they have generally subscribed. While things like a rigorous focus on Scripture, the independence of individual congregations, and religious liberty are Baptist distinctives, which they uphold over against challenges within the broader umbrella of the Christian faith and from outside the faith, Baptists have not tended to promote a view of economic affairs that can really be called Baptist.

The Baptists emerged from among the Puritans. In an age that predated Marx and more modern theories of redistribution, it is not surprising that the Puritans emphasized clean living, hard work, and Christian charity. It is likely they would have rejected social welfare systems of the type seen today on the belief that indiscriminate charity does more harm than good and such programs do nothing to reform poor moral choices. At the same time, they shared traditional Christian reservations against predatory forms of capitalism such as charging high interest, inflating the cost of goods to increase profits, and taking advantage of crises and scarcity to make bargains one-sided.[32] They inhabited a world in which expected social norms constrained what businessmen could do, which tempered the harsher consequences of capitalism.

In the middle of the nineteenth century, strongly influenced by Adam Smith's *The Wealth of Nations*, Baptist pastor and president of Brown University Francis Wayland wrote a popular textbook on political economy that promoted free market ideas, probably the closest thing Baptists have to a historic Baptist contribution to economic thought.[33] At different times and places, many Baptists have accepted the free market view of the world in part, perhaps, because of its easy fit with Baptist voluntarism. However, one can also find notes of dissent and sometimes powerful moves in a different direction from other Baptists from the nineteenth century to today.

While Baptists have rarely promoted outright socialism (at least in the mass), they have enthusiastically supported movements that would subordinate market forces to demands for moral reform. The first major effort of this type was the attempt to ensure businesses were closed on Sundays to preserve the Sabbath as a day of rest and worship.[34] While Baptists did not approve of requiring people to belong to church, tithe, attend, have the churches supported by taxes, etc., they have often tried and succeeded in leaving the day available for obedience to one of God's fundamental commands.

The second major effort was to forbid the production, sale, and consumption of alcoholic beverages. Attempting to ban a commercial product with such wide acceptance and historical pedigree constituted a major

---

[32] Leland Ryken, *Worldly Saints: The Puritans As They Really Were* (Grand Rapids: Zondervan, 1986), 173–86.

[33] Francis Wayland, *The Elements of Moral Science* (New York: Cooke, 1835).

[34] David W. Bebbington, *The Dominance of Evangelicalism: The Age of Spurgeon and Moody* (Downers Grove, IL: IVP, 2005), 239–40.

attack on the prerogatives of market capitalism.[35] While the Bible does not ban the consumption of alcohol outside of an admonition not to be drunk, it is possible to understand the attack on alcohol for its negative effects on men as breadwinners, its connection to spousal abuse, and its capacity to undermine the rational and moral agency of the person who drinks to excess. It is no surprise that alcoholism can often be accompanied by sexual infidelity, the use of prostitutes, and gambling—all constituting a web of social pathology that spreads through a community. Adam Smith noted that preachers who had the poor for an audience often proclaimed a stern moral message because all understood that while the wealthy could afford their errors, a workingman could be undone by his.[36] Clearly, alcoholism had a major negative social impact in the nineteenth and early twentieth centuries. And it is probably no coincidence that one of the first major developments following women's suffrage in the United States was the passage of an amendment to the Constitution banning alcohol.

More ambitious and holistic than the Sabbath and temperance movements was the Social Gospel thinking of Walter Rauschenbusch and others. Rauschenbusch was a Baptist pastor in Hell's Kitchen. Like many with a mind for reform in that era, Rauschenbusch saw American capitalism as something predatory in nature, placing him at the opposite end of the spectrum from Francis Wayland. Rauschenbusch thought competitive capitalism was, in effect, the opposite of Christianity's focus on love, mercy, and service. If business were an island, he maintained the church should send missionaries to it! From his perspective, a focus on unhindered capitalism had left the business part of the social order unregenerate. As a result, workers were being exploited for subsistence wages, products had the lowest

---

[35] David W. Bebbington, *Baptists through the Centuries: A History of a Global People* (Waco, TX: Baylor University, 2010), 127.

[36] Gertrude Himmelfarb highlighted this part of Smith's analysis in *One Nation, Two Cultures: A Searching Examination of American Society in the Aftermath of Our Cultural Revolution* (New York: Vintage, 2001), 3–5.

quality producers could get away with, and unscrupulous operators might even have sold poisonous or unsafe goods merely to squeeze out extra cents of profit.[37]

Although some businessmen would argue that Christian principles are extraneous to commerce, Rauschenbusch thought a moral analysis was exactly what was needed. While he conceded competition had a positive impact in clearing out inefficiencies, he insisted that the reign of competition is ultimately a reign of fear leading to a race to the moral and ethical bottom as all prioritize their own survival over the good of others. In part, this moral devolution had been enabled by the development of the corporate form, which put the organization as an isolating shield between producers and the public.[38] Individuals could hide behind the corporate shield if anything went wrong rather than suffering the consequences personally. Then, they could go on to start a new corporation to repeat abuses all over again with a clean slate.

Rauschenbusch thought it was exactly the role of the government to interfere with competition in the interests of safety and humane treatment. Although Rauschenbusch and his Social Gospel are often criticized by conservative coreligionists, it should not be missed that what he called for was not so different than the drives for Sabbath observation and temperance. The scope of his vision was simply more holistic.

The natural impulse from conservatives has been to dismiss Rauschenbusch as a Communist, a Socialist, or a theological liberalizer with no interest in the real, life-changing encounter between the individual and Christ. But that would not be fair. Rauschenbusch was neither a doctrinaire Socialist nor a preacher thinking only about legislation. He wanted to see the lordship of Christ extended to business both through the moral regulation of the activity and the conversion of human beings engaged in

---

[37] Walter Rauschenbusch, *Christianizing the Social Order* (New York: Macmillan, 1912).

[38] Rauschenbusch, *Christianizing the Social Order.*

commerce. It is true that he used the language of evolution ("the polliwog who needs to become a frog"), but he also spoke of the kingdom of Christ and the movement of the Holy Spirit in individual lives.[39]

From all of this, one can perhaps draw the inference that Baptists have generally agreed that it is legitimate to bring moral and spiritual principles to bear upon the economy and the government's regulation of it. When that should be done, the degree to which it should be done, and what justifications are necessary to support the infringement are points of debate to the present day inside and outside of the church. Baptists have typically not made political economy a point of separation, though they may become excited in arguing about it.

Regarding Southern Baptists (the largest body of Baptists in the world), the approach to political economy has mostly been conservative. Some Baptist writers have expressed their distress at the lack of desire of most Baptists to follow Rauschenbusch's lead and view reigning economic regimes more critically or pursue reform more energetically.[40] The reality is that when laissez-faire was dominant, a great many Southern Baptists leaned that way. And when big government was popularized in the US by a figure such as Franklin D. Roosevelt, many Southern Baptists surely voted for him and his program as FDR dominated the South electorally in each of his four presidential campaigns. When former "New Dealer" Ronald Reagan embraced small government while fighting the Soviet Union's collectivist (and officially atheist) model, many Southern Baptists supported him.[41]

The matter has perhaps been summed up best by the Baptist US Congressman Lawrence Brooks Hays in his remarks to the Baptist World

---

[39] Rauschenbusch, n.p.

[40] For a good example, see John Lee Eighmy, *Churches in Cultural Captivity: A History of the Social Attitudes of Southern Baptists* (Knoxville: University of Tennessee, 1987), 57–92.

[41] A great many Southern Baptists will recognize this same pattern in their own families with the Silent Generation voting for FDR and Democrats almost throughout their lives and Baby Boomers shifting toward Reagan and the Republicans.

Alliance in Copenhagen in 1947. While he insisted that Baptists could not compromise on religious liberty (though they believe Christian truths can beneficially inform law), he noted, "We do not identify our faith with governmental or economic patterns." He went on to say Baptists will tend to trust the state when it comes to "borderland issues" such as "the taxing of our wealth." Baptists, in his view, tend to trust popular governments "to deal honorably and justly with its constituency" and have found that promise fulfilled. If the state respects individual conscience, then there is room for prudence to shape the rest.[42]

Hays's view is not surprising in light of traditional Baptist priorities, which have tended to lean heavily in the direction of evangelism, missions, and religious liberty (which is strongly related to evangelism and missions) rather than toward developing a Protestant equivalent for Catholic social thought. Maximum flexibility regarding political arrangements paves the way for the acceptance by foreign governments of missionaries and for the acceptance of the gospel by people who do not feel the gospel is simply a cover for smuggling in ideological control of some kind.

Implications: What Does It Mean for Baptist Witness and Baptist Activism in the World?

Because the primary Baptist concerns are pure, voluntary worship and obedience uncoerced and uncorrupted by the state, evangelism and missions aimed at bringing people from around the world into relationship with Jesus Christ, and the regular study of God's Word, it is highly preferable that the state be limited in important ways. The limitation of the state itself makes sense in Christian terms given the example of the apostles' insistence on following God rather than men and drawing out the implications of the parable of Caesar's coin (previously discussed).

---

[42] Lawrence Brooks Hays, "Baptists and World Tasks," in *The Life of Baptists in the Life of the World*, ed. Walter B. Shurden (Nashville: Broadman, 1985), 138.

If Baptists (and other Christians) subscribe to the idea that all true political authority comes from God, then they cannot simply accept that a king's will (or any other secular authority) is law, full stop. Rather, Christians must perform an analysis of the type Martin Luther King Jr. described in his "Letter from Birmingham Jail" (or, for that matter, by Augustine or Thomas Aquinas to whom King referred). A law must be just if it is to be a law at all.[43] Otherwise, it may be little better than a command based on force as if issued from the mafia or a rogue squadron of mercenaries, as Augustine famously wrote.[44]

While it may be relatively clear to many that a free market in abortion represents a clear moral evil or that the unhindered exchange of human beings in the sex trade is a wrong that must be resisted, there are many closer questions with far-ranging consequences that attract active debate, but that cannot truly hope to count upon the support of Scripture for a definitive answer.

What can be discerned? The Bible demands simple procedural justice at a minimum, which is to say that theft, fraud, and breaking commitments are forbidden. Transparent, equal legal justice is also required. The wealthy should not be able to use their money to prevail unjustly in court and gain the favor of officials. We in the West tend to move on too easily from procedural justice, treating it as a ho-hum affair, but many people (in fact, many of the bottom billion) live without the kind of guarantees and prohibitions on bribery that Westerners tend to take for granted. Procedural justice is often pushed aside for the more ambitious "social justice," but justice in the rules and operation of the legal system is a grand accomplishment.

---

[43] See Martin Luther King Jr., "Letter from Birmingham Jail," April 16, 1963, available online from the African Studies Center–University of Pennsylvania, https://www.africa.upenn.edu/Articles_Gen/Letter_Birmingham.html.

[44] Augustine, *The City of God: Volume 1* (Edinburg: T&T Clark, n.d.), book 4, chap. 4, https://www.gutenberg.org/files/45304/45304-h/45304-h.htm.

It also seems clear that individuals, the church, and even the law (looking at the Old Testament) should take account of the poor through some form of provision. But regarding provision, these are broad guidelines that can be interpreted in a myriad of ways, especially those that touch upon politics.

The outlines are general in nature. Where systems are spelled out as with Israel's laws forgiving debt and requiring gleaning, they are tied to a particular kind of agricultural system that has largely disappeared from the earth. While Christians have suggestive ideas, the specifics in the modern world are not easily discerned. Does the Bible say the degree to which a national government should restrict or promote free trade with other nations? Can Christians produce Scriptures suggestive of the appropriate structure and rate of taxation or of whether one should tax income, consumption, capital gains, etc.? Does the Bible tell how generous the social safety net must be and to what degree it must be public versus private? The text does not provide these answers.

The requirement to love one's neighbor can help form a Baptist public disposition in a democratic world. Because all have a role to play in the Romans 13 authority of government, all are responsible for how his or her participation is stewarded. In political economic terms, the goal is to balance liberty, equality, and system performance in ways that lead to human flourishing for fellow citizens.

Systems that emphasize equality (especially the collectivist ones) present dangers in terms of generating less wealth and tend to infringe upon human rights such as freedom of speech and religious liberty (important for Baptists who place a high premium on conscience). That means Baptists cannot give in to a tyranny that would tell them to specify a general desire for benevolence and equality and then empower the government to achieve it. Not only is it quite difficult to figure out the specifics, but there is also the struggle against the power of sin that drags even highly idealistic systems down into abuses of power and privilege for the political elite. This sin problem complicates the goal of using government to morally regulate business because the power to regulate for good reasons can degenerate into rent-seeking behavior and regulatory capture that end up simply marrying government and corporate power over against the public interest.

The critical thing to note in all of this is that most of the questions involved in political economy—especially when talking about the economies of modern, developed nations—are prudential questions. In other words, we are not dealing with theological points about which there often can be no compromise, such as the question of the resurrection of Jesus Christ. Political economic questions are highly amenable to compromise and experimentation. The Baptist ideal referred to by Hays of not identifying the faith with particular patterns of political economy is wise for a church seeking to reach people in a wide variety of cultures all over the world. That itself is the core of a Baptist political economy.

Conclusion

From a Baptist and Christian perspective, something like Milton Friedman's impartial referee or umpire function of the government in the economy and business is a required minimum. The legal "playing field" should be an even one with the same set of rules applying to everyone. Force and fraud should be prevented from interfering with voluntary exchanges of value between persons and organizations.

The big question, which is the same question that addresses itself to every free person with a say in the matter, is the degree to which something more than the impartial referee and punisher of force and fraud is needed. Specifically, Baptists and Christians should ask whether the Bible indicates something more is needed. There is little doubt that the political economy of Israel is suggestive of measures that act to level the economic playing field (forgiveness of debts and restoration of land) and to provide for the poor (gleaning). The degree to which Israel's theocracy is normative is open to debate, but it is important to note these laws hit upon more than ceremonialism and, therefore, would seem to offer moral guidance.

The New Testament, while giving a view into an early church practicing an exceptional amount of sharing, does not say much about political economy other than giving the challenging ethic of neighbor love. If we are to love our neighbor, that duty would seem to imply that love extends into the way we order our political lives together. Too many, however, assume this neighbor love translates into some kind of collectivism. That leap is not as easily made as many believe because there are too many negative examples of how collectivist approaches reduce wealth and lead to human rights abuses and of how economic centralization leads to political repression.

The complex reality suggests that the general Baptist approach of not identifying closely with any particular social and economic pattern outside of insisting upon rights of conscience and religious liberty is a sound one. Mostly, political economy, as argued in the introduction, is a matter of operating with a relatively well-established modern consensus featuring capitalism and private property as significant features, but open to modification around the edges. Figuring out what that looks like is far more prudential than many would admit. It is likely that different systems work well in different types of settings, depending on geography, culture, ethnicity, pluralism, homogeneity, natural resources, religious beliefs, geopolitics, and more. The difficulty of the task does not mean we should abandon it, but humility should be a hallmark of our quest as we try to figure out how best to love our neighbors through political economy.

25

Just War and Baptist Political Theology

By Paul D. Miller

The first thing to be said about the Baptist contribution to just war thinking is there is not much of a Baptist contribution to just war thinking. Baptists have been notable for their diversity—their inconsistency, even—on war: espousing pacifism, justifying war, participating in war, and defending conscientious objection. The just war tradition is, by reputation, Roman Catholic property. Augustine of Hippo is often (inaccurately) said to be the founder of just war thinking. The tradition's most famous texts in historical theology belong to Thomas Aquinas, Francisco de Vitoria, and Francisco Suárez—two Dominicans and a Jesuit. Its renaissance in the twentieth century was due in part to the efforts of another Jesuit, John Courtney Murray, and to a pair of pastoral letters by the US Conference of Catholic Bishops in 1983 and 1993. Just war thinking often relies on appeals to natural law, which is also (wrongly) thought to be a Roman Catholic mode of thought (see chapter 19).

Some Protestants made important contributions to just war thinking dating as far back as Alberico Gentili (1552–1608), an Italian Protestant jurist and refugee who took up teaching and legal work as an exile in Oxford and London and who wrote Europe's first textbook on international law (he was probably an Anglican). Yet even then, Baptists have hardly been noticeable. The twentieth-century renaissance in just war thinking was led by Paul Ramsey, an American Methodist, ethicist, and professor at Princeton. Jean Bethke Elshtain, an ethicist and philosopher at the University of Chicago, made important contributions to just war scholarship; she was a lifelong Lutheran who converted to Catholicism late in life. Today's strongest Christian voices in just war scholarship include James Turner Johnson, who has a background in the Disciples of Christ and Methodism, and Nigel Biggar, an Anglican. The closest just war thinkers to the Baptist tradition are also its younger voices, including Marc LiVecche and Eric Patterson, both of whom have a variety of denominational influences and have spent time in Baptist churches but have gravitated toward Presbyterian congregations. Consequently, my work on just war did not make explicitly Baptist arguments or cite leading Baptist thinkers.[1]

Other scholars have noted the absence of a strong Baptist voice in just war thinking and, in parallel, a notable diversity in Baptists' response to and participation in war. "Baptist responses to war have represented a spectrum ranging from absolute rejection of war and participation in war to full participation with the proclamation of divine blessing and authority," according to Tim Demy.[2] Nathan Finn noted, "The twentieth century

---

[1] Paul D. Miller, *Just War and Ordered Liberty* (Cambridge: Cambridge University, 2021).

[2] Timothy Demy, "Praying for Peace but Preparing for War," in *Just War and Christian Traditions*, ed. Eric Patterson and J. Daryl Charles (Notre Dame, IN: University of Notre Dame, 2022).

witnessed considerable diversity in how Baptists approached questions of war and peace, normally depending upon world events at any given time."[3] John Smyth, Walter Rauschenbusch and Henlee Barnette (chapter 11), and Harry Emerson Fosdick were pacifists, drawing on the anabaptist influence on Baptist thought, along with Martin Luther King Jr. (chapter 13), at least later in his life. Within the same tradition, Thomas Helwys (chapter 2), Roger Williams (chapter 3), and Billy Graham (chapter 15) were not. *The Second London Confession of Faith* (1689) affirms that the magistrate may "wage war upon just and necessary occasions,"[4] and that Christians may participate in government service, including military service. By contrast, the 1833 New Hampshire Baptist confession makes no mention of war one way or the other. The Southern Baptist Convention's *Baptist Faith and Message*—in its 1925, 1963, and 2000 versions—calls on Christians to pray for peace and "do all in their power to put an end to war,"[5] but it neither affirms nor condemns just war principles. Probably the most common Baptist response to war is to affirm the right of individuals to claim conscientious objection and refrain from participating in war because of the historic Baptist emphasis on the freedom of conscience—though even then, Roger Williams, of all Baptists, disagreed.

Why the silence? The historical focus of Baptist political thought on religious freedom, and relative neglect of just war, is understandable considering the Baptist experience of being persecuted for conscience's sake by Anglicans in England, Congregationalists in New England, and Episcopalians in the South. As a persecuted community that did not enjoy cultural or political power in the seventeenth through early nineteenth

---

[3] Nathan Finn, in *Baptists and War: Essays on Baptists and Military Conflict, 1640s–1990s*, Canadian Baptist Historical Society Series, vol. 2, ed. Gordon L. Heath and Michael A. G. Haykin (Eugene, OR: Wipf and Stock, 2015), 221.

[4] Second London Baptist Confession of Faith (1689), chap. 24, par. 2, TGC website, https://www.thegospelcoalition.org/publication-online/second-london/.

[5] See "Comparison Chart," sec. XVI, SBC website, accessed October 29, 2022, https://bfm.sbc.net/comparison-chart/.

centuries, Baptists focused their political thought on the issue in which they had direct personal experience and had suffered the most injustice, and they developed a doctrine about the *limits* of state power. For the same reason, there is not much historic Baptist reflection on the *proper use* of state power. Just as Christians in the early church during the Roman imperial era were politically outcast and did not produce theology explaining what government was for or how Christians ought to use power, so too Baptists did not spend much time reflecting on what to do with state power, including its role in warfare.

The Argument

Despite their relative absence from the canonical texts in just war thinking, Baptists have ample experience thinking about war, sovereignty, and justice. It is through Baptists' lived historical experience during war and political crises that one can see their de facto political theology and doctrine of just war. In fact, a review of British and American Baptists' response to and participation in war shows *two* theologies of war battling for supremacy within the Baptist tradition.

First, Baptists' emphasis on religious disestablishment and liberty of conscience predisposed them to define justice as a matter of political liberty, or at least to believe that liberty was an essential precondition for justice. Put another way, Baptists' political theology has always been preferential to republican or democratic forms of government to the point of equating justice with republicanism. That is why, unlike older Christian denominations, "Baptists have almost always eschewed the resort to violence to impose Christianity on anyone," according to Anthony Cross, because that would violate their republican and democratic sympathies.[6] The implication for just war is straightforward. Baptists believed wars fought

---

[6] Anthony R. Cross, "Baptists, Peace, and War: The Seventeenth-Century Foundations," in *Baptists and War: Essays on Baptists and Military Conflict,*

for republican principles—for the defense and vindication of *res publica,* the public body—were just; those fought for other causes were not. This amounts to an implicitly republican just war tradition that is a distinctively Baptist outgrowth of the broader Christian and Augustinian tradition of just war thought. It substantially overlaps with my argument in *Just War and Ordered Liberty,* and I will argue in the conclusion that it represents the best way forward for a distinctively Baptist contribution to the broader Christian tradition of just war thinking.

But a second theology of war also emerges from this history. In some cases, Baptists equated the fate of their own nation with the fate of republican principles to the extent of defining justice as the victory of their nation. In other cases they stretched "Christianity" to encompass slavery. And in a few cases, Baptists joined other Christian voices throughout history in baldly calling for holy war for the true faith. In these cases, Baptists fought wars not to defend the commonwealth or vindicate liberty, justice, or republicanism, but to see the triumph of their nation, race, or church. Nationalism, slavery, and crusading amount to a repudiation of just war principles in favor of different kinds of holy war.

The contrast between these two visions of war shows a weakness in Baptist political theology: the lack of an explicitly Baptist theology of war until recently has left Baptists susceptible to prevailing cultural winds. A more rigorous and explicitly Baptist appropriation of the just war tradition—as some recent Baptist thinkers have attempted, including Carl F. H. Henry, Daniel Heimbach, Albert Mohler, Bruce Ashford, Timothy Demy, J. Daryl Charles, Ergun and Emir Caner, and myself—will help reformulate the best of Baptist political theology, making clear the connection between just war and ordered liberty while building stronger bulwarks against the Baptist temptation toward pacifism, on the one hand, and crusading, on the other.

1640s–1990s, ed. Gordon L. Heath and Michael A. G. Haykin (Eugene, OR: Pickwick, 2015), 16.

Baptists in British and Early American Wars

Baptists were republicans from the beginning. A few were pacifists, but considering their close ties to the Puritans, it is unsurprising that "Baptists actively fought on the Parliamentarians' side during the two phases of the English civil wars (1642–46 and 1648–49),"[7] and served in high office in Oliver Cromwell's republican government. They saw in the Puritan republic the opportunity to advance disestablishment and religious freedom. Some were so high-ranking and invested in the cause as to sign King Charles's death warrant and participate in his execution. These high-ranking Baptists were later excluded from the general pardon and executed in turn in 1660, after the monarchy's restoration. Baptists were so devoted to the republican cause that they were actively involved in several plots to overthrow the monarchy in the later seventeenth century. They saw the partial victory of their ideals in the 1688–89 Glorious Revolution: the Toleration Act, affirmed by the newly enthroned King William III, did not disestablish the Anglican Church, but it did affirm freedom of worship for nonconforming Christian sects. Baptists were one of the act's main beneficiaries.[8]

Similarly, American Baptists sided overwhelmingly with the Revolutionary cause at the end of the eighteenth century.[9] Baptist minister Samuel Stillman gave voice to a typically Baptist approach to the Revolution in an election-day sermon in Boston 1779, ostensibly on Matt 22:21: "Give, then, to Caesar the things that are Caesar's, and to God the things that are God's." Stillman managed to derive a full set of republican principles from the text because, at the outset, he understood Jesus to be saying that we ought "to render such obedience to Caesar, or to the civil magistrate, *as would be consistent with the natural and the civil rights of men*" (emphasis

---

[7] Cross, 17.

[8] Cross, 17, 23.

[9] Hight C. Moore, "The Baptists and the American Revolution: Nothing Original; All Is Reflected Light—Balzac," *Peabody Journal of Education* 23, no. 1 (1945): 43–54.

added). From that important addendum, Stillman was able to draw the legal and political equality of all men, the foundation of government based on popular consent, the need for a bill of rights, the inviolability of the rights of conscience, the need for "free and frequent" elections, "the right of a trial by jury," and the institution of private property. Stillman argued that government is no government if it fails to abide by these principles, and the people are within their right to ignore its laws and resist its authority. "That no laws are obligatory on the people, but those that have obtained a like consent. Nor are such laws of any force, if, proceeding from a corrupt majority of the legislature, they are incompatible with the fundamental principles of the government, and tend to subvert it." The right of war follows: if anyone violates another's natural rights, he "is an usurper, puts himself into a state of war, and may be opposed as a common highwayman."[10]

Baptists throughout the colonies agreed with Stillman. "During the American Revolution, there were about 97 Baptist churches in the colonies, and the total Baptist population was less than 10,000. Baptists overwhelmingly supported the colonists' fight for freedom," in large part because they rightly believed American freedom from British political tyranny would mean Baptist freedom from Congregationalist and Anglican religious tyranny. The few Baptist Tories—like Morgan Edwards, pastor of First Baptist Church in Philadelphia at the time of the Revolution—are noteworthy for their dissent from the otherwise overwhelming Baptist consensus in favor of the Revolution.[11] George Washington affirmed Baptists'

---

[10] From the same foundation, Stillman argued for the abolition of slavery and the recognition of the equal humanity and equal natural rights of Africans. "Shall we hold the sword in one hand to defend our just rights as men; and grasp chains with the other to enslave the inhabitants of Africa?—Forbid it heaven! . . . MAY the year of jubilee soon arrive, when Africa shall cast the look of gratitude to these happy regions, for the TOTAL EMANCIPATION of HER SONS!" Samuel Stillman, "A Sermon Preached before the Honorable Council," May 26, 1779, Evans Early American Imprint Collection, https://quod.lib.umich.edu/e/evans/N13070.0001 .001/1:4?rgn=div1;view=fulltext.

[11] Demy, "Praying for Peace."

wartime patriotism in a 1789 letter to the United Baptist Churches of Virginia: "While I recollect with satisfaction that the religious Society of which you are Members, have been, throughout America, uniformly, and almost unanimously, the firm friends to civil liberty, and the persevering Promoters of our glorious revolution; I cannot hesitate to believe that they will be the faithful Supporters of a free, yet efficient general Government."[12] Baptists were almost entirely identified with the American cause and with its republican principles.

But the equation of justice with republicanism carried an obvious danger when there was only one significant republican nation in the world. Baptists could and did equate the fate of the American nation with their cherished republican principles. During the War of 1812, American Baptists believed "a war with British North America was about more than maritime rights, economic concerns, or even nationalism; it was about an understanding of how God planned to use America to manifest his divine plan," according to one scholar. Baptists' faith in God's plans for America was "not simply about national pride in the political system," but rather about America's role in protecting religious freedom, being a model for the nations, and enabling missionary activity. "National character was of supreme importance because only a Christian America could properly spread the message of individual freedom to other nations still struggling under oppressive political and religious tyranny."[13]

However, for many Baptists this was a distinction without a difference. Because America uniquely protected the principles Baptists most cherished, many came to believe "America occupied a special or favored place in God's purposes . . . the sacred nature of the American nation

---

[12] George Washington, "From George Washington to the United Baptist Churches of Virginia," May 1789, https://founders.archives.gov/documents /Washington/05-02-02-0309.

[13] James Tyler Robertson, "A House Uniting: Americans, Baptists, and the War of 1812," in *Baptists and War*, Pickwick ed., 92, 60, 63, 64, 93, 81.

meant that the defense of the land was lauded as a noble enterprise." Thus, while lamenting the death and destruction of war, Baptists largely supported America's second war with Britain, but on subtly different, less republican grounds than the first war. "The fate of the land was thematically paired with the biblical stories of Israel, so when scores of Redcoats landed it was easy to turn to the tales of apocalyptic judgment to find out what message the Baptists could deliver to embattled Zion." They interpreted the war through the lens of Israel's story: national sin was followed by punishment and national calamity, but national repentance would lead to divine blessing.[14]

Although some Baptists dissented from the war frenzy of 1812 (including Isaac Backus),[15] the beginnings of nationalism and crusading creeping into Baptists' views of American warfare can be seen (though we should recognize that Baptists were hardly alone in this during the era when a truly national American identity first began to take shape). A similar sentiment was evident again in the next American war. After having swollen in numbers following the Second Great Awakening and found a sympathetic culture in the democratizing atmosphere of the Jacksonian age, Baptists were no longer on the fringe of American society, and they began to identify more closely with the American experiment just when Americans were growing supremely confident in their "Manifest Destiny" as God's New Israel to overspread the continent with their brand of Protestant liberty. During the war with Mexico (1846–1848), "Southern Baptists and Methodists championed it as a straightforward crusade against Latin Catholicism,"[16] reflecting Protestant nativism, American nationalism, and a rare instance in which some Baptists advocated war for religion.

---

[14] Robertson, 92, 60, 63, 64, 93, 81.

[15] Andrew Preston, *Sword of the Spirit, Shield of Faith: Religion in American War and Diplomacy* (New York: Anchor, 2012), loc. 2763, Kindle.

[16] Preston, loc. 3486, Kindle.

Baptists and the American Civil War

The Baptist understanding of war underwent a profound transformation in the American Civil War. The Civil War was also a Baptist Civil War, one fought on the battlefields and among theologians about the nature of sovereignty, the meaning of the American experiment, and just causes for war. Both sides used republican arguments, in keeping with past Baptist practice. But both sides changed and came to rely on other, more explicitly religious arguments. Northerners initially argued war was justified to defend the Union and its principles of republicanism, but through the war they came to believe war was justified for America to fulfill God's purposes as his chosen nation and vanguard of human liberty. Southern Baptists argued war was justified, like their Northern counterparts, to defend principles of republicanism, but they also argued it was a religious crusade to defend the biblical institution of slavery.

In the late eighteenth and early nineteenth centuries, most Americans, North and South, generally agreed that slavery was bad, even if Southerners would have said it was an allowable, necessary evil. By the 1840s, Southern theologians, including Baptists, were arguing that slavery was a divinely ordained positive good. John Leland, for example (chapter 6), argued in 1789 that slavery was a "horrible evil" and called for its abolition; but by 1839 he argued it was "humane, just, and benevolent" because it led to the Christianization and civilization of Africans.[17] This Southern theological trend led them into conflict with their Northern counterparts, who maintained their belief in slavery's evils. That is why Baptists, like Methodists and Presbyterians, split over slavery before the nation did. There were enough white Baptist abolitionists—like David Barrow, pastor of a Baptist church in Kentucky and author of an 1807 antislavery book—to prompt Baptist defenders of slavery to break away and form their own convention, which

---

[17] "John Leland: Evolving Views of Slavery, 1789–1839," *Bruce T. Gourley* (blog), http://www.brucegourley.com/writings/lelandslavery1.htm.

they did in 1845. African American Baptists made their own case in other ways, such as the Baptist layman Nat Turner, leader of his eponymous slave rebellion in 1831.

Southern Baptists, led by theologians like James Furman and James Boyce, came to argue that the defense of slavery was a just cause for war because they claimed slavery was a biblically ordained institution. "Slavery forms a vital element of the Divine Revelation to man," preached Ebenezer W. Warren, pastor of First Baptist Church in Macon, Georgia, in January 1861. That is why the South Carolina Baptists declared two years later that Northerners "assume that slavery is a sin and therefore ought to be abolished. We contend that it is a Scriptural institution. The very nature of the contest takes the point in dispute out of the category of politics, and delegates it to the sphere of Christianity. We are really contending for the precepts of religion." Southern Baptists, probably like most Southerners, came to justify the Civil War as a holy war for (their version of) Christianity.[18] The Confederacy was deliberately more explicit about establishing itself on "Christian" principles than the US Constitution had been, and Southern Christianity fused with Southern patriotism such that the two reinforced each other and became essentially indistinguishable. Alabama's Baptist convention called for secession before any state legislature did, as did most Baptist newspapers in the South.[19] South Carolina's secession convention in December 1860 was held in a local Baptist church, an appropriate symbol of Southern Baptist political theology during the war, which embraced a fusion of church and state and justified holy war in their common defense.

Some Southern theologians took a different approach, stressing republican principles instead of biblical ones. A key secessionist argument was

---

[18] Quoted in Bruce Gourley, "Yes, the Civil War Was about Slavery," Baptists and the American Civil War, February 8, 2017, http://civilwarbaptists.com/featured/slavery/.

[19] W. Harrison Daniel, "The Southern Baptists in the Confederacy," *Civil War History* 6, no. 4 (1960): 389–401.

that the Confederacy was rooted in, and a continuation of, the American Revolution. The Confederates argued they stood in an unbroken line with the Founding Fathers and cast their secession in the republican terms of state sovereignty, popular sovereignty, and federalism. That enabled Southern Christians—including Baptists like Jeremiah Bell Jeter, pastor of First Baptist Church in Richmond—to preach sermons in support of a war for republican principles, not (mainly) a war to sustain slavery. In some cases, the two lines of argument went together: in 1863 the SBC pledged to "render a hearty support to the Confederate Government in all constitutional measures to secure our independence," which was a republican argument, but also mourned "the death of that noble Christian warrior, Lieut. Ga. T. J. Jackson," who had just been killed by friendly fire at the battle of Chancellorsville.[20]

Northerners made a similar argument, tying the war to republicanism. Northerners equated republicanism with the continuation of the Union— Senator Daniel Webster of Massachusetts famously declared "Liberty and Union, now and forever, one and inseparable!" in an 1830 speech—and plainly believed they had just cause to preserve the Union by force. They saw secession as an attack on the United States, in response to which the North's response was a war of self-defense. Northern Baptists almost certainly joined the rest of the North in this argument. (President Lincoln was careful to orchestrate events such that Confederates fired the first shots of the war at Fort Sumter, strengthening the North's case that it was fighting a war of self-defense).

But it was almost impossible to argue that the war was for republican principles while ignoring the fate of slavery, which Northerners and abolitionists had spent decades arguing were incompatible. In the North and in the postwar reunited nation, Lincoln "helped solidify—even re-create—the

---

[20] "Resolution on Peace," May 1, 1863, quoted in Jerry Sutton, *A Matter of Conviction: A History of Southern Baptist Engagement with the Culture* (Nashville: B&H, 2008), 69, 70.

link in the American mind between Christianity and republicanism," in Preston's assessment.[21] Lincoln simplified the matter with the Emancipation Proclamation in 1863, but in doing so he also transformed the moral and political purpose of the war and introduced a temptation to view the war as a crusade for liberty. In this, the Civil War wrought profound changes to American Christianity and its political theology, including for Baptists. "Based partly on Lincoln's rechristening of America's civil religion and partly on the moral absolutism of preachers in the victorious North, Civil War faith helped form the ideological core of US foreign policy into the twentieth century."[22]

This "Civil War faith" is what helped Americans make sense of the carnage and believe that it served a higher purpose; but it also distorted their political theology after the war—though it may be difficult to recognize that because the Union did, of course, have just cause. But politicians and theologians could, and did, express the wrong reasons for the right cause. "The adoption of emancipation occurred alongside the transformation of the conflict from limited war to total war, even holy war," because Northern clergy "sanctified, in the most explicitly religious terms both the Northern cause and the United States itself."[23] The faith came to rest on the idea that America had a unique role as "God's chosen nation" to accomplish his benevolent purposes on earth, which meant America had a mission to spread liberty and alleviate suffering around the world. Some Baptists joined in this newfound messianic belief in America's mission. Henry Clay Fish, pastor of First Baptist Church in Newark, New Jersey, saw America's global mission in the outcome of the Civil War. In November 1863, he told his congregation, "In this struggle we stand for the world, we represent the world. For the world, freedom lives or dies here and now!"[24]

---

[21] Preston, *Sword of the Spirit*, loc. 3765, Kindle.

[22] Preston, loc. 3817.

[23] Preston, locs. 3765, 3863, 3956.

[24] Quoted in Harry S. Stout, *Upon the Altar of the Nation: A Moral History of the Civil War* (New York: Penguin, 2006).

In the Civil War, one can see both doctrines of war at play: both sides claimed the defense of republicanism a just cause of war, and both sides came to claim the holy war doctrine, which viewed the advancement of America's God-ordained mission (the North) or the defense of biblical slavery (the South) a just cause. In the end, the Civil War became a religious crusade for both sides. "American clergy on both sides of the Civil War sanctified their cause and demonized the other, in effect calling for their countrymen to wage total, holy war," according to Preston.[25] The war intensified popular religion and cemented its centrality in American life. Total war was justified because the stakes were existential; that, in turn, pressed preachers and politicians to reach for a deeper moral meaning to sanctify the struggle.

Baptists and the World Wars

American nationalism reached a high pitch at the turn of the twentieth century. Although most Americans opposed entry into World War I before 1916, President Woodrow Wilson (a Presbyterian whose father helped found the Southern Presbyterian Church in 1861) led a rapid change in national sentiment as he took the nation to war in 1917. He described the war in apocalyptic terms and America's mission in messianic language. American clergy followed suit, including some Baptists. "The Great War quickly assumed apocalyptic significance for most Christians, but for many conservative Protestants it seemed to be literally true," according to Preston.[26]

The SBC passed a resolution pledging "our loyal and sacrificial support" for the United States' entry into the Great War in May 1917.[27] Zane Batten, secretary of the Northern Baptist Convention's War Commission, wrote, "This war for the destruction of injustice and inhumanity is a holy

---

[25] Preston, *Sword of the Spirit*, loc. 3746, Kindle.
[26] Preston, Kindle location 5889.
[27] "Resolution on Peace," May 1, 1917, SBC website, https://www.sbc.net /resource-library/resolutions/resolution-on-peace-4/.

crusade and a continuation of Christ's sacrificial service for the redemption of the world."[28] John Straton, pastor of Calvary Baptist Church in New York, made a reasonably careful case for war against Germany because of its autocracy and denial of religious freedom, yet overstepped when he argued that Americans believe "the voice of the people is the voice of God" and the rival American and German systems "are the practical expressions of the forces of good and evil."[29] Others, such as the Fundamentalist Presbyterian Billy Sunday, went much further in describing the Great War as a holy war. The First World War was likely the nadir of just war thinking and the crest of holy war enthusiasm in American religion.

Baptists, like other Christians, split on how best to achieve peace in the aftermath. The famous industrialist and philanthropist John D. Rockefeller Jr., an ecumenically minded Baptist, supported the League of Nations and believed it was the best chance for lasting peace. J. C. Masse, a fundamentalist Baptist preacher and opponent of modernism in the Northern Baptist Convention, opposed it because it meant the United States, "a professedly Christian nation," would be entering a covenant with "nations that are altogether pagan."[30] After the war and the failure of the League of Nations treaty, widespread public disillusionment with the League's aims and purpose arose, along with cynicism about the role arms manufacturers played in perpetuating it. A de facto pacifism took hold of much of American opinion. The Northern Baptist Convention passed a resolution essentially affirming pacifism in 1922, stating that war "is barbarous, wasteful and manifestly contrary to every Christian ideal and teaching."[31] The SBC did not go quite so far, but it still expressed suspicion of arms manufacturing, endorsed a non-aggression pact, and called for the US to join the World

---

[28] Quoted in Preston, *Sword of the Spirit*, Kindle loc. 5817.

[29] Quoted in Preston, Kindle loc. 5869.

[30] Quoted in Preston, Kindle loc. 6668.

[31] "American Baptist Resolution on the Abolition of War," Northern Baptist Convention, 1922, https://www.abc-usa.org/wp-content/uploads/2019/02/WAR.pdf.

Court in 1935; opposed the US military buildup in 1936; called for a disarmament conference in 1937; called for a halt to trade in military resources with Japan in 1939; and expressed support for conscientious objection to military service in 1940.[32]

Some Baptists and evangelicals recognized the danger before most of the American public. William H. Houghton, an ordained Baptist pastor and president of the Moody Bible Institute, argued against pacifism on biblical grounds in the pages of *Moody Monthly* in April 1937, more or less reinventing the wheel of just war thinking. He warned in 1938 of the likelihood of another war and in November 1939 of Hitler's aggression and hostility to religion. "Long before many Americans were willing to consider it their business, [Houghton and others] were comparing the Nazis to the worst villains of history and prophecy."[33] By 1941, public opinion had turned. The Battle of Britain, among other things, helped persuade Americans that the war was probably inescapable. In May the SBC endorsed the military buildup and affirmed that "some things are worth dying for; and if they are worth dying for they are worth living for; and if they are worth living for they are worth defending even unto the death" and that "it were better to be dead than to live in a world dominated by the ideals of these modern dictators."[34] By May 1943, eighteen months into the American war effort, the SBC affirmed that Southern Baptists "as loyal citizens of the United States are cooperating and participating in all branches of the present war," while calling on the government to begin planning

---

[32] See "Resolution on Peace," May 1, 1935; "Resolution on Peace and War," May 1, 1936; "Resolution on Peace and War," May 1, 1937; "Resolution on America's and China's Invasion," May 1, 1939; and "Resolution Concerning War and Peace," June 1, 1940, on the SBC website. The page for each resolution can be viewed by visiting "Resources in Resolutions" at https://www.sbc.net/resource-library/resolutions and filtering by year.

[33] Timothy Padgett, *Swords into Plowshares: American Evangelicals on War, 1937–1973* (Bellingham, WA: Lexham, 2018), 33.

[34] "Resolution on Peace," May 1, 1941; see note 32.

how to establish conditions of lasting peace after the war.[35] The Northern Baptist Convention similarly passed resolutions endorsing the war effort, though with restrained language.

Perhaps chastened by their whiplash-like shift from pacifism to militarism and back again before, during, and after the First World War, American Christians seemed less apt to view the Second World War as a holy crusade or describe the justice of its cause in holy war terms. Perhaps counterintuitively, it may have helped that the Nazi Germany and Imperial Japanese threat was so enormous: while the enormity of their crimes might have tempted Christians to equate them with the kingdom of darkness, the universality of the threat they posed to all humanity—including Jews in Europe and countless millions of non-Christians across Asia—made it easier for Christians to see the war as a war for the defense of the common good, not for the advancement of one nation or faith. Prominent evangelical commentators had no "qualms about identifying the Allies with the cause of justice in the world" and still often mingled faith and patriotism, "yet they did so without conflating this mission with [the] cause of the church" and "never devolved into any kind of 'my country, right or wrong'" attitude.[36] Houghton "several times used his position at *Moody* to cool war frenzy" by exhorting his readers to love their enemies and reminding them of the humanity of the Germans and Japanese. "Hitler and Hirohito are entirely wrong, of course," Houghton wrote in June 1944, "but that doesn't mean that of necessity we are entirely righteous."[37] Baptists, along with other Christians, rediscover just war during and after World War II.

That may also explain why church leaders felt ready to express their concern—and, for some, their outrage—at the use of nuclear weapons against Japan to end the war. "Among the nation's clergy, an overwhelming majority responded to the atomic bombs with trepidation, fear, and

---

[35] "Resolution on Peace," May 1, 1943. See note 32.
[36] Padgett, Kindle locs. 800, 1167.
[37] Padgett, Kindle locs. 1087, 1215.

moral outrage" and not just among pacifist or leftist denominations, according to Preston.[38] Carl F. H. Henry, writing in 1952, years after the bombing, expressed unease about it and asked pointed questions about the US government's ability to use nuclear weapons ethically.[39] Henlee Barnette rejected just war altogether, arguing in the early 1960s that nuclear weapons made war intrinsically unjust (chapter 11). Many fundamentalist and conservative Christians saw in the advent of nuclear warfare the means by which Armageddon might come about and usher in the end of the world. Despite widespread criticism from across the religious spectrum about the use of nuclear weapons, President Harry Truman never expressed any public doubts about their use—and his was the most prominent Baptist voice in the debate.

Billy Graham and Martin Luther King Jr. on Vietnam

The renaissance in just war scholarship began in earnest after World War II, largely because of that war. Theologians from across Christian denominations saw the need to reacquaint themselves with their tradition's tools for assessing the justice or injustice of war in the aftermath of the most catastrophic war in history and the introduction of the most destructive weapons in history. Baptists were almost entirely absent from the conversation. They certainly participated in debates about war, specifically the war in Vietnam, but those debates generally did not make use of the just war tradition.

Southern Baptists and other conservative Baptist associations were generally, although not unanimously, supportive of the war in Vietnam, yet decreasingly so as the war dragged on; the American Baptist and Progressive National Baptist Conventions opposed it. "Like Americans in general, Baptists in the United States were divided over the Vietnam War," according

---

[38] Preston, *Sword of the Spirit*, Kindle loc. 8757.
[39] Padgett, Kindle loc. 2558ff.

to Nathan Finn.[40] The SBC passed at least nine resolutions on Vietnam from 1966 to 1973: a 1967 resolution was the most stridently supportive; none outright condemned the war; most called for peace but specified a just peace that respected the rights of all Vietnamese.[41]

Yet the grounds for either support or opposition were almost never framed in just war terms. The anti-war position was usually indistinguishable from pacifism: opposition to all war as intrinsically immoral rather than an argument the US lacked just cause to intervene in Vietnam. As for those supportive of the war, according to one scholar, Southern Baptists "based their unwillingness to publicly criticize military actions in Southeast Asia on the historic Baptist commitment to the separation of church and state. Simply put, it was not the place of the church to concern itself with military strategy," and their silence was indistinguishable from a passive acceptance of the state's war policy.[42] Baptists have, of course, seen no problem with their churches concerning themselves with other areas of policy, including slavery in the nineteenth century (both for and against), child labor and workplace safety in the early twentieth century, and abortion today. The curious recusal from commentary on the justice or injustice of war was, from the standpoint of the just war tradition, a dereliction of duty.

The Baptist approach to the Vietnam War, and their failure to use just war thinking, was illustrated by a disagreement between the two most famous Baptists of the mid-twentieth century: Billy Graham and Martin Luther King Jr. Billy Graham was a fierce, uncompromising, and vocal Cold Warrior. He hated Communism and preached against it so much that, according to one biographer, "Next to the gospel message, by his own recollection, he preached about it more than anything else." Graham

---

[40] Nathan A. Finn, "Baptists and the War in Vietnam," in *Baptists and War: Essays on Baptists and Military Conflict, 1640s–1990s*, ed. Gordon L. Heath and Michael A. G. Haykin (Eugene: Pickwick, 2015), 204.

[41] "Resolution on Peace," June 1, 1967, SBC website, https://www.sbc.net/resource-library/resolutions/resolution-on-peace-10/.

[42] Finn, "Baptists and the War in Vietnam," 207.

argued on one occasion that "Communism is a fanatical religion that has declared war upon the Christian God," rhetoric even Carl Henry would echo, albeit in a more scholarly tone. Henry "suggested that it was even more than a civic duty to America; it was the religious duty to God for Christians to oppose Communism." The danger is that such rhetoric could lead uncareful minds to view the Cold War as a holy war to defend the true faith and equate the United States with justice, the antithesis of just war thinking.[43]

Graham's view was widely shared by politically conservative Baptists, many of whom also opposed Communism because of the obstacles Communist governments erected to missionary activity. "Throughout the 1950s, evangelicals continued their backing of the American Cold War effort, but they occasionally rebuked the government, not for overly aggressive initiatives but for inadequate reactions to Communist moves," according to one scholar.[44] (Henry, by contrast, kept up a steady drumbeat of critiques against America's moral failings throughout the Cold War and clearly did not view it as a holy war). Americans and Christians had plenty of reason to oppose Communism, of course, but framing that opposition in holy war rather than just war terms—like the North's case for the Civil War after 1863—misunderstood the proper grounds for war and probably helped excuse the Cold War's excesses.[45]

---

[43] Grant Wacker, *America's Pastor: Billy Graham and the Shaping of a Nation* (Cambridge: Belknap, 2014). For excerpt, see "Billy Graham's Vietnam," February 22, 2018, https://harvardpress.typepad.com/hup_publicity/2018/02/billy-grahams -vietnam-grant-wacker.html. Padgett, Kindle location 2845, 3302.

[44] Padgett, Kindle loc. 178.

[45] "Billy Graham's Vietnam." Graham was correct to note the antithesis between atheist Communism and Christianity, but that is not why a (secular) government ought to oppose it. A government ought to oppose Communism because it is a violation of justice, not Christianity, and a violation of the dignity of all people, not just Christians. The case is similar to the North's theory of war during the Civil War. We can agree with the conclusion—the war was just—but disagree with the rationale, which turned the conflict into a religious war.

When the United States went to war against Communist North Vietnam, "in public, with rare exceptions, [Graham] stood shoulder to shoulder with Presidents Johnson and Nixon," in support of the war effort. Graham clearly thought the United States had just cause to defend South Vietnam against Communist aggression, an argument which could, in principle, be cast in just war terms (Henry essentially made that argument in a 1965 editorial in *Christianity Today*).[46] But that does not mean Graham was thinking in just war terms, particularly considering his tendency to treat the broader Cold War as a veritable holy war in defense of Christianity. In April 1969 he sent President Nixon a lengthy private memo offering suggestions for the war effort. One suggestion involved bombing civilian infrastructure to deprive the north of its economic livelihood, which one biographer judged "made little sense morally, for it surely violated Christian principles of just war as well as the Geneva Conventions." Graham later distanced himself from the war: he moved from "support for the administration's policies in the mid-1960s to professed neutrality, born of deep uncertainty, by the time the U.S. involvement ended in 1973," though without a clear statement of why his views changed. Later in life he repudiated his support for the war.[47]

By contrast, Martin Luther King Jr. condemned the Vietnam War in a famous April 1967 speech. He believed that the war took time, attention, and resources away from the cause of civil rights; that the draft disproportionately hurt the poor; that war was inconsistent with his ethic of nonviolence at home; that the war was poisoning the soul of America; that his commissions as a minister and as a Nobel laureate obligated him to work for peace; and that the war violated the brotherhood of all mankind. Taken to their logical conclusion, King's grounds for opposing the Vietnam War amounted to a principled case for pacifism, a stance King had apparently evolved toward as the logical conclusion of his domestic

---

[46] Carl F. H. Henry, "Halting Red Aggression in Viet Nam," *Christianity Today* (April 23, 1965).

[47] "Billy Graham's Vietnam."

commitment to nonviolence. Like Graham, King did not frame his argument in just war terms.

King added to his main case specific accusations against the United States and South Vietnam that could be interpreted in just war terms, as a case against the US having just cause or right intention and violating proportionality and discrimination. King detailed American war crimes and excesses, blamed the United States for the failure of the Geneva Accords, and blamed Diem's authoritarianism for the rise of the Vietcong. He was convinced that any further American involvement in Vietnam would not be based on noble intentions because, he believed, America sided with the rich and wreaked havoc on the world's poor. King further argued that the United States was using its military to protect overseas investments. King's arguments here could be interpreted as a just war argument, except that King did not apply the same scrutiny to North Vietnam, passing over its war crimes, authoritarianism, and corruption and its violations of the Geneva Accords in silence, which suggests King was not truly applying a just war framework so much as borrowing its language to condemn a war he had already decided was unjust on pacifist grounds.[48]

Post–Cold War: Baptists Discover the Just War Tradition

Scholarly interest in the just war framework exploded in the post–Cold War era. It is also the era in which we finally see serious Baptist engagement with just war thinking. The earliest such engagement came from Carl F. H. Henry, cofounder of the National Association of Evangelicals, the Evangelical Theological Society, and *Christianity Today*. As probably the foremost Baptist theologian of the twentieth century as well as an active

---

[48] Martin Luther King Jr., "Beyond Vietnam—A Time to Break Silence," American Rhetoric Online Speech Bank, April 4, 1967, https://www.american rhetoric.com/speeches/mlkatimetobreaksilence.htm.

public intellectual and advocate for greater evangelical activism, Henry probed the intersection of faith and politics with greater care and scholarship than most. Even before the end of the Cold War, Henry engaged with just war thinking. In a 1967 editorial on Vietnam, Henry asked, "How familiar are we with the traditionally formulated criteria of a just war, and do these justify American participation in Viet Nam on moral grounds?" He briefly described the criteria in a footnote (and credited the summary to a Catholic text), apparently the first Baptist engagement with the just war tradition in the post–World War II era.[49]

Later, Henry examined and rejected the pacifist and quietist interpretation of the Bible in his magnum opus, *God, Revelation and Authority* (published between 1976 and 1983). Pacifism and quietism (or political nonparticipation) "seems to imply that Christians ought to not strive for an end to slavery . . . or for an end to military aggression by predatory powers," Henry argued. "This seems like a sophisticated way of saying that soul-salvation (the church) has nothing to do with responsibility for the larger body (the world)." To the contrary, Henry believed "it is the Christian's duty to support government as an instrumentality for preserving justice and restraining disorder," including through force. Henry specifically noted that the image of the "sword" in Romans 13 is an image or symbol of war the apostle Paul affirmed. Beyond that, Henry did not cite or draw on the just war literature or previous theologians in the just war tradition.[50]

Shortly after Henry showed the way for a Baptist appropriation of just war thinking, a Christian policymaker helped institutionalize just war thinking in US government policy and, later, further develop its theology from a Baptist perspective. While serving on the White House staff, Daniel Heimbach, a Vietnam War veteran with a PhD in law, politics, and

---

[49] Carl F. H. Henry, "Viet Nam: A Moral Dilemma," *Christianity Today* (January 20, 1967): 27–28.

[50] Carl F. H. Henry, *God, Revelation and Authority: Volume IV*, God Who Speaks and Shows: Fifteen Theses, Part Three (Waco: Word, 1979), 534–35.

Christian ethics, helped integrate just war thinking in George H. W. Bush's wartime decisions during the Gulf War, after which he served as Deputy Assistant Secretary of the Navy. Heimbach subsequently moved to academia as a professor of Christian ethics at Southeastern Baptist Theological Seminary and has continued to reflect on the intersection between Baptist theology and statecraft.[51]

In October 2002, in the run-up to the next war with Iraq, Richard Land, then head of the SBC's Ethics and Religious Liberty Commission, sent President George W. Bush an open letter arguing that preemptive war against Iraq met the requirements of just war theory. Cosigned by four other prominent evangelical leaders, Land's letter argued that a war against Saddam Hussein's regime would be defensive because of Hussein's past record of aggression against neighboring countries and Iraqi civilians. Land praised Bush's intent to bring liberty to Iraqis and agreed with Bush's assessment that Iraq had flouted all previous international commitments and thus proven war was necessary as a last resort.[52]

Heimbach disagreed: he argued the just war tradition originally limited the just cause for war to a response to actual (not potential) wrongdoing and, thus, disagreed with the Bush administration's case for preemption in Iraq. He argued the war in Iraq was permissible to enforce the terms of the 1991 armistice (similar to James Turner Johnson's argument),[53] not as a matter of preemptive defense against possible future Iraqi aggression.[54]

---

[51] Daniel R. Heimbach, "The Bush Just War Doctrine: Genesis and Application of the President's Moral Leadership in the Persian Gulf War," in *From Cold War to New World Order: The Foreign Policy of George H. W. Bush,* ed. Meena Bose and Rosanna Perotti (Westport: Greenwood, 2002), 443–44.

[52] "The So-Called 'Land Letter,'" October 3, 2002, https://web.archive.org /web/20190705081813/https://waynenorthey.com/wp-content/uploads/2017/06 /The-Land-Letter.pdf.

[53] James Turner Johnson, *The War to Oust Saddam Hussein: Just War and the New Face of Conflict* (Lanham: Rowman and Littlefield, 2005).

[54] Daniel R. Heimbach, "Distinguishing Just War from Crusade: Is Regime Change a Just Cause for Just War?" in *War in the Bible and Terrorism in the*

Interestingly, Land's letter did not raise any questions of justice after war, the responsibilities of reconstruction and stabilization, or the work of peace building, the issues that turned out to be the most consequential of the Iraq war. The disagreement between Land and Heimbach is probably the first time two Baptist theologians have carried on a debate about war explicitly within the framework and categories of the just war tradition.

Albert Mohler, president of the Southern Baptist Theological Seminary, published a similar just war analysis and defense of preemption in 2004.[55] In arguing for the war in Iraq, Heimbach, Land, and Mohler accurately reflected the views of their denomination: in late March 2003, 87 percent of white evangelicals believed going to war in Iraq was the right decision.[56] The SBC, in this era now firmly aligned with the political Right and the Republican Party, passed resolutions in 1991 in support of the Gulf War; in 2003 in support of the Iraq War; and in 2002 and 2006 in support of the War on Terror.[57]

In recent years Mohler invoked the just war framework on his popular podcast *The Briefing* in discussing the Syrian Civil War, North Korea, drones, the atomic bombing of Hiroshima, nuclear deterrence, and nuclear

---

Twenty-First Century, ed. Richard S. Hess and Elmer A. Martens (University Park: Eisenbrauns, 2008), 79–92. Heimbach does Cicero an injustice by claiming he advanced a justification for empire. In fact, Cicero used his understanding of just war to *criticize* the Roman Empire. Heimbach also relies heavily on Augustine for his argument against preemption, but later thinkers in the same tradition gave some qualified support for it.

[55] Albert Mohler, "Is War Ever Justified? A Reality Check," *Albert Mohler* (blog), April 19, 2004, https://albertmohler.com/2004/04/19/is-war-ever-justified -a-reality-check.

[56] "War Concerns Grow, but Support Remains Steadfast," Pew Research Center, April 3, 2003, https://www.pewresearch.org/politics/2003/04/03/war-concerns-grow -but-support-remains-steadfast/.

[57] "Resolution on Operation Desert Storm," June 1, 1991; "On the War on Terrorism," June 1, 2002; "On the Liberation of Iraq," June 1, 2003; "On Prayer for the President and the Military," June 1, 2006. All SBC resolutions are available on the SBC website, https://www.sbc.net/resource-library/resolutions.

weapons.[58] Bruce Ashford, professor of theology and culture and former provost at Southeastern Baptist Theological Seminary, similarly wrote a fourteen-part series of articles on just war in 2020, reviewing its intellectual history, distinguishing it from jihad, and applying it to terrorism, asymmetrical warfare, drones, and special operations.[59] Heimbach devoted the most academic attention to it in a chapter of his new text, *Fundamental Christian Ethics,* reviewing the history of just war thinking from Christian and non-Christian sources, exploring its biblical basis, rebutting pacifism, distinguishing just war from crusade, and offering a lengthy case study analyzing torture and interrogation with just war categories.[60]

The post–Cold War ferment likely represents the most focused Baptist engagement with the just war tradition ever—likely fueled by greater Baptist ecumenism and willingness to engage with and borrow from other traditions, including Catholicism, something that would have scandalized Williams, Smyth, and Backus.

---

[58] Albert Mohler, April 25, 2017, in *The Briefing* (podcast), https://albertmohler .com/2017/04/25/briefing-04–25–17; Mohler, August 11, 2017, in *The Briefing* (podcast), https://albertmohler.com/2017/08/11/briefing-08–11–17; Mohler, August 7, 2020, in *The Briefing* (podcast), https://albertmohler.com/2020/08/07/briefing -8–7–20; Mohler, June 15, 2021, in *The Briefing* (podcast), https://albertmohler.com /2021/06/15/briefing-6–15–21.

[59] See Bruce Ashford, "To Fight or Not to Fight?," Bruce Ashford website, February 24, 2020, https://bruceashford.net/2020/to-fight-or-not-to-fight-that-is -the-question-ethics-of-warfare-series.

[60] Daniel R. Heimbach, *Fundamental Christian Ethics* (Nashville: B&H Academic, 2022), chapter 11. See also the following recent works on just war from Baptist writers (with thanks to Daniel Heimbach for highlighting these works): Ergun Mehmet Caner and Emir Fethi Caner, *Christian Jihad: Two Former Muslims Look at the Crusades and Killing in the Name of Christ* (Grand Rapids: Kregel, 2004); J. Daryl Charles, *Between Pacifism and Jihad: Just War and Christian Tradition* (Downers Grove, IL: IVP, 2009); J. Daryl Charles and Timothy J. Demy, *War, Peace, and Christianity: Questions and Answers from a Just-War Perspective* (Wheaton, IL: Crossway, 2010).

Conclusion

The recent engagement highlights the need for more scholarly and theological reflection on what Baptists distinctively have to offer to Christian thinking about war. Baptists have, like other Christians, sometimes espoused pacifism and sometimes preached holy war. But the best of Baptist political theology, as reflected in our lived experience in wartime, is not only aligned with the Christian just war tradition, but it is a distinctive, organic, and positive contribution to it. The doctrine of just war is a near-perfect fit with Baptist political theology. Indeed, just war is a *better* fit with the Baptist tradition than the high church traditions from which it sprang. It is precisely the Baptist emphasis on the disestablishment of the church from the state that lays the strongest groundwork for the waging of wars for the *common* good and the strongest safeguards against crusades and wars for religion. Baptists, more than any other Christian tradition, have emphasized that conversion must come from a free, conscious, rational movement of the soul; there is no compulsion in matters of faith and, thus, no role for the state in matters of religion. That is the bedrock of the doctrine of religious freedom and disestablishment—and it is on the same grounds that we reject the doctrine of holy war and affirm the doctrine of just war.

The just war doctrine came to its clearest definition in contrast to the (false) doctrine of holy war, which was widely prevalent during the Wars of Religion. Advocates of just war doctrine rejected the idea of holy war, war to defend or propagate the true faith, for the same reason Baptists reject state compulsion in matters of faith at home. State power must be separate from inner conscience. If the state cannot compel in matters of faith at home, neither can it do so on the international stage. Baptists, more than anyone, understood this doctrine and its implications at home, in domestic policy and Constitutional design. While Baptists were not at the forefront of applying the same insight to international affairs, we should recognize that the just war inheritance is ideally suited to the architecture of Baptist political theology and its emphasis on disestablishment. Just war is the disestablishment of the church from warfare. The church still speaks about war and seeks to hold the state accountable for its conduct of war: we articulate principles of justice by which the state ought to conduct its wars. But the church does not fight war and does not expect the state to fight for the church's parochial interests. We seek to use war, when necessary, in the service of justice for all—for the common good and for principles of peace and justice as discoverable in the natural law—not for the defense of the faith as found in Scripture.

Finally, Baptists' emphasis on republicanism can be seen as an authentic development in just war thinking, one that is distinctive to our tradition but a genuine contribution to the broader Christian thought. Older just war thinking tended to describe war as just when it vindicated the common good and principles of peace, justice, and order. To that, Baptists add *liberty*, and they call the institutionalization of those principles together *republicanism*. Republicanism is another word for a system of *ordered liberty*. Baptists, then, have an answer that is both more concise and more specific to the questions of just war. When is war just? The violent disruption of ordered liberty is the "injury" in response to which force may be used and war may be justly waged. What does justice require? Justice requires the vindication and restoration of ordered liberty in, through, and after warfare.

26

Baptists and American Evangelical Identity

By Barry Hankins

The problem in discussing Baptists and evangelical identity begins with the problem of evangelical identity. What is it? Evangelicals have no pope, no magisterium, no institutional headquarters—not even a convention or association, as nearly all Baptists have. In short, there is no one to define what an Evangelical is or to police the membership of the group. For historians, however, a near consensus concerning evangelical identity existed for a quarter century. That consensus was built on the Bebbington Quadrilateral, which defined evangelicals as Protestant Christians marked by (1) conversionism ("the belief that lives need to be changed"); (2) activism ("the expression of the gospel in effort"); (3) biblicism ("a particular regard for the Bible"); and (4) crucicentrism ("a stress on the sacrifice of Christ on the cross"). These have always been subject to debate, and a few historians have challenged whether there even is such a thing as evangelicalism. Still, in 2014, the twenty-fifth anniversary of the quadrilateral, there were scholarly sessions at professional conferences reflecting on its use and value.[1]

British historian David Bebbington first articulated the quadrilateral in his 1989 book *Evangelicalism in Modern Britain*.[2] When he wrote the definition, he believed he was merely summarizing what everyone already knew and agreed on, and that may have been true at some subconscious, intuitive level. But the explicit articulation of this definition proved so concise and insightful that it took hold among scholars and laypeople alike. Today, if one goes to the website of the National Association of Evangelicals, a page contains a video in which a variety of evangelical leaders—male, female, white, and people of color—articulate in their own words one or more aspects of the quadrilateral in answer to the question that appears above the video: "What is an Evangelical?" The quadrilateral itself then appears in bullet-point form in the third paragraph beneath the video.[3]

While Bebbington intended the quadrilateral as a phenomenological definition with theological implications, some historians believe it privileges the latter too much. The efficacy of the quadrilateral is that it allows scholars to bring together a diverse, wide array of people who have almost nothing in common in terms of race, class, political views, country of origin, and so forth. The fact that the quadrilateral is transhistorical, however, gives some historians pause, as it groups together evangelicals over nearly three centuries. Recently, in the face of white evangelicals becoming a political near-monolith within the Republican Party, scholars have

---

[1] The papers from the American Society of Church History session and those from the Conference on Faith and History session were published as "Roundtable: Re-Examining David Bebbington's 'Quadrilateral Thesis," *Fides et Historia* 47, no. 1 (Winter/Spring 2015): 44–96.

[2] David Bebbington, *Evangelicalism in Modern Britain: A History from the 1730s to the 1980s* (Grand Rapids: Baker, 1989), 2–3. Bebbington listed the four components in the order I am using them.

[3] "What Is an Evangelical?", National Association of Evangelicals, accessed November 13, 2020, https://www.nae.net/what-is-an-evangelical/.

begun to question whether there might be something other than theology holding them together. This debate increased in intensity as a reported 80 percent of white evangelicals supported Donald Trump when he ran for president in 2016,[4] a man whose life has accentuated none of the theological aspects of evangelicalism while violating nearly everything evangelicals have stood for concerning personal morality. Evangelical support for Trump might lead one to side with Lord Shaftesbury: "I know what constituted an Evangelical in former times. I have no clear notion what constitutes one now."[5] Such uncertainty seems even stronger today than when Bebbington used Shaftesbury's quote to introduce the quadrilateral in 1989.

As part of this new debate over evangelical identity, in 2018 historian John Fea asked on his blog, "Should we retire the Bebbington Quadrilateral?" When the blog post appeared, Fea was putting the finishing touches on his book *Believe Me: The Evangelical Road to Donald Trump*. There, Fea argued that white evangelical support for Trump is the logical outgrowth of evangelical politics based on "fear, the pursuit of worldly power, and a nostalgic longing for a national past that may have never existed in the first place."[6] Going further than Fea in *Believe Me* is historian and Calvin University

---

[4] Sarah Pulliam Bailey, "White Evangelicals Voted Overwhelmingly for Donald Trump, Exit Polls Show," *Washington Post*, November 9, 2016, https://www .washingtonpost.com/news/acts-of-faith/wp/2016/11/09/exit-polls-show-white -evangelicals-voted-overwhelmingly-for-donald-trump/.

[5] Quoted in Bebbington, *Evangelicalism in Modern Britain,* 1–2. For a compelling response to the media's use of the term "evangelical" and its coverage of evangelical support for Trump, see Thomas S. Kidd, *Who Is an Evangelical?: The History of a Movement in Crisis* (New Haven: Yale University, 2019).

[6] "Should We Retire the 'Bebbington Quadrilateral'?," *The Way of Improvement Leads Home* (blog), January 4, 2018, https://thewayofimprovement.com/2018/01 /04/should-we-retire-the-bebbington-quadrilateral/. This blog has since been discontinued and the article itself moved to Current, at https://currentpub.com/2018 /01/04/should-we-retire-the-bebbington-quadrilateral/. See also John Fea, *Believe Me: The Evangelical Road to Donald Trump* (Grand Rapids: Eerdmans, 2018), 7.

professor Kristin Kobes Du Mez. She has issued the most serious challenge to the Bebbington Quadrilateral to date in her 2020 book *Jesus and John Wayne: How White Evangelicals Corrupted a Faith and Fractured a Nation.* Du Mez makes no claim to supplant the quadrilateral. Rather, she challenges the efficacy of any transhistorical definition, arguing that over the past quarter century something other than theology has come to define white evangelicals. "Today, what it means to be a 'conservative evangelical' is as much about culture as it is about theology," she writes.[7] Du Mez then traces the increasing emphasis on (1) Christian masculinity, (2) patriarchy, (3) nationalism, and (4) militarism as presented in a vast array of evangelical literature from the 1980s forward. These four elements could be taken as a new quadrilateral, but it may be more descriptive to call this the Du Mez Patrilateral, signifying the centrality of patriarchy and masculinity in her interpretation and the way power manifests itself through these cultural and political features of white evangelicalism. Like Fea, she finds evangelical support for Trump to be no aberration. As she writes, "It was, rather, the culmination of evangelicals' embrace of militant masculinity, an ideology that enshrines patriarchal authority and condones the callous display of power, at home and abroad."[8]

For the framework of the rest of this chapter, I will use the Bebbington Quadrilateral and the Du Mez Patrilateral as two poles on either end of a continuum that defines evangelicalism at this moment in history. The key question will be where do Baptists, especially Southern Baptists, fit into an evangelical framework that consists of both Bebbington theologically and Du Mez culturally? I focus on Southern Baptists for two reasons. First, they are the largest of the Baptist groups, by far. Second, as they have worked through their evangelical identity, they have become the clearest example of what an Evangelical is.

---

[7] Kristin Kobes Du Mez, *Jesus and John Wayne: How White Evangelicals Corrupted a Faith and Fractured a Nation* (New York: Liveright, 2020), 9–10.

[8] Du Mez, 3.

The Southern Baptist Struggle for Evangelical Identity—Part 1

It is not altogether clear when Southern Baptists began to think about their relationship to evangelical identity, but a reasonable place to start is with the work of E. Y. Mullins in response to the fundamentalist-modernist controversy in the Northern Baptist Convention (NBC), which peaked from 1922 to 1924 but had been building since the 1890s. That controversy ostensibly pitted theological modernists against Fundamentalists, but there was a range of theological positions on each side. On the side led by the modernists were many who retained evangelical beliefs, something very much like the Bebbington Quadrilateral, along with more thoroughgoing theological liberals such as Harry Emerson Fosdick. On the fundamentalist side were militant separatists like William Bell Riley and evangelical Baptist denominationalists like Curtis Lee Laws. Laws actually coined the term "fundamentalist" in 1920 but later had little to do with a movement led by the likes of Riley and John Roach Straton, both of whom wanted to fight a theological battle within the NBC and a culture war against evolution and Catholicism outside.[9]

As the fundamentalist-modernist controversy unfolded in the NBC, Mullins worked to head off a similar rift in the SBC by carving out a theology that was orthodox and evangelical theologically without being fundamentalist. He retained the supernatural elements of conversion and crucicentrism, but he also incorporated a good dose of the experiential facets of the faith that emanated from Friedrich Schleiermacher and theological modernism, as well as some elements of higher criticism of Scripture. This has led some to question Mullins's biblicism. The same could be said of Augustus H. Strong among Northern Baptists. Still, both theologians sought to retain much of nineteenth-century evangelical theology against

---

[9] Thomas S. Kidd and Barry Hankins, *Baptists in America: A History* (New York: Oxford University, 2015), 183–95.

the thoroughgoing critique made by modernists or the militant defense of the faith led by Fundamentalists.[10]

It is possible to frame the tension between Baptist denominationalists such as Laws and Mullins on the one hand and Fundamentalists like Riley and J. Frank Norris on the other along the quadrilateral-patrilateral continuum. Laws and Mullins tried to fashion a theological Baptist identity that would include those in their respective denominations who embraced the basic evangelical tenets of their faith—i.e., something akin to the Bebbington Quadrilateral. Riley, and especially Norris, were culture warriors long before the term existed—so much so that they were more inclined to make common cause with non-Baptists on evolution, Catholicism, militant foreign policy, and blatant Christian nationalism than they were to cooperate with their own denominational compadres on issues of theology. Just to highlight Norris, his masculinity, patriarchy, and militant approach to everything led to all manner of public battles that ran over into his shooting and killing a Catholic businessman in his own church office, multiple accusations of sexual harassment, at least one credible accusation of sexual assault, and militant anti-Communism. Not to shortchange Riley, while there was no hint of sexual impropriety in his career, as he moved from the twenties to the thirties, he marginalized the women he had once touted as preachers and evangelists in favor of a male-only ministry. Then, during the last decade of his life he trafficked in conspiratorial anti-Semitism. Both Norris and Riley believed they were, in the words of Laws, "doing battle royal for the faith," but this very fact makes one wonder what that faith was, or at least what its essence was. It often looked a good bit more like Du Mez's Christian

---

[10] While there are many sources on Mullins, a good place to start would be Edgar Young Mullins, *The Axioms of Religion: A New Interpretation of the Baptist Faith* (Philadelphia: Judson, 1908). For Strong see, Grant Wacker, *Augustus H. Strong and the Dilemma of Historical Consciousness* (Macon: Mercer University, 1985).

masculinity, patriarchy, nationalism, and militarism than the Bebbington Quadrilateral.[11]

Even as Mullins tried to remain highly theological, tooling along the Bebbington end of the continuum, he could not resist tying Baptist identity to American democracy. In his highly influential book *The Axioms of Religion*, the "religio-civic axiom" made no reference to Scripture or theology but rather to the First Amendment to the US Constitution. "We may regard American civilization as a Baptist empire," he claimed, "for at the basis of this government lies a great group of Baptist ideals."[12] Meanwhile, Mullins's contemporary, Southern Baptist statesman George Truett, made one of the most famous speeches in Southern Baptist history from the steps of the US Capitol in 1920. While he extolled as a Baptist virtue the separation of church and state, he was already on record nearly equating Baptist identity and American democracy, exclaiming to a Baptist World Alliance meeting in 1911, "The triumph of democracy, thank God, means the triumph of Baptists everywhere."[13] While neither Mullins nor Truett were being patriarchal or particularly masculine here, they both, at least on occasion, seemed to tie Baptist identity to America's political ideals, at least mirroring, however dimly, a more explicit Christian nationalism that would come from the likes of Riley and Norris.[14]

---

[11] For Norris, see Barry Hankins, *God's Rascal: J. Frank Norris and the Beginnings of Southern Fundamentalism*, 2nd ed. (Knoxville: University of Tennessee, 2022); for Riley, see William Vance Trollinger Jr., *God's Empire: William Bell Riley and Midwestern Fundamentalism* (Madison: University of Wisconsin, 1990).

[12] Mullins, *The Axioms of Religion*, 255. Quoted in Kidd and Hankins, *Baptists in America*, 182. For a full discussion of Mullins and George Truett's views in this regard, see Christopher L. Canipe, *A Baptist Democracy: Separating God from Caesar in the Land of the Free* (Macon, GA: Mercer University, 2011).

[13] George Truett, *God's Call to America* (New York: George H. Doran, 1923), 19. Quoted in Kidd and Hankins, *Baptists in America*, 178. This line of argument comes from Canipe, *A Baptist Democracy*.

[14] As Canipe puts it, the wall of separation became a mirror. See *A Baptist Democracy*, 152.

Fast-forward to 1976, and one can see the beginning of a new struggle over evangelical identity within Southern Baptist history. That year,
Jimmy Carter was running for president. A devoted Southern Baptist
Sunday school teacher, Carter referred to himself as "born-again" and as
an "evangelical." The press and media did not know what to make of this.
As *New York Times* religion reporter Kenneth Briggs reflected later, most
people had little idea what an Evangelical was, and those who did had
views that hearkened back to the Scopes trial of 1925—"a backwoods
yahoo-ism that they found very distasteful."[15] In an attempt to clarify matters, *NBC Nightly News* anchor John Chancellor started the March 23
broadcast by saying in reference to the notion of being "born again": "We
have checked on the religious meaning of Carter's profound experience. It
is described by other Baptists as a common experience, not something out
of the ordinary. Being reborn does not mean having a vision or hearing
the voice of God."[16]

Foy Valentine of the SBC's Christian Life Commission (CLC), the forerunner of today's Ethics and Religious Liberty Commission, would have
none of what he saw as a conflation of evangelicalism and Southern Baptist
identity. Little more than a week before the election, *Newsweek* magazine
declared 1976 "The Year of the Evangelicals" in an issue with a cover that
read "Born Again!" at the top and "The Evangelicals" just below mid-page.
Valentine's famous statement appeared on page seventy-six: "Southern
Baptists are not evangelical," he said. "That's a Yankee word." He went on to
say that Southern Baptists have their "own traditions, our own hymns, and
more students in our seminaries than they have in all theirs put together."

---

[15] Quoted in William Martin, *With God on Our Side: The Rise of the Religious
Right in America* (New York: Broadway Books, 1996), 149–50.

[16] Among other places to find the text and video of Chancellor's comments,
see "The Roots of Evangelicals' Political Fervor," October 29, 2018, https://www
.retroreport.org/transcript/the-roots-of-evangelicals-political-fervor/. Chancellor's
statement can be viewed on the video in this link at 1:48.

Then came the crux of Valentine's complaint: "We don't share politics or their fussy fundamentalism, and we don't want to get involved in their theological witch-hunts."[17]

In this odd and offhanded way, politics ("we don't share politics") has been part of the question of Southern Baptists and evangelical identity since the 1970s, along with "fussy fundamentalism" and "theological witch-hunts," which could have been a reference to fundamentalist J. Frank Norris and his ilk. In other words, without using the terms Christian masculinity, patriarchy, nationalism, and militarism, Valentine was in some ways viewing Northern evangelicalism as a combination of "theological witch-hunts" and a certain kind of politics.

Ironically, just three years earlier, when Valentine spoke at the now-famous Thanksgiving Workshop on Evangelicals and Social Concern in Chicago, he spoke of evangelicals as "we." His address was subsequently published in a collection of essays reflecting on *The Chicago Declaration of Evangelical Social Concern*. "Really, now," he asked, "who are we evangelicals interested in Christian social concern?" Two paragraphs later he made it even more explicit: "We are evangelical Christians," he wrote, following with "We are neither inordinately proud nor especially ashamed that we are evangelical Christians. This is just who we are."[18] Valentine called out and rejected the hyper-individualism of some evangelicals that would concentrate on personal salvation and ignore social sin. Social sins that Valentine said evangelicals could not ignore included "ecological

---

[17] Kenneth L. Woodward et al., "Born Again! The Year of the Evangelicals," *Newsweek* (October 25, 1976): 76. For an analysis of Valentine's statement, see Joel Carpenter, "Is 'Evangelical' a Yankee Word?: Relations Between Northern Evangelicals and the Southern Baptist Convention in the Twentieth Century," in *Southern Baptists and American Evangelicals: The Conversation Continues*, ed. David S. Dockery (Nashville: B&H, 1993), 78–99.

[18] Foy Valentine, "Engagement—the Christian's Agenda," in *The Chicago Declaration*, ed. Ronald J. Sider (Carol Stream: Creation House, 1974), 58–59.

rape, militarism, white racism, sexism, poverty in the midst of plenty, crime, consumer exploitation by business, inflation, unemployment, over-population, and the like."[19]

At this point, Valentine is calling out as sin some of what Du Mez sees as central to white evangelicalism in the twenty-first century—militarism, white racism, and sexism. Still, Valentine's address was thoroughly evangelical in the Bebbington Quadrilateral sense. He cited Scripture multiple times (biblicism), spoke repeatedly of the need for conversion and regeneration (conversionism), and explicitly referenced the cross of Christ (crucicentrism). Moreover, the thrust of his address was evangelical social concern (activism).[20] It appears, then, that Valentine was quite comfortable with evangelical identity at the Chicago meeting in 1973 when the politics were right, or perhaps one should say left, and he was quite comfortable with Carter's brand of politics. But in response to the "born-again" phenomenon swirling around Carter, the media tended to reduce evangelicalism to conversion alone, and that was a tent far too broad for Valentine's evangelicalism.

Another Baptist Evangelical at the Thanksgiving workshop was Carl F. H. Henry, who, like Valentine, became one of the original signers of the Chicago Declaration. Over a mere four pages, Henry lauded the declaration for steering a course distinct from either secular ideologies or mainline ecumenical efforts. The declaration did so, first, by retaining the "new birth" (conversionism) in the face of mainline criticism that individual conversion was something of a distraction from social concern. A second contribution of the Chicago declaration, Henry argued, was keeping Scripture central (biblicism). "Insofar as the Chicago Declaration spoke," he argued, "it attempted to do so in a specifically biblical way." Henry viewed the declaration as having steered a course between "a theology of revolutionary

---

[19] Valentine, 63.
[20] Valentine, 62.

violence or of pacifistic neutrality in the face of blatant militarist aggression" and "such fanfare as 'capitalism can do no wrong' or 'socialism is the hope of the masses.'"[21]

Twenty-six years before the 1973 Chicago declaration, Henry had published *The Uneasy Conscience of Modern Fundamentalism*.[22] Using the term in the broadest sense to include all evangelicals, in this little book he lamented fundamentalism's turn away from social concern toward an exclusive emphasis on individual salvation. "A predominant trait, in most Fundamentalist preaching," Henry wrote, "is this reluctance to come to grips with social evils."[23] Social evils he cited repeatedly throughout the book were similar to Valentine's: "aggressive warfare, racial hatred and intolerance, the liquor traffic, exploitation of labor or management." Unlike Valentine, Henry never wavered in his evangelical identity. As a Northerner, Northern Baptist, and then after the late 1950s a Southern Baptist, he never saw any tension between Baptist and evangelical identity, and thus he would become a mentor to Southern Baptist conservatives during the Conservative Resurgence of the 1980s and 1990s.

It did not take long for evangelicals and most Southern Baptists to sour on President Jimmy Carter. There is even a question of how fervently they supported him in the first place.[24] Famously, in 1979, Baptist Fundamentalist

---

[21] Carl F. H. Henry, "Reflections," in *The Chicago Declaration*, ed. Ronald J. Sider (Carol Stream: Creation House, 1974), 127–31.

[22] Carl F. H. Henry, *The Uneasy Conscience of Modern Fundamentalism* (Grand Rapids: Eerdmans, 1947).

[23] Henry, 18.

[24] See, for example, J. Brooks Flippen, *Jimmy Carter, the Politics of Family, and the Rise of the Religious Right* (Athens: University of Georgia, 2011), 104. Flippen claims Gerald Ford received 9.6 million votes of "self-described" evangelicals, while Carter received 6.4 million. Tracking the evangelical vote was uncommon in 1976, so the actual numbers or percentages that year are suspect. That said, there is a consensus that Carter's support among conservative Protestants declined during his presidency and that Reagan won roughly 63 percent of the evangelical vote in 1980.

Jerry Falwell Sr., a member of the fundamentalist Baptist Bible Fellowship International (BBFI), launched the Moral Majority as evangelicals coalesced around Republican candidate Ronald Reagan. Reagan was not much of an evangelical himself, at least publicly, but Southern California evangelicals had begun to support him in the 1960s when he ran for governor because they shared his conservative political philosophy. Falwell and the Moral Majority became a venue through which Reagan's evangelical candidacy became national. Soon, a handful of other organizations collectively became known as the New Religious Right, then just the Religious Right, and by the 1990s the Christian Right, as evangelicals from California to Virginia coalesced around Reagan.[25]

As a Fundamentalist, Falwell touted the Bebbington Quadrilateral and even the militant defense of it, especially the defense of biblicism in the form of biblical inerrancy. As a leader of a social movement, however, his Moral Majority fit squarely into the Du Mez Patrilateral. Beginning in the mid-1970s, he worked to shore up American patriotism, organizing "I Love America" rallies across the country. Moral Majority planks included a strong national defense, patriarchal families, and a virulent anti-Communism that would have made J. Frank Norris proud, which is fitting given that Falwell once said he was trained by men who were trained by Norris. As Du Mez points out, Falwell spoke of the church as "an army equipped for battle," Sunday school as an "attacking squad," and Christian radio as "the artillery."[26]

Meanwhile, as the Moral Majority led in the development of what was then called the New Religious Right and as evangelicals became

---

[25] For Southern California evangelicals rallying around Reagan in the 1960s, see Darren Dochuk, *From Bible Belt to Sunbelt: Plain-Folk Religion, Grassroots Politics, and the Rise of Evangelical Conservatism* (New York: W. W. Norton, 2011). For the movement of evangelicals into the Republican Party and the rise of the Christian Right, see Daniel K. Williams, *God's Own Party: The Making of the Christian Right* (New York: Oxford University, 2010).

[26] Quoted in Du Mez, *Jesus and John Wayne*, 99.

the Republican party's most reliable voting bloc, the Southern Baptist Convention was undergoing a thorough transformation. Moderate leaders like Valentine were replaced by conservatives like Richard Land as the Christian Life Commission (CLC) became the Ethics and Religious Liberty Commission (ERLC). The presidency of the SBC went from being something of an honorary position to a highly contested office, the winner of which got to appoint members of the Committee on Committees, which in turn appointed members of the boards of the SBC's agencies and seminaries. The rallying cry of this Conservative Resurgence was theological, but politics was near the center as well, particularly abortion and religion's role in public schools, as were the complementarian view of marriage and the role of women in pastoral ministry.[27]

One might say the resurgence was a convergence—of the Bebbington Quadrilateral and the Du Mez Patrilateral. Complementarianism in the home and male-only leadership in the churches joined with a vigorous conservative politics that came to be called "culture war" by the 1990s. For example, as soon as the SBC's flagship, the Southern Baptist Theological Seminary in Louisville, came under conservative control in 1993, new president R. Albert Mohler Jr. instituted hiring requirements that included biblical inerrancy and the theological position that women cannot serve as pastors, a position that was added to the SBC's confession of faith, *The Baptist Faith and Message*, in 2000. The complementarian position that women should be "graciously submissive" to their husbands had been added in 1998.[28]

As the resurgence unfolded, the identity debate over the term "evangelical" began anew. What did it mean to be an evangelical, and why had moderates, represented by Valentine, been so reluctant to adopt the term?

---

[27] See Barry Hankins, *Uneasy in Babylon: Southern Baptist Conservatives and American Culture* (Tuscaloosa: University of Alabama, 2002).

[28] Hankins, 81–83 and 214–28.

The Southern Baptist Struggle for Evangelical Identity—Part 2

The conservatives leading the resurgence began to openly identify themselves as evangelicals, some citing the influence of Carl Henry as well as the non-Baptist guru of evangelical cultural engagement Francis Schaeffer.[29] As this happened, Southern Baptist and evangelical scholars revisited the question of Baptists and evangelical identity, and as they did so, they attempted to keep the conversation centered on what would soon become the Bebbington Quadrilateral. In 1983, theologian James Leo Garrett Jr. of Southwestern Baptist Theological Seminary joined with historian and Southern Baptist Theological Seminary professor E. Glenn Hinson in a written debate published as *Are Southern Baptists "Evangelicals"?* Neither scholar identified with the resurgence, and Hinson was an ardent opponent, and target, of the conservatives.[30]

Garrett led off by summarizing the reluctance of Southern Baptist moderates to identify as evangelicals—their resistance to being associated with fundamentalism, resistance to interdenominational movements, and preference for the terms "conservative" and "evangelistic" rather than "evangelical." Over two chapters, Garrett carefully laid out "Who Are the Evangelicals?" and "What Evangelicals Believe and Practice." Then he articulated where Southern Baptists have positioned themselves theologically over their history, including a seven-point refutation of Valentine's notorious statement. Garrett concluded there was no other place to put Southern Baptists, so he called them "denominational Evangelicals." Writing pre-Bebbington, Garrett built on Richard Quebedeaux's three-fold definition to create his own quintilateral: "Southern Baptists are denominational Evangelicals," he wrote. "They belong to and exemplify the great heritage of [1] Scriptural

---

[29] Hankins, 14–40.

[30] James Leo Garrett Jr., E. Glenn Hinson, and James E. Tull, *Are Southern Baptists "Evangelicals"?* (Macon: Mercer University, 1983).

authority, [2] Christocentric doctrine, [3] gospel proclamation, [4] experience of grace, and [5] evangelistic endeavor which is Evangelicalism."[31]

Hinson countered Garrett's argument by first acknowledging that Evangelicals were quite a bit like Southern Baptists, and this was what made them "a danger."[32] Why were they dangerous to Southern Baptists? Citing evangelical theologian Bernard Ramm, Hinson argued that "Evangelicals . . . let nothing stand above what they consider the objective Word of God found in the Scriptures." By contrast, Hinson responded, "[Baptists] have insisted that faith must be free and voluntary if it is to be genuine and responsible faith, that there is no objective word apart from uncoerced human response."[33] Throughout his argument, Hinson reiterated this notion that "[Baptist] refers to that version of Christianity which places the priority of voluntary and uncoerced faith or response to the Word and Act of God over any supposed 'objective' Word and Act of God."[34] Garrett's most trenchant response to Hinson was when he pointed out that Hinson's source for evangelical identity was Ramm, and Ramm was a Baptist. "How," Garrett asked, "can the theology of this lifelong Baptist be rightly taken as the antithesis of Baptist beliefs?" Garrett answered his own question, "It is possible because Hinson has imputed to Baptists his own view that places religious experience above the Bible as a source of religious truth."[35]

The year after the publication of *Are Southern Baptists "Evangelicals"?*, in a footnote in a book by the same publisher (Mercer), Leonard Sweet referred to the Garrett-Hinson debate as "one of the stranger exchanges about whether a denomination is 'evangelical.'"[36] But Southern Baptists

---

[31] Garrett, Hinson, and Tull, 125–26. For Garrett's quick refutation of Valentine, see pp. 119–20.

[32] Garrett, Hinson, and Tull, 165–66.

[33] Garrett, Hinson, and Tull, 166.

[34] Garrett, Hinson, and Tull, 173–74.

[35] Garrett, Hinson, and Tull, 202.

[36] Leonard I. Sweet, "The Evangelical Tradition in America," in *The Evangelical Tradition in America*, ed. Leonard I. Sweet (Macon: Mercer University, 1984), 85 n. 306.

were not done probing their identity, and as they did they adhered to a Bebbington-like definition. In 1993, David Dockery edited *Southern Baptists and American Evangelicals: The Conversation Continues*.[37] By the time this volume appeared, the Conservative Resurgence was nearly complete, and there was a growing consensus that agreed with Garrett from a decade before. Southern Baptists were evangelical but with their own unique history, which made them evangelical but different. Dockery edited another volume titled *Southern Baptist Identity* that appeared in 2009. The subtitle, *An Evangelical Denomination Faces the Future*, indicated how the debate had evolved since the Garrett-Hinson book in 1983. The question was no longer "Are Southern Baptists 'Evangelicals'?" but how Southern Baptists as evangelicals should do theology and live in the culture.

As Southern Baptist conservatives forged a consensus on their being evangelical, they also became a major force in the culture wars. Following Valentine's retirement from the Christian Life Commission in 1987, there was a brief interim under another executive director before Richard Land took the reins. The CLC was changed to the Ethics and Religious Liberty Commission and became the voice of the SBC on church-state issues as well as political witness and activism—pro-life causes especially, but also matters of race, electoral politics, and many others. By virtue of his energy, intellect, and sheer presence, Land turned the ERLC into arguably the most influential Christian political organization in America. During the presidency of George W. Bush, Land was among the most visible evangelical political leaders in the country, helping to launch the "I Vote Values" campaign in 2004. A central feature of that effort was a voter registration drive in which he traveled the country in a bus with his photo and the "I Vote Values" motto plastered on the side.[38]

---

[37] David S. Dockery, ed., *Southern Baptists and American Evangelicals: The Conversation Continues* (Nashville: B&H, 1993).

[38] See for example, Jill Waggoner, "SBC's Richard Land Launches iVoteValues.com and iLiveValues.com," February 8, 2008, https://erlc.com/resource-library/press-releases/sbcs-richard-land-launches-ivotevalues-com-and-ilivevalues-com/. This article reviews the original launching of "I Vote Values" in 2004. See also

Slightly less visible, but just as influential, was Albert Mohler. After becoming president of the Southern Baptist Theological Seminary, he emerged as a theologically sophisticated voice for evangelical Southern Baptists in the culture wars. While Land lobbied Congress and spoke with presidents, Mohler developed a major following on his blog, *The Briefing,* and appeared often on major newscasts. When the SBC revised *The Baptist Faith and Message* in 1998 to include the complementarian clause on wifely submission, for example, it was Mohler who landed on CNN's primetime news program *Larry King Live* to explain complementarian views on marriage.[39]

Land and Mohler, along with a handful of other Southern Baptist conservatives less visible to the broader public, were deeply influenced by evangelical authors Carl F. H. Henry and Francis Schaeffer. Reading both in their youth, they learned from Schaeffer the importance of the evangelical social witness to a culture that was no longer Christian. From Henry, they became aware of how a social witness could be and should be deeply informed by theology. This awareness of the need for a Christian

---

David Kirkpatrick, "The 2004 Campaign: Strategy; Bush Allies Till Fertile Soil, Among Baptists, for Votes," *New York Times,* June 18, 2004, https://www.nytimes .com/2004/06/18/us/2004–campaign-strategy-bush-allies-till-fertile-soil-among -baptists-for-votes.html and "USCIRF: Richard Land Appointed to Commission by Senator Bill Frist," United States Commission on International Religious Freedom, July 26, 2005, https://www.uscirf.gov/news-room/releases-statements/uscirf-richard -land-appointed-commission-senator-bill-frist-replacing.

[39] Many years ago, I viewed Mohler on *Larry King Live,* June 12, 1998, James P. Boyce Centennial Library, Southern Baptist Theological Seminary, videotape. I do not know if the video is still accessible. A handful of Mohler's appearances on national news shows are available on YouTube, but not this one. For a recent controversy over the June 1998 appearance, see Jonathan Merritt, "Al Mohler, Southern Baptist Leader, Says He Was 'Stupid' to Defend Slavery in 1998 CNN Interview," Religion News Service, May 15, 2020, https://religionnews.com/2020/05/15/al -mohler-southern-baptist-leader-says-he-was-stupid-to-defend-slavery-in-1998 –cnn-interview/. For my discussion of the "submission statement," see Hankins, *Uneasy in Babylon,* 213–28.

political and cultural engagement was aided by experiences outside the South that alerted them to America's growing secularization—Land at Princeton University and then Oxford, and Mohler in south Florida with non-Southern transplants and an evangelical megachurch down the street from his own. While a doctoral student at Southern Seminary, Mohler became friends with Henry, counting the evangelical stalwart as a personal mentor. Land, meanwhile, referred to Henry as the most influential theologian of the twentieth century.[40]

The George W. Bush presidency constituted heady years for evangelicals. As Land liked to say, the Reagan administration returned his phone calls, Bush 41 would as well, but "not as quickly and sometimes not quite as receptively." The Clinton administration would not take his calls, but in the Bush 43 White House, "They call us, and they say, 'What is your take on this?'"[41] Land lauded Bush as speaking in evangelical terms more than any president in his lifetime, which extended from Eisenhower forward, including even Reagan. "Let me be very clear about this," he said in a *Frontline* interview during Bush's reelection campaign of 2004. "We need to vote our values, our beliefs and our convictions. We shouldn't be endorsing candidates. We should be looking for candidates who endorse us."[42]

It seemed that Land and other evangelical leaders of the Christian Right were experiencing under Bush what they had called for in 1998. In March of that year, frustrated by the lack of commitment to evangelical causes Republicans were showing, conservative guru Paul Weyrich summoned twenty-five leaders to Washington to discuss strategy. "The go-along, get-along strategy is dead," Land told those gathered. "No more engagement. We want a wedding ring, we want a ceremony, we want a consummation of the

---

[40] For a longer discussion of the influence Henry and Schaeffer had on Southern Baptists, see Hankins, *Uneasy in Babylon*, 21–40.

[41] "The Jesus Factor: Interview Richard Land," Frontline, February 4, 2004, https://www.pbs.org/wgbh/pages/frontline/shows/jesus/interviews/land.html.

[42] "The Jesus Factor: Interview Richard Land."

marriage."[43] This marriage to the Republican cause, consummated during the Bush years, contributed more than anything else to the perception that "evangelical" was becoming a political term. It would become increasingly difficult for Land and others to adhere to the Bebbington Quadrilateral's theological definition.

From the Bebbington Quadrilateral to the Du Mez Patrilateral

During the Southern Baptist controversy, the SBC conservatives worked hard to keep the focus on theology, insisting as they did that all positions in the denomination be held by avowed biblical inerrantists. Still, even during the years they were consolidating their control, the role of women in home and church loomed significant, as did issues of cultural engagement such as abortion, religious liberty, and race. It was assumed the Bebbington Quadrilateral, plus patriarchy in home and church, plus a pro-life stance on abortion equaled Southern Baptist evangelicalism. This made Southern Baptists relatively typical among American evangelicals, and it meant there is at least a soft patriarchy baked into evangelical theology. In public life, however, there was nothing soft about Southern Baptist evangelicalism. As it was expressed increasingly in the form of political battles against the Left, many Southern Baptists moved steadily toward something akin to the Du Mez Patrilateral with its emphasis on culture war over theology.

Following George W. Bush's presidency, evangelicals increasingly portrayed themselves along lines articulated by sociologist Christian Smith in his 1998 book, *American Evangelicalism: Embattled and Thriving*.[44] During

---

[43] Quoted in Laurie Goodstein, "Religious Right, Frustrated, Trying New Tactic on G.O.P.," *New York Times*, March 23, 1998, https://www.nytimes.com /1998/03/23/us/religious-right-frustrated-trying-new-tactic-on-gop.html.

[44] Christian Smith, *American Evangelicalism: Embattled and Thriving* (Chicago: University of Chicago, 1998).

the Obama years some leaders seemed to argue that evangelicals were embattled and no longer thriving, in fact under siege. Land's criticism of the first African American president increased steadily over Obama's first term. At one point he likened the Affordable Care Act (Obamacare) to Nazism, then softened his views after being confronted by the Anti-Defamation League.[45] With regard to the steady march of gay rights and gay marriage, he said on his radio program that "down in the grade school levels, they're recruiting people for homosexual clubs. . . . It's really child abuse, that's what it is."[46] By 2012, he was promoting any Republican in the presidential primaries, arguing, as the *New York Times* titled his online op-ed, "The Bottom Line Is to Beat Obama."[47]

Land's criticism of the president led eventually to his ouster from the ERLC when he made insensitive and racially charged comments following the killing of Trayvon Martin. Martin was a seventeen-year-old African American visiting his aunt in Florida when he was followed and then shot and killed by a self-styled neighborhood watchman named George Zimmerman. On March 23, 2012, amid national debate over the tragedy, Obama remarked that if he had a son, he would look like Trayvon Martin. A week later Land responded on his call-in radio show, *Richard Land Live!*, claiming that Obama

---

[45] "Richard Land Apologizes for Using Nazi Analogy," *Nashville Post* (blog), October 11, 2009, https://www.nashvillepost.com/home/blog/20426277/richard-land-apologizes-for-using-nazi-analogy No longer accessible. See also Bob Allen, "SBC Leader Apologizes for Nazi Analogy," Baptist Standard, October 16, 2009, https://www.baptiststandard.com/archives/2009–archives/sbc-leader-apologizes-for-nazi-analogy/.

[46] Kyle Mantyla, "Land: Gay Activists Seek Full-Blown 'Sexual Paganization of Society,'" *Right Wing Watch*, September 26, 2011, https://www.rightwingwatch.org/post/land-gay-activists-seek-full-blown-sexual-paganization-of-society/. I would not have believed this charge or cited this source without the audio clip of Land saying this on his radio program: https://youtu.be/vCI9lzoI9_c.

[47] Richard Land, "The Bottom Line Is to Beat Obama," *New York Times*, April 1, 2012, https://www.nytimes.com/roomfordebate/2011/12/13/have-evangelicals-lost-their-sway/the-bottom-line-is-to-beat-obama.

was exploiting the Trayvon Martin tragedy to "gin up the black vote." He followed by saying that Black activists Jesse Jackson and Al Sharpton, both ministers, were fomenting "a mob mentality" and that a Black man is "statistically more likely to do you harm than a white man."[48] For Land, it seemed as if even a tragic killing of an unarmed Black teen was cause not for lament but for culture war, and his African American brothers in Christ took note. Black SBC leaders such as Dwight McKissic and Fred Luter, the latter on the cusp of becoming the first African American SBC president, responded to Land's comments with outrage, as did some white SBC leaders.[49] The criticism gave way to a reprimand of Land by the ERLC Board of Trustees. The trustees noted the irony of Land's comments given his "long career of work on racial reconciliation," a clear reference to Land's leadership on the SBC racial reconciliation resolution of 1995. Land issued an apology, but it was not enough, especially when the racial incident dovetailed with charges of on-air plagiarism, which led to a second reprimand from the trustees and the cancellation of his radio program. Land resigned as head of the ERLC shortly thereafter.[50]

---

[48] For the Obama quote, see David A. Graham, "Quote of the Day: Obama: 'If I Had a Son, He'd Look Like Trayvon," *The Atlantic* (online), March 23, 2012. https://www.theatlantic.com/politics/archive/2012/03/quote-of-the-day-obama-if-i-had-a-son-hed-look-like-trayvon/254971/; for reports of other Land comments, including the statistical comment on Black men, his apology, and his eventual departure, see Morgan Feddes, "Richard Land's Comments on Trayvon Martin Investigated by SBC," *Christianity Today*, April 20, 2012, https://www.christianitytoday.com/news/2012/april/richard-lands-comments-on-trayvon-martin-investigated-by.html. See also, Associated Press, "Baptist Leader Criticizes Trayvon Martin Support," *Newsday*, April 14, 2012. https://www.newsday.com/news/nation/baptist-leader-criticizes-trayvon-martin-support-1.3660945+&cd=1&hl=en&ct=clnk&gl=us; and Art Toalston, "Trustees Reprimand Land, Halt Radio Program over Comments," Baptist Press, June 1, 2012, http://www.bpnews.net/37942.

[49] Greg Horton, "Did Land Write His Apology for Racially Charged Remarks?," Good Faith Media, May 23, 2012, https://www.ethicsdaily.com/did-land-write-his-apology-for-racially-charged-remarks-cms-19628/.

[50] Art Toalston, "Trustees Reprimand Land, Halt Radio Program over Comments," Baptist Press, June 1, 2012, http://www.bpnews.net/37942. For the plagiarism, see Sarah Posner, "Baptist Blogger Who Discovered Land Plagiarism

Land's cultural demise came in the context of his combative, politically incorrect culture war against a president evangelicals believed facilitated and emboldened anti-Christian forces. By that time, media attention to evangelicals centered almost entirely on leaders engaged in culture wars. Land was succeeded at the ERLC by Russell Moore. While Moore continued much of Land's work, especially surrounding religious liberty and pro-life causes, he also represented a generational change in outlook about how evangelicals should approach politics. Moore's position, outlined adeptly in his book *Onward: Engaging the Culture without Losing the Gospel,* is that evangelicals need to stop seeing themselves as a "moral majority," but instead as a prophetic minority living in a pagan culture.[51] Moore's book can be viewed as resistance to the notion that evangelical identity is primarily about culture war.

As the Trump era commenced, the generational shift from Land to Moore seemed to become a contest between SBC culture warriors exuding the Du Mez Patrilateral and those who wanted to get back to missions and evangelism, the conversionism and activism planks of the Bebbington Quadrilateral. Land had clearly set the template for a militant, culture-war approach to public life, and Robert Jeffress of First Baptist Dallas would take on that role. Easily the most visible Trump-supporting culture warrior, Fox News made Jeffress a regular contributor, seemingly portraying him as the voice of evangelicals. He gave an April 2016 interview where he said, "Frankly, I want [for president] the meanest, toughest son of a gun I can find. And I think that's the feeling of a lot of evangelicals."[52] One would be

---

Says Investigation Is 'Unprecedented,'" *Religion Dispatches,* April 23, 2012, https://religiondispatches.org/baptist-blogger-who-discovered-land-plagiarism-says -investigation-is-unprecedented/. Land got the material from Jeffrey T. Kuhner, "Obama Foments Racial Division," *Washington Times,* March 29, 2012, https:// www.washingtontimes.com/news/2012/mar/29/obama-foments-racial-division/.

[51] Russell Moore, *Onward: Engaging the Culture without Losing the Gospel* (Nashville: B&H, 2015), 3–25.

[52] Julie Lyons, "Robert Jeffress Wants a Mean 'Son of a Gun' for President, Says Trump Isn't a Racist," *Dallas Observer,* April 5, 2016, https://www.dallasobserver

hard-pressed to find a more John Wayne–like statement than this, reeking as it does of machismo and militarism. Largely in response to Jeffress's comments, Alan Bean of *Baptist News* wrote an article titled "Jesus and John Wayne: Must We Choose?" With Bean's blessing, Du Mez had her book title. In the article, Bean wrote, "Men like Wayne and Trump represent white male manhood in all its swaggering glory," and he called Jeffress "the most outspoken proponent of Jesus/John Wayne dualism."[53] Appearing with Trump multiple times on the campaign trail, sometimes offering opening prayers, Jeffress said that America needed "a strong man to protect its citizens against evil-doers."[54] As for moral qualms evangelicals might have about supporting a thrice-married serial adulterer who bragged in an *Access Hollywood* tape about what amounted to sexual assault, Jeffress argued that evangelicals were under no illusions they were voting for a "choir boy." "I am getting sick and tired of these namby-pamby, pantywaist, weak-kneed Christians who say they are going to stay home in November out of moral principle," he said as the election approached. "Will you please tell me what great moral principle there is in the universe that would allow a pro-abortion, anti-religious liberty candidate like Hillary Clinton to become the president?"[55]

Arrayed on the other side of the Trump campaign, and by implication perhaps against John Wayne as well, were influential if less famous Southern Baptist evangelicals. Chief among them were Russell Moore, Al Mohler, and

---

.com/news/robert-jeffress-wants-a-mean-son-of-a-gun-for-president-says-trump-isnt-a-racist-8184721.

[53] Alan Bean, "Jesus and John Wayne: Must We Choose?," *Baptist News Global*, October 31, 2016, https://baptistnews.com/article/jesus-and-john-wayne-must-we-choose/#.YUoAlKBOn65. Bean acknowledges that he borrowed the title of his article from a song by the Bill Gaither Vocal Band.

[54] Quoted in Du Mez, *Jesus and John Wayne*, 258.

[55] Quoted in Gregory Tomlin, "Jeffress: Christians Who Don't Vote for Trump Are 'Hypocrites' and 'Fools,'" *Christian Examiner*, September 13, 2016, https://www.christianexaminer.com/article/jeffress-christians-who-dont-vote-for-trump-are-hypocrites-and-fools/51055.htm.

J. D. Greear, who served as SBC president from 2018 to 2021. In 2016, in the wake of the *Access Hollywood* tape, Moore said in response to evangelical support for Trump, "The damage done to the gospel witness this year will take longer to recover from than those 1980s televangelist scandals."[56] Appearing on *CNN Tonight*, Mohler made a similar claim: "When it comes to Donald Trump," he told CNN show host Don Lemon, "evangelicals are going to have to ask a huge question: Is it worth destroying our moral credibility to support someone who is beneath the baseline level of human decency?"[57] By 2020, Mohler had changed his position, endorsing Trump largely because the president's Supreme Court nominations made it more likely that *Roe v. Wade* might be reversed.[58]

Throughout his presidency, which ran for three of Trump's four years in office, Greear was troubled that evangelicals had come to be known primarily as Trump supporters. In a 2019 interview with Margaret Hoover, host of PBS's *Firing Line*, he argued that Southern Baptists were putting too much emphasis on politics and urged them to get back to the Great Commission—i.e., evangelism. Here he was touting none other than the conversionism and activism planks of the Bebbington Quadrilateral. Then, as if he were self-consciously pushing back against the Du Mez Patrilateral, he said Southern Baptists need to get back to "who we are." And who are Southern Baptists, according to Greear? Not culture warriors, but rather, as he put it, "a community that welcomes in the stranger, that advocates for the vulnerable. We're people who, yes, we have political convictions, but our

---

[56] Quoted in Sarah Eekhoff Zylstra, "Why Trump Tape Caused Only One Evangelical Leader to Abandon Him," *Christianity Today* (online), October 10, 2016, https://www.christianitytoday.com/news/2016/october/why-trump-tape-cause -evangelical-leader-switch-wayne-grudem.html.

[57] Southern Seminary, "Albert Mohler Discusses Trump and Evangelicals on CNN Tonight–October 11, 2016," YouTube Video, 8:05, October 12, 2016, https://www.youtube.com/watch?v=exvuCgWiIGk&feature=youtu.be.

[58] R. Albert Mohler Jr., "Christians, Conscience, and the Looming 2020 Election," *Albert Mohler* (blog), October 26, 2020, https://albertmohler.com/2020 /10/26/christians-conscience-and-the-looming-2020-election.

main message is about a savior who gave his life so that people could be for-given and live eternally and not about a kingdom we can set up on earth."[59] He didn't sound much like John Wayne or Donald Trump.

Such obvious pushback against Trump and his SBC supporters put Greear, along with Moore, squarely in the crosshairs of a new group called the Conservative Baptist Network. CBN seemed genuinely perturbed, not only with the anti-Trump stance but with the racial justice emphasis of the never-Trump Southern Baptists as well. Such a position seemed to put the SBC in line with progressives and Black Lives Matter protests rather than the Republican Party. The CBN seemed poised to keep the SBC aligned with the Republican Party of Trump, the exact opposite of what Greear and Moore had been advocating.

The 2021 SBC presidential election seemed to be a referendum on the quadrilateral versus patrilateral. Which way would the denomination move: deeper into the culture wars or back toward evangelism, missions, and to a lesser extent a social justice stance that would have warmed Foy Valentine's heart? Alabama pastor Ed Litton, known for his efforts on the issue of racial reconciliation, appeared as the candidate most like Greear. He was nomi-nated by the only African American SBC president, Fred Luter.[60] Clearly, Litton was the candidate representing those wanting to move the SBC beyond its Trump-supporting identity within white evangelicalism. As if to make the choice as stark as possible, pastor Mike Stone ran essentially as the CBN's candidate. One of the express purposes leading to the founding of the

---

[59] "J. D. Greear," *Firing Line with Margaret Hoover*, September 7, 2018, http://www.pbs.org/wnet/firing-line/video/jd-greear-v5dt98/. I address Southern Baptists, Trump, and the 2021 SBC presidential election in a forthcoming book chapter. See Barry Hankins, "From Uneasy to Conflicted: Southern Baptist Leaders in an Age of Trump," in *Southern Baptists Re-Observed*, ed. Keith Harper (Knoxville: University of Tennessee, 2022).

[60] See Bob Smietana, "Alabama Pastor Ed Litton, Known for Racial Reconciliation Work, Joins SBC Presidential Race," *Religion News Service*, January 21, 2021, https://religionnews.com/2021/01/21/alabama-baptist-pastor-ed-litton -known-for-work-on-racial-reconciliation-joins-crowd-sbc-presidential-race/.

CBN was its desire to thwart "worldly ideologies infiltrating the Southern Baptist Convention, including Critical Race Theory, Intersectionality, and other unbiblical agendas deceptively labeled as 'Social Justice.'"[61] Stone was also the former head of the SBC Executive Committee, which had investigated Russell Moore, ostensibly to gauge whether his anti-Trump activities were alienating SBC congregations.[62] On the eve of the 2021 SBC annual meeting, Moore resigned from the ERLC and left the SBC altogether. Mohler was also a candidate in 2021, as was a fourth person, Randy Adams of the Northwest Baptist Convention. Stone and Litton finished 1–2 in the four-person race; then Litton won the runoff, suggesting perhaps that most of the denomination hopes to re-embrace the quadrilateral rather than the patrilateral as the defining elements of its identity. Mohler's inability to get traction for his presidential bid, meanwhile, suggests how difficult it is to be a culture warrior who nevertheless attempts to adhere to a theological definition of evangelical. Denouncing Trump in the name of theological integrity in 2016, then supporting the president in 2020, quite possibly alienated or at least confused a good number of Southern Baptists on either end of the quadrilateral-patrilateral spectrum.

So where does this leave us? Seemingly settled once and for all during the Conservative Resurgence, the nature of Southern Baptist evangelical identity is no longer so clear—but that is because evangelical identity itself is now up for debate. Are white evangelicals held together by theology or politics, Christian belief or culture war? As we have seen, there are Southern Baptist leaders who want to continue as allies of a Trumpian Republican

---

[61] "Statement: The Conservative Baptist Network Strongly Supports President Trump's Action Against CRT," Conservative Baptist Network, September 5, 2020, https://conservativebaptistnetwork.com/statement-the-conservative-baptist-network-strongly-supports-president-trumps-action-against-crt/.

[62] Bob Smietana, "Southern Baptist Leader Russell Moore Faces Investigation for Anti-Trump Comments," *The Christian Century*, March 9, 2020, https://www.christiancentury.org/article/people/southern-baptist-leader-russell-moore-faces-investigation-anti-trump-comments.

party. Others want to step back from culture war and return to an emphasis on missions and evangelism, with a less partisan approach to social justice issues like racial reconciliation. Despite recent events, Southern Baptists are clearly arrayed across the spectrum from the quadrilateral to the patrilateral. To paraphrase Lord Shaftesbury, "I know what constituted [a Southern Baptist] Evangelical in former times. I have no clear notion what constitutes one now."

Conclusion

The Weaknesses and Future of Baptist Political Theology

By Andrew T. Walker and Paul D. Miller

The Weaknesses of Baptist Political Theology?

What are the weaknesses of Baptist political theology? To answer this question, we must address weaknesses in both Baptist political *thought* and Baptist political *practice*.

Recognizing the failings of past practice is, sadly, all too easy. Some Baptists were apologists for slavery, owned slaves, participated in the slave trade, fought for the Confederacy, were members of the Klan, and defended Jim Crow. They argued the Bible supported their view and made racism and slavery part of their political theology. Similarly, some Baptists adopted an idolatrous vision of the United States, blurred the lines between church and state, called America a chosen nation, and viewed its wars as holy crusades.

Does that mean racism and national chauvinism are baked into the core of Baptist identity? There are good reasons for rejecting that conclusion. Racism and national chauvinism were—again, sadly—common in American life; Baptists were hardly their only boosters. Baptists' complicity with such sins cannot be a simple function of Baptist identity or Baptist theology when plenty of non-Baptists fell into the same sins—and when many other Baptists at the time rejected slavery and advocated for abolition or rejected "chosen nation" theology and defended religious liberty, decades before abolitionism or religious liberty went mainstream.

Baptists who invented theological justifications for racism, slavery, segregation, and crusading nationalism looked to the Bible for an *ex post facto* justification for a political position that they already had and that they prioritized over the Bible's message holistically understood. They were not biblical exegetes so much as propagandists cherry-picking biblical passages to use as fig leaves for their ideologies of power. Baptists' historic sin here is not that Baptist identity caused racism, but that Baptists' racism trumped their Baptist identity.

But that does not mean we can dismiss the sins of past Baptists' practice as irrelevant to the legacy of their political witness. That would be akin to the No True Scotsman fallacy. In this version—the No True Baptist fallacy—we say that Baptist political theology did not support racism or slavery. When faced with evidence that many Baptists in the past did in fact support them, we reply, "Well, no *true* Baptist supported racism and slavery." That leaves the question unanswered: Why did so many self-identified Baptists act against purported Baptist truths in favor of social and political evils? It is true that Baptist *theology* does not support such egregious sins, but we should still ask why Baptist *practice* often did.

The answer may lie in certain tendencies in Baptist life—indeed, in much of mainstream American Christianity. Americans are given to individualism. They think in terms of individual agency, choice, and action rather than structures, groups, or intergenerational legacies. They are also anti-elitist. They are suspicious of authority and expertise. And many

Protestant traditions have struggled since the sixteenth century with anti-nomianism because of their founding focus on avoiding a gospel of works. The result is that some evangelicals (including some Baptists) have preached and practiced a gospel of inward, individual salvation with few implications for social, cultural, and political life—a gospel shorn of its implications for relationships. Into that vacuum of political theology step other political theories—such as nationalism, racism, imperialism, and more—which then become the de facto political witness for Christians who know of no other orienting framework for political life.

These intellectual predispositions—individualism, anti-structuralism, antinomianism, even quietism—could be considered other weaknesses, or at least perennial temptations, of Baptist (or generally evangelical) political theology. As with racism and slavery, we can insist they are not necessary implications of Baptist theology, nor are Baptists uniquely guilty of them—but we also must admit they have often overlapped with Baptist political practice.

The essays in the final part of this volume are an effort to formulate a holistic Baptist political theology that is freed from past sins and (we hope) from the intellectual predispositions that weaken an otherwise strong framework. Our articulation of Baptist political theology takes inspiration from the best of the historic Baptist political witnesses, including the Baptists who understood the imperative for abolition and civil rights and, above all, who spent centuries arguing for and defending religious freedom and disestablishment. It is a Baptist political theology that understands the gospel's implications for all of social, cultural, and political life, including for bioethics, sexuality and gender, the environment, political economy, race and ethnicity, and war and peace.

Baptists and Republicanism

In recognizing that Baptist political theology can and should address itself to a broad range of political issues, we approach another truth. It is often said that Protestantism lacks a social theory, that Protestantism does not have a holistic approach to social, cultural, and political life. That, we think, is wrong. We do have a unifying vision, and Baptists are best positioned to make it explicit: as our history shows, some version of republicanism (with a small "r") is our social theory. We did not invent it (pagan Greeks and Renaissance Italian Catholics were republicans long before we were), but we adopted it and made it our own. Baptists—in making common cause with Cromwell and Parliament against the king; with the Patriots and revolutionaries against the Tories and the Crown; and with the United States against the kaiser, the Nazis, and the Soviets—have consistently identified the survival and success of republicanism with the cause of justice and peace in this world.

Classically, republicanism consisted in popular sovereignty, majoritarian government, minority protections, the rule of law, checks and balances among independent branches of government, and the priority of the common good—the "public thing" or *res publica*—over private gain. As discussed in chapter 25, Baptists have understood these institutions as the best available political outworking of justice, biblically understood. We love our neighbors politically when we build, maintain, participate in, and defend institutions, norms, polities, and constitutions that reflect a broadly republican orientation.

Identifying republicanism as the center of our political vision raises another possible difficulty. Republicanism may be our social theory, but twenty-first century American democracy has departed from the republican vision in many ways—especially in republicanism's cultural component. Republicanism is not just a set of political institutions. Republicanism rightly understood also has a cultural content and cultural theory to it. It is a culture engendered by an educated and informed citizenry, a spirit of fraternity among coequal citizens, a healthy patriotism and gratitude for the blessings of public life, a sense of honor for public service, and—above all—a vigilance against corruption, self-dealing, and the temptation to abuse the public trust for private gain.

It is increasingly difficult for a Baptist, or any Christian who shares this broad approach to political life, to defend the republican ideal and, simultaneously, our practice of democracy in America. Put another way, those who wish to defend the American experiment in free government cannot limit themselves to defending a few well-known institutions like elections and the Bill of Rights. Reducing free government to those institutions is too thin, too procedural, and too individualistic, focused exclusively on citizens' rights at the expense of citizens' responsibilities. We must rediscover our republican roots to understand and articulate the cultural component of it, which means articulating a sort of Christian republicanism. We must preach about how to practice the arts of public life and public service as a natural outflowing of our Christian duty to love our neighbors, work for justice, and aid in the flourishing of our fellow human beings.

As we do so, we face one final challenge: What is the relationship between the culture of republicanism and white Anglo-American culture? They are not the same—free government exists and thrives in essentially every major cultural bloc and region of the world, often with differences or adaptations that emerged from unique national histories. But we also must recognize that the Anglo-American articulation and institutionalization of republicanism starting in the eighteenth century has been the most influential in world history, by far, and that Baptist thought and practice is similarly indebted to the same history. Can we disentangle the culture of republicanism from our Anglo-American heritage? Can Baptists articulate our political theology without falling into cultural chauvinism, especially given the history of British and American racism?

These are the challenges for the next generation of Baptist thinkers. Understanding our history helps us understand our unique Baptist strengths even as we acknowledge our past failures and present weaknesses and temptations. We must have eyes to see the temptations—individualism, antistructuralism, antinomianism, and selective quietism because we have the privilege and responsibility to rearticulate a Baptist political witness across the full spectrum of social, cultural, and political life. And we do so in an increasingly pluralistic context that demands that we, to a far greater degree than our predecessors, work to understand and disentangle the relationship between Baptist theology and Anglo-American culture. Happily, Baptist theology has ample resources within it to meet these challenges.

Strengths for Contemporary Challenges

As of this writing, the prospects facing Baptists within a North American context seem to be either secular progressivism or a growing post-liberalism among some sectors of American conservatism. Baptist thought cuts against both grains. Baptist political theology insists upon (1) a positive vision for statecraft pursued for the common good in publicly intelligible ways via greater facility with the natural law (see chapter 19); (2) religious liberty for all (chapter 20); (3) rejecting any formal church-state establishment (4) while avoiding pietism, sectarian withdrawal, or state-sponsored secularism. Such a formula represents, in embryonic form, a program for further development.

First, concerning what undergirds the ordination of government to begin with, the furtherance of justice is inseparable from a positive vision for statecraft. Statecraft entails the responsible stewarding of power in the direction of truth and the common good and the disempowering of falsehood. This in no way ought to conflict with Baptist theology. It only means the responsible pursuit and stewardship of political power for just ends that serve all equally. A rightly ordered Baptist political theology will differentiate between coercive, arbitrary, and domineering manifestations of religion and those rooted in a broad and organic application of justice that aims to secure goods necessary for human flourishing.

Second, because Baptists believe the government is not empowered with any redemptive mission in mind, such a reality recognizes the legitimate claim non-Baptists have to participate in society. Such a reality is no invitation to relativism, but to mutual interrogation of the quality of one's views in service to justice and the common good. Baptist political theology must offer a positive account of the common good rooted in a firm vision that persons of all faiths and no faith have equal share in the decisions of how they are governed. This is an invitation to level-headedness and civility, not civil war carried out by ideological means.

Third, because of our commitment to disestablishment, Baptists must continually affirm the principle that the mission of the state given by God is not the mission of the church. Baptists must also remind those who are apt to use the apparatus of the state to directly further Christian ends that the state is no necessary handmaiden to the gospel.

Fourth, Baptist political theology is neither secular nor sectarian. It believes in the positive value of religion for shaping the moral ecology of its surrounding context.

Baptist public theology must remind society that a humane civil society requires mediating institutions that offer sources for moral authority and moral formation. Rooted in a vision for transcendence that neither instrumentalizes religion for the sake of social cohesion nor relegates it to the margins as an oppressive matrix, Baptists are well positioned to remind those in the surrounding context that both government and citizens alike are accountable to God for the decisions they make that impact our shared, common life.

To that end, Baptists are uniquely suited to use the language of natural law and develop the theology around it for public application. Because of our emphasis on disestablishment, we know better than most the necessity of discovering and articulating the common good we have with nonbelievers and people from different cultural backgrounds. This necessarily entails a greater development in Baptist natural law formulations.

Conclusion

"The grass withers, the flowers fade, but the word of our God remains forever" (Isa 40:8). God's eternal truth is perfect and never changes, but our understanding of it is another matter. The early church fathers argued for three centuries about the nature of the Trinity and the incarnation. It took another millennium for the Reformers to bring greater clarity to the doctrine of justification. The Bible's inerrancy was only fleshed out last century. God, in his providence, has allowed us to participate in the drama of theological work, unearthing new insights, finding sharper perspectives, or highlighting emerging questions in the light of new circumstances in human history.

That means this volume, as much as any book, is a product of its time. It is not the final word on Baptist political theology. We hope it is something like a road map showing where we came from, where we have traveled, and where we think the road leads next. It comes at a time of great tumult and change in the United States and around the world. Secularization seems to have finally caught up to America. Huge cultural and demographic changes are overtaking much of the developed world. New technologies have reset the horizon of what was even imaginable a generation ago. As the global population approaches 8 billion, it is unclear how much life the biosphere can support without breakdown. And, as always, wars and rumors of wars stalk the earth.

Grappling with these problems is the work of citizens and statesmen, educators and scholars, activists and institutions. As they confront an array of challenges old and new, the Baptist political witness is an invaluable resource. Rooted in natural law and God's creation design and seeing clearer than any other tradition the proper relationship of church to state, Baptists can speak in a pluralistic world across lines of culture, time, and sect about the common good. The goal of our public engagement, of course, is not to tout our relevance for its own sake, but to point beyond ourselves to a design for common flourishing. Our relevance and our ability to think clearly about those problems is an advertisement, a road sign pointing to the Author in whose creation we live, whose design is manifest in his Word, whose Word is our guide. It is a road worth traveling that leads to greater justice, peace, and flourishing in this life and to the face of God in the next.

SUBJECT INDEX

SCRIPTURE INDEX